Whitestein Series in Software Agent Technologies

Series Editors:
Marius Walliser
Monique Calisti
Thomas Hempfling
Stefan Brantschen

This series reports new developments in agent-based software technologies and agent-oriented software engineering methodologies, with particular emphasis on applications in various scientific and industrial areas. It includes research level monographs, polished notes arising from research and industrial projects, outstanding PhD theses, and proceedings of focused meetings and conferences. The series aims at promoting advanced research as well as at facilitating know-how transfer to industrial use.

About Whitestein Technologies

Whitestein Technologies AG was founded in 1999 with the mission to become a leading provider of advanced software agent technologies, products, solutions, and services for various applications and industries. Whitestein Technologies strongly believes that software agent technologies, in combination with other leading-edge technologies like web services and mobile wireless computing, will enable attractive opportunities for the design and the implementation of a new generation of distributed information systems and network infrastructures.

www.whitestein.com

Software Agent-Based Applications, Platforms and Development Kits

Rainer Unland
Matthias Klusch
Monique Calisti
Editors

Birkhäuser Verlag
Basel · Boston · Berlin

Editors:

Rainer Unland
Universität Gesamthochschule Essen
Fachbereich Mathematik und Informatik
Schützenbahn 70
D-45117 Essen

Monique Calisti
Whitestein Technologies
Pestalozzistrasse 24
CH-8032 Zürich

Matthias Klusch
German Research Center for Artificial
Intelligence,
Deduction and Multiagent Systems
Stuhlsatzenhausweg 3
D-66123 Saarbrücken

2000 Mathematics Subject Classification 68T35, 68U35

A CIP catalogue record for this book is available from the Library of Congress,
Washington D.C., USA

Bibliographic information published by Die Deutsche Bibliothek
Die Deutsche Bibliothek lists this publication in the Deutsche Nationalbibliografie;
detailed bibliographic data is available in the Internet at <http://dnb.ddb.de>.

ISBN 3-7643-7347-4 Birkhäuser Verlag, Basel – Boston – Berlin

© 2005 Birkhäuser Verlag, P.O. Box 133, CH-4010 Basel, Switzerland
Part of Springer Science+Business Media
Cover design: Micha Lotrovsky, CH-4106 Therwil, Switzerland
Printed on acid-free paper produced from chlorine-free pulp. TCF ∞
Printed in Germany

ISBN-10: 3-7643-7347-4
ISBN-13: 978-3-7643-7347-4

e-ISBN: 3-7643-7348-2

9 8 7 6 5 4 3 2 1

www.birkhauser.ch

Software Agent-Based Applications, Platforms and Development Kits

Rainer Unland
Matthias Klusch
Monique Calisti
Editors

Birkhäuser Verlag
Basel · Boston · Berlin

Editors:

Rainer Unland
Universität Gesamthochschule Essen
Fachbereich Mathematik und Informatik
Schützenbahn 70
D-45117 Essen

Monique Calisti
Whitestein Technologies
Pestalozzistrasse 24
CH-8032 Zürich

Matthias Klusch
German Research Center for Artificial
Intelligence,
Deduction and Multiagent Systems
Stuhlsatzenhausweg 3
D-66123 Saarbrücken

2000 Mathematics Subject Classification 68T35, 68U35

A CIP catalogue record for this book is available from the Library of Congress, Washington D.C., USA

Bibliographic information published by Die Deutsche Bibliothek
Die Deutsche Bibliothek lists this publication in the Deutsche Nationalbibliografie; detailed bibliographic data is available in the Internet at <http://dnb.ddb.de>.

ISBN 3-7643-7347-4 Birkhäuser Verlag, Basel – Boston – Berlin

© 2005 Birkhäuser Verlag, P.O. Box 133, CH-4010 Basel, Switzerland
Part of Springer Science+Business Media
Cover design: Micha Lotrovsky, CH-4106 Therwil, Switzerland
Printed on acid-free paper produced from chlorine-free pulp. TCF ∞
Printed in Germany

ISBN-10: 3-7643-7347-4   e-ISBN: 3-7643-7348-2
ISBN-13: 978-3-7643-7347-4

9 8 7 6 5 4 3 2 1   www.birkhauser.ch

Contents

Preface

Intelligent agents and multi-agent systems (MAS) represent the next big step in the development of next-generation software systems, especially when considering large scale distributed applications consisting of several sub-components with behavior that is increasingly difficult to predict. This is supported by important research and development results and reinforced by the increasing uptake of agent-based solutions and services for real-world industries. In fact, software agent technology successfully addresses a number of highly relevant issues, like efficient resource distribution, scalability, adaptability, maintainability, modularity, autonomy, self-sustainability, and decentralized control, by providing powerful concepts, metaphors and tools. The mentioned issues are often regarded as essential non-functional properties of emerging software architectures and systems.

The high importance of agent-related research and development can be seen from the fact that currently about 100 major projects are funded in Europe only - see http://www.agentlink.org/resources/agentprojects-db.php - and more than 100 academic and commercial software tools are publicly advertised - see http://www.agentlink.org/resources/agent-software.php. And these numbers are still growing. As a result of the enormous efforts the stage of maturation has reached a level, which encourages commercial players to increasingly adopt multi-agent systems concepts and technologies for the development of a variety of real-world applications in different domains such as logistics, e-commerce, and entertainment. In this perspective, concrete agent-driven research and development results (such as applications, platforms, and development kits) substantially contribute to promote the technology and increase its exploitation for industrial solutions.

This book provides a first and comprehensive overview of existing software agent development kits, environments, and applications. It is intended to be of particular use for those who want to assess the maturity and state-of-the-art of applied software agent technology. Both the software engineering and the user perspective are covered by a carefully selected set of contributions reporting on prominent examples of agent development environments, platforms, and toolkits and deployed agent-based applications from various different application areas. In particular, most of them have been either successfully demonstrated to the public at the agent technology exhibition of the first German conference for Multi-Agent system TEchnologieS (MATES 2004) in Erfurt, or won the prestigious system innovation award of the international workshop series on Cooperative Information Agents (CIA). Since this book concentrates on implemented systems most of them are available on the Internet. Thus, at the end of each paper you will find all relevant information about where to get the software on the Internet (if it is available) and whom you may contact in case of questions.

Contents

The book consists of seven chapters. The assignment of papers to chapters has been a hard choice, since many papers fall into several categories. However, we believe the final layout is the most reasonable one.

The first three chapters (with eight papers altogether) present toolkits for the development of multi-agent systems. The toolkits are subdivided into three categories: platforms, development environments, and frameworks. An *agent platform* is intended as the set of middleware components supporting the development of (distributed) multi-agent applications. It provides all basic services, like agent life-cycle management, communication, tasks scheduling, security, etc., to easily initialize and run multi-agent systems. A *development environment* usually supports all phases in multi-agent system engineering, which comprises requirements engineering, system design, development and deployment. *Agent frameworks* provide a high-level programming environment consisting of a multi-agent system skeleton that allows the programmer to easily extend it to a full-fledged MAS application. Toolkits can also be differentiated according to their focus of support. In general, it is possible to distinguish between middleware- and reasoning-oriented systems. In this latter case, one emphasizes rationality and goal-directedness support for agent development.

The first chapter focuses on agent platforms and starts with the paper *The JADE Platform and Experiences with Mobile MAS Applications* by Fabio Bellifemine, Giovanni Caire, Giosuè Vitaglione, Giovanni Rimassa, and Dominic Greenwood. JADE is a well-known and well-established Java-based and FIPA-compliant agent platform. The paper gives a comprehensive overview about the basic concepts of JADE. Furthermore, it shows how JADE can be used on mobile networks. Finally, it discusses possible application domains for JADE. The second paper *A-globe: Agent Development Platform with Inaccessibility and Mobility Support* by David Šišlák, Martin Rehák, Michal Pechoucek, Milan Rollo, and Dušan Pavlicek presents *A-globe*, a streamlined lightweight platform for MAS development, which operates on normal PCs as well as on PDAs. After a comprehensive introduction into the basic features of *A-globe* it is compared to some other agent platforms. The next section concentrates on simulation support since *A-globe* provides a special infrastructure for environmental simulation. The third paper in this chapter *Supporting Agent Development in Erlang through the eXAT Platform* by Antonella Di Stefano and Corrado Santoro motivates and presents first the agent programming language Erlang. Then the agent programming platform eXAT that is based on Erlang is discussed. eXAT especially emphasizes the implementation of agent intelligence, behavior, and communication.

The second chapter is dedicated to development environments. The paper *Living Systems® Technology Suite* (LS/TS) by Giovanni Rimassa, Monique Calisti, and Martin E. Kernland describes the LS/TS set of components for the development and deployment of products and systems based on software agent technology and autonomic computing. The paper not only gives a comprehensive overview about the architecture and functionality of this package, but also discusses the challenges that were to be addressed in order to develop the proposed software methodology and infrastructure. The second paper by Vladimir Gorodetsky, Oleg Karsaev, Vladimir Samoylov, Victor Konushy, Evgeny Mankov, and Alexey Maly-shev presents the *Multi-Agent System Development Kit* (MASDK), a comprehensive software tool kit for the development, implementation, and deployment of multi-agent systems. The paper mainly concentrates on the development process, which is heavily influenced by the Gaia methodology. It is conducted with the help of a number of integrated editors (e.g., for the model, protocol, ontology, behavior, and state transition development), which are described in detail. The third paper *An Integrated Development Environment for Electronic Institutions* by Josep Lluís Arcos, Marc Esteva, Pablo Noriega, Juan Antonio Rodríguez-Aguilar, and Carles Sierra presents a methodology and an integrated development environment for engineering multi agent systems as electronic institutions. The latter defines a set of artificial constraints that articulate agent interactions, defining what they are permitted and forbidden to do. It defines a normative environment where heterogeneous (human and software) agents can participate by playing different roles and can interact by means of speech acts. The integrated use of these tools is illustrated using as an example the double auction market.

The third chapter starts with the paper *Jadex: A BDI-Agent System Combining Middleware And Reasoning* by Lars Braubach, Alexander Pokahr, and Winfried Lamersdorf. The presented system Jadex relies on an arbitrary given agent platform, e.g. JADE, however, extends it by providing tools to model agent rationality and goal-directedness. Its reasoning engine supports cognitive agents by exploiting the BDI model. It permits to explicitly model such features as beliefs, plans, goals or capabilities. The CAFnE toolkit is presented in the paper *Component Agent Framework For Non-Experts (CAFnE) Toolkit* by Gaya Jayatilleke, Lin Padgham. and Michael Winikoff. The vision of the authors is not only to support developers in the initial application development but also to provide a framework that facilitates domain experts themselves in making modifications to a deployed system, in order for it to better fit needs which are identified as the system is used. The system is introduced and its functionality is explained with the help of an example system.

The forth chapter comprises two papers that show how Web-Services can be integrated into agent technology. The paper *The WSDL2Agent Tool* by László Zsolt Varga, Ákos Hajnal, and Zsolt Werner presents a bipartite tool for this purpose. The WSDL2Jade part of the tool generates code for a proxy agent that makes the Web service available in a multi-agent environment. The WSDL2Protégé part of the tool translates a WSDL description to a Protégé project in order to support its semantic enrichment. It generates a project file for the Protégé ontology engineering tool in which the ontology of the Web service can be visualized, edited, or exported to various formats. The second paper *WS2JADE: A Tool for Run-Time Deployment and Control of Web Services as JADE Agent Services* by Xuan Thang Nguyen, Ryszard Kowalczyk, Mohan Baruwal Chhetri, and Alasdair Grant presents the WS2JADE framework. It permits the easy integration of Web services into the JADE agent platform. In particular, the technical aspects of the run-time deployment and control of Web services as agent services are discussed. The Web service - agent integration capabilities of WS2JADE are demonstrated with simple examples of Web service management including service discovery, composition, and deployment with JADE agents.

Chapter five concentrates on *Tool Support for Agent Communication and Negotiation.* The paper by Tibor Bosse, Catholijn M. Jonker, Lourens van der Meij, Valentin Robu, and Jan Treur presents SAMIN, *A System for Analysis of Multi-Issue Negotiation.* The agents in this system conduct one-to-one negotiations, in which the values across multiple issues are negotiated on simultaneously. The paper shows how the system supports both automated and human negotiation. To analyze such negotiation processes, the user can enter every formal property deemed useful into the system and use the system to automatically check this property in given negotiation traces. The paper also shows how to deal with incomplete information and presents some experimental results about human multi-issue negotiation. F*uzzyMAN: An Agent-Based E-Marketplace with a Voice and Mobile User Interface* by Frank Teuteberg and Iouri Loutchko focuses on the conceptual foundations and the architecture of an agent-based job e-Marketplace that supports mobile negotiations. The negotiation model is based on many negotiation issues, a fuzzy utility scoring method, and simultaneous negotiation with many negotiation partners in an environment of limited negotiation time. The paper discusses FuzzyMAN's architecture, agents, negotiation model, and mobile and voice user interfaces. Heikki Helin and Mikko Laukkanen deal in their paper with *Efficient Agent Communication in Wireless Environments.* They propose a layered model of agent communication in the context of the FIPA agent architecture. For each layer of this communication stack an efficient solution for wireless agent communication is presented. Furthermore, the paper thoroughly analyzes the performance of agent communication in slow wireless environments.

Chapter six contains two papers about tool kits for mobile agents. The paper *AMETAS - The Asynchronous MEssage Transfer Agent System* by Michael Zapf presents a development and runtime environment for creating and running mobile, autonomous agents under Java 2. AMETAS defines three kinds of application components: agents, user adapters, and services. Services are able to wrap system-dependent resource accesses and provide functional enhancements while user adapters integrate the human user into the agent environment. Techniques of mediation are used to realize open applications; i.e. applications with an ever-changing set of components. The discussed security system prevents illegal access between users and defines the access control to resources. The other paper *Tracy: An Extensible Plugin-Oriented Software Architecture for Mobile Agent Toolkits* by Peter Braun, Ingo Müller, Tino Schlegel, Steffen Kern, Volkmar Schau, and Wilhelm Rossak presents a kernel-based tool kit that only provides fundamental concepts and functions common to all toolkits and abstracts from all of their possible services. In particular, although Tracy was developed as a mobile agent toolkit, its kernel abstracts from all issues related to agent mobility, delegating this to an optional service implementation. This makes it possible to replace Tracy's migration service with another implementation and even to have two different migration services in parallel. Service implementations are developed as plug-ins that can be started and stopped during run-time. The paper first discusses the set of fundamental services. Then it is shown how they are realized in Tracy.

Chapter seven comprises three papers that are related to agent-based applications. Each of these papers also covers a research issue, however, discusses its solution on the basis of an application. *The Packet-World: A Test Bed for Investigating Situated Multi-Agent Systems* by Danny Weyns, Alexander Helleboogh, and Tom Holvoet presents as application area the packet world. The research aim of the paper is to discuss how to model a distributed application as a set of co-operating autonomous entities (agents), which are situated in an environment. The Packet-World is used as a test bed to explore and evaluate a broad range of fundamental concepts and mechanisms for situated MASs. The paper elaborates on the structure of the environment, agents' perception, flexible action selection, protocol-based communication, execution control and timing, simultaneous actions and several forms of stigmergy. *Decommitment in a Competitive Multi-Agent Transportation Setting* by Pieter Jan 't Hoen, Valentin Robu, and Han La Poutre discusses the decommittment issue on the basis of a large-scale logistics setting (freight forwarding) with multiple, competing companies. It is shown in the paper that decommitment as the action of foregoing of a contract for another (superior) offer can reach higher utility levels in case of negotiations with uncertainty about future opportunities. The paper *Teamworker: An Agent-Based Support System for Mobile Task Execution* by Habin Lee, Patrik Mihailescu, and John Shepherdson shows how a multi-agent based computer cooperative support system known as TeamWorker can help to overcome the difficulties faced by mobile workers. Each mobile worker is assigned a personal agent that can assist her/him during the working day through appropriate service provision (based on current work context), and through monitoring work progress to anticipate and undertake required actions on the user's behalf. A detailed presentation of the TeamWorker system is given, including the benefits provided for a real life mobile business process.

As this book is a collaborative effort, the editors would like to thank foremost the contributing authors for their outstanding contributions, and the reviewers and publisher for their invaluable help and assistance during the whole project. We also would like to thank Dr. Stefan Göller from Birkhauser Publishing Ltd. for his outstanding support in producing this book.

In summary, we hope that this book will be of substantial benefit for students, software engineers, computer scientists, researchers (both academic and industrial), and IT experts, who are keen to learn about the deployment of software agent technology for engineering complex solutions and systems.

Enjoy the reading!

Monique Calisti, Matthias Klusch, Rainer Unland
Zürich - Saarbrücken - Essen
Spring 2005

The JADE Platform and Experiences with Mobile MAS Applications

Fabio Bellifemine, Giovanni Caire, Giosuè Vitaglione,
Giovanni Rimassa and Dominic Greenwood

Abstract. This paper draws a perspective about a software platform for multi-agent systems, called JADE. JADE is an Open-Source Java middleware very popular in the MAS research and development community, counting a lively and active user base. Here we will describe the JADE architecture, the main features provided by the platform, and some application domains from the Open Source community.

1. Introduction

JADE [1] is a middleware for the development of distributed multi-agent applications. According to the multi-agent systems approach, an application based on the JADE platform is composed of a set of cooperating agents, which can communicate with each other through message exchange. Each agent is immersed within an environment that can be acted upon and from whom events can be perceived. Intelligence, initiative, information, resources and control can be fully distributed on mobile terminals as well as on computers in the fixed network. The environment can evolve dynamically and agents appear and disappear in the system according to the needs and the requirements of the applications.

JADE provides the basic services necessary for distributed peer-to-peer applications in the fixed and mobile environment allowing each agent to dynamically discover others and to communicate with them. From the application point of view, each agent is identified by a unique name and provides a set of services. It can register and modify its services and/or search for agents providing given services, it can control its life cycle and, in particular, communicate with all other peer agents by exchanging asynchronous messages, a widely accepted communication model for distributed and loosely-coupled software components. Communication between the agents, regardless of whether they are running in the wireless or in the wireline network, is completely symmetric with each agent being able to both initiate an interaction and respond to it. JADE is fully developed in Java and is based of the following driving principles:

☐ *Interoperability*. JADE is compliant with the FIPA specifications [2]. As a consequence, JADE agents can interoperate with other agents, provided that they comply with the same standard.

☐ *Portability*. JADE provides a homogeneous set of APIs that are independent from the underlying network and Java edition. More in details, the JADE run-time provides the same API for the J2EE, J2SE and J2ME environment and it has been designed and optimized for low footprint and memory requirements.

☐ *Ease of use and faster time-to-market*. The set of APIs has been designed with the goal of reducing the time to market for developing applications; therefore, they aim to hide the complexity of the middleware behind a simple and intuitive set of APIs.

☐ *Pay-as-you-go philosophy*. Programmers do not need to use all the features provided by the middleware. Features that are not used do not require programmers to know anything about them neither they add computational overhead.

After this introduction, the paper is organized as follows. Next chapter describes the high level components of the architecture. Then the evolution of distributed kernel on which the platform is based upon is analyzed and the new architecture based on a set of distributed coordinated filters is presented. Next chapter presents some of the most interesting platform-level services. Then, the split container architecture is presented and how it is suitable for mobile networks and devices, including how the platform is able to guarantee MSISDN-based[1] identification of the peers. A categorization of the application domains where the platform and this technology provides highest payoff is then presented and, finally, the Open Source Community, the JADE Board, and the future roadmap are presented.

2. JADE Architecture

JADE includes both the libraries (i.e. the Java classes) required to develop application agents and the run-time environment that provides the basic platform-level services and that must be active on the device before agents can be executed. Each instance of the JADE run-time is called *container* (since it "contains" agents). The set of all containers is called *platform* and provides a homogeneous layer that hides from agents the complexity and the diversity of the underlying tiers (hardware, operating systems, types of network, JVM) as depicted in Figure 1.

For bootstrapping and FIPA compliance purposes, one among these containers is labeled as *Main Container*; it must be the first to start up and all other containers

---

[1] MSISDN stands for "Mobile Subscriber ISDN Number". Basically it is the phone number of the SIM-card in the mobile phone.

register with it at bootstrap time. The Main Container has the following specific responsibilities:

☐   It manages the *Container Table* (i.e. the set of all the nodes that compose the distributed platform).

☐   It manages the *Global Agent Descriptor Table* (i.e. the set of all the agents hosted by the distributed platform, together with their current location).

☐   It manages the *Message Transport Protocols Table* (i.e. the set of all deployed message transport endpoints, together with their deployment location).

☐   It hosts the platform *Agent Management Service* (*AMS*) agent, mandated by FIPA specifications as unique white page and life-cycle management agent.

☐   It hosts the platform *Default Directory Facilitator* (*DF*) agent, mandated by FIPA specifications as default yellow page management agent.

All the above operations are essential for correct and FIPA-compliant platform operation. Unfortunately, this also entails that, from a fault tolerance perspective, the Main Container is a sensible part of the platform, and a single point of failure for many tasks. For this purpose, the replication service, described in the followings, allows to monitor and replicate the main container responsibilities.

Its distributed architecture allows deploying JADE platforms that run across multiple Java editions, from powerful servers to small mobile devices. The limited memory footprint, in fact, allows installing JADE on all mobile phones provided that they are Java-enabled. JADE is compatible with the J2ME CLDC/MIDP environment and it has already been extensively used on the field over GPRS network with several commercial mobile terminals. The JADE run-time memory footprint, in a MIDP1.0 environment, is around 45 KB, but can be further reduced until 20 KB using the ROMizing technique, i.e. compiling JADE together with the JVM [3]. JADE is extremely versatile and therefore, not only it fits the constraints of environments with limited resources, but it has already been integrated into complex architectures such as .NET or J2EE [4] where JADE becomes a service to execute multi-party proactive applications.

3. Platform Kernel

The platform is built on top of a distributed kernel that supports basic platform-level operations such as message delivery and agent life-cycle management. The current kernel architecture can be considered as the third generation of the kernel. The first generation of JADE had a monolithic distributed kernel and was only able to operate in the J2SE environment. The second generation had to target the whole spectrum of Java editions (from Micro-Edition to Enterprise Edition) and introduced the idea of having many platform profiles, that allowed choosing whether to include a feature or not. Though flexible enough, this second-generation kernel had a fixed feature set. Even if most features (agent mobility, event management, platform security) could be turned on or off, the kernel did not allow easy extension by including new platform-level services. In order to effectively address the more demanding requirements gathered from the first JADE-based systems, and also in order to promote an application model based on seamlessly situated agents, a third generation of JADE kernel was conceived and built.

This section outlines the resulting architecture, highlighting the design rationale backing up the major choices made.

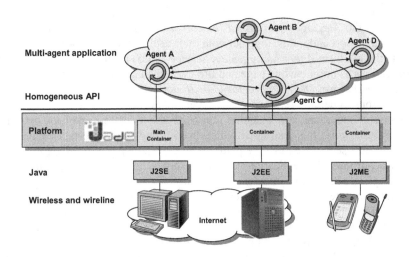

Fig. 1. JADE Distributed Architecture

3.1 Ideas and motivations

The first, natural direction in designing the third generation JADE kernel was to strive for finer-grained modularity of the kernel features. Moreover, an open-ended set of kernel-level feature sets was envisaged, and a flexible deployment strategy was essential in targeting the hybrid wireless/wireline network.

The first abstraction, adopted in order to give an extensible structure to the JADE kernel, is the *Service*. A JADE service groups together a set of features according to their conceptual cohesion, and is the kernel-level unit of deployment. Some sample JADE kernel services are agent management, agent mobility and event notification. These services closely correspond to the second-generation feature sets, but now they comply with a generic and extensible model that allows many more services to be developed and eases creating more complex ones, such as some of the services that will be described in the next sections.

The second abstraction adopted to achieve the seamless distribution of agents in the platform is the *Container*. This concept was kept from the previous kernel versions, but now it has an enhanced semantics. While in first- and second-generation kernels a JADE container was meant to contain only agents, now a third-generation container holds both agents and services.

From the previous requirements and the design vision, a set of desiderata for the new architecture was obtained:
1.   Different services can be composed together.
2.   Any subset of the available services can be deployed at any given container, possibly adding/removing a service during normal platform operation.
3.   Some services can be present only on a subset of the platform containers or can be present with different service levels at different containers.
4.   The services can run on the various Java editions supported by JADE, possibly with a graceful degradation on the more resource constrained devices.

3.2 The distributed coordinated filters architecture

Part of the inspiration needed to shape the new architecture was drawn from the research area about aspect-oriented programming [5]. The main tenet of aspect orientation is to promote separation of concerns, by writing software code as a collection of independently written aspects, expressing a different concern each.

Aspects, though written separately, will then be combined together to yield the final application. The process of combining together the different aspects according to some rules is called aspect weaving. The aspect-oriented approach basically stems from a programming language viewpoint, and the first works such as AspectJ [6] use source code translators to perform compile-time aspect weaving. Another option would be to perform run-time aspect weaving through some kind of component composition technique; among these dynamic approaches, a pioneering work was made by Aksit and others [7] with the proposal of composition filters as a way to transparently extend object systems.

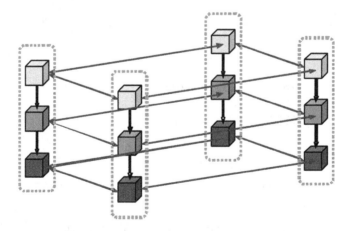

Fig. 2. Distributed coordinated filters architecture of the JADE Kernel.

In Java-based aspect languages and systems, a third option is viable and has become very popular, that is, classload-time aspect weaving. Due to the lack of support in J2ME and considering that JADE struggles to provide all its features to users through nothing more than a Java API, the third generation JADE kernel architecture took the biggest inspiration from the composition filters approach. Basically each object is provided with two filter chains: an incoming chain whose filters are invoked whenever the object receives a method call, and an outgoing chain whose filters are invoked whenever the object is about to call some other object's method itself.

By mixing the composition filters approach with the distribution of services across containers, we obtained the *Distributed Coordinated Filters* architecture, sketched in Figure 2.

In the figure above, every color refers to a specific kernel service, and every dotted line encloses a container. This means that, in the depicted example, the distributed platform has three services deployed on four containers. The various kernel operations are represented by commands, which flow across services in their container as shown by the vertical arrows. This accounts for the filtering aspect, just like in the original composition filters model. The horizontal arrows show that a single service (say, the one at the bottom) is actually distributed on several network nodes. We call *Slice* the part of a service that resides on a given node; the colored cubes in Figure 2 are exactly the service slices. Service slices and their interaction account for the distribution and coordination aspect in our model.

The UML diagram in Figure 3 shows the general layout of the resulting solution.

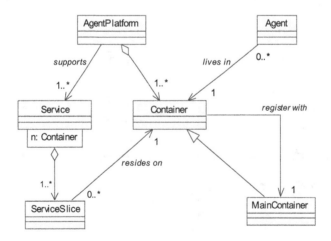

Fig. 3. Main elements of the JADE Kernel.

4. Platform Services

The architecture of the JADE kernel enables the deployment of platform-level services at run-time: each container can be deployed with the necessary services, such as communication, replication, persistence, or security. Programmers can also implement and deploy their own application-specific services, where needed.

The agent class usually accesses these platform-level services via a *Service Helper* that exposes all the methods available to the agent. In some cases (e.g. for the communication service), the methods are exposed by the Agent class itself, partly because of backward compatibility, partly because of easiness of use.

For the sake of brevity, this section does not report the full list of available services but just some of the most relevant and representatives.

4.1 Communication Service

In order to communicate, an agent just sends a message to a destination agent. Agents are identified by a name (no need for the destination object reference to send a message) and, as a consequence, there is no temporal dependency between communicating agents. The sender and the receiver could not be available at the same time. The receiver may not even exist (or not yet) or could not be directly known by the sender that can specify a property (e.g. "all agents interested in football") as a destination. Because agents identifies each other by their name, hot change of their object reference are transparent to applications. Despite this type of communication, security is preserved, since, for applications that require it, JADE provides proper mechanisms to authenticate and verify "rights" assigned to agents. When needed, therefore, an application can verify the identity of the sender of a message and prevent actions not allowed to perform (for instance an agent may be allowed to receive messages from the agent representing the boss, but not to send messages to it). All messages exchanged between agents are carried out within an envelope including only the information required by the transport layer. That allows, among others, to encrypt the content of a message separately from the envelope.

The communication service is instantiated, by default, on every JADE container and it makes transparent to agents the location of communicating end points. Each agent owns a private queue that is filled by the communication service with incoming messages. Agents can access this private queue via any arbitrary combination of the following methods: polling-based, timeout blocking-based (i.e. blocks until a message arrives or until the given timeout expires), message-template based (i.e. it gets the first message in the queue that matches the passed message template).

The structure of a message complies with the ACL language defined by FIPA [2] and includes fields, such as variables indicating the context a message refers-to and timeout that can be waited before an answer is received, aimed at supporting complex interactions and multiple parallel conversations. As a matter of fact, in order to further support the implementation of complex conversations, JADE provides a set of skeletons of typical interaction patterns to perform specific tasks, such as negotiations, auctions and task delegation. By using these skeletons (implemented as Java abstract classes), programmers can get rid of the burden of dealing with synchronization issues, timeouts, error conditions and, in general, all those aspects that are not strictly related to the application logic.

An analysis and a benchmark of Scalability and Performance of the JADE Message Transport System is reported in [8].

4.2 Security Service

Security in JADE is, by nature, distributed and enabled by a set of services delineated by function. Those services are *Authentication*, *Permission* and *Encryption*, described as follows:

The *Authentication Service* ensures that any user starting a JADE platform or container is legitimate within the computational system and takes responsibility for her actions, so as to be authorized to create agents within that platform. Being legitimate in the case of JADE authentication implies that the user is known to the system by having at least one valid identity and associated password. Authentication does not however imply any guarantees of behavior, this is managed by the Permission Service. The authentication mechanism itself is based on the *Java Authentication and Authorization Service* (*JAAS*) API [9] that enables enforcement of differentiated access control on system users. JAAS provides a set of de facto *LoginModules*; with the Unix, NT and Kerberos modules implemented in the current. The Unix and NT modules are Operating System dependent and are designed to use the identity of the user extracted from the current Operating System session. The Kerberos module is system independent in operation, but requires system-specific configuration prior to use. Such login modules usually require the user to enter some information as credentials, such as passwords or smart-cards. A variety of input methods have already been provided, including text, GUI and command-line, the latter available primarily for authenticating users on remote containers. The default configuration is such that if the user fails to be correctly authenticated, the system will exit and issue appropriate messages.

Due to authentication, all components (containers and agents) in a JADE platform must be owned by an authenticated user. As an extension of this, the *Permission Service* provides a layer of control over the actions that agents can perform, either permitting or denying them according to stated rules. It is thus possible to selectively grant access to platform services or application resources. This ultimately implies that permissions can be used to influence the structure of relationships between agents interacting within and across JADE platforms. The rules are typically stated in a system files according to standard JAAS policy file syntax [9], extended with a special policy model providing enhancements specifically useful to distributed agent applications. Two types of policy files can be used to grant permissions to agents: (1) The *MainContainer policy file* that specifies platform-wide permissions, e.g. "Agents owned by user Bob can kill agents owned by user Alice". (2) *Container policy files* that specify container-specific permissions, e.g. "Agents owned by user Bob can kill agents owned by user Alice on the local container"). Container policy files can also regulate access to local resources (JVM, file system, network, etc.).

Finally, message privacy and integrity is managed by the *Encryption Service*, which provides reasonable security guarantees when sending a ACL messages between agents on the local, or a foreign, platform. Signatures are used to both ensure the identity of a message originator and the integrity of a message (confidence that data has not been tampered with during transmission). Encryption is used to ensure privacy of the message by protecting message data from eavesdropping (confidence that only the intended receiver will be able to read the clear message). In JADE both signature and encryption always apply to the entire payload of a message in order to protect all the information contained in the slots of the ACL message (content, protocol, ontology, etc.). The security-related information (such as the signature, the algorithm or the key) is placed into the envelope. Users themselves do not need to deal with the actual signature and encryption mechanisms, but just need to request a message to be signed or to check whether a received message has been signed. If some problems occur whilst signing, encrypting, verifying or decrypting a message, the message is discarded and a failure notice is returned to the sender.

4.3 Agent Management and Migration Service

The Agent Management service provides support for managing the life cycle of agents. Each agent owns and controls its thread of execution, and life-cycle transitions can only be initiated by the agent or requested to the AMS (provided that the requestor has the needed permissions). The platform takes care of hiding the object reference of the agent in order to avoid other agents, or other objects of the system, to take control and directly manipulate an agent by calling its public methods. Notice that these two features (i.e. owning the thread and keeping private the object reference) are needed in order to meet the agent autonomy requirement that each platform is requested to guarantee.

In the J2SE and Personal Java environments, JADE supports mobility of code and of execution state so that an agent can stop running on a host, migrate its code and state on a different remote host, and restart its execution from the point it was interrupted (actually, JADE implements a form of *not-so-weak* mobility because the stack and the program counter cannot be saved in Java). This functionality allows distributing computational load at runtime by moving agents to less loaded machines without any impact on the application. In a similar way, agent cloning is support in order to clone agent state and code.

4.4 Replication Service

To keep JADE fully operational even in the event of a failure of the Main-Container, a Main Replication Service was included in the latest versions of the platform. With this service is then possible to start any number of Main Container nodes, which will arrange themselves in a logical ring so that whenever one of them fails, the others will notice and act accordingly. Ordinary containers will be able to connect to the platform through any of the active Main Container nodes; the different copies will evolve together using cross-notification. Without Main Container replication, JADE platform has a star topology, while enabling Main Container replication turns the topology into a ring of stars, as shown in Figure 4.

In the fault-tolerant configuration two or more Main Container nodes are arranged in a ring, and each node is monitoring its neighbour: if the node Main-Container-1 fails, the node Main-Container-2 will notice and inform all the other Main Container nodes, so that a smaller ring can be rebuilt with the surviving nodes.

Peripheral containers can be arbitrarily spread among the available Main Container nodes. Any single peripheral container is connected to exactly one node and in absence of failures it is completely unaware of all the other copies. When a Main Container node fails, there will generally be some orphaned peripheral containers. They will attach themselves to another one among all the Main Container nodes present in the platform.

JADE supports two policies in distributing the Main Container list to peripheral containers. A first option is to enable detection of changes to the list and notify peripheral containers. A second option is to pass the address list to peripheral containers at start-up time, avoiding notification traffic towards peripheral containers when the fixed list of Main Container nodes is known beforehand.

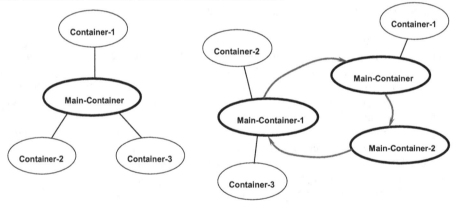

Fig. 4. Star topology (left) and ring of stars topology (right)

4.5 Message-Content Management Service

When an agent A communicates with another agent B, a certain amount of information I is transferred from A to B by means of an ACL message. Inside the ACL message, I is represented as a content expression consistent with a proper content language (e.g. SL) and encoded in a proper format (e.g. string). Both A and B have their own (possibly different) way of internally representing I. Taking into account that the way an agent internally represents a piece information must allow an easy handling of that piece of information, it is quite clear that the representation used in an ACL content expression is not suitable for the inside of an agent. In order to facilitate the creation and handling of messages content, JADE provides support for automatically converting back and forth between the format suitable for content exchange (including String, sequence of bytes, XML and the *Resource Description Framework*, RDF), and the format suitable for content manipulation (i.e. Java objects). This support is integrated with *Protégé* [10], an ontology creation graphical tool that allows also importing/exporting ontology in several formats, including the *Web Ontology Language (OWL)*.

This support for content languages and ontologies automatically performs all the necessary message format marshaling (and unmarshaling) as well as a number of semantic checks to verify that I is a well-formed piece of information, i.e. that it complies with the rules (for instance that the age of Giovanni is actually an integer value) of the ontology by means of which both A and B ascribe a proper meaning to *I*.

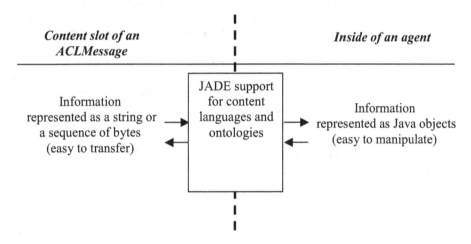

Fig. 5. JADE support for content management.

The conversion and check operations are carried out by a content manager helper object. The content manager provides a convenient interfaces to access the conversion functionality, but actually just delegates the conversion and check operations to an ontology (i.e. an instance of the `Ontology` class included in the `jade.content.onto` package) and a content language codec (i.e. an instance of the `Codec` interface included in the `jade.content.lang` package). More specifically, the ontology validates the information to be converted from the semantic point of view while the codec performs the translation into strings (or sequences of bytes) according to the syntactic rules of the related content language

Notice that JADE is opaque to the underlying inference engine system, if inferences are needed for a specific application, and it allows programmers to reuse their preferred system. It has been already integrated and tested with *Java Expert System Shell (JESS*

[11]) and some Prolog environments; moreover, a separate academic add-on is available, which supports building rational agents [12].

4.6 Persistence Service

Another important aspect that needs to be considered in order to support server-side applications is persistent data management. Nowadays the dominant infrastructure for this is a relational DBMS, with more recent extensions towards a less structured data model (mainly binary data and text).

The persistence-related features were divided into two categories. First, there are system-level features, such as persistently storing agents and whole containers; then, there are application-level features concerning the persistent storage of application-specific entities. In designing JADE Persistence Service, the focus for the API was kept on system-level features, with the rationale of avoiding redundant API wrapping, relying instead directly on some chosen persistence Java API for application-level features.

The chosen persistence engine turned out to be *Hibernate* [13], for a number of reasons among which its plain persistent component model and its powerful object-oriented query language were prominent. Using Hibernate data mapping capabilities, a model of the relevant JADE system-level entities (agents, containers, messages and others) was made. Then, a basic graphical tool was developed to allow easy management of persistent storage and both API-level and ACL-level access was granted to application programmers. The Persistence Service is distributed as an add-on to the main JADE package and is currently being evaluated and tried out by the JADE user community.

4.7 Other services

Several other platform-level services are available and the expandability of the kernel will facilitate several more to be implemented in the future.

For instance, a *Logging Service* is available that exploits the capabilities of the `java.util.logging` package in order to enable management of per-class logging levels and logging handlers (e.g. different file names and file formats). A graphical tool, the `LogManagerAgent`, also allows modifying at run-time the logging configuration of each class, features that is very useful for on-the-site debugging.

Of course, the platform also includes a naming service (ensuring each agent has a unique name) and a yellow pages service that can be distributed across multiple hosts. Federation graphs can be created in order to define structured domains of agent services.

5. JADE for Mobile Networks

Usage of JADE on mobile networks and resource-constrained mobile terminals needs the platform to properly address new non-functional issues, such as the memory and processing power limitations of mobile devices and the characteristics of wireless networks, specifically the commonplace *General Packet Radio Service* (*GPRS*) in terms of bandwidth, latency, intermittent connectivity and IP addresses variability. Inter-container communication cannot be anymore assumed to be stable, persistent, and reliable as connectivity may suddenly drop because of dead spots.

The *Split Container* execution mode faces these limitations by executing only a very small part of the container (called *front-end*) on the mobile terminal. The remaining part (called *back-end*) runs somewhere in the fixed network. As depicted in Figure 6, the front-end provides to agents living on the mobile phone the same APIs as a normal container: that makes the split container execution completely transparent to application agents. Similarly, a back-end behaves for the rest of the platform exactly as a normal container does: that makes the split container execution completely transparent to the rest of the platform. The front-end and the back-end are linked together by means of a permanent connection. The front-end just communicates with the back-end that, instead, is responsible for interacting with the rest of the platform. When the front-end of a split container is launched on a mobile device, it first needs to create its back-end on a host in the fixed network. In order to do that, it requires a normal JADE container to act as a mediator and to serve back-end creation requests. Any JADE container can act as mediator for several split containers, the only limitation being the number of connections that a single host is able to keep opened.

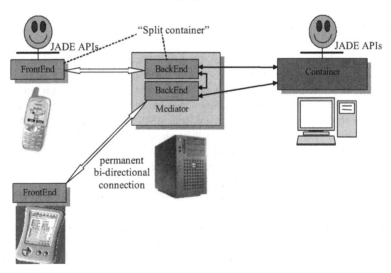

Fig. 6. Split container architecture.

The split container approach provides a number of advantages:

☐   Most of the container functionality (such as hosting the services and registering with the Main container) is delegated to the back-end. As a consequence, the front-end can be extremely lightweight and save resources for applications agents. Using obfuscation techniques, as described in [3], we were able to reduce the JADE footprint down to 43 Kbytes.

☐   The front-end is able to detect a drop down of the connection with the back-end (e.g. because the user entered a dead spot), react, and automatically recover it, as soon as possible.

☐   Both the front-end and the back-end can implement a store and forward mechanism so that any message, that was tried to exchange when the connection was temporarily down, is automatically buffered and delivered as soon as the connection is restored.

☐   The IP address of the device is hidden by the back-end to the rest of the platform. Therefore a change of the device IP address is completely transparent to the applications and to the rest of the platform.

☐   Last but not least, the split container approach allows the platform provider (likely the telecom operator) to keep control on the applications and the services provided over the platform. In fact, though completely peer-to-peer from a logical point of view, the communication between two agents on mobile devices always passes through the back-ends of the split containers. By plugging ad hoc services in the back-ends, the operator is in fact able to implement e.g. application-specific event-based logging, billing, priority assignment mechanisms based on the user subscription.

5.1 The PDP context manager module

Multi-agent applications need to face the peer discovery problem, i.e. how a peer becomes aware of other peers to communicate with. Typically, this is solved by means of some sort of white pages and yellow pages services that require each peer to register and successively search for other peers. Mobile devices, however, are intrinsically identified by their user phone number, i.e. the MSISDN (Mobile Station International ISDN Number). For this reason, all mobile applications involving people whose phone numbers are known a-priori (e.g. applications involving a group of people) should not require any peer discovery mechanism: a peer acting on behalf of a user should be addressable by simply specifying the phone number of that user.

JADE supports this MSISDN-based identification by means of the PDP (Packet Data Protocol) context manager module. When a mobile phone attaches to the GPRS network, it communicates with the operator's SGSN (Serving GPRS Support Node) to request the creation of a PDP context. This is a logical association between the mobile phone and the network, including aspects such as routing, QoS and billing. The mobile phone request is passed to the GGSN (Gateway GPRS Support Node) to verify the GPRS account and assign an IP address to a new PDP Context. In general, the authentication is performed by using a RADIUS server connected to the GGSN. The

JADE PDP context manager is a software module able to interact with the RADIUS Server. When a back-end creation is requested, the JADE container, which is acting as mediator, interrogates this module and gets back the MSISDN corresponding to the IP address the request comes from. In this way, JADE can use the device MSISDN to identify the starting split container and possibly force any agent starting on that container to comply with proper name space conventions based on the MSISDN. For example, an agent implementing a chat application may be named *<device msisdn>-chat* so that its name is known a priori by other chat agents on other devices. The PDP context manager module complies with a simple and well defined interface so that the actual implementation can be modified or even replaced depending on the operator network topology.

Besides offering an intrinsic peer identification mechanism, the integration with the RADIUS Server also allows exploiting the GPRS authentication to authenticate JADE nodes. The advantage of this is threefold:

☐   It is secure enough from the operator point of view since it relies on its standard authentication mechanism.

☐   It allows the operator to easily manage access control lists of users/phone-number authorized to join the platform.

☐   It does not require users to enter additional username and password to launch JADE based applications on their mobile devices.

6. JADE Application Domains

One of the main goals in developing a middleware is to maintain a high degree of openness and flexibility, making it applicable in as many different application domains as possible. We propose hereafter a first general categorization with no scientific completeness but just to provide a general understanding of the effectiveness of JADE. The highest payoff of adopting Agent Technology is expected in those cases where an interaction between numerous elements is required, and where an autonomous and dynamic adaptation to complex relations is needed.

6.1 Mobile applications

The focus here is supporting users on the move with a "personal agent" that helps its owner. Its goal is to facilitate the search and discovery of information through the interaction with other peers, being both other people and "service providers". In general, JADE agents are extremely suited to act in the context of Mobile PIM – Personal Information Management: their ability of autonomous and proactive acting and seamless communications allows conceiving applications for everyday life organization, like meeting organizer, info search or services negotiation.

Several examples illustrate the strengths of JADE peers acting as assistants for travelers, being private tourists or mobile workers. Other applications have been developed in the mobile work or sales support systems, in which agent duties are task and information sharing and exchange. In the entertainment field, JADE middleware can either be the base for multiparty gaming applications, in which a real interaction between players is offered, or can be the building block for an enhanced kind of mobile community where peer-to-peer communication allows richer relationships amongst members.

BTexact uses the JADE platform, and the LEAP add-on for mobile terminals, for its application supporting the coordination and the activities of a mobile workforce, including the distributed scheduling of jobs, job management on the fly, travel and knowledge management, and location-based coordination [14]. *Telecom Italia LAB* uses JADE for developing new mobile VAS (Value Added Services) for nomadic micro-communities over Java-enabled mobile phones.

6.2 Internet applications

In the Internet domain several application concepts based on agent technology have been proposed during the years, as the main concept has been to beneficiate from the increased connectivity, in terms of bandwidth and relations amongst people.

JADE-based systems allow end users to deal with the complexity and number of opportunities, and to exploit the possibility to seamlessly access remote resources and services. Key elements in JADE-based applications designing are direct communication support, smart information retrieval capabilities and negotiation techniques. Starting from these basic principles, various sectors have been considered such as e-learning or e-healthcare, and in general all the contexts of e-commerce/e-trading have been tackled. Moreover many of the considerations put forward in the mobile environment can been easily extended to a fixed consumption, allowing an integrated organisation of the personal and working life between PC and mobile devices. Lastly, the entertainment sector has been analysed starting from the obvious consideration on community services, multiparty gaming and content sharing applications.

Whitestein Technologies AG uses the JADE platform in the health care field, in collaboration with *Swisstransplant*, the Swiss National Transplant Coordination centre for organ transplants, for an agent-based system for decision-making support in organ transplant centers. By combining agent technology, constraint satisfaction techniques and JADE capabilities, Whitestein implemented the *Organ Transplant Management (OTM)* solution [15].

6.3 Corporate applications

The intelligent agents approach is an evident choice for business applications striving to enhance company productivity and efficiency. The point is easing collaboration and cooperation between systems and people in order to achieve better results. Many different examples of the usage of agent technology have been provided already in order to support company processes: when it comes the time to share information or coordinate tasks the deployment of JADE-based system becomes very effective and useful.

Instances have been proposed in "soft contexts", such as knowledge management and personnel administration or in general for the support to decision making processes. Other proposals have come in "harder" environments, including companies core processes, like logistic or production: valuable demonstrations concern systems for factory control, exploiting JADE capabilities in optimising tasks and coordinating resources. Interestingly enough, some JADE applications exceed even company boundaries supporting activities amongst different businesses: the ability of agents in the negotiation and information retrieval amongst services and resource providers leads to the construction of JADE-based supply-chain or e-procurement products.

6.4 Machine-to-Machine applications

In those cases where communication peers are machines instead of humans, JADE features can be exploited at its best. Autonomy and proactivity of agents play a crucial role in the management of complex systems: when the number of elements and the complexity of the relations raise, the opportunity of a distributed control significantly simplifies system operations.

Complex algorithms and heavy elaborations, typically concentrated in a single central point can be spread among agents, increasing overall efficiency and system performance and reducing the risks connected with this concentration, thus increasing system fault tolerance and scalability.

Classical examples in this context are automatic control or traffic management systems, but the helpfulness of JADE approach can go down in more depth: several studies are under way in order to extend P2P agents paradigm to network management, with the concept of peers mapping onto network equipments and interacting amongst them for resources optimizations and system control.

Finally it's interesting to cite the extensive application of agent models for simulation uses. The concept of numerous elements acting independently but together in the environment in which they are part of, easily applies to several contexts, from different science sectors (for instance biology, ecology and natural science in general) to social and economic studies.

Rockwell Automation implemented the *Manufacturing Agent Simulation Tool* (*MAST*) [16] for the manufacturing control sector. The tool shows agents for basic material-handling components (e.g. a manufacturing cell, a conveyor belt, an AGV, etc.) capable of mutual collaboration on the product transportation via the exchange of messages. Agents are able to deal at run-time with dynamic changes and exceptional cases, such as failure detection and recovery, change of the layout of the factory's shop floor, addition/removal of components or their interconnections.

6.5 JADE Community

The evolution strategy of the JADE project, since its beginning, is based on a collaborative intent aimed at focusing the interest of an ever-growing community of users and developers. This community revolves around two focal points: the open source project and the JADE Governing Board.

JADE is, in fact, distributed open source under the LGPL license. The aim of this license is to facilitate the creation of an open and effective platform with the help of a user community, while allowing everybody to base the business upon the applications. At the time of writing, more than 60,000 official downloads and several contributions from some tens of different companies and academic institutions have been counted, including complete subsystems (the so-called *JADE add-ons*), but much more are welcome and expected.

The JADE Governing Board [1] is a not-for-profit agreement between a set of companies, all sharing the intent and the effort of promoting the evolution of this software tool and its adoption by the mobile telco industry as a java-based de-facto standard middleware for agent-based applications. The JADE Board governs and implements the evolution of the software deciding which features should be added next. At the time of writing, the Board is composed of 5 members: *TILAB*, *Motorola*, *Whitestein Technologies AG*, *Profactor GmbH*, *France Telecom*. Each member of the JADE Board has the advantage of contributing and voting about priorities, technical and strategic decisions about the evolution of the JADE Project. Board members shall agree with the governing rules and commit to a minimal amount of resources for development and promotion of JADE. The Board is open to all companies and organizations with a concrete business interest in JADE and that commit to its development and promotion.

7. Conclusions and Future Roadmap

The paper presented the architecture of the JADE platform with particular details on the new kernel, realized as a set of distributed coordinated filters. This new kernel enables composition of platform-level services and great extensibility and adaptivity to the requirements of the deployment environment. The specific case of the mobile networks and terminals has been presented by showing how the split container execution mode allows meeting the peculiar requirements of that deployment environment and the PDP context manager module has been described, that enables support for MSISDN-based identification. As any healthy software infrastructure, JADE is still evolving while trying to balance the need for change with the requirement to protect its users from backward-incompatible modifications.

In order to manage the ever-increasing size and evolution of the project, a Governing Board was created as a not-for-profit agreement between companies that commit to the development and promotion of the platform. At the time of writing, the four main goals/directions of the project are the followings. The first goal is to consolidate the software platform by increasing the strength of features such as scalability, performance, robustness, security, integration with Web Services and network apparatuses; two new releases per year are expected to be distributed. The second goal is to develop new functionalities and integrate them into the middleware. In particular, the Board is already developing an intelligent communication layer based upon a semantics interpreter able to exploit the formal semantics of the FIPA Agent Communication Language. New developments are also planned on the collaboration and organization layers for improving the organization view of the multi-agent system. The third important goal is to further increase the level of participation and commitment of the Open Source Community. The Web-based infrastructure of the project will be extended with a sourceforge-like system what will enable each member of the community to submit a workplan for a new project and, if approved by the Board, have its own working space, including the CVS repository, the mailing list, the bug-tracking, the forum, etc. Finally, the fourth goal is to broaden the scope and the size of the JADE Board by welcoming new members and new proposals.

References

[1]   The JADE Project Home Page. Available at http://jade.tilab.com
[2]   The Foundation for Intelligent Physical Agents. Available at http://www.fipa.org
[3]   M. Berger et.al.. *Porting Distributed Agent-Middleware to Small Mobile Devices*. Workshop on Ubiquitous Agents, AAMAS2002, Bologna, July 2002
[4]   D. Cowan, M. Griss, R. Kessler, B. Remick, B. Burg. A Robust Environment for Agent Deployment, *AAMAS 2002 - Workshop on Challenges in Open Agent Environments*, Bologna, Italy, July 2002
[5]   Aspect-Oriented Software Development. Available at http://aosd.net
[6]   G. Kiczales, E. Hilsdale, J. Hugunin, M. Kersten, J. Palm, W. G. Griswold, "An Overview of AspectJ", In *Proc. ECOOP 2001*, Budapest, pp. 327-353, June 2001.
[7]   M. Aksit, K. Wakita, J. Bosch, L. Bergmans, A. Yonezawa. "Abstracting Object Interactions Using Composition Filters". Proceedings of the *ECOOP 1993 Workshop on Object-Based Distributed Programming*, pp. 152-184, Springer-Verlag.
[8]   G. Vitaglione, E. Cortese, F. Quarta, P. Vrba. Scalability and Performance of the JADE Message Transport System. Analysis of suitability for Holonic Manufacturing Systems. *EXP - In Search of Innovation (Special Issue on JADE)*, Vol 3, Nr. 3, Telecom Italia Lab, Turin, Italy, September 2003, pp. 52-65.
[9]   Java Authentication and Authorization Service (JAAS),http://java.sun.com/products /jaas
[10]   Protégé, available at http://protege.stanford.edu
[11]   Jess, the Expert System Shell for the Java Platform. Available at http://herzberg.ca.sandia.gov/jess
[12]   A. Pokahr, L. Braubach, W. Lamersdorf. Jadex: Implementing a BDI-Infrastructure for JADE Agents. *EXP - In Search of Innovation (Special Issue on JADE)*, Vol 3, Nr. 3, Telecom Italia Lab, Turin, Italy, September 2003, pp. 76-85.
[13]   The Hibernate Project Home Page. Available at http://www.hibernate.org
[14]   The mPower Project Home Page. Available at http://research.btexact.com/islab/IBSRpublic/MPower.html
[15]   M. Calisti, P. Funk, S. Biellman, T. Bugnon. A Multi-Agent System for Organ Transplant Management. Available at http://www.whitestein.com/resources/papers/wssat03-organtrans.pdf
[16]   P. Vrba, MAST: Manufacturing Agent Simulation Tool, *EXP - In Search of Innovation (Special Issue on JADE)*, Vol 3, Nr. 3, Telecom Italia Lab, Turin, Italy, September 2003.

Fabio Bellifemine, Giovanni Cairem and Giosuè Vitaglione
Telecom Italia LAB
Service Platforms
Via G. Reiss Romoli 274
10148 Turin
Italy
e-mail: {fabio.bellifemine, iovanni.caire, iosue.vitaglione}@tilab.com

Giovanni Rimassa and Dominic Greenwood
Whitestein Technologies AG
Pestalozzistrasse 24
8032 Zürich
Switzerland
e-mail: {gri, dgr}@whitestein.com

Information about Software

Software is available on the Internet as
- ( )   prototype version
- (X) full fledged software (under LGPL license), version no: 3.3
- (X) full fledged software (under commercial license), version no: 3.3
- ( )   Demo/trial version
- ( )   not (yet) available

Internet address: http://jade.tilab.com
Description of software: JADE is a middleware for the development of distributed multi-agent applications. It is available both for J2SE and J2ME Java platform. Download address: http://jade.tilab.com

Contact person for question about the software:
Name: Fabio Bellifemine
email: jade-board@avalon.cselt.it

$\mathcal{A}$-globe: Agent Development Platform with Inaccessibility and Mobility Support

David Šišlák, Martin Rehák, Michal Pěchouček,
Milan Rollo and Dušan Pavlíček

Abstract. At present several Java-based multi-agent platforms from different developers are available, but none of them fully supports agent mobility and communication inaccessibility simulation. They are thus unsuitable for experiments with large scale real-world simulation. In this chapter we describe architecture of $\mathcal{A}$-**globe**, fast, scalable and lightweight agent development platform with environmental simulation and mobility support. Beside the functions common to most agent platforms it provides a position-based messaging service, so it can be used for experiments with extensive environment simulation and communication inaccessibility. Simple benchmarks that compare the $\mathcal{A}$-**globe** performance against other available agent platforms are also included.

1. Introduction

In this chapter we present $\mathcal{A}$-**globe** [2], an agent platform designed for fast prototyping and application development of multi-agent systems. $\mathcal{A}$-**globe** provides the same level of services as JADE, COUGAAR, FIPA-OS, JACK (see Section 3 for comparisons and references). Besides presentation of the system itself, we will describe several application scenarios. The main focus of the $\mathcal{A}$-**globe** developers has been given to the following applications domains:

- **simulation**, especially simulation of the multi-agent environment and collective behavior of large communities
- **scalability**, high-number of fully fledged and fully autonomous agents, that are loosely coupled with *lightweight infrastructure*
- **agent migration** persistence and code and state migration within the communication network as much as physical reallocation of the computational host and thus modelling of partial and non-permanent *communication inaccessibility*[13].

The platform provides functions for residing agents, such as communication infrastructure, store, directory services, migration function, deploy service, etc. Communication in $\mathcal{A}$-globe is very fast and the platform is relatively lightweight.

$\mathcal{A}$-globe platform is FIPA [6] compliant on the ACL level while it does not support the FIPA specification for inter-platform communication, as the addressing and transport-level message encoding were simplified. Interoperability is not necessary for development of the closed systems, where no communication outside these systems is required. This is the case of e.g. agent-based simulations. For large scale scenarios the interoperability also brings problems with system performance where memory requirements, communication speed may become the bottleneck of an efficient collective operation.

$\mathcal{A}$-globe is suitable for real-world simulations including both static and mobile units (e.g. logistics, ad-hoc networking simulation), where the core platform is extended by a set of services provided by Geographical Information System (GIS) and Environment Simulator (ES) agent. The ES agent simulates dynamics (physical location, movement in time and others parameters) of each unit.

In this chapter you will learn about the architecture and more technical details about the $\mathcal{A}$-globe multi-agent platform (see Section 2), the comparison with different available platforms will be provided (see Section 3). The last section of this chapter will be devoted to simulation and two implemented simulation scenarios (see Section 4).

2. System Architecture

The system integrates one or more agent platforms. The $\mathcal{A}$-globe design is shown in Figure 1. Its operation is based on several components:

- **agent platform** – provides basic components for running one or more agent containers, i.e. container manager and message transport layer (section 2.1);
- **agent container** – skeleton entity of $\mathcal{A}$-globe, ensures basic functions, communication infrastructure and storage for agents (section 2.2);
- **services** – provide some common functions for all agents in one container;
- **environment simulator (ES) agents** – simulates the real-world environment and controls visibility among other agent containers (section 4.1);
- **agents** – represent basic functional entities in a specific simulation scenario.

Simulation scenario is defined by a set of actors represented by agents residing in the agent containers. All agent containers are connected together to one system by the GIS services. Beside the simulation of dynamics the ES agent can also control communication accessibility among all agent containers. The GIS service applies accessibility restrictions in the message transport layer of the agent container.

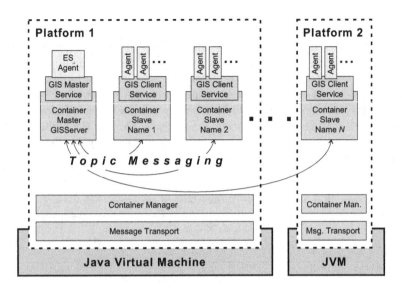

FIGURE 1. System Architecture Structure

2.1. Agent Platform

The main design goals were to develop the platform as lightweight as possible and to make it easily portable to different operating systems and devices (like PDA). The platform is implemented as an application running on Java Virtual Machine (JVM 2 edition 5.0 or higher is required). Several platforms can run simultaneously (maximum 1000) on one computer, each in its own JVM instance. When a new agent container is started, we can explicitly specify in which platform it will be created and run.

The platform ensures the functionality of the rest of the system using two main components:

- **Container Manager.** One or more agent containers can run within single agent platform. Container Manager takes care of starting, execution and finishing of these containers. Containers are mutually independent except for the shared part of the message transport layer. Usage of single agent platform for several containers running on one computer machine is beneficial because it rapidly decreases system resources requirements (use of single JVM), e.g. memory, processor time, etc.
- **Message Transport.** The platform-level *message transport* component ensures an efficient exchange of messages between two agent containers running in a single agent platform (single JVM).

2.2. Agent Container

The agent container hosts two types of entities that are able to send and receive messages: agents and services. Agents do not run as stand-alone applications. Instead, they are executed inside the agent containers, each agent in its own separate thread. The schema of general agent container structure is shown in Figure 2. Container provides the agents and services with several low level functions (message transport, agent management, service management). Most of the higher level container functionality (agent deployment, migration, directory facilitator, etc.) is provided as standard container services.

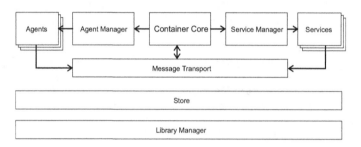

FIGURE 2. The Agent Container Structure

The agent container components are:

- **Container Core.** The Container Core starts up and shuts down all container components.
- **Store.** The purpose of *Store* is to provide permanent storage through interface which shields its users from the operating system's filesystem. It is used by all container components, agents and services. Each entity in the agent container (agent, service, container components) is assigned its own virtual storage, which is unaffected by the others. Whenever an agent migrates, its store content is compressed and sent to the new location.
- **Library Manager.** The Library Manager manages the libraries installed in the container and monitors which agents/services use which library.
- **Message Transport.** The Message Transport is responsible for sending and receiving messages from and to the container.
- **Agent Manager.** The Agent Manager takes care of creation, execution and removal of agents on the container. It creates agents, re-creates them after platform restart, routes the incoming messages to the agents, packs the agents for migration and removes agent's traces when it migrates out of the platform or dies.
- **Service Manager.** The Service Manager takes care of starting and stopping the services present in the agent container and their interfacing to other container components. The user can start, stop and inspect the services using a GUI. There are two types of services – user services and system services.

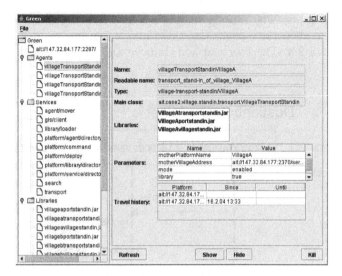

FIGURE 3. Container GUI: Agent Information

The system services are automatically started by the container and form a part of the container infrastructure (agent mover, library deployer, directory services etc.). The system services cannot be removed. The user services can be started by the user or any agent/service. The user services can be either permanent (started during every container startup) or temporary (started and stopped by an agent). In contrast to agents the services are not able to migrate to other containers.

The *container name* must be unique inside one system built from several containers. This name is also used for determination of the specific store subdirectory for the agent container and is registered with the *Environment Simulator Agent*.

2.2.1. Container GUI. The *agent container* has a graphic user interface (GUI), which gives the user an easy way to inspect container state and to install or remove its components (agents, services and libraries). The GUI could be shown or hidden both locally and remotely (by message). The GUI screen shot is shown in figure 3.

The window has two parts. The tree on the left side shows names of agents, services and libraries present on the container. The right side shows detailed information about the object selected in the tree. Moreover, the agents and services are allowed to create their own GUI without any restrictions.

2.2.2. Library Manager. The *Library Manager* is responsible for the libraries installed in the agent container and monitors the use of these libraries by agents and services. Descriptor of each agent or service specifies which libraries the agent/service requires. The Library Manager is also responsible for automatic library migration when the agent using this library migrates, as described in the dedicated section 2.3. The user can add, remove and inspect libraries using the container GUI.

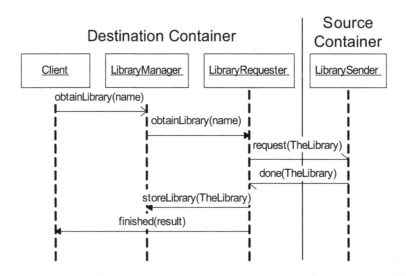

FIGURE 4. Library Deployment Sequence Diagram

Every new loaded library in 𝒜-**globe** container internally uses the library name constructed from the original library name and SHA-1 hash [1] of the library content. The loaded library is automatically labelled with unique version label constructed as `ver{ver_num_in_the_container}@{container_name}`. This way, two different libraries with same file name can be used in parallel within a single 𝒜-**globe** platform. The library can be removed before a class loader opens it. After opening, it can not be removed from the runtime environment. It can be only removed at 𝒜-**globe** restart.

Class loader is defined for each agent and service. If an agent/service doesn't use any special library, it uses a bootstrap class loader. The bootstrap class loader locates classes only in the name space defined in the path specified by the starting `CLASSPATH` parameter or manifest `CLASSPATH` parameter in the JAR library used by Java runtime. If an agent/service uses specific libraries, it has to define its own class loader which tries to load classes in specified libraries. However, even the agent specific class loader always prefers classes defined by the bootstrap class loader. Therefore, default classes can not be "overridden" - it has no sense to define own `java.lang.String` class because it will never be actually loaded. In 𝒜-**globe**, each agent (service) class loader defines agent/service class resolving *name space*. The migration process and the message transport layer always use respective *name space*.

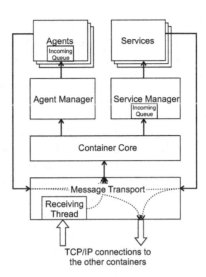

FIGURE 5. Message Flow

Therefore, several agents with different versions of the same main class can run in a single agent container.

2.2.3. Message Transport. The *Message Transport* is responsible for sending and receiving messages. Shared TCP/IP connection for message sending is created between every two agent containers hosted on different agent platforms when the first message is exchanged between them. Messages between two agent containers running in the same agent platform are passed via the platform-level *message transport* component. The message flow inside the container is shown in figure 5.

The message structure respects FIPA-ACL [7]. Messages are encoded either in XML or Byte64 format. Message content can be in XML format or String. The structure of each message content in XML format is described by Document Type Definition (DTD). For coding and decoding XML messages the Java APIs for XML Binding (JAXB) [10] package is used. For transport, all binary data (e.g. libraries, serialized agents, etc.) is encoded using the open source Base64 coding and decoding routines.

The *message transport* layer takes care that all message are serialized (marshaled) and deserialized (unmarshaled) in the appropriate class name space depending on the sender and receiver agent/service's class loader.

Agent may receive messages without using conversation discrimination (all messages incoming to this agent are processed in one method), otherwise it must use the *conversation manager* with tasks.

2.2.4. Conversation Manager and Tasks. Usually, an agent deals with multiple jobs simultaneously. To simplify the development of such agents, $\mathcal{A}$-globe offers *tasks*. A task is able to send and receive messages and to interact with other tasks.

The Conversation Manager takes care of every message received by the agent to be routed to the proper task. The decision, to which `Task` a message should be routed, depends on the massage `ConversationID`. The `ConversationID` should be viewed as a 'reference number'.

2.2.5. Agents. The agents are autonomous entities with a unique name and an ability to migrate. There is a separate thread created for each agent. A wrapper running in the thread executes the agent body. Whenever an agent enters an error state or finishes its operation, the control is passed back to the wrapper, which handles the situation. The return value of the agent state is used to determine agent's termination type (die, migrate, suspend). Therefore, potential agent failures are not propagated to the rest of the agent container. Agents could be deployed to remote containers.

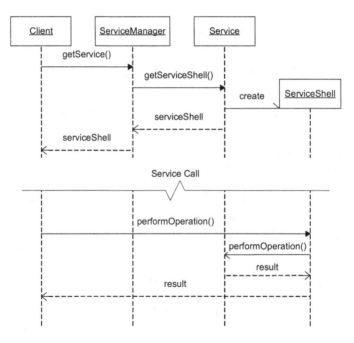

FIGURE 6. Service Shell Operation

2.2.6. Services. The services are bound to a particular container by their identifier. The same service may be present at several containers and can be also deployed to remote containers. Services handle the requests coming in two forms - as messages or local interface calls.

The agents (and services or container components) have two ways to communicate with a service. Either via normal messages or by using the *service shell*. The service shell is a special proxy object that interfaces service functions to a client. The UML sequence diagram of service shell creation and use is shown in Figure 6.

The advantage of the service shell is an easy agent migration (for migration description see section 2.3): while the service itself is not serializable, the service shell is. When an agent migrates, the shell serializes itself with the information what service name it was connected to. When the agent moves to the new location, the shell reconnects to the same service at the new location. When a service is shut down, it notifies it's shells so that they refuse subsequent service calls.

There are several common services described in the table 1. These services are automatically started by the agent container and provide common functions for all agents.

SERVICE NAME	DESCRIPTION
`container/command`	Service through which the container core remotely receives commands (show/hide GUI, shutdown)
`container/directory`	It provides extended white pages and directory pages services. It supports inaccessible environment and uses visibility updates provided by ES Visibility servers. The service is automatically started on every client container.
`container/library/directory`	Provides searching of library matching some search criteria
`container/deploy`	Service responsible for starting an agent from agent info record
`gis/master`	Master side of Environment Simulator service
`gis/client`	Client side of Environment Simulator service

TABLE 1. System services description

2.2.7. Agent/Service Naming and Addressing. The agent name is globally unique and is normally generated by the platform during agent creation. The service name is unique only within one agent container (services cannot migrate) and is specified by the service creator. The address has the following syntax:

aglobe://platform_ip:port/[agent|service]/name.

2.3. Agent Migration and Cloning Procedure

In order to successfully migrate, the agent has to support serialization. The *Library Manager* takes care that all necessary libraries are transferred with the agent code. The migration sequence is shown in Figure 7.

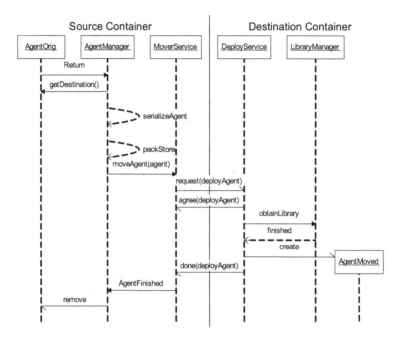

FIGURE 7. Agent Migration

All exceptions that might occur during the process are properly handled and the communication is secured by timeouts. If the migration cannot be finished for any reason, the agent is re-created in its original container.

If the **done** message is successfully sent by the agent destination container but never received by the source container, two copies of the agent emerge. If the **done** message is received by the source container, but the agent creation fails at the destination container, the agent is lost. These events can never be fully eliminated due to the possible communication inaccessibility, but maximum caution was given to minimize their probability.

When the migrating agent uses external libraries, the library manager service (see Section 2.2.2) moves the necessary libraries not available on the new container on behalf of the migrating agent. The migration process makes use of the Java programming language features - serialization and externalization. Whenever an agent migrates or a new agent(service) is deployed, the Library Manager checks which libraries (including the library version) are missing on the container and obtains them from the source container. The inter-platform functionality of the Library Manager is realized though the service **library/loader** (this service is present on every agent container). Library deployment sequence diagram is shown in Figure 4.

Agent cloning is analogous to the agent migration. The procedure differs only in two points - the clone created on the remote can have a different name, specified by the agent and the original agent is not removed at the end of the operation.

2.4. Sniffer Agent

The Sniffer Agent is an on-line tool for monitoring all messages and their transmission status (delivered or not-reachable target). This tool helps find and resolve communication problems in the system during the development phase.

The sniffer can be started only on an agent container where *gis/master* service is running. After the sniffer starts, all messages between agents and services inside any container or among two agent containers are monitored. Messages can be filtered by the sender or receiver of the message. All messages matching the user-defined criteria are shown in the sniffer GUI, as shown in Figure 8. The message transmission status is visualized by the type of line. The color of the message corresponds to the message performative.

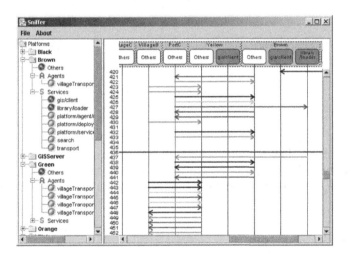

FIGURE 8. The sniffer

2.5. Communication Analyzer

The sniffer agent provides a detailed overview of the communication between agents. However, the amount of details provided by the sniffer, combined with the column alignment of agents makes the global view of the interactions in the community difficult to grasp. Quite often, we prefer to clearly see the intensity of interactions between agents, rather than the details of individual communications. This is exactly the service provided by the *communication analyzer*, as shown in Figure 9. Communication Analyzer presents selected agents, filtered by a regular expression, in a circle. Messages exchanged between agents influence the color and the width of the links between communicating agents. In order to keep the image updated, old messages fade away progressively and only the recent ones are visible. Such visualization tool is important especially in situations with limited accessibility, where the fragmentation of the community can be readily perceived. For example in ACROSS scenario (see paragraph 4.2), we can observe the average number of agents participating in auctions or the lack of communication with agents that are not considered to be trustful by others.

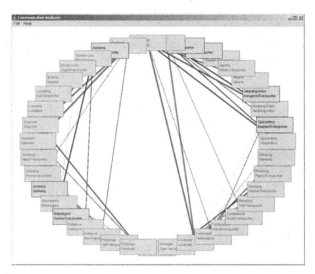

FIGURE 9. The Communication Analyzer user interface. Note that two disjoint parts of the agent system can be clearly observed, indicating possible communication failure.

3. Platform comparison

This section presents the results of comparison of available JAVA-based agent development frameworks evaluated by an industry expert Pavel Vrba from Rockwell Automation Research Center in Prague [21], which were carried out in a cooperation with the Gerstner Laboratory.

    These benchmarks were focused especially on the platform performance which is a crucial property in many applications. Detailed description of the particular features is beyond the scope of this chapter. Firstly, the particular benchmark criteria, which the agent platform should provide are identified (e.g. small memory footprint and message sending speed). These benchmarks were carried out for the following agent platforms[1] - JADE [9, 3], FIPA-OS [17], ZEUS [11], JACK [8] and

---

[1]GRASSHOPPER's licence does not allow to use it for benchmarking and other comparison activities.

A-globe [2]. Shall be noted that the platforms feature various special capabilities that are out of scope of the comparison (e.g. BDI capability in JACK). These features can have an impact on the investigated performance measures.

JAVA-based Agent Development Toolkits/Platforms - Benchmark Results						
April 2004, Rockwell Automation in Prague						
PIII, 600MHz, 256MB	Message sending - average roundtrip time (RTT)					
Agent Platform	agents: 1 pair messages: 1.000 x ⇆		agents: 10 pairs messages: 100 x ⇆		agents: 100 pairs messages: 10 x ⇆	
	serial [ms]	parallel [s]	serial [ms]	parallel [s]	serial [ms]	parallel [s]
JADE v3.1	0,8	0,36	7,5	0,19	76,3	0,49
JADE v3.1 1 host, 2 JVM, RMI	10,3	4,92	111,9	6,35	1 190,5	7,14
JADE v3.1 2 hosts, RMI	5,79	3,30	68,8	3,71	770,3	2,48
FIPA-OS v2.1.0	28,6	14,30	607,1	30,52	2 533,9	19,50
FIPA-OS v2.1.0 1 host, 2 JVM, RMI	20,3	39,51	205,2	12,50	✗	✗
FIPA-OS v2.1.0 2 hosts, RMI	12,2	5,14	96,2	5,36	✗	✗
ZEUS v1.04	101,0	50,67	224,8	13,28	✗	✗
ZEUS v1.04 1 host, 2 JVM, ?	101,7	51,80	227,9	✗	✗	✗
ZEUS v1.04 2 hosts, TCP/IP	101,1	50,35	107,6	8,75	✗	✗
JACK v3.51	2,1	1,33	21,7	1,60	221,9	1,60
JACK v3.51 1 host, 2 JVM, UDP	3,7	2,64	31,4	3,65	185,2	2,24
JACK v3.51 2 hosts, UDP	2,5	1,46	17,6	1,28	165,0	1,28
AGlobe v1.0	0,3	0,10	2,8	0,04	28,4	0,09
AGlobe v1.0 1 host, 2 JVM, TCP/IP	2,4	0,33	24,6	0,88	242,7	0,98
AGlobe v1.0 2 hosts, TCP/IP	2,2	0,33	13,9	0,31	96,5	0,44

TABLE 2. Message delivery time results for selected agent platforms

3.1. Message Speed Benchmarks

The agent platform runtime, carrying out interactions, should be fast enough to ensure reasonable message delivery times. The selected platforms have been put through a series of tests where the message delivery times have been observed under different conditions.

In each test, the so called *average roundtrip time* (avgRTT) is measured. This is the time period needed for a pair of agents (let's say A and B) to send a message from A to B and get reply from B to A. The roundtrip time is computed by the agent A when a reply from B is received as a difference between the receive time and the send time. This message exchange was repeated several times (depending on the type of experiment) and the results were computed as an average from all the trials.

The overall benchmark results are presented in the Table 2. A more transparent representation of these results in the form of bar charts is depicted in Figure 10.

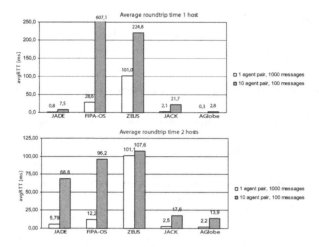

FIGURE 10. Message delivery time - serial test results

Three different numbers of agent pairs have been considered: 1 agent pair (A-B) with 1000 messages exchanged, 10 agent pairs with 100 messages exchanged within each pair and 100 agent pairs with 10 messages per pair. Moreover, for each of these configurations two different ways of executing the tests are applied.

In the *serial* test, the A agent from each pair sends one message to its B counterpart and when a reply is received, the roundtrip time for this trial is computed. It is repeated in the same manner N-times (N is 1000/100/10 according to the number of agents). The *parallel* test differs in such a way that the A agent from each pair sends all N messages to B at once and then waits until all N replies from B are received.

Different protocols used by agent platforms for the inter-platform communication are mentioned: Java RMI (Remote Method Invocation) for JADE and FIPA-OS, TCP/IP for ZEUS and $\mathcal{A}$-**globe** and UDP for JACK. Some of the tests, especially in the case of 100 agents, were not successfully completed mainly because of communication errors or errors connected with the creation of agents. These cases are marked by a special symbol.

3.2. Memory requirements benchmark

This issue is mainly interesting for deploying agents on small devices like mobile phones or personal digital assistants (PDAs) which can have only a few megabytes of memory available. This issue is also important for running thousands of agents on one computer at the same time. Approximate memory requirements per agent can be seen in Figure 11.

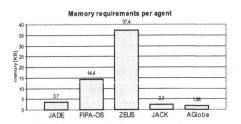

FIGURE 11. Approximate memory requirements per agent

4. Simulation

$\mathcal{A}$-**globe** platform is primarily aimed at large scale, real world simulations with fully fledged agents. To support this goal, it includes a special infrastructure for environmental simulation. We will now describe this infrastructure, together with two scenarios implemented using the platform, where we emphasize the concepts used in the simulation of two very different environments for a multi-agent system.

4.1. Simulation support in $\mathcal{A}$-globe

While designing the simulations in $\mathcal{A}$-**globe** platform, we use agents not only to play roles in the simulated world - *actor agents* but we also use them to implement the world where the actor agents act. The agents used for the world simulation are all located in a dedicated master container and are called *Environment Simulation* agents.

These agents only rarely use messages to communicate with actor agents. Instead, they communicate via *topic messaging* - container-to-container messaging specifically reserved for environmental simulation, as shown in Figure 12.

Topic messaging is managed by GIS Service - a special service that is a part of the $\mathcal{A}$-**globe** platform and can be started in a container by specifying an appropriate startup parameter. This parameter value determines whether the container is a *master*, server side container or a *client* - normal container with actor agents.

Client agents subscribe with GIS client service to receive various topics. If such a topic is received by the container, it is distributed to all subscribed agents. Note that all agents in the container receive the same value - this is appropriate in our opinion, as the environment perception shall be identical for all collocated agents. In addition, the agents who wish to act on the environment can submit topics to the GIS service. These topics are then sent to all ES agents in the master container subscribed to receive the topic.

In the nominal configuration, each ES agent manages an internal model of the environment, updates the model with the actions received from actors and submits the environment status to actors in their containers. Each ES agent can handle one or more topics and one topic can be handled by more then one agent.

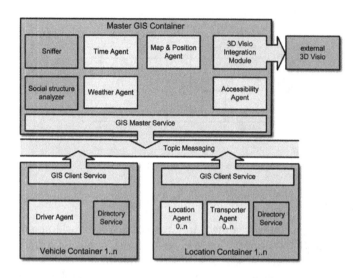

FIGURE 12. Topic messaging in $\mathcal{A}$-**globe**

Specialized ES agents can also subscribe to receive local topics from other ES agents. Typically, many specialized ES agents can receive position information from position agent and use this data to submit appropriate localized environment information to agents.

This approach scales fairly well with the community size. However, when the environment becomes more complex, it is often not economic to handle the environment simulation in the ES agents as the interactions become too cumbersome and internal models too complicated. In this case, the server can use an appropriate GIS server with an ES agent wrapper for simulation purposes. The ES agent(s) is then responsible only for obtaining the information from the appropriate layers of the GIS server and submitting them to corresponding topics. The use of the GIS server is not without a cost - the integration with wrapper agent is rarely flawless and shall be avoided for simple environments.

ES agent can be responsible for nearly any simulation layer, depending on the wishes of the developers. However, a privileged place between ES agents is occupied by *accessibility agents*, who control the existence of communication links between containers holding the actors. Their prominence is caused by the fact that the platform messaging layer is integrated with these agents through predefined topics and any attempt to send a message to an agent in an inaccessible container is automatically unsuccessful.

There are several ES agents implemented and some of them are provided as a part of the $\mathcal{A}$-**globe** platform package for optional use:

Agent Containers — aglobe://147.32.84.177:1775/agent/MatrixESAgent

	Moon	Earth	Mercury	Mars	Venus
Moon	✓	✓			✓
Earth	✓	✓			
Mercury			✓	✓	
Mars			✓	✓	
Venus	✓				✓

FIGURE 13. Platform Visibility Matrix

- **Manual (Matrix) ES Agent** This agent provides simple user-checkable visibility matrix, as shown in Figure 13. The user simply checks which containers can communicate together and which can not.
- **Distance-based ES Agent** This agent is a fully automatic environment simulator. It receives positions of mobile agent containers representing mobile units in virtual world and automatically controls accessibility between them. The visibility is controlled by means of the simulation of the short range wireless link. Therefore each container can communicate only with containers located inside the predefined radius limit. As the containers move, connections are dynamically established and lost.

Other visibility agents can be implemented for each specific simulation, provided that they respect the ontologies and protocols that apply for them.

4.2. ACROSS – Agent Complex Reasoning Simulation System

To illustrate the concepts of the platform design presented above, we will present the ACROSS scenario that uses the above features to create a relatively rich world where diverse types of agents can interact. Currently, we use this scenario as a common base for multiple research projects, where we need to investigate interactions between a relatively high number of fully-fledged agents.

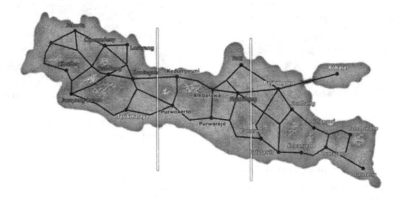

FIGURE 14. ACROSS scenario. The geography of the island is modelled after the real Java island in Indonesia, with necessary simplifications.

In our scenario, figure 14, we solve a logistics problem in a non-collaborative environment with self-interested agents. Agents that are part of the scenario have no common goals and their cooperation is typically financially motivated.

We have three types of information about each agent [15]. *Public information* is available to all agents in the system. It includes the agent identity, services proposed to other agents and other relevant characteristics it wishes to reveal. *Semi-private information* is the information which the agent agrees to share with selected partners in order to streamline their cooperation. In our case, resource capacity cumulated by resource type is shared within transporters' alliances (see below). *Private information* is available only to agent itself. It contains detailed information about agent's plans, intentions and resources.

The following types of agents participate in the scenario as actors:

Location Agents: Location agents represent population and natural resources, figure 15 (a). They create, transform or consume resources. As most location agents are unable to completely cover the local demand, they acquire the surplus goods from other locations through one round, sealed bid auctions organized by buyers according to the FIPA CNP protocol [5]. As most Location agents are physically remote, it is necessary to transport the acquired goods from the provider to the buyer. In order to do so, location agents contract ad-hoc coalitions of transporter agents to carry the cargo, figure 16.

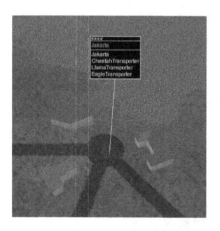 

FIGURE 15. (a) – Location and 3 Transporter agents in a village container; (b) – a Driver agent in a car container

Transporter Agents: Transporter Agents are the principal agents in our scenario. They use their resources - vehicles, driven by *Driver agents* - to transport the cargo as requested by location agents. As a normal request exceeds the size that may be handled by a single transporter, transporters must form one-time coalitions in order to increase the coverage and thus to be chosen in the auctions. All transporter agents are self-interested and they don't wish to cooperate with all other transporters. They only pick the partners that are compatible with their private preferences. The compatibility is checked using the public information available about the potential partner and agents' private preferences.

While answering the calls for proposals, the agents must form the coalitions relatively fast and efficiently to submit their bid before timeout elapses. Therefore, they use the concept of alliances, discussed in [15], to make the process more efficient. Alliances are groups of agents who agree to exchange the semi-private information about their resources in order to allow efficient pre-planning before starting the coalition negotiation itself. Using the pre-planning, negotiation can directly concentrate on optimization issues, rather than starting from resource query, saving valuable time and messages.

Driver Agents: Driver Agents drive the vehicles owned by Transporter agents, figure 15 (b). They handle path planning, loading, unloading and other driver duties.

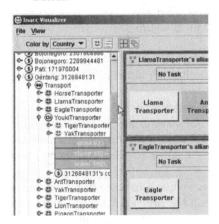 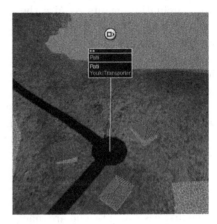

FIGURE 16. Location agents contract ad-hoc coalitions of transporter agents to carry the cargo

Numbers of agents actually used can vary from project to project, but the basic configuration uses 25 Location agents, each of them in separate container, 25 Transporter Agents distributed among Location agents' containers and 65 Driver Agents, each with its own container. Besides these "active" agents, we do need several services per container to implement platform functions like GIS, directory or migration management. With the latest optimizations, this configuration runs on a single PC, greatly facilitating the experiments.

Besides the agents mentioned above, several other agents are used for world simulation purposes, as described in 4.1. ACROSS scenario is managed by the following agents:

NodePod Agent simulates the positions and movements of all agent containers (see 2.2) in the simulated world. ACROSS world containers are positioned in the graph. Location agents are placed in a selected node, while the vehicle containers move through the graph following the edges - roads. For each moveable container, at least one agent in this container must be able to communicate the decisions about future directions to the NodePod agent and to handle events generated by the NodePod upon arrival to the graph node. NodePod doesn't take any part in road planning or decision making - it plainly simulates the movements of agent container support on the map following the orders from the Driver agents.

For large scale scenarios, we prefer to handle the movements of agents in a central simulation element, rather than in the container itself. This approach, even if slightly less flexible while adding new agents, pays off thanks to the important savings in the number of messages necessary to run the simulation. In most cases, we require the movements to be smooth, requiring at least 10 simulation steps per second. If the movements are managed in a distributed manner, the system would require 600 messages per second just to report the positions of containers. Besides the sheer number of messages, we must take into account the fact that many simulation agents require the knowledge of all agent's position in order to generate their output (for example accessibility). Synchronization then becomes an important issue.

Besides the communication with driver agents, the NodePod agent also provides the updated positions of all containers to all other simulation agents in the master container, especially to the Visibility Agent.

Accessibility Agent is an ES agent that simulates the accessibility between the agent containers. It uses the position data received from NodePod ES agent to determine the distance, updates the data with stochastic link failures specified by the configuration parameter and sends the updates to the containers whose accessibility has changed.

We shall note that the two types of inaccessibility - distance based or caused by the link failures - have very different effects on the processes in the community. In the first case, agents who are inaccessible cannot start any direct interaction and this translates into the suboptimal performance of the system, according to the standard economic theories. On the other hand, if the inaccessibility is stochastic, the interactions can indeed start, but the actors must be aware of the possibility that the link can be broken at any time. Therefore, the agents must adopt an appropriate method for inaccessibility resolution, such as use of stand-ins (see [18]), social knowledge or adopted interaction protocols.

Weather Agent maintains the model of the weather in the various parts of the environment. The weather is generated once per each simulation day and submitted to all Location containers. It is then used to adjust the production or consumption of various resources.

Two additional modules are currently integrated with *NodePod* agent. The **3D visualizer** module ensures the selection and formatting of the data for the external visualizers. Besides the pure position data, this module receives the status messages from agents and displays them in the appropriate visualizers. Due to the intensive data flow between this module and external visualizers, we were forced to implement an efficient binary protocol for message sending. The **time module** controls the speed at which the simulation runs. It maps the real time to physical simulation step, therefore influencing the basic pace at which the system runs. Besides this fundamental parameter, we can modify the second parameter, that maps the simulation step to simulation day, used to trigger the recurrent agents' actions, such as production or commercial exchanges.

Commercial Visualizer agent visualizes the auctions, including all bids and selected winners, together with the coalitions of transporters that handle the transportation, as shown in figure 17. It also presents the alliances and their formation described above. In contrast to Sniffer or Communication analyzer agents, this agent is scenario dependent. This makes its integration with other scenarios non-trivial, but the specificity makes the presentation efficient and understandable.

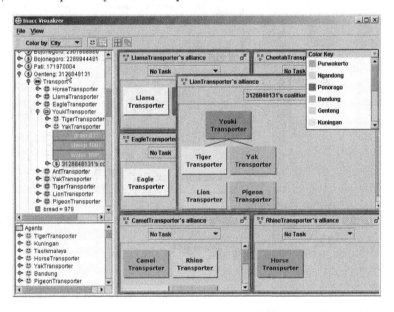

FIGURE 17. The commercial visualizer GUI

Other ES agents may include for example a Bandit agent, implementing the adversarial actions in the environment, or other various project dependent simulators and visualizers.

4.3. Naimt – Naval Automation and Information Management Technology

Features of the 𝒜-globe platform were also verified on the simulation of identification/removal of mines situated in given area using a group of autonomous robots. This simulation was developed within the Naval Automation and Information Management Technology (NAIMT) project. This software simulation of real-life hardware robots was required to enable scalability experiments and efficient development and verification of embedded decision making algorithms.

The goal of the group of robots is to search the whole area, detect and remove all mines located there. To allow mine removal a video transmission path must be established between the base (operated by human crew that gives the robot a permission to remove the mine) and the robot who has found the mine. Typically, relying via the other robots is necessary, because the video transmission range is limited (e.g. wi-fi connection or acoustic modems in underwater environment). Figure 19 shows an example of robots transmitting a video to base. In this scenario two types of communication accessibility are included:

- **High bandwidth** accessibility, necessary for video transmissions, very restrained.
- **Signaling** accessibility, used for coordination messages and position information, is higher than video accessibility, but remains limited.

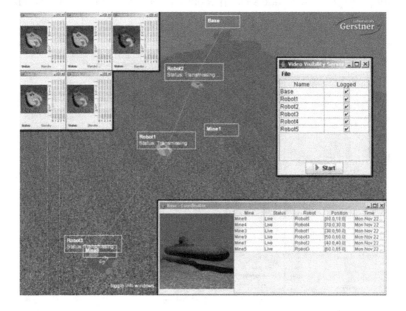

FIGURE 18. Relayed communication (link between the robot and base through 4 relays)

All robots in the simulation are autonomous and cooperative. Their dedicated components (coordinators) negotiate in peer-to-peer manner when preparing the transmission path. *A*-**globe** ES agent and GIS services are utilized during this phase to inform the robot about others within its video transmission range.

Each robot consists of several components, implemented as *A*-**globe** agents running within one agent container:

- **Robot Pod** simulator, computing robot moves and updating its position with GIS server via GIS service.
- **Mine Detector** simulator, providing the decision-making components with information about found mines.

- **Video** data acquisition and transmission element. This subsystem creates the data feed form the source provided by the simulation and prepares transmission path by remotely spawning one-use transmission agents along the path. Video is then transmitted as a stream of binary encoded messages.
- **Robot Coordinator** implementing search algorithm, transmission coalition establishment and negotiation.

We are using three different approaches to distributed coordination in fixing the ad-hoc data transmission feed. The most straightforward are the approaches relying on a single agent mastering the planning process. Upon finding the mine, it requests the other visible robots to move to a specific positions so that a high-bandwidth transmission link between the mine and the base is established. In two variants of this approach, we may emphasize either the communication quality or the minimization of other robots' actions disturbance. When we optimize the communication quality, relay robots tend to be placed on the join between the mine and the base so that the distance between the relays is minimized and minimal possible number of robots is used. On the other hand, when we try to minimize the impact on relay robots' own plans, relays are spread in the area between the transmission origin and target, in the proximity of their original areas. In the third approach, the control over the feed planning is not centralized, but rather passed along the communication link relays when the connection is constructed. This approach is well adopted for the environments where the communication is limited and the knowledge necessary for feed building is not common, but rather distributed among robots.

Generality of the $\mathcal{A}$-**globe** technology has been proved when migrating the technology to the robocup soccer environment. The GIS server and ES agents managing the position of the robots have been replaced by the information from the robocup soccer camera. Similarly the nodepod agent has been directly coupled with the hardware of the robocup soccer robots.

5. Acknowledgement

Authors wish to express acknowledgement to Rockwell Automation Research Center in Prague for mutually beneficial cooperation in the platform evaluation process. $\mathcal{A}$-**globe** agent platform was developed within the project "Inaccessibility in Multi-Agent Systems" (contract no.: FA8655-02-M-4057). The NAIMT deployment has been supported in part by ONR project no.: N00014-03-1-0292.

6. Conclusion

$\mathcal{A}$-**globe** agent platform supports communication inaccessibility, agent migration and deployment on remote containers. These features make $\mathcal{A}$-**globe** a well suited platform for simulation and implementation of physically distributed agent systems with applications ranging from mobile robotics to environmental surveillance by

FIGURE 19. Relayed communication as simulated by Robocup soccer robots. Robot movements and positions are derived from hardware inputs. Base is in the upper-left corner.

sensor networks. $\mathcal{A}$-**globe** was designed as streamlined lightweight platform which will operate on classical (PC) as well as mobile devices (PDA).

FIPA compliance was not considered a key feature for the simulation-oriented platform the $\mathcal{A}$-**globe** is. However, in the course of the embedding process we are currently planning to implement a dedicated platform service providing FIPA compliance for external communication to cover the gap. Key features the platform currently presents are full mobility support (2.3) and environmental simulation support and platform-level inaccessibility control (4.1). The main driving force of the platform development is the emphasis on easy simulation support and sharp separation between the simulation parts and agent code. Agents that are developed and validated in the simulated environment can be then easily deployed in the real environment, where the GIS service will provide access to the local sensors instead of the simulated values.

The ACROSS scenario is currently exploited with the Agent Technology Group for investigating diverse research concepts in collective decision-making. We study primarily various techniques for coping with agents' communication and coordination in inaccessible and adversarial environments. The **remote presence** techniques include primarily the *stand-in agent* technology [16], [12], [18], while the **remote awareness** concept includes mainly the methods for agents *social knowledge* maintenance and *acquainted models* (e.g. the Tri-base Acquaintance Model [14]).

The ACROSS scenario is used as a benchmark for testing the agents meta-reasoning capacities. The meta-reasoning agents are monitoring the communication exchange in order to reconstruct agents private knowledge. Meta-reasoning in collaborative environments is used mainly for optimization of agents collective behavior [19], [20]. The tri-base acquaintance model has been extended recently for representation of agents' mutual trust and used for formation of trusted and semi-trusted coalitions.

Within the NAIMT scenario, the 𝒜-**globe** agents have been used mainly for studying the concept of distributed coordination in partially inaccessible environment. Various techniques of distributed planning, coordination and ad-hoc data transmission processes are currently being investigated [4].

References

[1] FIPS PUB 180-1. Federal standard 180-1: Secure hash standard. http://www.itl.nist.gov/fipspubs/fip180-1.htm, 1995.

[2] A-Globe. A-Globe Agent Platform. http://agents.felk.cvut.cz/aglobe, 2004.

[3] F. Bellifemine, G. Rimassa, and A. Poggi. Jade - a fipa-compliant agent framework. In *Proceedings of 4th International Conference on the Practical Applications of Intelligent Agents and Multi-Agent Technology*, London, 1999.

[4] J. M. Bradshaw, A. Uszok, R. Jeffers, and N. Suri. Representation and reasoning for daml-based policy and domain services in kaos and nomads. In *Autonomous Agents and Multi-Agent Systems (AAMAS 2003)*, Melbourne, Australia, 2003. New York, NY: ACM Press.

[5] FIPA. Fipa contract net interaction protocol specification. Foundation for Intelligent Physical Agents, http://www.fipa.org/specs/fipa00029, 2002.

[6] FIPA. Foundation for intelligent physical agents. http://www.fipa.org, 2004.

[7] FIPA-ACL. Fipa agent communication language overview. Foundation for Intelligent Physical Agents, http://www.fipa.org/specs/fipa00037, 2000.

[8] M. Fletcher. Designing an integrated holonic scheduler with jack. In *Multi-Agent Systems and Applications II.*, Manchester, 2002. Springer-Verlag, Berlin.

[9] JADE. Java Agent Development Framework. http://jade.tilab.com, 2004.

[10] JAXB. JAVA API for XML Binding. http://java.sun.com/xml/jaxb, 2004.

[11] H. Nwana, D. Ndumu, L. Lee, and J. Collis. Zeus: A tool-kit for building distributed multi-agent systems. *Applied Artificial Intelligence Journal*, 13(1):129–186, 1999.

[12] M. Pěchouček, M. Dobíšek, J. Lažanský, and V. Mařík. Inaccessibility in multi-agent systems. In *Proceedings of International Conference on Intelligent Agent Technology*, pages 182–188, 2003.

[13] M. Pěchouček, V. Mařík, D. Šišlák, M. Rehák, J. Lažanský, and J. Tožička. Inaccessibility in multi-agent systems. final report to Air Force Research Laboratory AFRL/EORD research contract (FA8655-02-M-4057), 2004.

[14] M. Pěchouček, V. Mařík, and O. Štěpánková. Role of acquaintance models in agent-based production planning systems. In M. Klusch and L. Kerschberg, editors, *Co-operative Infromation Agents IV - LNAI No. 1860*, pages 179–190, Heidelberg, July 2000. Springer Verlag.

[15] M. Pěchouček, V. Mařík, and J. Bárta. A knowledge-based approach to coalition formation. *IEEE Intelligent Systems*, 17(3):17–25, 2002.

[16] M. Pěchouček, M. Rehák, M. Rollo, D. Šišlák, and J. Tožička. Solving coordination inaccessibility in coalition operations. In *Knowledge Systems for Coalition Operatioins 2004*, pages 19–36. CTU, Prague, 2004.

[17] S. Poslad, P. Buckle, and R. Hadingham. The fipa-os agent platform: Open source for open standards. In *Proceedings of 5th International Conference on the Practical Applications of Intelligent Agents and Multi-Agent Technology*, pages 355–368, Manchaster, 2000.

[18] M. Rehák, M. Pěchouček, J. Tožička, and D. Šišlák. Using stand-in agents in partially accessible multi-agent environment. In *Proceedings of Engineering Societies in the Agents World V (to appear)*, October 2004.

[19] S. Russel and E. Wefald. *Do the Right Thing: Studies in Limitted Rationality*. The MIT Press, Cambridge, MA, 1991.

[20] J. Tožička, J. Bárta, and M. Pěchouček. Meta-reasoning for agents' private knowledge detection. In M. Klusch, S. Ossowski, A. Omicini, and H. Laamanen, editors, *Cooperative Information Agent VII – Lecture Notes in Computer Science, LNAI 2782*, Heidelberg : Springer-Verlag, 2003.

[21] Pavel Vrba. Java-based agent platform evaluation. In Mařík, McFarlane, and Valckenaers, editors, *Holonic and Multi-Agent Systems for Manufacturing*, number 2744 in LNAI, pages 47–58. Springer-Verlag, Heidelberg, June 2003.

Information about Software

Software is available on the Internet as
- ( ) prototype version
- (•) full fledged software (freeware), version no.: 2.2
- ( ) full fledged software (for money), version no.:
- ( ) Demo/trial version
- ( ) not (yet) available

Internet address:
    Description of software: Agent Platform *A*-**globe**
    Download address: http://agents.felk.cvut.cz/aglobe

Contact person for question about the software:
    Name: David Šišlák
    E-mail: sislakd@feld.cvut.cz

David Šišlák, Martin Rehák, Michal Pěchouček,
Milan Rollo and Dušan Pavlíček
Gerstner Laboratory©
Czech Technical University in Prague
Technická 2, Prague 6, 166 27 Czech Republic
e-mail: {sislakd, rehakm1, pechouc, rollo, pavlicd}@feld.cvut.cz

Supporting Agent Development in Erlang through the eXAT Platform

Antonella Di Stefano and Corrado Santoro

Abstract. This work describes a new approach for writing multi-agent systems considering the use of the Erlang programming language. An analysis of the features of this language is provided, which shows that Erlang characteristics allow a programmer to easily model and implement agent systems. Then, a new agent programming platform, called **eXAT**—*erlang eXperimental Agent Tool*—will be described. This platform has been designed by the authors to support agent development and deploying with Erlang; the aim is to provide an all-in-one environment, allowing an agent designer to program *agent intelligence*, *agent behavior* and *agent communication* with a single language.

Keywords. Rule-based agents, agent platforms, multi-agent systems, Erlang.

1. Introduction

To date, in the field of agent programming platforms and languages, two main trends are registered [4]; many *platforms* are written using existing well-known programming languages, such as Java or C++ [16, 1, 60, 9], while, on the other hand, ad-hoc *agent programming languages* have been proposed [59, 48, 61, 56, 45, 49], able to map agent-specific characteristics to native constructs. In the authors' opinion, both of these approaches suffer of the same *incompleteness* problem. Platforms typically realized with existing imperative languages often need to integrate additional tools, able to model and handle other important aspects of agent programming, like the intelligence. These additional tools are based on programming languages and models strongly different than those of the platform. For example, rule-production systems [2, 3, 7], which are often integrated together with Java platforms, are based on a declarative/logic constructs. Another example is JADEX [55], the BDI [57] extension for JADE [16], which forces the agent programmer to use XML and OQL. As a result, to develop a complete multi-agent application, the programmer is forced to deal with several and heterogeneous languages and programming methodologies. As an alternative, agent programming languages [23, 59, 48, 61, 56, 45, 49] are rich of agent-specific constructs but lack statements and libraries needed for general-purpose applications. These languages are specifically designed to model and implement agent's mind, reasoning process and behaviors. For this reason, they provide constructs to specify beliefs, intentions and plans, to map actions deriving from the arrival of an ACL message, to formalize the agent's reasoning process, etc. But, on the other hand, these languages do not provide functions or libraries for e.g. building user interfaces, writing network/Internet communication protocols, handling generic data in form of strings or byte sequence, etc. Therefore, the integration of other environments is often needed to build a complete software system. As a result, writing the various aspects of the same multi-agent application adopting a number of different languages not only needs more sophisticated and elaborated design strategies, but often introduces inefficiencies, since e.g. data needs to be converted when transferred from the domain of a language to another.

The approach suggested by the authors is to combine, in a single programming language, the ability of offering a general-purpose environment, with language constructs and a programming philosophy able to express all the main agent-related features. It was not necessary to design a new programming language, but *Erlang* [14, 12, 8] has demonstrated to be a language very promising for the development of agent systems [31]. Apart authors' research [28, 30, 29], the Erlang language has gained interest, in the agent community: it is cited in the "Agent Software" list of the Agentlink web site [4] and some of its characteristics (message reception and matching semantics) have inspired some concepts and constructs of other agent programming language [48, 49]. A recent work [62] has proposed an Erlang-based BDI tool.

This Chapter deals with the reasons that make Erlang suitable for modeling all the aspects of multi-agent systems. To evaluate the real effectiveness of using Erlang in agent system implementation, an agent platform has been realized, called **eXAT**—*erlang eXperimental Agent Tool* [6, 58, 28, 30, 29][1]. Such a platform (which is itself completely written in Erlang) provides an all-in-one environment to program *agent intelligence*, *agent behavior* and *agent communication*. The Chapter is structured as follows. Section 2 gives a brief overview of the Erlang language, showing its syntax and main peculiarities; we also discuss the reasons that led us to consider this language an interesting instrument to model and design agent systems. Section 3 summarizes of the basic working scheme of the eXAT platform and its components, sketching the agent model it supplies. An in-depth description of the functionalities of eXAT is dealt with in Sections 4, 5 and 6, while Section 7 provides a qualitative comparison of eXAT with some other agent platforms and agent programming languages. Section 8 concludes the Chapter.

---

[1]The platform is available through a BSD-style license and can be downloaded at http://www.diit.unict.it/users/csanto/exat/.

2. Erlang for Agents

2.1. Overview of the Language

Erlang is a functional language developed at Ericsson laboratories [14, 50, 8]. It was initially designed with the aim of having a flexible language and runtime environment to implement the control system of telephone exchange equipments [12, 15]; the language was then extended in order to make it general-purpose.

Erlang derives from Prolog and borrows from this language the syntax, the data types and the ability of handling symbols, but not the semantics: while Prolog is logic, Erlang is *functional*. Erlang programming is based on *functions* that can have multiple *clauses*. Each function clause can also have a *guard*, i.e. a boolean expression representing a pre-condition to be met in order to activate the clause. When a function is called, the matching clause (that also makes the guard true, if present) is executed. Figure 1 reports a sample Erlang source that shows some of the main features of the language. As it is shown in the Figure, each Erlang source file, called *module*, starts with a declaration of the module name (which must be the same of the source file) and the list of "exports", that is the list of functions, each with its arity[2], which can be called by other modules. Then we have the declaration and implementation of each function with the relevant clause. Each function clause ends with a semicolon (;) while the last clause ends with a dot (.).

As for data, data types and variables, Erlang uses the same rules of Prolog. A constant is represented with a (untyped) number or an *atom*, which is a lowercase literal or any literal enclosed within single quotes (e.g. hello, 'wants-to-do'). Variables are instead represented with uppercase literals. This syntax is used, in the

---

[2]number of arguments of the function.

```
-module (samples). % Module declaration
-export ([fact/1, foo/2, sum/1, match_inform/1, execute/2]).
% List of function callable by another module

fact (N) when N == 0 -> 1;
fact (N) -> N * fact (N - 1).

foo (hello, X) -> io:format ("Say 'Hello ~w'\n", [X]);
foo (goodbye, X) -> io:format ("Say 'Goodbye ~w'\n", [X]);
foo (_, X) -> io:format ("woops!\n").

sum ([]) -> 0
sum ([H | T]) -> H + sum (T).

match_inform ([$(,$i,$n,$f,$o,$r,$m,$ | T]) -> true;
match_inform (X) when islist (X) -> false.

execute ({X, 'wants-to-do', Y}, {Y, 'is-feasible'}) -> % .. do something
execute (_,_) -> false.
```

FIGURE 1. Some Examples of Erlang Code

specification of function clauses, to indicate if a parameter, given when the function is invoked, must match an actual value or it has to be bound to a variable; in clause specification, the symbol "_" plays the role of a wildcard (see functions `fact` and `foo` in Figure 1). Basic Erlang types include also *lists* and *tuples*. Lists, syntactically represented with square brackets $[term_1,term_2,\ldots,term_n]$, are handled using the Prolog-style statement `[H|T]` = *List* (see the `sum` function in Figure 1, that sums all the elements of a list). Erlang tuples are instead sequence of terms enclosed in graph brackets, i.e. $\{term_1,term_2,\ldots,term_n\}$; operations allowed on tuples are (*i*) to separate elements, (*ii*) to get the length and (*iii*) to read the nth element. Erlang also handles *strings*, which are treated as lists where each element is the ASCII code of each character. String processing is thus performed using list matching expressions. As an example, the function `match_inform` in Figure 1 returns "true" if the argument is a string that begins with (`inform`[3].

Even if Erlang is syntactically similar to Prolog, it features many differences not only in semantics but also in other aspects, such as the concurrency and programming model. Erlang programs are composed of a set of *isolated processes* that share nothing and communicate one another by means of messages exchanged using smart and flexible language constructs. The process model and communication abstraction are derived from CSP [46] and π-calculus [52]; however a programmer is not forced to deal with such process calculi to design programs: a complete set of library modules hides the details of the process model, facilitating the development of concurrent Erlang programs. The Erlang concurrency constructs also handles distribution transparently, by allowing a seamless communication among processes belonging to different network nodes: the language constructs to perform data exchange do not change if processes are remote instead of local.

In addition to the cited characteristics, Erlang programs feature portability, since they are compiled in platform-independent (bytecoded) executable files that can directly run using the Erlang virtual machine[4]. The Erlang runtime environment is also quite complete since it provides a very large number of libraries, comparable to those of other more famous languages[5].

2.2. Why Erlang?

This Section briefly discusses the reasons leading to choose Erlang for implementing agent systems. Section 7, instead, will compare other agent platforms/languages with the eXAT/Erlang approach.

The first reason is tied to the *agent model*. By definition [44, 64], an agent *senses* the environment and *acts* onto it on the basis of the inputs and its internal *state*; thus, an agent behavior can be expressed by means of a function like

$$(Act, NewState) = f(Sense, CurrentState) \qquad (1)$$

---

[3]The symbol $x is a shortcut for the representation of the ASCII code of the letter x.
[4]The Erlang environment is provided for many platforms, such as Windows, Linux, BSD, Solaris, VxWorks, etc.
[5]See the documentation provided in the Erlang web site [8].

```
(action1, state1) = f(event1, start)
(action2, stop)   = f(event2, start)
(action3, stop)   = f(event3, state1)
```

FIGURE 2. A Finite-State Machine and its specification using a function with several clauses

Since, in the agents' world, *Act*, *NewState*, *CurrentState* and *Sense* are discrete variables, functions like (1) call for the use of the *finite-state machine* (FSM) abstraction for a representation of agent behavior, and *functions with multiple clauses* for a concrete specification and implementation of such an agent behavior. We can represent a FSM with a directed graph, where *vertexes* represent states and *edges* represent events triggering actions that lead to another state; using this representation, each function clause written as (1) is indeed the specification of a state transition, as the example in Figure 2 reports[6]. Such a model can be easily implemented in Erlang by means of a direct one-to-one mapping of the (agent) model provided by (1) to native language constructs, i.e. an Erlang function with several clauses. As a reference, Figure 3 reports the realization, in Erlang, of the FSM in Figure 2. The reader can appreciate the 1 : 1 mapping of the function *f* to its implementation (in this case, the "action" is not a specific value returned by the function, but each action is implemented in the body of the function); the listing also shows the function **execute_fsm** that concretely executes our FSM by picking next event, calling function **f** and recursively calling itself (until the state **stop** is reached). For reference, Figure 4 shows a (possible) Java implementation of the same FSM: we can see that transitions are "hidden" in the body of the

---

[6] In the graph representing a FSM, we used the UML notation that indicates the initial state with an edge exiting from a filled circle and the final state with an edge leading to a filled double circle.

```
-module (sample_fsm).
-export ([run/0]).

f(event1 , start) ->   % ... write the implementation of 'action1'
    state1;
f(event2 , start) ->   % ... write the implementation of 'action2'
    stop;
f(event3 , state1) ->  % ... write the implementation of 'action3'
    stop.

execute_fsm (stop) -> ok;
execute_fsm (CurrentState) -> Event = get_next_event(),
    NextState = f(Event , CurrentState), execute_fsm (NextState).

run() -> execute_fsm (start).
```

FIGURE 3. Erlang implementation of the FSM in Figure 2

```
public class SampleFSM {
  int EVENT1 = ...;
  int EVENT2 = ...;
  int EVENT3 = ...;
  int START = ...;
  int STATE1 = ...;
  int STOP = ...;
  int f(int event, int state) {
    switch (state) {
      case START:
        switch (event) {
          case EVENT1: do_action1(); return STATE1;
          case EVENT2: do_action2(); return STOP;
        }
        break;
      case STATE1:
        switch (event) {
          case EVENT3: do_action3(); return STOP;
        }
    }
  }
  public void run() {
    int currentState = START;
    while (currentState != STOP) {
      int event = get_next_event();
      currentState = f(currentState, event);
    }
  }
}
```

FIGURE 4. A possible Java implementation of the FSM in Figure 2

switches of method f and not clearly visible as in Figure 3. Surely, we could also consider a more "formally correct" Java implementation that maps events, states and actions to classes/objects, and thus provides an object-based framework for FSM specification and execution; but this would imply several source files, a lot of code lines (more than those of the Erlang listing) and the needing of handling an object model that could be complex. This is due to the fact that each concept in Java (as in many other O-O languages) must be mapped onto an object, and this often results in a framework with many classes. On the other hand, symbolic languages, like Erlang, can represent concrete concepts directly with symbols, thus facilitating the engineering and also reducing the lines of code to be written and debugged. Moreover, the mechanism for identifying the function clause that matches a call (which we exploit in specifying and executing a FSM) is provided natively by Erlang: any other language not offering the same feature could implement something similar with a library, but can neither overcome the limitations of the language nor introduce new constructs[7].

---

[7] This is true if we do not consider the possibility of building an interpreter, for function clauses, which is implemented on the top of an existing language; but this is the same as defining and using *another* language for our FSM specification and implementation. Thus, in this case, we should evaluate the new language built and not the language used to write the interpreter.

A second reason for choosing Erlang is the *concurrency and programming model*. Erlang programming philosophy is based on decomposing a problem into *tasks*, associating each task to a single Erlang process, and making processes communicate in order to achieve the goal of the problem. Languages featuring this characteristic are called by Joe Armstrong—one of the inventors of Erlang— *Concurrent-Oriented Programming Languages (COPL)*. He claims in [13] that "We often write programs that model the world or interact with the world. Writing such programs in a COPL is easy. First we perform an analysis, which is a three-step process: 1. We identify all the truly concurrent activities in our real-world activity; 2. We identify all the message channels between the concurrent activities; 3. We write down all the messages which can flow on the different channels. Now we write the program. The structure of the program should exactly follow the structure of the problem." The reader can easily find, in this citation, many characteristics in common with multi-agent system programming and design [64, 65, 66]. For example, engineering a multi-agent system using the Gaia methodology [63, 66] implies to derive, from a description of the system to be designed, (*i*) the *roles* to be played by the various agents, then (*ii*) charge each roles with one or more tasks, and finally (*iii*) identify the *interactions* that have to occur among agents playing roles.

Other reasons making Erlang attractive are related to both its similarity with Prolog and its built-in capability of identifying the function clause to be activated (*function clause matching*). Such characteristics can be exploited for programming both agent intelligence and agent behavior with the same language. As for the former aspect, the design and implementation of agent intelligence should be supported by a suitable artificial intelligence tool, such as a rule-production system. To this aim, in many currently available agent platforms, which are mainly Java-based, an integration with tools such as JESS [2], CLIPS [3] or Drools [7] (or other ad-hoc approaches [55]) is mandatory. In this sense, Erlang function clauses and clause matching mechanism are very suited to support the specification of *pre-conditions* activating *actions* (coded in the body of the function), in the perfect style of rule-production systems. As an example, see the function `execute` in Figure 1: here the first function clause can be seen as a pre-condition, like a Prolog predicate, that triggers something. Such a characteristic eases the implementation of expert systems or rule-production engines supporting agent reasoning. Moreover, this aspect, and in particular the matching capability, if related to the agent model based on FSM, can be used, when designing the behavior of an agent, to specify the conditions triggering change of state.

All the above argumentations highlight that Erlang possesses many interesting features for the implementation of software agents; however, such a language does not itself provide a complete runtime environment for the execution of agent-based applications, but it only supports specific aspects of agent design and implementation. Behaviors expressed with multiple functions clauses need a suitable engine to support their (autonomous) execution. Similarly, using functions clauses as pre-conditions for rules is not sufficient to realize an expert system: an appropriate library able to process these rules, also supporting a knowledge base, is mandatory. This is supplied by eXAT, an agent platform realized by the authors to provide a complete runtime environment, that will be described in the following Sections.

3. An Overview of the eXAT Platform

eXAT is an agent platform that allows multi-agent application programming using only the Erlang language; it provides a suitable support to realize *agent intelligence*, *agent behavior* and *agent collaboration*. These main aspects rely on eXAT agent's model, which is sketched in Figure 5 and described below.

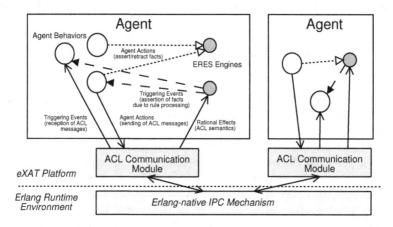

FIGURE 5. Agent Model in eXAT

As the Figure reports, the main components of an eXAT agent are the *ERES engines*, which implement agent's intelligence, and the *behaviors*, which implement agent's computation. Such components are able to interact with the *ACL Communication Module*, which is provided by the platform to support message exchanging among agents. All components of an agent and the ACL Communication Module influence each other as briefly sketched below. An in-depth description of the functioning and usage of such modules is instead provided in the subsequent Sections.

ERES engines are rule processing systems supporting agent reasoning through an Erlang library called ERES [5]. Each engine has its own *rules* and a *knowledge base* that stores a set of *facts*; each fact is specified with an Erlang tuple or a list. The knowledge base of an ERES engine, when associated to an agent, is thus able represent the "mental state" of such an agent. Rules are written as function clauses and rule processing is based on checking that one or more facts, with certain patterns, belong to the knowledge base and then executing the guarded action or asserting new facts. An agent may use different ERES engines, each implementing a different reasoning process; this can be used for the engineering of reasoning processes that appear separated at initial design stage. In this case, the agent's mental state can be considered composed of the facts stored in the knowledge bases of all the engines associated to the agent. The ERES module will be fully described in Section 4.

Agent behaviors, expressed by using Erlang functions with multiple clauses describing a FSM, implement the actions an agent has to perform to achieve its goal and are processed by the behavior execution module of eXAT. Agent behaviors are subject to both the *agent's mental state* and the occurrence of *external events*; these represents *triggers*, for the FSM, that cause action execution and state change. Triggers relevant to agent's mental state refer to the presence of one or more facts in a given ERES engine. External events refer instead to the arrival of an ACL message. Behavior engineering is made flexible by allowing a designer to compose behaviors *in sequence*—to support serial activities—or *in parallel*—to support multiple concurrent activities (e.g. handling of multiple simultaneous interactions). Moreover, the concept of inheritance, typical of the object-oriented programming paradigm, is introduced in eXAT to allow the *specialization (extension)* of a behavior by means of re-definition of one or more elements of the FSM mapping function. To this aim, eXAT provides a library that, together with supporting such a specialization, adds object-orientation capabilities to Erlang, thus allowing *classes* to be written and *objects* to be instantiated as in Java/C++. This feature combines the advantages of functional and object-based programming in order to offer an agent development environment more flexible than that of provided by a traditional object-oriented language. Behavior engineering and functioning will be dealt with in Section 5.

To make agent collaboration possible, eXAT agent behaviors use the service provided by the ACL module, which is responsible to support exchanging, composition, parsing and matching of ACL messages, according to the FIPA standard [38]. A set of functions are used to send and receive FIPA speech acts and bind the reception of a specific message to a behavior event. The communication module is able not only to trigger actions on the basis of the reception of a message but also to concretely influence and check the agent's mental state, following message exchanging and according to FIPA-ACL semantics [38]. This is an important contribution with respect to other agent platforms, which require this link to be made "by hand" by agent designers. Messaging and semantic support will be described in Section 6.

```
-module (sample).
-export ([rule/3, purchasing/3]).
-rules ([parents, purchasing]).

parents (Engine, {'child-of', X, Y}, {female, Y}) ->
    eres:assert (Engine, {'mother-of', Y, X});
parents (Engine, {'child-of', X, Y}, {male, Y}) ->
    eres:assert (Engine, {'father-of', Y, X}).

purchasing (Engine,
            ['has-goal', Agent, [purchasing, Good, Price]],
            ['balance-of', Agent, Balance])
            when (Balance - Price) > 3000) ->
    eres:assert (Engine, [intends, Agent, [purchase, Good]]).
```

FIGURE 6. Some Sample Productions Rule in ERES

4. Supporting Intelligence with ERES

As introduced above, the ERES library supports the concurrent execution of multiple rule-processing engines. Each engine works on its own *Knowledge Base (KB)*, which stores a set of facts, and with one or more *Production Rules*. Each rule is an Erlang function clause (the clause represents a predicate applied to the *KB*) and its body can contain any Erlang statement as well as functions to manipulate the *KB* of the engine, i.e. asserting another fact or retracting an existing fact. A rule is expressed using the following form:

func_name (Engine, FP_1, FP_2, ..., FP_n) when *predicate* ->
    Body of the rule action

Here Engine is the (name of the) ERES engine the rule belongs to and FP_1, FP_2, ..., FP_n are patterns matching facts: if the *KB* contains facts that match all the patterns of the rule, the latter is activated and the function body is executed.

Such a rule specification model perfectly reflects the syntax and semantics of well-known rule production systems [3, 2, 7]. As an example, let us suppose we want to implement the following rule: *If X is the child of Y and Y is female, then Y is X's mother; otherwise, if Y is male, then Y is X's father*. This rule can be written using the two clauses of the function parents in Figure 6, given that we represent the relations "child of", "mother of", "father of" and the "gender" respectively with the Erlang tuples {'child-of', X, Y}, {'mother-of', X, Y}, {'father-of', X, Y} and {female, X}, {male, X}. As another example, the function purchasing in Figure 6 says that if an agent has the goal of purchasing an item and the agent's remaining balance is greater than 3000 €, then the agent intends to buy that item.

Rules are pre-processed by the ERES module when the engine is started. This aims at building a data structure suitable for efficiently finding rule clauses to be fired, should a fact be asserted or retracted. The technique employed is a variation

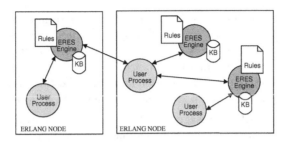

FIGURE 7. ERES Engines and User Processes

of the Forgy's RETE algorithm [33] and exploits Erlang matching capabilities to perform the *selection* and *join* operations[8].

An additional features of ERES is the capability of realizing *blackboard architectures* [24]. An ERES engines with no production rules can in fact behave as a Linda tuple space [20], and thus used to perform coordination among activities of an agent or among different agents that would not use message exchanging[9]. This is an important additional characteristic of the platform since it provides a native means to support many well-known agent coordination models [53, 19, 25, 54, 22].

From the runtime point of view, as Figure 7 reports, each ERES engine runs on a separate Erlang process. A set of APIs is provided to allow user processes to interact with running engines; such primitives include creating/destroying an engine, adding a new rule, manipulating existing rules, asserting/retracting a fact, checking for the presence of one or more facts with a given pattern, waiting for the assertion of a fact with a given pattern, obtaining all the facts of the *KB*, etc. (see [5, 58] for more details). According to Erlang distribution model, each ERES engine can be also accessed by Erlang processes running on different network nodes (see Figure 7).

5. Engineering Agent Behaviors

As introduced in Section 3, the overall computation of an agent is programmed in eXAT by means of a set of *behaviors*, each modeled as a finite-state machine. This philosophy is similar to that of other agent platforms [16, 1], but behavior engineering is made more flexible in eXAT thanks to the integration of object-oriented and functional/symbolic programming concepts.

An eXAT behavior is programmed using a set of Erlang functions that express what are the *events* that, bound to certain *states*, trigger the execution of certain *actions* and the change of *state*. Since an event is in general characterized by an associated data, each event is defined by specifying its *type* and a *data pattern*, the

---

[8]See the citation for the details on the RETE algorithm.
[9]To this aim a set of Linda-like primitives (*out, in, inp, rd* and *rdp*) is also provided by the ERES module.

latter indicating the template to be matched by the data in order to activate the
event itself. For example, the "arrival of an *inform* speech act" is an event whose
type is "arrival of any ACL message" and whose pattern specifies a matching between the performative name and the "inform" constant. This separation between
event types and data patterns allows behaviour specialization and promotes reuse,
as it will be detailed in Section 5.2. Event types handled by eXAT are:

- **Reception of an ACL message** (event type *acl*). The data pattern is a specification of how the triggering message has to be formed.
- **Expiry of a given timeout** (event type *timeout*). The data pattern is the
  timeout value in milliseconds.
- **Assertion of fact(s)** (event type *eres*). The data pattern specifies the template
  of the fact(s) that has to be asserted, in a given ERES engine, in order to
  trigger the event.
- **A silent (spontaneous) event** (event type *silent*). This event type has no
  associated data.

An eXAT behavior, expressed by modeling the FSM with a directed graph as
reported in Section 2.2, is represented by means of the following three functions,
action, *event* and *pattern*:

$$
\begin{aligned}
&action : StateName \rightarrow \text{setof } (EventName, ActionProcedure) \\
&event : EventName \rightarrow (EventType, PatternName) \\
&pattern : PatternName \rightarrow PatternSpecification \\
&EventType \in \{silent, eres, acl, timeout\}
\end{aligned}
\tag{2}
$$

Function **action** returns the information related to the edges exiting the state name
(vertex) given as parameter; each information is composed of the *name of the event*
and the procedure implementing the *action* (the new state reached by the edge
after action execution is encoded by using an API function, called in the body of
action implementation). Function **event** gives, for each event name, the *event type*
and the *name of the associated data pattern*. Finally, function **pattern** returns, for
each pattern name, the relevant pattern specification, which is dependent of the
type of the event tied to the pattern itself.

It can be easily noted that the model above is different than that of formula (1), however its semantics is the same: we have only separated the various
parts of a FSM in order to make specialization possible by means of inheritance.
As it will be detailed in Section 5.2, such a specialization process will imply to
change only one or more values returned by one or more functions in (2) of a
behavior already designed.

As an example of behavior engineering in eXAT, we report in Figure 8 a simple FSM with its implementation (ignore, for the moment, the Self parameter,
which is passed to all the functions reported in the listing, because its meaning
will explained in Section 5.2). As it can be noted, two clauses for action have

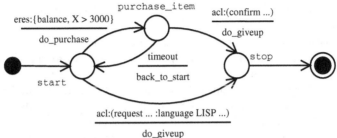

```
-module (sample1).
-export ([action/2, event/2, pattern/2, ...]).

action (Self, start) -> [{start_to_purchase_event , do_purchase},
                         {start_to_stop_event , do_giveup}];
action (Self, purchase_item) ->
                    [{purchase_to_start_event , back_to_start},
                     {purchase_to_stop_event , do_giveup}].

event (Self, start_to_purchase_event) -> {eres, balance_pattern};
event (Self, start_to_stop_event) -> {acl, request_pattern};
event (Self, purchase_to_start_event) -> {timeout , timeout_value};
event (Self, purchase_to_stop_event) -> {acl, confirm_pattern}.

pattern (Self, balance_pattern) -> {my_engine, get,
                                   {balance , fun (X) -> X > 3000 end}};
pattern (Self, request_pattern) -> [#aclmessage {speechact = request,
                                                 language = 'LISP' }];
pattern (Self, timeout_value) -> 1000;
pattern (Self, confirm_pattern)-> [#aclmessage {speechact = confirm}].

do_purchase (Self, Event , Data , StateLeft) ->
    % perform action ...
    % ... and set next state
    object:do (Self, purchase_item).

back_to_start (Self, Event , Data , StateLeft) ->
    % set next state
    object:do (Self, start).

do_giveup (Self, Event , Data , StateLeft) ->
    % perform finalization ...
    % ... and stop behaviour
    object:stop (Self).
```

FIGURE 8. A sample behavior in eXAT

been used, one for each behavior state name (state `stop` is the final state in which the behavior is ended). Four clauses (the same of the number of transitions) are instead used for functions `event` and `pattern`. The example also shows the way in which patterns are specified: `balance_pattern` is an ERES pattern indicating the assertion of fact $\{balance, X\}$, with $X > 3000$, while `request_pattern` specifies instead the matching of a "request" ACL message whose content field is expressed in LISP. Pattern specification also allows complex matching expressions, by means of the use of 'fun' Erlang constructs, which define lambda functions (see the balance_pattern in Figure 8).

As the listing shows, each action is implemented in the function whose name is specified in the behavior structure (do_purchase, back_to_start and do_giveup in the example); the parameters given to these functions indicate, in order, the event fired, the actual data bound to that event and the name of the FSM state in which the event occurred. Action implementation has the responsibility of setting the next state of the FSM; this is performed by using eXAT functions object:do or object:stop, to respectively change the FSM's state and terminate the behavior.

5.1. Composing Behaviors

The finite-state machine abstraction used to develop agent behaviors is a common (and simple) way to express agent computations. However, in the case of engineering complex agent applications, the behaviors of involved agents could be complex as well, thus needing a FSM composed of a large number of states and transitions. Such a situation could present several difficulties during development stage. In principle, the use of a single (even large) FSM could be not enough when an agent computation has to be composed of concurrent activities, e.g. agents handling multiple and concurrent interactions. Secondly, in many situations, parts of an overall agent computation, which have been already designed, could be reused in another different agent application (this is the case instance of standard FIPA interaction protocols [43], such as the contract-net [39], the request protocol [41], the English auction [40], etc.)[10]. Such considerations lead us to engineer an overall agent computation through small and ready-to-use *components*, each one implementing a simple and basic behavior, to be arranged *in sequence*—to support serial activities—or *in parallel*—to support multiple concurrent activities[11].

eXAT supports such a model by allowing the specification, in the body of an action function, of the next behavior to be executed or the set of behaviors that have to concurrently run. This is achieved by means of the function agent:behave, which takes, as argument, a behavior name or a list of behavior names. Serial execution is supported by a sequence of agent:behave function calls, and specifying, in each call, one of the behaviors to be executed[12]; parallel execution is instead achieved by specifying the behaviors to be concurrently started in a list given as the parameter of a single agent:behave function call. This function is synchronous, that is, it triggers (sub-)behaviors execution and then waits for their completion.

As an example, the top of Figure 9 reports a behavior with two state transitions. The first transition is tied to the assertion of the fact {*action, purchase*}, which triggers (sub-)behavior **b1**; when the latter's execution ends, behavior **b2** is

---

[10]But reuse could be considered also for behavior patterns not strictly related to standard interaction protocols.
[11]This approach is equivalent to using subroutines and co-routines in traditional imperative languages and it is also used in some agent platforms currently available, such as JADE [16].
[12]The execution order is obviously the same as the order of the function calls.

started; then the state goes again to start. The second transition, tied to the reception of a request speech act, triggers the parallel execution of behaviors **b3** and **b4**. Here the reader can note, in the listing, the use of the function agent:behave to specify the sub-behaviors to be executed.

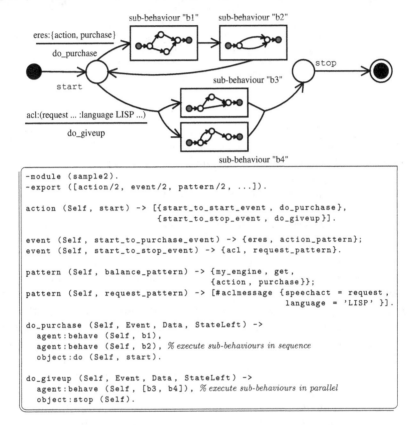

```
-module (sample2).
-export ([action/2, event/2, pattern/2, ...]).

action (Self, start) -> [{start_to_start_event, do_purchase},
                         {start_to_stop_event, do_giveup}].

event (Self, start_to_purchase_event) -> {eres, action_pattern};
event (Self, start_to_stop_event) -> {acl, request_pattern}.

pattern (Self, balance_pattern) -> {my_engine, get,
                                    {action, purchase}};
pattern (Self, request_pattern) -> [#aclmessage {speechact = request,
                                                 language = 'LISP' }].

do_purchase (Self, Event, Data, StateLeft) ->
  agent:behave (Self, b1),
  agent:behave (Self, b2), % execute sub-behaviours in sequence
  object:do (Self, start).

do_giveup (Self, Event, Data, StateLeft) ->
  agent:behave (Self, [b3, b4]), % execute sub-behaviours in parallel
  object:stop (Self).
```

FIGURE 9. Behavior Composition

5.2. Specializing Behaviors

Behavior composition, performed according to the concepts above, allows the "as-is" reuse of the code of an existing behavior in several multi-agent applications. However, in some cases, a behavior could not be designed so general to allow its reuse for a specific purpose, but some changes need to be applied. In order to make reuse possible also in these cases, eXAT allows behavior engineering using an object-orient approach and, in particular, by means of virtual inheritance. Such a concept is applied to create a new behavior b', derived from b, that transforms the FSM of b according to the following possibilities:

1. Adding new states and transitions;

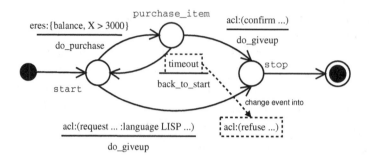

FIGURE 10. Behavior Extension

2. Removing existing states and/or transitions;
3. Modifying existing states and/or transitions by changing:
   (a) the state reached by a transition;
   (b) the action procedure bound to a transition;
   (c) the event type bound to a transition;
   (d) the data pattern bound to a transition;
   (e) one or more elements of a data pattern.

Figure 10 depicts an example of such an extension: here we considered the reuse of the FSM of Figure 8 by changing the timeout event into the arrival of a "refuse" speech act.

Supporting such an extension concept is made possible in eXAT thanks to the provided "object" module, which introduces object-orientation in Erlang programs; this module is intended for writing classes with attributes and methods, also featuring virtual inheritance as in Java or C++. The object model provided is similar to that of Java. A class is declared and implemented in a single Erlang module (corresponding indeed to a single source file); it must define and export the extends function, returning the name of the ancestor class/module[13]; then functions declared in the module can be treated as *methods* by adding another parameter, called Self, in function declaration: this parameter represents the object's instance within which the method is invoked and plays the same role of the this keyword in C++ and Java. According to Erlang style, a method can have multiple clauses and guards, and they play a fundamental role also in deriving child classes: methods feature a fine grained overriding model, because we can override all clauses of a method (the whole method), a single clause of a method, or even add another clause to method. This characteristic provides a very flexible and expressive programming environment and it is an important feature that cannot be obtained with a traditional object-oriented programming language[14].

---

[13]This function may be not declared if the class/module has no ancestors.
[14]For instance, C++, Java or Python allow the definition of methods with different prototypes and default parameters, but this is not the same as having different *clauses*.

```
-module (sample1_extended).
-export ([extends/1, event/2, pattern/2]).

extends () -> sample1.

event (Self, purchase_to_start_event) -> {acl, refuse_pattern}.

pattern (Self, refuse_pattern) -> [#aclmessage {speechact = refuse}].
```

FIGURE 11. Listing of the Behavior of Figure 10

Behavior engineering in eXAT exploits this Erlang-based object-oriented pro-gramming capability: each behavior is indeed a *class*, all defined functions—action, event, pattern and the functions implementing the actions—are methods[15], and behavior extension is performed by deriving that class and accordingly overriding one or more methods or method clauses. In particular, FSM modifications at items (1) and (2) of the list above (adding and removing states and transitions) can be achieved by overriding existing (or adding new) clauses of the action method or of the methods implementing the actions. Item (3a) can be realized by overriding a method implementing the action. Finally, items (3b–e) can be implemented by suitably overriding methods action, event, pattern or one of their clauses.

It is now easy to show how the behavior extension of Figure 10 can be im-plemented. The code is reported in Figure 11 and shows how easy is to add the desired feature: we extended the sample1 behavior in Figure 8 by overriding the event clause relevant to the transition to be modified and then adding the needed ACL pattern.

Behavior extension in eXAT allows the redefinition of not only single method clauses, as it has been shown, but also *single elements* of data returned by action/2, event/2 and pattern/2 functions. This ability, called *partial redefinition*, means to change only some elements of the data returned by a function, e.g. one of the couples {*event, action*} bound to a certain state, the *event* of such a couple, the *event type* or the *pattern name* bound to a certain event, one element of a data pattern, etc. As an example, if we would design a behavior like that of Figure 11 but for agents that speak only "Prolog", we need to accordingly change *only the language slot* of ACL patterns. This is made possible in eXAT by means of the use of the function acl:refine that allows a single pattern specified in the ancestor class to be refined: in our example, as reported in Figure 12, this function is used to add a matching value for the "language" slot in ACL messages. Such a partial redefinition capability implies a very flexible control on behavior engineering. This feature is made possible thanks to the intrinsic characteristics of Erlang and is hard to obtain with a traditional object-oriented language[16].

---

[15]This is the reason why the sample codes in Figure 8 and 9 report function declarations with Self as the first parameter.

[16]Indeed it could require a very complex object model to try to achieve a similar—but not the same—flexibility.

```
-module (sample1_extended_prolog_speaking).
-export ([extends/1, pattern/2]).

extends () -> sample1_extended.

pattern (Self, request_pattern) ->
  acl:refine (Self, request_pattern, 1,
              #aclmessage {language = 'Prolog'});
pattern (Self, refuse_pattern) ->
  acl:refine (Self, refuse_pattern, 1,
              #aclmessage {language = 'Prolog'}).
```

FIGURE 12. A more specialized behavior

6. Messaging and Semantics

eXAT agents interact through the exchange of ACL messages, in accordance with the FIPA-ACL standard [38]. While message reception is performed by means of the specification of an ACL message pattern that triggers an action in a behavior, message sending is done through a set of functions of the eXAT "acl" module, each function specialized to send a different speech act type and named like the speech act it sends. So we have functions acl:inform, acl:cfp, acl:confirm, acl:request, etc. All these functions take, as parameter, the message to be sent, encoded in an Erlang form[17]. In the current version of eXAT, such messages are sent using messaging primitives and the transport protocol natively provided by the Erlang runtime system, so (at the moment) interactions are possible only among eXAT agents. Interaction with agents running on other kind of platforms is currently not supported, but a new eXAT release is under development[18], which will provide standard FIPA message transport protocols [37, 36] and message encoding [34, 35].

Since messaging relies on Erlang standard communication primitives, from the point of view of the Erlang runtime, an agent is seen as a process whose registered name corresponds to the name of the agent set by the programmer[19]. This means that agent naming and addressing follow, in the current release of eXAT, the same rules of process addressing in Erlang: a local agent is referred using its name, while a remote agent is referred using a concatenation of its name, the sign "@" and the name of the remote site in which the agent lives.

The messaging modules of the eXAT platform not only provide a simple means to exchange messages with the right syntax, but they are also able to support *message semantics*. According to FIPA-ACL specification [38], eXAT includes automatic checking of the *feasibility precondition (FP)* and the *rational effect (RE)*

---

[17]In particular, the Erlang record #aclmessage is defined, where each field corresponds a slot of a standard ACL message, i.e. sender, receiver, content, language, etc.

[18]We plan to release this new version by June 2005.

[19]In Erlang, each process may be registered with a literal name so that message addressing is performed using the registered name of the receiving process.

relevant to each speech act sent. This is made possible by (*i*) providing an Erlang-based syntax of SL sentences [42] and (*ii*) using an ERES engine (and in particular the relevant Knowledge Base) as a representation of the mental state of an agent, storing Erlang-translated SL sentences as facts[20]. Such a combination allows *FP*s to be checked by looking at what is stored in the KBs representing the mental state of sender and receiver agents, while *RE*s can be supported by suitably updating these KBs.

The use of ACL semantics in agent programming is an important support for the engineering of "really rational" agents. In such agents, the deliver of a message, on the basis of the semantics, is able to change receiver's mental state; therefore, agent reaction can be programmed on the basis of the semantic effect the message has onto agent's mental state [18, 17, 26]. As it is known, this ensures a decoupling between messages and agent actions, allowing an agent to decide, on the basis of its autonomous reasoning process, what to have to do when a message is received. Such an ACL semantics support gives more autonomy and interaction awareness to agents, and also allows a more flexible agent engineering. As an example, let us suppose that we would like to design an agent that does something when "it knows that a sentence is true"; let us also suppose that the sentence can be asserted by either the agent's reasoning process or the arrival of an inform message that explicitly asserts the sentence. As in both cases the effect is "believing that the sentence is true", exploiting automatic processing of ACL semantics provided by eXAT implies to write a behavior where the trigger is exactly what we need: the assertion of the fact representing the sentence in the ERES engine representing the agent's mental state. Without such a built-in semantic support, we should have used two triggers in the behavior—thus provoking a loss of generality—or add another behavior that mimics inform *RE*—thus burdening the agent design and implementation processes.

7. Related Work

Today there are many agent platforms and languages [4], so comparing eXAT with all of them is quite difficult; we will instead concentrate our attention only on some of the most widely known. In the following, we will distinguish approaches that employ agent programming languages designed ad-hoc and agent platforms built on the top of existing (and general purpose) programming languages. We already dealt with the incompleteness problem of both approaches in Section 1, which was the main reason driving us to search for an alternative; for this reason, we will describe here only the differences the chosen agent languages and platforms present with respect to our Erlang/eXAT approach.

---

[20]The translation from SL to Erlang is simple: each SL sentence, represented as a list "(a b c ...)" is translated into an Erlang list, i.e. "[a, b, c, ...]", while a parameter such as ":paramname paramvalue" is translated into the Erlang tuple "{paramname, paramvalue}".

7.1. Agent Programming Languages

The concept of software systems written using processes (agents) interacting through the exchange of messages is not only a base of Erlang but also of some agent programming languages. This basic model is derived from formal approaches, such as CCS [51], π-calculus [52] and actor model [11]. The agent programming languages April [48] and Go! [49] follow these models. April is a symbolic language for concurrent programming; not only its process model is similar to that of Erlang, but also message matching constructs follow the same Erlang rules. Go! is instead April enriched with logic functionalities, such as knowledge base representation and (concurrent) reasoning capabilities, as in Parlog [23]. Go! allows a designer to define *functions*, *Prolog-like predicates* and *queries*, i.e. the Prolog "goals". Agent programming in Go! is thus basically logic/declarative and supported by many language constructs; it also allows to define *objects* as knowledge base elements, like in CLOS [47] or CLIPS [3].

Agent0 [59], PLACA [61], AgentK [27] and 3APL [45] are high-level languages for the design of goal-oriented agents. They are based on the BDI model [57] and provide constructs for defining beliefs, intentions, plans, obligations, capabilities, etc. Some of them integrate an agent communication language [32, 38] to allow interoperability with other agents.

A different philosophy is instead the base of APL [21] and JACK [10]. Both support the BDI model but the language is mainly Java-based, that is, it extends/integrates Java and provides a compiler that transforms the source code into Java executables. APL has its own grammar (similar to that of Java) which presents ad-hoc statements to define agents with their beliefs, plans and goals; it also allows Java constructs and standard JRE libraries in agent developing. JACK, instead, extends the Java language by adding some constructs to define the agent-specific features needed by the BDI model.

The programming model of these approaches is different than that of eXAT, which instead clearly separates the behavioral part from the agent's intelligence, allowing the programmer to intervene on both. This means that eXAT provides a "low-level" agent programming philosophy, in which the programmer can control all agent parts with a grain finer than that of the cited languages, whose processing mechanisms are built-in and not visible to (nor manageable for) the designer. Indeed, an higher-level programming platform could be also obtained by integrating eXAT with Erlang-based BDI tools, such as [62].

7.2. Agent Platforms

Among the agent platforms available today, it is worthwhile considering those which comply with the FIPA agent interoperability standard [43]. For this reason, here we will deal with JADE [16] and FIPA-OS [1], which are the most widely known (Java-based) FIPA compliant platforms. Both take care of agent interoperability and behavioral aspects but do not provide any support for agent intelligence: it must be implemented by integrating external tools [2, 7, 55]. Also

ACL semantics is not supported and must be done (by hand) by the programmer when needed[21].

As for behavior engineering, JADE supports FSM-based behaviors with inheritance and specialization. JADE behaviors are based on computations (*sub-behaviors*) tied to each FSM state; such a computation specifies the action an agent has to do when it reaches that state; the computation must also check and generate the events that fire transitions to another state. A similar approach is provided in FIPA-OS. Here computations are encapsulated into Task objects, each having the responsibility of catching an event (i.e. the arrival of a message) and starting another Task to perform the action and wait for the next event.

In both platforms, sub-behaviors (or Tasks) are strongly tied to the specific FSM for which they are designed; eXAT instead provides a separation between FSM structure and the tied computations: event generation and handling is not a task of a user-defined computation but a native mechanism provided by eXAT, while agent actions, that are bound to transitions, specify what agent has to do after event occurrence. Such kind of structure allows an existing FSM to be used with other actions—by overriding the methods defining the actions—or to use the actions in another context—by calling the action method from another behavior[22].

8. Conclusions

In this Chapter, a new approach for multi-agent system implementation with the Erlang language has been described, supported through eXAT, a new experimental Erlang-based agent platform. The choices of developing a new platform and employing Erlang have been motivated, by showing how the main characteristics of this language can be exploited for agent implementation. On this basis, a model for engineering agent behaviors has been provided, which considers the use of multiple finite-state machines whose events may be bound to ACL message reception as well as be the result of a reasoning process of the agent. Behavior engineering is also made flexible by allowing FSM composition and specialization. Such concepts are altogether made available in eXAT by means of suitable libraries that permit to design, with the same programming language and tool, agent intelligence, agent behavior and agent communication. The advantages of the proposed approach are clearly stated through the whole Chapter; eXAT characteristics have been also compared to those of some other existing platforms and agent programming languages.

Acknowledgment

This work has been partially supported by the "WEBMINDS" FIRB research project of the Italian MIUR.

---

[21] JADE board announced a new version of JADE with a native support of ACL semantics, but this version has not been released yet (at the time this paper was written).

[22] A deeper comparison between eXAT and JADE, which includes also some code snippets, is provided, for reader's interest, in [28, 30, 29, 31].

Information about Software

Software is available on the Internet as
        (*) prototype version
Internet address: http://www.diit.unict.it/users/csanto/exat/
        Description of software: Erlang-based Agent Platform
        Download URL: http://www.diit.unict.it/users/csanto/exat/download.html
Contact person for question about the software:
        Name: Corrado Santoro
        email: csanto@diit.unict.it

References

[1] http://fipa-os.sourceforge.net/. FIPA-OS Web Site., 2003.

[2] http://herzberg.ca.sandia.gov/jess/. JESS Web Site, 2003.

[3] http://www.ghg.net/clips/CLIPS.html. CLIPS Web Site, 2003.

[4] http://www.agentlink.org/resources/agent-software.php, 2004.

[5] http://www.diit.unict.it/users/csanto/eres.html. ERES Web Site, 2004.

[6] http://www.diit.unict.it/users/csanto/exat/. eXAT Web Site, 2004.

[7] http://www.drools.org. Drools Home Page, 2004.

[8] http://www.erlang.org. Erlang Language Home Page, 2004.

[9] http://www-2.cs.cmu.edu/~softagents/, 2004.

[10] http://www.agent-software.com, 2004.

[11] C. Agha and C. Hewitt. *Concurrent Programming using Actors*. MIT Press, 1987.

[12] J. L. Armstrong. The development of Erlang. In ACM Press, editor, *Proceedings of the ACM SIGPLAN International Conference on Functional Programming*, pages 196–203, 1997.

[13] J. L. Armstrong. Making Reliable Distributed Systems in the Presence of Software Errors. *PhD Thesis, Swedish Institute of Computer Science, Stockholm, Sweden*, 2003.

[14] J. L. Armstrong, M. C. Williams, C. Wikstrom, and S. C. Virding. *Concurrent Programming in Erlang, 2nd Edition*. Prentice-Hall, 1995.

[15] Joe Armstrong and Robert Virding. Erlang - An Experimental Telephony Programming Language. In *XIII International Switching Symposium*, May 27-June 1, Stockholm, 1990.

[16] F. Bellifemine, A. Poggi, and G. Rimassa. Developing multi-agent systems with a FIPA-compliant agent framework. *Software: Practice and Experience*, 31(2):103–128, 2001.

[17] Federico Bergenti. Formalizing the Reusability of Agents. In Andrea Omicini, Paolo Petta and Jeremy Pitt, editor, 4th *International Workshop Engineering Societies in the Agents World (ESAW 2003)*. Springer, 2003.

[18] Federico Bergenti and Agostino Poggi. A Development Toolkit to Realize Autonomous and Inter-operable Agents. In 5th *International Conference on Autonomous Agents (Agents 2001)*, Montreal, Canada, 2001.

[19] G. Cabri, L. Leonardi, and F. Zambonelli. Mobile-Agent Coordination Models for Internet Applications. *IEEE Computer*, 33(2), February 2000.

[20] N. Carriero and D. Gelernter. Linda in Context. *Comm. ACM*, 32(4), April 1989.

[21] J. Chang-Hyun and K. M. Geroge. Agent-based Programming Language: APL. In *2002 ACM Symposium on Applied Computing*, Madrid, Spain, 2002.

[22] P. Ciancarini, R. Tolksdorf, F. Vitali, D. Rossi, and A. Knoche. Coordinating Multi-agent Applications on the WWW: A Reference Architecture. *IEEE Transaction on Software Engineering*, 24(5), 1998.

[23] Keith Clark and Steve Gregory. PARLOG: Parallel Programming in Logic. *ACM Transactions on Programming Languages and Systems*, 8(1):1–49, January 1986.

[24] Philip R. Cohen, Adam Cheyer, Michele Wang, and Soon Cheol. Baeg. An Open Agent Architecture. In Micheal N. Huhns & Munindar P. Singh, editor, *Readings in Agents*, pages 197–204, 1997.

[25] M. Cremonini, A. Omicini, and F. Zambonelli. Coordination and access control in open distributed agent systems: The TuCSoN approach. In António Porto and Gruia-Catalin Roman, editors, *Coordination Languages and Models*, volume 1906 of *LNCS*, pages 99–114. Springer-Verlag, 2000.

[26] M. Dastani, J. van der Ham, and F. Dignum. Communication for Goal Directed Agents. In Marc-Philippe Huget, editor, *Communication in Multiagent Systems - Agent Communication Languages and Conversation Policies*, pages 239–252. LNCS, 2003.

[27] W. H. E. Davies and P. Edwards. Agent-K: an Integration of AOP and KQML. In Y. Labrou and T. Finin, editors, *CIKM'94 Workshop on Intelligent Information Agents*, Anaheim, CA, 1994.

[28] Antonella Di Stefano and Corrado Santoro. eXAT: an Experimental Tool for Programming Multi-Agent Systems in Erlang. In *AI*IA/TABOO Joint Workshop on Objects and Agents (WOA 2003)*, Villasimius, CA, Italy, 10–11 September 2003.

[29] Antonella Di Stefano and Corrado Santoro. eXAT: A Platform to Develop Erlang Agents. In *Agent Exhibition Workshop at Net.ObjectDays 2004*, Erfurt, Germany, 27–30 September 2004.

[30] Antonella Di Stefano and Corrado Santoro. Designing Collaborative Agents with eXAT. In *ACEC 2004 Workshop at WETICE 2004*, Modena, Italy, 14–16 June 2004.

[31] Antonella Di Stefano and Corrado Santoro. On the Use of Erlang as a Promising Language to Develop Agent Systems. In *AI*IA/TABOO Joint Workshop on Objects and Agents (WOA 2004)*, Turin, Italy, 29–30 October 2004.

[32] T. Finin and Y. Labour. A Proposal for a New KQML Specification. Technical Report TR-CS-97-03, Computer Science and Electrical Engineering Dept., Univ. of Maryland., 1997.

[33] C.L. Forgy. Rete: a fast algorithm for the many pattern/many object pattern match problem. *Artificial Intelligence*, pages 17–37, 1982.

[34] Foundation for Intelligent Physical Agents. FIPA ACL Message Representation in Bit-Efficient Encoding Specification —No. SC00069G, 2002.

[35] Foundation for Intelligent Physical Agents. FIPA ACL Message Representation in XML Specification—No. SC00071E, 2002.

[36] Foundation for Intelligent Physical Agents. FIPA Agent Message Transport Protocol for HTTP Specification—No. SC00084F, 2002.

[37] Foundation for Intelligent Physical Agents. FIPA Agent Message Transport Protocol for IIOP Specification—No. SC00075G, 2002.

[38] Foundation for Intelligent Physical Agents. FIPA Communicative Act Library Specification—No. SC00037J, 2002.

[39] Foundation for Intelligent Physical Agents. FIPA Contract Net Interaction Protocol Specification—-No. SC00029H, 2002.

[40] Foundation for Intelligent Physical Agents. FIPA English Auction Interaction Protocol Specification—-No. SC00031F, 2002.

[41] Foundation for Intelligent Physical Agents. FIPA Request Interaction Protocol Specification—-No. SC00026H, 2002.

[42] Foundation for Intelligent Physical Agents. FIPA SL Content Language Specification—-No. SC00008I, 2002.

[43] Foundation for Intelligent Physical Agents. http://www.fipa.org, 2002.

[44] Stan Franklin and Art Graesser. Is it an Agent, or just a Program?: A Taxonomy for Autonomous Agents. In *Third International Workshop on Agent Theories, Architectures, and Languages (ATAL)*. Springer-Verlag, 1996.

[45] K.V. Hindriks, F.S. de Boer, W. van der Hoek, and J.-J.Ch. Meyer. Agent programming in 3APL. *Autonomous Agents and Multi-Agent Systems*, 2(4):357–401, 1999.

[46] C.A.R. Hoare. *Communicating Sequential Processes*. Prentice Hall International, 1985.

[47] Sonya E. Keene. *Object-Oriented Programming in Common Lisp*. Addison-Wesley, 1989.

[48] Frank McCabe and Keith Clark. April: Agent Process Interaction Language. In N. Jennings and M. Wooldridge, editor, *Intelligent Agents*. Springer, LNCS 890, 1995.

[49] Frank McCabe and Keith Clark. Go! - A Multi-Paradigm Programming Language for Implementing Multi-Threaded Agents. *Annals of Mathematics and Artificial Intelligence*, 41(2-4):171–206, August 2004.

[50] Mickaël Rémond. *Erlang - Programmation*. Eyrolles, 2003.

[51] R. Milner. *Communication and Concurrency*. Prentice Hall International, 1989.

[52] R. Milner. *Communicating and Mobile Systems: the Pi-Calculus*. Cambridge Univ Press, 1999.

[53] Andrea Omicini, Alessandro Ricci, Mirko Viroli, Marco Cioffi, and Giovanni Rimassa. Multi-agent infrastructures for objective and subjective coordination. *Applied Artificial Intelligence*, 18(9/10):815–831, October/December 2004.

[54] G. P. Picco, A. Murphy, and Roman G.-C. LIME: Linda Meets Mobility. In D. Garlan and Los Angeles (USA) J. Kramer, eds., editors, *21th Intl. Conference on Software Engineering (ICSE '99)*, May 1999.

[55] A. Pokahr, L. Braubach, and W. Lamersdorf. Jadex: Implementing a BDI-Infrastructure for JADE Agents. *Telecom Italia Journal: EXP - In Search of Innovation (Special Issue on JADE)*, 3(3), Sept. 2003.

[56] A. S. Rao. AgentSpeak(L): BDI agents speak out in a logical computable language. In *Agents Breaking Away*, pages 42–55. Springer-Verlag, LNAI 1038, 1996.

[57] A. S. Rao and M. P. Georgeff. Modeling Rational Agents within a BDI-Architecture. In R. Fikes J. Allen and E. Sandewall, editors, 2nd *International Conference on Principles of Knowledge Representation and Reasoning (KR'91)*. Morgan Kauffman, 1991.

[58] Corrado Santoro. *eXAT: an Experimental Tool to Develop Multi-Agent Systems in Erlang - A Reference Manual*. Available at `http://www.diit.unict.it/users/csanto/exat/`, 2004.

[59] Y. Shoham. AGENT-0: A Simple Agent Language and its Interpreter. In 9th *National Conference of Artificial Intelligence*, Anaheim, CA, 1991. MIT Press.

[60] K. Sycara, M. Paolucci, M. van Velsen, and J. Giampapa. The RETSINA MAS Infrastructure. *Special joint issue of Autonomous Agents and Multi-Agent Systems Journal*, 7(1 and 2), July 2003.

[61] S. R. Thomas. The PLACA Agent Programing Language. In N. Jennings and M. Wooldridge, editor, *Intelligent Agents*. Springer, LNCS 890, 1995.

[62] Carlos Varela, Carlos Abalde, Laura Castro, and José Gulias. On Modelling Agent Systems with Erlang. In 3rd *ACM SIGPLAN Erlang Workshop*, Snowbird, Utah, USA, 22 September 2004.

[63] M. Wooldridge, N. Jennings, and D. Kinny. The Gaia Methodology for Agent-Oriented Analysis and Design. *Journal of Autonomous Agents and Multi-Agent Systems*, 3(3), 2000.

[64] M. J. Wooldridge. *Multiagent Systems*. G. Weiss, editor. The MIT Press, April 1999.

[65] F. Zambonelli, N.R. Jennings, A. Omicini, and M.J. Wooldridge. Agent-oriented software engineering for Internet applications. In A. Omicini, F. Zambonelli, M. Klusch, and R. Tolksdorf, editors, *Coordination of Internet Agents: Models, Technologies, and Applications*, chapter 13, pages 326–346. Springer-Verlag, March 2001.

[66] Franco Zambonelli, Nicholas R. Jennings, and Michael Wooldridge. Developing multiagent systems: The gaia methodology. *ACM Trans. Softw. Eng. Methodol.*, 12(3):317–370, 2003.

Antonella Di Stefano and Corrado Santoro
University of Catania, Engieering Faculty
Viale Andrea Doria, 6
95125 - Catania, ITALY
e-mail: {ad, csanto}@diit.unict.it

Living Systems® Technology Suite

Giovanni Rimassa, Monique Calisti and Martin E. Kernland

Abstract. This chapter presents and discusses the Living Systems Technology Suite, LS/TS, a solution for the development and deployment of products and systems based on software agent technology and autonomic computing. LS/TS comprises a software development methodology and a Java-based agent platform with development tools. The focus of this paper is on the LS/TS agent platform: the concepts, API and development tools that support the design and implementation of multi-agent systems are described and discussed. This chapter also lists a few significant challenges that a middleware for multi-agent systems has to face, and also shows how each one of them is addressed by the LS/TS agent platform.

Keywords. agent middleware, development tools, run-time environment, development methodology.

1. Introduction

In recent years, Agent Oriented Software Engineering (AOSE) has been increasingly adopted to provide solutions able to flexibly adapt in real-time to changing and unforeseen run-time conditions and fluctuations in the ever more complex and dynamic business world. However, in order to meet today's stringent IT requirements, a comprehensive and solid approach to agent-based software design, development and deployment is needed. In this perspective, we have conceived and developed the Living Systems Technology Suite, LS/TS, a comprehensive approach, including a development methodology and a Java-based set of components and tools, for the professional development and deployment of products and solutions based on software agent technology.

Before starting to develop agent-based solutions around 2000, we carried out a comprehensive analysis of the prevailing research in agent technologies as well as available platforms, tools, and methodologies, and put the result in contrast to our comprehensive experience with real-world IT projects and the related customer expectations. While agent technologies were progressing, they had to meet an established industrial IT world, with many stable, mission-critical systems and networks in place that had grown over years, corporate IT strategies with defined product sets from major players and vendors, and huge investments in systems and know-how, resulting in challenging requirements for the still young agent technologies with respect to basic product quality, in particular regarding reliability and failover, performance and scalability, security; business functionality, eg. transactions, sessions, persistence; system administration functionality, eg. configuration and diagnostic tools; migration and extension capabilities of existing operational systems; integration with, and interfaces to, currently operational systems, products, and solutions; re-use of peoples know-how and experience, and organizational and administrative procedures and tools; and adherence to industry standards.

By then, J2EE EJB application servers represented a state-of-the-art technology fitting the above requirements and expectations. However, it was evident that J2EE could not be universal environment for any application domain, but that J2SE support was also necessary. The *Living System® Technology Suite* , discussed in this paper, provides a solution that strives to fulfill the above challenging requirements.

The rest of this chapter is organized as follows. Section 2 summarizes today's main business challenges and requirements in term of IT support. While, as discussed, agent technology provides powerful concepts and techniques to build effective solutions, it is also clear that several challenges lie ahead for agent-based computing. The overall LS/TS architecture, presented in Section 3, has been conceived with the aim to meet such challenges. To this purpose we defined the *common agent layer* as a way to express agent abstractions providing the foundation of the LS/TS programming model, discussed in Section 3.1, and we decomposed the overall LS/TS package into a development suite and and run-time suite, both presented in Section 3. Section 4 lists the engineering challenges posed by the LS/TS goals and the market expectations, and details how LS/TS tackles each of them. Finally, in Section 5, we discuss in more depth important features of LS/TS by motivating our choices and highlighting future work before concluding the paper with Section 6.

2. Challenges for Agent-Based Computing

In today's complex and rapidly transforming markets, business organizations have to face a variety of challenges, which can impose significant changes to their business processes and structures. The main requirements, common to a large majority of industries including telecommunications, logistics, financial services, manufacturing, healthcare, have been induced by several factors:

- *Liberalization and market deregulation* have been triggering fierce competition leading to the need for quick and flexible reactions to customers expectations and requirements. On the other hand, despite self-interest, many business

organizations must often dynamically coordinate to achieve a comprehensive service offering.

- *High exposure to variability.* Many businesses work under increasingly dynamic conditions, in which the diversity of constraints to be satisfied is not always known a priori. This requires the capability to adapt business strategies and solutions and often to operate in real-time (or nearly real-time) mode.
- *Growing diversity in market demand.* This trend has been causing higher differentiation and shorter life-cycle of offered products and services. As a major consequence, business process management is becoming increasingly complex.
- *Explosion of available data.* The extension of business horizons can produce an exponential growth of information to be processed, which is often heterogeneous and distributed. This can become a quite challenging task especially in real-time (or near to real-time) operational mode.

These factors translate into business organizations demanding more frequent adaptation from their software systems and hardware infrastructures, which are often highly distributed, must be able to gather, analyze and visualize vast amounts of data, interoperate with a large number of diverse technologies and tools, and integrate different business processes at both intra- and inter-enterprise levels. In particular, IT solutions are expected to provide easy adaptation of applications and content to accommodate heterogeneous users expectations, backgrounds and roles.

The problem is that today's operational IT systems are usually based on traditional technologies unable to provide the required flexibility to meet the above business needs. As a result, new software design, development and integration approaches are being pursued. As a key approach, agent technology provides powerful metaphors, concepts and techniques for conceptualizing, designing and implementing effective solutions meeting current business needs [21]. Agents facilitate one-to-one mapping of real world business models into system components, can act as smart decision making support elements in complex, dynamic, and networked markets and can be delegated responsibility for performing tasks that would be otherwise very difficult, time consuming, costly or just infeasible for humans. Various recent examples of industrial uptake of agent technology can be found in [1].

3. LS/TS Overview

One of the major goals of LS/TS is to provide agent technology relevant abstractions without introducing proprietary language extensions or even a new programming language. As the base for LS/TS, the Java programming language was chosen due to several reasons such as the wide acceptance and use of the language as well as its portability. The agent-specific abstractions are implemented using standard language capabilities, thus LS/TS applications are pure Java applications. LS/TS provides a Java library named *Core Agent Layer*, CAL, with implementations of these new abstractions.

LS/TS provides a comprehensive development tool suite, the mentioned CAL library, and a sound methodology. The Development Suite of LS/TS is based on the *Eclipse* Java IDE [7]. This allows the agent technology relevant abstractions to be managed on the tool level, by providing a new kind of view on the agent application. This approach enables developers to directly handle these new abstractions, while keeping the compiled Java application in line with the mainstream and open development tool suite for the Java platform.

The methodological support consists of the UML-based *Agent Modeling Language*, AML, and a comprehensive software development process called the *Agent-oriented Development Methodology*, ADEM. AML [5] is a semi-formal visual modeling language for specifying, modeling and documenting systems that incorporate concepts drawn from multi-agent systems theory[1].

3.1. The LS/TS Programming Model

The LS/TS architecture can be divided into two separate parts according to when and by whom each component is used. On the one hand, the *Development Suite* comprises the tool chain used by software developers at system construction time. The *Run-Time Suite*, instead, is defined by all the LS/TS pieces working as an integrated whole to aid application users and administrators at system operation time. LS/TS is available in different editions, Personal, Business, and Enterprise, as further explained in Section 3.2.

Figure 1 shows that there is a *conceptual layer* that belongs neither to the development nor to the runtime domains. Rather, such a layer ties together the two and ensures the conceptual integrity of both the developer artifacts (system models and source code) and the user artifacts (actual executable modules, user interfaces and user documentation). This conceptual layer hosts the *programming model* of LS/TS.

This programming model's most general component is the aforementioned *Common Agent Layer*, CAL. Beyond being independent of the LS/TS Edition to be applicable for J2SE and J2EE, the CAL is also open extensible.

The most general component belonging to LS/TS programming model is the *Common Agent Layer*, CAL. Beyond being edition independent due to the aforementioned challenge, the CAL also needs to be open and extensible.

The reason for this is that the notion of agency can be extremely general and encompasses a whole host of biological, artificial and software entities. A lot of very concrete and precisely defined agent models have been proposed by researchers [11, 20, 10, 4], but sticking to a concrete agent model was felt to clash with LS/TS goal of being widely applicable.

The chosen approach was instead a feature-based one, where a set of characteristic properties are considered, and different software components are labelled

---

[1]For more detailed information on AML please refer to:
http://www.whitestein.com/pages/solutions/meth.html

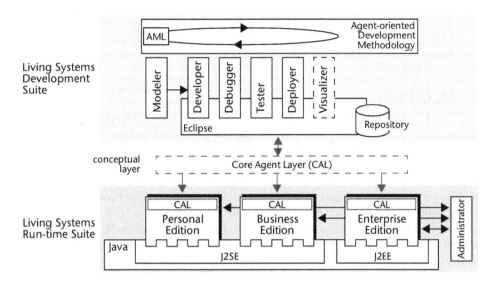

FIGURE 1. The overall structure of LS/TS

differently according to which properties they possess and which ones they do not. *Autonomy* is perhaps the most significant feature of software agents, so the degree of autonomy can be taken as the discriminating factor to impose some structure on this classification.

The CAL contains three different agent types as the basic design elements, having different properties each and providing a different set of functionality. Depending on the specific research area, researchers agree or disagree about the agenthood of some of these types; the interested reader can refer to [17] to see a not very recent but still fundamentally valid commentary concerning what is considered to be an agent by different research groups. However, it is important to remark that the taxonomy adopted in LS/TS is more motivated by application requirements than from a systemic analysis of the multi-agent system research.

The three agent types supported by the CAL are as follows:

1. The *Autonomous Agent* represents a control element of the application logic, able to sense its surroundings, act on them and also to coordinate with other agents. This kind of agent, even when taken in its simplest form, exhibits a high enough degree of autonomy to comply with the criteria of the *weak agent definition* [22]. More powerful agent models, gifted with reasoning capabilities and complying with the *strong agent definition* by [22] can be built on this groundings.

2. The *Servant Agent* offers a view on application services and reactive functionality, thereby exposing what are essentially passive computational units as a part of the overall multi-agent system.

3. The *Data Agent* aggregates data according to meaningful clusters, thus providing units of description that can be made to match relevant concepts of the application domain or of the social organization chosen for the multi-agent application.

3.2. LS/TS Editions

LS/TS addresses deployment variability by providing three different run-time environments, each for a different deployment scenario. The run-time environment is the habitat of the agents and provides a messaging infrastructure, lookup services, persistency services, etc. The messaging infrastructure enables asynchronous message passing between the autonomous agents, which are the participants in this peer-to-peer communication. The *Federation* feature of the run-time environment allows connection to several other run-times. These run-times then form a group, called a Federation. Within a *Federation* the agents can reach each other by peer-to-peer messaging, no matter on which physical machine they actually reside (more on the *Federation* feature can be found in Section 4.2).

The Enterprise Edition, is executed on J2EE application servers. Thus, the run-time benefits from the features of the J2EE application server, such as connectivity with other systems, transactions, resource management, etc.

The Business Edition runs on the Java 2 Standard Edition, and offer maximum programming flexibility while still ensuring powerful runtime services such as resource control and monitoring or platform federation.

The Personal Edition is intended for technology exploration, solution prototypes, and lightweight, personal applications. This edition does not provide database connectivity. As part of the Development Suite the PE can serve as entry level development environment, but is not licensable for production use.

Each run-time environment is able to execute any LS/TS agent application, due to the unifying CAL layer. Each of the environments provides the full functionality of CAL with differences in implementation sophistication.

This provides an easy upgrade to one of the other run-time environments based on prevailing business and deployment needs. The three environments differ regarding functionality for areas such as transaction management, client access, fail-safe operation, clustering, and resource management.

3.3. The LS/TS Development Suite

The development suite, as shown in Figure 1, consists currently of five tools, four of them are based on the Eclipse platform. The *Modeler* is based on Enterprise Architect, a UML modelling tool from Sparx Systems [8]. With the Modeler tool, the user creates a model of the agent application using AML. The created model described by class, interaction, activity and state diagrams is then exported to an intermediate format based on XML which is the input for the subsequent tools.

The *Developer* is the main design and implementation tool for the application programmer. It is an extension to the standard Eclipse Java programming environment, providing specific navigators, views, and manipulators of the Java code for the LS/TS agents. The Developer can import AML models from the Modeler and automatically create the appropriate code structure. This template code is then ready to be filled with the corresponding business logic of the application. Extended search capabilities allow systematic discovery of specific *Agent Logic* components, to explore who is the sender of a specific message, who is the receiver of a specific message, etc.

The *Debugger* is an extension to the standard Eclipse Java debugger, with direct support of the agent abstractions of the CAL and the logic of the agents. As an example, it is possible to add a breakpoint to an agent that is only triggered if a specific message sent from an agent arrives, or if an agent reads or writes a specific value from its *Agent Data Storage*.

The *Tester* supports unit testing of single agents and their logics. It consists of helper classes and mock objects that ease the creation of unit tests for LS/TS specific agent logic.

Once an agent application has been implemented, the developer has to package it with the necessary third-party libraries, meta information about the agent application, and run-time environment specific information. All this is handled by the *Deployer*, a set of features integrated in the Developer tool. Here the decision has to be made, on which edition of the run-time environment one wants to deploy the agent application.

The operation of the run-time environment is assisted by the *Administrator*, a tool which helps to visualize and control the ongoing execution of the application. It is possible to see a list of the messages throughout the platform, both before they are processed and after they have been delivered. An *Inspector* provides a view of agent state, life-cycle management of an agent (e.g. stopping an agent), etc.

4. Addressing Challenges with LS/TS

The market expectations put forward in Section 2 pose a set of non-trivial requirements and constraints for a software infrastructure and methodology such as the one offered by LS/TS. From a software engineering perspective, the following technical challenges have to be faced:

1. *Supporting agent technology relevant abstractions throughout the software life-cycle, despite the assumptions made by traditional development environments.* The main clash here comes from the fact that traditional stepwise software development methods and systems heavily decouple data flow, execution flow and configuration flow and therefore cannot be effectively used to preserve agent concepts and abstractions across the entire software life-cycle. The effectiveness of agent technology is largely reliant upon the capability to hide low-level technical details by capturing the application logic into abstractions that can be understood by both users and developers.

2. *Providing comprehensive coverage of different application domains and deployments.* Because of the diversity of business requirements and the need to integrate applications into different execution environments it is challenging to provide a solution that can offer an effective trade-off between these aspects.

3. *Augmenting the application semantics with agent concepts (such as pro-activity, asynchronous communication, etc.), while being hosted and acting within the standard deployment solutions currently popular within IT environments.* Providing effective support to corporate customers with a new and more flexible approach such as agent technology cannot be achieved without paying careful attention to the whole system and legacy software integration.

4. *Supporting a range of dynamic software component interactions in complex environments, where different kinds of entities exist (agents, resources, artifacts, etc.) with varying degrees of autonomy.* While modeling multi-agent applications, one should avoid the pitfall of attributing agent properties to domain elements that do not really have them, out of conceptual bias. This *'everything is an agent'* attitude can needlessly complicate applications and systems.

5. *Reconciling component autonomy and pro-activity with component manageability.* Those elements that actually end up being realized as autonomous agents must not jeopardize the overall application predictability and should also grant effective manageability of the deployed systems. This challenging aspect is still an important open research topic [18], [19].

The Living System Technology Suite has been conceived and developed with these issues in mind. In the following we aim at showing how the different software engineering challenges outlined above are addressed by LS/TS features and architecture.

4.1. Bringing Agent Abstractions to Developers

The first goal for a middleware trying to support a new way of building software is, quite naturally, to provide a well defined yet easy to use way to express relevant concepts through software constructs. Among the concepts that define and characterize the multi-agent system approach to software development, the most important one to be considered is of course the *Autonomous Agent* concept, which is directly expressed by LS/TS. Figure 2 shows the Autonomous Agent within the context of LS/TS runtime environment.

Its higher level of autonomy makes the Autonomous Agent very powerful as it can plan its own execution. In combination with the other agent types listed in Section 3.1, the Autonomous Agent can be used to control the execution of complex agent applications. The programming model of LS/TS autonomous agents is a natural one for software components that exhibit weak agency. An autonomous agent, as it is perceived by LS/TS application developers, has the following features.

- *Continuous execution.* An autonomous agent follows a life-cycle such that it is always running from its creation to its termination.
- *Long-term state.* An autonomous agent has state that captures its history (past perceptions and actions); such state has a lifetime that is longer than any single conversation or process the agent is involved in.
- *Procedural autonomy.* An autonomous agent does not rely on external threads of control to execute its code; rather, it can choose when and whether to take action or observe its environment.
- *Message exchange.* An autonomous agent can send and receive messages to set up interactions with other peers.

While this programming model is natural and offers good abstractions to the programmers developing multi-agent applications, a straightforward, naive implementation would fail to have the non-functional properties (scalability, robustness, etc.) that are required if an agent platform is to effectively tackle the challenges described at the beginning of Section 4.

Therefore, LS/TS Autonomous Agents have a composite structure, fostering separation of concerns and allowing different levels of functionality in different deployment environments. The Autonomous Agent consists of three components, as illustrated in Figure 2.

1. The *Agent Meta Information.*
2. The *Agent Data Storage.*
3. The *Agent Logic.*

The Agent Meta Information holds all the pieces of information that are necessary to maintain the properties of the Autonomous Agent programming abstraction. Such information includes, for example, the agent identity. The Agent Data Storage keeps the long term agent state, and can leverage persistent storage facilities when available. The Agent Logic contains all application relevant information and functionality of the Autonomous Agent. This includes the agent capabilities (i.e. what the agent can do) and the structure of the complex tasks it can perform (composite actions and perceptions, interaction protocols, and the like).

This means that the Agent Logic defines the type of the agent (TravelAgent, StockTradingAgent, etc.). Between agents of the same type (i.e., same functionality, e.g. many stock trading agents that trade stocks in the name of their user/owner), the only thing that would be different is the Agent Data Storage, which contains the agent's private information (e.g. stocks to trade, preferred prices, trading strategy, stock owners contact information) and the Agent Meta Information which determines the identity of the agent instance.

Another noteworthy aspect depicted in Figure 2 is the relationship between an Autonomous Agent and the Agent middleware hosting it. Due to its active nature, an LS/TS Autonomous Agent exposes features to the Agent middleware but also uses some other ones provided by the LS/TS runtime.

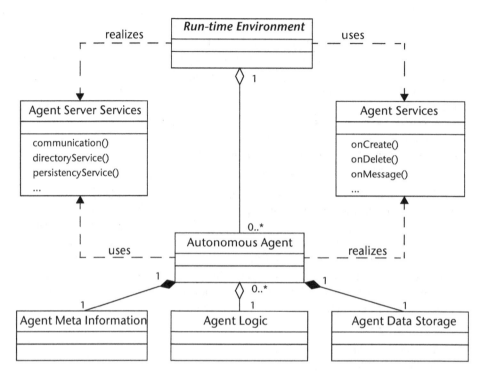

FIGURE 2. Autonomous Agent and its relationship with the hosting Agent middleware

Each Autonomous Agent provides a generic set of services, which is the interface to the agent middleware: The *life-cycle services* (Agent Services in Figure 2) allow the agent middleware to control the execution of the agents and allow the agent to execute appropriate logic when the state of its life-cycle changes. *on-Create()* triggers the code that needs to be executed when the agent is created. This is often some initialization sequence or sometimes even empty. *onDelete()* triggers the code that needs to be executed when the agent is destroyed. This can be some clean up code, closing down open connections, or making transient data persistent. On the other hand, the run-time environment exposes some services for Autonomous Agents to use, such as message based communication, a directory service and, depending on the concrete deployment configuration, persistence facilities.

The *Message Dispatching Agent Logic*, MDAL, is the default agent logic provided by LS/TS to Autonomous Agent developers. It is expected to be effective for a large set of application domains and environments, but can be extended or replaced by the developer thanks to the open and extensible nature of the CAL. In addition, other agent logic modules (eg. goal-oriented) will be available as part of the LS/TS offering in the future.

The MDAL allows for both message-triggered and conversation-triggered behaviour specification. Messages whose semantics are to be interpreted within a wider scope (an agent conversation or any complex interaction) are named *context messages*, whereas isolated messages that do not belong to an extended interaction are called *non-context messages*.

The *ContextSelector* and the *ContextFactory* components work together to create contexts on demand and to dispatch to existing contexts those messages that are recognized as being a follow-up to an already started interaction. However, the real core of the MDAL is the *MessageHandler* class. The Message Handler implements some application logic that is triggered by a specified message.

An interaction with other agents can be handled by the Message Handler. The interaction can take the form of a conversation where a sequence of communicative acts on some topic is executed. The delivery of a message created by a communicative act is the message that is handled by the Message Handler. The handling of the incoming message can include the sending of a reply to the counterpart agent (*continuation* of the conversation). All received messages that belong to the same conversation are handled in the same context by the same Message Handler.

A fundamental aspect of agent interaction is to support composability of basic conversations to yield aggregate ones. This feature is also required to enable goal directed, plan executing agents that are not provided with exhaustive solutions to their tasks but rather with building blocks and composition rules. LS/TS supports interaction composability within the MDAL by the possibility to set up a parent-child relationship between the Message Handlers.

The parent Message Handler can activate a new Message Handler and declare it as a child. This causes the execution of the parent Message Handler to be suspended until the execution of the child Message Handler is completed. When the child Message Handler has completed execution the parent Message Handler is automatically notified.

This type of relationship between handlers allows an easy implementation of nested activities or interactions. For example, agent A is interacting with agent B. At some point in this interaction agent B needs to obtain information from agent C and cannot continue the interaction with A until it has the information from C. Agent B can obtain this information only by starting an interaction with agent C. Hence, a nested interaction with C is started. The interaction with A is suspended, while the interaction with C is in progress.

4.2. Supporting Multiple Deployments and Domains

The second challenge presented above mentions different deployment scenarios with specific requirements. The main way LS/TS copes with this challenge is by making available the three aforementioned editions (see Section 3.2) that allow tailored deployment and subsequent extensibility. Moreover, some more detailed deployment options are available. In the following, three possible situations are presented, and for each one of them the solution with a LS/TS run-time environment is described.

- *Persistent Deployment.* In real-world production deployments, a strong emphasis is often put on avoiding data loss. For this first requirement, the Enterprise Edition of LS/TS offers the possibility to execute the agents in a persistent mode where the messages and the Agent Data Storages are kept persistent. In addition, XA transactions are used to ensure that this data stays in a consistent state. The result is that the agent application will not lose any data, even if the JVM should crash. After restarting the application server and the Enterprise Edition run-time, the agent application continues to run as if nothing happened.
- *Application-transparent Clustering.* Often, the scenario presented above is enough, however, a few production deployments require that the application has a 24/7 uptime, meaning that it is constantly available. This requirement can be met by running the Enterprise Edition in a clustered setup in order to achieve failover capabilities. One possible setup is to have two run-time nodes running on two different machines, both connected to the same JMS server and database. Should one node fail, another one will take over after a few milliseconds. The agent application will continue to run as though nothing happened, as the relevant data of the application is persistent on the database. This scenario, like the previous one, is transparent to the agent application.
- *Application-visible Federation.* To further extend the application reach, instead of simply adding more resources while still keeping the application model of a single big and powerful machine hosting the whole application, the *LS/TS Federation* feature can be exploited. This allows a set of loosely coupled LS/TS run-time nodes to communicate with each other and to exchange messages. Autonomous Agents and connected clients still see the individual run-time, however, messages for agents not found on the run-time will be forwarded to the other nodes in the Federation. LS/TS Federation enables applications with a dynamic, non client/server deployment schema where agents and the nodes hosting them can appear and disappear freely during normal system operation, thus harnessing the true power and flexibility of agent technology.

Another feature that adds to the flexibility of the run-times is their internal structure which consists of a microkernel, where functionality such as the messaging infrastructure and directories is built as services that are loaded at startup time. Thus, the run-time can be configured at startup time with a suitable set of services, and several flavors of the same service can be available. The Personal Edition and the Business Edition have both the same microkernel, but mostly different services.

The above list shows how LS/TS supports a multi-faceted set of deployment configuration, that vary not just with respect to the host Java edition, but also with the non-functional properties desired for the application and even with the distribution semantics (e.g. transparently replicated or visibly federated).

4.3. Extending Traditional Runtime Environments

As mentioned in Section 3, the LS/TS product offering comprises three different run-time environments, the *Personal Edition*, the *Business Edition*, and the *Enterprise Edition*. The Personal Edition is meant for prototyping and explorations and is also embedded within the Development Suite so that simple applications can be immediately executed, including directly in the Debugger. The Business Edition is based on J2SE [13], just like the Personal Edition, however, it contains more features and a more sophisticated implementation.

The Enterprise Edition is based on J2EE [14] and needs a J2EE application server to run. Being hosted by an application server without exploiting proprietary mechanisms implies that LS/TS Enterprise Edition only requires an application server compliant with the EJB 2.0 specification [9]. The specification does not allow the management of own threads of execution, as this resource should be controlled by the application server. The consequence of this constraint is that an LS/TS agent cannot have its own execution thread.

Supporting the autonomous agent abstraction and programming model, while complying with J2EE imposed restriction results in an architecture where agents do not exclusively own a thread. Threads are kept outside the agents and are given to them when they need to execute some of their behavior. Each agent in turn gives up its thread when it has finished with it.

A thread is passed to an agent whenever a new message arrives; moreover, the agent application developer can register recurring notifications and define the interval of how often these notifications should be delivered. Thus, the Autonomous Agent never exclusively owns a thread for processing, but receives a thread for processing when appropriate. The effect is similar with agent systems where the agent exclusively owns the thread, because on the processor level, the threads themselves receive a limited time-slice for processing which is scheduled by the Java Virtual Machine (JVM) and by the operating system.

Another constraint of the EJB 2.0 specification led to a design decision common to all LS/TS run-times, namely to have only one message queue for all agent-to-agent messages. The alternative would have been to equip every agent with its on message inbox, however this was not feasible due to performance reasons as the inboxes would have been required to persist inside the J2EE application server.

With the decision to have only one message queue, it was also possible to use JMS as the messaging infrastructure. This allows the option to have the messages persisted and handled by JMS. In addition, there is XA transaction support available for JMS messaging which brings the benefits mentioned above of incurring no data loss.

Business and Enterprise Editions of LS/TS are equipped with resource management capabilities. The Enterprise Edition profits from the underlying application server whereas the Business run-time has its own resource management service. Because of this resource management service, a virtually unlimited number of agents and messages can be sustained by the run-time environment.

Another issue that pertains to this challenge is integrating agent applications or agent technology in general into existing solutions. One possible method to achieve integration these days is to be accessible as a Web Service for other IT systems. This can be achieved by using the Web Service Gateway (WSG) which is included in the LS/TS offering. By configuring the WSG, specific Autonomous Agents can be exposed as Web Services with a defined interface. Which agent and how it is exposed is a question of the configuration. The agent does not need any special special functionality as the Web Service call is transferred to a message. Thus, for the agent the Web Service request seems like just another request from another Autonomous Agent. The WSG runs independently of the run-time in a separate servlet container, as it is based on the AXIS implementation of Apache [2].

A similar approach is chosen for the integration of external client application that are not Web Services. Here, LS/TS provides a Java client library which allows the client to connect to the run-time and send and receive messages just as another agent. The connectivity is reached through synchronous RMI calls which are managed inside the run-time and there transformed to asynchronous message passing to the other agents. The identification of the client contains enough information such that the agent is able to discover if the sender of a message is another Autonomous Agent or an external client.

4.4. Covering the Autonomy Spectrum

When modeling real-world problems in complex application domains, agents are an important concept to use, but they are by no means the only one. Rather, an agent is quite a rich software component, so that several application parts cannot comply with the requirements of even the weak definition of agency.

The Common Agent Layer accommodates not only Autonomous Agents as the components applications are built from, but also Servant and Data Agents, as listed in Section 3.1. Figure 3 shows a conceptual taxonomy of the agent types supported by the CAL.

The intermediate (i.e. non leaf) nodes of the inheritance tree depicted in the figure represent conceptual entities and are not provided as actual Java classes of the LS/TS API. It is worth noticing how a first differentiation is made between *synchronously accessed* and *asynchronously accessed* agents. Far from being just a low-level synchronization issue, this distinction marks the very first step that differentiates autonomous software components from reactive objects that obey *Design by Contract* [16]. In [16] it is clearly shown how an asynchronous rendezvous between components (a *separate feature call* in Eiffel parlance) significantly weakens the assumptions that can be made about program behaviour, thereby loosening the coupling between components and increasing their autonomy.

Moreover, the conceptual taxonomy diagram shows that Autonomous Agents can freely use (i.e. interact with) both other Autonomous Agents and simpler data and servant agents. This highlights how Autonomous Agents mostly play the role

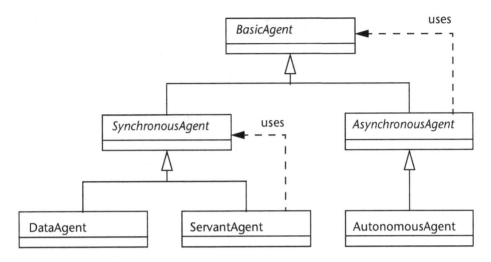

FIGURE 3. The conceptual taxonomy of agents in the CAL

of control supervisors, overseeing the behaviour of less autonomous components, enacting meta-level policies that result in a software system that possesses the *self-CHOP* qualities that are, e.g. advocated by *autonomic computing* proponents [15]. As shown by the loop in the diagram, an Autonomous Agent can also exert a relationship of command on another Autonomous Agent, thereby yielding support for social organization modeling.

The Servant Agent and the Data Agent are rather similar in the access patterns they allow. A *Lookup Service* is provided by the agent platform to contact data and servant agents and then, a specific interface, dependent on the actual kind of data or computation, is adopted. The Autonomous Agent, as described in 4.1, offers instead a full fledged abstraction for those application components that need to exhibit agency traits such as proactivity and interactive ability.

4.5. Managing Software Autonomy

Multi-agent systems are an approach to software construction that fosters loose coupling and asynchronicity among components. While this is effective to develop flexible applications in complex and highly dynamic environments, care has to be taken not to compromise other needs in the area of control and management of running applications.

The previously cited resource control features of LS/TS are a first, important measure to put limits and constraints to what agents can do in term of resource acquisition and consumption. However, powerful and effective support must also be provided to system administrators, even more so in IT departments of larger businesses where system management can easily become a daunting task without proper help.

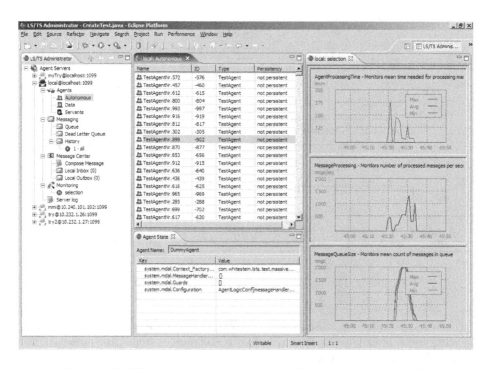

FIGURE 4. Monitoring resource usage and inspecting agents with
the Administrator

The tool that allows managing an instance of LS/TS run-time environment
suite is the *Administrator*. The Administrator supports the operation of the run-
time, which is valuable during debugging, but also important for monitoring a
production deployment. The monitoring allows the gathering of data from the run-
time which concerns the application and the run-time itself (e.g. average processing
time of each agent per incoming message, number of messages in the message
queue, heap memory used, etc.). A special service collects this information during
run-time and the individual statistics can be turned on and off at run-time. In
this way, an operator can peek into the running application on demand without
consuming too many resources throughout the lifetime of the agent application, as
the additional information collection process is quite a costly operation regarding
CPU and memory resources. A feature that is valuable also for debugging purposes
is the Agent Data Storage inspector which shows the key-value pairs of the state
of the agent. Figure 4 illustrates these two features.

Another useful feature which is used during debugging is the so called message
history, which collects the messages that are processed by agents or clients. It is
possible to graphically visualize the peers of this messaging communication and
to inspect what kind of messages were sent (see Figure 5). The life-cycle of the
Autonomous Agent can be controlled as well, so in case e.g., too much resources

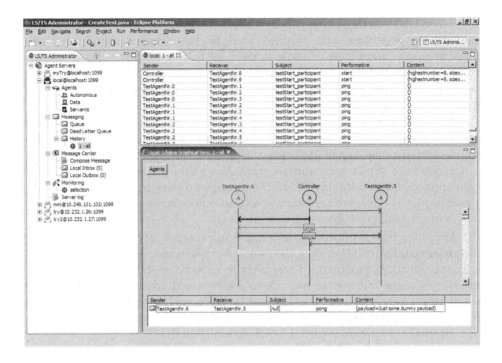

FIGURE 5. Browsing the message history with the Administrator

are used by a particular agent, it can be stopped. The Administrator provides the necessary functionality to achieve this, by e.g., monitoring the processing time or by inspecting the messages sent, the operator can then in special cases decide to stop the processing of an Autonomous Agent.

5. Discussion and Future Work

This section will discuss a few relevant topics stemming either from the LS/TS architecture, features, or both. One first very important issue is the extent to which non-autonomous entities should be considered when conceiving and designing a middleware for multi-agent systems.

The multi-agent system approach draws conceptual inspiration from fields as diverse as philosophy of language, social sciences and biology. Such a wide array of inputs produce a very rich model for software applications. Within this model there are a lot of entities that are not autonomous but still play a critical role in affecting the overall system behavioural and non-functional properties. Some of these entities are *social roles*, *organizational units*, *coordination artifacts*, *goals* and *mental states*.

The ADEM methodology supports most if not all of the above mentioned non-autonomous entities at the modeling level; but this richness has to be matched at the implementation level by some support for more than just software agents. It is from this perspective that the LS/TS hierarchy of agent types can be better understood: Servant Agent and Data Agent provide a simple way to implement *agent wrappers* when interfacing with external systems.

Moreover, the LS/TS runtime itself, with its microkernel and service based internal architecture provides a powerful means to embed non-autonomous components within a multi-agent application. Currently the LS/TS services only serve as a middleware deployment unit to grant Java multi-edition support; however it is expected that a suitable API will be placed into these services to have them appear as part of the agent environment so that autonomous agents can effectively sense and act (and possibly coordinate) through LS/TS services.

Managing the clash between autonomy and control, as cited in Section 4, is the fundamental principle driving the resource management in LS/TS. The goal is to have applications programmed according to an agent-centric view where *agents manage resources*, but also to have them administered according to a platform-centric view where *platforms manage agents*. When such a goal is used to inspire the concurrency model of the middleware, the cooperative intra-agent multitasking with externalized threads used in LS/TS naturally ensues.

While generally applicable in the vast majority of cases, the adopted threading model could be unsuitable for some specific situations where an agent is to be tightly bound to its perception and action channels, possibly with some response time constraints. The issue is currently taken into account for some further evolution of LS/TS; a first natural option would then be to have a special kind of Autonomous Agent that has special status and is allowed to use one or more Java threads permanently.

A second, less obvious, possibility would be to build a more flexible model of agent perceptions and actions so that synchronization and timing constraints can be attached to them, and have perceptor and effector components that can enforce these constraints. Proceeding in this way, irregularities in the threading model are pushed towards the agent/environment boundary so that the pollution of the CAL model is minimized. Such an approach could also be applied to soft or even hard real-time applications (if a suitable RTOS and realtime JVM are available), because the real-time sensitive activities (e.g. periodic sampling from a set of sensors with a rate-monotonic scheduling) would then be embedded in suitable perceptors.

The interaction model exposed by the LS/TS platform is generic and only comprises the fundamental messaging and scheduling features needed by software agents. This choice does not commit to a specific agent model beyond ensuring the basic agency properties, and allows the construction of heterogeneous multi-agent systems where agents in different social positions have different internal architectures.

Currently, work is being undertaken at Whitestein to provide a set of higher level features that will comprise new subsystems of LS/TS development and run-time suites. These subsystems will provide ready-made support for semantic communication in term of pre-defined communicative acts, ontology description frameworks and interaction protocol specification. The same attention to open standards that pervades LS/TS today also applies to the upcoming work, so special care is being taken to leverage public efforts such as the W3C Semantic Web activity.

The ongoing work so far deals with the application programming and middleware levels of software development. In the near future, the strategy of relying on the Java platform and refraining from using or inventing other programming languages will be retained although the authors are aware of interesting efforts in this area [6], [12].

6. Concluding Remarks

Dynamic markets are pressing for more dynamic and flexible IT solutions able to:

- Adapt, when circumstances change, their behavior by means of learning capabilities, continuous monitoring of the environment, reactive and proactive actions.
- Customize offered products/services so that they better fit to specific users, places, times and events by acquiring and making use of context-relevant information.

Agent technology provides powerful abstractions and techniques for conceptualizing, designing and implementing effective solutions. However, in today's highly demanding IT environments, this requires a solid approach to designing, developing and deploying agent-based applications and systems.

This chapter introduced the Living System Technology Suite (LS/TS), which has been conceived and implemented in the perspective of supporting professional development of adaptive agent-based solutions for today's dynamic and complex business context. Beyond presenting the conceptual foundation of LS/TS and describing its various components, the main challenges faced during its development have been discussed as well as the consequent choices made to meet them.

Acknowledgments

The authors wish to thank Stefan Brantschen and Thomas Haas for their valuable and precious contribution, support and guidance during the overall LS/TS development project, and Dominic Greenwood for his precious suggestions and comments on this paper.

Many thanks also to the whole LS/TS development team, namely Branislav Hladky, Pavol Bernhauser, Milan Michalicek, Herbert Vojcik, Milos Volauf, Peter Nather, Attila Strba, and Juraj Dzifcak, for their valuable work and efforts.

References

[1] Agentlink News, *Industrial Uptake of Agent Technology.* Issue 16, December 2004

[2] Web Services Axis.
http://ws.apache.org/axis/

[3] Brantschen, S. and Haas, T. *Agents in a J2EE World.* Agentlink News #9, April 2003

[4] Brooks, Rodney A. *Intelligence without Representation.* Artificial Intelligence, 47:139159, 1991.

[5] Červenka, Radovan, Trenčanský, Ivan, Calisti, Monique and Greenwood, Dominic *AML: Agent Modeling Language. Toward Industry-Grade Agent-Based Modeling.* AAMAS 2004 workshop on Agent Oriented Software Engineering (AOSE), July 2004, New York, USA.

[6] Dastani, M., Van Riemsdijk, B., Dignum, F., and Meyer, J.J. *A Programming Language for Cognitive Agents: Goal Directed 3APL.* Proceedings of the First Workshop on Programming Multiagent Systems: Languages, frameworks, techniques, and tools (ProMAS03). Melbourne, 2003.

[7] Eclipse web site.
http://www.eclipse.org/

[8] Enterprise Architect, Sparx System web site.
http://www.sparxsystems.com/

[9] Enterprise JavaBeans Technology documentation.
http://java.sun.com/products/ejb/docs.html

[10] Fischer, Klaus, Müller Jörg P., and Pischel, Markus. *Unifying Control in a Layered Agent Architecture.* Agent Theory, Architecture and Language Workshop 95:240-252, Montreal, August 1995.

[11] Jamali, Nadeem, Thati, Prasannaa and Agha, Gul A. *An Actor-based Architecture for Customizing and Controlling Agent Ensembles.* IEEE Intelligent Systems 14:2(38-44)

[12] *Jason: A Java-based agentSpeak interpreter used with saci for multi-agent distribution over the net.*
Available at http://jason.sourceforge.net/

[13] Java 2 Platform, Standard Edition (J2SE).
http://java.sun.com/j2se/

[14] Java 2 Platform, Enterprise Edition (J2EE).
http://java.sun.com/j2ee/

[15] Kephart, J.O. and Chess D. M. *The Vision of Autonomic Computing.* Computer, 36(1):4152, 2003.

[16] Meyer, Bertrand *Object Oriented Software Construction, 2nd Ed.* Prentice Hall, 1997

[17] Petrie, Charles J. *Agent-Based Engineering, the Web, and Intelligence.* IEEE Expert, 11:6(24-29). IEEE Press, 1996.

[18] Proceedings of the AAMAS-03 Workshop on *Autonomy, Delegation, and Control: From Inter-agent to Organizations and Institutions,* July 2003, Melbourne, Australia.

[19] Proceedings of the IJCAI-2001 Workshop on *Autonomy, Delegation, and Control: Interacting with Autonomous Agents,* August 2001, Seattle, USA.

[20] Rao, Anand S., and Georgeff, Michael P. *BDI-Agents: from Theory to Practice.* Proceedings of the First Intl. Conference on Multiagent Systems. San Francisco, 1995

[21] Rajdou, Navi. *Adaptive Agents Boost Supply Network Flexibility.* Forrester Report, March, 2002.

[22] Wooldridge, Michael, and Jennings, Nicholas R. *Intelligent Agents: Theory and Practice.*
Knowledge Engineering Review, 10:2(115-152). Cambridge Journals, 1995.

Information about Software

Software is available on the Internet as
( ) prototype version
( ) full fledged software (freeware), version no.:
(X) full fledged software (for money), version no.:
(X) demo/trial version
( ) not (yet) available

Internet address:
Description of software: http://www.whitestein.com/pages/solutions/ls_ts.html
Download address:

Contact person for question about the software:
Name:
email: lsts@whitestein.com

Giovanni Rimassa
Whitestein Technologies AG
Pestalozzistrasse 24
8032 Zurich
Switzerland
e-mail: gri@whitestein.com

Monique Calisti
Whitestein Technologies AG
Pestalozzistrasse 24
8032 Zurich
Switzerland
e-mail: mca@whitestein.com

Martin E. Kernland
Whitestein Technologies AG
Pestalozzistrasse 24
8032 Zurich
Switzerland
e-mail: mek@whitestein.com

Multi Agent System Development Kit

Vladimir Gorodetsky, Oleg Karsaev, Vladimir Samoylov,
Victor Konushy, Evgeny Mankov and Alexey Malyshev

Abstract. Recent advances in the area of multi–agent technology are attracting a growing attention and interest of both scientific community and industry. This interest is stipulated, on the one hand, by the steadily increasing capabilities of multi-agent technology that offers a new paradigm and powerful means for design of large scale distributed intelligent systems, and, on the other hand, by the practical needs of industry to have a reliable and efficient technology to cope with new challenges of practice. At present, one of the most important research challenges is elaboration of powerful methodologies for agent-based systems engineering and development of efficient software tools supporting implementation and deployment of the multi-agent systems. The paper presents one of such tools, Multi–Agent System Development Kit, based on and implementing *Gaia* methodology that supports the complete life cycle of multi-agent system engineering, implementation and deployment, and insures the integrity of all the solutions produced by designers at different stages of the development process.

1 Introduction

Although agent-oriented software engineering has been a subject of intensive research for over a decade, it has not yet reached the level of maturity required for it to be rated as an industrial technology. By now a lot of MAS software tools have been developed. Among them, the well-known and highly popular are AgentBuilder [20], Jack [18], JADE [3], ZEUS [9], FIPA-OS [13], agentTool [11], etc. An almost complete list of such software tools can be found in ([24], [25]). Nevertheless, in spite of the rich theoretical achievements in the area, there practically exist no Multi-Agent System (MAS) software tools capable of supporting the complete life cycle of industrial MAS comprising analysis, design, implementation, deployment and maintenance.

A capabilities study of the existing software tools allows to see a number of common disadvantages considerably decreasing their performance and degree of maturity. The first of such disadvantages to be mentioned, and a substantial one, consists in insufficient usage of the experience accumulated within the object–oriented approach and the existing (at least, de-facto) "standards" developed for the analysis, design and implementation stages that are commonly used in the information technologies [6]. The major source of it is the fundamental mismatch between the methods and the abstract conceptions used by the object-oriented approach [6], on the one hand, and by the agent-oriented approach ([22, 23]) on the other hand, explicitly shown in [21]. A number of initiatives is being currently undertaken to overcome this mismatch and to find an efficient solution. Among them, the most promising one is the initiative being jointly undertaken by two leading international organizations focused on standardization in the area of new information technologies, FIPA and OMG, as a part of project *Agent UML* [1].

Another considerable disadvantage of the existing MAS software tools is a weak consistency of the solutions produced at the consecutive stages of a MAS application life cycle. As for this, a certain growth of research activity can be observed in the development of methodologies aimed at supporting the above mentioned consistency of the MAS life cycle, including the analysis, design, implementation, deployment and maintenance aspects. Some well-known methodologies of such kind are Gaia [21], MESSAGE [7], MaSE [12], Prometheus [19], Adelfe [4], Tropos [14], PASSI [8]. The core of the integrity maintenance problem is the necessity to automatically maintain the consistency of the solutions being produced at the different stages of the MAS development process. For example, while implementing MAS, it is necessary to strictly conform to the solutions produced at the analysis and design stages. Rational Rose software tool supporting an information system object-oriented analysis, design and implementation, can serve as a guiding line for this purpose. Comparison of MAS development tools and methodologies can be found in ([5], [10]).

This paper presents the Multi-Agent System Development Kit (MASDK) that was a subject of research and development during the last four years. The first and second versions of MASDK [15] were practically used for fast prototyping of several MAS applications in different problem domains [16, 17]. The experience accumulated during this period as well as recent advances and trends in MAS methodology and technology made clear the fundamental drawbacks of the earlier versions and gave way to forming sound requirements for the next version of MASDK, version 3.0.

For this version design some new trends and achievements in the agent-oriented software engineering methodology have been taken into account. In particular, the basic methodological principles of the Gaia methodology [21] have been implemented. Indeed, Gaia methodology consists of two basic stages of MAS development that are (1) analysis and (2) design. The analysis is aimed at reaching *"an understanding of the system and its structure (without reference to any implementation detail)"* [21]. This stage assumes development of abstract solutions and notions related to the system organization, i.e. identification of MAS tasks, description of role models, and interaction model [21]. An objective of the design stage is *"to transform the abstract models derived during the analysis stage into models at a sufficiently low level of abstraction that they can be easily implemented"* [21]. This stage assumes formal specification of agent models, service models, and acquaintance model.

MASDK 3.0 software tool is currently being assessed and evaluated by means of developing of a number of multi-agent systems, e.g., for intrusions detection in computer network, for situation assessment and for business activity monitoring.

This paper describes the MASDK 3.0 software tool, and with a certain focus on its correlation with the Gaia methodology. Section 2 outlines MASDK 3.0 software tool, technology supported by it, and abstract agent architecture. Section 3 covers the overall view of the specification structure of multi-agent systems developed using MASDK, outlines development methodology and its mapping with Gaia one. The analysis and design stages, supported by MASDK and carried out through usage of a number of specialized graphical editors are considered in section 4. Section 5 outlines the implementation and deployment stages. Section 6 considers one of the most important problems of any MAS technology which consists in maintaining consistency of solutions produced at various technology stages; it is also shown in the section how the consistency is insured within a technology supported by MASDK. Related works and comparison of MASDK with some other tools is presented in Section 7. In conclusion the paper basic results are summarized.

2   Outline of MASDK 3.0 Software Tool and Technology Supported

MASDK 3.0 software tool consists of the following components (Fig.1): (1) System core which is a data structure designed for XML-based representation and storing of MAS formal specification; (2) Integrated set of graphical editors supporting the user's activity aimed at formal specifying of the MAS under development; (3) Library of C++ classes, comprising what is usually called Generic agent, corresponding to the reusable

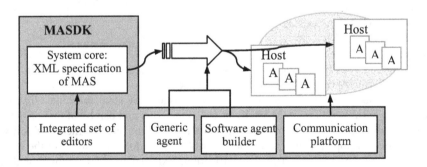

Fig. 1. MASDK software tool components and their interaction

component common for all agents; (4) Communication platform to be installed in the computers, in the network, that are involved in the MAS being designed, and (5) Builder of software agent instances, that carries out (i) generation of source and executable codes of software agents in C++ language and (ii) deployment of software agents over the earlier installed communication platform.

Generalized architecture of the agents developed using MASDK is shown in Fig.2. It includes the following basic components:

> ➢ invariant (reusable) component called *Generic Agent*,
> ➢ agent behavior model,
> ➢ mental model of agent,
> ➢ set of agent services represented in terms of state machines, and
> ➢ library of auxiliary application-oriented functions.

The *Generic agent* component which is the basic class for all agents is a reusable component of MASDK environment (Fig.1). This component can be thought of as *engine* that realizes a common (reusable) scenario of agent operation. It comprises the general functions that 1) support sending and receiving of messages, 2) initiate respective services of agents, control of their execution and process of interruptions depending on the current states of agents, 3) provide the interaction agents with human users, 4) provide access to agents' data storages, etc.

The Agent behavior model, Mental model and *State machines* are intended for problem-oriented specification of agent. The agent behavior model specifies the states associated with providing the agent with respective services, the models of services being specified as state machines. The mental models comprise specification of notions, data storage structure, and the initial data and knowledge possessed by the agent. All three mentioned classes of

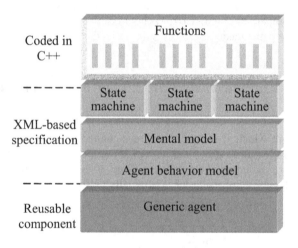

Fig. 2. Agent architecture

components are developed by a designer using the *integrated set of editors* (Fig.1) and stored in *system core* (Fig.1) as *XML*-based specifications.

The *Functions* specify agent operation in the states of state machines. They are coded in the usual way, i.e., in MASDK in C++ language, and can be of one of the two varieties: *scripts* and *external functional components*. Scripts are fragments of software code that are developed using corresponding MASDK editors and stored in the system core as entries of MAS XML-based specification. External functional components are developed out of the MASDK environment and viewed as components the execution of which is initiated by the agent during execution of scripts.

A specification of MAS in MASDK includes specifications of *agents* and *agent classes*. Agents of each class have a common specification of the components comprising the architecture of agent (Fig.2), except for the content of mental models, in particular – the initial data and the knowledge possessed by the agents.

Software implementation of agents is performed by the *Software agent builder* component (Fig.1) in automatic mode. For each agent class, the software agent builder executes the three successive tasks:

1. Generation of the source C++ code of the problem–oriented components of agent class, i.e. of the *Agent behaviour model* and all *State machines*. The main goal of this task is transformation of *XML*-based specifications of these components into source code in C++ on the basis of *XSLT* technology.

2. Compilation of the C++ code of agent class into an executable code. For this procedure the following components are used as inputs:

   ➤ Source C++ code of the problem–oriented components produced by the task 1;
   ➤ Source C++ codes of particular functions;
   ➤ *Generic agent* components, which are reusable components of MASDK.

   In case of an error, the generator analyses the compilation output file and localizes the state machine, also indicating the state which contains the error. If a syntax error is made by a designer who was responsible for specifying the algorithm of the agent behavior, the generator indicates the name of the state machine, its state and the number of the row, in which the designer made the error.

3. Building the data storage (storages) specified in mental models of the agent class.

3 Methodology of MAS development

A MAS development process in MASDK can be technologically divided in to three stages. At the first stage a detailed design of the MAS is developed. In particular, this stage assumes the development of the models described in Gaia methodology [20], namely – role models, interaction model, agent models, service models, and acquaintance model. At that the service models of agent classes are described in greater detail than it is done with Gaia methodology. All activities at this stage are entirely carried out by the *integrated set of editors (ISE)* and the results (the detailed design of the MAS) are stored at the *system core* component in special XML-based language. The second stage consists in programming the particular components that can be derived from the detailed design of the MAS developed at the previous stage. The third stage consists in compiling and building the software agents.

Thus, almost all development process is carried out based on the *ISE* component; so, let us discuss this component and the respective methodology of application systems development in detail. The set of editors comprising the *ISE* component can be divided into three categories (Fig.3): 1) the set of editors (*MAS model, Protocol, Ontology* editors) aimed at describing abstract concepts and system organization, 2) the set of editors (*Agent class behavior model, State machine, State, Private ontology* editors) designed for description of concrete concepts and design of agent classes, and 3) the set of editors (*Agents' configuration and Agent mental model* editors) aimed at building and deployment of the agents.

The enumerated set of editors provides the following methodology for MASs development that starts from the two initial stages (*analysis* and *design*) which are parts of Gaia methodology [21].

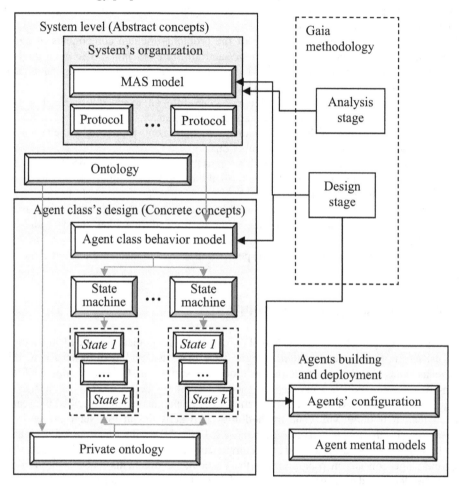

Fig. 3. Structure of graphic editors in MASDK and their mapping with Gaia methodology

1) *Analysis.* The development process is initiated with the requirements statement and the results of *role* and *interaction* models specification that comprise *an organizational model* of the MAS. The respective activities are supported by the *MAS model* and the *Protocol* editors.

2) *Design.* According to Gaia methodology the objective of this stage assumes development of *agent, service* and *acquaintance* models. The agent model development assuming determination of agent classes and instances of each from them is carried out using the *MAS model* and the *Agents' configuration* editors. The service models are

developed using the *Agent class behavior model* editor and the acquaintance model with the aid of the *MAS model* one.

3) *Ontology description.* Domain ontology description is specified by means of the *Ontology* editor and initially[1] can be developed in parallel with stages 1 and 2. However there are relations between the models presupposes a certain sequence of their development. In particular, a detailed specification of communication acts of the protocols at later phases of development implies specifying of messages contents in terms of ontology notions. It means the respective notions of ontology have to be specified for doing it. The first three stages are designed for describing abstract concepts of the application system. The concrete concepts are developed through the following sequence of stages.

4) *State machine development (Service development).* Each service identified at the design stage (stage 2) is developed as a state machine using *State machine* and *State* editors. At that, such a state machine is described at the level of states and transitions between them without minor details of states implementation. A service is associated with respective protocols and activities and, consequently, development of a state machine assumes relating each state to either communication act of some protocol or one of the activities. One communication act is related to only one state, while one activity can be related to several states. Transitions between states describe the scenario of the service execution.

5) *Private ontology development.* Private ontology is required for specification of the notions used for describing the agent class mental model. At that, it involves private notions of the agent class and the notions inheriting ones from the shared ontology developed at stage 3. Private ontology development also assumes specifying a data storage scheme (or several storage schemes) of agent class.

6) *Agents initial mental model.* This stage consists in describing initial data and knowledge of the agents. It must be noted that at the previous stages (namely – 4, 5) the agent classes have been specified and the agents of each class have no specifics except for their names. Therefore, the initial mental models of agents are their specifics that single out the agents of each class.

7) *Agent classes components programming.* Components of each agent class that have to be specified in the usual way (in case of MASDK environment it consists in developing a code in C++ language) are identified as a result of stage 3 execution. All of them are either scripts of agent classes' behavior in particular states of state machines or invoked from these scripts as external components.

8) *Agents code generating.* This function is executed automatically by *Software agent builder* component (Fig.1).

9) *Agents configuration and deployment.* This stage assumes specifying the locations of agents, deploying of the agent according to the results, and filling in the storages of the agents with their initial mental models developed at stage 6.

---

[1] Development process in MASDK can have iterative character. It means each model developed in process of MAS development can be refined repeatedly.

Thus a development of MAS in MASDK is generally reduced to development of mentioned problem-oriented components. It is carried out using of graphical editors through which the respective *XML*-based templates stored in system core are filled in. These graphical editors and structure of respective components are considered in the following section.

4   Integrated system of editors

MAS specification comprises a set of interrelated components that are developed based on respective template types and stored in the system core. Set of these components comprising MAS specification are depicted in the environment browser a screenshot of which with an abstract example is shown in Fig.4. Specification of each MAS includes the following components:

➢ Domain *ontology*;

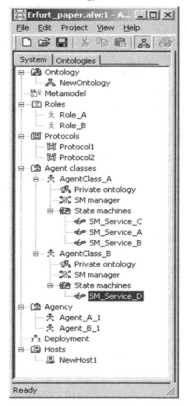

Fig. 4. Browser and System core content

➢ *Meta model* of MAS describing its organization, namely – names of the identified roles, agent classes, protocols and relations between them;
➢ Description of *role models*;
➢ Specification of *protocols*.

Model of each agent class comprises the following models:

➢ *Private ontology* describing the notions and storages of mental model;
➢ *SM Manager (State Machines manager)* describing list of service names and scenarios of their execution;
➢ Set of *state machines*, each of them specifying respective service;
➢ Initial mental model of each *agent* from the class;
➢ *Deployment* model describing configuration of agents and their locations;
➢ *Host* model describing necessary data of the hosts where agents are located.

The integrated editors system consists of seven basic graphic editors corresponding to the respective classes of components constituting the specification of MAS under development. It means that the components of each class are developed using respective graphic editor (the main editor). Let us remark that according to the methodology of MAS development in MASDK described in section 3, a designer uses the same editors at all different stages of a process. Using a graphic editor implies using several auxiliary editors. These are used for specifying specific details of the components and not dealt with in detail in the paper.

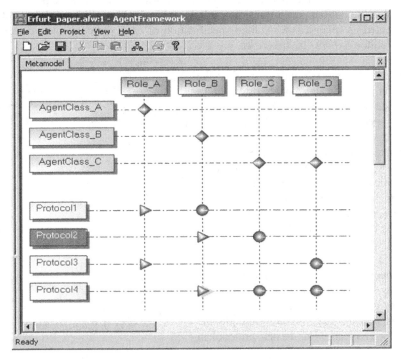

Fig. 5. MAS model editor

4.1 MAS model editor

MAS model editor (Fig.5) and related to it the auxiliary editors (dialogs) are designed for description of the MAS organization, and they also support carrying out of the two initial stages of the development process: analysis and design partially. At the analysis stage these editors are used for specifying role and interaction models. The set of roles identified/found at this stage is presented in the upper part of the model editor window. In the current version of MASDK a model of each role is specified in the auxiliary editor according to the template which is an accessory of Gaia methodology as high-level (textual) description. A formal specification of this template for graphic representation of the role models has been developed and after implementation of the respective editor it will be integrated in MASDK environment.

Description of an interaction model is implemented using two editors. The MAS model editor allows to describe a high-level representation of this model. Such a representation assumes listing of all interaction protocols, specification of all participants of each protocol, and pointing out the roles that initiate these protocols. It is presented in the bottom part of the editor window (Fig.5). The initiators of the protocols are presented as triangles. A detailed specification of each protocol is executed using another editor which is described in the section 4.2.

High-level representation of the interaction model in the model editor allows for considering additional useful tasks related to the specification of this model. In particular, one of these tasks deals with the possibility of describing the MAS behavior on the whole. This task is reduced to investigation of possible relations between protocols and using them for describing meta-scenarios of the MAS behavior. It is viewed as one of the possible improvements of MASDK environment in future. However, the current version already allows to analyze some aspects of this task. Presentation of the rectangles denoting protocols in proper order, and using different colors gives way to show protocols nesting. E.g., in the example the protocol 2 is specified as nested protocol in protocol 1.

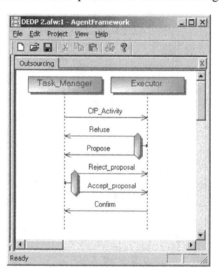

Fig. 6. Protocol editor

The above results, including the information about the found roles, the interaction protocols, mapping of the roles to the protocols and the textual description of the role models are used for defining the agent models, namely – the agent classes. According to the methodology this is considered to be a task of the design stage. The set of agent classes and assignment of roles to them are shown in the middle part of the MAS model editor window. Let us notice that any agent class may be able perform one or several roles. E.g., in the example, the agent class 3 is mapping two roles while two other agent classes are one-to-one mapping roles 1 and 2.

4.2 Protocol Editor

Detailed description of the roles interaction protocols is one of the key tasks of the analysis stage. Realizing the extremely high importance of this task was evidently one of the motives for the Agent UML project ([1], [2]) having been jointly initiated by FIPA and OMG. The project goal consists in extension of the UML language to agent-based system specification language, and one of the focuses of this Project is development of a language specially designed for specification of agent interaction protocols [2].

MASDK 3.0 includes a graphic editor of protocols. An example of a protocol graphic representation in Fig.6 within the window of editor in question is *Contract Net Protocol*. The current version of the implemented editor makes use of some basic constructs of Agent UML project. In particular, the basic capabilities of the roles interaction protocol are as follows: 1) the protocol is specified as a modified sequence diagram (Fig.6); 2) the message exchange scheme is specified using *AND*, *OR* and *XOR* connectors; 3) the participants of interaction protocols are roles; 4) the specification of message classes is implemented in ACL language. Some of the constructs being considered in Agent UML project and not included in current version of the protocol editor are several *life lines* of a role and *nested protocols*. The first construct (several life lines of a role) will be included in the next version of the protocol editor. Specification of the nested protocols in MASDK is not regarded as a task being solved using the protocol editor. The interaction model in MASDK is specified at two levels and with usage of two editors respectively. The first level of an interaction model is specified using MAS model editor (Section 4.2), and detail specification of each protocol is carried out using protocol editor. At that, specification of nested protocols is a task related to the first level with usage of MAS model protocol. This possibility is described in Section 4.1.

4.3 Ontology editor

A sample snapshot of the window of this editor is given in Fig.7. It aims at introducing the shared application ontology notions and the relations between them, and at specifying the private ontologies of agent classes. Description of the notions assumes introducing attributes for them and specification of the attributes domains.

The classes of relations are important characteristics of the ontology editor. At that, including them in MASDK suggests availability of respective mechanisms in the environment that have to provide for solving a number of tasks in which introduced relations are used. In particular, these mechanisms have to provide for solving the following tasks:

> ➢ Insuring correctness of the relations specifications, i.e. checking of constraints specific for particular classes of relations, e.g., introducing an inheritance between notions should prohibit cycles generation.
> ➢ Support of data storage structures generation aimed at storing the agent classes mental models.
> ➢ Providing the necessary syntactic expressiveness of the agents' mental model specification language and an object–oriented style of access to the data storages.

The existing version of MASDK includes the mechanisms that allow to implement these functions for processing inheritance relations. In the course of this processing, both single and multiple inheritance relations between the ontology notions are considered. Development and implementation of the mechanisms of this kind for other classes of relations (inclusion, association, etc) is in progress now, this task being considered as a high priority.

The inheritance relations between the classes of ontology notions described using a respective graphic editor are depicted by arrows between the notions belonging to this relation (Fig.7).

This editor is also used as the editor of agent class private ontology. Besides the abilities and functions discussed above, it is also able to perform the following functions.

Since private ontology of an agent class can include not only specific notions but some notions of the shared part of the application ontology as well, the application ontology editor has to be able to select a subset of the application ontology notions in order to use them in the private ontology of an agent class. This function is the first additional one.

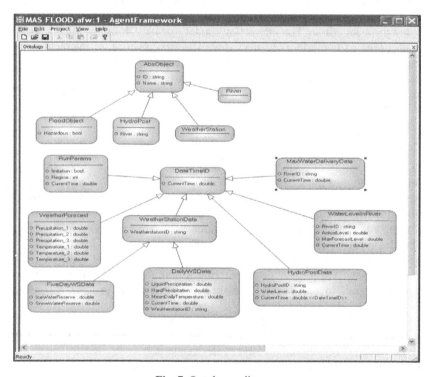

Fig. 7. Ontology editor

The second additional function of the application ontology editor supports specification of the storage structure for the agent class mental model. To realize this function, specification of the notions and relations of the agent class private ontology is carried out. Later, while generating agent class instances, this specification is used for automated generation of respective storages for data and knowledge. The resulting data structures can be either relational data bases or XML files.

4.4   Agent Class Behavior Model Editor

Agent class behavior model is designed for listing a set of agent class services and for specifying scenarios of their execution. A MAS model specification comprising the role models, the interaction model, and the assignment of roles to the agent classes form a basis for deriving a set of services for each agent class. Specification of agent class behavior model is carried out using graphic editor whose screenshot along with an abstract example of the model is shown in Fig.8. It should be noted that this editor only describes the name and conceptual description of services.   More detailed formal specification of each service is carried out as a state machine model, and to do this a state machine editor described in Section 4.5 is used.

The main objective of the model consists in specifying scenarios of the derived services execution. It implies specifying the respective components defining the types of events initiating execution of services, and actions that can be or has to be performed during execution of the respective services. The model template includes the following kinds of such components.

Input protocols

This component lists the protocols in which the agent class under development is a participant and not an initiator. It is worth noting that this subset of protocols is derived

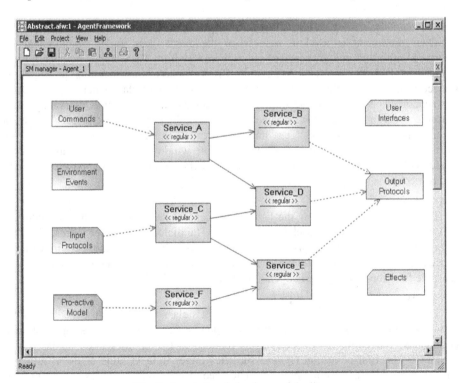

Fig. 8. Agent class behavior model editor

from MAS model automatically. Based on the above this component specifying is reduced to mapping of each protocol from the list to respective service. This activity is carried out through the auxiliary dialog related to this component, and in the window of agent class behavior model editor such relations are shown as arrows between the *Input protocols* component and the respective services. Each protocol from the list is one-to-one mapping respective service. At that each mapping implies the certain information for the service (state machine) development. It has to comprise states for processing of all protocol's communication acts, and the first protocol's act triggers execution of the service (state machine).

Output protocols

This component contains the list of the protocols in which the agent class under development is indicated as initiator. This component specifying is reduced to carrying out same activities as those being executed for *Input protocol* component specifying. This subset of protocols is automatically derived from the MAS model; each protocol from the list is one-to-one mapping respective service (state machine). This activity is carried out through the auxiliary dialog related to this component, and in the window of agent class behavior model editor such relations are shown as arrows between the respective services and the *Output protocols* component. Each mapping implies that the state machine realizing the service has to comprise states for processing of all protocol's communication acts.

User commands

This component is used in case when the agent class under development has interface with user, and any services are triggered by him. The component specifying is reduced to 1) listing of user commands, 2) their one-to-one mapping to respective services (state machines), and 3) identifying states of agent class when the commands are accessible. Mechanism providing for a usage of the commands is realized as a reusable function of the generic agent component. In particular, it selects accessible commands depending on the agent state and presents them in the user interface of the *Portal* component described in Section 5. In the window of the agent class behavior model editor such relations are shown as arrows between the *User command* component and respective services.

User Interfaces

This component represents the list and conceptual description of the user interface dialogs initiated by the agent class in question. The dialogs can either represent certain information for user or imply his response, e.g., while receiving certain data for subsequent operation. Mechanism supporting a usage of such dialogs is realized as a reusable function of the generic agent component as well.

Pro-active model

This component specifies possibility of agent's class to initiate an execution of any services without environmental impacts like, e.g., receiving messages or user commands. The component specifying is reduced to listing rules like *"When ... if ... then ..."*. The first condition (*When*) specifies either time instants or event initiating checking of the second condition (*if*). The second condition specifies the agent class mental state in which the service (state machine) indicated in the third part of the rule (*then*) has to be executed. The component specifying is carried out through the auxiliary dialog, and in the window of agent class behavior model editor such relations are shown as arrows between the *Pro-active model* component and the respective services. Mechanism providing for checking of these rules and initiating of the services is realized as a reusable function of the generic agent component as well.

Environment events and Effects

If agent is operating within an external environment then it can receive data from any external equipment (e.g., sensors) or/and their control. In this case it is necessary to specify interaction between agent class and external equipment, and the Environment events and Effects components are used then. These components specifying consists in 1) listing of interaction acts, 2) their mapping to the respective services, and 3) specifying the interface trough which data exchange is executed. Carrying out the latter task is reduced to specifying of mechanisms supporting information receiving from and sending to external equipment and algorithms of such information processing. Such mechanisms are rather application dependent and therefore they have to be specified "ad hoc", however, the generic agent component includes some reusable solutions which can be used for doing it.

Developing scenarios of the services execution implies specifying two kinds of relations: relations between components described above and services, and relations between services. The latter kind of relations is used to specify the following two cases:
  ➢   synchronous initiation of nested services, and
  ➢   asynchronous initiation of any service.

Synchronous initiation of a nested service *B* by a service *A* means the following scenario of their execution. Execution of the service A is interrupted after initiation of the service *B*, and continued after the service *B* accomplishment. At that the service *A* can use the results of the service *B* execution; the service can be considered as nested one in the following two cases: 1) when it provides for the execution of some other services, and 2) when it provides for the operation of an agent class related to any protocol. Asynchronous initiation of the service *B* by the service *A* can be considered if the results of the service *B* execution are not required for the service *A* execution. At that if some services are triggered by any service asynchronously then they will be executed in parallel.

The following relation existing between liveness properties of a role model in Gaia methodology [21] and graphic notation used for specifying of the agent class behavior mode 1 are worth noting. On the one hand, "the atomic components of a liveness expression are either *activities* or *protocols*" [21]. On the other hand, components that are used for specifying of an agent class behavior model denote *protocols, services* (some of them associated with activity execution), *acts of agent class interaction with user* and *with external equipment*. At that, a liveness expression includes the operators: "*x followed by y*", "*x or y occurs*", "*x and y interleaved*", which can be specified via respective kinds of relations between components and services in the agent class behavior model. All above described relations between the liveness expressions and the agent class behavior models are used at the design stage of MAS development, and allow to account for the results received at the analysis stage.

4.5 State Machines Editor

Specification of the agent class services is carried out in terms of state machines. This comprises the following activities: (1) specification of the set of state machine states; (2) specification of transitions and conditions determining the transition choice depending on the agent current state; (3) specification of the state machine (agent) behavior in each particular state.

The first and second activities are executed by a designer of MAS. These activities are supported by graphic editor given in Fig.9. The third activity, on the contrary, is executed by a programmer trough respective dialogs.

It should be noted that agent class behavior model, state machines and their states can be considered as different levels of description of agent class behavior. At that, agent class behavior model (Section 4.4) aims at describing agent class's behavior on the whole. State machines are used to describe partial scenarios of agent classes, and states of state machines are used to describe partial functions executed within respective scenarios. Thus, the editor of state machines can be considered the graphic editor of partial behavior scenarios of agent classes.

Specification of state machine can use specific functions that perform actions of

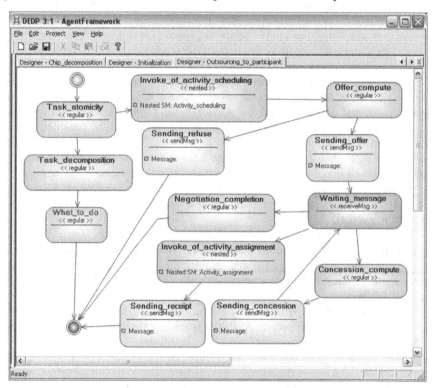

Fig. 9. State machine editor

several specific classes, such as processing of one or more input messages, sending one or several messages, waiting for a response, invoking asynchronous process, initiating other state machine, etc. Specification of the functions of a kind can be based on the use of respective reusable components. Since functions in MASDK are described in terms of partial states, the environment includes several pre-defined different templates of states that are used to specify functions of respective classes. States specified according to different templates are highlighted in the window of an editor by different colors (Fig.9).

Initial sketch of each state machine can be developed automatically. Component that carries out this activity uses as input data solutions developed at the previous stages of system development. In particular, it analyzes agent class behavior model, and if the state machine under development is mapped to a protocol, analyzes specification of this protocol and generates states aimed at processing the protocol's communication acts. At the following step, a designer develops in detail the above initial sketches of the state machines inserting auxiliary states and updating transitions scheme.

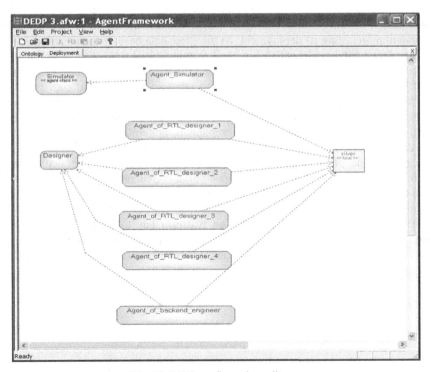

Fig. 10. MAS configuration editor

5 Deployment

Deployment of MAS consists in carrying out the following functions:
  ➢ Specification of the MAS configuration,
  ➢ Specification of initial states of agent mental models, and
  ➢ Generation and installation of software agents in the computer network according to the MAS configuration.

MAS configuration is specified using graphic editor given in Fig.10. This editor is used for specification of the following data about agents: (1) agent's unique name; (2) indication of agent class, whose instance is the software agent, and (3) the host name and its Internet address where the software agent in question has to be situated. For example, Fig.10 shows a configuration where six agents are instances of two agent classes (one agent of the first class and five agents of the second class). The configuration assumes that agents are situated in a single host.

It is important, that while having a set of agent classes developed an arbitrary number of different MAS configurations can be generated. They can differentiate in the number of agents of different classes and their allocation within Internet.

Specification of initial states of agent mental models is the next step of MAS implementation preceding its deployment. At this step, data base of each agent destined for storing of its mental model is filled in, thus, forming initial state of its mental model. It is necessary to recall that the scheme of the aforementioned data base is given in terms of notions of private ontology of the respective agent class. The above activity can be carried out either through invariant user interface, which is not depended from a agent class storage schemes, or through interfaces tuned to peculiarities of the MAS in question, i.e., tailored for them. The last version is preferable when the number of private ontology notions and/or relations between them is too large.

Executable code of the MAS of determined configuration is generated through special functional component of *Software agent builder*. Generation procedure results in filling in the initial states of software agents mental models.

Before the deployment of MAS (installation of the software agents) within the particular computer network, communication platform has to be installed. For this purpose, a reusable component of MASDK called *Portal* is installed in all the computers where MAS is deployed. Installation of *Portal* is supported by a special function of the MASDK environment.

Communication platform is destined to support the message passing (both local and remote) between MAS agents. It is important that the same communication platform can support operation of several multi-agent systems. Messages are transmitted between agents by portals these agents run on. TCP/IP is used to pass messages between agents. A message is represented as an XML with a proprietary structure. At the moment not an external message transmission protocol is supported.

Portal is provided with a user interface (Fig.11), that supports the following functions:

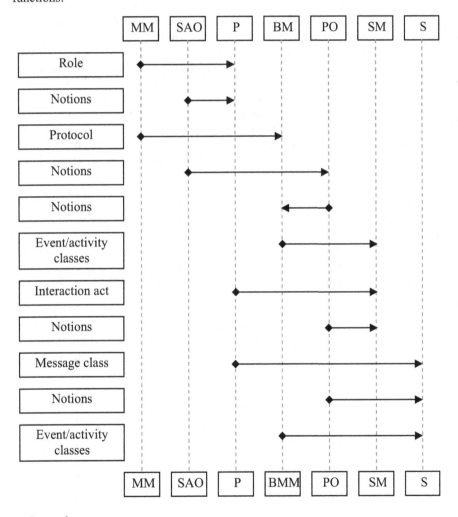

Legend:
MM – mental model of MAS, *SAO* –shared application ontology,
P – protocol, *BM* – agent class behaviour model,
PO – private ontology of an agent class, *SM* – state machine, *S* – state of SM

Fig. 11. Scheme of interrelations between components

> ➤ Initiating and shutting down the agents of a selected MAS;
> ➤ Visualization of the available user commands of operating agents and activation of their performance.

6 Maintenance of MAS Consistency

An important problem of MAS development is the consistency maintenance. If consistency of the MAS project components is not maintained in the development process then total development efforts and costs can considerably increase. It should be noted that the MAS design processes can potentially be well structured, thus, allowing development of special mechanisms intended for consistency maintenance. Such a possibility is based on the use and evolution of abstract notion classes utilized in the methodology. Particularly, the list of these notion classes within MASDK environment includes: role, protocol (communication acts, classes of messages), agent class, auxiliary components of agent class behavior model (see subsection 4.4), state machine (state, specialized state class), ontology notions. The use of these abstract notions basically allows regarding the design process as specification of instances of the above abstract notions and establishing different interconnections between them. While establishing such interconnections, it is necessary to meet a certain set of requirements and constraints that are independent of application domain. Scheme of main interconnections between components used in MASDK is depicted in Fig.12. This provides a possibility to well maintain the MAS consistency.

Within the MASDK 3.0 environment a special component called *Master* is used to practically exploit the above opportunity. It operates in two modes: (1) *Consistency checking* and (2) *Design mastering*. In the first mode, *Master* provides a designer with the list of consistency violations of various kinds, e.g., "*Communication act of the protocol <name_of_the_act> is not provided with the respective function on the agent class side*". While operating in the second mode, *Master* supports the necessary ordering of MAS design processes in the top-down style. At certain phases of design process this mode of operation allows *Master*, while accounting for already produced

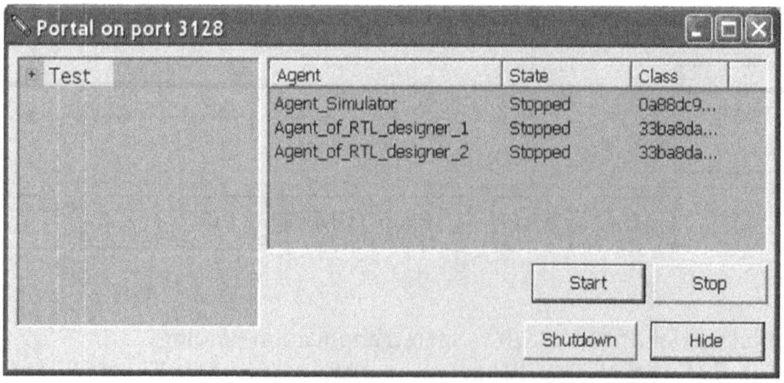

Fig. 12. User interface of the Portal component

solutions, to automatically generate certain new solutions or their parts. For instance, if behavior model of an agent class is specified, *Master* can initiate generation of the respective set of states of state machine implementing the above behavior model.

7 Related Work

There are many tools for MASs development and each tool has its own features. We selected only tools that support visual designing and development. In the following sections we compare MASDK against 4 most known for us tools meeting the mentioned criterions.

7.1 agentTool

agentTool [11] is a tool for analyzing, designing and implementing multi-agent systems by MaSE methodology. In contrast to MASDK, the analysis phase in agentTool starts from defining goals and use cases that should help to discover roles in the target MAS. MASDK doesn't have analogues to goals and use cases. In agentTool after that each role is assigned goals it is responsible for and tasks are defined to achieve these goals. MASDK doesn't have an analogue to a task.

Then in both tools protocols are defined, but in agentTool only two roles can participate in a protocol. In contrast to agentTool, in MASDK a protocol is detailed down to communication acts. In agentTool it is also possible to define communication acts but only for agent classes irrelatively of any protocol. In both tools agent classes are defined by roles they play.

Then in agentTool each agent class is refined by defining components it consists of. Those components as communication acts are specified using a finite state automaton. In MASDK this step is performed in "SM Manager" editors that have more formal structure and advanced facilities (see details in the corresponding chapter).

At the end agentTool generates Java classes for agents and communication acts, which have to be filled in with implementation code. MASDK has built in editors for entering all required implementation code in C++ and allows to generate source code in C++ and to build executable modules. Also, MASDK has facilities to install a built MAS.

Thus from our point of view agentTool has more expressive capabilities for analyzing and designing but those for implementation are incomplete. MASDK allows to develop a MAS ready for running but relationships between designing and implementation details aren't so clear.

7.2 PTK

PTK supports MAS development by PASSI [8] methodology. It is implemented as a Rational Rose plug-in and uses UML for step-by-step designing and development multi-agent systems.

PTK has good facilities to support all stages of MAS development. Development in PTK starts from problem domain analysis and from functional decomposition of the target MAS. Then roles, protocols and agent classes are discovered. In contrast to MASDK, PTK has good facilities for the analysis of functionality of the target MAS and for distribution of functions between roles and agents.

An ontology in PTK is described by two diagrams: Domain Ontology and Communication Ontology. For each communication user has to define an ontology, a language and a protocol. In MASDK interactions between agents are fully described for roles these agents play.

Every agent in PTK is described as a class. Agents' behavior is displayed in one or more activity diagrams. However those diagrams have no affect on the classes. In MASDK agents' structure and behavior are specified using state machines which are automatically transformed into executable modules. PTK also delivers template agents with corresponding facilities. Finally PTK generates classes for agents, tasks and ontology which should be completed in the Pattern Repository tool. Agents created in PTK can be executed on FIPAOS or JADE.

From our point of view the design phase in PTK is more clear and useful for unskilled users but MASDK provides with more convenient facilities for implementation and deployment.

7.3 JACK

JACK [18] is a full-scale environment for MAS development using Java. It supports MAS development accordingly with BDI agent's model.

Analysis and design is performed in this tool using BDI concepts: Capability, Event, Plan, Agent. However there is no considerable distinction between analysis and design stages which can be done iteratively like in MASDK, because both systems support integrity. In contrast to MASDK, JACK was designed for reactive intelligent agents development. It allows to create variants of a plan to react on events. Those plans are used by the engine implemented in the generic agent for searching a way to reach a goal. In MASDK State Machine is an analogue of the plan but there is no an analogue to Capability (MASDK has some properties of Capability which are in the Role concept). MASDK is more useful when the system behavior and agents coordination with detailed description of protocols should be specified explicitly. There are no protocols in JACK but messages are treated as a kind of events. Both tools support full specification of implementation details.

Thus both systems support full development cycle with iterative modifications. MASDK is more useful for systems with a strict coordination but JACK for reactive systems. Comparing to JACK, MASDK has more advanced system of graphic editors but language constructions in JACK are more elaborated.

7.4 Zeus

Zeus [9] is mostly intended for development of MASs concerning planning and especially distributed planning problems. A proprietary methodology with FIPA protocols support is used in Zeus.

Development of a MAS in Zeus starts with Ontology description. Zeus allows to use single inheritance between notions and specify notion attributes with simple or user-defined types (JavaObjects). Similar functionality is also implemented in MASDK.

Then in Zeus agents are specified and the ontology notions are linked to them (MASDK has Private Ontology as an analogue). Protocols (any protocol can be one of 6 predefined types) and strategies are indicated for the agents. MASDK doesn't have an analogue to the 'strategy' concept. Zeus doesn't support further detailing of agents but in MASDK there are SM-Manager and State Machine Editors for that purposes.

At the next step project tasks are specified with connection to ontology notions and with execution restrictions. MASDK doesn't have an analogue to a task.

At last Zeus generates Java source code for the target MAS. It is possible to choose target platform: UNIX or Windows.

Thus Zeus with its planning problems orientation gives an opportunity to concentrate more on a problem domain than on interactions between agents. In contrast to Zeus, in MASDK the designing phase is supported more deeply but protocols should be created from scratch using corresponding editors. Also, MASDK has no explicit analogue of the 'task' concept.

8 Conclusion

MASDK environment presented in the paper possesses a number of practically important advantages allowing to noticeably decrease efforts and costs associated with the development of MASs of wide range. Among them, the most important ones are the following:

1) Development process is carried out according to well grounded methodology, in our case the *Gaia* methodology, whose abstract notion classes determined at the analysis stage are further specialized and developed in depth at the stages of design and implementation.

2) Graphical style of the development process supported by a number of user friendly editors of MASDK provides for clear and easy understandable presentation of MAS and its components along the whole development process. Together with the thorough and clear methodology graphical style provides for productive and effective cooperation between designer and programmer during the whole life cycle of MAS development.

3) Due to well structured set of abstract notion classes used in analysis and design processes, the MASDK environment provides for checking and maintenance of integrity of the development results at all stages of the process.

4) Representation of interaction protocols that is a key task in any MAS specification is particularly based on solutions involving the existing experience of object-oriented approach whose main solutions are considered now as de-facto standards in information technology.

5) One of the most important ideas of MASDK is reusability of solutions. *Generic agent* library, that integrates reusable solutions/software components, practically implements the reusability idea, thus, reducing development process to the specification of application-oriented data and knowledge.

Currently the MASDK software tool is basically implemented and is validated based on development of MASs in such problem domains as information fusion and situation assessment, computer network security, agent-based business activity simulation and monitoring.

Acknowledgment

We wish to thank European Office of Aerospace Research and Development of the USAF (EOARD) and the Russian Academy of Sciences, Department of Information Technology and Computer Science (Project 4.3) for support granted.

We also thank Cadence Design Systems Ltd. for its realistic assessment of the MASDK capabilities and its industrial perspectives as part of a joint project. It helped to determine needs and directions of further improvement of the platform and to prove the advanced solutions implemented.

References

1. Agent UML: http://www.auml.org/
2. Bauer, B., Muller, J. P., and Odell, J.: Agent UML: A Formalism for Specifying Multiagent Interaction. In: Ciancarini, P. and Wooldridge, M. (eds): Agent-Oriented Software Engineering, Springer-Verlag, Berlin, (2001) 91-103
3. Bellifemine, F., Caire, G., Trucco, T., and Rimassa, G.: Jade Programmer's Guide. JADE 2.5 (2002) http://sharon.cselt.it/projects/jade/
4. Bernon, C., Gleizes, M.P., Peyruqueou, S., and Picard, G.: Adelfe, a methodology for Adaptive Multi-Agent Systems Engineering. In: Third International Workshop "Engineering Societies in the Agents World" (ESAW-2002), Madrid, (2002)
5. Bitting, E., Carter, J., and Ghorbani, A. A.: Multiagent Systems Development Kits: An Evaluation. In: Proceedings of the 1st Annual Conference on Communication Networks & Services Research, Moncton, Canada, (2003) 80-92
6. Booch, G.: Object-Oriented Analysis and Design, 2nd ed., Addison-Wesley: Reading, MA, (1994)

7. Caire, G., Leal, F., Chainho, P., Evans, R., Garijo, F., Gomez, J., Pavon, J., Kearney, P., Stark, J., and Massonet, P.: Agent-oriented analysis using MESSAGE/UML. In: Wooldridge, M., Ciancarini, P., and Weiss, G., (editors): Second International Workshop on Agent-Oriented Software Engineering (AOSE-2001), (2001) 101-108
8. Cossentino, M., Sabatucci, L., Sorace, S., and Chella, A.: Patterns reuse in the PASSI methodology. In: Fourth International Workshop Engineering Societies in the Agents World (ESAW'03), London, UK (2003) 294-310
9. Collis, J. and Ndumu, D.: Zeus Technical Manual. Intelligent Systems Research Group, BT Labs. British Telecommunications. (1999)
10. Dam, K. H., and Winikoff, M.: Comparing Agent-Oriented Methodologies. In: Proceedings of the Fifth International Bi-Conference Workshop on Agent-Oriented Information Systems (At AAAMAS-03), Melburn (2003)
11. DeLoach S. and Wood, M.: Developing Multiagent Systems with agentTool. In: Castelfranchi, C., Lesperance Y. (Eds.): Intelligent Agents VII. Agent Theories Architectures and Languages, 7th International Workshop, LNCS. Vol.1986, Springer Verlag, (2001)
12. DeLoach, S. A., Wood, M. F., and Sparkman, C. H.: Multiagent systems engineering. In: International Journal of Software Engineering and Knowledge Engineering, 11(3), (2001) 231-258
13. FIPA-OS: A component-based toolkit enabling rapid development of FIPA compliant agents. http://fipa-os.sourceforge.net/
14. Giunchiglia, F., Mylopoulos, J., and Perini, A.: The Tropos software development methodology: Processes, Models and Diagrams. In: Third International Workshop on Agent-Oriented Software Engineering, Jula (2002)
15. Gorodetski, V., Karsaev, O., Kotenko, I., and Khabalov, A.: Software Development Kit for Multi-agent Systems Design and Implementation. In: Dunin-Keplicz, B., Navareski, E. (Eds.): From Theory to Practice in Multi-agent Systems. Lecture Notes in Artificial Intelligence, Vol. # 2296, (2002) 121-130
16. Gorodetski, V., Karsaev, O., and Konushi, V.: Multi-Agent System for Resource Allocation and Schedulling. In: Lecture Notes in Artificial Intelligence, Vol. # 2691, (2003) 226-235
17. Gorodetsky, V., Karsaev, O., and Samoilov, V.: Multi-agent Technology for Distributed Data Mining and Classification. In: Proceedings of the IEEE Conference Intelligent Agent Technology (IAT-03), Halifax, Canada, (2003) 438-441
18. Jack. Jack intelligent agents – version 3.1, agent oriented software. Ltd., Australia, http://www.agent-software.com.au .
19. Padgham, L. and Winikoff, M.: Prometheus: A pragmatic methodology for engineering intelligent agents. In: Proceedings of the OOPSLA 2002 Workshop on Agent-Oriented Methodologies, Seattle, (2002) 97-108
20. Reticular Systems Inc: AgentBuilder An Integrated Toolkit for Constructing Intelligent Software Agents. Revision 1.3. (1999) http://www.agentbuilder.com/.
21. Wooldridge, M., Jennings, N.R., and Kinny, D.: The Gaia Methodology for Agent-Oriented Analysis and Design. In: Journal of Autonomous Agents and Multi-Agent Systems, Vol.3. No. 3 (2000) 285-312
22. Woldridge, M.: Agent-based software engineering, In: IEEE Proc. Software Eng, 144(1), (1997) 26-37
23. Woldridge, M., and Jennings, N. R.: Pitfalls of agent-oriented development. In: Proc. Second Int. Conf. On Autonomous Agents (Agents 98), Minneapolis/St Paul, MN, (1998) 385-391
24. http://www.agentbuilder.com/AgentTools/index.html.
25. http://www.agentlink.org/resources/agent-software.php

Information about software

Software is available in the Internet as:

- ( ) prototype version
- ( ) full fledged software (freeware), version no.:
- ( ) full fledged software (for money), version no.:
- ( ) Demo/trial version
- (x) not (yet) available

Contact person for question about the software:

Name: Oleg Karsaev
email: ok@mail.iias.spb.su

Oleg Karsaev
Laboratory of Intelligent Systems
St. Petersburg Institute for Informatics and Automation
14 Line, 39, St. Petersburg, 199178
Russia
email: ok@mail.iias.spb.su

An Integrated Development Environment for Electronic Institutions

Josep Lluís Arcos, Marc Esteva, Pablo Noriega, Juan Antonio Rodríguez-Aguilar and Carles Sierra

Abstract. There is an increasing need of methodologies and software tools that ease the development of applications where distributed heterogeneous entities can participate. Multi-agent systems, and electronic institutions in particular, can play a main role on the development of this type of systems. Electronic institutions define the rules of the game in agent societies, by fixing what agents are permitted and forbidden to do and under what circumstances. The goal of this paper is to introduce an integrated development environment that supports the engineering of electronic institutions.

Keywords. electronic institutions, multi-agent systems, software engineering.

1. Introduction

Multi agent systems (MAS) are systems composed of autonomous agents which interact in order to satisfy their common and/or individual goals. A main feature of MAS is that the communication occurs at knowledge level and that they use flexible and complex interactions among their components. Thus, the design and development of MAS suffer from all the problems associated to the development of distributed concurrent systems and the additional problems which arise from having flexible and complex interactions among autonomous entities [12]. The complexity of designing multi-agent systems increases when we focus on open systems [10]. Open multi agent systems are those in which the participants are unknown in advance and can change over time. These systems are populated by heterogeneous agents, generally developed by different people using different languages and architectures, representing different parties, and acting to maximise their own utility. In order to cope with these problems appropriate methodologies that allow the analysis and design of agent systems and software tools that support their development life cycle are needed [12, 11].

Human societies successfully deal with similar issues by deploying institutions [16] that establish how interactions of a certain sort will and must be structured within an organization. Institutions represent the rules of the game in a society, including any (formal or informal) form of constraint that human beings devise to shape human interaction. Therefore, they are the framework within which human interaction takes place, defining what individuals are forbidden and permitted and under what conditions. Furthermore, human institutions not only structure human interactions but also enforce individual and social behaviour by obliging everybody to act according to the norms.

Hence, we advocate for the introduction of their electronic counterpart, namely *electronic institutions* (EIs) [15, 19, 6], to establish the rules of the game in agent societies. An EI defines a set of artificial constraints that articulate agent interactions, defining what they are permitted and forbidden to do. An EI defines a normative environment where heterogeneous (human and software) agents can participate by playing different roles and can interact by means of speech acts [22]. Our actual experience in the deployment of actual-world MAS as EIs [20, 4] allow us to defend the validity of this approach. Notice though, that as noted in [6, 19] we believe that engineers need to be supported by well-founded tools. Hence, in this paper we introduce an integrated development environment for EIs that supports engineers through all the stages of the design and development of MAS.

As a case study we will use through this paper the Double Auction Market [8]. In this institution trader agents participate for selling and buying different commodities. The institution offers participating traders a brokering service in which trader agents can register which commodities they are interested on selling and buying. Therefore, when there are some trader agents interested in one commodity the institution realises a double auction to facilitate the trading.

The paper is structured as follows. In section 2 we describe the components of our EI model. From section 3 to 7 we outline the different stages for engineering EIs and how the different software tools that we have developed support them. Finally, in sections 8 and 9 we describe the related work and draw some conclusions.

2. Electronic Institutions. Fundamental Concepts

In this section we present a short description of electronic institutions (for further details refer to [15, 19, 6]). To define an electronic institution it is necessary to define a common language that allows agents to exchange information, the activities that agents may do within the institution and the consequences of their actions. Our model of electronic institutions is based on four principal elements: a dialogical framework, a set of scenes, a performative structure, and a set of normative rules.

The dialogical framework defines the valid illocutions that agents can exchange and the participant roles as well as their relationship. By sharing a dialogical framework, we enable heterogeneous agents to exchange knowledge with other agents. In the most general case, each agent immersed in a multi-agent environment is endowed with its own inner language and ontology. In order to allow agents to successfully interact with other agents we must address the fundamental issue of putting their languages and ontologies in relation. For this purpose we propose that agents share what we call the *dialogical framework*. EIs establish the acceptable illocutions by defining the ontology (vocabulary) —the common language to represent the "world"— and the common language for communication and knowledge representation. Moreover, the dialogical framework defines the possible participating roles within the EI and the relationships among them. Each role defines a pattern of behaviour within the institution, and any agent within an institution is required to adopt some of them. The identification and regulation of roles is considered as part of the formalisation process of any organisation [21]. In the context of an EI, we distinguish between two types of roles: *internal* and *external*. The internal roles can only be played by what we call *staff* agents, i.e. the agents that belong to the institution. We can regard them as the electronic version of the workers in human institutions. Since an institution delegates its services and duties to the internal roles, an external agent can never play an internal role.

The activities in an electronic institution are the composition of multiple, distinct, possibly concurrent, dialogic activities, each one involving different groups of agents playing different roles. For each activity, interactions between agents are articulated through agents group meetings, which we call *scenes*, that follow well-defined communication protocols. In fact, no agent interaction within an EI takes place out of the context of a scene. We consider the protocol of each scene to model the possible dialogic interactions between roles. In other words, scene protocols are patterns of multi-role conversation. Then, they can be multiply instantiated by different groups of agents. A distinguishing feature of scenes is that they allow agents, depending on their role, either to enter or to leave a scene at some particular moments(states) of an ongoing conversation.

A scene protocol is specified by a directed graph whose nodes represent the different states of the conversation and the arcs are labelled with illocution schemes or timeouts that make the conversation state evolve. Thus, at each point of the conversation, it is defined what can be said, by whom and to whom. As we want the protocol to be generic, state transitions cannot be labelled by grounded illocutions, instead illocution schemes have to be used, where, at least, the terms referring to agents and time must be variables while the other terms can be variables or constants. Thus, the protocol is independent of concrete agents and time instants. Moreover, arcs labelled with illocution schemes can have some constraints associated which impose restrictions on the valid illocutions and on the paths that the conversation can follow. This allows, for instance, to specify that in an auction scene following the English auction protocol, buyers' bids must be always greater than the last submitted bid.

While a scene models a particular multi-agent dialogic activity, more complex activities can be specified by establishing relationships among scenes which are captured in the performative structure. In general, the activity represented by a performative structure can be depicted as a collection of multiple, concurrent scenes. Agents navigate from scene to scene constrained by the rules defining the relationships among scenes. In order to capture the relationship between scenes we use a special type of scenes: *transitions.* The type of transition allows to express agents synchronisation, choice points where agents can decide which path to follow or parallelisation points where agents are sent to more than one scene. Transitions can be regarded as a type of routers in the context of a performative structure. Moreover, the very same agent can be possibly participating in multiple scenes at the same time. Likewise, there may be multiple concurrent executions of a scene. Therefore we must also consider whether the agents following the arcs from one scene to another are allowed to start a new scene execution, whether they can choose to join just one or a subset of the active scenes, or even join all the active scenes.

A performative structure can be regarded as a network of scenes whose connections are mediated by transitions that determine the role flow policy among different scenes. That is, *how* agents depending on their role can move among the different scenes and *when* new conversations can be started. Finally, an initial and a final scene determine the entry and exit points of the institution respectively.

Agent actions in the context of an institution have consequences, usually in the shape of compromises which impose obligations or restrictions on dialogic actions of agents in the scenes wherein they are acting or will be acting in the future. The purpose of normative rules is to affect the behaviour of agents by imposing obligations or prohibitions. Notice that since we are considering dialogic institutions the only actions we consider are the utterance of illocutions. Therefore, we can refer to the utterance of an illocution within a scene or when a scene execution is at a concrete state. The intuitive meaning of normative rules is that if illocutions are uttered in the corresponding scene states, and some predefined expressions are satisfied, then other illocutions satisfying other expressions must be uttered in the corresponding scene states in order to fulfil the normative rule.

To summarise, the notions above picture the regulatory structure of an EI as a "workflow" (performative structure) of multi-agent protocols (scenes) along with a collection of (normative) rules that can be triggered off by agents' actions (speech acts). Notice too that the formalisation of an EI focuses on macro-level (societal) aspects, instead of on micro-level (internal) aspects of agents.

3. Engineering Electronic Institutions

Next we detail the steps to be followed when engineering and subsequently executing institutions. These steps cover the engineering of both the institutional rules and the participating agents. Thus, we propose the engineering of EIs through the following stages:

- *Specification.* Formal specification of the institutional rules. In other words, a formal specification of EIs concepts introduced in section 2. The result is a precise description of the kinds and order of messages that agents can exchange, along with a collection of norms to regulate their actions.

- *Verification.* Once specified an institution, it should go through a verification process before opening it to participating agents. This step is twofold. There is a first verification process focusing on static, structural properties of the EI specification. A second verification process follows concerned with the expected dynamic properties of the EI. We advocate that the dynamic verification of EIs should be done by means of simulation, with the aim of exploring the institution performance with different populations of agents. The institution designer should analyse the results of the simulation and eventually introduce changes in the specification if they differ from the expected ones.
- *Agent generation.* Once the institution specification is validated, it can be made available for agent participation. At this point, agent designers have to implement their agents. We want to remark that we do not impose restrictions on the type of agents that can participate in the institution. Hence, agent designers can choose the language and architecture that better fulfill their goals.
- *Execution & Analysis.* An EI defines a normative environment that shapes agent interactions. As an institution will be populated at execution time by heterogeneous and self-interested agents, we cannot expect that these agents will behave according to the institutional rules encoded in the specification. For this purpose, we advocate that the institution should be executed via an infrastructure that facilitates agent participation, while enforcing the institutional rules. Furthermore, it is important to give support to the monitoring of EIs executions to detect agents' misbehaviours and unexpected situations.

In order to facilitate the engineering of EIs we have developed a set of software tools that give support to all the above-mentioned steps. These tools are integrated in the Electronic Institutions Integrated Development Environment (EIDE). EIDE allows for engineering both the institutional rules and the participating agents. EIDE is composed of the following tools:

ISLANDER: A graphical tool that supports the specification and static verification of institutional rules.

SIMDEI: A simulation tool to animate and analyse *ISLANDER* specifications. In other words, SIMDEI supports the dynamic verification of *ISLANDER* specifications.

aBUILDER: An agent development tool that, given an *ISLANDER* specification from an EI, generates agent skeletons. The generated skeletons can be used either for EI simulations supported by *SIMDEI* or for actual executions of the institution supported by *AMELI*.

AMELI: A software platform to run EIs. The platform facilitates agent participation in the institution while enforcing the institutional conventions. Electronic institutions specified with *ISLANDER* are run by *AMELI*.

Monitoring tool: A tool that permits the monitoring of EI executions run by *AMELI*. It graphically depicts all the events occurring during an EI execution.

In what follows we describe how the different EIDE tools are employed for the engineering of EIs. In order to illustrate how the different tools work, we use the Double Auction Market.

4. Specification and Verification via ISLANDER

The specification and static verification of EIs is supported by *ISLANDER* [7]. As to the specification of EIs, the tool combines both graphical and textual specifications. More precisely, the tool permits the graphical specification of the roles and their relationships, the scene protocols, and the performative structure. We believe that graphical specifications facilitate the work of agent designers as they are easier to create and to understand. In order to textually define the remaining elements of a specification, the tool structures the way in which it has to be introduced. Whenever possible, pop-down menus are used. This is used for fields that contain references to other specified elements and for fields whose value is one out of a predefined set. This facilitates the designer's work because he has only to select the element from a list and thus reduces typing errors.

ISLANDER supports the static verification of specifications by checking their structural correctness. Thus, the tool carries out the following verifications:

- **Integrity.** The tool checks that cross references among the different elements of the specification are correct. In other words, it checks that each element which is referenced is actually defined.
- **Liveness.** It checks that agents will not be blocked at any point of the performative structure, that each scene is reachable for each of its roles, and that agents can always reach the final scene from each scene.
- **Protocol Correctness.** It checks that scene protocols are correctly specified. That is, that each state of the graph is accessible from the initial state, that a final state is reachable from each state and that the labels of the different arcs are correctly specified according to the scene dialogical framework.
- **Normative rules correctness.** It checks that normative rules are specified correctly and that agents can fulfill them. The later means that agents can reach the scenes where they have to utter the illocutions for fulfilling each normative rule.

Figure 1 depicts the graphical user interface of *ISLANDER*. The menus contain the general operations of the application and they are similar to other applications. For instance, the file menu contains options to save the current specification, and open a new one, while the insert menu pemits the user to insert a new EI component on the current specification. The tool bar contains icons for a quick access to the operations. There is also a specific icon that activates the verification process. On the *project structure pane* the user can see all the elements and sub-elements that belong to the current specification ordered by category. It

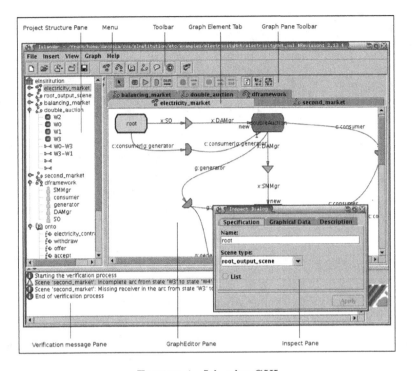

FIGURE 1. Islander GUI

permits the user to navigate among them. When he changes the selection the other panes are modified appropriately in order to show the information of the selected element or sub-element. The *graph editor pane* supports the edition of the graphical components of EIs, namely the edition of the graphical component of performative structures, dialogical frameworks and scenes. The user can edit the different graphs and modify them using the mouse. The graph editor pane is used for the creation and modification of the graph topology while the textual information associated to the graph is introduced and modified using the *inspect pane*. For instance, the graph pane is used for adding a new node to the graph but the name of the node is introduced using the inspect pane. Furthermore, the inspect pane is used for the specification of the rest of the elements of an EI. Finally, the *verification message pane* at the bottom of the figure, is used for showing the errors when the user activates the verification of the current specification. Moreover, *ISLANDER* allows the user to move to the element containing the error by simply selecting the error message text. When a user selects an error all the panes of the application are modified in order to show the element containing the error. Once an EI has been specified and verified, the user can export the institution to XML, employed at further stages of the development cycle.

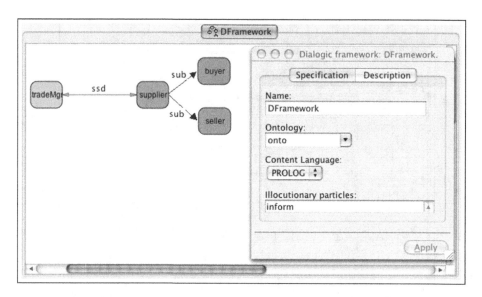

FIGURE 2. Double Auction Dialogical Framework

Summarising, *ISLANDER* supports the specification of EIs, facilitating the designer's work by combining graphical and textual specifications. Furthermore, the verification process permits checking the correctness of the specifications. The result of this stage is a sound, unambiguous and correct specification of the institutional rules. In the next subsections we present the specification of the double auction market using *ISLANDER*.

4.1. Specifying the Double Auction Market

4.1.1. Dialogical Framework. Figure 2 depicts the specification of the Double Auction Market dialogical framework. Notice that there are four different roles, namely: *tradeMgr*, *trader*, *buyer* and *seller*. They are specified graphically using the graph editor pane. In order to differentiate between the internal and external roles, internal roles are displayed in yellow, while external roles are displayed in brown. Hence, we can see that there is only one internal role (*tradeMgr*), whereas there are three external roles (*trader*, *buyer* and *seller*). The *tradeMgr* role will be played by a staff agent in charge of the brokering service and in charge of starting and realising the double auctions. The rest of the roles will be played by the external agents entering the institution for buying and selling commodities.

Furthermore, there are also some relationships among roles. On the one hand, the *tradeMgr* and the *trader* roles are incompatible (denoted by the *ssd* relation in figure 2) meaning that agents cannot play both roles within the institution. On the other hand, the *trader* role subsumes (denoted by the *sub* relation in figure 2) the *buyer* and *seller* roles, meaning that agents authorised to play the trader role can also play the buyer and seller roles.

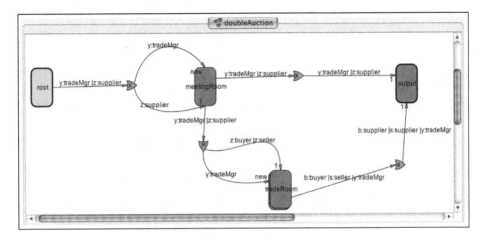

FIGURE 3. Double Auction Performative Structure

Finally, the specification contains the definition of the rest of the elements of a dialogical framework, namely: the ontology, the content language and the illocutionary particles. Concretely, the specification defines that the institution ontology is the *DAOntology*, that the content language is PROLOG and that the illocutionary particles are *inform*, *failure* and *request*.

4.1.2. Performative structure. Figure 3 shows the specification of the performative structure of the Double auction market as shown by *ISLANDER*. Its activities are represented by the *meetingRoom* scene, where traders are matched by the trade manager based on their interests in commodities, and the *tradeRoom* scene, where a Double auction is run to rule the trading. Observe that trading agents switch their role to either buyer or seller when moving from the *meetingRoom* to the *tradeRoom*. Notice too that while there is a sole execution of the *meetingRoom* scene, multiple executions of the *tradeRoom* scene may occur, being dynamically created depending on trading agents' interests. Finally, the *root* scene and the *output* scene represent the institution's entry and exit points.

4.1.3. Double Auction Scene. Figure 4 depicts the specification of the double auction scene where commodities are traded following a double auction protocol. In this protocol agents playing the buyer and seller roles have some time to submit their offers, which are matched later on to decide which transactions are done.

The first issue to address when specifying a scene is the definition of the roles that can participate in it and size of their populations. In this scene can participate agents playing the *tradeMgr*, *buyer* and *seller* roles. The scene requires the participation of exactly one agent playing the *tradeMgr* role, while there are no constraints on the number of agents playing the *buyer* and *seller* roles (zero is the default value for the *Max* field for a role meaning that there is no limit on the number of agents that can participate playing the role). We can also observe

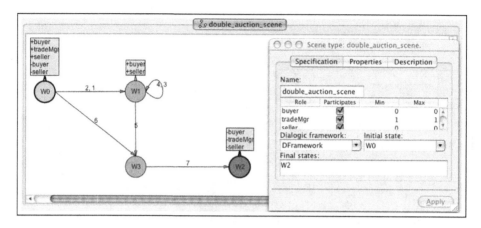

FIGURE 4. Double Auction scene

that the dialogical framework, that will be used to construct the illocution schemes labeling the arcs of the scene protocol, is the *DoubleAuctionDF*.

On the right part of the figure we can observe the specification of the scene protocol introduced using the graph editor panel. The following labels are associated to the arcs:

1   *inform(?s:seller, ?t:tradeMgr, offer(?offer))*
2   *inform(?b:buyer, ?t:tradeMgr, demand(?demand))*
3   *inform(?s:seller, ?t:tradeMgr, offer(?offer))*
4   *inform(?b:buyer, ?t:tradeMgr, demand(?demand))*
5   *[5000]*
6   *[5000]*
7   *inforn(?t:tradeMgr,all,performed_contracts(?contract))*

The scene starts at its initial state $w0$ where buyers and sellers can start to submit their offers, labels 1 and 2. Notice that after the first offer is made the scene will evolve to state $w1$, where they can continue submitting offers, labels 3 and 4, until the timeout specified by label 5 expires making the scene evolve to $w3$. Furthermore, the connection from $w0$ to $w3$ labeled also with a timeout guarantees that the scene will not be blocked if there are no offers. Once at state $w3$ the *tradeMgr* calculates the contracts matching buyers and sellers offers using the rules of the double auction protocol. The scene concludes when the *tradeMgr* announces the contracts, label 7, making the scene evolve to its final state $w2$.

Finally, in the figure it can be observed that buyer and seller agents can enter the scene at states $w0$ and $w1$, while they can leave the scene at the states $w0$ and $w2$. Complementarily, the *tradeMgr* agents can enter the scene at $w0$ and can leave it at $w2$.

5. Dynamic verification via SIMDEI

While *ISLANDER* permits the static verification of EIs, their dynamic verification is done via simulation. The purpose of the simulation is to study the dynamic behaviour and performance of the specified institution under different circumstances. For instance, in the case of the double auction the institution designer could simulate the performance of the system with different populations of buyer and seller agents.

Simulations of EIs can be run by means of the *SIMDEI* simulation tool that we have developed over REPAST [1]. Before running the simulation institution designers must develop different type of agents playing the different institution roles. This process is partially supported by the *aBUILDER* tool as explained in the next section. It is a task of the institution designers to develop types of agents, as similar as possible to the ones that will populate the institution when it will be open to external agents. Once agents have been developed simulations can be executed thanks to the *SIMDEI* simulation tool to conduct *what-if analysis*. The institution designer is in charge of analyzing the results of the simulations and return to the specification stage if they differ from the expected ones.

6. Agent development via aBUILDER

Once the institution has been specified and verified, it is time for designing the agents. Notice that within an institution we distinguish between the internal roles played by the staff agents and the external roles played by the external agents. Since staff agents are those in which the institution delegates their services and duties, they are necessary for the correct execution of the institution. Thus, it is a task of institution designers to develop them. On the contrary, external agents playing the external roles must be developed by the parties that they will represent. At this point we want to remark that we do not impose restrictions on the type of agents which can participate in the institution. Agent designers can choose the language and architecture that is better to fulfill their goals as well as they can use any software tools that facilitate their work. Therefore, it is not mandatory for them to use the *aBUILDER* tool.

Agent development is partially supported by the *aBUILDER* tool. Notice that an EI specification defines what agents can do within the institution but it does not define how agents must take their decisions. For instance, the specification of the double auction market defines how and when buyer and seller agents can submit their offers on the double auction scene, but it is a decision of every agent to decide which offers to submit. Of course, this will depend on each agent preferences and on their decision making mechanisms, which are probably different for each agent. Given an EI specification *aBUILDER* allows for defining agent skeletons

---

[1] http://repast.sourceforge.net

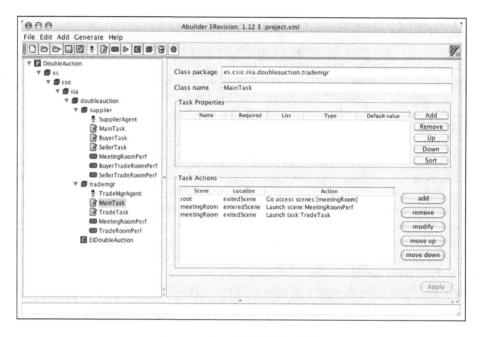

FIGURE 5. *aBUILDER* GUI

that must be later on completed by agent designers with the decision making mechanisms.

The current version of the *aBUILDER* tool permits to define agents composed by tasks and behaviours. On the one hand, tasks define general activities for an agent and each one can involve the participation in different scenes. On the other hand, a behaviour defines what an agent will do within a scene. In other words, a behaviour defines which information an agent stores from the received messages, and which utterances it utters. Therefore, the tasks determine how agents will be moving among the performative structure scenes, while the behaviours define what agents will do within the different scenes.

In order to specify a task an agent designer has to define what the agent has to do when leaving and entering scenes. On the one hand, it has to be specified which scene to join next or which task to launch when the agent leaves a scene. On the other hand, it has to be specified which behaviour to launch when the agent enters the scene. In order to know the different scenes and the rest of the institutional rules, the *aBUILDER* tool is capable of loading EIs specification as generated by *ISLANDER*.

Figure 5 depicts the graphic user interface of the *aBUILDER* tool to design agents for the Double Auction market. We can see on the left part the agents being defined. Notice that the tool permits the definition of multiple agents at the same time. In this case, two types of agents are defined, namely: *traderAgent* and

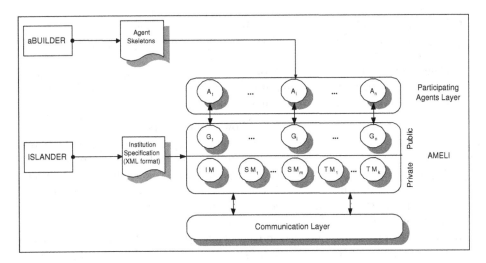

FIGURE 6. Electronic institution architecture

tradeMgrAgent. We can also observe the tasks and behaviours defined for each of them. For instance, for the tradeMgr two tasks (*MainTask* and *TradeTask*), and two behaviours (*MeetingRoomPerf* and *TradeRoomPerf*) are defined. When a user selects any of them, its information is shown and can be modified on the right part of the *aBUILDER* graphic user interface. Concretely, in figure 5 the information shown on the right part correspond to the *MainTask* of the *tradeMgrAgent*, which is the task that will be executed when it will enter in the institution. It can be observed that three actions are defined within this task. The first one defines that the agent will go to the *meetingRoom* scene when leaving the *root* scene. The second one defines that the *MeetingRoomPerf* behaviour will be launched when entering the *MeetingRoom* scene. Finally, the third one specify that the *TradeTask* task will be launched when leaving the *MeetingRoom* scene.

Once all the tasks and behaviours have been specified the tool permits the generation of code standing for agent skeletons for the different types of agents. In the current version the code is generated in JAVA. The generated code is capable to navigate through the institution performative structure and scenes, launching the specified tasks and behaviours at the defined points. However, they must be filled up with the decision making mechanisms before to send them to the institution.

Summarising, given an EI specification the *aBUILDER* tool supports the definition of different types of agents and the generation of agent skeletons.

7. Execution and Analysis

7.1. Execution via AMELI

As depicted in figure 6, our architecture is composed of the following layers:

- **Participating agent layer.** The agents taking part in the institution.
- **Social layer (AMELI).** An infrastructure that mediates and facilitates agents' interactions while enforcing the institutional rules.
- **Communication layer.** In charge of providing a reliable and orderly transport service. The current implementation can either use JADE [1] or a publish-subscribe event model as communication layer.

Notice that unlike approaches that allow agents to openly interact with their peers via a communication layer, we advocate for the introduction of a social layer (*AMELI*) which mediates agent interactions at run time. On the one hand, *AMELI* provides participating agents with information about the current execution. For instance, information about the participating agents within a scene execution. On the other hand, it enforces the institutional rules to the participating agents. At this aim, *AMELI* keeps track of the execution state, and uses it along with the institutional rules encoded in the specification to validate agents actions.

As we can observe in figure 6 *AMELI* is composed of the following types of agents:

- **Institution Manager (IM).** It is in charge of starting an EI, authorising agents to enter the institution, as well as managing the creation of new scene executions. It keeps information about all participants and all scene executions. There is one institution manager per institution execution.
- **Transition Manager (TM).** It is in charge of managing a transition controlling agents' movements towards scenes. There is one transition manager per transition.
- **Scene manager (SM).** Responsible for governing a scene execution (one scene manager per scene execution).
- **Governor (G).** Each one is devoted to mediating the participation of an agent within the institution. There is one governor per participating agent.

Since external agents can only communicate with their governors, we can regard *AMELI* as composed of two layers: a *public* layer, formed solely by governors; and a *private* layer, formed by the rest of *AMELI* agents, not directly accessible to external agents. Furthermore, all these agents collaborate to guarantee the correct evolution of an EI execuution.

Finally we want to outline the main features of our architecture:

- **Domain independent** *AMELI* can be used for the deployment of any specified institution without any extra coding. For this purpose, agents composing *AMELI* load institution specifications as XML documents generated by *ISLANDER*. Thus, the implementation impact of introducing institutional changes amounts to the loading of a new (XML-encoded) specification.
- **Agent-architecture neutral** Participating agents are only required to be capable of opening a communication channel with their governors.
- **Scalable** When employing JADE, the agents composing *AMELI* can be readily distributed among different machines

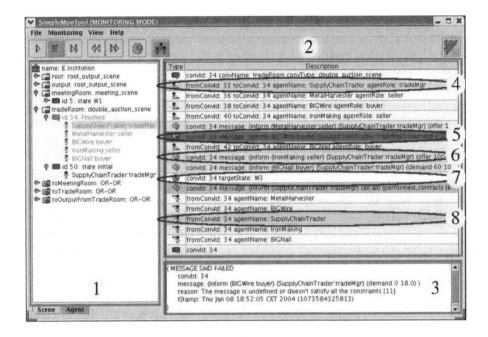

FIGURE 7. Double auction market monitoring

- **Communication neutral** Participating agents regard our architecture as *communication neutral* since they are not affected by changes in the communication layer.

The execution of an EI starts with the creation of an Institution Manager. Once up, the institution manager activates the initial and final scenes launching a scene manager for them. Thereafter, external agents can begin submitting to the institution manager their requests to join the institution. When an agent is authorised to join the institution, it is connected to a governor and admitted into the initial scene. From there on, agents can move around the different scene executions or start new ones according to the EI specification and the current execution state.

7.2. Execution Monitoring

An EI execution can be monitored thanks to the *monitoring tool* that depicts graphically all the events occurring at run time. Fairness, trust and accountability are the main motivations for the development of a monitoring tool that registers all interactions in a given enactment of an electronic institution [15, 19]. Giving accountability information to the participants increases their trust in the institution. This is specially important for electronic institutions where people delegate their tasks to agents. Furthermore, the tool permits them to analyse their agent(s) behaviour within the institution in order to improve it. From the point of view of the institution designers, the tool is useful for testing the system and the staff agents before making the institution available to external agents. Furthermore, when the institution is running it can be used to detect unexpected situations and fraudulent behaviours of external agents.

The monitoring tool displays all the interactions occurring in the different scene and transition executions, along with agents' movements among scenes. Figure 7 shows the monitoring of an execution of the Double Auction market. Frame 1 contains a list of the institution's scenes and transitions along with their executions. The list includes a single execution of the *meetingRoom* scene (*id 5*) at state *W1*. Furthermore, there are two different executions of the *tradeRoom* scene: one ongoing execution (id 50 at the initial state), and a finished one (id 34). The figure shows that while five agents (a trade manager –*tradeMgr*, two buyers, and two sellers) have participated in scene execution 34, a single agent (a trade manager) is waiting for buyers and sellers to join in scene execution 50. According to section 7.1, there is a scene manager agent per ongoing scene execution (e.g. id 5, 50). Besides, no scene manager agent is required any longer for scene execution 34 since it is finished. Furthermore, there is one transition manager agent per transition. Frame 2 depicts the events occurring during scene execution 34: agents' entrance (e.g. label 4), the utterance of valid (e.g. label 6) and wrong (e.g. label 5) illocutions, transitions caused by timeouts (e.g. label 7), agents' exit (e.g. label 8). We must remind the reader that the coordinated activity of the scene manager of the scene execution and the participating agents' governors guarantee that all these events abide by the scene specification. To illustrate the control of *AMELI* agents, frame 3 visualises an illocution rejected because a constraint in the specification is violated when buyer *BIGWire* attempts at submitting a demand of 0 units at 18 EUR. Since the scene manager evaluates the illocution as not valid, *BIGWire* is informed by its governor about the failed action.

Finally we wan to remark that the tool also allows for the monitoring of the participation of an agent within the institution. In this case, it shows the scenes in which the agent has taken part, along with the messages that it has exchanged.

8. Related Work

Recently, a number of MAS methodologies —e.g. GAIA [26], Tropos [9], or [23] to name a few— have been proposed. Most MAS methodologies are based on strong agent-oriented foundations, however, while offering original contributions at the design level, they tend to be unsatisfactory on a development level because of the lack of support to their design and implementation. Furthermore, most MAS methodologies are agent-centered rather than community or socially-centered, hence focus more on the internal aspects of agent functionality than on the interaction aspects.

There are some agent infrastructures such as DARPA COABS [3] and FIPA compliant platforms such as JADE [1] that deal with many issues that are essential for open agent interactions —communication, identification, synchronization, matchmaking— that can be used as building blocks for the development of open multi-agent systems. These building blocks are arguably too distant from organisation-centered patterns or social structures.

A different —and interesting— approach to a unified MAS development framework are the protocol-centered approaches. The proposal by Hanachi [2] allows for specifications of interaction protocols that need to be subsequently compiled into a sort of executable protocol brokers called moderators. In Tropos, the specifications are transformed into agent skeletons that must be extended with code, similar to the *aBUILDER* tool presented here. However, at execution time there is no mechanism to ensure that agents follow the specification of the system.

Although some proposals agree on the need of adopting a social stance, as far as we can tell the formal definition of organization-centered patterns and social structures in general, along with their computational realization, remain largely undeveloped (as noted in [26]).

In addition to these infrastructures and methodologies just mentioned, some agent research has focused on the introduction of social concepts such as organizations (e.g. [18],[5]),or institutions (e.g. [25]), [14], [13]). Nonetheless, to the best of our knowledge there are no tools supporting their computational realization, nor a proper engineering methodology directly associated with them.

A promising line of work is the one adopted by Omicini and Castelfranchi (e.g. [17]). It postulates some significant similarities with our EI approach: focus on the social aspects of the interactions, a unified metaphor that prevails along the development cycle, and the construction of tools to implement methodological ideas. They discuss *coordination artifacts* and propose to develop them as devices to wrap agents so that their interactions in a given MAS are subject to that MAS protocol and keep an accurate picture of the interaction context[2]. While their proposal mentions other conceptual design levels —and, consequently, other devices— the actual development of the methodology and the associated tools appears to be still rather tentative.

Finally, we believe that the most similar approach to ours is the one taken in [24], where the authors take a declarative stance to specify both EIs and their participating agents. Thus, Vasconcelos et al. propose a declarative means to represent EIs whereby they can carry out automatic checks for desirable properties. They also show how to exploit an EI specification to *synthesise* agents that conform to the specification.

---

[2]These coordination artifacts are essentially what we call *governors*.

9. Conclusions

In this chapter we have presented a technology that we have developed to address the challenges of building open multi-agent systems. We do not claim to be dealing with open systems in their full complexity, but rather addressing a restricted —albeit significant enough— type of openness: that present in interactions that involve autonomous, independent entities that are willing to conform to a common, explicit, set of interaction conventions. We will call these *a-open systems*[3]. We argue that this type of multi-agent systems can be effectively designed and developed as electronic institutions. Similarly, to human institutions in human societies, EIs define the rules of the game in agent societies, establishing what agents are permitted and forbidden to do. In other word, an EI structures the valid interactions that agents may have as well as defining the consequences of those interactions. Therefore, an EI defines a normative environment that constraints agents interactions at run time.

In order to cope with the complexity of engineering EIs, we early identified the importance of developing software tools which give support to their design, development and subsequent execution. Therefore, through this paper we have presented an Electronic Institutions Integrated Development Environment (EIDE) that supports the engineering of EIs. Through the paper we have presented the different tools that compose EIDE, and we have illustrated how they work using as an example the Double Auction Market. Notice, that we advocate that EIs engineering must start with a formal specification of the institutional rules supported by *ISLANDER*. The result is a sound and unambiguos definition of the institutional rules. Furthermore, *ISLANDER* also supports the static verification of specifications, while dynamic verification is done via simulation using the *SIMDEI* tool. Although, we do not impose constraints on the type of agents that can partcipate in an EI, their design and development is partially suppported by the *aBUILDER* tool. Finally, EIs can be executed thanks to *AMELI*, which facilitates agent participation within an EI, while enforcing the institutional rules. A main feature of *AMELI* is that it can be used for the execution of any specified instituion without any extra coding. Furthermore, EI executions can be monitored using the monitoring tool. To conclude, we want to point out that EIDE has proven to be highly valuable in the development of actual-world e-commerce applications such as the Multi-Agent System for Fish Trading (MASFIT) [4].

For further information and software downloads, the interested reader should refer to http://e-institutions.iiia.csic.es.

10. Acknowledgements

Marc Esteva enjoys a Fulbright/MECD postdoctoral scholarship FU2003-0569. The research reported in this paper is partially supported by the Spanish CICYT

---

[3]Openness is limited by the *dscription* to the conventions.

project Web-i (2) (TIC-2003-08763-C02-01). The authors would like to thank the IIIA Technological Development Unit's programmers for their valuable contribution to the development of EIDE.

References

[1] F. Bellifemine, A. Poggi, and G. Rimassa. Developing multi-agent systems with jade. In C. Castelfranchi and Y. Lesperance, editors, *Intelligent Agents VII*, number 1571 in Lecture Notes in Artificial Intelligence, pages 89–103. Springer-Verlag, 2001.

[2] C. Sibertin-Blanc C. Hanachi. Protocol moderators as active middle-agents in multi-agent systems. *Journal of Autonomous Agents and Multiagent Systems*, 8(2), March 2004.

[3] Control of agent-based systems. http://coabs.globalinfotek.com.

[4] Guifré Cuní, Marc Esteva, Pere Garcia, Eloi Puertas, Carles Sierra, and Teresa Solchaga. Masfit: Multi-agent systems for fish trading. In *16th European Conference on Artificial Intelligence (ECAI 2004)*, Valencia, Spain, August 2004.

[5] V. Dignum. *A Model for Organizational Interaction*. PhD thesis, Dutch Research School for Information and Knowledge Systems, 2004. ISBN 90-393-3568-0.

[6] M. Esteva. *Electronic Institutions: from specification to development*. PhD thesis, Universitat Politècnica de Catalunya (UPC), 2003. IIIA monography Vol. 19.

[7] M. Esteva, D. de la Cruz, and C. Sierra. Islander: an electronic institutions editor. In *Proceedings of AAMAS 2002*, pages 1045–1052, 2002.

[8] Daniel Friedman and John Rust, editors. *The Double Auction Market: Institutions, Theories, and Evidence*. Addison-Wesley Publishing Company, 1991. Proceedings of the Workshop on Double Auction Markets held June, 1991, Santa Fe, New Mexico.

[9] F. Giunchiglia, J. Mylopoulos, and A. Perini. The tropos software development methodology: Processes. Technical Report 0111-20, ITC-IRST, November 2001.

[10] C. Hewitt. Offices are open systems. *ACM Transactions of Office Automation Systems*, 4(3):271–287, 1986.

[11] Carlos A. Iglesias, M. Garijo, and J. C. Gonzalez. A survey of agent-oriented methodologies. In J. P. Muller, M. Singh, and A. S. Rao, editors, *Intelligent Agents V*, Lecture Notes in Artificial Intelligence. Springer-Verlag, 1999.

[12] Nicholas R. Jennings, Katia Sycara, and Michael Wooldridge. A roadmap of agent research and development. *Autonomous Agents and Multi-agent Systems*, 1:275–306, 1998.

[13] Ismail Khalil-Ibrahim, Gabriele Kotsis, and Wieland Schwinger. Mapping abstractions of norms in electronic institutions. In *Twelfth International Workshop on Enabling Technologies: Infrastructure for Collaborative Enterprises*, pages 30–35, Linz, Austria, June 2003.

[14] Henrique Lopes-Cardoso and Eugénio Oliveira. Virtual enterprise normative framework within electronic institutions. In *5th International Workshop on Engineering Societies in the Agents World*, Toulouse, October 2004.

[15] Pablo Noriega. *Agent-Mediated Auctions: The Fishmarket Metaphor*. Number 8 in IIIA Phd Monograph. 1997.

[16] D. North. *Institutions, Institutional Change and Economics Perfomance*. Cambridge U. P., 1990.

[17] Andrea Omicini, Alessandro Ricci, Mirko Viroli, Cristiano Castelfranchi, and Luca Tummolini. Coordination artifacts: Environment-based coordination for intelligent agents. In *Third International Joint Conference on Autonomous Agents and Multi-agent Systems (AAMAS'04)*, pages 286–293, New York, USA, July 19-23 2004.

[18] H. Parunak and J. Odell. Representing social structures in uml. In *Agent-Oriented Software Engineering II. LNCS 2222*, pages 1–16. Springer-verlag edition, 2002.

[19] Juan A. Rodríguez-Aguilar. *On the Design and Construction of Agent-mediated Electronic Institutions*. PhD thesis, Universitat Autonoma de Barcelona, 2001. Also as IIIA Monograph N. 14.

[20] Juan A. Rodríguez-Aguilar, Pablo Noriega, Carles Sierra, and Julian Padget. Fm96.5 a java-based electronic auction house. In *Second International Conference on The Practical Application of Intelligent Agents and Multi-Agent Technology(PAAM'97)*, pages 207–224, 1997.

[21] W. R. Scott. *Organizations: Rational, Natural, and Open Systems*. Englewood Cliffs, NJ, Prentice Hall, 1992.

[22] J. R. Searle. *Speech acts*. Cambridge U.P., 1969.

[23] A. Sturm, D. Dori, and O. Shehory. Single-model mehtod for specifying multi-agent systems. In *Proceedings of AAMAS 03*, pages 121–128, Melbourne, Australia, 2003.

[24] W. W. Vasconcelos, D. Robertson, C. Sierra, J Esteva, M. Sabater, and Wooldridge M. Rapid prototyping of large multi-agent systems through logic programming. *Annals of Mathematics and Artifical Intelligence*, 41:153–169, 2004.

[25] Javier Vázquez-Salceda. *The Role of Norms and Electronic Institutions in Multi-Agent Systems*. Whitestein Series in Software Agent Technology. Birkhäuser Verlag AG, Switzerland, 2004.

[26] F. Zambonelli, N. Jennings, and M. Wooldridge. Developing multiagent systems: The gaia methodology. *ACM Transactions on Software Engineering and Methodology*, 12(3):317–370, 2003.

Information about Software
Software is available on the Internet as

    (X) prototype version
    ( ) full fledged software (freeware), version no.:
    ( ) full fledged software (for money), version no.:
    ( ) Demo/trial version
    ( ) not (yet) available

Internet address: http://e-institutions.iiia.csic.es
Description of software:
    The electronic institutions development environment (EIDE) is a set of tools aimed at supporting the engineering of intelligent distributed applications as electronic institutions. Software agents appear as the key enabler technology behind

the electronic institutions vision. Thus, electronic institutions encapsulate the co-ordination mechanisms that mediate the interactions among software agents representing different business parties. The EIDE allows for engineering both electronic institutions and their participating software agents. Notably, the EIDE moves away from machine-oriented views of programming toward organizational-inspired concepts that more closely reflect the way in which we may understand distributed applications. It supports a top-down engineering approach: firstly the organization, secondly the individuals. The EIDE is composed of:

ISLANDER.: A graphical tool that supports the specification of the rules and protocols in an electronic institution.

AMELI.: Software platform to run electronic institutions. Once an electronic institution is specified with ISLANDER is ready to be run by AMELI without any programming.

aBUILDER.: Agent development tool.

SIMDEI.: Simulation tool to animate and analyze specifications created with ISLANDER prior to the deployment stage.

Download address: http://e-institutions.iiia.csic.es
Contact point for question about the software:
   email: eide@iiia.csic.es

Josep Lluís Arcos
Artificial Intelligence Research Institute, IIIA
Spanish Council for Scientific Research, CSIC
08193 Bellaterra, Barcelona, Spain.
Voice: +34 93 580 95 70 Fax: +34 580 96 61
e-mail: `arcos@iiia.csic.es`

Marc Esteva
(uiuc) Graduate School of Library and Information Science
University of Illinois at Urbana-Champaign
501 E. Daniel Street, Champaign, IL 61820
Voice: +1 217 265 0235 Fax: +1 217 244 3302
e-mail: `esteva@uiuc.edu`

Pablo Noriega
Artificial Intelligence Research Institute, IIIA
Spanish Council for Scientific Research, CSIC
08193 Bellaterra, Barcelona, Spain.
Voice: +34 93 580 95 70 Fax: +34 580 96 61
e-mail: `pablo@iiia.csic.es`

Juan Antonio Rodríguez-Aguilar
Artificial Intelligence Research Institute, IIIA
Spanish Council for Scientific Research, CSIC
08193 Bellaterra, Barcelona, Spain.
Voice: +34 93 580 95 70 Fax: +34 580 96 61
e-mail: `jar@iiia.csic.es`

Carles Sierra
Artificial Intelligence Research Institute, IIIA
Spanish Council for Scientific Research, CSIC
08193 Bellaterra, Barcelona, Spain.
Voice: +34 93 580 95 70 Fax: +34 580 96 61
e-mail: sierra@iiia.csic.es

Jadex: A BDI-Agent System Combining Middleware and Reasoning

Lars Braubach, Alexander Pokahr and Winfried Lamersdorf

Abstract. Nowadays a multitude of different agent platforms exist that aim to support the software engineer in developing multi-agent systems. Nevertheless, most of these platforms concentrate on specific objectives and therefore cannot address all important aspects of agent technology equally well. A broad distinction in this field can be made between middleware- and reasoning-oriented systems. The first category is mostly concerned with FIPA-related issues like interoperability, security and maintainability whereas the latter one emphasizes rationality and goal-directedness. In this paper the Jadex reasoning engine is presented, which supports cognitive agents by exploiting the BDI model and is realized as adaptable extension for agent middleware such as the widely used JADE platform.

1. Introduction

Today various different agent platforms are available providing support for the development of agent applications [21]. As agent orientation is a very broad field covering topics concerning inter alia agent organizations, agent behaviour as well as messaging it becomes obvious that most of these platforms focus on specific objectives and therefore cannot address all important aspects of agent technology equally well. Two important categories of platforms are middleware- and reasoning-oriented systems.

The first category is mostly concerned with FIPA-related issues that address interoperability and various infrastructure topics such as white and yellow page services. Hence agent middleware is an important building block that forms a solid foundation for exploiting agent technology. Most middleware platforms intentionally leave open the issue of internal agent architecture and employ a simple task oriented approach [2, 15, 32]. In contrast, reasoning-centered platforms focus on the behaviour model of a single agent trying to achieve rationality and goal-directedness. Most successful behaviour models are based on adapted theories coming from disciplines such as philosophy, psychology or biology. Depending on the level of detail of the theory the behaviour models tend to become complicated and can result in architectures and implementations that are difficult to use. Especially when advanced artificial intelligence and theoretical techniques such as deduction logics are necessary for programming agents, mainstream software engineers cannot easily take advantage of agent technology.

In this paper the Jadex agent framework is presented, which builds upon an existing middleware agent platform and supports easy to use reasoning capabilities. It adopts the BDI model [5] and combines it with state-of-the-art software engineering technologies like XML and Java. In the following, section 2 motivates the need for agent-oriented middleware. In section 3 reasoning approaches for agents are sketched and the BDI fundamentals regarding the individual concepts and their interrelationships are described. Section 4 explains the design and implementation of the Jadex system by detailing the abstract architecture and several implementation aspects. In section 5 the approach taken by Jadex is classified and compared to other approaches - in particular to the JACK agent framework. A summary and an outlook describing ongoing work and planned extensions conclude the paper.

2. Agent Middleware

Typically *middleware* in the field of distributed systems is seen as "[...] network-aware system software, layered between an application, the operating system, and the network transport layers, whose purpose is to facilitate some aspect of cooperative processing. Examples of middleware include directory services, message-passing mechanisms, distributed transaction processing (TP) monitors, object request brokers, remote procedure call (RPC) services, and database gateways." [1]

As agent orientation builds on concepts and technology of distributed systems middleware for agents is equally important for the realization of agent-based applications. Thereby, the term *agent middleware* is used to denote common services such as message passing or persistency management usable for agents. The paradigm shift towards autonomous software components in open, distributed environments requires on the one hand new standards to ensure interoperability between applications. On the other hand new middleware products implementing these standards are needed to facilitate fast development of robust and scalable applications. Agents can be seen as application layer software components using middleware to gain access to standardized services and infrastructure.

The Foundation for Intelligent Physical Agents (FIPA) [28] is an international non-profit organization providing standards for heterogeneous interacting agents and multi-agent systems. Since 1997 a number of specifications have been released which are replaced or updated regularly. The work on specifications focuses on

---

[1] http://iishelp.web.cern.ch/IISHelp/iis/htm/core/iigloss.htm

application as well as on middleware aspects. Specifications related to applications provide systematically studied example domains with service and ontology descriptions. The middleware-related specifications address in detail all building blocks required for an abstract agent platform architecture. This includes mechanisms for agent management, as well as infrastructure elements such as directory services and message delivery. Besides, there are extensive specifications on the syntactic and semantic layer of agent communication. This concerns inter alia the format and meaning of individual messages as well as the standard interaction protocols providing a unified basis for agent communication and interaction.

The FIPA specifications have been implemented in a number of agent platforms [2, 15, 32] and interoperability among those platforms has been shown, for example in the agentcities network.[2] In addition to the FIPA specifications, several platforms also address further middleware issues and provide specialized solutions, e.g. for security, persistency, or mobility. Although the available middleware platforms therefore provide a solid basis for developing open, interoperable agent systems, not all important aspects of agent development are supported equally well. The middleware platforms provide generic abstractions for application independent distribution and communication issues, but most of them realize a simple task-based agent model. This approach allows decomposing the overall agent behaviour into smaller pieces and attaching them to the agent as needed. Additionally, the tasks themselves can be implemented in an object-oriented language such as Java allowing the software developer to easily start using the agent paradigm. Once agent applications become more complex, another abstraction layer is needed to support the implementation of high-level decision processes inside the agents. Such abstractions are provided by cognitive agent architectures as described in the next section.

3. Reasoning for Agents

To build agents with cognitive capabilities, several theories from different disciplines like psychology, philosophy and biology can be utilized. Most cognitive architectures are based on theories for describing behaviour of individuals. The most influential theories with respect to agent technology are the Belief-Desire-Intention (BDI) model [5], the theory of Agent Oriented Programming (AOP) [31], the Unified Theories of Cognition (UTC leading to SOAR) [20, 23] and the subsumption theory [9]. Each of these theories has its own strengths and weaknesses and supports certain kinds of application domains especially well. The Jadex reasoning engine is based on the BDI model due to its simplicity and folk psychological background as explained further in the following section.

---

[2]http://www.agentcities.net

3.1. BDI Foundations

The BDI model was conceived by Bratman as a theory of human practical reasoning [5]. Its success is based on its simplicity reducing the explanation framework for complex human behaviour to the *motivational stance* [13]. This means that the causes for actions are always related to human desires ignoring other facets of human cognition such as emotions. Another strength of the BDI model is the consistent usage of folk psychological notions that closely correspond to the way people talk about human behaviour.

Beliefs are informational attitudes of an agent, i.e. beliefs represent the information, an agent has about the world it inhabits, and about its own internal state. But beliefs do not just represent entities in a kind of one-to-one mapping; they provide a domain-dependent abstraction of entities by highlighting important properties while omitting irrelevant details. This introduces a personal world view inside the agent: the way in which the agent perceives and thinks about the world.

The motivational attitudes of agents are captured in *desires*. They represent the agent's wishes and drive the course of its actions. Desires need not necessarily be consistent and therefore may not be achieved simultaneously. A "goal deliberation" process has the task to select a subset of consistent desires (often referred to as *goals*). Actual systems and formal theory mostly ignore this step (with the exception of 3APL [11, 12]) and assume that an agent only possesses non-conflicting desires. In a goal-oriented design, different goal types such as achieve or maintain goals can be used to explicitly represent the states to be achieved or maintained, and therefore the reasons, why actions are executed [8]. When actions fail it can be checked if the goal is achieved, or if not, if it would be useful to retry the failed action, or try out another set of actions to achieve the goal. Moreover, the goal concept allows to model agents which are not purely reactive i.e., only act after the occurrence of some event. Agents that pursue their own goals exhibit pro-active behaviour.

Plans are the means by which agents achieve their goals and react to occurring events. Thereby a plan is not just a sequence of basic actions, but may also include more abstract elements such as subgoals. Other plans are executed to achieve the subgoals of a plan, thereby forming a hierarchy of plans. When an agent decides on pursuing a goal with a certain plan, it commits itself (momentarily) to this kind of goal accomplishment and hence has established a so called *intention* towards the sequence of plan actions. Flexibility in BDI plans is achieved by the combination of two facets. The first aspect concerns the dynamic selection of suitable plans for a certain goal which is performed by a process called "meta-level reasoning". This process decides with respect to the actual situation which plan will get a chance to satisfy the goal. If a plan is not successful, the meta-level reasoning can be done again allowing a recovery from plan failures. The second criteria relates to the definition of plans, which can be specified in a continuum from very abstract plans using only subgoals to very concrete plans composed of only basic actions.

Algorithm 1 BDI-interpreter, taken from [29]

```
BDI-interpreter
Initialize-state();
repeat
    options := option-generator(event-queue);
    selected-options := deliberate(options);
    update-intentions(selected-options);
    execute();
    get-new-external-events();
    drop-successful-attitudes();
    drop-impossible-attitudes();
end repeat
```

3.2. BDI Realization

The foundation for most implemented BDI systems is the abstract interpreter proposed by Rao and Georgeff (see algorithm 1) [29]. At the beginning of every interpreter cycle a set of applicable plans is determined for the actual goal or event from the event queue. Thereafter, a subset of these candidate plans will be selected for execution (meta-level-reasoning) and will be added to the intention structure. After execution of an atomic action belonging to some intention any new external events are added to the event queue. In the final step successful and impossible goals and intentions are dropped. Even though this abstract interpreter loop served as direct implementation template for early PRS systems [18], nowadays it should be regarded more as an explanation of the basic building blocks of a BDI system. Several important topics such as goal deliberation and the distinction between goals and events are not considered in this approach.

4. Jadex Realization

The following sections present the motivation, architecture and execution model of the newly developed reasoning engine Jadex (see also [27]). Details about the integration of the reasoning engine into the platform are described in a separate section. Afterwards some tools are introduced which offer extended support for agent debugging.

4.1. Motivation and Project Background

In the context of the MedPAge project the need for an agent platform was identified that would support FIPA-compliant communication with a high-level agent architecture such as BDI. The MedPAge ("Medical Path Agents") project is part of the German priority research programme 1083 *Intelligent Agents in Real-World Business Applications* funded by the Deutsche Forschungsgemeinschaft (DFG). In cooperation between the business management department of the University of Mannheim and the computer science department of the University of Hamburg,

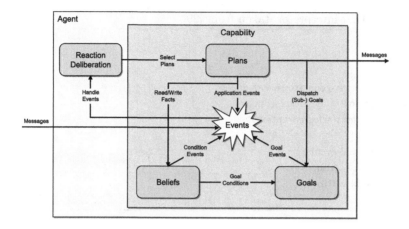

FIGURE 1. Jadex abstract architecture

the project investigates the advantages of using agent technology in the context of hospital logistics [24, 25]. The Jadex project started in December 2002 to provide the technical basis for MedPAge software prototypes developed in Hamburg.

Addressing the need for an agent platform that supports both middleware and reasoning, the approach chosen was to rely on an existing mature middleware platform, which is in widespread use. The JADE platform [3] focuses on implementing the FIPA reference model, providing the required communication infrastructure and platform services such as agent management, and a set of development and debugging tools. It intentionally leaves open much of the issues of internal agent concepts, offering a simple task-based model in which a developer can realize any kind of agent behaviour. This makes it well suited as a foundation for establishing a reasoning engine on top of it. While the agent platform is concerned with external issues such as communication and agent management, the reasoning engine on the other hand covers all agent internals. Therefore the architecture is to a large extent independent from the underlying platform.

4.2. Architecture Overview

In Fig. 1 an overview of the abstract Jadex architecture is presented. Viewed from the outside, an agent is a black box, which receives and sends messages. Incoming messages, as well as internal events and new goals serve as input to the agent's internal reaction and deliberation mechanism. Based on the results of the deliberation process these events are dispatched to plans selected from the plan library. Running plans may access and modify the belief base, send messages to other agents, create new top-level or subgoals, and cause internal events. The reaction and deliberation mechanism represents the only global component within Jadex. All other components are contained in reusable modules called capabilities.

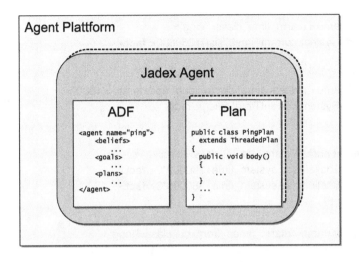

FIGURE 2. Composition of a Jadex agent

4.2.1. Agent Definition. To create and start an agent, the system needs to know the properties of the agent to be instantiated. The initial state of an agent is determined among other things by the beliefs, goals, and the library of known plans. Jadex uses a declarative and a procedural approach to define the components of an agent (see Fig. 2). The plan bodies have to be implemented as ordinary Java classes that extend a certain framework class, thus providing a generic access to the BDI specific facilities. All other concepts are specified in a so called Agent Definition File (ADF) using an XML language that follows the Jadex meta-model (described in [26]) specified in XML schema and allows for creating Jadex objects in a declarative way. Within the XML agent definition files, the developer can use expressions to specify designated properties. The language for these expressions is Java extended with OQL constructs that facilitate e.g. the specification of queries. In addition to the BDI components, some other information is stored in the definition files such as default arguments for launching the agent or service descriptions for registering the agent at a directory facilitator.

The reaction and deliberation mechanism is generally the same for all agents. The behaviour of a specific agent is therefore determined solely by its concrete beliefs, goals, and plans. In the following each of these central concepts of the Jadex BDI architecture will be described in detail.

4.2.2. Beliefs. One objective of the Jadex project is ease of usage. Therefore Jadex does not enforce a logic-based representation of beliefs. Instead, ordinary Java objects of any kind can be contained in the beliefbase, allowing reuse of classes generated by ontology modeling tools or database mapping layers. Objects are stored as named facts (called beliefs) or named sets of facts (called belief sets). Using the belief names, the beliefbase can be directly manipulated by setting, adding, or

```
01   <belief name="alarm_time" class="long">
02     <fact>System.currentTimeMillis()+360000</fact>
03   </belief>
04
05   <belief name="system_time" class="long" updaterate="1000">
06     <fact>System.currentTimeMillis()</fact>
07   </belief>
08
09   <beliefset name="alarm_times" class="long">
10     <fact>$beliefbase.system_time+360000*2</fact>
11     <fact>$beliefbase.system_time+360000*3</fact>
12   </beliefset>
13
14   <beliefset name="alarm_times_from_db" class="long">
15     <facts>Database.queryAlarmTimes()</facts>
16   </beliefset>
```

FIGURE 3. Belief and belief set examples

removing facts. A more declarative way of accessing beliefs and beliefsets is provided by queries, which can be specified in an OQL-like language [4]. The beliefs are used as input for the reasoning engine by specifying certain belief states e.g. as preconditions for plans or creation conditions for goals. The engine monitors the beliefs for relevant changes, and automatically adjusts goals and plans accordingly. E.g. a belief change can trigger a goal's creation or drop condition, or render the context of a plan invalid leading to a plan abort.

In Fig. 3 some example belief and belief set declarations are depicted that e.g. could be usable for realizing some kind of alarm clock agent. The belief "alarm_time" (lines 1-3) represents time in milliseconds and therefore requires its value being of the Java class "long". It provides already an initial fact (line 2) that will be initialized at the agent start-up. Hence the alarm time is set to one hour in the future. For being able to check whether the alarm time has been reached a dynamic "system_time" belief is declared. Using an updaterate for this belief leads to continuous reevaluations of the belief value (here every second). For representing more than a single alarm time a belief set can be employed. The "alarm_times" belief set (lines 9-12) declares two alarm times as initial facts. Note that these facts are only evaluated once and access the belief "system_time" from the beliefbase by using the reserved variable "$beliefbase". If the number of initial facts is unknown, it is also possible to retrieve those values dynamically. E.g. the belief set "alarm_time_from_db" queries a database to retrieve its initial facts.

4.2.3. Goals. Jadex follows the general idea that goals are concrete instantiations of an agent's desires. For any goal it has, an agent will more or less directly engage into suitable actions, until it considers the goal as being reached, unreachable, or not desired any more. Unlike most other systems, Jadex does not assume that all adopted goals need to be consistent to each other. To distinguish between just adopted (i.e. desired) but not yet active goals and actively pursued goals, a goal lifecycle is introduced which consists of the goal states *option*, *active*, and *suspended* [8]. When a goal is adopted, it becomes an option that is added to the agent's desire structure. A deliberation mechanism is responsible for managing the state transitions of all adopted goals (i.e. deciding which goals are active and which are just options). Some goals may only be valid in specific contexts determined by the agent's beliefs. When the context of a goal is invalid it will be suspended until the context is valid again.

Based on the general lifecycle described above, Jadex supports four types of goals, which exhibit different behaviour with regard to their processing as explained below. A *perform* goal is directly related to the execution of actions. Therefore the goal is considered to be reached when some actions have been executed, regardless of the outcome of these actions. An *achieve* goal is a goal in the traditional sense, which defines a desired outcome without specifying how to reach it. Agents may try several different alternative plans, to achieve a goal of this type. A *query* goal is similar to an achieve goal. Its outcome is not defined as a state of the world, but as some information the agent wants to know about. For goals of type *maintain*, an agent keeps track of the desired state, and will continuously execute appropriate plans to re-establish the maintained state whenever needed. More details about goal representation and processing in Jadex can be found in [8].

Fig. 4 shows some goal declarations picking up the alarm clock agent example again. For realizing the alarm functionality of the agent a "notify_user" achievement goal (lines 5-10) is declared. It has the purpose to notify the user when the alarm time has been reached. Hence, it has a creation condition that leads to a goal instantiation when the alarm time is due (lines 6-8). The goal will be satisfied, when the user is aware of the alarm (e.g. represented by a belief "user_notified"), which may be signaled to the agent by pressing some button of the alarm clock. This is intuitively expressed with the goal's target condition (line 9). If the user does not respond to the alarm, the goal will be retried every ten minutes (cf. retrydelay and exlude settings).

In response to this goal some plan has to be executed. Such a plan could e.g. notify the user by playing one of her favorite songs. To achieve this the plan has to ensure that the favorite song is available (e.g. as mp3 file) as well as it will be played. For retrieving the favorite song a "retrieve_song" query goal can be used (lines 12-15), which requires as input the name of the song to retrieve (line 13) and gives back the song location (line 14). Note, that the direction attribute is used to declare the "song" parameter as return value. Subsequent plans could handle a "retrieve_song" goal e.g. by simply fetching it from a local directory or by downloading it from the internet. For playing the song a "play_song" goal (lines 1-3) is provided. This goal is very simply as it just has one input parameter for

```
01   <performgoal name="play_song">
02     <parameter name="song" class="MediaLocator"/>
03   </performgoal>
04
05   <achievegoal name="notify_user" retrydelay="600000" exclude="never">
06     <creationcondition>
07       $beliefbase.system_time==$beliefbase.alarm_time
08     </creationcondition>
09     <targetcondition>$beliefbase.user_noti ed</targetcondition>
10   </achievegoal>
11
12   <querygoal name="retrieve_song">
13     <parameter name="song_name" class="String"/>
14     <parameter name="song" class="MediaLocator" direction="out"/>
15   </querygoal>
16
17   <maintaingoal name="keep_clock_adjusted">
18     <maintaincondition>
19       Math.abs($beliefbase.system_time-$beliefbase.reference_time)<500
20     </maintaincondition>
21   </maintaingoal>
```

FIGURE 4. Goal examples

the song file. Suitable plans supporting different sound formats could be provided
to actually play the music.

In addition to the alarm functionality, a "keep_clock_adjusted" maintenance
goal (lines 17-21) could be used to ensure that the clock is in line with a reference
time. Therefore, a maintain condition is defined that is valid as long as system and
reference time do not differ more than 0.5 secs (line 19). Whenever this condition is
violated the goal will become active and trigger plan executions for synchronizing
the system clock.

4.2.4. Plans. The reasoning engine handles all events such as the reception of a
message or the activation of a goal by selecting and executing appropriate plans.
Instead of performing planning from first principles for each event, BDI systems
like Jadex use the plan-library approach to represent the plans of an agent. For each
plan a plan head defines the circumstances under which the plan may be selected
and a plan body specifies the actions to be executed. In Jadex, the most important
parts of the head are the goals and/or events which the plan may handle and a
reference to the plan body. Additionally, a context condition as well as variable
bindings can be specified in the plan head.

The agent programmer decomposes concrete agent functionality into separate
plan bodies, which are predefined courses of action implemented as Java classes.

```
01   /** Plan skeleton for an application plan. */
02   public class SomePlan extends jadex.runtime.Plan {
03
04       public void body() {
05           // Plan code.
06       }
07
08       public void passed() {
09           // Optional cleanup code in case of a plan success.
10       }
11       public void failed() {
12           // Optional cleanup code in case of a plan failure.
13       }
14       public void aborted() {
15           // Optional cleanup code in case the plan is aborted.
16       }
17   }
```

FIGURE 5. Plan body skeleton

Object-oriented techniques and existing Java IDEs can be exploited in the development of plans. Plans can be reused in different agents, and can incorporate functionality implemented in other Java classes e.g., to access a legacy system. To access functionality of the Jadex system, a Java API is provided for basic actions such as sending messages, manipulating beliefs, or creating subgoals.

The basic structure of a plan body is shown in Fig. 5. The plan body is a Java class that extends the Jadex framework class "Plan" and hence has access to the BDI specific methods provided by the Plan API. The domain specific behaviour of the plan will be placed inside the mandatory body method (lines 4-6). Additionally, the three methods passed() , failed() and aborted() are provided allowing a plan to perform clean up operations (lines 8-16). These methods are invoked automatically with respect to the plan's final success state. If the body() method runs through the passed() method is called, whereas the failed() method is called when an uncatched exception occurs within the body() method. Finally, the aborted() method is called, when plan processing was interrupted from outside. Two different abort cases can be distinguished, either when the corresponding goal succeeds before the plan is finished (i.e. its target condition is fulfilled) or when the plans root goal is dropped.

As an example for a plan declaration in Fig. 6 the plan head (top, lines 1-6) and plan body (bottom, lines 1-10) of a "notification" plan suitable for the above described alarm clock agent are presented. The plan head is very simple in this case and consists only of the obligatory body expression (line 2) that describes how a plan body is created at runtime and how it is triggered (line 4). As the

```
01   <plan name="notify">
02     <body>new Noti cationPlan()<body/>
03     <trigger>
04       <goal ref="notify_user"/>
05     </trigger>
06   </plan>
```

```
01   public class Noti cationPlan extends Plan{
02     public void body(){
03       IGoal retrieve = createGoal("retrieve_song");
04       retrieve.getParameter("song_name").setValue("Jingle Bells");
05       dispatchSubgoalAndWait(retrieve);
06       IGoal play = createGoal("play_song");
07       play.getParameter("song").setValue(retrieve.getParameter("song").getValue());
08       dispatchSubgoalAndWait(play);
09     }
10   }
```

FIGURE 6. Plan head and body example

trigger refers to the "notify_user" goal type it is applicable for each goal instance of that type. The plan body is a Java class named "NotificationPlan" that extends the Jadex framework class "Plan". Inside the mandatory body() method the plan creates and dispatches a "retrieve_song" (lines 3-5) and a "play_song" goal (lines 6-8). The plan will fail when either of the subgoals fail, because subgoal failures raise BDI exceptions that need explicitly to be caught if the plan wants to proceed execution in an error case.

4.2.5. Capabilities. For the purpose of reusability, Jadex supports a flexible module-concept called capabilities [10], which enables the packaging of functionally related entities (beliefs, goals and plans) into a cluster. A capability definition, written as a separate XML document, is therefore very similar to an agent definition, and usually represents a certain application functionality required by several different agents (e.g., a generic negotiation mechanism). A capability provides a separate namespace for the elements contained within, and therefore avoids name-clashes with other capabilities. Agents can be composed of any number of capabilities, that in turn may contain subcapabilities. For advanced settings it is even possible to add or remove single capabilities at runtime.

Each capability exhibits to the superordinated capability a clearly defined interface by distinguishing e.g. between goals or beliefs that can be used from the outside, and those that are only visible to the capability itself. A fundamental difference to the original capability concept of Busetta et al. is that to be used, an element of an inner capability must be explicitly referenced in the scope of the outside capability or agent (see Fig. 7). Any concrete element is internal per

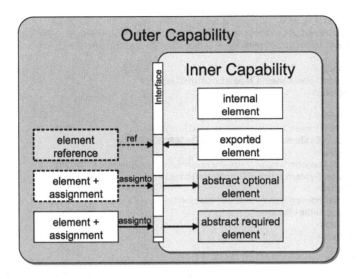

FIGURE 7. Capability concept

default, meaning that it is visible only in the capability it is defined in. For example internal beliefs are only accessible from plans that share the same scope (capability) as the beliefs. To make an element accessible from the outer capability it needs to be exported. Note that this only expresses the possibility to be used from the outer capability. If the outer capability wants to use the exported element it has to explicitly declare this by defining a place-holder (called reference) for the original element. When for example a plan of the outer capability wants to access an exported belief of the inner capability, the outer capability needs to define a belief reference. This reference, acting as a proxy of the original element at runtime, has to be supplied with its own symbolic name. To support usability, for the user (e.g. a plan) it is transparent whether the element is a reference or a concrete element because a unified view for both is provided.

Besides concrete elements a capability may also include abstract elements that either require an element assignment from the outer capability or not (required vs. optional). If an element is abstract and optional the functionality of the enclosing capability does not depend on that element and can be used without an assignment for the element. Otherwise it is mandatory to provide an assignment. E.g. abstract beliefs are a possibility to add knowledge into a capability from the outside. A detailed description about the adapted capability concept can be found elsewhere [7].

4.2.6. Complete Example Agent. In Fig. 8 the complete type declaration of a simple alarm clock agent (as introduced in the last section) is depicted. It has the ability to notify a user at a specified alarm time by playing a song. In the agent tag

```
01 <agent xmlns:xsi="http://www.w3.org/2001/XMLSchema-instance"
02  xsi:noNamespaceSchemaLocation="http://jadex.sourceforge.net/jadex.xsd"
03  name="Alarmclock" package="jadex.examples.alarmclock">
04
05  <imports>
06   <import>javax.media.MediaLocator</import>
07  </imports>
08
09  <beliefs>
10   <belief name="alarm_time" class="long">
11    <fact>System.currentTimeMillis()+360000</fact>
12   </belief>
13   <belief name="system_time" class="long" updaterate="1000">
14    <fact>System.currentTimeMillis()</fact>
15   </belief>
16   <belief name="user_notified" class="boolean">
17    <fact>false</fact>
18   </belief>
19  </beliefs>
20
21  <goals>
22   <achievegoal name="notify_user" retrydelay="600000" exclude="never">
23    <creationcondition>
24     $beliefbase.system_time==$beliefbase.alarm_time
25    </creationcondition>
26    <targetcondition>$beliefbase.user_notified</targetcondition>
27   </achievegoal>
28   <querygoal name="retrieve_song">
29    <parameter name="song_name" class="String"/>
30    <parameter name="song" class="MediaLocator" direction="out"/>
31   </querygoal>
32   <performgoal name="play_song">
33    <parameter name="song" class="MediaLocator"/>
34   </performgoal>
35  </goals>
36
37  <plans>
38   <plan name="notify">
39    <body>new NotificationPlan()</body>
40    <trigger><goal ref="notify_user"/></trigger>
41   </plan>
42   <plan name="hd_retrieve">
43    <body>new HardDiskRetrievePlan()</body>
44    <trigger><goal ref="retrieve_song"/></trigger>
45   </plan>
46   <plan name="web_retrieve">
47    <body>new WebRetrievePlan()</body>
48    <trigger><goal ref="retrieve_song"/></trigger>
49   </plan>
50   <plan name="play">
51    <body>new PlaySongPlan()</body>
52    <trigger><goal ref="play_song"/></trigger>
53   </plan>
54  </plans>
55 </agent>
```

FIGURE 8. Example agent definition

(lines 1-3) the type name "Alarmclock" and package name "jadex.examples.alarm-clock" are defined. Additionally, the URL to the Jadex schema is declared for validation purposes.

It consists of beliefs (lines 9-19) for the "alarm time" (lines 10-12), the dynamic "system time" (lines 13-15) and a flag indicating if the user has responded to the notification (lines 16-18). The goals section (lines 21-35) contains the top-level goal "notify user" (lines 22-27) which is created when the alarm time has been reached. Additionally, the two subgoal types for retrieving (lines 28-31) and playing a song (lines 32-34) are provided. The plans section (lines 37-54) contains the corresponding plans that are capable of handling the goals. Note, that two different plans are specified to handle a "retrieve song" goal. As no priorities are specified for these plans, the order of declaration determines the execution order. This means, only if the song could not be located on the hard disk (hd_retrieve plan, lines 42-45) it will be tried to load the song from the internet (web_retrieve plan, lines 46-49).

Together with the plan bodies (not shown here), the example provided in this section can directly be executed. Therefore it is only necessary to compile the plan classes with a normal Java compiler. Having started the JADE platform, the Jadex remote monitoring agent (rma) allows for starting Jadex agents simply by selecting agent models (ADFs) from a file-chooser.

4.3. Execution Model

For a complete reasoning engine several different components are necessary. The core of a BDI architecture is obviously the mechanism for plan selection. Plans not only have to be selected for goals, but for internal events and incoming messages as well. To collect the incoming messages and forward them to the plan selection mechanism a specialized component is needed. Another mechanism is required to execute selected plans, and to keep track of plan steps to notice failures. In Jadex, all of the required functionality is implemented in cleanly separated components. The relevant information about beliefs, goals, and plans is stored in data structures accessible to all these components.

Fig. 9 shows the interrelations between those components. The functional elements of the execution model can also be found in the abstract BDI interpreter presented in section 3.2. The difference between Jadex and the abstract interpreter is, that in Jadex these functionalities are carried out independently by three distinct components (message receiver, dispatcher, and scheduler).

The message receiver has the purpose to take messages from the platform's message queue and create Jadex message events which are placed in the event list (similar to the get-new-external-events() operation of the abstract interpreter). The dispatcher continuously consumes the events from the event list and builds the applicable plan list for each event (corresponds to the option-generator() function). This is done by checking for all plans if the considered event or goal triggers the plan and additionally if the plan's pre- and context conditions are valid. Corresponding plans are added to the list of applicable plans. In a subsequent step, the

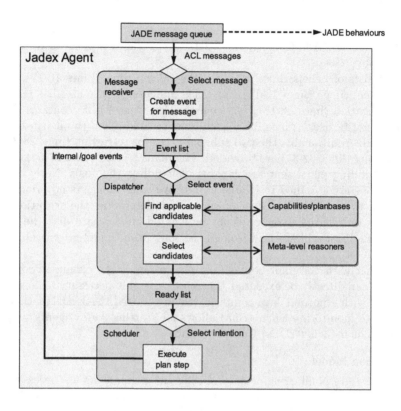

FIGURE 9. Jadex execution model

dispatcher selects plans to be executed (similar to the deliberate(options) operation) by possibly utilizing meta-level reasoning facilities. This means that if more than one plan is principally applicable for the given event or goal the decision process is delegated to a user-defined meta-level reasoning plans. The meta-level reasoner has the task to rank the plan candidates with respect to domain-dependent characteristics.

The selected plans are placed in the ready list after associating the selected plans to the corresponding events or goals, like it is done in update-intentions(selected-options). This makes the plan aware of the goal or event to handle and allows for reading goal or event details from within the plan body.

Finally, the scheduler takes the plans from the ready list and executes them (corresponds to the execute() operation). Thereby, execution of plans is done stepwise, which means that only one plan step of a single plan is executed uninterruptedly. In contrast to the original approach, in which pre-defined actions are used as plan steps, Jadex introduces the notion of *dynamic plan steps*, which will interrupt a plan whenever relevant internal changes occur. Internal changes are considered

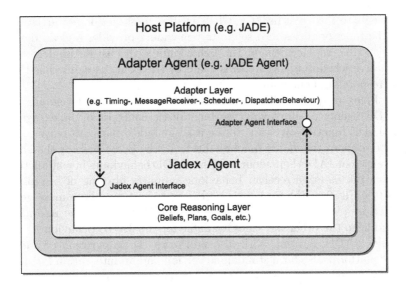

FIGURE 10. Integration mechanism

as relevant when such changes have side-effects, e.g. if a belief change triggers the creation of a new goal.

Note, that the drop-impossible/successful-attitudes() operations of the abstract interpreter are not part of the execution model, because in Jadex those operations are carried out on-the-fly, whenever there are relevant changes in the agent's beliefs.

4.4. JADE Integration

The integration of the Jadex BDI reasoning engine into JADE follows a generic mechanism depicted in Fig. 10. It consists mainly of three distinct layers: The *Host Platform* (here JADE), an *Adapter Agent* and the *Jadex Agent* which encapsulates the BDI reasoning engine. The host platform is only capable to execute agents of a certain type (here JADE agents). Therefore, a Jadex agent has to be wrapped into an adapter agent which is generically done by providing necessary services for the Jadex agent as well as for the adapter agent through small interfaces. Both sides are aware of the other side only in terms of these interfaces to minimize dependencies. In general the *Jadex Agent Interface* offers methods for performing reasoning steps, whereas the *Adapter Agent Interface* provides notification and message sending facilities.

The JADE adapter agent has the purpose to create an instance of the Jadex engine with an agent definition file, which will be interpreted by the Jadex agent to initialize its state. The above mentioned components are implemented in three JADE behaviours of the adapter agent using functionalities from the reasoning layer. In addition, there is a simple timing behaviour with the purpose to add timeout events to the event list (e.g. when awaited messages do not arrive). Implementing the functionalities into separate behaviours provides a clean design and allows for flexible replacement of the behaviours with custom implementations, e.g. alternative scheduling mechanisms could be tried out, using modified versions of the corresponding behaviours.

The Jadex project facilitates a smooth transition from developing conventional JADE agents to employing the mentalistic concepts of Jadex agents. All available JADE functionality can still be used in Jadex plans. Moreover, it is possible to use some of the Jadex functionality e.g., the belief base or the goal base, from conventional JADE behaviours. To use JADE behaviours in conjunction with Jadex plans the message receiver behaviour supports filtering of incoming ACL messages (see Fig. 9 at the top). It is necessary to sort out those messages which are handled by plans and therefore have to be dispatched to the internal Jadex system and keep the other messages available for the JADE behaviours.

Besides JADE, current work also addresses the integration of Jadex into other host platforms. So far a standalone version and an integration for the DIET platform [22] have been successfully realized. Support for other kinds of middleware such as J2EE is also feasible.

4.5. Tool Support

The tool support for the Jadex BDI reasoning engine mainly focuses on the debugging phase. For the development of Jadex agents ordinary Java IDEs such as Eclipse can be used as plans are written in plain Java. For the creation of agent definition files an XML editor is necessary, e.g. the XML-Buddy plug-in for Eclipse. Provided that a sophisticated XML editor supporting strict schema validation is used, editing becomes very comfortable as auto-completion can be utilized and additionally specification errors are already reported at design time.

For the documentation of agent applications the Jadexdoc tool has been developed (see Fig. 11). It is based on the Javadoc tool and extends it with agent specific characteristics. For all application relevant agent and capability definition files, documentation is generated that summarizes the BDI attitudes and provides links to all used capabilities as well as ordinary Java classes (e.g. a belief class) for which normal Javadocs are provided. Hence the tool enables an integrated view for agent applications consisting of agents and objects.

As a Jadex agent is still a JADE agent, all available tools of JADE can also be used to develop Jadex agents. Most of the JADE platform deals with the external view of an agent, which does not differ between conventional JADE agents and Jadex agents. E.g. the JADE sniffer agent allows for observing agent communications by visualizing the message respective protocol-based interactions and the dummy agent can be used to comfortably enter and send messages. Only the JADE introspector agent is of limited use, because it only shows the four Jadex standard behaviours and not the agent's plans. To enable a comfortable testing of Jadex agents three new tool agents have been developed: the BDI introspector, the logger agent and the tracer tool.

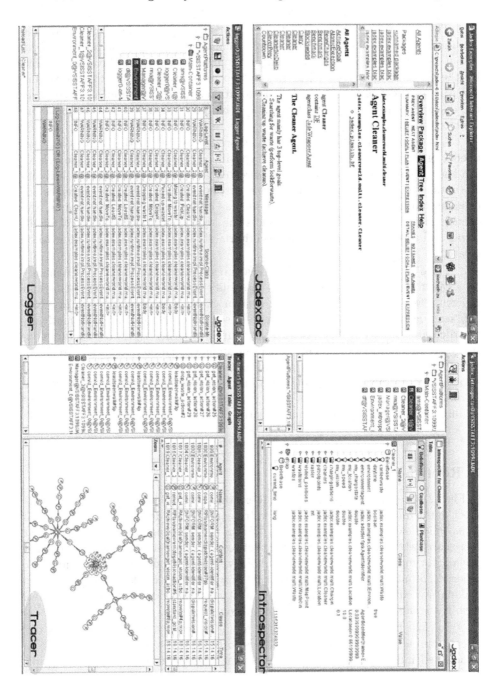

FIGURE 11. Tool screenshots

The introspector's purpose is twofold. First, it supports the visualization and modification of the internal BDI concepts thus allowing inspection and reconfiguration of an agent at runtime. Secondly, it simplifies debugging through a facility for the stepwise agent execution. In the step mode it is possible to observe and control each event processing and plan execution step having detailed control over the dispatcher and scheduler. Hence it can be easily figured out what plans are selected for an event or goal.

A big problem in debugging agent systems consists in the amount and sequence of outputs the agents produce typically on the console. With the help of the logger the agent's outputs can be directed to a single point of responsibility at runtime. In contrast to simple console outputs, the logger agent preserves additional information about the output such as its time stamp and its source (the agent and method). Using these artifacts the logger agent offers facilities for filtering and sorting messages by various criteria allowing a personalized view to be created.

Third tool meant to support the debugging phase is the tracer. Based mainly on ideas from [19] the tool offers the possibility to trace the dynamic behaviour of agents, which means that relevant system changes like reading/writing a belief, sending/receiving a message, pursuing some goal or plan are automatically recorded and displayed. For visualization purposes either a graph structure consisting of interconnected system changes or an agent-centered tree view are available. The tool can inter alia be used to understand why an agent has performed some action (e.g. executed a plan), because the causes for the action are preserved. Additionally, the graph-based visualization can be used to detect unwanted actions (failures) within regular behaviour patterns.

5. Related Work

In Fig. 12, a general overview of several existing agent platforms is given with respect to the dimensions application area (research vs. industrial use) and technical focus (middleware vs. BDI approach).[3] From this classification can be seen that there currently is almost no connection between middleware and BDI systems. Especially for industrial use of agent technology, it is of importance that middleware aspects like interoperability and security as well as aspects for rational decision making are equally well supported. Against this background, a combination of both research strands seems to be a promising approach.

To close the gap between middleware and reasoning two fundamentally different approaches exist. One possibility is to build agent platforms on top of an established industry standard for component oriented software engineering like

---

[3]References to all depicted agent platforms can be found on the Jadex project page: http://vsis-www.informatik.uni-hamburg.de/projects/jadex/links.php

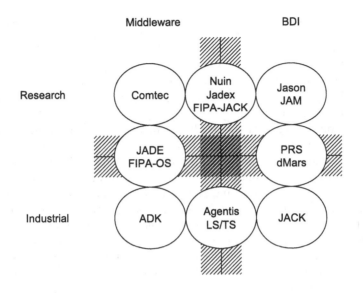

FIGURE 12. Classification of Agent Platforms

Java J2EE and therefore integrate agent technology in application server environments. Typical representatives for this approach are Agentis[4] and Whitestein's LivingSystems technology suite (LS/TS).[5] The other possible approach is based on existing (FIPA-compliant) middleware agent platforms and enhances them with BDI-specific characteristics. Examples for this approach are Nuin [14] and Jadex. In addition, with FIPA-JACK [33] a research approach exists, which enhances the commercial JACK platform with FIPA communication capabilities.

Both integration techniques have different advantages and disadvantages, hence there is not a single predominant solution. General advantages of the application server approach are that industry-grade tools are available and can be utilized to ensure several business critical properties like availability and fault-tolerance. In addition, also development and management tools can be reused to a certain degree. The main drawback of this approach is that it relies on standards for software components that have some similarities with agents, but still need to be adapted to the agent paradigm. On the contrary, using existing agent middleware as the foundation for reasoning has the advantage of being in line with the FIPA-agent standards, but the available tools do not offer the same degree of maturity yet. Due to the primary application domain of Jadex in which FIPA-compliant communication is an essential criterion, Jadex originally took the latter approach and is currently realized as a loosely coupled add-on to a middleware agent platform. Nevertheless, Jadex uses a generic integration mechanism

[4]http://www.agentissoftware.com/
[5]http://www.whitestein.com/

(as described in section 4.4) that allows for flexible adaptation to other kinds of middleware.

Jadex and JACK

Concerning the available BDI-concepts, Jadex has many similarities with the commercial JACK agent platform [17]. Therefore, Jadex will be compared with JACK in the following in more detail.

On the conceptual level the JACK agent platform strictly adopts the BDI interpreter cycle by Rao and Georgeff (see section 3.2) and provides a new agent programming language (JAL) extending Java with BDI-specific file types (agents, capabilities, events, beliefs, plans) and declarative statements. Therefore all of the aforementioned file types including the plans are realized as JACK Framework classes which have to be extended to build an application. JACK programs are compiled to normal Java files with a precompiler and can subsequently be translated to Java classes using the normal Java compiler. In addition to agent-centered BDI concepts, JACK also supports agent teams with the SimpleTeams approach [16]. The runtime infrastructure of JACK consists of an environment for agent execution and proprietary message transport. Management agents for yellow and white pages services are not available. Further on, JACK offers tool support for the development of agents with an integrated development environment (IDE) including a graphical plan editor which allows for visual plan construction. Debugging agent applications is alleviated with runtime tools for stepwise plan execution and observing agent communications.

In contrast to JACK, Jadex does not adhere to the traditional BDI interpreter in a strict manner, but defines separated responsibilities for the important parts of the deliberation cycle. Also different from JACK, Jadex does not define a new agent programming language, but uses a BDI metamodel defined in XML-schema for agent definition and pure Java as implementation language for plans avoiding the need for a precompiler. Jadex supports the same core BDI concepts (except the team concepts) as JACK and additionally introduces several extensions. Most interesting is the extension concerning explicit goal types, which alleviates the disadvantage of treating goals only in the form of simple events [8] and which is the basis for goal deliberation. Because Jadex runs on top of JADE it exhibits all of its middleware features such as FIPA-compliant communication, management agents for yellow and white pages services, security and persistency mechanisms. The same applies for tool support, which means that all of the JADE tools can be used with Jadex agents as well. Furthermore, Jadex provides additional debugging support with the debugger and logger tools, but currently lacks visual tools for agent development.

6. Conclusion and Outlook

This article presents an approach to the integration of an agent middleware with a reasoning engine to combine the advantages of both strands. A motivation for agent-oriented middleware and an overview of the BDI model was given, and the design and realization of the Jadex BDI engine as an extension to the widely used JADE agent platform was described. The Jadex system allows for the construction of rational agents, which exhibit goal-directed (as opposed to task-oriented) behaviour. The construction of Jadex agents is based on well-established software engineering techniques such as XML, Java and OQL enabling software engineers to quickly exploit the potential of the mentalistic approach. The Jadex project is also seen as a means for researchers to further investigate which mentalistic concepts are appropriate in the design and implementation of agent systems. In addition to its usage in context of the MedPAge project in Hamburg, several other institutes have used Jadex to implement research systems. E.g., the Technical University of Karlsruhe has used Jadex to implement an experimental system for representing norms in multi-agent systems [30] and at the Delft University of Technology, Jadex was used realize a personal travel assistant application [1].

The current version is Jadex 0.931, which can be freely downloaded under LGPL license from the project homepage http://jadex.sourceforge.net/. It is termed a beta stage release, what means that it has reached considerable stability and maturity to be used in practical settings. Ongoing work currently focuses on two aspects of the system: Extensions to internal concepts and additional tool support. On the conceptual level extensions to the basic BDI-mechanisms are developed, such as support for planning, teams, and goal deliberation. In contrast to other BDI agent systems Jadex supports an explicit and declarative representation of goals. It is planned to utilize this explicit representation by improving the BDI architecture with a generic facility for goal deliberation which alleviates the necessity for designing agents with a consistent goal set. Additionally, the explicit representation allows investigating task delegation by considering goals at the inter-agent level.

Work on tools mainly addresses the usability of agent technology as a mainstream software engineering paradigm. The tool support of Jadex currently focuses on the testing phase supplying debugger, logger and tracer agents. To achieve a higher degree of usability it is planned to support the design phase as well with a graphical modeling tool based on the MDA-approach. Additionally, tools for documenting agents and deployment of multi-agent applications are being developed [6].

Acknowledgement

This work is partially funded by the German priority research programme 1083 *Intelligent Agents in Real-World Business Applications*.

References

[1] M. Beelen. Personal Intelligent Travelling Assistant: a distributed approach. Master of science thesis, Knowledge Based Systems group, Delft University of Technology, 2004.

[2] F. Bellifemine, G. Caire, and G. Rimassa. JADE: The JADE platform for mobile MAS applications. In *Net.ObjectDays 2004: AgentExpo*, 2004.

[3] F. Bellifemine, G. Rimassa, and A. Poggi. JADE – A FIPA-compliant agent framework. In *4th International Conference on the Practical Applications of Agents and Multi-Agent Systems (PAAM-99)*, pages 97–108, London, UK, December 1999.

[4] M. Berler, J. Eastman, D. Jordan, C. Russell, O. Schadow, T. Stanienda, and F. Velez. *The Object Data Standard: ODMG 3.0*. Morgan Kaufmann Publishers Inc., 2000.

[5] M. Bratman. *Intention, Plans, and Practical Reason*. Harvard University Press, Cambridge, Massachusetts, 1987.

[6] L. Braubach, A. Pokahr, K.-H. Krempels, and W. Lamersdorf. Deployment of Distributed Multi-Agent Systems. In *Fifth International Workshop on Engineering Societies in the Agents World (ESAW 2004)*, 2004.

[7] L. Braubach, A. Pokahr, and W. Lamersdorf. Extending the Capability Concept for Flexible BDI Agent Modularization. In *Proceedings of the Third Workshop on Programming Multiagent Systems: Languages, frameworks, techniques, and tools (ProMAS05)*, 2005.

[8] L. Braubach, A. Pokahr, D. Moldt, and W. Lamersdorf. Goal Representation for BDI Agent Systems. In *Proceedings of the Second Workshop on Programming Multiagent Systems: Languages, frameworks, techniques, and tools (ProMAS04)*, 2004.

[9] R. Brooks. A Robust Layered Control System For A Mobile Robot. *IEEE Journal of Robotics and Automation*, 2(1):24–30, March 1986.

[10] P. Busetta, N. Howden, R. Rönnquist, and A. Hodgson. Structuring BDI Agents in Functional Clusters. In N. R. Jennings and Y. Lespérance, editors, *Intelligent Agents VI, Proceedings of the 6th International Workshop, Agent Theories, Architectures, and Languages (ATAL) '99*, pages 277–289. Springer, 2000.

[11] M. Dastani and L. van der Torre. Programming BOID Agents: a deliberation language for conflicts between mental attitudes and plans. In *Proceedings of the Third International Joint Conference on Autonomous Agents and Multi Agent Systems (AAMAS'04)*, 2004.

[12] M. Dastani, B. van Riemsdijk, F. Dignum, and J.-J. Meyer. A Programming Language for Cognitive Agents: Goal Directed 3APL. In *Proceedings of the First Workshop on Programming Multiagent Systems: Languages, frameworks, techniques, and tools (ProMAS03)*, 2003.

[13] D. Dennett. *The Intentional Stance*. Bradford Books, 1987.

[14] I. Dickinson and M. Wooldridge. Towards practical reasoning agents for the semantic web. Technical Report HPL-2003-99, Hewlett Packard Laboratories, 2003.

[15] Emorphia Limited. *FIPA-OS V2.1.0 Distribution Notes.*, 2001.

[16] A. Hodgson, R. Rönnquist, and P. Busetta. Specification of Coordinated Agent Behavior (The SimpleTeam Approach). In *Proceedings of the Workshop on Team Behaviour and Plan Recognition at IJCAI-99, Stockholm, Sweden*, 1999.

[17] N. Howden, R. Rönnquist, A. Hodgson, and A. Lucas. JACK Intelligent Agents - Summary of an Agent Infrastructure. In *Proceedings of the 5th ACM International Conference on Autonomous Agents*, 2001.

[18] F. Ingrand, R. Chatila, R. Alami, and F. Robert. PRS: A High Level Supervision and Control Language for Autonomous Mobile Robots. In *Proc. of the IEEE Int. Conf. on Robotics and Automation*, pages 43–49, Minneapolis, April 1996.

[19] D. Lam and K. Barber. Debugging agent behavior in an implemented agent system. In *Second International Workshop on Programming Multi-Agent Systems at the Third International Joint Conference on Autonomous Agents and Multi-Agent Systems*, pages 45–56, New York, NY, July 20 2004.

[20] J. F. Lehman, J. E. Laird, and P. S. Rosenbloom. A gentle introduction to Soar, an architecture for human cognition. *Invitation to Cognitive Science*, 4, 1996.

[21] E. Mangina. Review of Software Products for Multi-Agent Systems. http://www.agentlink.org/resources/software-report.html, 2002.

[22] P. Marrow. The DIET project: building a lightweight, decentralised and adaptable agent platform. *AgentLink News*, 12:3–6, April 2003.

[23] A. Newell. *Unified Theories of Cognition*. Harvard University Press, 1990.

[24] T. O. Paulussen, N. R. Jennings, K. S. Decker, and A. Heinzl. Distributed Patient Scheduling in Hospitals. In G. Gottlob and T. Walsh, editors, *Proceedings of the Eighteenth International Joint Conference on Artificial Intelligence (IJCAI-03)*. Morgan Kaufmann, 2003.

[25] T. O. Paulussen, A Zöller, A. Heinzl, A. Pokahr, L. Braubach, and W. Lamersdorf. Dynamic Patient Scheduling in Hospitals. In M. Bichler, C. Holtmann, S. Kirn, J. Müller, and C. Weinhardt, editors, *Coordination and Agent Technology in Value Networks*. GITO, Berlin, 2004.

[26] A. Pokahr and L. Braubach. *Jadex User Guide, Release 0.921*, 2004.

[27] A. Pokahr, L. Braubach, and W. Lamersdorf. Jadex: Implementing a BDI-Infrastructure for JADE Agents. *EXP – in search of innovation*, 3(3):76–85, 2003.

[28] S. Poslad and P. Charlton. Standardizing Agent Interoperability: The FIPA Approach. In M. Luck et al., editor, *9th ECCAI Advanced Course, ACAI 2001 and Agent Links 3rd European Agent Systems Summer School, EASSS 2001, Prague, Czech Republic, July 2001*, pages 98–117. Springer-Verlag: Heidelberg, Germany, 2001.

[29] A. Rao and M. Georgeff. BDI Agents: from theory to practice. In V. Lesser, editor, *Proceedings of the First International Conference on Multi-Agent Systems (IC-MAS'95)*, pages 312–319, San Francisco, CA, USA, 1995. The MIT Press: Cambridge, MA, USA.

[30] T. Schubert. Normen zur Überwachung und Steuerung autonomer Multi-Agenten Systeme. Diplomarbeit, Institut für Programmstrukturen und Datenorganisation, Fakultät für Informatik, Universität Karlsruhe (TH), 2004. (in German).

[31] Y. Shoham. Agent-oriented programming. *Artificial Intelligence*, 60(1):51–92, 1993.

[32] Tryllian Solutions B.V. *The Developer's Guide*, 2004.

[33] K. Yoshimura. FIPA JACK: A plugin for JACK Intelligent Agents. Technical report, RMIT University, 2003.

Information about Software

Software is available on the Internet as:

( ) prototype version
(x) full fledged software (freeware), version no.: 0.931
( ) full fledged software (for money), version no.:
( ) Demo/trial version
( ) not (yet) available

Internet address:

Description of software: http://jadex.sourceforge.net
Download address: http://sourceforge.net/projects/jadex

Contact person for question about the software:

Name: Lars Braubach / Alexander Pokahr
email: {braubach — pokahr}@informatik.uni-hamburg.de

Lars Braubach, Alexander Pokahr and Winfried Lamersdorf
Distributed and Information Systems Group
Computer Science Department, University of Hamburg
Vogt-Kölln-Str. 30, 22527 Hamburg
Germany
e-mail: {braubach, pokahr, lamersd}@informatik.uni-hamburg.de

Component Agent Framework for Non-Experts (CAFnE) Toolkit

Gaya Jayatilleke, Lin Padgham and Michael Winikoff

Abstract. Developing agent-oriented systems is still a difficult task. However, a component-based approach can help by supporting both modular modification of existing systems and construction of new systems from existing parts. Component Agent Framework for non-Experts (CAFnE) is such a framework that uses concepts from model-driven development and component based software engineering to allow domain experts to easily assemble agent systems. Here we look at the implementation of the framework in the form of the CAFnE toolkit that provides the domain experts with the necessary tools to build and modify agent applications.

1. Introduction

Agents are a powerful technology with many significant applications, both demonstrated and potential [12, 13]. However, building and modifying agent systems currently requires substantial expertise in one or more agent development platforms. The complex domains where agents are used often have requirements that change as the understanding of the system grows. Agent systems are inherently modular and well suited to the gradual development of the system as specialised situations are recognised and appropriate behaviour specified. Typically domain experts (e.g. meteorologists, scientists, accountants) or users identify and require these changes once the system is deployed. The need for an agent software developer to make these modifications slows down the evolution of the system, as well as increasing the cost. Our vision is to develop a framework that facilitates domain experts themselves in making modifications to a deployed system, in order for it to better fit needs which are identified as the system is used. This paper describes the Component Agent Framework for non-Experts (CAFnE) Toolkit which supports

This work was supported by the Australian Research Council (Linkage Grants LP0347025 and LP0453486) in collaboration with the Australian Bureau of Meteorology and Agent Oriented Software Pty. Ltd. We would also like to thank the reviewers for their valuable comments.

this ongoing modification of an application by domain experts. The Toolkit is also used by developers in the initial application development. The motivation for this work comes from the experience in working with several groups of domain experts and in particular the meteorologists we worked with in developing a weather alert system described in [16].

The Toolkit is based on an underlying framework where agent systems are made up of well defined small components, with structured support for modifying or adding these in well defined ways. For example, assume that we have a definition for a goal, which is based on a description of the world in terms of a set of attributes. A domain expert wishing to add a new goal could then be presented with a menu of the attributes from which to choose a combination that specifies the goal state. In order to build plans to achieve this goal, the domain expert can be presented with the set of existing actions and (sub)goals which affect the relevant attributes.

The components within our framework are of a relatively fine granularity in order to support the domain experts in the required ways. Unlike components in traditional Object Oriented Software Engineering, these are not reusable binary units of composition, as supporting code reuse is not our primary objective. The purpose of our components is to allow structured and guided modification of an application in appropriate ways.

Some of the components we use (e.g. plans, agents, goals) are an integral part of existing agent development platforms, but others (e.g. actions, protocols, environment) are more implicit. Making them explicit in our tool assists the agent software developer in building well structured applications that lend themselves to ongoing modification as the application develops in scope and complexity.

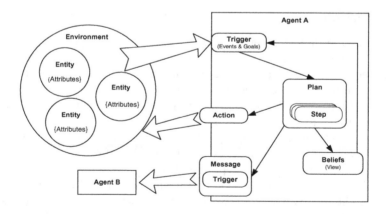

FIGURE 1. Simplified model of an agent in our framework

Our starting point for component definition was the SMART framework of Ashri and Luck [15]. However we have modified and extended this framework based on a case study of a meteorological application, typical of the kind of system we aim to support. We have excluded the SMART component types that correspond to core functions of an agent platform, such as the action selection function. Such components are provided by the agent platform and are not usually modified by application developers, let alone domain experts, so are irrelevant for our purposes. Definitions of the application-specific component types, such as goals and plans, have been modified in some cases based on our explorations of actual needs within the example meteorology application. Figure 1 shows this simplified model of an agent that we use in our framework. The components in this model are described in section 2.

In describing the CAFnE toolkit we draw on the meteorology application to illustrate and exemplify the functionality of CAFnE. We provide a brief description of this application in order to support our later examples. In the rest of the paper we then describe our underlying component model, the CAFnE toolkit and how it is used to both build and modify an agent system. Finally we compare our work to that of others and describe areas of ongoing and future work.

1.1. Meteorology Alerting System

Currently, human forecasters receive a large range of information from many sources such as radar, automated weather stations, lightning, and volcanic ash advisories. The weather alert system[1] [16] aims to reduce the information overload experienced by human forecasters by filtering information and automatically generating a range of alerts.

The system receives information from a range of sources including:

- Automated Weather Stations (AWS) which produce regular readings including temperature, pressure, and wind speed and direction.
- Terminal Aerodrome Forecasts (TAF) which are regularly-issued forecasts for airports, and contain pressure and temperature predictions.
- Thunderstorm alerts.

The system is structured as an open agent system implemented in JACK^{TM} [5] where each agent subscribes to information sources. For example, one of the agent types subscribes to AWS and TAF information, and checks for consistency between the forecasts (TAF) and the actual weather readings (AWS). If a significant inconsistency is detected it sends an alert event. Forecasters' GUIs subscribe to alert events. Example situations that result in alerts are inconsistencies between forecasts (TAF) and data readings (AWS) and extreme weather conditions such as high wind speed or thunderstorms.

---

[1]The weather alert system is part of the research project *Open Agent Architectures for Intelligent Distributed Decision Making* which is funded by the Australian Research Council (Linkage Grant LP0347025, 2003-2005) and is joint work with the Australian Bureau of Meteorology (Australia's national weather service, *www.bom.gov.au*) and Agent Oriented Software Pty. Ltd. (*www.agent-software.com*).

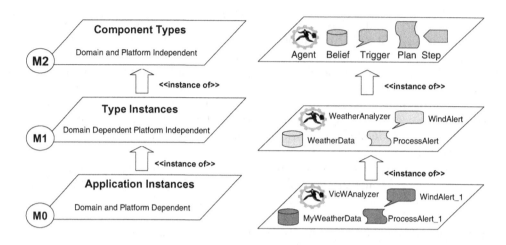

FIGURE 2. Layered Component Definitions

The key issues include ensuring that the system is resilient to various forms of failure (i.e. is robust); reducing "alert pollution", that is trying to avoid over-loading the human forecasters with too many alerts whilst ensuring that essential information is delivered; and ensuring that the system is extensible.

This application has in fact undergone a range of developments since the initial implementation, and we are in the process of modelling these in CAFnE as they occurred in practice, as a form of partial evaluation of the toolkit.

2. Understanding the Toolkit

In order to understand how the CAFnE toolkit works, it is important to have an idea about the underlying model that the toolkit is based on.

2.1. Component Model

Based on the simplified agent model shown in Figure 1 and the outcome of the analysis of the weather application (refer to section 1.1) we found a basic set of components that can be used to define and build an agent application. This set of component types comprise: *attribute, entity, environment, goal, event, trigger, plan, step, belief* and *agent*. In order to use these basic component types in a way that resolves the issues stated in section 1, we adopt a model driven approach.

The components are defined in a layered manner similar to the levels M0, M1 and M2 defined in the Model Driven Architecture (MDA) of the Object Management Group (OMG). Figure 2 shows the levels in our model (left side) and examples of entities in each layer (right side). The name of the corresponding MDA level name is given in a circle. It is important to note that we have not defined our levels using the Meta Object Facility (MOF) on which the MDA is based on [14]. A rigorous comparison of the MDA levels and our levels is out of the scope of this paper and we leave it as future work.

At the meta-meta level (M2 equivalent) we define the domain-independent generic component types found in our study. These generic types are then used in the meta level (M1 equivalent) to define domain dependent component types. For example, using the M2 level component type *Agent* we can define a *WeatherAnalyzer* type at the M1 level in the meteorology application domain. The M0 level defines the runtime components of the system which are bound to a domain as well as a runtime platform. These components are defined based on the M1 level type instances using instantiation. For example an instance of the *WeatherAnalyzer* type could be created at runtime as *VicWAnalyzer*.

We use XML DTD and XML as languages for providing definitions at the M2 and M1 levels respectively[2]. The reasons for selecting XML as the definition language for components are three fold. As stated earlier, our interest is in defining components at a descriptive level rather than at a platform level. For this XML provides an inherently structured language for specifying the anatomy of each component. This is also one of the reasons for deciding against a formal language such as Z ("Zed") [21] (used by SMART for defining its components) which is more suitable for defining process than structure. Secondly, using technologies such as XSLT (XSL-Transformations) it is easier to transform the XML definitions of the components to executable code. This process is shown in Figure 3. The XML component definitions generated by the top level development tool can be converted into executable code of an existing agent programming language by the *Transformation module*. This way we are able to leverage an existing agent platform for executing our component agents. For example, in our initial implementation of CAFnE, we are transforming the component definitions to JACK agent language [5] code. Thirdly, XML is well supported by tools and is also well established in mainstream software engineering.

In the rest of the section we provide the XML DTD definitions and a brief description of each base component type (M2 level). Interested readers can find a more comprehensive description and examples in [11].

2.1.1. Attributes, Entities and Environments: A defining characteristic of agents is that they are situated in an environment (usually highly dynamic). Therefore we need an effective way to model and represent the Environment. Our definition of an Environment is with respect to an agent in the system and not with respect to an observer of the system. SMART provides two environment definitions: as a set of Attributes; or as a set of Entities, where an *Entity* is a group of Attributes. Based on the above we define an Attribute type as a tuple:

```
<!ELEMENT Attribute (%ID;)>
<!ATTLIST Attribute Type CDATA #REQUIRED>
<!ENTITY % ID "(#PCDATA)">
```

---

[2]See http://www.w3.org/TR/2004/REC-xml-20040204/ for a specification of XML and DTD

Where *ID* refers to a *unique identifier* used to identify an Attribute. *Type* refers to the domain the Attribute value belongs to. An Entity can be defined as being a collection of Attributes:

```
<!ELEMENT Entity (Attribute)+>
<!ATTLIST Entity ID CDATA #REQUIRED>
```

2.1.2. Goals: A goal can be seen as a set of attributes that describes a desired state of the world that the agent needs to bring about, so long as a failure condition is not satisfied [23]. Hence a Goal can be defined as:

```
<!ELEMENT Goal (Attributes, Success?, Failure?)>
<!ELEMENT Attributes (Attribute+)>
<!ELEMENT Success (#PCDATA)>
<!ELEMENT Failure (#PCDATA)>
<!ATTLIST Goal ID CDATA #REQUIRED>
```

Where *ID* is a "Goal Identifier" used to identify a goal and *Success* and *Failure* are (optional) boolean expressions that state the success and failure conditions of the Goal respectively.

2.1.3. Events: An Event is a notification of a certain state of the agent or of its environment. Based on our definitions, an Event type can be defined as:

```
<!ELEMENT Event ((Attributes|Entities)+, Step?)>
<!ELEMENT Attributes (Attribute+)>
<!ELEMENT Entities (Entity+)>
<!ELEMENT Step (#PCDATA)>
<!ATTLIST Event ID CDATA #REQUIRED>
```

where the *Attributes* and *Entities* describe the state being notified by the Event and the optional Step (see section 2.1.5 for Step definition) provides a way to specify a reflexive action. A reflexive action is when an action is executed directly as a result of an event occurrence without invoking a plan.

We also define a *Trigger* which invokes a plan (see section 2.1.4 for the definition of a plan). A Trigger can be either an *Event* or a *Goal*, This is only an addition to our terminology and not a component in its own right.

2.1.4. Plans: A Plan responds to a predefined Trigger (i.e. achieves a Goal or handles an Event) by executing a sequence of "steps" (a step is a generalised form of an action defined in section 2.1.5). Based on this definition we represent a Plan as:

```
<!ELEMENT Plan (Context, Steps)>
<!ELEMENT Context (#PCDATA)>
<!ELEMENT Steps (Step+)>
<!ATTLIST Plan ID CDATA #REQUIRED>
<!ATTLIST Plan Trigger_ID CDATA #REQUIRED>
```

Where *Context* is a boolean expression that specifies the state in which this plan is applicable and *Steps* specify the sequence of steps to be executed by the plan. The parameters *ID* and *Trigger_ID* refer to the identifier of the plan and the identifier of the Trigger being handled by the plan respectively.

2.1.5. Steps: A Step is an atomic process that changes the internal or external environment of the agent. This is a generalisation of an Action which in our model is a special Step type that changes the external environment. Other Step types include belief revision, firing sub goals, messaging and logical conditions. A Step can be formalised as below:

```
<!ELEMENT Step (Input*, Output*, Instructions, Outcome)>
<!ELEMENT Input (Attribute+)>
<!ELEMENT Output (Attribute+)>
<!ELEMENT Instructions (#PCDATA)>
<!ELEMENT Outcome (#PCDATA)>
<!ATTLIST Step ID CDATA #REQUIRED>
<!ATTLIST Step Type (action | trigger | revision ...) #REQUIRED>
```

Where *Input* specifies which Attributes are required to carry out the step (e.g. WindSpeed). *Output* specifies a set of attributes that will be bound to values as a result of the step execution. *Outcome* is a post condition of the step represented as a boolean expression in terms of the beliefs. *Instructions* specify the execution process of the step; i.e. the code that implements the step.

2.1.6. Beliefs: An agent's Beliefs are used to store the agent's view of its environment, as well as its internal state. We use the relational model to structure the Attribute tuples that represent beliefs. Hence a Belief set can be defined as:

```
<!ELEMENT Belief (Attribute+, Keys)>
<!ELEMENT Keys (Key+)>
<!ELEMENT Key (#PCDATA)>
<!ATTLIST Belief ID CDATA #REQUIRED>
```

Where the set of *Attributes* (denoted by *Attribute+*) defines a tuple in the Belief set and the *Keys* define a subset of the attributes that acts as a key.

2.1.7. Agent: An agent in our framework is a collection of triggers (goals and events), plans and beliefs. Hence an agent type in our model can be defined as below:

```
<!ELEMENT Agent (Triggers+, Plans+, Beliefs+)>
<!ELEMENT Triggers (Handles*, Posts*)>
<!ELEMENT Handles (Event_ID | Goal_ID)+>
<!ELEMENT Posts (Event_ID | Goal_ID)+>
<!ELEMENT Event_ID (#PCDATA)>
<!ELEMENT Goal_ID (#PCDATA)>
<!ELEMENT Plans (Plan_ID)+>
<!ELEMENT Plan_ID (#PCDATA)>
<!ELEMENT Beliefs (BeliefSet_ID)+>
<!ELEMENT BeliefSet_ID (#PCDATA)>
<!ATTLIST Agent ID CDATA #REQUIRED>
```

2.2. Toolkit Design

The CAFnE (Component Agent Framework for non-Experts) toolkit that supports the above model driven components, consists of three main modules.

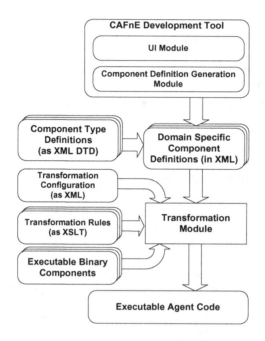

FIGURE 3. An Overview of the Component Toolkit

1. UI Module
2. Component Definition Generation (CDG) Module
3. Transformation Module

The *UI Module* allows the user to easily specify domain specific instances (i.e. M1 level components) of the base component types, with minimal or no use of complex programming constructs. Although we use an XML based specification to define these components, the users do not write XML or require any XML knowledge. We believe that, in addition to having a simple and clear set of component definitions, a smart GUI plays a major role in making agent development more accessible to non-experts. Although the *UI Module* of the currently implemented prototype is limited in this aspect, we intend to improve it in the future. A more detailed example of how the *UI Module* is used to encode an agent application is covered in section 3.

The *Component Definition Generation (CDG) Module* is responsible for generating the appropriate XML specifications for the components defined by the users via the *UI Module*. In other words, the output of the *CDG Module* is an XML file that complies to a specific DTD for each component that the user has defined using the *UI Module*.

Example: Consider an Event type instance called "envWindData" that notifies an agent about the wind speed at a given location on a given date and time. Following is the XML specification for this event generated by the *CDG Module*.

```
<Event ID="envWindData">
  <Attributes>
    <Attribute Type="String">Location</Attribute>
    <Attribute Type="int">WindSpeed</Attribute>
    <Attribute Type="String">Date</Attribute>
    <Attribute Type="String">Time</Attribute>
  </Attributes>
</Event>
```

The *CDG Module* saves each component specification as an XML file named as "[component ID].XML". In an actual CAFnE project these files are saved under a special folder named "Definitions" inside the relevant project folder.

The *Transformation Module* is one of the key apparatus in our model driven component based development. It is used to transform the platform independent XML specifications to an executable agent language code. In a nutshell, this is achieved by applying a set of XML-Transformations (XSLT) to the XML component specifications generated by the *CDG Module*. However, it is not a straight forward process as writing a set of XSLT scripts. The main challenge is the number of transformations required to obtain the relevant target platform constructs from the XML component specifications. One issue is that there is not always a one-to-one relationship between a CAFnE component and a target platform construct. This is mainly due to the variations in existing BDI agent platforms such as JACK and Jadex. For example, to implement a Goal defined in CAFnE, both an event and a plan in JACK are required. Therefore the *Transformation Module* needs to know which transformations are to be applied to a given component specification to obtain the required target platform constructs. One way to achieve this is to hard code this into the *Transformation Module*. This has the obvious disadvantage of needing a separate *Transformation Module* for each target platform. We have taken a different approach, where transformation settings for a given target platform are provided as input to the *Transformation Module*. This is shown in Figure 3 as "Transformation Configuration" which is an XML file that specifies the transformations applicable for a given component specification and also some of the output details as file name extensions. A part of a 'Transformation Configuration" file for generating JACK agent language code is shown below:

```
<Transformation>
  <module type="Agent">
    <T outputExt="agent" prefix="" xslFile="agent.xsl"/>
  </module>
  <module type="Plan">
    <T outputExt="plan" prefix="" xslFile="plan.xsl">
      <Filter xslFile="Plan_Beliefs.xsl"/>
```

FIGURE 4. A Simple Transformation

```
    <Filter xslFile="Plan_Trigger.xsl"/>
    <Filter xslFile="Plan_Revision.xsl"/>
    <Filter xslFile="Plan_Message.xsl"/>
    <Filter xslFile="Plan_Action.xsl"/>
  </T>
</module>
<module type="Event">
  <T outputExt="event" prefix="" xslFile="event.xsl"/>
  <T outputExt="plan" prefix="" xslFile="step_Plan.xsl"/>
</module>
  ...
  ...
</Transformation>
```

A `<module>` tag refers to the component type the transformation is applicable to and a `<T>` tag contains the details of of the transformation for a given `<module>`. The "xslFile" attribute in the `<T>` tag points to the XSLT script that needs to be applied by the *Transformation Module*. The output of applying a single transformation listed by a `<T>` tag is a single file in the target agent platform (see Figure 4).

A `<Filter>` tag refers to a filter (cascaded transformation) process within a transformation. This is useful in breaking an otherwise long, complex transformation into small manageable transformations. This helps a developer who has to write these transformations, to easily decompose them into smaller transformations. For example, in the above configuration file, a Plan type is transformed to JACK code using five cascaded transformations, listed as filters, that each transforms a specific aspect of the Plan specification to JACK agent language code. Both types of transformations (i.e. direct and filter based) are implemented in the CAFnE *Transformation Module* using the Xalan-Java library for XSLT and XPath [3]. The XSLT script "event.xsl" shown in Figure 4 is listed below to give the reader an idea of a simple XSLT script in CAFnE used for generating JACK agent language code.

```
<xsl:stylesheet xmlns:xsl="http://www.w3.org/..." version="1.0">
<xsl:output method="text" indent="no"/>

<xsl:template match="Event">
public event <xsl:value-of select="@ID"/> extends MessageEvent
```

---
[3] http://xml.apache.org/xalan-j/

```
{
    #set behavior ApplicableChoice first;

<xsl:apply-templates select="Attributes"/>
    public boolean _$pseudo;
<xsl:variable name="attNum">0</xsl:variable>

    #posted as
    fire(<xsl:for-each select="//Attributes/Attribute">
        <xsl:value-of select="@Type"/> a<xsl:number count="Attribute"/>
        <xsl:if test="position()!=last()">, <xsl:text>&#x20;</xsl:text>
        </xsl:if> </xsl:for-each>, boolean _pseudo)
        {
        <xsl:for-each select="//Attributes/Attribute">
        <xsl:value-of select="."/>=a
        <xsl:number count="Attribute"/>;
        </xsl:for-each>_$pseudo=_pseudo;
        <xsl:if test="not(boolean(//Event/Step))">
        _$pseudo=false;
        </xsl:if>
        }
}
</xsl:template>
<xsl:template match="Attributes">
    <xsl:apply-templates select="Attribute"/>
</xsl:template>

<xsl:template match="Attribute">
    public <xsl:value-of select="@Type"/><xsl:text>&#x20;</xsl:text>
    <xsl:value-of select="."/>;</xsl:template>
</xsl:stylesheet>
```

A developer needing to transform a CAFnE application to a specific agent platform (e.g. Jadex [18]) needs to write a new set of XSLT scripts and update the "Transformation Configuration" file to reflect the applicable transformations for each component type to obtain the correct set of executable code. Once these files are provided, a non-Expert using the CAFnE tool can specify, generate and transform component definitions via the same CAFnE user interface.

3. Using the CAFnE Tool to Build and Modify Agents

In this section we take a more detailed look at the *UI Module* of the CAFnE toolkit. First we look at the steps involved in building an agent application using the toolkit. Then we look at five detailed examples of how an existing CAFnE based agent application can be easily modified using the tool.

3.1. Building an Agent Application

Building an application within the CAFnE framework can be broken down into four broad steps. It is important to note that CAFnE does not enforce a particular methodology for arriving at a design for the agent application. However due to its foundations in BDI principles, we recommend the use of a mature methodology which supports the design of BDI agents, such as Prometheus[4][17] to be used as a guideline. The four steps are as follows:

1. Visual Modeling
2. Component Encoding
3. Transformation
4. Compilation in target platform

3.1.1. Step 1: Visual Modeling: The first step in developing an agent system in our framework is to design the overall structure of the multi-agent system, and of the agent types in the system. The most effective way to achieve this is to use a tool that allows visual manipulation of components. The current version of CAFnE *UI Module* does not provide this facility yet and hence we use the Prometheus Design Tool (PDT)[5] for this purpose. We intend to integrate the visual modeling aspects of the PDT into the CAFnE tool in the future.

Using the visual modeling features provided, a user can design an agent application by manipulating the various components visually. As we have provided a clear set of component types and their relationships, it is easier to integrate them visually to obtain a skeleton application based on component type instances. Providing the finer internal details of the components is achieved in step 2, Component Encoding.

PDT allows the user to drill down and look at the definitions diagrammatically at various levels. While it is not feasible to describe the many features of PDT here, we provide an overview of how the Weather Alert application is designed in PDT.

Example 1: Designing of the Weather Alert System
The current version of the Weather Alert system built using the CAFnE framework is a simpler version of the system described in section 1.1, which is the one currently being deployed. The system consists of three types of Agents:

- **WeatherAnalyzer**: This Agent type receives wind speed readings as an Event type called envWindData from the environment. The WeatherAnalyzer agent type processes this data by firstly classifying the Strength of the wind speed as HIGH, MID or LOW based on a set of threshold values stored in a beliefset. Secondly by looking at past wind readings stored in a beliefset, it also determines if the wind speed is increasing or decreasing (referred to as WindTrend). Finally, it sends these details to an Alerter agent type using an Event (called NotifyWindData).

---

[4]While Prometheus is not intended for non-experts, using it as a guide in the design process can help in the systematic development of an agent system
[5]PDT is a supporting design tool for the Prometheus agent development methodology; it is freely available from http://www.cs.rmit.edu.au/agents/pdt

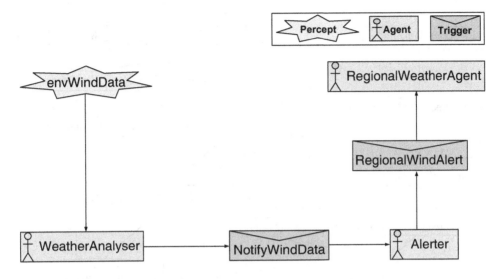

FIGURE 5. Application Overview

- **Alerter**: This Agent type is responsible for notifying the various regions[6] under the weather system's surveillance. Each of these regions are represented by an Agent of type RegionalWeatherAgent. The Alerter Agent notifies the RegionalWeatherAgent Agents of the wind level based on a notification criteria for each region. For example, an alert is sent to the RegionalWeatherAgent for the Victoria region if there have been no alerts sent in the past 10 minutes and if the wind speed is both HIGH and increasing.
- **RegionalWeatherAgent**: These Agents represent each region under the Weather system's watch. At present, these Agents are responsible for displaying an alert to the meteorologist, formatted based on the severity of the alert.

We used the visual modeling utilities in PDT to design the above application. The resulting system overview diagram is shown in Figure 5. The three types of Agents in the system and events passed between them are also shown. A drilled down view of the Agent type *Weather Analyzer* with its internal components is shown in Figure 6.

3.1.2. Step 2: Component Encoding: The objective of this step is to provide the finer details of the components identified in visual modeling phase. This is done using the CAFnE *UI Module* shown in Figure 7.

The main window of the CAFnE *UI Module* shown in Figure 7 is populated with the component definitions from our Weather Alert System. It is important to understand the functions of the two tree-view windows on either side of the main window. The tree window on the right (called the "Agent World") lists all

---

[6]The regions are the various states of Australia.

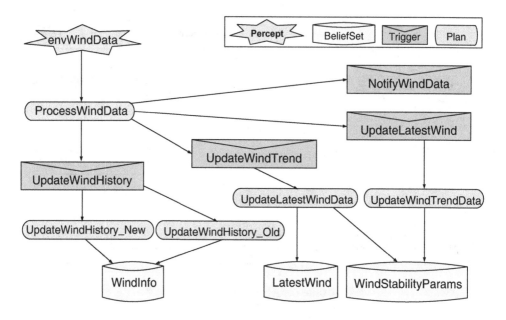

FIGURE 6. WeatherAnalyzer Agent

the Attributes and Steps used by the agent application. These are the two basic
component types which the other component types (such as Plans, Events, Goals,
and Agents) are based on.

Attributes can be added and updated freely (using the *New* menu option) by
a user. It is essential that all Attributes used in the application are defined prior to
usage. Grouping of Attributes as Entities is not supported in the current version
of the toolkit and will be included in the future.

The bottom half of the right tree window lists all the Steps used in the
application. As can be seen, Steps are categorized as one of *Belief Steps* (which can
add, read, update or remove information in belief data), *Message Steps* (including
a send step for sending messages), *Trigger Steps* (including raise and subgoal
steps for firing triggers in asynchronous and synchronous modes), *Logical Steps*
(include condition step for expressing boolean expressions) and *Action Steps*. All
Step categories apart from Action are generic to all agent applications. Hence
those are built into the CAFnE tool. However Action Steps are domain specific
since they are concerned with the environment in which the application is run.
Therefore Actions need to be provided for each application-domain separately.

Action steps can encapsulate complex executable code, which is normally developed by expert developers. The idea here is for an expert developer to provide
the non-Expert with a set of domain specific Action Steps that can be utilized in

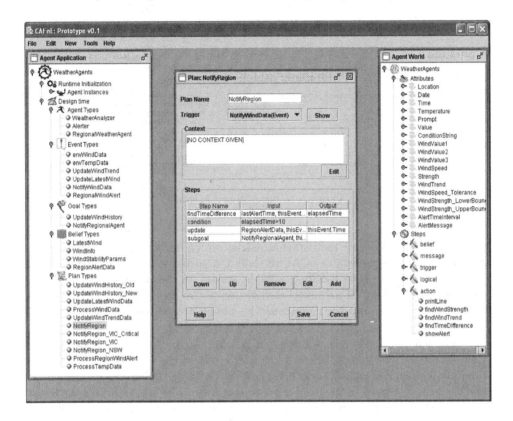

FIGURE 7. CAFnE Toolkit

formulating plans[7]. Therefore Actions (Steps in general) provide a level of granularity for the non-experts to encode plans that can solve domain problems, without delving into complex programming. However, the framework does allow the use of target platform code (as in Java or JACK) as Steps. This provides the flexibility for the users who can program in these languages. In the current version, each action is implemented as a Java class. The framework does not enforce a certain way of creating Actions as long as they can be invoked within a Plan and adhere to the Step definition given in Section 2.

Figure 8 shows the XML Step definition for *findWindStrength* action and its Java class implementation. The *findWindStrength* Step is used to find the Strength of a wind speed reading by comparing the speed to an upper bound value (above which the Strength is set to HIGH) and a lower bound value (below which the Strength is set to LOW). For each input and output Attributes of the Action, there is a corresponding *set* or *get* method in the class. Further, each Action class

---

[7]There might be cases where Actions can be reused across domains. In either case, Actions need to be developed by an expert developer.

```
<Step ID="findWindStrength" Type="action">
    <Input>
        <Attribute Type="int">WindSpeed</Attribute>
        <Attribute Type="int">WindStrength_LowerBound</Attribute>
        <Attribute Type="int">WindStrength_UpperBound</Attribute>
    </Input>
    <Output>
        <Attribute Type="String">WindStrength</Attribute>
    </Output>
</Step>
```

XML Definition of *findWindStrength* Action

```
public class findWindStrength {
    private int WindStrength_LowerBound;
    private int WindStrength_UpperBound;
    private String WindStrength;
    private int WindSpeed;

    public findWindStrength() {...}
    public void setWindSpeed(int wSpeed){...}
    public void setWindStrength_LowerBound(int lBound){...}
    public void setWindStrength_UpperBound(int uBound){...}
    public String getWindStrength(){...}

    public void execute(){...}
}
```

Java implementation of *findWindStrength* Action

FIGURE 8. Step Specification

contains a special *execute* method that carries out the processing required by the Action. All Actions used by the CAFnE toolkit are listed in a file named *Steps.xml*, which the toolkit uses to list the available actions. A developer who requires to add new Actions to CAFnE needs to first create the necessary Java classes and then include entries into the *Steps.xml* file, similar to the one on the left side of Figure 8.

The left hand side tree window (called the "Agent Application") in Figure 7 shows the various component instances, grouped at the top level based on the time of the development phase when they are defined. Under *Design Time* you find the type instances of the five base component types (*Plan, Belief, Goal, Event* and *Agent*). Under *Runtime Initialization* you find the definitions for the run-time instances of Agent types. This window provides easy access to all the component instances in the application for maintenance purposes. Some of the many features available to users when defining these component instances are discussed in examples below. As stated in section 2.2, the component instances defined here are saved as XML files in the relevant project folder.

Once all the component type instances defined in the visual modeling step are encoded as CAFnE constructs using the *UI Module*, the application is ready to be transformed. The two examples given below show how the CAFnE *UI Module* is used to create an Event and an Agent.

Example 2: Defining the Event type NotifyWindData

The Event type *NotifyWindData* is used by the Agent type *WeatherAnalyzer* to notify the Agent type *Alerter* of the recently received wind data (see Figure 5). *NotifyWindData* needs to contain data about the location, date, time, strength and wind trend of the recent wind reading. Hence it needs to contain the Attributes that represent these different data.

The Event type creation frame in CAFnE *UI Module* is shown in Figure 9, which can be invoked via the "Tool" sub menu on top main menu bar. As all the Attributes are defined, a user only has to provide an Event name and then

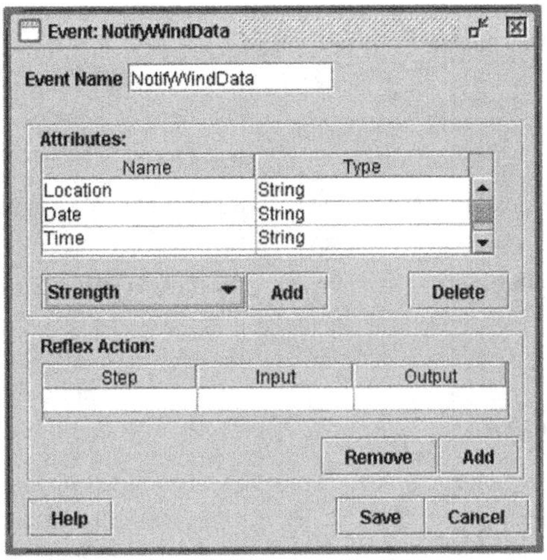

FIGURE 9. Event type creation frame

select the necessary Attributes from the drop down menu in the frame. Further, a user can also select a single action as a Reflex action for an Event as explained in Section 2.1 under the Step definition. The resulting XML specification for this Event type is given below:

```
<Event ID="NotifyWindData">
   <Attributes>
      <Attribute Type="String">Location</Attribute>
      <Attribute Type="String">Date</Attribute>
      <Attribute Type="String">Time</Attribute>
      <Attribute Type="String">WindStrength</Attribute>
      <Attribute Type="String">WindTrend</Attribute>
   </Attributes>
</Event>
```

Example 3: Defining the Agent type WeatherAnalyzer

The Agent type *WeatherAnalyzer* is the key processing Agent type in the Weather application. It receives data from the environment and redirects it to other Agents after performing some pre-processing. As can be seen on the design diagram in Figure 6, the *WeatherAnalyzer* Agent type has several Plans, Events and Belief-Sets.

The CAFnE toolkit provides a single frame interface (shown in Figure 10) to easily define an Agent type. The approach taken here is to define an Agent type by selecting the Triggers and Plans used by the agent. The rest of the dependent component types used by the Agent type are automatically derived by the tool based on the dependencies. This allows a user to think of an Agent type in terms of the Triggers and Plans it uses, without worrying about the other components.

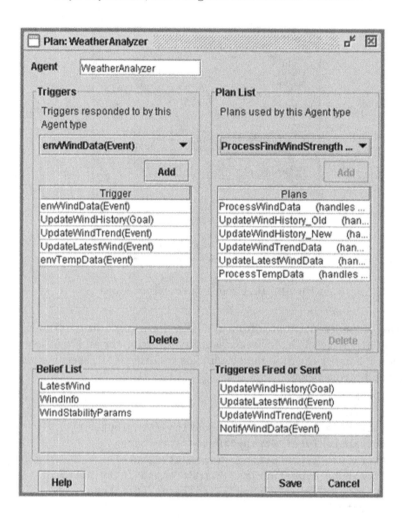

FIGURE 10. Agent type creation frame

For instance, when the user selects the Trigger *UpdateWindHistory* as one of the Triggers handled by the *WeatherAnalyzer* agent type, the tool automatically adds the two Plans and the BeliefSet needed to achieve this (see Figure 6 to see the relationship between the *UpdateWindHistory* Event and the relevant Plans and BeliefSets).

3.1.3. Step 3: Transformation: The *Transformation* step applies the transformation process described in section 2.2 to the XML files generated in the *Component Encoding* step. This process is integrated into the toolkit and is accessible via the "Tools" menu. The Transformer module included in the current version of CAFnE toolkit only supports the JACK agent language. Hence the result of the transformation step is a set of JACK language source files saved in a folder named "Runtime" inside the corresponding CAFnE project folder.

3.1.4. Step 4: Compilation in target platform: If the transformation step completes without any errors, then the agent application is ready to be compiled into executable code. This process will depend on the target language used by the users. For our current version we use the JACK agent language compiler which is accessible via the "Compile" button in the Transformation window or through an operating system shell window. Once the application is successfully compiled, it can be run by calling the appropriate start up command as required by the runtime platform and the agent application.

3.2. Modifying the Weather Alert System

Most of the time the non-Experts who use agent systems are faced with situations requiring modifications to be made to an existing system, rather than building agent applications from scratch[8]. Therefore the underlying concepts of CAFnE and the toolkit are developed keeping this aspect in mind. The clear internal and external structures of the components make it easy for a non-Expert to modify them easily, without delving into programming.

In the rest of the section we look at two examples of simple modifications made to the Weather Alert system using the CAFnE tool.

Example 4: Adding a new Agent type instance

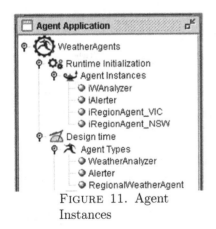

FIGURE 11. Agent Instances

Assume an instance of the Weather Alert system with a single instance of the *WeatherAnalyzer* Agent type (refer to Example 3 for details of this Agent type). In an environment where a vast number of wind data events is generated rapidly, it makes more sense to have more than one instance of this agent type to handle the environment data. This provides a load balancing mechanism that allows for efficient handling of wind data. However the number of Agent instances required can not be correctly estimated at design time and a better indicator of this is the responsiveness of the system at runtime. Therefore a user might need to add instances of *WeatherAnalyzer* Agent type to maintain a desired level of responsiveness, once the system is in use[9].

---

[8]This aspect was highlighted in detail in the Introduction section
[9]While this process can be automated, we look at the more simple solution of manually adding Agent instances

The existing instances of Agents are listed on the left side tree window of the CAFnE *UI Module* (See Figure 11) under *Agent Instances*. A new Agent instance can be added using the "Tool" menu. The Agent instance creation frame is shown in Figure 12 (left side window). A user only needs to give a name for the instance (i.e. iWAnalyzer2) and then select from a drop down list the type of the instance (i.e. WeatherAnalyzer). When an Agent type is selected, the tool lists the BeliefSets used by the Agent type under the "Beliefs" pane. If these BeliefSets need to be populated with an initial data set, the user can do so by clicking on the "Edit Data Set" button and then using the frame shown on the right side of the Figure 12. This provides an easy way to enter and modify any start up data required by the agent.

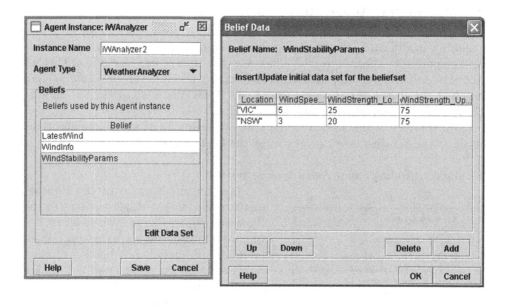

FIGURE 12. Creating an Agent type instance

Example 5: Modifying the ProcessWindData Plan

Plans are the means of specifying processes in our model of agents and hence are the component type most likely to be modified by users to obtain new forms of behaviors from agents. Here we look at changing the plan called *ProcessWindData* used by the *WeatherAnalyzer* Agent type.

The *ProcessWindData* plan handles the Event type *envWindData* that it receives from the environment (see Figure 6 on page 182). As can be seen in Figure 6, the *ProcessWindData* Plan fires three internal Events (*UpdateWindHistory, UpdateWindTrend* and *UpdateLatestWind*) and an external Event (*NotifyWindData*) sent to the Agent type *Alerter* (see Figure 5). The purpose of the internal Events is to update some BeliefSets and calculate the Strength and WindTrend values (see the description of the *WeatherAnalyzer* in Example 1 for the meaning of Strength and WindTrend). The external Event *NotifyWindData* is used to notify the *Alerter* Agent type of the Strength and WindTrend of the most recent wind reading.

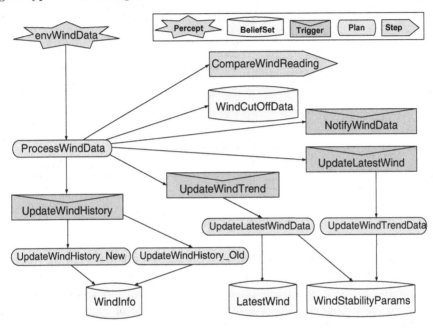

FIGURE 13. Modified WeatherAnalyzer Design

The above version of the *ProcessWindData* Plan sends a notification to the *Alerter* Agent type regardless of how low the wind reading from the environment is. This causes an unnecessary number of messages, which can be reduced by modifying the *ProcessWindData* plan. The proposed change is, not to send a notification if the wind reading is less than a predefined lower bound value. To make this *cut off* process more streamlined, the lower bound value is selected based on the location of the wind data.

The first step in making this change is to modify the agent design to reflect the changes. We do this by modifying the *WeatherAnalyzer* Agent type design using our visual modeling tool (i.e. PDT). The modified design is shown in Figure 13 (note the changes compared to Figure 6).

Once the design is changed, it can be encoded in CAFnE components using the *UI Module*. As can be seen we need a new BeliefSet named *WindCutOffData* that should contain the Attributes *Location* and *WindSpeed_CutOff*. Using the process shown in Example 1, a user can create the new BeliefSet. Once the new BeliefSet is added, it can be populated using the data entry feature available in the Agent instance creation process (see Example 4).

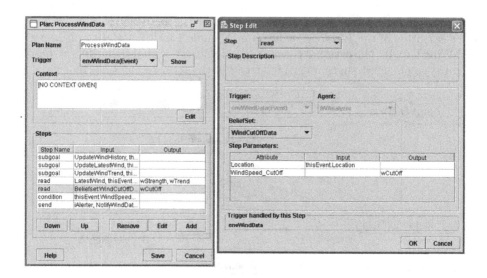

FIGURE 14. Plan Edit

To edit the *ProcessWindData* Plan, a user needs to double click on the Plan name in the left tree window. This invokes a Plan edit frame similar to the one shown on the left side of Figure 14. Now the user can add the new Steps by clicking the "Add" button. The frame on the right side of Figure 14 shows the screen for adding/editing a Step. Here it shows the screen for adding the "read" Step for reading the cut off value (given as *wCutOff*) for the given region (given as *thisEvent.Location*) from the new *WindCutOffData* beliefset. Similarly a logical Step for comparing the *wCutOff* value with the current wind speed reading (given as *thisEvent.WindSpeed*) can also be added. It is important to note that the Step addition screen is made easier with the user only needing to select values from drop down lists most of the time.

A partial XML specification for this new Plan, generated by the tool is given below. We have only listed the six Steps, leaving out the specifics of the inputs. The `<Plan>` tag includes the identifier and the Trigger handled by this plan. The `<Context>` tag which defines the plan context is set to *true* in this case to indicate that this will respond to the *envWindData* event, unconditionally. All the Steps executed in this plan are included under the `<Steps>` tag as `<Step>` elements.

```
<Plan ID="ProcessWindData" Trigger_ID="envWindData">
  <Context>true</Context>
  <Steps>
    <Step ID="subgoal" Type="trigger">
      <Trigger>UpdateWindHistory</Trigger>
      <Inputs>
        <Input ID="Location" Type="String">thisEvent.Location</Input>
        <Input ID="Date" Type="String">thisEvent.Date</Input>
```

```
          <Input ID="WindSpeed" Type="int">thisEvent.WindSpeed</Input>
        </Inputs>
      </Step>
      <Step ID="subgoal" Type="trigger">
        <Trigger>UpdateLatestWind</Trigger>
      </Step>
      <Step ID="subgoal" Type="trigger">
        <Trigger>UpdateWindTrend</Trigger>
      </Step>
      <Step ID="read" Type="belief">
        <BeliefSet>WindCutOffData</BeliefSet>
      </Step>
      <Step ID="condition" Type="logical">
      </Step>
      <Step ID="send" Type="message">
        <Trigger>NotifyWindData</Trigger>
        <Destination>iAlerter</Destination>
      </Step>
    </Steps>
</Plan>
```

4. Related Work

Component Based Software Engineering is a well-established technology within object-oriented software engineering [10], and has also been explored in relation to Agent Oriented Software Engineering. However none of the approaches that we have seen have provided the right combination of simplicity and expressivity to support non-experts in modification of evolving agent applications in the way that we envision. Agent component systems such as dMARS [7], PARADIGMA [1], DESIRE [3], JAF [22], Jadex [18] and others [8, 20] have focused on making agent *architectures* modular, rather than on making applications developed using these architectures modular. These approaches make it easier to change the core functionality of the agent architecture such as how the agent selects actions and how the agent perceives the world. However, they do not support domain-oriented structuring and changes of an agent application through components as in developing a weather event monitor agent from existing weather-related components. In other words they are not intended for non-experts. Another common problem faced in using these systems is the loosely defined nature of components such as *actions*. While most of these systems use *actions* as the primitive atomic behaviours used by agents (frequently contained in Plans), they do not provide a definition for a self-contained *action* at the implementation level. For instance, in dMARS, where there is clear semantics for an action, they are implemented as *action formulae* [4], which are not easy for a non-expert to use. Another important aspect missing in these systems is the lack of a clear definition for the Environment the agent is embedded in. Most of the time it is left to the agent developer to come up with a model for the environment. In CAFnE we provide a means for defining the Environment with a set of Attributes and provide a way to easily refer to them within other components. This simple referential model allows non-Experts to visualise the agent application and the Environment as one rather than creating separate models.

The SMART framework [15] on which PARADIGMA [1] is based provides an extensive set of components for defining an agent. However we find that some of these are not relevant for our purpose, as they define underlying infrastructure components such as *AgentPerception* and *AgentState*, rather than those required for a particular application. Other components are not defined in sufficient detail, or in a way that facilitates their use for building and modifying applications. These include components such as *Actions*, *Plans* and *Events*. We have however taken aspects of the SMART framework as a starting point and further developed or modified these in line with what we perceive as necessary for providing the concrete implementation support desired.

Another category of work has focused on providing agent toolkits with general purpose agent components for expert agent programmers. This category includes toolkits such as ABLE (Agent Building and Learning Environment) [2] and ZEUS [6]. Both these tools provide graphical interfaces with an extensive set of components mostly comprising core processing elements such as communication, learning and planning based on Java. ZEUS provides more support for multi agent communication and collaboration while ABLE specialises in agent learning. These prepackaged components help the expert to rapidly develop agent systems via component reuse. However they can only be used by expert programmers who are skilled in object-oriented languages such as Java and agent concepts. Therefore these tools do not provide an answer to our problem of supporting non-expert users.

The only work that we are aware of that develops a component framework aimed at applications, rather than agent architectures, is [9]. This work views each agent as consisting of a number of Activity components, where an activity is basically a tree of Decision components leading to a Behaviour component. Although this work is promising, defining an agent with only Activity, Decision and Behaviour components seems too limited in implementing complex agent systems. For example, it is not clear how agent beliefs (i.e. agent's view of the world) are maintained and also how proactive (goal-oriented) behaviour can be implemented. As a whole, it is not clear how the three component types can be used to implement flexible behaviours as supported by architectures such as the Belief Desire Intention (BDI) architecture [19].

5. Conclusion and Future Work

This paper described the "Component Agent Framework for non-Experts (CAFnE)" and the toolkit that implements it. CAFnE provides a model-driven component-based approach for building and modifying agent systems, mainly targeting the domain expert users with a limited knowledge in agent programming. While there has been other work done on component based agent systems, our focus is on two main areas. Firstly, our aim is to provide a structured and an easy to use set of components for the use of non-experts. Secondly, our components are at a level that describes an agent application rather than an agent architecture. In other words, our interest is not in components that contribute to an execution platform of agents (which is an area for expert developers). CAFnE provides a set of basic component types, namely *attribute, entity, environment, trigger (goal, event), plan, step, belief* and *agent* that can be used to build an agent application. In order to use these components to build and modify agents, we provide the CAFnE toolkit. The current prototype version of the CAFnE toolkit contains methods for easily defining and modifying an agent system without delving into complex agent programming.

There are four directions for future work. Firstly, we intend to improve the *UI Module* of the CAFnE toolkit by adding new features such as integrated visual modeling (now done using PDT). Secondly, there are aspects of the underlying framework that can be improved. One such area that we regard as essential is an easy to use mechanism to define and implement protocols for inter-agent communication. Other important platform changes include a richer Plan language for controlling Step execution and transformation modules to support other BDI execution platforms such as Jadex. Thirdly, we will investigate ways in which the effects of a change to an application can be explored and visualised. Finally, we intend to evaluate the effectiveness of CAFnE by providing a group of meteorologists with an extended version of the Weather Alert system and asking them to make changes to the system. If they are able to successfully make changes, without any intervention from a programmer, then we will consider the approach to be highly successful. Initial indications are that this seems very possible.

References

[1] R. Ashri, M. Luck, and M. d'Inverno. Infrastructure support for agent-based development. *Foundations and Applications of Multi-Agent Systems, LNAI2403*, pages 73–88, 2002.

[2] J. Bigus, D. Schlosnagle, J. Pilgrim, W. Mills, and Y. Diao. ABLE: A toolkit for building multiagent autonomic systems. *IBM Systems Journal*, 41(3):350–371, 2002.

[3] F. M. Brazier, C. M. Jonker, and J. Treur. Principles of component-based design of intelligent agents. *Data Knowledge Engineering*, 41(1):1–27, 2002.

[4] A. Brenton. The dMARS plan language reference manual (dMARS v1.6.12). Technical report, Australian Artificial Intelligence Institute, 1996.

[5] P. Busetta, R. Rönnquist, A. Hodgson, and A. Lucas. JACK Intelligent Agents - Components for Intelligent Agents in Java. Technical report, Agent Oriented Software Pty. Ltd, Melbourne, Australia, 1998. Available from http://www.agent-software.com.

[6] J. Collis and D. Ndumu. The zeus agent building toolkit: Zeus technical manual (release 1.0). Technical report, British Telecommunications PLC, 1999.

[7] M. d'Inverno, D. Kinny, M. Luck, and M. Wooldridge. A formal specification of dMARS. In M. Singh, A. Rao, and M. Wooldridge, editors, *Intelligent Agents IV: Proceedings of the Fourth International Workshop on Agent Theories, Architectures, and Languages*, pages 155–176. Springer-Verlag LNAI 1365, 1998.

[8] K. Erol, J. Lang, and R. Levy. Designing agents from reusable components. In *Proceedings of the Fourth International Conference on Autonomous Agents*. Barcelona, Spain, 2000.

[9] H. J. Goradia and J. M. Vidal. Building blocks for agent design. In *Fourth International Workshop on AOSE*, pages 17–30. AAMAS03, July 2003.

[10] G. T. Heineman and W. T. Council. *Component-Based Software Engineering: Putting the Pieces Together*. Addison-Wesley Publishing Company, ISBN: 0-201-70485-4, 2001.

[11] G. Jayatilleke, L. Padgham, and M. Winikoff. Towards a component-based development framework for agents. In *Proceedings of the 2nd German Conference on Multiagent System Technologies (MATES)*, Erfurt, Germany, 05 2004. Springer.

[12] N. Jennings and M. Wooldridge. Applications of intelligent agents. In N. R. Jennings and M. J. Wooldridge, editors, *Agent Technology: Foundations, Applications, and Markets*, chapter 1, pages 3–28. Springer, 1998.

[13] N. R. Jennings. An agent-based approach for building complex software systems. *Communications of the ACM*, 44(4):35–41, April 2001.

[14] A. Kleppe, J. Warmer, and W. Bast. *MDA Explained, The Model Driven Architecture: Practice and Promise*. Addison-Wesley Publishing Company, ISBN: 0-321-19442-X, 2003.

[15] M. Luck and M. d'Inverno. *Understanding Agent Systems*. Springer, ISBN 3540419756, 2001.

[16] I. Mathieson, S. Dance, L. Padgham, M. Gorman, and M. Winikoff. An open meteorological alerting system: Issues and solutions. In *Proceedings of the 27th Australasian Computer Science Conference*, Dunedin, New Zealand, Jan. 2004.

[17] L. Padgham and M. Winikoff. *Developing Intelligent Agent Systems: A Practical Guide*. John Wiley and Sons, ISBN 0-470-86120-7, 06 2004.

[18] A. Pokahr and L. Braubach. Jadex: User guide (release 0.92). Technical report, Distributed Systems Group, University of Hamburg, Germany, 05 2004.

[19] A. S. Rao and M. P. Georgeff. BDI-agents: from theory to practice. In *Proceedings of the First Intl. Conference on Multiagent Systems*. San Francisco, 1995.

[20] N. Skarmeas and K. L. Clark. Component based agent construction. *International Journal on Artificial Intelligence Tools*, 11(1):139–163, 2002.

[21] J. M. Spivey. *The Z Notation: A Z Reference Manual*. Prentice Hall International, 1989.

[22] T. Wagner, B. Horling, V. Lesser, J. Phelps, and V. Guralnik. The Struggle for Reuse: Pros and Cons of Generalization in TÆMS and its Impact on Technology Transition. *Proceedings of the ISCA 12th International Conference on Intelligent and Adaptive Systems and Software Engineering (IASSE-2003)*, July 2003.

[23] M. Winikoff, L. Padgham, J. Harland, and J. Thangarajah. Declarative & procedural goals in intelligent agent systems. In *Proceedings of the Eighth International*

Conference on Principles of Knowledge Representation and Reasoning (KR2002), Toulouse, France, Apr. 2002.

Gaya Jayatilleke
School of Computer Science and Information Technology,
RMIT University,
GPO Box 2476V, Melbourne, VIC 3001, Australia
Tel: +61 3 9925 3781

e-mail: gjayatil@cs.rmit.edu.au

Lin Padgham
School of Computer Science and Information Technology,
RMIT University,
GPO Box 2476V, Melbourne, VIC 3001, Australia
Tel: +61 3 9925 3214

e-mail: linpa@cs.rmit.edu.au

Michael Winikoff
School of Computer Science and Information Technology,
RMIT University,
GPO Box 2476V, Melbourne, VIC 3001, Australia
Tel: +61 3 9925 9651

e-mail: winikoff@cs.rmit.edu.au

The WSDL2Agent Tool

László Zsolt Varga, Ákos Hajnal and Zsolt Werner

Abstract. The WSDL2Agent tool is used to help the integration of existing web services into agent based systems. The input to the WSDL2Agent tool is the WSDL file of a web service and the tool provides two types of output. The WSDL2Jade part of the tool generates code for a proxy agent that makes the web service available in multi-agent environment. The WSDL2Protégé part of the tool generates project file for the Protégé ontology engineering tool in which the ontology of the web service can be semantically enriched, visualized, or exported to various formats. In this paper we present the technical details of the code generators and the application scenario of the tool.

1. Introduction

The creation and popularity of web services are growing rapidly, and recently, web service interface is more and more often provided for internet services in addition to the traditional web interface. Interest in agent technology is also increasing both in the field of research (grid, semantic web, AI) and industry (ontology modelling, service integration). This motivated us to create the WSDL2Agent tool, which can be used in the integration of existing web services into agent based systems. This way we help to bridge the gap between existing non-agent systems and agent systems. With the help of this tool existing web services can be integrated into agent systems and agents will have access to a wide range of existing services. Moreover agent system developers may concentrate on adding intelligent functions to these services by combining and extending them. The idea of using agents to enable advanced operational modes of web services is advocated by several researchers [1][2] and also by the Web Services Architecture specification of the W3C [3].

The WSDL2Jade tool is applicable to create proxy agents for arbitrary web services. The proxy agent is able to accept client agent requests to invoke the web service, call the web service, and send the web service results back to the client agents (illustrated in Figure 3). The proxy agent thus wraps the web service invocation code into an agent shell and operates like a FIPA agent: it can be deployed on an agent platform, communicates with other agents using FIPA standard Agent Communication Language (ACL) [4], and has a public ontology that defines the messages it understands.

The WSDL2Protégé tool is applicable to create Protégé [5] project file from the WSDL file of an arbitrary web service. This project file can then be opened in the Protégé knowledge-base modelling environment, where the ontology of the original WSDL document can be prepared and edited (as shown in Figure 2). In addition, Protégé is able to export the ontology in various formats, such as RDF, OIL, DAML+OIL, or OWL. Using the Ontology Bean Generator plug-in [6] of Protégé an agent skeleton can be created from the Protégé project file.

The main contribution of this paper is the detailed description of a technology to integrate web services into agent systems, the implementation of the technology in the WSDL2Agent tool, applying the tool to the Google web service as well as demonstrating in a simple application how an agent can integrate existing web services and add new functionality to them by combining them. As we will see in the related work section, these contributions are novel.

In section 2 we shortly sum up the background information needed to use the WSDL2Agent tool. In section 3 we describe how to use the WSDL2Agent tool. Based on this information you can generate your own code on the web site of the tool. Section 4, 5 and 6 describe in detail how the WSDL2Agent tool generates code. You will need this information to understand, possibly modify and deploy the generated code. Section 4 describes how the WSDL2Agent tool reads and interprets WSDL files. Section 5 describes how the WSDL2Jade tool generates the code, while section 6 details how the WSDL2Protégé tool generates the project file. Section 7 shows a demo agent system integrating web services. Section 8 discusses related work and section 9 concludes the paper.

2. Background

In this section we are going to introduce web services, agents, the JADE agent platform and the Protégé knowledge engineering environment, because the WSDL2Agent tool builds on them.

2.1 Web Services and the WSDL

The purpose of web services [3] is to provide some document or procedure-oriented functionality over the network. The web service is an abstract notion of certain functionality, the concrete piece of software implementing the web service is called provider agent, while other systems that wish to make use of the web services are called requester agents. Requester agents can interact with the provider agent via message exchange using SOAP (Simple Object Access Protocol) messages typically conveyed over HTTP. The interface of the web service is described in machine-readable format by a WSDL (Web Services Description Language) document. It defines the service as a set of abstract network end-points called ports and a set of operations representing abstract actions available at these ports. For each operation the possible input and output messages are defined and decomposed into parts. The data types of parts are described using the XSD (XML Schema Definition) type system, which may be either built-in XML data types or custom, even nested structures: complex types or arrays. The abstract definitions of ports, operations, and messages are then bound to their concrete network deployment via extensibility elements: internet location, transport protocol, and transport serialization formats.

The definition of the web service interface in the WSDL is encapsulated by a single <definitions> element in which the <service> element contains the internet address of the web service in the location attribute of the <soap:address> element. The <portType> element consists of the list of the operations (<operation> elements) provided by the web service, for which input and output message types are associated via the <input> and <output> elements. Message types are described by individual <message> elements; each containing a list of named parts with either a built-in XML type or a complex type. Complex types must be defined in the <types> section of the WSDL that may form structures or arrays. Finally, the <binding> element of the WSDL is applicable to specify the encoding style and namespace for each operation input and output message.

2.2   Agents

The notion of agent emerged from many different fields including economics, game theory, philosophy, logic, ecology, social sciences, computer science, artificial intelligence and later distributed artificial intelligence. In all these fields an agent is an active component that behaves intelligently in a complex environment to achieve some kind of goal. Experts from the different fields tend to agree that the most important characteristics of agents are those which are defined by Wooldridge and Jennings [7]. First of all an agent is a computer system situated in some environment. The agent is reactive, which means that it is capable of sensing its environment and acting on it. The agent can autonomously act in its environment and make decisions itself. The agent has design objectives and can decide itself how to achieve them. While taking the decisions the agent is not just passive, but can take initiatives towards its goals. The agent has social abilities and can interact with the actors in its environment.

The need for interoperable agent communication created the Foundation for Intelligent Physical Agents (FIPA) [8] standardization body. The aim of FIPA is to develop software standards for heterogeneous and interoperating agents and agent systems, in order to enable the interworking of agents and agent systems operating on platforms of different vendors in industrial and commercial environments. As a result of the FIPA standardization activity, many research labs and industrial organizations started to develop competing agent platforms independently all over the world. FIPA standard agent platforms provide an environment where agents can be deployed and with the help of the agent platform services they can interact with other agents on any

FIPA standard agent platform in a FIPA conformant way achieving agent communication level interoperability.

Agents are starting to become highly relevant to bodies such as the World Wide Web Consortium (W3C) and the Global Grid Forum (GGF). The convergence between grid and agents is of interests, because agent systems require robust infrastructure and Grid systems require autonomous, flexible behaviours [9]. Developments such as web services and semantic web services [10][11] also investigate many of the issues which have already been addressed by agent technologies.

2.3 JADE

JADE (Java Agent DEvelopment Framework, http://jade.tilab.com/) is a software framework that complies with the FIPA specifications and provides a middleware to help in the implementation of multi-agent systems. The agent platform is fully implemented in Java. Software agents also written in Java can be deployed and run in JADE. The agent platform can be distributed across machines and the configuration can be controlled via a remote GUI. In addition to JADE's core functionality, a set of graphical tools are available which support the debugging and deployment phases. For agent developers JADE provides libraries through which agents can easily communicate with other agents due to the built-in message handling, composition and decoding functionalities.

We chose JADE as the target platform for the proxy agent in the WSDL2Agent tool because of the above features, and also because this agent platform is the most widely used, as shown by the statistics of the Agentcities worldwide testbed. Chosing JADE as the target platform does not put much restriction on the deployment of the generated agents. Although the generated proxy agent (described in section 5) is required to run in JADE, client agents wishing to communicate with the proxy agent can still run on any FIPA compliant platform.

2.4 Protégé

Protégé (http://protege.stanford.edu/) is an ontology engineering tool developed at Stanford Medical Informatics, and though it has historically been used in the area of biomedical applications, nowadays it is widely used as knowledge-base modelling environment in different application areas as well. Since Protégé's internal model is based on a meta model similar to the object-oriented and frame-based systems, it is basically applicable to design and represent ontologies consisting of classes (frames), properties (slots), property characteristics (facets and constraints), and instances. With Protégé, designers can build, edit, maintain, and visualize ontologies representing the formal model of the knowledge domain on a graphical user interface, which tasks would require large amount of manual work otherwise, especially in the case of real-world applications. In addition, due to the extensibility of the platform, Protégé can import existing ontologies from, and export a Protégé ontology to various formats (such as CLIPS, XML, UML, OIL, DAML+OIL, RDF, OWL) via plug-ins.

3.   Using WSDL2Agent

In this section we are going to describe the engineering process of the integration of web services into agent system and then how you can use the WSDL2Agent tool to generate the code for this process.

3.1   Engineering Process

The architecture of web service integration into agent systems is shown in Figure 1. Each Web Service is represented by a Proxy Agent. The Proxy Agent is able to receive web service invocation requests in FIPA Agent Communication Language (ACL), invoke the web service using the Simple Object Access Protocol (SOAP) and then return the result in FIPA ACL. These proxy agents basically have the same functionality as the web service, but they are able to communicate in FIPA ACL. In order to add autonomous and proactive features to web services, we imagine that an Agent with Agent Logic is also developed. The Agent with Agent Logic is the client agent of one or more Proxy Agents and provides intelligent services to the Client Agent which might be either a user interface agent or any other agent in the agent system.

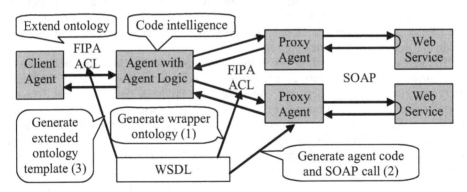

Fig. 1. Web services integrated into agent systems

The two most important software components in our agent system implementation are the ontology code and the agent code. The ontology code implements the way the agents encode, decode and interpret the content of ACL messages. The agent code implements the actions taken by the agent. In the case of the Proxy Agents there are direct mappings from web service definitions to ontology code and web service invocation to agent code, because the Proxy Agent converts the web service protocol to ACL messages and the only type of action it takes is the web service invocation. These mappings are described in section 5. The WSDL2Agent tool generates the code for the ontology between the Proxy Agent and the Agent with Agent Logic (indicated with No. 1 in Figure 1), as well as the code of the Proxy Agent (indicated with No. 2 in Figure 1).

While communicating with its clients, the Agent with Agent Logic will use an ontology similar to the wrapper ontology possibly extended with a few other concepts, actions and elements, because the Agent with Agent Logic also uses the web service results. The WSDL2Protégé tool generates a template for the ontology between the Agent with Agent Logic and its clients (indicated with No. 3 in Figure1). The Ontology Bean Generator can be used to generate the code template of the Agent with Agent Logic. The agent logic has to be added by the developer both to the extended ontology and the Agent with Agent Logic.

3.2   Generating Code with WSDL2Agent

The WSDL2Agent tool is available on-line at the internet location http://sas.ilab.sztaki.hu:8080/wsdl2agent. You can upload your WSDL file to the tool in two different ways: either by specifying the URL of the file, or directly uploading the file itself. Then select the output you need: either WSDL2Jade to generate the code for the Proxy Agent and its ontology, or WSDL2Protégé to generate the Protégé project files for the template of the extended ontology.

3.2.1   WSDL2Jade Output

The WSDL2Jade tool web application returns the generated files in a zipped archive. Section 5 will describe how these files are generated. Here we give you a summary of the files in order to give you an overview. You may want to come back here and read again this description after reading section 5.

The *webserviceontology* directory in the archive contains the Java files belonging to the ontology, which is further decomposed into *service/port/operation* directory hierarchy in order to separate AgentAction, Predicate and Concept classes corresponding to different operations (and to avoid file name conflict). In the case of complex types a separate *service/port/operation/soap* directory contains the Java classes needed by the SOAP-based communication. And finally, the *webserviceontology/service* directory contains the WebServiceOntology.java file that registers the ontology of the web service, and the common ErrorPredicate.java file.

The code of the proxy agent is placed in the *webserviceagent* directory, and two batch files are provided in the root directory to help in compiling (compile.bat) and running (run.bat) the proxy agent. The WSDL2Jade tool automatically replaces the (potential) Java keywords in the WSDL (by appending the "_value" suffix to such strings) resulting in syntactically correct Java sources. The compilation also creates a jar archive of the ontology which can be published to client agents wishing to contact the proxy agent.

The web page of the WSDL2Agent tool describes how to write a test client agent to invoke the services of the wrapper agent. You can directly copy and paste the code of a test client agent from the documentation section of the web site.

3.2.2 WSDL2Protégé Output

The WSDL2Protégé tool generates a Protégé project that consists of three files called: webservice.pprj, webservice.pont, webservice.pins. To load the project into Protégé, open the file webservice.pprj. The project contains ontology elements, classes (a.k.a. frames) describing the communication with the web service. In order to be able to use the Ontology Bean Generator plug-in, the generated web services ontology complies with the predefined ontology hierarchy of the Ontology Bean Generator. Figure 2 shows an ontology generated by WSDL2Protégé loaded into Protégé. After editing this ontology you can generate an agent code template using the Ontology Bean Generator plug-in.

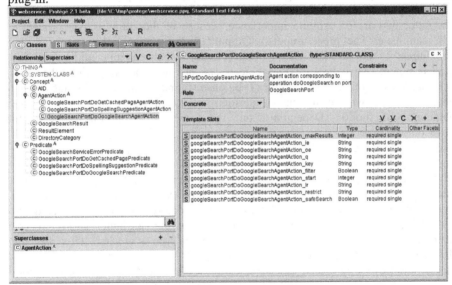

Fig. 2. The model in Protégé visual development environment

4. WSDL Parsing

In this section we describe how the WSDL2Agent tool builds an internal model of the web service description in the WSDL file. The WSDL2Jade and WSDL2Protégé tools use this internal model to generate code. In order to be able to process any WSDL file, the most critical is the parsing of complex and array types.

All parsing takes place in org.sztaki.wsdl2jade.WsdlParser, which is supported by some helper classes mostly for storing data. The processing starts with a call to one of parseWsdlFile(), parseWsdlURI() or parseWsdlInputStream(), depending on the physical source of the WSDL. All the three methods return an org.sztaki.wsdl2jade.Wsdl instance, after reading in the WSDL definition (javax.wsdl.Definition) from the source and calling processDefinition() in the same class.

The processDefinition() processes the <definitions> element of the WSDL, and builds the WSDL model in the memory, which is then returned as result. In the outermost loop, it iterates through the services javax.wsdl.Definition. Inside of the loop, there is another loop iterating over the ports. It reads the <soap:address location=""> extensibility element from the port body; the binding; sets transport and style of the port; gets the operations of the newly-read binding. As there can be more than one operations associated with a binding, it iterates over them. It sets the soap action for the operation, sets soap:body encodingStyle and namespace of the port and processes the input and output parts by calling processInputAndOutputParts().

The latter two are of extreme importance because of the complex type system a WSDL can have. The processInputAndOutputParts() processes all <part>'s of the passed <input> / <output> tags. Uses a boolean to decide between input and output. The method is not recursive because Part objects can not reference (contain) other Part objects, unlike with the case of ComplexType objects (and <complexType> tags). This is where we decide whether the part in question is a complex type or an array (or the combination of both). Depending on this, we give a further call to processComplexType().

The processComplexType() is passed a newly created ComplexType instance and a String denoting the "name" attribute of a <complexType> in the WSDL file. We search for this <complexType> in the entire XML document. Upon finding it, we decide whether it's an array declaration or a standard <complexType> with <elements> (see section 5.4 on array handling). In both cases, the enclosed type information is read and if any <element> (or, in the case of an array declaration, the <attribute> tag) references another <complexType>, another instance of ComplexType is created. After that, the method is recursively called back.

Please note that we do exactly the same as in processInputAndOutputParts() before starting recursion over with the slight difference that we have a Hashtable instead of a pair of Strings to be set because parts and complex types are inherently the same.

5.   The WSDL2Jade Tool

The WSDL2Jade tool is applicable to create a proxy agent, which is able to accept client agent requests, call a web service, and send the web service results back to the client agent. The proxy agent, wrapping the web service invocation code into an agent shell, works like an ordinary agent: it can be deployed in an agent platform and it communicates with other agents using FIPA ACL. The code generated by the WSDL2Jade tool uses the FIPA SL content language [12] supported by JADE. In multi-agent systems web services can be accessed easily by simply communicating with the proxy agent. Agent programmers can thereafter focus on the agent logic, which results in faster and more reliable development, since they do not have to implement occasionally complicated SOAP web service invocation code each time an agent wishes to use web services.

The WSDL2Jade tool is available on the internet, and developers only need to submit the WSDL file of the web service (or its URL) to get the complete Java sources composing the proxy agent. After compilation, the proxy agent can be deployed in the JADE agent platform. The ontology of the proxy agent can be published for potential client agents, who are then able to communicate with the proxy agent: compose requests and interpret reply messages, that is, to use web services. Figure 3 illustrates how the proxy agent interacts with client agents and the web service.

Fig. 3. The interaction of the proxy agent, the client agent, and the web service

The web service data types defined in the WSDL are mapped to ontology data types. The concrete mapping is discussed in the next sections. The web service invocation is mapped to an ACL message of FIPA REQUEST type corresponding to an agent action. The returned web service result is mapped to an ACL message of FIPA INFORM type corresponding to a predicate in the ontology. The proxy agent receives the FIPA REQUEST, interprets it according to the ontology, invokes the web service on the port defined in the WSDL, encodes the result of the web service invocation into a FIPA INFORM of the ontology and returns the result.

The codes presented in the next sections are generated by the WSDL2Jade tool for the web services of Google. The interface of the services is defined by the WSDL description located at http://api.google.com/GoogleSearch.wsdl. The Google Web API consists of three operations called doGoogleSearch, doGetCachedPage, and doSpellingSuggestion. The doGoogleSearch operation is applicable to search in Google's index of web pages by submitting a query string (and search parameters) for which Google sends the set of search results back. The doGetCachedPage operation returns the cached contents of a specified URL when Google's crawlers last visited the page; and finally, the doSpellingSuggestion operation can be used to obtain spell correction for the submitted expression. For more information about Google web services refer to [14].

5.1   The Agent Code

The source code of the proxy agent can be divided into two main sections: agent setup code and ontology code described in the following section. After parsing the submitted WSDL file and building an internal model, the WSDL2Jade tool is capable of generating all the sources automatically, by adapting a previously constructed internal code skeleton using the actual information in the WSDL. The source code complies with the guidelines of the JADE [13] Programmer's Guide.

The agent code is contained by the generated Java class called *WebServiceName*Agent (where *WebServiceName* is the name attribute of the service element in the WSDL), which is responsible to start the proxy agent in the agent platform. In the *setup* method, the proxy agent registers the language (the FIPA standard SL *codec*), registers the ontology, and specifies the *behaviour* of the agent (addBehaviour), defining its life-cycle (e.g. OneShotBehaviour, CyclicBehaviour) and functionality. The corresponding part of the source code of the proxy agent generated for the Google web services [14] is illustrated below:

```
class GoogleSearchServiceAgent extends Agent {
  ContentManager manager = getContentManager();
  void setup() {
    manager.registerLanguage(new SLCodec());

manager.registerOntology(WebServiceOntology.getInstance
());
    addBehaviour(new HandleRequestBehaviour(this));
  }
```

The behaviour of the agent is determined by the inner class called HandleRequestBehaviour, which extends JADE's CyclicBehaviour so that the agent accepts messages in infinite loop. In the *action* method of the HandleRequestBehaviour class the agent handles the incoming messages. In accordance with standards used in agent technology and considering the protocol of web service message exchange, a client request message has to be mapped to the FIPA REQUEST type message, and the proxy agent's answer message conforms with the FIPA INFORM type message, respectively. In JADE, REQUEST type messages contain a single Java object implementing JADE's AgentAction interface, and INFORM messages contain an object implementing the Predicate interface. Since a web service may contain several operations (these are the actual functions that can be invoked) the WSDL2Jade tool assigns a unique *OperationName*AgentAction - *OperationName*Predicate pair of classes to each operation (where *OperationName* string is the name attribute of the operation element in the WSDL).

When a client request message arrives (and the *action* method is invoked), the proxy agent can thus decide which web service operation has to be called by simply matching the incoming AgentAction class instance (which is the *ContentElement* object extracted from the message) against potential AgentAction classes assigned to different operations:

```
void action() {
  ACLMessage msg =

receive(MessageTemplate.MatchPerformative(ACLMessage.RE
QUEST));
  ContentElement ce =
manager.extractContent(msg).getAction();
    if (ce instanceof DoGoogleSearchAgentAction)...
    if (ce instanceof DoGetCachedPageAgentAction)...
    if (ce instanceof DoSpellingSuggestionAgentAction)...
```

The proxy agent can then create a call object (in the appropriate if branch), set the matching operation name (the name attribute of the related operation element in the WSDL), and from the AgentAction class it can read and add the required input parameters to the call object (*params.add*). This sequence corresponds to a standard web service call using SOAP. Note that since field types in the AgentAction class sent in the ACL message may be incompatible with the types required by Apache Axis SOAP implementation (used by the proxy agent), instead of the ordinary getter methods the generated _SOAP postfixed getter methods are applied here, which return data with type conforming to Axis (detailed in the next section). The operation can be invoked after setting the internet address of the web service (*setTargetEndpointAddress*), which can be found in the location attribute of the soap:address element:

```
org.apache.axis.client.Call call =
service.createCall();
call.setOperationName(new QName("urn:GoogleSearch",
"doGoogleSearch"));
params.add(ce.getKey_SOAP());
params.add(ce.getQ_SOAP());
...
call.setTargetEndpointAddress(
    new URL("http://api.google.com/search/beta2"));
...
resp = call.invoke(paramsObject);
```

If the web service call is successful (no exception is thrown), a new Predicate object is created representing the related operation output into which the web service result (*resp* object) is written. Finally, an INFORM message is constructed with the Predicate object (*fillContent*), and sent back to the client agent (*createReply*). The proxy agent, like in the case of reading the input parameters, uses the generated _SOAP postfixed setter method to write the received SOAP-type data into the ACL-compatible Predicate class.

```
DoGoogleSearchPredicate result = new
DoGoogleSearchPredicate();
result.setReturn_value_SOAP(resp);
ACLMessage answerMsg = msg.createReply();
answerMsg.setPerformative(ACLMessage.INFORM);
manager.fillContent(answerMsg, result);
send(answerMsg);
```

If the web service call fails for some reason, an error message, containing a dedicated ErrorPredicate class (with the description of the *AxisFault*) is returned.

5.2   XML Data Types in ACL Messages

The data types and data structures used by web service inputs and outputs are described by the WSDL file using XML Schema [15] language. We chose the Apache Axis implementation of SOAP to invoke and pass parameters to (or receive from) the web service in the proxy agent. Accordingly, Java sources (classes and field types) representing the XML types in the WSDL have to conform to the JAX-RPC specification [16] defining the XML-Java bindings. For example, in the case of a 'string' XML type, Axis assumes a java.lang.String object representation of the data used in the interaction with web service. Note that these bindings apply to the communication between the proxy agent and the web service.

On the agent side, however, data types used in the ACL messages have to be matched against the data types available in JADE, which supports five (symbolic) types called: STRING, INTEGER, FLOAT, BOOLEAN and DATE. As with the XML-Java bindings in Axis, JADE also prescribes how these symbolic data types have to be represented in the underlying Java code: STRING corresponds to String, INTEGER can be implemented by either Integer or Long, FLOAT can be either Float or Double, BOOLEAN corresponds to Boolean, and, finally, DATE must be implemented by java.util.Date class.

When creating the WSDL2Jade tool we had to decide how to represent XML types in JADE messages; and how to translate SOAP to ACL messages, and vice versa. In Table 1 we summarized the XML-JADE type mapping used by the WSDL2Jade tool.

Note that these associations may result in imprecise translation in some cases (e.g. integer, decimal) due to the limited number of data types available in JADE. (The encoding of such data types in strings would change the original semantic that we tried to avoid.) In practice, however, this mapping is still applicable to convert SOAP and ACL messages satisfactorily.

As an example, part of the XML definition of the input message of the *doGoogleSearch* operation is shown below:

```
<message name="doGoogleSearch">
  <part name="key" type="xsd:string"/>
  <part name="start" type="xsd:int"/>
  <part name="filter" type="xsd:boolean"/>
  ...
</message>
```

Table 1. XML-JADE type mapping

XML (WSDL)	JAVA REPRESEN-TATION(AXIS)	JADE ONTOLOGY	JAVA REPRE-SENTATION (JADE)
string	java.lang.String	STRING	java.lang.String
integer	java.math.BigInteger	INTEGER	java.lang.Long
int	java.lang.Integer	INTEGER	java.lang.Integer
long	java.lang.Long	INTEGER	java.lang.Long
short	java.lang.Short	INTEGER	java.lang.Integer
decimal	java.math.BigDecimal	INTEGER	java.lang.Long
float	java.lang.Float	FLOAT	java.lang.Float
double	java.lang.Double	FLOAT	java.lang.Double
boolean	java.lang.Boolean	BOOLEAN	java.lang.Boolean
byte	java.lang.Byte	INTEGER	java.lang.Integer
dateTime	java.util. GregorianCalendar	DATE	java.util.Date
base64Binary	byte[]	STRING	java.lang.String
hexBinary	byte[]	STRING	java.lang.String
unsignedInt	java.lang.Long	INTEGER	java.lang.Long
unsignedShort	java.lang.Integer	INTEGER	java.lang.Integer
unsignedByte	java.lang.Short	INTEGER	java.lang.Integer
time	java.util. GregorianCalendar	DATE	java.util.Date
date	java.util. GregorianCalendar	DATE	java.util.Date
anySimpleType	java.lang.String	STRING	java.lang.String

The WSDL2Jade tool generates the following AgentAction class wrapping the above input parameters:

```
class DoGoogleSearchAgentAction implements AgentAction{
    java.lang.String key = null;
    void setKey (String param) { key = param; }
    String getKey () { return key; }
    String getKey_SOAP () {
        String jadeSlot = this.key;
        String soapSlot = jadeSlot;
        return soapSlot;
    }
    java.lang.Integer start = null;
    ...
    java.lang.Boolean filter = null;
    ...
```

As it is seen, in the AgentAction class (used in the incoming ACL messages) fields are created with names corresponding to the name attribute of the part element and with type corresponding to the JADE Java type associated to the XML type in the WSDL. In addition to the simple getter and setter methods (used by JADE) for each field a _SOAP postfixed getter method is generated through which the proxy agent can access the data contained in the field in the Java type required by Axis (although in this example JADE and XML Java types coincide). In the case of an incoming message the proxy agent can thus easily pass web service input parameters to Axis using the _SOAP getter methods.

Similarly, in the Predicate classes (used in the answer ACL messages) _SOAP setter methods are generated by the WSDL2Jade tool, which expect SOAP Java type input parameters and set the related JADE type field. The proxy agent in this way can directly fill JADE type fields with SOAP Java type web service results.

Note that *base64binary* and *hexBinary* XML types, are represented by strings in the ACL messages, which contain the base64 encoded form of the original byte arrays (by convention). The encoding/decoding is performed automatically by the proxy agent. This is illustrated in the doGetChachedPagePredicate class:

```
class DoGetCachedPagePredicate implements Predicate {
  java.lang.String return_value;
  void setReturn_value (String param) { return_value =
param; }
  String getReturn_value () { return return_value; }
  void setReturn_value_SOAP (byte[] soapSlot){
    String jadeSlot = new String
            (starlight.util.Base64.encode(soapSlot));
    this.return_value = jadeSlot;
  }
}
```

5.3   Complex Type Concepts

In the case of simple web services, operation inputs and outputs can be wrapped completely in the fields of the related AgentAction or Predicate classes. In the <types> section of the WSDL file, however, web service providers may define custom structures composed of built-in XML types or further complex types (nested to arbitrary depth). Since such compound data structures cannot be represented by a single, primitive Java type, separate Java classes are created by the tool for each complex type. The Java type of the field corresponding to an input or an output parameter in the AgentAction/Predicate classes can be a basic Java type (as listed in Table 1), or a reference to a Java class representing the compound structure, depending on whether it is a built-in XML type or a complex type message part.

For example, in the WSDL file of Google web services we can find the following complex type definitions for ResultElement and DirectoryCategory:

```
<types>
  <xsd:complexType name="ResultElement">
    <xsd:element name="summary" type="xsd:string"/>
    <xsd:element name="URL" type="xsd:string"/>
    <xsd:element name="directoryCategory"
           type="typens:DirectoryCategory"/>
    . . .
  </xsd:complexType>
  <xsd:complexType name="DirectoryCategory">
    <xsd:element name="fullViewableName"
                      type="xsd:string"/>
    . . .
  </xsd:complexType>
  . . .
</types>
```

The WSDL2Jade tool generates the following two classes (getter and setter methods are omitted here):

```
class ResultElement implements Concept {
  java.lang.String summary = null;
  java.lang.String uRL = null;
  DirectoryCategory directoryCategory = null;
  . . .
}
class DirectoryCategory implements Concept {
  java.lang.String fullViewableName = null;
  . . .
}
```

Note that, Java classes belonging to complex types have to implement JADE's Concept interface (instead of AgentAction or Predicate interfaces), but fields are generated in the same way as was described at the AgentAction and Predicate classes.

Since web services can interpret structures containing SOAP Java types only, when a data structure needs to be forwarded to the web service (or structured web service results need to be sent back to the client agent), the proxy agent has to translate whole structures. For this reason the WSDL2Jade tool actually generates two classes for each complex type: one corresponding to the structure that can be used in ACL messages (shown above) and one corresponding to the structure that can be used in SOAP messages containing SOAP Java types only. To avoid confusion, these latter classes are named with a _SOAP postfix. Fields in these classes are named in the same way as in the corresponding JADE classes, but contain SOAP Java type fields (according to the associations in Table 1).

To make the conversion of whole objects easier for the proxy agent, in JADE classes two additional methods are generated: *getSOAPClone* and *set_SOAP*. Through them, a complete SOAP type clone object can be obtained from the set of JADE type fields, and all the JADE type fields can be filled from a SOAP type counterpart object. Both of these methods execute a sequence of elementary type conversions steps for class fields (as described before). Proxy agents can thus read and write structured data as easily as obtaining and setting primitive JADE and SOAP Java type fields.

The source code of the _SOAP classes belonging to *ResultElement* and *DirectoryCategory* complex types are shown below (getter and setter methods are omitted here)

```
class ResultElement_SOAP {
  java.lang.String summary = null;
  java.lang.String uRL = null;
  DirectoryCategory_SOAP directoryCategory = null;
  ...
}
class DirectoryCategory_SOAP {
  java.lang.String fullViewableName = null;
  ...
}
```

The *getSOAPClone, set_SOAP* methods of the ResultElement class is illustrated below (ommitting the previously listed fields here):

```
class ResultElement implements jade.content.Concept {
  ResultElement_SOAP getSOAPClone () {
    ResultElement_SOAP clone=new ResultElement_SOAP();
    clone.summary = this.getSummary_SOAP();
    clone.uRL = this.getURL_SOAP();
    clone.directoryCategory =
this.getDirectoryCategory_SOAP();
    ...
    return clone;
  }

  void set_SOAP(ResultElement_SOAP param) {
    setSummary_SOAP(param.summary);
    setURL_SOAP(param.uRL);
    setDirectoryCategory_SOAP(param.directoryCategory);
    ...
  }
  ...
}
```

5.4   XML Arrays and ACL Lists

Web service operations may require or return arrays of data as input or output parameters. Such structures of the web service are also declared in the <types> section of the WSDL file, where either arrays of built-in XML types or arrays of complex types can be declared. They can even be multi-dimensional.

In ACL SL messages, however, we cannot use arrays (there is no such structure), therefore we have to represent arrays used in SOAP messages by lists in JADE. In the corresponding Java classes the WSDL2Jade tool therefore assigns list type fields (implemented by jade.util.leap.ArrayList) to array type elements in the WSDL. The type of the objects wrapped by the list is the JADE Java type corresponding to the built-in

XML type (or the Java class created for the complex type) of which the array is composed. For example, in the case of int[] array in the WSDL, the corresponding list is allowed to contain java.lang.Integer objects.

In contrast to the ordinary getter and setter methods (operating simply on ArrayLists) the get_SOAP/set_SOAP methods expect and return arrays of the related SOAP Java type objects (corresponding to the built-in XML type). These are used in the communication with the web service. The latter methods, on the one hand, create arrays from lists, or lists from arrays, respectively; and, on the other hand, perform the elementary type conversions for each object (SOAP-JADE) contained in the array or list depending on the direction of the transformation. Note that in the case of an array of complex types the elementary type conversion uses the get_SOAPClone/set_SOAP methods of classes assigned to complex types. The proxy agent can thus access array type objects as simple as in the scalar case, produce web service required arrays from lists, and create lists from the web service result arrays.

For example, the following array of complex type declaration can be found in GoogleSearchResult complex type:

```
<xsd:complexType name="GoogleSearchResult">
 <xsd:element name="resultElements"
type="typens:ResultElementArray"/>
 . . .
 </xsd:complexType>

<xsd:complexType name="ResultElementArray">
 <xsd:complexContent>
  <xsd:restriction base="soapenc:Array">
   <xsd:attribute ref="arrayType"
arrayType="typens:ResultElement[]"/>
   <xsd:attribute ref="soapenc:arrayType"
        wsdl:arrayType="typens:ResultElement[]"/>
 . . .
 </xsd:complexType>

<xsd:complexType name="ResultElement">
 . . .
 </xsd:complexType>
```

The generated source code implementing WSDL arrays as lists is shown below:

```
class GoogleSearchResult implements Concept {
  ArrayList resultElements = null;
  void setResultElements (ArrayList param)
    { this.resultElements = param; }
  ArrayList getResultElements () { return
this.resultElements; }
  void setResultElements_SOAP (ResultElement_SOAP[]
param) {...}
  ResultElement_SOAP[] getResultElements_SOAP () {...}
```

The WSDL2Jade tool is also capable of processing multi-dimensional array declarations in the WSDL, although they occur rarely in practice. Multi-dimensional arrays are represented by lists of lists in the JADE, where each list contains lists corresponding to the representation of one lower dimensional array. For example, the two-dimensional array int[][] is represented by a list of objects each containing a list of java.lang.Integer objects. Since *ArrayLists* cannot be nested directly in JADE (it is not possible to register such structures in the ontology), each list has to contain dedicated objects which may then wrap further lists inside. The two-dimensional integer array is thus represented by a list of *Integer1DArray* objects, where an *Integer1DArray* object contains a single list type field containing java.lang.Integer objects. These intermediate array-wrapper classes (such as *Integer1DArray*) are also created by the tool automatically. As described in the case of one-dimensional arrays, the related _SOAP getter and setter methods are generated in the multi-dimensional case as well. They expect and return multi-dimensional arrays of SOAP Java types in this case.

5.5   Agent Ontology and Registration

The set of Java classes corresponding to web service inputs (AgentActions), outputs (Predicates), and complex types used in web service messages (Concepts) is called the ontology of the proxy agent (and also the ontology of the web service).

When the proxy agent starts up, it has to register its ontology first to be able to serialize/deserialize objects in agent messages by JADE. In the ontology registration code each class has to be added to JADE's knowledge base by submitting the class name and schema type (among of AgentActionSchema, PredicateSchema, ConceptSchema) information, and each field has to be specified in the registered classes by submitting the field name, symbolic field type (such as STRING, INTEGER, or the referenced schema name) and cardinality data (in the case of lists; optional otherwise). Note that cardinality attribute is also used to indicate optional elements in the WSDL (minOccurs="0").

A part of the ontology registration code (WebServiceOntology.java) generated by the WSDL2Jade for Google web services is shown below:

```
class WebServiceOntology extends Ontology {
  WebServiceOntology (Ontology base) {
    add(new AgentActionSchema
        ("GoogleSearchPortDoGoogleSearchAgentAction"),
        DoGoogleSearchAgentAction.class);
    as=(AgentActionSchema) getSchema
        ("GoogleSearchPortDoGoogleSearchAgentAction");
    as.add("key", (PrimitiveSchema)
getSchema(BasicOntology.STRING),
        ObjectSchema.OPTIONAL);
    ...
}
```

6.   WSDL2Protégé

The WSDL2Protégé tool can be used to create the model of the web service ontology for the submitted WSDL file in the form of a Protégé project file, which can then be opened in Protégé knowledge engineering environment. The model can be visualized and edited on demand, furthermore, JADE agent code can be generated using the Ontology Bean Generator plug-in. Protégé is also applicable to export the web service ontology to various formats, such as RDF, OIL, DAML+OIL, or OWL.

The WSDL2Protégé tool utilises the same WSDL parser as the WSDL2Jade tool, but generates a different output from the WSDL description. In this section we will focus on the Protégé file generation part, therefore the description will be shorter to reduce space.

6.1   The Model

The generated Protégé ontology follows the pattern of the ontology generated by the WSDL2Jade tool. For input and output messages the conversion assigns Protégé frames (corresponding to classes) with slots (corresponding to fields) representing message parts. Frames assigned to operation input messages are called AgentActions, and frames created for output messages are called Predicates in accordance with the conventions used in agent technology and the WSDL2Jade tool. Since frame and slot names must be globally unique in the knowledge domain, frame names are composed of the port name and operation name strings (in the WSDL) which is followed by either the AgentAction or Predicate strings. Slot names start with the container frame name and this is followed by the part name as specified in the WSDL file. Web service invocation faults are represented by the ErrorPredicate frame.

6.2   XML Data Types and Protégé slots

Protégé supports four basic types for slots: BOOLEAN, FLOAT, INTEGER, STRING (and a type called ANY, which can hold a value with any basic type). This implies that message parts and complex type elements in the WSDL have to be represented by such slot types.

In Table 2 we summarized the designed Protégé slot representations of the built-in XML types (using ANY where the XML type cannot be represented correctly in Protégé) used by the WSDL2Protégé tool.

6.3   Complex Type Frames

Complex types defined in the WSDL are represented by frames with slots corresponding to the contained elements. Since complex type names are unique in the WSDL, frame names get the name attribute of the complex type simply, but slot names must still be prefixed with the container frame name. To message parts and complex type elements referring to another complex type in the WSDL the WSDL2Protégé tool assigns slots with a special type called CLASS and restricts the slot's Allowed Parents facet to the frame corresponding to the referenced complex type. Other built-in XML type elements in complex type definitions are represented simply by slots with type associated according to Table 2.

Table 2. XML-Protégé type mapping

XML (WSDL)	Protégé slot type
string	STRING
integer	INTEGER
int	INTEGER
long	INTEGER
short	INTEGER
decimal	INTEGER
float	FLOAT
double	FLOAT
boolean	BOOLEAN
byte	INTEGER
dateTime	ANY
base64Binary	ANY
hexBinary	ANY
unsignedInt	INTEGER
unsignedShort	INTEGER
unsignedByte	INTEGER
time	ANY
date	ANY
anySimpleType	ANY

6.4   XML Array and Multiple Cardinality Slots

Array type fields in the WSDL are represented by slots with multiple cardinality (available in Protégé as a slot attribute), as with the list representation of arrays used by the WSDL2Jade tool. In the case of a one-dimensional array a single, multiple cardinality slot is created with type corresponding to the type of the array elements. For n-dimensional arrays, however, intermediate frames have to be created to represent 1, 2, ..., n-1 dimensional arrays where each frame contains a single, multiple cardinality, CLASS type slot referencing to the frame corresponding to the one-lower dimensional array (except for the one-dimensional case). For example, in the case of a two-dimensional integer array, an intermediate frame called Int1DArray is created with an INTEGER type, multiple cardinality slot, and the slot corresponding to the 2-dimensional array is implemented by a multiple cardinality, CLASS type slot with Allowed Parents: Int1DArray.

6.5   The Structure

Frames are organized in a predefined structure required by the Ontology Bean Generator plug-in to be able to generate JADE code. In this structure all the frames of the ontology are the child classes of a special frame called Concept. Frames representing complex types are directly inherited from Concept. Frames corresponding to operation input messages are the subclasses of the dedicated frame called AgentAction (which is a child class of Concept), frames representing operation output messages are the subclasses of the frame called Predicate (also extending Concept). Finally, a so-called AID class instance must be present for the successful agent code generation with the Ontology Bean Generator plug-in.

Figure 2 in section 3 shows the model generated by the WSDL2Protégé tool for Google web services in Protégé visual development environment. As it is seen in Figure 2, three AgentAction frames and three Predicate frames are created for the web service operations of the Google web services. Other frames representing complex types (GoogleSearchResult, ResultElement, DirectoryCategory) are inherited from the abstract Concept frame. Slots within the frames got a unique name and the associated Protégé type in accordance with Table 2. The cardinality of the slots is also set: single in the scalar case, but multiple in the case XML of arrays.

If we export the generated ontology from Protégé into OWL format, then we can publish the ontology. Part of the OWL representation of the *GoogleSearchPortDoGoogleSearchAgentAction* agent action together with the *key* property is the following:

```
<owl:Class
rdf:ID="GoogleSearchPortDoGoogleSearchAgentAction">
 <rdfs:subClassOf>
  <owl:Class rdf:about="#AgentAction"/>
 </rdfs:subClassOf>
</owl:Class>

<owl:FunctionalProperty rdf:ID=
    "googleSearchPortDoGoogleSearchAgentAction_key">
 <rdfs:range

rdf:resource="http://www.w3.org/2001/XMLSchema#string"/
>
 <rdf:type

rdf:resource="http://www.w3.org/2002/07/owl#DatatypePro
perty"/>
 <rdfs:domain

rdf:resource="#GoogleSearchPortDoGoogleSearchAgentActio
n"/>
</owl:FunctionalProperty>
```

The return value of the *GoogleSearchPortDoGoogleSearchAgentAction* agent action is the *GoogleSearchPortDoGoogleSearchPredicate*. Its OWL representation as generated by the WSDL2Agent tool and exported from Protégé is the following:

```
<owl:Class
rdf:ID="GoogleSearchPortDoGoogleSearchPredicate">
 <rdfs:subClassOf rdf:resource="#Predicate"/>
</owl:Class>
<owl:ObjectProperty rdf:ID="googleSearchPort
                DoGoogleSearchPredicate_return_value">
 <rdf:type rdf:resource=
 "http://www.w3.org/2002/07/owl#FunctionalProperty"/>
 <rdfs:domain rdf:resource=
     "#GoogleSearchPortDoGoogleSearchPredicate"/>
 <rdfs:range rdf:resource=
     "http://www.w3.org/2002/07/owl#Class"/>
 <protege:allowedParent
rdf:resource="#GoogleSearchResult"/>
</owl:ObjectProperty>
```

7. Web Service Integration Demo Application

WSID (Web Service Integration Demo) system [17] composed of agents and web-services illustrates the application concept of the WSDL2Agent tool. The Google web service used in the previous sections demonstrates how the proxy agent is generated, while the WSID system shows how an agent can integrate existing web services and add new functionality to them by combining them.

The WSID Agent uses two existing web services: the FinancialFunctions web service and the NumberSpeller web service, both of them publicly available [18]. The FinancialFunctions web service provides several different operations to calculate some finance related numeric information such as deposit future value, deposit present value, etc., according to the submitted input parameters (value, rate, payment, etc.). The NumberSpeller web service simply transforms the submitted integer number to a spell form in the specified language. The Intelligent Financial Agent (IFA) adds to existing financial web services the possibility to make textual reports in the user's language by combining it with the NumberSpeller web service.

The WSID system is shown in Figure 4. The IFA has a web front-end, but client agents can also directly access its services.

Both web services have their own wrapper agent in the agent system. The user can select from a web page the financial operation which he wants to do and the language for the textual report. This information is sent to the central node of the system: the Intelligent Financial Agent. The IFA first invokes the FinancialFunction Wrapper Agent and then, after having received the numeric result, sends it to the NumberSpeller Wrapper Agent. This way the IntelligentFinancial agent is able to provide a financial textual report in the user's language on the web page.

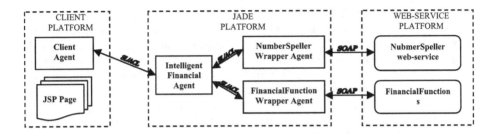

Fig. 4. The web service integration demonstration application architecture

8. Related work

Our work was partly stimulated by similar work within the Integrating Web Services Working Group of the Agentcities project [19] as well as an initiative for a similar interest group of the World Wide Web Consortium. This working group proposed a gateway approach [21][1] for the problem of agent and web services integration, and decomposed the problem into two parts: 1) software agents utilize web services, 2) software agents offer web services. The WSDL2Jade tool was implemented independent of the gateway approach in order to allow the deployment of mass amount of agents in the Agentcities testbed from existing web service applications. Moreover the WSDL2Jade tool is the first and most elaborated implementation to generate proxy agents for the utilisation of web services. It is expected that the JADE system will include similar component in the future.

The WSDL2Protégé part of the tool can be used to generate the basis for the Web Service Modelling Framework (WSMF) elements of semantic web services [11]. The WSDL2Protégé tool helps to translate a WSDL description to a Protégé project file and load in into Protégé where a semantic enrichment can be done easily. Once the semantic enrichment is complete, the goal repository, the ontology of the content language for the communication between proxy agents and mediators, as well as the skeleton of a proxy agent code can be derived [22].

The WSDL2DAMLS tool described in [20] can also be used to migrate web service descriptions to semantic web service descriptions, because it can directly generate a DAML-S description form a WSDL file. The WSDL2DAMLS tool also needs human intervention, because the WSDL file does not contain the needed semantic information. Although the WSDL2DAMLS tool produces a DAML-S file, it does not support the creation of the elements of the WSMF model.

9. Conclusions

The WSDL2Agent tool helps to integrate existing web services into agent systems. It was developed to help the deployment of mass amount of agent systems in the Agentcities worldwide testbed [19]. The WSDL2Jade part of the tool is the first and most elaborated implementation to generate proxy agents for the utilisation of web services. The WSDL2Protégé part is the only tool to translate a WSDL description to a Protégé project in order to support its semantic enrichment. In this paper we gave a detailed technical insight into the operation and usage of the tool.

The WSDL2Agent tool can link agent systems to other technologies as well. We have investigated in [22] how the tool can be used to migrate web services into the semantic web services world [10][11]. The WSDL2Agent tool is useful in grid environments as well. Users have reported to use the WSDL2Agent in grid systems by converting GWSDL files into WSDL descriptions and then applying the WSDL2Agent tool on the WSDL files. This way WSDL2Agent helps the integration of grid applications into agent systems. The WSDL2Agent tool therefore becomes more and more important by supporting the integration of existing systems (either web services or grid applications) into agent applications.

We are planning to investigate how to give better support for semantic web services and grid applications. Currently WSDL2Agent supports WSDL1.1. Support for the recently published WSDL 2.0 specification is also planned.

Acknowledgement

The authors wish to acknowledge the collaboration of the partners in the projects where the development of WSDL2Agent was started. These partners are AITIA Rt., Széchényi National Library, T-Systems Dataware Ltd., and the core partners of the Agentcities project. We also thank Eric Pantera for developing the WSID application.

László Zsolt Varga, Ákos Hajnal, Zsolt Werner
Computer and Automation Research Institute
Kende u. 13-17
1111 Budapest
Hungary
e-mail: {laszlo.varga|ahajnal|werner}@sztaki.hu

References

[1] Lyell, M., Rosen, L., Casagni-Simkins, M., Norris. D.: "On software agents and web services: Usage and design concepts and issues" In Proc. of the 1st International Workshop on Web Services and Agent Based Engineering, Sydney, Australia, July 2003.

[2] Maximilien, E.M., Singh, M.P.: "Agent-based architecture for autonomic web service selection" In Proc. of the 1st International Workshop on Web Services and Agent Based Engineering, Sydney, Australia, July 2003.

[3] Web Services Architecture, W3C Working Group Note 11 February 2004, http://www.w3.org/TR/2004/NOTE-ws-arch-20040211/

[4] Foundation for Intelligent Physical Agents: "FIPA ACL Message Structure Specification", http://www.fipa.org/specs/fipa00061/, (2002)

[5] Gennari, J., Musen, M., Fergerson, R., Grosso, W., Crubézy, M., Eriksson, H., Noy, N., Tu. S.: "The evolution of Protégé-2000: An environment for knowledge-based systems development" International Journal of Human-Computer Studies, 58(1):89-123, 2003.

[6] van Aart, C.J., Pels, R.F., Giovanni C. and Bergenti F.: "Creating and Using Ontologies in Agent Communication" Workshop on Ontologies in Agent Systems 1st International Joint Conference on Autonomous Agents and Multi-Agent Systems, 2002.

[7] Wooldridge, M., Jennings, N.R.: "Intelligent Agents: Theory and Practice" The Knowledge Engineering Review, 10(2), 115-152., 1995

[8] Dale, J., Mamdani, E.: "Open Standards for Interoperating Agent-Based Systems" In: Software Focus, 1(2), Wiley, 2001.

[9] Foster, I., Jennings, N. R., Kesselman, C.: "Brain meets brawn: Why Grid and agents need each other" Proceedings of the 3rd International Conference on Autonomous Agents and Multi-Agent Systems, New York, USA, 8-15., 2004.

[10] OWL-S Coalition "OWL-S 1.1 Release" http://www.daml.org/services/owl-s/1.1/ 2004

[11] Bussler, C., Maedche, A., Fensel, D.: "A Conceptual Architecture for Semantic Web Enabled Web Services" ACM Special Interest Group on Management of Data: Volume 31, Number 4, Dec 2002.

[12] Foundation for Intelligent Physical Agents: "FIPA SL Content Language Specification", http://www.fipa.org/specs/fipa00008/, (2002)

[13] Bellifemine, F., Poggi, A., Rimassa, G.: "JADE - A FIPA-compliant agent framework", In Proc. of the Fourth International Conference and Exhibition on the Practical Application of Intelligent Agents and Multi-Agents (PAAM'99), London, UK, (1999) pp. 97-108.

[14] Google Web API, http://www.google.com/apis/

[15] W3C Working Draft "XML Schema Part 1: Structures", "XML Schema Part 2: Datatypes", http://www.w3.org/TR/xmlschema-1/, http://www.w3.org/TR/xmlschema-2/

[16] WebServices – Axis, http://ws.apache.org/axis/

[17] Web Service Integration Demo, http://sas.ilab.sztaki.hu/wsid/

[18] Alphabeans web services (See the "Run the demos" section at the URL below.) http://www-106.ibm.com/developerworks/webservices/demos/alphabeans/

[19] Willmott, S.N., Dale, J., Burg, B., Charlton, P., O'brien, P.: "Agentcities: A Worldwide Open Agent Network", Agentlink News 8 (Nov. 2001) 13-15,

http://www.AgentLink.org/newsletter/8/AL-8.pdf

[20] Paolucci, M., Srinivasan, N., Sycara, K., Nishimura, T.: "Toward a Semantic Choreography of Web Services: From WSDL to DAML-S" Proc. of the First International Conference on Web Services (ICWS'03), Las Vegas, Nevada, USA, June 2003, pp 22-26.

[21] Agentcities Task Force. Integrating Web Services into Agentcities Recommendation. http://www.agentcities.org/rec/00006/actf-rec-00006a.pdf, 2003.

[22] Varga, L.Z., Hajnal, A., Werner, Z.: "An Agent Based Approach for Migrating Web Services to Semantic Web Services", Lecture Notes in Computer Science Vol. 3192, C. Bussler, D. Fensel (Eds.), Artificial Intelligence: Methodology, Systems, and Applications 11th International Conference, AIMSA 2004, Varna, Bulgaria, September 2-4, 2004, Proceedings, pp. 371-380., ISBN-3-540-22959-0

Information about Software

Software is available on the Internet as
prototype version

Internet address:
Description of software: The WSDL2Agent tool is available on-line on the Internet. The input to the WSDL2Agent tool is the WSDL file of a web service. The WSDL file can either be uploaded to the web site of the tool or specified with an URL. The tool provides two types of output in a downloadable zip file. The WSDL2Jade part of the tool generates the code of a proxy agent that makes the web service available in multi-agent environment. The WSDL2Protégé part of the tool generates project file for the Protégé ontology engineering tool in which the ontology of the web service can be visualized, edited or exported to various formats.

Online availability address: http://sas.ilab.sztaki.hu:8080/wsdl2agent/

Contact person for question about the software:
email: wsdl2agent@sas.ilab.sztaki.hu

WS2JADE: A Tool for Run-time Deployment and Control of Web Services as JADE Agent Services

Xuan Thang Nguyen, Ryszard Kowalczyk,
Mohan Baruwal Chhetri and Alasdair Grant

Abstract. Web services and software agent technologies are two areas that have attracted substantial research and industry interests in recent years. On the one hand, the Web services technology is gaining popularity because of its well-defined infrastructure aiming at enabling interoperability among heterogenous applications. On the other hand, the agent technology aims at providing intelligent autonomous capabilities for distributed components. A combination of these two technologies could create an environment where Web services and agents can employ and compliment each others' strengths. In this chapter, we propose a framework called WS2JADE for integrating Web services and the JADE agent platform. In particular, the technical aspects of run-time deployment and control of Web services as agent services with WS2JADE are presented. We relate our framework to other solutions in the area and show how new emerging Web services management technologies can be used with WS2JADE for enabling Web services management with agents. The management capabilities are demonstrated with simple examples of using WS2JADE for service discovery, composition and deployment with JADE agents.

1 Introduction

With the emergence of Web service standards, the universal interoperability between distributed applications is fast becoming a reality. Web services follow a loosely coupled integration model and use industry-standard protocols to facilitate the seamless integration of heterogeneous systems within and across organisations. While the Web service technology offers many distinctive advantages and benefits, it still has certain limitations potentially hindering its broader adoption in more complex applications. In particular it involves the limited support for the management of the discovery, composition and execution of Web services (e.g. [1, 18, 24, 25]).

The agent technology offers abilities of intelligent operations, interactions and cooperation between autonomous components that can be used in automating management tasks and business processes, and has also been recognized as a promising technology for managing Web services [9, 10, 17, 25]. However, because Web services and agents were originally developed separately with different standards and specifications their integration is not straightforward. Realising the benefits of integrating these two technologies, significant research has been carried out in this direction. The Agentcities Web Service Working Group's project [4] is an example of such an effort aiming at addressing the issue of Web services and agents integration. More recently, Agentcities has also created openNet [26] that provides a test-bed environment for integrating software agents, Web services and Semantic Web services. The integration of software agents and services in general has been proposed by Luck et al. [20] as one of the major tasks for the agent community. The main obstacles in integrating Web services and agents are the mismatches in description and communication used by these two technologies. One way to overcome these obstacles can be a proxy-based integration approach that allows the two technologies to evolve in parallel without imposing any restrictions on either, providing the gateway to bridge the Web services and agents.

Web services can work across organizations and be composed to create new Web services. There are business scenarios in which many Web services from different administration domains need to be tied together in cross-organisational business processes or complex composite applications. Consequently, Web services management becomes a complex task that requires a high level of intelligent capabilities and automation support. The emerging Web services management technologies, such as WS-Management [1] and Web Services Distributed Management (WSDM-MUWS [24], WSDM-MOWS [25]), define additional interfaces for Web services needed for their management. However they do not specify the management mechanisms, i.e. 'how', 'when' or 'why' these Web services can be managed. The agent technology is well poised to fulfil this role and support Web services with the required management mechanisms. If agents were able to interact with Web services, the agent technology could be integrated into the Web service management model effectively and used to manage Web services.

In this paper, we propose a framework for integrating Web services and FIPA compliant software agents, which offers many advantages over previous solutions. Specifically it enables run-time deployment and control of Web services as agent services. The management of Web service discovery, composition and execution can be performed both at the agent service and the Web service levels. Section 2 overviews the related work in the area of integrating Web services and agent technologies. Section 3 presents the proposed framework called WS2JADE and its technical aspects. Section 4 discusses the need for Web service management and current standards available for Web service management. It also discusses how and why agent technology, and in particular WS2JADE can support Web service management. Section 5 demonstrates the specific capabilities of WS2JADE with simple examples of Web service management including service discovery, composition and deployment with JADE agents. Finally, concluding remarks and an outline of the future work are presented in Section 6.

2   Related Work

The agents and Web services communication, and a synthesis of the agents and Web services have been addressed in a number of works. In [11], the authors discuss the "agentification" for Web services, in which the legacy systems could be re-engineered into agent-based Web services. In [10] an agent-based architecture is proposed for the selection and composition of Web services. The trend of using agents to monitor and control Web services composition has been increasing recently, evidenced by a number of other publications (e.g. [12, 27, 28]). In most of those works however, agents do not conform to any specific standard and details of using agents to invoke Web services are not formally described. The general assumption is that any agent can request any Web service by acting as the Web service's client. In practice, if this assumption held then the agents' code would need to contain the Web service invocation code. For FIPA-compliant agent systems, this also means that in addition to agent communication languages, the agents' programmer need to consider the low level details of Web services invocation. There have been attempts to provide a framework in which agents and Web services, with separation of concerns in their implementations, can communicate with each other. A symmetric integration of Web services and FIPA-compliant agent platforms has been proposed in [4] as a high-level architectural recommendation from the Agentcities [3]. It is the fact that Web services were developed without the concept of agents (i.e. FIPA agents) and can exist without agents. The symmetric architecture takes this into consideration and also that many Web service clients may have autonomous characteristics of agents without conforming to the FIPA specifications. A proxy-based approach allows the two platforms to be evolved in parallel without imposing any restrictions on each other.

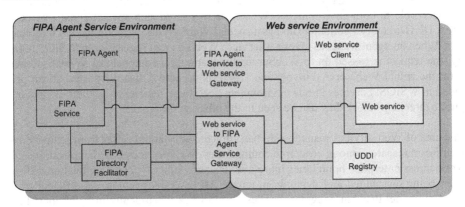

Fig. 1. FIPA Agents – Web services Integration Architecture [4]

A FIPA agent service environment can exist in parallel with a Web service environment as depicted in Figure 1 [4]. The *"FIPA Agent Service to Web service Gateway"* on the border between the two environments allows a FIPA agent to access Web services by translating ACL messages into Web service invocations. In the other direction, the

"Web Service to FIPA Agent Gateway" exposes and registers agent services in UDDI Registry Server so that any Web service client can use them. Following the Agentcities recommendations, two separate solutions have been proposed to solve two ends of the problems for the FIPA compliant JADE agent system. One solution exposures Web services to JADE agents [19] and JADE agent services to Web services [7, 8, 33]. Whitestein Technology has proposed WSAI (Web Service agent Integration) [33] and WSIGS (Web Service Integration Gateway Service) [7], and has already released the tool WSAI as an open source code in its first version. WSIGS is under development and its architecture has been published in [7] and [8]. WSDL2JADE has been released by Sztaki [19] as an online program that converts WSDL file to JADE classes. It takes a Web service address as an input and generates outputs of JADE agent code and agent ontology for the Web service. However, there is no run-time deployment capability.

WSAI [33] allows Web service clients to use JADE agents' services. In order to do this, WSDL files are generated for these agent services. Technically, at this stage WSDL files are created manually from the agents' behaviors. It also requires "interface agents" to communicate with a target agent. These "interface agents" are created and destroyed per Web service client invocation of the agent service. However it appears that the practicability of WSAI is limited. This is because of the default single-threaded mode of JADE agent, and the asynchronous and stateful nature of agent communication do not fit well in the current implementation stage of Web service communication model, which is stateless and mostly synchronous. There have been discussions of asynchrony versus synchrony in agents and Web services in [4]. WSIGS [7] is under development at the writing time of this paper. WSIGS proposes an architecture for the bi-directional integration without special agents, and provides a set of codecs that do the translation between the agents' ACL (Agent Communication Language) and Web services' calls. To be visible in both environments, WSIGS is registered as a special agent service in FIPA DF (Directory Facilitator) and as a special Web service endpoint in UDDI directories. When an agent wants to invoke a service (Web service) registered in WSIGS registry, the request is passed on to WebServiceInvocation, a component of WSIGS, to perform the actual Web service invocation. There is no active discovery mechanism provided in WSIGS. Services in one environment need to be registered by their owners in a public directory before they can be seen in the other environment.

The area of Web services management has attracted substantial effort from industry and significant research among academic communities. Web services-based applications can work across enterprise boundaries more now than any other types of applications. However, being distributed and dynamic in nature, Web services require an efficient management model that can integrate seamlessly and work dynamically in a distributed environment. There have been two main approaches in tackling this problem and they are complimentary to each other. In the first approach, management is done through Service Level Agreement (SLA) or service contracts. This approach assumes that control over Web services is not visible to external managers and service management is enforced through agreement terms (rewards, penalty, preference, etc) specified in the contracts. Current work on this approach can be found in [15] and [37]. In the second approach, external mangers can exert direct control over a Web service. For this to happen, the Web service that needs to be managed must expose some manageability interfaces. This approach is the latest emerging management model from industry, supported for example by two specifications, Web Services Distributed Management (WSDM) [22] originally from HP and WS-Management [1] from Microsoft. At this initial stage, WS-Management and WSDM appear to overlap in a number of aspects.

WS2JADE proposed in this paper aims at enabling seamless and dynamic Web services and agent technology integration, and is geared for agent-based management of Web services. To do this, it utilizes useful features from emerging Web service management models; especially Web services based management models like WSDM and WS-Management. It provides facilities to integrate with future implementation of WSDM and WS-Management, and offers the deployment of Web services as agent services at run-time. It is the first step towards the ultimate goal of automation of Web service management using agents. WS2JADE does not automatically provide intelligent algorithms for Web services management. However, it provides a gateway for the existing management algorithms to be employed in the multi-agents environment. With WS2JADE, an overlay management network of agents can be formed to manage the Web services network and communicate with the underlying management of Web services.

3   WS2JADE: Web Services-Agents Integration

This section describes the proposed approach for the integration of Web services and JADE agents with WS2JADE. From an architectural perspective, WS2JADE, in accordance with [4], forms a gateway between a Web service and FIPA agent service. As depicted in Figure 2 there are two distinct layers in WS2JADE: the interconnecting layer and the management layer. These two layers provide facilities to connect the Service Oriented Layer (Web services) and the JADE agent layer together.

The layer which contains entities that directly and dynamically interconnect Web services and agents is the Interconnecting Layer. The management layer, being static, creates and manages those dynamic interconnecting entities. In WS2JADE, the interconnecting entities consist of special agents, ontology and protocol specifications. We call these special agents WSAG (Web Service Agents). WSAG are the agents capable of communicating with and offering Web services as their own services. The combination of the static and dynamic layers is a distinct feature of WS2JADE as compared to earlier tools mentioned in the previous section. The WS2JADE management layer is capable of active service discovery, and automatically generating and deploying WSAG at runtime. It is an improvement over WSDL2JADE since it can automate the agent deployment process. Instead of being passive like WSIG, the WS2JADE is designed to actively discover Web services and generate equivalent Web services if required. Also, each WSAG is multi-threaded to take an advantage of supporting concurrent requests of Web services and has its own Web service invocation module.

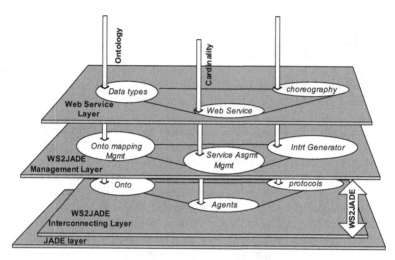

Fig. 2. WS2JADE layer mapping

Figure 2 shows that WS2JADE management can be looked at from a different perspective as a layer which is capable of projecting the Web services (or any service-oriented environment) layer into the JADE agent layer. The result of this projection is represented by the interconnecting entities. As depicted in that figure, three mappings are carried out by WS2JADE during the projection: ontology mapping, interaction mapping, and assignment mapping. These mappings are handled by three main components

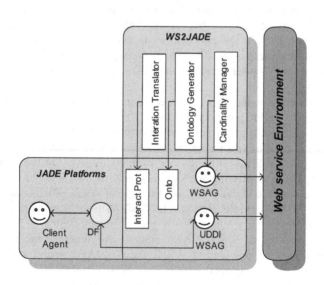

Fig. 3. WS2JADE components

that form the WS2JADE management layer: *ontology generation and management* component, *interaction translation* component, and the *service assignment management* component. These components interact with each other and provide the WS2JADE management part as shown in Figure 3.

Figure 3 presents the different components within WS2JADE system and how they are linked to JADE agent system. The vertical rectangular box depicts WS2JADE, the horizontal one depicts JADE. Note that the overlap between WS2JADE and JADE consists of components in the WS2JADE interconnecting layer: generated interaction protocols, ontologies, and WSAG. Figure 3 also illustrates a scenario for WS2JADE operation, in which a client agent searches for some service on DF. The DF can trigger WS2JADE to look up for available services in the Web service environment. If some Web services are found, their corresponding ontology and interaction models are generated. Also, a WSAG capable of accessing the Web service is generated. This WSAG registers the Web service as its service on DF, and communication between the client agent and this WSAG can start if the client agent wants the service. The following subsections discuss each WS2JADE component in more details.

3.1 Ontology Generation and Management

The ontology generator is responsible for ontology generation and ontology management. It translates data and its structure from Web service WSDL interfaces into meaningful information for agents. A detailed explanation of WSDL can be found in WSDL specification [9]. WSDL describes abstract concepts and concrete entities. The abstract concepts are port type, operation, message and data type. The concrete entities are data encoding style, transport protocol and network address. In WS2JADE, the abstract concepts are relevant for the ontology mapping management as agents need to know how to invoke the operations of a Web service. The concrete entities are handled by the interaction generator and management component. WS2JADE ontology generator and management component converts Web services' data types, and the operation inputs and outputs into the agent ontologies. The corresponding WSDL port type is tagged in the structure of the ontologies. Since JADE is implemented in Java, JADE ontologies are often represented as Java classes, which are convenient for JADE agent's manipulation and processing. Alternatively, it can be in other formats such as RDFS [34] and OWL [35] for interoperability with other FIPA compliant agent platforms provided that there are suitable codec plug-ins. Our WS2JADE toolkit supports JADE native ontology and OWL. To generate ontologies in Java, a WSDL data type is converted to a concept in agent ontologies. Two concepts are generated for each WSDL operation. One is for the operation input message and the other is for the output message. WSDL data types can be built-in XML types. The list of built-in simple XML data types are defined in the XML schema specification [29]. We map these built-in simple data types to Java primitives that are supported by JADE ontology representation. For XML data types that are not built-in, special customized Java classes are used, for examples, Beans, Enumeration Holders and Facet classes.

The following is an example of generated ontology for a XML type Enumeration defined as:

```
<s:simpleType name="Mode">
        <s:restriction base="s:string">
        <s:enumeration value="On" />
        <s:enumeration value="Off" />
        </s:restriction>
</s:simpleType>
```

The generated ontology concept in a Mode class extends from JADE Concept class:

```
public class Mode implements jade.content.Concept{
ModeFacet facet=null;
java.lang.String enumEle;
        public Mode(){}
        public java.lang.String getEnumEle(){return enumEle;}
        public void setEnumEle(java.lang.String enumIn){
          this.enumEle = enumIn;
        }
}
```

This Mode class has a facet defined as in ModeFacet class, which restricts the value of enumEle slot in Mode concept to one of values in the xml Enumeration.

```
public class ModeFacet implements jade.content.schema.Facet{
public void validate(jade.content.abs.AbsObject abs,
jade.content.onto.Ontology onto) throws
jade.content.onto.OntologyException {
try {
        jade.content.abs.AbsPrimitive p =
jade.content.abs.AbsPrimitive) abs;
        boolean valid = false;
        java.lang.String    obj=p.getString();
        if(obj.equals("On"))
        valid = true;
        if(obj.equals("Off"))
        valid = true;
        if (!valid) {
```

```
            throw new jade.content.onto.OntologyException("Facet
    restriction violated");

                }

            }

            catch (Exception e) {

            throw new
    jade.content.onto.OntologyException("Invalid Facet Object",
    e);

                }

            }

        }
```

Generating an ontology in the OWL format is simpler than in Java classes because OWL and WSDL both use XML. Similar to JADE ontology generation approach, data types and messages in WSDL are mapped to concepts in OWL. There is a one-to-one relationship between concepts in the ontologies generated in Java and OWL. OWL is still very new and subjected to changes; however we share the belief that it will continue to play an important role in Semantic Web with an increasing support from agent communities.

In addition to the ontology generation, the ontology management is important in WS2JADE. WS2JADE organises generated ontologies in an efficient way. For data types that can be shared among different Web services, the corresponding generated ontology concepts are shared and form a common ontology base. This means that every time a new Web service is presented as an agent service, part of the existing ontology base and domain knowledge can be reused for this new service. Also, this allows the ontologies to be structured in a manageable way.

3.2 Interaction Translation

The interaction translation component handles the conversion from Web service communication into agent communication. Specifically, it converts Web service transport messages into ACL envelopes, and Web service interaction patterns into agent protocols. These correspond to two sub-functionalities: language translation and interaction pattern conversion.

3.2.1 Language Translation

To translate Web service transport messages (commonly SOAP) into agent ACL messages, the SOAP envelope is first projected into the Java language and then into ACL. We do not translate SOAP directly into ACL for two reasons. Firstly, we want to reuse our generated ontologies and the existing Java implementations of SOAP. Secondly, we want to make use of the agent's capabilities to understand and process the messages according to its own logic (in addition to language translation) before forwarding them.

This is best done by translating SOAP and ACL into Java – the native language for JADE.

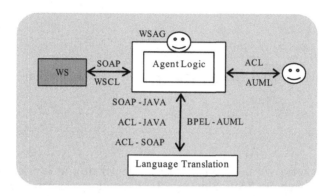

Fig. 4. Language Translation

Figure 4 shows that when a WSAG receives a SOAP message, it uses the Language Translation component to convert this message directly to ACL and send to the client agent. It can also perform some reasoning and modification on the message by converting the message to Java classes before any translation into ACL. In the Language Translation part of the interaction translation component, Axis' JAX-RPC (Java API for XML based Remote Procedure Call [30]) implementation and an extension of JADE ontology package are used to support SOAP to JAVA translation. Axis is one of the most popular open source implementations of SOAP today. On the one hand, JAX-RPC, led by Sun, is a specification of Web Service Invocation framework in Java. In JAX-RPC specification, at the client side, Java to XML translation in remote method call is done through a mapping from Java client stubs to the SOAP message representation. On the other hand, in JADE, information represented in JADE ontology-supported classes (Java objects) can be converted to different ACL content languages, including SL and LEAP. We can see from Figure 4, that language translation is leveraged by the reuse of many existing technologies instead of reinventing the wheel. SOAP-ACL translation is done by piping SOAP-JAVA and ACL-JAVA translation together. The main task of the language translation component is to map the Axis stubs to JADE ontologies. However, due to the restrictions of JADE ontology and JAX-RPC classes it is not easy to convert data between them. In particular, an automation of the conversion process for any data types is difficult. Hence, we use special classes which represent the ontology facets to preserve precisions in the conversion process. There has been a similar discussion in [19] for Sztaki's WSDL2JADE. Complex data mapping in WS2JADE (for example mapping of Axis Holder and Enumeration types to JADE ontology concepts and classes) is done recursively through simple data type.

3.2.2 Interaction Pattern Translation

In the interaction pattern translation component, WS2JADE focuses on choreography. By "choreography" we mean the required patterns of interactions among parties. It is in contrast to "orchestration" that describes how a composite Web service is constructed from other atomic services. For a composite Web Service, choreography is obtained by looking from an outsider's perspective. It tells the Web service clients different steps of how to use a composite service.

We have mapped simple interactions implicitly described in WSDL documents into standard FIPA interaction protocols [14]. Web service (WSDL version 1.2) provides four types of operations: one-way, request-response, solicit-response, and notification. In the one-way operation, a Web service client sends a request without receiving any response from the Web service. In the request-response, the client sends a request and receives a response synchronously. In the solicit-response, the Web service sends a solicit request to the client and receives a response. In the last type, notification, the Web service notifies the client without receiving any response. These four types of Web service operations lead to three common interaction patterns in practice: request-response, solicit-response, and subscribe-notification. The request-response and solicit-response interaction patterns correspond to those of Web service operation types. The subscribe-notification interaction describes the conversation style in which a client registers to the Web service in order to receive notifications when some event occurs. Table 1 summarizes the mapping of these interactions styles to agent protocols. More information on FIPA Request Interaction protocol and Subscribe Interaction protocol can be found in [14].

Table 1. Interaction pattern mapping

Web Service Interaction Patterns	Agent Protocols
Request-Response	FIPA Request Interaction Protocol
Solicit-Response	FIPA Request Interaction Protocol
Subscribe-Notification	FIPA Subscribe Interaction Protocol

3.3 Service Assignment Management and Service Discovery

The Service Assignment Management component is responsible for the cardinality mapping and service deployment management. The cardinality mapping manages M:N relationship between Web services and WSAG. Offering the same Web services on different WSAG allows better load balancing and reduces probability of service access failure when some WSAG are down. Offering more than one Web service on a proxy agent allows related Web services to be grouped together. The cardinality mapping of M:N permits a number of Web services can be offered and duplicated as services of different WSAG. This relationship is managed through a registry that keeps records as triples of the Web service, a WSAG that offers this Web service, and a new name for the Web Service in the agent platform. The service assignment management also provides a tool for deploying and destroying WSAG. It assigns Web services to a WSAG informing it which ontologies should be used for the newly assigned Web Service. If an assigned Web service is reported to be no longer available, the service deployment management removes the service from the list of the offered services of WSAG and from the DF.

The Service Discovery component is designed to discover Web services. It is essentially a piece of software that can use Web service discovery protocols and translate the received information into agent service descriptions for the DF. As mentioned earlier, we prefer an active discovery model rather than waiting for services to be registered. At the time of this writing, Web service discovery protocol is complex and subject to change with the latest revised version of WS-Discovery [17] specification which uses multicast protocols. Traditional Web service discovery mechanism of UDDI shares a common model with agent DF in the sense of accessing the directory. However, UDDI has evolved away from the concept of a "Universal Business Directory" that represented a master directory of publicly available services as DF still is. Most P2P based and multicast discovery protocols prove that requesting service providers to register the services is not always the case. Because UDDI implementations are widely available at this stage, in WS2JADE version 1.0 the Web services discovery is available as a UDDI proxy agent. This agents supports special discovery services which can be configured to proxy to any UDDI version 2 servers, including Microsoft and IBM UDDI inquiry servers.

3.4 Remarks

As mentioned earlier and discussed in [4], the main difficulties in integration of Web services and FIPA compliant agent platforms are the mismatches in communication and descriptions. These are summarized in Tables 2 and 3, respectively. For translation from a Web service to an agent service, WS2JADE handles these mismatches through its different components. Although the current version of WS2JADE is operational and offers many advantages over other tools, it can still be improved in a number of areas.

For example to increase the ontology reuse and avoid redundancy, the semantic mapping management component can be extended to detect semantic equivalence of two syntactically different generated concepts and keep one of them only. In [14], the authors focus on this topic and outline some approaches to achieve this. The current version of WS2JADE has not yet implemented that specific feature but future versions will include it.

Table 2. Communication Mismatch

FIPA agent communication	W3 Web Service communication
ACL/IIOP+HTTP	SOAP/HTTP
Asynchronous	Synchronous/Asynchornous
Stateful	Stateless

Another area is the interaction pattern translations. Web Service Choreography Description Language (WS-CDL) [36] has been under development for some time. WS-CDL is considered as a layer above WSDL in the Web service technology layer hierarchy. It describes a set of rules to explain how different partners may act in a conversation. W3C recommends it as a necessary complement to BPEL and programming languages like Java that only describe one endpoint, and not the whole system of interaction.

Table 3. Description Mismatch

FIPA Agent Service	W3 Web Service
Name – Name of the service	Names of services, port types, operations, etc.
Type – Type of the service	Type – Container of data type
Protocols – List of supported protocols	Message – Abstract, typed definition of data
Ontologies – List of supported ontologies	Operation – Abstract description of action
Languages – List of supported content languages	Port Type – Abstract set of operations
Ownership – The owner of the service	Binding – Protocol & data format specs for a port type
	Port – Single endpoint as combination of a binding and a port type.

In the WS2JADE approach, we plan to convert BPEL4WS and WS-CDL (however not at this stage of WS-CDL development) into agent Unified Modeling Language (AUML [5]) for the overall protocol representation in UML template. AUML is an extension of UML language for agents and has been used as a standard language to describe FIPA interaction protocols. The interaction translation will keep generated AUML documents in its protocol specification repository which can be looked up by client agents (or the client agents' designers) before using the service. In this version of WS2JADE we have not implemented the translation of WSCL to AUML. One reason for this is the instability and immaturity in Web Service Choreography as evidenced by the suppression of WSCI (Web Service Choreography Interface) and WSCL (Web Service Choreography Language) [2] by WS-CDL [36] which is still in the first draft version.

4   Management of Web Services

In this section we first discuss existing standards for the management of Web services and how these standards can be implemented. Then we discuss why agents are suited for Web service management and how agent systems, in particular JADE, can fit into emerging management models and take advantage of them by using WS2JADE.

4.1. Web Services Management Frameworks with Web Services

Web services represent vital resources for any business organization and are prevalently used to carry out business processes and transactions between businesses or within an enterprise. When they interact with other Web services, they form a logical network which can be distributed across enterprises. From the business organization's view point, the ability to manage such a logical network, and automate and integrate various internal functions is very critical in order to provide Web service security, usability and reliability. In order to achieve this, there is a need for standards and tools which allow the management of Web services. At present, there are very few standards which address the management of business processes or the underlying application services they rely on. The very nature of Web services makes this task (of managing Web services) all the more challenging. Some of the characteristics of Web services which contribute to this challenge include *distributed nature, extensibility, standardization and discovery* [22].

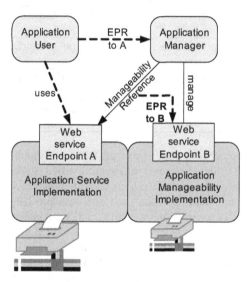

Fig. 5. Management of a Web service or a resource exposed as a Web service using a Web service [22]

Hewlett-Packard has proposed the Web Services Management Framework (WSMF) which is a logical architecture for the management of resources [22]. Extending this work further, with the support from other companies including IBM and DELL, HP has released the Web Services Distributed Management (WSDM) specification which defines how the management of any resource can be accessed via web service protocols – Management Using Web Services (MUWS) [24] and how Web services can be managed using Web services – Management of Web Services (MOWS) [25]. The specification was submitted to Organization for the Advancement of Structured Information

Standards (OASIS) and has been accepted as a standard. Microsoft, in collaboration with various IT companies has released its own SOAP-based protocol for managing systems (including Web services) called Web Services for Management (WS-Management) [1]. WS-Management shares the basic idea with WSDM in identifying a manageable resource and communicating with it.

As shown in Figure 5, each time a resource is exposed as a Web service or a Web service is made available, it also provides a reference to its manageability endpoint. The Application Manager can find this reference to the Application Manageability Implementation, and then performs management actions on the application by exchanging messages with Web service endpoint B (manageability endpoint). In more complex scenarios, the Application Manager can find out the relationships among different application processes from their manageability interfaces and use them as the inputs for a more dynamic management algorithm.

4.2 Enabling Web Service Management with WS2JADE

This part discusses the application of agent technology for Web service management and WS2JADE capability in integrating with emerging Web services based management models. This discussion is a significant departure from previous discussions on how Web services can be accessed and used by agents since management functionalities discussed so far are on the agent service level. In this part, we discuss how agent-based management can be carried out on the Web services level.

A management system, in general, requires some level of automation. In an ideal situation, it should be able to diagnose faults and take appropriate correction actions. A software agent is an autonomous software entity or computer system situated in some environment. Therefore a management system itself or its sub-components shares the fundamental characteristic of an agent. As a result, modelling management systems as agents or agent systems is a natural choice. There have been many management systems with agents. Examples are Sun's Java Management Extension (JMX) [31]-a new feature in version 5.0 of Java 2 platform and McAfee's ePolicy Orchestrator [21] software. In JMX, a given resource is instrumented by Java objects known as Managed Beans, or MBeans. These MBeans are registered and managed by management agents, known as JMX agents. The specification provides a set of services for JMX agents to manage MBeans. In ePolicy Orchestrator, Anti-Virus software on client PCs are monitored by a set of agents for possible virus outbreaks. In these examples, the management environments in which the managed objects (MBeans, Anti-Virus software) reside do not scale up globally. In particular, the environment is limited to Java programming languages for JMX and to a local computer for ePolicy Orchestrator. Consequently, the management agents in these local environments do not need to follow well-defined standards. However, Web services environment can span organizational boundaries, and hence, its management agents, if implemented, should exhibit social capabilities with a common global standard such as FIPA specifications so that coordination can take place at a level. web services management is a broad term which covers different areas such as

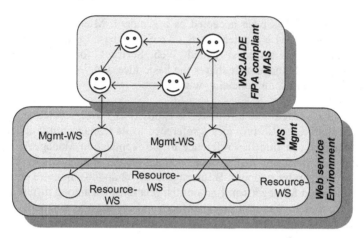

Fig. 6. WS2JADE for WS Management

access mechanism (authentication, authorization, etc), provisioning (SLA management, execution monitoring, etc), and composition (composition structure, conversation relationships, etc). As mentioned before, the MUWS 1.0 specifications define how to represent and access manageability interfaces of resources as Web services. The MOWS 1.0 specification defines how to consider Web services as resources and how to describe and access that manageability interfaces using MUWS. They together provide the Web services managers with one set of protocols and semantic instrumentation to manage Web services based applications and processes across enterprise and organizational boundaries. However, to what extent a manageability interface can be exposed to external managers and how the Web services managers coordinate and manage their Web services efficiently and intelligently are not in the scopes of these specifications. In other words, while these web service management standards define the interfaces needed for managing a web service, they do not specify 'how, 'when' or 'why' a web service should be managed. If we look at the attributes of software agents, we can see that they are often characterized by their 'intelligent and social capabilities' and exhibit autonomous, goal-driven behaviour. Hence multi-agent systems fit into the web service management picture provided they can use the manageability interface. The agents can coordinate, cooperate and negotiate on how much visibility of a management interface should be exposed, and make plans of how to manage Web services. Direct Web service manipulations are supported by management infrastructures which implement WSDM or WS-Management. Figure 6 presents this Web services management model with the support from WS2JADE. In the top layer of WS2JADE and FIPA compliant MAS, available AI techniques can be implemented and distributed among FIPA compliant agents, these agents communicate with WS2JADE agents to get access to the manageability interfaces of manageable Web services in the second layer of Web service Management. They then coordinate and manage the Web services in the bottom layer. Note that these are logical layers. In some implementation, services in the Web service management layer can be the same with services in the bottom layer.

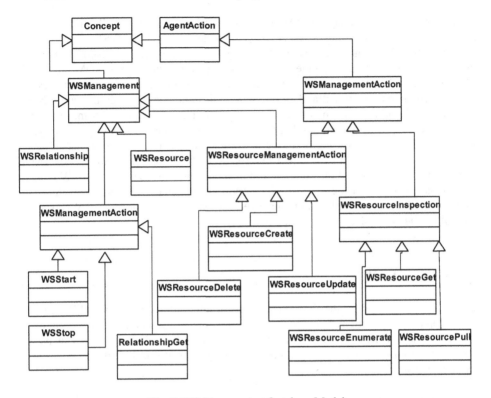

Fig. 7. WS Management Ontology Model

We believe a Web based management of Web services model, such as WSDM or WS-Management, has a great potential to be widely adopted by software vendors in the future. Hence, we have implemented an ontology base for Web services management in WS2JADE. The ontology structure was designed after a careful review of both WSDM and WS-Management specifications to combine common and important management elements in these specifications. Figure 7 partially presents this ontology structure. As illustrated from the figure, WSResource and WSRelationship are important concepts for Web service management. They extend from the WSManagement concept which serves as a root concept of all other content elements. WSResource defines a distinct type of management attributes exposed by a manageable Web service. WSRelationship class represents relationships between two Web services or two Web services resources. At the lowest level, three types of relationships are defined: *includesOf, dependsOn* (between two Web services), and *correlatesWith* (between two Web services resources). *"includesOf"* relationship between two Web services means that the first Web service is composite and it has the second Web service in its composition structure. *"dependsOn"* relationship keeps track of relationships hidden by virtualization process. A *"correlatesWith"* relationship indicates a correlation between property values of two Web services' resources. WSManagementAction is the root concept where all other management actions subclass from. These management actions include WSResourceCreate, WSResourceDelete, and WSResourceUpdate which correspond to resource management functions of creating, deleting, and setting a resource in WSDM and WS-Management. Also, for resource enumerations, WSResourceEnumerate establishes the resource enumeration context and WSResourcePull iterates over an enumeration result set. Depending on how much control over a service that a manageability interface has, the Web service management ontology can be further extended. FIPA compliant agents and WS2JADE agents use the ontology to communicate on Web service management related information. Whether a direct control of Web service is required, WS2JADE agents translate the control information into management actions available in WSDM or WS-Management. With the help of Web service management ontology and the management model outlined in Figure 6, management reasoning and access for Web service control can be decoupled and handled separately.

5   Demonstration

This section demonstrates the Web service - agent integration capabilities of WS2JADE with simple examples of Web service management including service discovery, composition and deployment with JADE agents. It describes how Web services can be accessed and used by JADE agents and how other agents can use this advantage to build value-added services in composition.

The Find-and-Bind example demonstrates Web services discovery and deployment by JADE agents. A client agent searches for Web services on the UDDI agent in WS2JADE and then accesses and uses these Web services through a newly generated agent. The new agent is created, deployed, and registered in the DF (Directory Facilitator) by WS2JADE at run time. It offers services equivalent to the Web services in terms of functionalities except that they can be used by other agents. Then we demonstrate an example for building a composite service from different Web services with the use of WS2JADE. In our scenario, three agents have a plan on how to compose different Web services to form a valued-added service. It uses WS2JADE to discover Web services and then bind these Web services to the abstract services in the plan. Sample Web services used in this demonstration are Amazon Web Service, PayFriend and GlobalTransports Web service. A client agent can search for and view different items from Amazon, pay for them through PayFried service and order with GlobalTransports Web service.

5.1. Deployment of Web Services as JADE Agent Services

WS2JADE provides a tool for deploying and controlling Web services as agent services. This tool is provided through the combination of the service assignment mapping and the interaction pattern management components. It allows JADE agents to deploy Web services on the fly. The libraries which enable this tool are found in the *cia-*

mas.wsjade.management package while the main class for the graphical user interface is *ciamas.wsjade.management.utils.Admin*. The deployment of Web services with WS2JADE is explained in the remainder of this section.

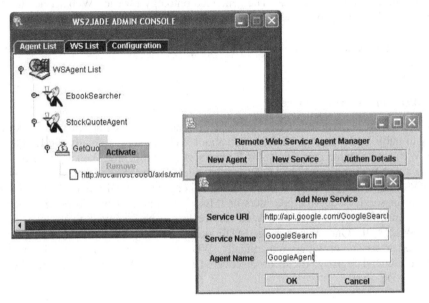

Fig. 8. WS2JADE Admin Console showing service deployment interfaces.

At first, the gateway agent container is started and the WSAG agents are deployed on it. Once the WSAG agents have been created, they are ready to deploy Web services as agent services. After the Web services have been deployed as agent services, they are ready for use by client agents. Each time a Web service is deployed as a JADE agent service, ontology packages are generated and compiled. These ontology packages can then be sent to a public Web server where they are available for download and use by the client agents. As mentioned before, at this stage ontologies are available as Java classes (JADE native ontology) and as OWL files.

Since the WSAG (essentially JADE) agents are multithreaded, they can offer/service multiple Web services at the same time. During the deployment of these Web services, each service is assigned a different agent-service name. The agent-service name can be the same as the Web service. If two WSAG agents deploy the same Web service, they must use different names. The screen shots in Figure 8 show two WS2JADE consoles: one is for local and the other is for remote management. Local management means that WS2JADE's WSAG agents are deployed to run on the local machine. Remote management allows an administrator to activate/deactivate the WSAG agents and control their services remotely. Remote management also requires correct authentications. Authentication details are stored in *.authen* file under WS2JADE root folder. As can be seen from the screenshot, in the left console for the local management, the agentList tab shows the deployed WSAG agents named *EbookSearcher, StockQouteagent* along with the services they provide namely *Ebook* (hidden) and *GetQoute* services. The WSList tab (its content is invisible in the screenshot) shows the list of deployed Web services along with their WSDL address. The generated ontology for each Web service in OWL format can be viewed by clicking on the agent providing the service. In the right console for the remote management, the Google Web service at http://api.google.com/GoogleSearch.wsdl is deployed as a service of a WSAG agent named GoogleAgent.

5.2 Discovery of Web Services

The Universal Description, Discovery and Integration (UDDI) specifications define a way to publish and discover information about Web services. Actually the UDDI itself is a Web service which provides SOAP interfaces for publishing Web services and querying about Web services. The UDDI inquiry interface in WSDL format is published by UDDI.org and can be found at http://www.uddi.org. The UDDI registry can be used to search for services, service providers or tModels by name or by browsing categorizations. Since the UDDI itself is a Web service, it can be deployed as an agent service with WS2JADE. Once this is done, JADE agents can then query this agent service for services or service providers dynamically. Whenever a new Web service is registered with the UDDI registry, it can be discovered by the WSAG agent upon inquiry by a client JADE agent.

The interaction flow is illustrated in the Figure 9. From the client agent side, it needs to do a search on UDDI agent (step 1) for a wanted Web service (e.g. Google). After getting search results back (step 2) from UDDI agent, the client agent, based on its own reference, determines a service it wants to use and queries the WSManager agent on how to use this Web service. The WSManager agent informs the client the address of the agent which can offer a proxy service of this Web service (step 4). The client now can start to use the service (step 5 and 6). To examine what happen inside WS2JADE, as mentioned before, WS2JADE proxies the MS UDDI (step 1A) through UDDI agent as default to fulfil the client request at step 1. After step 3, the WS Manager creates a new agent and deploys a new agent service that is a proxy of the wanted Web service. The WS Manager also registers this agent on the DF. The address of this agent is returned back to the client agent. WS invocation is again done indirectly through the proxy service of the newly generated agent. The UDDI agent can also be configured to use UDDI servers different than Microsoft's one.

The screenshots in Figure 10 show the interface for a client Agent which can do the search for a service with key words for the service name, business name, or tModel. This WSAG agent has deployed the Microsoft test UDDI which is available at http://test.uddi.microsoft.com and hence, clients can query this UDDI agent for details about different services and service providers. As can be seen, a search for services starting with Google returned 4 results.

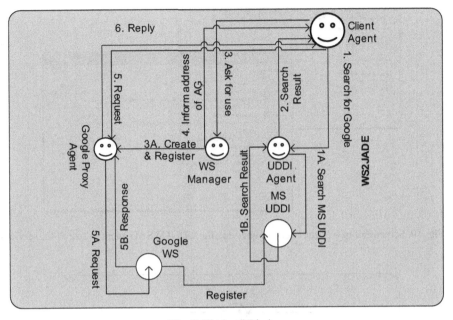

Fig. 9. Find and Bind

The client agent now can use the remote service deployment capability of WS2JADE to request for a wanted Web service to be deployed as an agent service. This can be done by making a request to the Manager agent as shown in figure 8 as explained previously. The Manager agent, after successfully deploying the Web service, informs the client agent the address of the targeted agent and the location of the ontology used to access the service.

5.3 Composition of Web Services

A user can enter keywords that are used in search requests on Amazon and can add items returned in the search results to a remote shopping cart. When they have finished adding items to the shopping cart they can pay for the items and organize delivery. This demonstration is a next step of the previous one. We have a scenario in which three agents: P , A, and G, have a composition plan for offering online item purchase. Such a plan needs to take into account online payment transaction and product delivery. In the plan, P is responsible for client payment. A is responsible for shopping cart. G is responsible for item delivery. The interaction sequence is depicted in Figure 11. First, the client agent searches for the products and add them to its shopping cart (step 1 and 2, repeated). Once the client agent does a checkout, agent A informs it payment details with agent P. The client agent then contacts P to do payment. After the payment is made, agent P informs agent A whether the payment is successful (step 6.1). If it is, agent A sends a message to agent G and asks for item delivery.

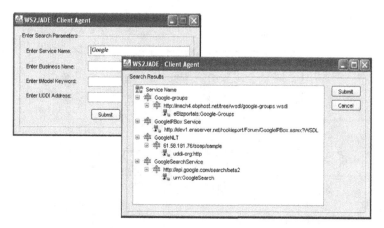

Fig. 10. Screenshot of a client interface querying the UDDI WSAG agent to search for services

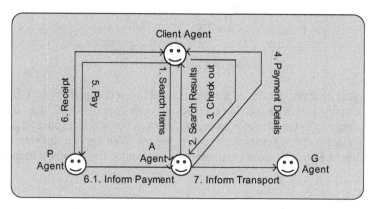

Fig. 11. Composition Plan

At the abstract level, no concrete implementation of services is described in the plan. Because the main purpose of this demonstration is to show how Web services can be invoked and composed by agents, we focus on the interaction sequences only and assume that the plan is encoded in some format that the agents can understand. The services these agents are going to use are Web services. The agents P, A, and G, based on the requirements of their own services, try to find and bind Web services. How this can be done with WS2JADE is explained in the first demonstration. Hence, we skip these steps and assume that after find-and-bind steps, agent P becomes a proxy of PayFriend Web service, agent A becomes a proxy of Amazon Web service, and agent G becomes a proxy of GlobalTransport Web service as depicted in Figure 12. The composite service now can now be executed. Since this is merely a demonstration, transactions are preferably not committed. PayFriend Web service and GlobalTransport Web service are developed by us to emulate essential functionalities in the interfaces of PayPal and

Global Transport Web services, however, without real transactions to any banks. Pay-Friend and GlobalTransport Web services and Amazon Web service can be found at:

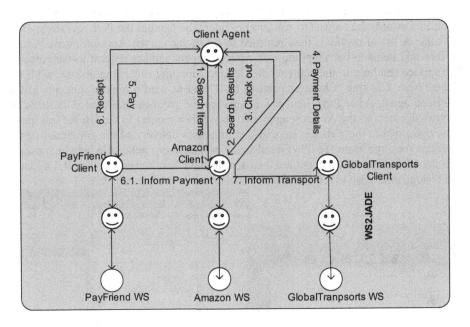

Fig. 12. Composition Service

PayFriend Address:
http://mercury.it.swin.edu.au:8080/axis/services/PayFriend?wsdl
GlobalTransport Address:
http://mercury.it.swin.edu.au:8080/axis/services/GlobalTransports?wsdl
Amazon Web Service Address:
http://soap.amazon.com/schemas2/AmazonWebServices.wsdl

Additional information of PayPal and GlobalTransport Web services are provided in the links below. To use the PayPal service, users need to subscribe to PayPal developer network for a developer key.

PayPal Web service:
https://www.paypal.com/cgi-bin/webscr?cmd=p/pdn/devcentral_landing-outside
Global Transport Web service:
http://transportal.russia.webmatrixhosting.net/default.aspx?static=webservices

The screenshots in Figure 13 show the enactment of a composite Web service. The se-quences can be explained as following. A user can enter keywords that are used in search requests on Amazon and can add items returned in search results to a remote shopping cart. When they have finished adding items to the shopping cart they can pay for the items and organize delivery. The screenshots in Figure 13 and 14 show the result of a composite service invocation by the Client agent. The user clicks 'Search' triggering the Client to send a request to the Amazonagent to search Amazon. The Amazonagent then forwards the request to AmazonProvider who handles the Web service invocation calls. A list of results is then returned to the client via the Amazon agent. A user can then add items to the shopping cart, which triggers another request to the Amazon Web service resulting in the contents of a remote shopping cart being updated with the selected item. Clicking 'Checkout' causes the Client to send a request message to the PayFriend agent. After PayFriend has completed the payment transaction it sends an acknowledgement to the Amazon agent that forwards a request to the GlobalTransports agent who invokes the web service call that organises delivery of the purchased items. A receipt message from the PayFriend agent and delivery acknowledgment message from the GlobalTransports agent are then sent to the Client agent and the GUI updated with dialogs indicating to the user that the transaction is complete.

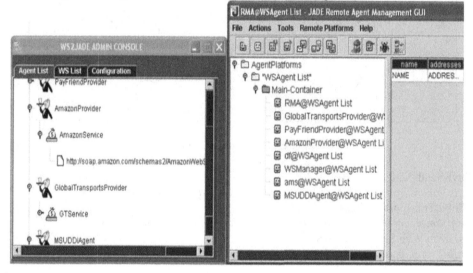

Fig. 13. Screenshot showing a composite service offered by different WSAG agents

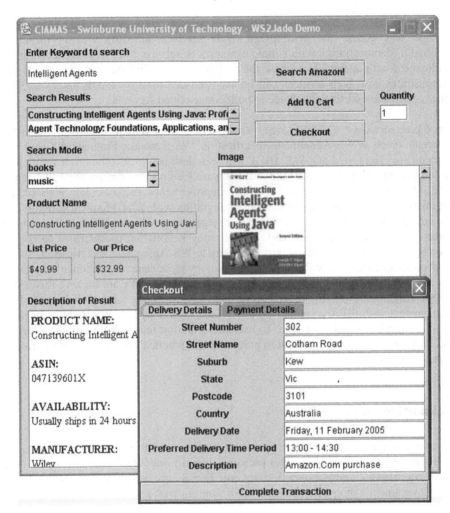

Fig. 14. Screenshot showing the result of a composite service invocation by the Client agent

6. Conclusion

The paper presents a framework and toolkit called WS2JADE for integrating Web services and JADE agents. In contrast to other solutions like WSDL2JADE or WSIGS, WS2JADE provides facilities to deploy and control Web services as agent services at run time for deployment flexibility and active service discovery. WS2JADE also provides a management ontology base for integrating with any future implementations of emerging distributed WS management standards which employ Web services such as

OASIS's WSDM. The future of intelligent agents with autonomous capabilities, which manage and access the widespread Web services infrastructure, is promising. WS2JADE demonstration with simple examples of service discovery, composition and deployment with agents shows how the toolkit achieves first steps in that direction. It demonstrates how Web services can be accessed and used by JADE agents and how other agents can take this advantage to build value-added services.

Since Web services is a volatile area with rapid changes and many specifications in WS-* domain (such as WS-Agreement Specification, WS-Resource Framework) need to be implemented and tested out, WS2JADE has been designed to accommodate future plug-in components. However, there are still software features and design areas that require new solutions, implementations or further improvements. In particular, Web services negotiation, semantic processing, and full integration with WSDM specification will be our next focus for WS2JADE. Web services negotiation will give WS2JADE agents the ability to read, understand contracts, and employ negotiation mechanisms to contract Web services and their compositions according to WS-Agreement specification. Semantic processing capability will improve the ontology management component in structuring ontology trees and possibly merging related ontologies. We are looking forward for a wide adoption of WSDM or WS-Agreement specifications for a global level of WS management with FIPA compliant agent systems. We hope that WS2JADE can be applied in more real-world examples to make contribution into agent-based Web services and business process management in particular and practical applications of multi-agent systems in general.

Acknowledgments

This work is part of the Adaptive Service Agreement and Process Management in Services Grid project CG060081. This project is proudly supported by the *Innovation Access Programme - International Science and Technology* established under the Australian Government's innovation statement, *Backing Australia's Ability*.

References

1   A., Arora, et al, Web Services for Management (WS-Management) available at http://www.intel.com/technology/manage/downloads/ws_management.pdf accessed on 6th April 2005.

2   A., Banerji, et al, Web Services Conversation Language (WSCL) 1.0, available at http://www.w3.org/TR/2002/NOTE-wscl10-20020314/ accessed on 25th April 2005

3   agentLink, European Co-ordination Action for agent-based computing, available at http://www.agentlink.org/ accessed on 25th April 2005

4   Agentcities Web Services Working Group, "Integrating Web services into agentCities", Technical Recommendation available at http://www.agentcities.org/rec/00006/ accessed on 25th April 2005

5   B. Bauer, J.P Muller, and J. Odell, agent UML: formalism for specifying multiagent soft-
     ware systems, in agent-Oriented Software Engineering, Ciancarini, P. and Wooldridge, M.,
     Editors. LNCS, Vol 1957, 2001, Springer, pp. 207-221.

6   WS2JADE, Web services to agents http://www.it.swin.edu.au/centres/ciamas, accessed on
     24th April 2005.

7   D. Greenwood, M. Calisti, "An Automatic, Bi-Directional Service Integration Gateway", In
     The 1st International workshop on Web Services Agent-Based Engineering (WSABE'
     2004) held in conjunction with The 3rd International Joint Conference on Autonomous
     Agents and Multi-Agent Systems, New York, USA, 2004. Available at
     www.agentus.com/WSABE2004/program/, accessed on 25th April 2005.

8   D. Greenwood, M. Calisti, "Engineering web service - agent integration", IEEE Systems,
     Cybernetics and Man Conference, the Hague, Netherlands, Oct, 2004, pp.1918-1925

9   E. Christensen et al., Web Service Description Language (WSDL 1.1), available at
     http://www.w3.org/TR/wsdl , accessed on 5th April 2005.

10   E.M. Maximilien and M.P. Singh, "Agent-based architecture for autonomic web service
     selection". In The 1st International Workshop on Web Services and Agent-based Engineer-
     ing (WSABE'2003) held in conjunction with The 2nd International Joint Conference on
     Autonomous Agents and Multi-Agent Systems, Melbourne, Australia, 2003. Available at
     www.agentus.com/WSABE2003/program/maximilien.pdf, accessed on 25th April 2005.

11   F., Cheng, H., Guo, B., Xu, "Agentification for Web Services", Proc. 28th Annual Interna-
     tional Computer Software and Applications Conference (COMPSAC'04) ,Hong Kong, Sept
     2004, pp.514-519

12   F., Ishikawa, N., Yoshioka, Y., Tahara, S., Honiden, "Mobile agent System for Web Ser-
     vices Integration in Pervasive Networks", International Workshop on Ubiquitous Comput-
     ing (IWUC 2004), April, 2004, Porto, Portugal, pp.38-47

13   F., Ishikawa, N., Yoshioka, Y., Tahara, S., Honiden, "Toward Synthesis of Web Services
     and Mobile agents", In Proc. of the 2st International Workshop on Web Services and agent
     Based   Engineering   (WSABE'04),   New   York,   2004.   Available   at
     http://www.agentus.com/WSABE2004/program/.

14   Foundation for Intelligent and Physical agents. Interaction Protocol Specification,
     http://www.fipa.org/repository/ips.php3

15   H. Ludwig, "Web Services QoS: External SLAs and Internal Policies: Or, How Do We
     Deliver What We Promise?", Proc. 4th IEEE Int'l Conf. Web Information Systems Eng.
     Workshops, IEEE CS Press, 2003, pp. 115–120.

16   I., Foster, N.R., Jennings, C., Kesselman, "Brain Meets Brawn: Why Grid and agents Need
     Each Other", The Third International Joint Conference on Autonomous agents and Multi
     agent Systems, AAMAS'04, July, 2004, New York, USA, pp.8-15.

17   J.,Beatty, et al., Web Services Dynamic Discovery (WS-Discovery) available at
     http://msdn.microsoft.com/ws/2004/10/ws-discovery/, accessed on 24th April 2005.

18   J., Cao, et al., Composing Web Services Based on agents and Workflow, M. Li et al.,
     (Eds.), GCC2003, Springer-Velag Berlin Heidelberg, 2004, pp 948-955.

19   L. Zs. Varga,Á. Hajnal, "Engineering Web Service Invocations from agent Systems". Pro-
     ceedings of the 3rd International Central and Eastern European Conference on Multi-agent
     Systems, CEEMAS 2003, Prague, Czech Republic, June, 2003, pp. 626-635.

20   M., Luck, P., McBurney, C., Preist, "Agent Technology: Enabling in Next Generation
     Computing", Sections 4.5.2, agentLink, 2003, pp. 23-26.

21   McAfee, McAfee® ePolicy Orchestrator®, available at
     http://www.mcafeesecurity.com/au/products/mcafee/mgmt_solutions/epo.htm, accessed on
     24th April 2005.

22   N., Catania et al. An Introduction to WSDM-MOWS and WSDM-MUWS available at http://devresource.hp.com/drc/specifications/wsdm/index.jsp, accessed on 24th April 2005.

23   N. Cavantzas et al. Web Services Choreography Description Language Version 1.0, http://www.w3.org/TR/2004/WD-ws-cdl-10-20041012/, accessed on 24th April 2005.

24   OASIS TC, Web Services Distributed Management: Management Using Web Service (MUWS 1.0) Part 1 & 2, OASIS standard at http://www.oasis-open.org/committees/tc_home.php?wg_abbrev=wsdm, accessed on 24th April 2005.

25   OASIS TC, Web Service Distributed Management: Management of Web Services (WSDM-MOWS) 1.0, OASIS standard at http://www.oasis-open.org/committees/tc_home.php?wg_abbrev=wsdm, accessed on 24th April 2005.

26   OpenNet Test-bed Initiatives: http://x-opennet.org/

27   P. Buhler, J.N. Vidal, and H. Verhagen, "Adaptive workflow= web services + agents", In Proc. of the International Conference on Web Services, Las Vegas, U.S.A, July 2003, pp. 131-137.

28   P. Buhler, J.N. Vidal, and H. Verhagen, "Enacting BPEL4WS Specified Workflows with Multi-agent Systems" , In Proc. of the 2st International Workshop on Web Services and agent Based Engineering, New York, 2004. Available at www.agentus.com/WSABE2004/program/, accessed on 24th April 2005.

29   P. V. Biron, K. Permanente, and A. Malhotra, XML Schema Part 2: Data types Second Edition, http://www.w3.org/TR/xmlschema-2/, accessed on 24th April 2005.

30   Sun Microsystems, Inc. Java API for XML-Based RPC (JAX-RPC), available at http://java.sun.com/xml/jaxrpc/index.jsp

31   Sun Microsystems, Inc. Java Management Extension (JMX), available at http://java.sun.com/products/JavaManagement/, accessed on 24th April 2005.

32   Telecom Italia Lab. JADE (Java Agent Development Framework), available at http://sharon.cselt.it/projects/jade/, accessed on 24th April 2005.

33   Whitestein Information Technology Group AG. Web services agent Integration Project available at http://wsai.sourceforge.net/index.html, accessed on 24th April 2005.

34   World Wide Web Consortium, RDF Vocabulary Description Language 1.0: RDF Schema, available at http://www.w3.org/TR/rdf-schema/, accessed on 24th April 2005.

35   World Wide Web Consortium, OWL Web Ontology Language Overview available at http://www.w3.org/TR/owl-features/, accessed on 24th April 2005.

36   World Wide Web Consortium, Web Services Choreography Description Language Version 1.0, available at http://www.w3.org/TR/2004/WD-ws-cdl-10-20040427/, accessed on 24th April 2005.

37   X., Gu, Klara N.N., Chang, C., Ward, "QoS-Assured Service Com-position in Managed Service Overlay Networks", in Proc. of 23rd IEEE International Conference on Distributed Computing Systems (ICDCS 2003), Providence, Rhode Island, May, 2003, p.194.

Information about Software

Software is available on the Internet as
- (x)   prototype version
- ( )   full fledged software (freeware), version no.:
- ( )   full fledged software (for money), version no.:
- ( )   Demo/trial version
- ( )   not (yet) available

Internet address:
Description of software:
http://www.it.swin.edu.au/centres/ciamas/tiki-index.php?page=ws2jade-proj
Download address:
http://www.it.swin.edu.au/centres/ciamas/tiki-index.php?page=ws2jade

Contact person for question about the software:
Name: Xuan Thang Nguyen
Email: xnguyen@ict.swin.edu.au

Xuan Thang Nguyen
Faculty of Information and Communication Technologies
Swinburne University of Technology
Melbourne VIC 3122, Australia.
e-mail: xnguyen@ict.swin.edu.au

Ryszard Kowalczyk
Faculty of Information and Communication Technologies
Swinburne University of Technology
Melbourne VIC 3122, Australia.
e-mail: rkowalczyk@ict.swin.edu.au

Mohan Baruwal Chhetri
Faculty of Information and Communication Technologies
Swinburne University of Technology
Melbourne VIC 3122, Australia.
e-mail: mchhetri@ict.swin.edu.au

Alasdair Grant
Faculty of Information and Communication Technologies
Swinburne University of Technology
Melbourne VIC 3122, Australia.
e-mail: 4103515@swin.edu.au

A System for Analysis of Multi-Issue Negotiation

Tibor Bosse, Catholijn M. Jonker, Lourens van der Meij,
Valentin Robu and Jan Treur

Abstract. This paper presents a System for Analysis of Multi-Issue Negotiation (SAMIN). The agents in this system conduct one-to-one negotiations, in which the values across multiple issues are negotiated on simultaneously. It is demonstrated how the system supports both automated negotiation (i.e., conducted by a software agent) and human negotiation (where humans specify their bids). To analyse such negotiation processes, the user can enter any formal property deemed useful into the system and use the system to automatically check this property in given negotiation traces. Furthermore, it is shown how, compared to fully closed negotiation, the efficiency of the reached agreements may be improved, either by using incomplete preference information revealed by the negotiation partner or by incorporating a heuristic, through which an agent uses the history of the opponent's bids in order to guess his preferences.

1. Introduction

Negotiation is a process by which a joint decision is made by two or more parties [9]. Typically each party starts a negotiation by offering the most preferred solution from the individual area of interest. If an offer is not acceptable by the other parties they make counter-offers in order to move them closer to an agreement. The field of negotiation can be split into different categories, e.g. along the following lines:

- one-to-one versus more than two parties
- single- versus multi-issues
- closed versus open
- mediator-based versus mediator-free

The research reported in this article concerns one-to-one, multi-issue, (partially) closed, mediator-free negotiation. For more information on negotiations between more than two parties (e.g., in auctions), the reader is referred to, e.g., [12]. In single-issue negotiation, the negotiation focuses on one aspect only (typically price) of the concept under negotiation. Multi-issue negotiation (also called multi-attribute negotiation) is often seen a more cooperative form of negotiation, since often an outcome exists that brings joint gains for both parties, see [10].

Closed negotiation means that no information regarding preferences is exchanged between the negotiators. The only information exchanged is formed by the bids. In partially open negotiation some information regarding preferences is exchanged, and in completely open negotiation all information is exchanged. More information about (partially) open negotiations can be found, e.g., in [7] and [10]. However, the trust necessary for open negotiations is not always available.

The use of mediators is a well-recognised tool to help the parties in their negotiations, see e.g., [6, 10]. The mediator aims for a deal that is fair to all parties. Reasons for negotiating without a mediator can be the lack of a trusted mediator, the costs of a mediator, and the hope of doing better than fair with respect to personal gain.

The literature on closed, multi-issue, one-to-one negotiation without mediators covers both systems to (partially) automate the negotiation process, and more analytic research focused on properties of the negotiation process and negotiation space. Based on a literature study and on our own analysis, a number of properties are presented here that focus largely on the dynamics of the negotiation process itself and on the results of the negotiation.

The SAMIN system presented in this paper has been developed to support and formally analyse such negotiation processes, i.e., multi-issue, (partially) closed, one-to-one negotiations without mediators. The system requires three types of input:

(1) a negotiation *trace* (or a set of traces)
(2) a set of *dynamic properties* considered relevant for the negotiation process
(3) the *negotiation profiles* of the participants

A *trace* is a sequence of bids by the negotiators. A *dynamic property* is an (informal, semi-formal or formal) expression that might or might not hold for a certain trace. An example of a simple dynamic property is bid-alternation, i.e., after communicating a bid to another agent, the agent remains silent until it has received a new bid from the other agent. A *negotiation profile* is a description of the preferences of the agent within the particular negotiation domain. The profiles together define the space of possible and efficient outcomes and are, therefore, essential for the creation of a complete analysis of the performance of a negotiator.

The most important measure of efficiency in bilateral negotiations, cf. [21], is

Pareto-efficiency. An outcome is said to be Pareto-efficient if the utility of any party cannot be improved without a loss of utility for another. The set of all Pareto-efficient outcomes form the Pareto-efficient frontier. The distance of an outcome to the Pareto frontier gives a measure of efficiency of a bid.

The SAMIN system consists of three components: an *Acquisition Component*, an *Analysis Component* and a *Presentation Component*. The Acquisition Component is used to acquire the input necessary for analysis. The Analysis Component performs the actual analysis, and the Presentation Component presents the results of the analysis in a user-friendly format.

SAMIN can check automatically whether selected properties hold for the traces under analysis. Such an analysis provides a means to improve bidding strategies and bidding protocols, both for human negotiators and for software agents in automated negotiation systems. Beside introduction of the SAMIN system, a subgoal of this paper is to report some results of such analyses, focusing both on human and automated negotiators. Regarding *human-human negotiation*, the results will be presented of applying SAMIN in the analysis of empirical traces obtained from an experiment in multi-issue negotiation about second hand cars. In the experiment the efforts of 74 humans negotiating against each other have been analysed using SAMIN. Regarding *automated negotiation*, SAMIN has been used to analyse the efficiency of the reached agreements by software agents, in order to improve the strategies of these software agents. To this end, a mechanism has been modelled in which agents are able to use any amount of incomplete preference information revealed by the negotiation partner. It is shown that the outcome of such a negotiation can be further improved by incorporating a "guessing" heuristic, by which an agent uses the history of the opponent's bids to predict his preferences. Experimental evaluation shows that the combination of using incomplete preference information with the guessing heuristic leads to agreement points close to or on the Pareto Efficient Frontier.

In Section 2 formalisation of negotiation process dynamics will be discussed in terms of negotiation states, transitions, and traces. Section 3 explains the formal specification of dynamic properties and presents example dynamic properties relevant for (partially) closed multi-issue one-to-one negotiations. The architecture of the SAMIN system is presented in Section 4. Section 5 illustrates how SAMIN can be used to analyse human negotiation processes. Some experiments in human multi-issue negotiation are described and analysed, and the results of the analysis are discussed. Next, Section 6 shows how SAMIN can be used to analyse automated negotiation processes. It is shown how software negotiators can be improved using two strategies (guessing and limited information sharing) that can be used alone, or in combination. Finally, Section 7 discusses related work, and Section 8 provides conclusions and some planned future work.

2. Formalising Negotiation Process Dynamics

Negotiation is essentially a dynamic process. To analyse those dynamics, it is, therefore, relevant to formalise and study dynamic properties of such processes. For example, how does a bid at a certain point in time compare to bids at previous time points? The formalisation introduced in this section is based on the notion of negotiation process state, negotiation transition and negotiation trace.

2.1 Formalising States of a Negotiation Process

The state of a (one-to-one) negotiation process at a certain time point can be described as a combined state consisting of two states for each of the negotiating agents: S = < S1, S2 > , where S1 is the state of agent A, and S2 is the state of agent B.
   Each of these states include,
   - the agent's own most recent bid
   - its evaluation of its own most recent bid
   - its evaluation of the other agent's most recent bid
   - the history of bids from both sides and evaluations

   To describe negotiation states a state ontology Ont is used. Example elements of this ontology are a sort BID for bids, and relations such as utility(A, b, v) expressing that A's overall evaluation of bid b is a real number v between 0 and 1. Based on this ontology the set of ground atoms At(Ont) can be defined. A state is formalised as any truth assignment: At(Ont) → {t, f} to this set of ground atoms. The set of all states described by this ontology is denoted by States(Ont).

2.2 Negotiation Transitions

A particular negotiation process shows a sequence of transitions from one state S from States(Ont) to another (next) state S' from States(Ont). A transition S → S' from a state S to S' can be classified according to which agents are involved. During such a transition each of the main state components (S1, S2) of the overall state S may change. The simplest types of transition involve a single component transition. For example, when one agent generates a bid, while the other agents is just waiting: a transition of type S1 → S1 or S2 → S2. Next come transition types where both components are involved. For example, when a communication from agent A to agent B takes place, changing the state S2 of agent B: a transition of type S1 x S2 → S2. Notice that in principle, also more complex transition types are possible, involving changes of both state components at the same time, i.e., S1 x S2 → S1 x S2. In organised cooperations between multiple agents the complexity of the types of transitions is often limited by regulation of the organisation. For example, in organised negotiation processes, usually it is assumed in the protocol that after communicating a bid to the other agent, the agent remains silent until it has received a new bid from the other agent (see the dynamic property 'bid alternation' in Sections 3 and further below). Such an assumption about the protocol implies that the transitions involved in the negotiation are only of the simpler types mentioned above.

2.3 Negotiation Traces

Negotiation traces are time-indexed sequences of negotiation states, where each successive pair of states is a negotiation transition. To describe such sequences a fixed *time frame* T is assumed which is linearly ordered. A *trace* $\mathcal{T}$ over a state ontology Ont and time frame T is a mapping $\mathcal{T}$: T → STATES(Ont), i.e., a sequence of states $\mathcal{T}_t$ (t ∈ T) in STATES(Ont). The set of all traces over state ontology Ont is denoted by TRACES(Ont). Depending on the application, the time frame T may be dense (e.g., the real numbers), or discrete (e.g., the set of integers or natural numbers or a finite initial segment of the natural numbers), or any other form, as long as it has a linear ordering.

3. Dynamic Properties of Negotiation Processes

This section presents a classification of dynamic properties of negotiation processes along with examples of each class. Before presenting the classification and the specific dynamic properties of negotiation, the formal method for specifying those properties is presented.

3.1 Specification of Dynamic Properties

Specification of dynamic properties of a negotiation process can be done in order to *analyse* its dynamics, for example to find out how certain properties of a negotiation process as a whole relate to properties of a certain subprocess, or to verify or evaluate a negotiation model. To formally specify dynamic properties that express characteristics of dynamic processes (such as negotiation) from a temporal perspective an expressive language is needed. To this end the *Temporal Trace Language* TTL is used as a tool; cf. [5], which is briefly defined as follows.

The set of *dynamic properties* DYNPROP(Ont) is the set of temporal statements that can be formulated with respect to traces based on the state ontology Ont in the following manner. Given a trace $\mathcal{T}$ over state ontology Ont, a certain state of the agent A during a negotiation process at time point t is indicated by state($\mathcal{T}$, t, A). In the third argument, instead of A also specific parts of A can be used, such as input(A), or output(A), which refer to observations and actions by A, respectively. These state indicators can be related to state properties via the formally defined satisfaction relation |=, comparable to the Holds-predicate in the Situation Calculus: state($\mathcal{T}$, t, A) |= p denotes that state property p holds in trace $\mathcal{T}$ at time t in the state of agent A. Based on these statements, dynamic properties can be formulated in a formal manner in a sorted first-order predicate logic with sorts T for time points, Traces for traces and F for state formulae, using quantifiers and the usual first-order logical connectives such as ¬, ∧, ∨, ⇒, ∀, ∃. As an example, consider the dynamic property bid alternation, which states that for all two different moments in time t1, t3, that A generates a bid, there is a moment in time t2, with t1 < t2 < t3, such that A received a bid generated by B. In formal TTL-format, this property is expressed as:

bid_alternation(γ:TRACE) ≡
∀ A, B: AGENT, ∀ b1, b3: BID, ∀ t1, t3: time :
t1 < t3 &
state(γ, t1, output(A)) |= to_be_communicated_to_by(b1, B, A) &
state(γ, t3, output(A)) |= to_be_communicated_to_by(b3, B, A)
⇒ ∃b2: BID, ∃t2: time : t1 < t2 < t3 &
state(γ, t2, input(A)) |= communicated_to_by(b2, A, B)

Usually for reasons of presentation dynamic properties are expressed in informal or semi-formal forms.

3.2 Classes and Examples of Dynamic Properties of Negotiation

The properties relevant for analysing the dynamics of (partially) closed multi-issue one-to-one negotiation, can be divided into the following types:

- **Bid properties** give some information about a specific bid. They are usually defined in terms of the negotiation space and the profiles of the negotiators. Bid properties concern, for example, the Pareto efficiency of a bid.
- **Result properties** are a subset of the set of bid properties, concerning only the last bid of a negotiation process (i.e., the final agreement).
- **Bid comparison properties** compare two arbitrary bids with each other. An example is domination: a bid b1 dominates a bid b2 with respect to agents A and B iff both agents prefer bid b1 over bid b2; see below for a formalisation
- **Step properties** are a subset of the set of bid comparison properties, concerning only the transitions between successive bids. Hence, they are restricted to the combinations of bids of one party that directly follow each other.
- **Limited interval properties** concern parts of traces. Basically, they state that each step in a certain interval satisfies a certain step property. For instance: a negotiation process is Pareto-monotonous for the interval [t1, t2] iff for all successive bids b1, b2 in the interval b2 dominates b1 (see below).
- **Trace properties** are a subset of the set of limited interval properties, concerning whole traces.
- **Multi-trace properties** compare the dynamics observed in more than one trace. An example is Better Negotiator: agent A is a better negotiator than agent B iff in more than 60% of the negotiations between A and B, the deal reached is more to the advantage of agent A than of agent B.
- **Protocol properties** specify certain constraints on the negotiation protocol. A specific instance is: over time the bids of negotiators A and B alternate.

Note that the first two types are basically *static properties*, whereas the other types are *dynamic properties*: they specify behaviour over time. In [1] for each of these types a number of properties are described in detail, both in informal and in formal notation. In this paper, only a small selection of relevant properties is presented.

configuration_differs(b1:BID, b2:BID) ≡

∃a: ISSUE, ∃v1, v2: VALUE :
value_of(b1, a, v1) & value_of(b2, a, v2) & v1 ≠ v2

This bid comparison property states that two bids b1 and b2 differ in configuration iff there is an issue that has a different value in both bids. For example, in bid b1 the value of the issue "color" is "red", whereas in bid b2 this value is "blue". Similar properties can be defined stating that two bids differ in configuration in at least x issues. This property can also be used as a building block to specify a step property, e.g. "in the view of agent A, agent B varies the configuration, but not the utility". Such a property are useful to find out what kind of opponent the negotiator is dealing with.

strictly_dominates(b1:BID, b2:BID, A:AGENT, B:AGENT) ≡
∀vA1, vA2, vB1, vB2 : real :
util(A, b1, vA1) & util(A, b2, vA2) & util(B, b1, vB1) & util(B, b2, vB2) ⇒ vA1 > vA2 & vB1 > vB2

This bid comparison property states that a bid b1 dominates a bid b2 with respect to agents A and B iff both agents prefer bid b1 over bid b2. This notion is related to Pareto Efficiency, see e.g., [10]. The property could also be changed to weakly_dominates by changing the > sign into the ≥ sign. Moreover, it can be used as a building block to specify step properties, limited interval properties (see the next property), and trace properties.

strict_pareto_monotony(γ:trace, tb:time, te:time) ≡
∀t1, t2: time, ∀A, B: AGENT, ∀b1, b2: BID :
[tb ≤ t1 < t2 ≤ te & is_followed_by(γ, A, t1, b1, B, t2, b2)]
⇒ state((γ, t2) |= strictly_dominates(b2, b1, A, B)

This limited interval property makes use of the previous property. It states that a negotiation process γ is strictly Pareto-monotonous for the interval [t1, t2] iff for all successive bids b1, b2 in the interval b2 dominates b1. By choosing for tb and te respectively the start and end time of the process, the property can be transformed into a trace property. Generally, traces that satisfy this property are not abundant in (human) real world multi-issue negotiations, since if the profiles of the two parties are strongly opposed (with emphasis on the same issues), even in multi-issue situations a gain for the one often implies a loss for the other. If, however, the profiles are less opposed, Pareto-monotony may occur.

pareto_inefficiency(γ:trace b:BID, A:AGENT, B:AGENT, ε:real) ≡
∀vA, vB : real :
util(A, b, vA) & util(B, b, vB) ⇒ pareto_distance(vA, vB) = ε

This bid property informally states that with respect to agents A and B, the Pareto inefficiency of a bid b is the number ε that indicates the distance to the Pareto Efficient Frontier according to some distance measure d in utilities. Here, d(b1, b2) is the distance between the bids b1 and b2 when viewed as points in the plane of utilities. The function to measure the distance in the plane can still be filled in, e.g., the sum of absolute differences of coordinates, or the square root of the sum of squares of the differences, or the maximum of the differences of the coordinates. The Pareto Efficient Frontier is the set of all bids b for which there is no other bid b' that dominates b. Hence, in case the Pareto Inefficiency of a bid is 0, there is no other bid that dominates it. By filling in the resulting agreement of a negotiation for bid b, the property is transformed into a result property. In general, determining the number ε for which this property holds is a good measure for checking the success of the negotiation process. In a similar way, the property nash_inefficiency can be formulated, which calculates the distance from a certain bid to the Nash Point. This is the point (on the Pareto Efficient Frontier) for which the product of both utilities is maximal, see e.g., [10].

4. The SAMIN Architecture

SAMIN is a Prolog-based software environment that has been designed at the Vrije Universiteit Amsterdam for the analysis of multi-issue negotiation processes. Section 4.1 describes the role SAMIN can take in an analysis setting of negotiation processes. Next, Section 4.2 presents a top level overview of the SAMIN architecture. Basically, the system consists of three components: an *Acquisition Component*, an *Analysis Component* and a *Presentation Component*. These components are described in more detail in Sections 4.3, 4.4, and 4.5, respectively.

4.1 SAMIN in its Environment

The SAMIN system has been designed to work together in interaction with a human analyst and either human or software agent negotiators. As depicted in Figure 1, the analyst determines the properties that SAMIN is to use in the analysis of negotiation processes. He or she can select (and if necessary adapt) properties from SAMIN's library, or can construct new properties with the help of SAMIN's special dynamic property editor. SAMIN can only analyse a negotiation process if it has access to the profiles used by the different parties, and the bids exchanged between the parties. SAMIN does not influence the negotiation while it is being carried out, it only observes either during the negotiation, or afterwards.

The analysis result of one or more negotiations is presented to the human analyst. The analyst can use that result for purposes within Cognitive Science (e.g., to analyse human negotiation processes and train human negotiators) or Artificial Intelligence (e.g., to improve the strategies of software agents). Interesting for the future might be to present the results directly after the conclusion of the negotiation to a software agent negotiator that is capable of learning so that the agent can use the result to improve its negotiation skill by itself. A negotiation process can be monitored directly by SAMIN (if the agents allow interfacing), or the negotiation trace can be written to a file and be analysed in hindsight by SAMIN. The current version of SAMIN is developed especially for closed multi-issue one-to-one negotiations, entailing that the only information exchanged between the negotiators are the bids.

The input required by SAMIN (see Figure 1) consists of properties, profiles, and traces of bids. Its output consists of an analysis that can be presented in a user-friendly format (see Section 4.4 and 4.5). As mentioned before, SAMIN offers the user both a library of properties to choose from and a dynamic property editor to create new properties. Profiles can be obtained in two ways. Either the negotiator presents a pre-specified profile to SAMIN or the negotiator can use SAMIN's interactive profile editor to create it in SAMIN. Pre-specified profiles have to be in a format recognised by SAMIN. The trace of bids required by SAMIN can be obtained by SAMIN monitoring the bids exchanged between the negotiators during the negotiation process. This only requires the bids to be in a format recognised by SAMIN and the possibility to "over-hear" the communication between the negotiators. Another possibility is that the bids exchanged during a negotiation process are stored in a special file. If the bid-traces are in the right format, SAMIN can perform analysis on one or on a combination of such traces after the negotiation has been completed. If the negotiators wish to do so, they can use SAMIN's bid ontology editor to define what a bid should look like, before entering the negotiation phase. Construction of bid ontology and the profiles is part of the pre-negotiation phase [10].

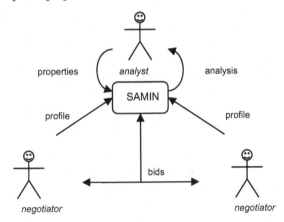

Figure 1. SAMIN in its environment

4.2 Top Level

At the top level, SAMIN consists of three components: an *Acquisition Component*, an *Analysis Component* and a *Presentation Component*, see Figure 2. Here, the solid arrows indicate data flow. The dotted arrows indicate that each component can be controlled separately by the analyst. The Acquisition Component is used to acquire the input necessary for analysis. The Analysis Component is used to perform the actual analysis (i.e., checking which properties hold for the negotiation process under analysis). Finally, the Presentation Component is used to present the results of the analysis in a user-friendly format. Furthermore, SAMIN maintains a library of properties, templates of properties, bid ontologies, and profile ontologies (not shown in Figure 2). The working of the three components will be described in detail in the next sections.

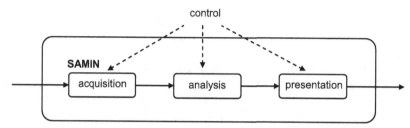

Figure 2. Global Overview of the SAMIN architecture

4.3 The Acquisition Component

The acquisition component is used to obtain the required input for the analysis. It consists of an *ontology editor*, a *dynamic property editor* and a *trace determinator*.

The ontology editor is used for the construction of bid ontologies and profile ontologies necessary to automatically interpret the bids exchanged by the negotiators, and to automatically interpret the profiles of the negotiators. The ontology editor is typically used to construct a bid ontology and a profile ontology, thus allowing the user to identify the issues to be negotiated, the values that each of these issues can take, and the structure of bids, in the bid ontology. Furthermore, in specifying the profile ontology the user identifies the possible evaluations that can be given to values, and the utility functions of bids.

The dynamic property editor supports the gradual formalisation of dynamic properties in TTL format. The editor offers a user interface that allows the analyst to construct dynamic properties, represented in a tree-like format.

The trace determinator can be used interactively with the analyst to determine what traces to use in the analysis. The user can interactively locate the files containing the traces to be checked. The traces themselves can be of three categories: (human) empirical traces, simulated traces, and mixed traces. An empirical trace is the result of an existing human negotiation process. A simulated trace is the result of an automated negotiation process. A mixed trace is the result of a human negotiating with a software agent. To support the acquisition of traces of all three types, a dedicated interface has been created for SAMIN.

4.4 The Analysis Component

The analysis component currently consists of a *logical analyser* that is capable of checking properties against traces. To this end, the tool takes a dynamic property in TTL format and one or more traces as input, and checks whether the dynamic property holds for the traces.

Traces are represented by sets of Prolog facts of the form *holds(state(m1, t(2)), a, true)* where m1 is the trace name, t(2) time point 2, and a is a state property as introduced in Section 3.1. The above example indicates that state formula a is true in trace m1 at time point 2. The Analysis Component basically uses Prolog rules for the predicate sat that reduce the satisfaction of the temporal formula finally to the satisfaction of atomic state formulae at certain time points, which can be read from the trace representation. Examples of such reduction rules are:

```
sat(and(F,G)) :- sat(F), sat(G).
sat(not(and(F,G))) :- sat(or(not(F), not(G))).
sat(or(F,G)) :- sat(F).
sat(or(F,G)) :- sat(G).
sat(not(or(F,G))) :- sat(and(not(F), not(G))).
```

In addition, if a dynamic property does not hold in a trace, then the software reports the places in the trace where the property failed.

4.5 The Presentation Component

The presentation component currently includes a tool that visualises the negotiation space in terms of the utilities of both negotiators. This *visualisation tool* plots the bid trajectory in a 2-dimensional plane, see Figure 3. The utilities are real values that indicate how a particular bid is evaluated by a negotiator. Details about the calculation of utilities are provided in the next Section.

In Figure 3, the seller's utility of a bid is on the horizontal axis, and the buyer's utility is on the vertical axis. The light area corresponds to the space of possible bids. In this area, each curve is a continuous line, corresponding to a different combination of discrete issues. The specific position on the line is determined by the continuous issue 'price'. Since in this particular domain 4 discrete issues with 5 possible values occur (see next section), there are already 625 (= 5^4) different curves. In this Figure, the sequences of actual bids made by both buyer (left) and seller (right) are indicated by the dark points that are connected by the two angular lines. The upper-left point indicates the buyer's first bid, and the lower-right point indicates the seller's first bid. The dotted line indicates the Pareto Efficient Frontier according to the profiles of the negotiating agents, and the short dark lines show the distance from each bid to this frontier. The small dot that is plotted on the Pareto Efficient Frontier (on the right) corresponds to the Nash Point. From this picture, it is clear that both negotiators make more and more concessions (their bids converge towards each other). Eventually, they reach a point that does not lie on the Pareto Efficient Frontier, but is rather close to it anyhow.

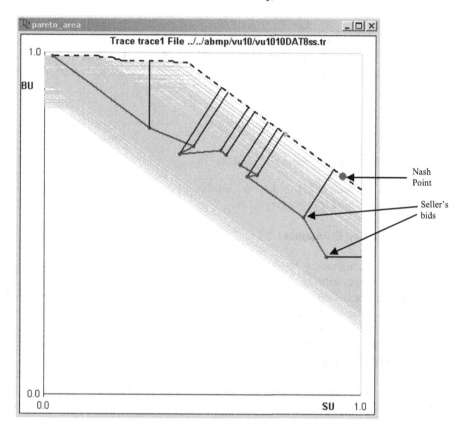

Figure 3. Visualisation Tool

5. Human Multi-Issue Negotiation Experiments

To illustrate the use of analysing human multi-issue negotiation processes, SAMIN has been applied in a case study. As mentioned in Section 4, the analysis component of SAMIN takes traces and formally specified dynamic properties as input and checks whether a property holds for a trace. Using automatic checks of this kind, some of the properties provided in Section 3 have been checked against empirical traces generated by students during practical sessions in multi-issue negotiation. The domain of the case study, a negotiation about second hand cars, is presented in detail in Section 5.1. Section 5.2 describes the setup of the experiments performed in the case study. The analytical results of the acquired traces will be shown in Section 5.3.

5.1 Domain: second hand cars

The protocol used in the experiments is an alternating-offers protocol. In this type of negotiation, a bid has the form of values assigned to a number of issues of the object under negotiation. Here, the object of negotiation is a particular second hand car. Within this domain, the relevant issues are cd_player, extra_speakers, airco, tow_hook and price. Consequently, a bid consists of an indication of which CD player is meant, which extra speakers, airco and tow hook, and what the price of the bid is. The goal of the negotiators is to find agreement upon the values of the four accessories and the price. Here, the price issue has a continuous value, whilst the other four issues have a discrete value from the set {good, fairly_good, standard, meager, none}. These values are assumed to be objective indicators from a consumer organisation, so there can be no discussion about whether a certain CD player is good or fairly good.

Before the negotiation starts, both parties specify their *negotiation profile*: for all issues with discrete values they have to assign a number to each value, indicating how satisfied they would be with that particular value for the issue (e.g. "I would be very happy to buy/sell a good CD player, a bit less happy with a fairly good CD player, ..." and so on). The buyer also has to indicate what is the maximum amount of money (s)he would be willing to spend. Moreover, both parties have to assign a number to each of the issues, indicating how important they judge that issue (e.g. "I don't care that much which CD player I will buy/sell"). Notice that this does not conflict with the above statements. An example negotiation profile for a buyer is shown in Figure 4. In addition to this negotiation profile, the seller is provided with a *financial profile*. This is a list of all issues, where for each issue it is indicated how much it costs, both to buy it and to build it into the car. Since we focus on closed negotiation, none of the profiles will be available for the other party. However, SAMIN has access to both profiles.

When both parties have completed their profiles, the negotiation starts. To help human negotiators generating their bids, the system offers a special tool that calculates the utility of a bid before it is passed to the opponent.

The utility U_B of a bid B is defined by the weighted sum over the issue evaluation values $E_{B,j}$ for the different issues denoted by: $U_B = \Sigma_j w_j E_{B,j}$. The weight factors w_j are based on the issue importance factors. Here scaling takes place (the sum of weight factors is made 1, and the evaluation values $E_{B,j}$ are between 0 and 1) so that the utility is indeed is between 0 and 1; for more details, see [4]. Since the negotiators have individual negotiation profiles, for each bid the seller's utility of the bid is different from the buyer's utility of the bid.

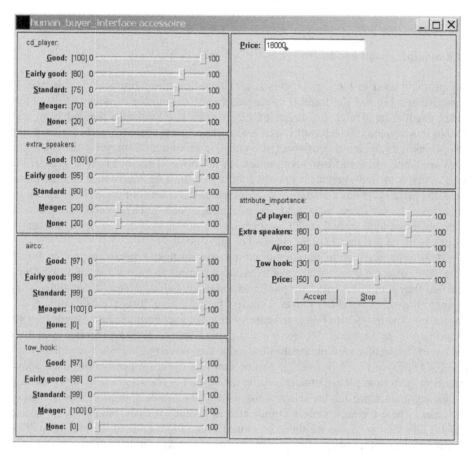

Figure 4. Example Buyer's Negotiation Profile

Besides for facilitating the bidding process, the profiles are used by SAMIN to analyse the resulting traces. For example, to check whether the property Pareto-Monotony
holds (i.e., "For each combination of successive bids b1, b2 in the trace, both agents
prefer bid b2 over bid b1"), the software must have a means to determine when an agent
"prefers" one bid over another.

5.2 Experimental setup

Participants. 74 subjects participated in the experiment, in three different sessions. All
sessions took place during a master class for students of the final classes of the VWO (a
particular type of Dutch High School). The age of the students mostly was 17 years, but
varied between 14 and 18 years. Most of them were males. In the first session, in March
2002, 30 students participated. In the second, in March 2003, 28 students participated.
In the third session, in November 2003, 16 students participated.

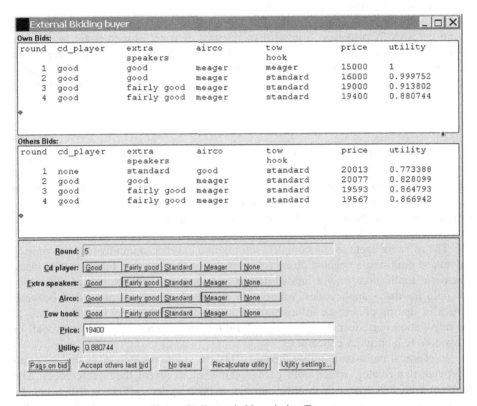

Figure 5. Example Negotiation Trace

Method. Before starting the experiment, the participants were provided some background information on negotiation, and in particular about multi-issue negotiation. Some basic negotiation strategies were discussed. In addition, the second hand car example was explained. Then they were asked to start negotiating, thereby taking a profile in mind (that had to be specified first) aiming at obtaining the best possible deal, without showing their own profile to the opponent. The negotiation process was performed using different terminals over a network, which allowed each participant to negotiate with another anonymous participant. All negotiators could input their bids within a special interface. The resulting negotiation traces were logged by the system, so that they could be re-used for the purpose of analysis. A screenshot of an example negotiation trace is depicted in Figure 5. This trace is shown from the perspective of the buyer. In the upper part of the window, the buyer's own bids are displayed, including the buyer's utility for each bid. In the middle part, the bids of the seller are displayed, including the buyer's utility for each bid. The lower part consists of the bidding interface, which allows the buyer to input his bid and pass it to the seller.

5.3 Results of the Human Experiments

Using the SAMIN prototype, a number of relevant dynamic properties for multi-issue negotiation (also see Section 3) have been checked against the traces that resulted from the experiments. The results indicate that humans find it hard to guess where the Pareto Efficient Frontier is located. Due to space limitations, the detailed results are not shown in this paper. The interested reader is referred to [1].

6 Using Incomplete Information

The above sections concentrate on the analysis of human negotiations. In the current chapter it is shown how SAMIN can be used to analyse software negotiations. To this end, a particular software agent for negotiation was implemented and its performance was evaluated using SAMIN.

The software agent uses incomplete information in order to improve the outcome of automated multi-issue negotiations. The rationale for this research line is that in many electronic applications only a limited degree of trust exists between parties. This does not hold for many applications, where only a limited degree of trust exists between parties in sharing preference information. The reasons for this may be endogenous to the negotiation (e.g., fear the other may abuse this information to get a better deal) or exogenous (e.g., privacy concerns).

In classical multi-issue-utility theory ([21]), the solution proposed is the use of an independent mediator, which both parties can trust to reveal their preferences. The problem with this approach in an electronic or open system setting is that it can be difficult to establish whether a mediator is indeed impartial or more trustworthy than the negotiation partner himself. For example, an agent may have no way of knowing if the solutions proposed by the mediator are not biased towards the other or that his preference information will not be stored and used for other purposes. By contrast, our approach is to use a distributed design, in which each agent computes its own bids, using the information available about the preferences of the opponent. We take into account two different types of (incomplete) information:

- Partial profile information, which is communicated by the negotiation partner himself in the beginning of the negotiation.
- Profile information, which can be deduced (learned) from successive bids during the negotiation itself. Here we start from the assumption that the way the negotiation partner is bidding may reveal something about his preferences. For this mechanism we use the term "guessing" to clearly show it is a heuristic.

In our current work we preferred the heuristic approach to designing automated negotiation, since we feel this allows more flexibility. This position is supported, among others, by [17] who clearly show that "what is required are agent architectures that implement different search mechanisms, capable of exploring the set of possible outcomes under both limited information and computation assumptions". However, this does not mean we ignore the results from game theory: they are present in both measuring the efficiency of reached agreements (e.g., Pareto-efficiency) and in analysing some properties of our mechanism (incentive compatibility properties). To analyse the effectiveness of the strategies and the impact of revealing small bits of information in the negotiation, the strategies were implemented and tested within the environment of the SAMIN system.

6.1 Background of the model

As in the human experiments, our negotiation follows an alternating-offers protocol. A bid in such a negotiation has the form of values assigned to a number of issues. If the negotiation is about the sale of a car, then the relevant issues are again: CD player, extra speakers, airco, tow hook, price. Thus, a bid consists of an indication of which CD player is meant, which speakers, airco and tow hook, and what the price of the offer is.

Although the examples given are based on this domain, our negotiation model and its description presented in this chapter are generic. Instantiations in other domains are possible and have been considered – for example an employer and employee negotiating about work shifts and overtime pay (work performed in collaboration with Almende B.V, Rotterdam).

The current model represents an extension of the negotiation model presented in [4]. This paper presents two main directions in which the model was adapted (in [14]), after the publication of the original research:

- A mechanism where the agents are allowed to exchange and take into account partial preference information from the negotiation partner was modelled.
- A novel "guessing" heuristic by which an agent can estimate the preferences of the other using his past bids was proposed and tested.

Both for the original work and the extension, the DESIRE design method and software environment [15] were used to design the agents. Although we also cover some elements of the existing model, we only do so very briefly, to allow more extensive explanations for the parts that were added or adapted from the original research. For further details readers are asked to consult [4, 14, 26].

Our negotiation model works by performing computations on two levels: the overall bid level and the issue level. This involves first evaluating the utility opponent's previous bid, and then planning the target utility for the own next bid. Finally, the configuration of the next bid will be selected such that it fits this target value. In the design of our agent, these steps are modelled as separate components and our presentation follows this structure.

6.2 Bid Utility Determination and Planning

The evaluation for each issue is computed based on an evaluation function, specified by the agent owner (user) in the beginning of the negotiation. This function takes the generic form eval: VS -> E, where VS is either a finite set of discrete values or an infinite set of continuous values, while $E = [0,1]$. For example, in our domain accessories have discrete values (quality levels, assigned an evaluation by the user), while issues such as mileage or price are continuous, and their utility is computed by a continuous function. Next, the utility of the opponent's previous bid is computed. The *overall utility* U_B of a bid B is taken as a weighted sum of the *issue evaluation values* $E_{B,j}$ for the different issues j: $U_B = \Sigma_j \ w_j \ E_{B,j}$. Here all weights w_j are normalized importance factors based on the raw importance factors p_k for the different issues (provided by the user through an interface in the beginning of the negotiation): $w_j = p_j / \Sigma_k p_k$

Finally a target evaluation is computed for the agent's next bid. For determination of the next bid's *target utility* TU the following formula is used: $TU = U_{BS} + CS$, with U_{BS} the utility of the agent's own last bid, and the concession step CS determined as: $CS = \beta (1 - \mu / U_{BS})^* (U_{BO} - U_{BS})$, where U_{BO} is the utility of the opponent's last bid, with respect to the agent's own utility function. Factor β stands for *negotiation speed*, while factor $(1 - \mu / U_{BS})$ expresses that the concession step will decrease to 0 if the U_{BS} approximates a minimal utility μ. The minimal utility is a measure of how far concessions can be made.

6.3 Issue Planning

The *Issue Planning* component is shown in Figure 6. Here, the arrows denote data flow. This component determines the values of issues for the next bid, in such a way that the utility of the next bid equals the target utility. This is done in two steps: first a target evaluation is computed per issue, based on the target evaluation planned for the whole bid. Next, issue values are chosen with the evaluation closest to the target evaluations (for all issues except price). The configuration of the next bid is then completed by selecting a value for price, such that the utility of the final bid fits exactly its target.

In order to make better directed concessions, in planning the target evaluation for each issue we take into account not only the own preference weight of the agent, but also the weight of the opponent. If the opponent is not willing to reveal her preference weight for some (or maybe all) issues, an estimation of these weights is computed in "Estimation of Opponent's Parameters" component. The role of the "Guess Coefficients" component is to analyse the way the opponent is bidding and to provide some extra information to be used for estimating these private preference weights.

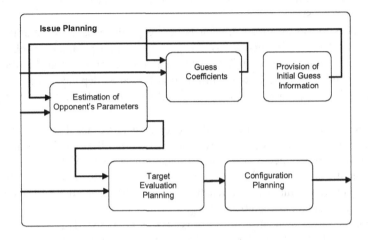

Figure 6. Internal composition of Issue Planning

6.3.1 Target Evaluation Planning

This component outputs a target evaluation for each issue in the next bid, based on the bid target value.

The target issue evaluation is determined in two steps. First a basic target issue evaluation for each issue is computed as:

$$BTE_j = E_{BS,j} + (\alpha_j / N) (TU - U_{BS})$$

In the above formula $E_{BS,j}$ represents the evaluation for issue j in the agent's own previous bid, U_{BS} the overall evaluation of the agent's previous bid, while TU represents the target utility for the next bid (as shown in Section 6.2). The parameter α_j is chosen as $\alpha_j = (1 - w_j)(1 - E_{BS,j})$, where the first parameter expresses the influence of the user's own importance factor, while the second factor assures that the target evaluation values remain scaled in the interval between 0 and 1. Parameter N is a normalization factor, defined as: $N = \Sigma_j w_j \alpha_j$. By this choice we ensure that the following relation always holds: $\Sigma_j w_j BTE_j = TU$ (for a full proof of this property we refer the reader to [4]).

The Basic Target Evaluation, however only takes into accounts the own preference weights of the agent. Using only this value would work, but tests showed that it leads to sub-optimal results, since the preferences of the other are not considered in any way when making concessions. To improve on this, the following solution was implemented. For each issue $j \in I$ (where I denotes the set of all issues) a Preference Difference Coefficient δ_j is computed as:

$$\delta_j = (W_{other,j} - W_{own,j}) / (W_{other,j} + W_{own,j})$$

This coefficient (scaled between -1 and 1) expresses how different the preferences of the two parties for each issue are. Positive values for δ_j denote a stronger preference of the negotiation partner for issue j, while negative values denote a stronger own preference for this issue.

The concession to be made in each issue $j \in I$ depends on a parameter called *configuration tolerance*, denoted as $\tau_j \in [-1,1]$. The tolerance parameter is chosen to be issue-specific, in order to better differentiate the amount of concessions between issues. Therefore, for each issue $j \in I$, the configuration tolerance depends on the preference difference coefficient of that issue, according to the following formula: $\tau_j = \tau_{gen} * (1 + \delta_j)$

Here the parameter τ_{gen} represents the general tolerance, used by the agent for all issues j. The general tolerance is always chosen between 0 and 0.5 and also gives a measure of how fast the agent is willing to make concessions. Values closer to 0 will denote an agent who is less willing to make concessions, while values closer to 0.5 will denote an agent who is interested to reach a deal quickly. Since $\delta_j \in [-1,1]$ the tolerance for any issue j is scaled between 0 and $2*\tau_{gen}$.

Finally, the target evaluation for each issue j is computed. This is done by taking into account both the basic target issue evaluation (as described above) and a concession to the issue evaluation from the previous bid of negotiation partner, as follows: $TE_j = (1 - \tau_j) \, BTE_j + \tau_j \, E_{BO,j}$

Here BTE_j is the basic issue evaluation for issue j and $E_{BO,j}$ is the evaluation for issue j from the opponent's previous bid. From the above formula, one can see that values of the configuration tolerance τ_j close to 0 signify that mostly the user's own importance factors are taken into account, while values close to 1 shows that maximum possible concession is made towards the other's value. And since τ_j depends directly on δ_j, it is the difference in preference for each issue that determines how much concession should be made.

Within the *Target Evaluation Planning* component we have assumed that the opponent's preference weights for an issue are known. However, if the other is not willing to share his weights for some (or all) issues, then they will need to be estimated.

6.3.2 Estimation of Opponent's Parameters and Guessing

The role of these components is to determine, for those issues for which the opponent was not willing to reveal his preference weights, an estimation of those weights (namely of the parameter $W_{other,j}$ needed in the equation above).

We denote by Iknown the set of issues for which the opponent was willing to reveal his importance weights in the beginning of the negotiation and by Iunknown the issues whose preference weights are kept private. Since all preference weights are normalised (see Section 6.2), the sum of weights for the private issues is computed as: $\Sigma_{j \in Iunknown} W_j = 1 - \Sigma_{k \in Iknown} W_k$.

For the issues with private weights, the remaining weight $\Sigma_{k \in Iknown} W_k$ needs to be divided between them. This is the goal of the guessing mechanism, which is more formally defined in [14]. Intuitively the idea is to divide the remaining weight based on the perceived concessions the opponent makes during the negotiation. Each discrete-valued issue is assigned a qualitative value from the set {good, fairly good, standard, meager, none}. Each party in the negotiation assigns to these values a numerical evaluation from 0 to 100, independent from the issue weight. For example, if "good" has for the buyer an evaluation of 100, and "standard" the evaluation 60, and the weight of the CD player issue is 60 out of a total of 300 (or normalised form 0.2), then a good CD player will bring an evaluation of 0.2*100=20 to the total utility, while a standard one an evaluation of 0.2*60=12. So a buyer that concedes during the negotiation, for the issue CD player, from "good" to "standard" makes a global utility concession of 8.

However, the Seller, in a closed negotiation setting does not know either the weight of the issue CD player, nor does he know the evaluations the Buyer has assigned to values such as "good", "fairly good" or "standard". However, he can compare concessions between issues, based on the fact that, for a certain price level, buyers always prefer better quality issues than worse ones.

For example, suppose two issues: CD player and Tow Hook have both unknown (i.e. not revealed) utility weights. Initially the Buyer asks for both issues the quality "good". However, for one issue, say CD player, she is only willing to concede from "good" to "fairly good", while for the other, say Tow Hook, she is willing to concede from "good" to "standard". The seller in this example can infer that the CD player is more important to this particular buyer than the Tow Hook, because a rational buyer gives in first in the issues which are less important to her.

A formal description of this mechanism, as well as the experimental results from the tests performed to validate our model are given here for reasons of space, but the interested reader is asked to consult [14].

6.4 An example negotiation trace

The model presented above was tested along several dimensions, such as:
- The number of issue weights revealed
- Whether guessing is used or not
- The choice for the issue importance factors
- The evaluations for the issue value levels

Due to space limitation, we do not give a full discussion of these results here. For a full discussion of our experimental results, we ask the reader to consult [14]. In this section we illustrate the functioning of our model through a complete example trace, as produced by our simulation tool. Tables 1 and 2 below describe the evaluations which are given by the 2 parties to their agents, though the input interface.

	Tow hook	Airco	Extra speakers	CD player	Price
BUYER	90	90	15	15	300
SELLER	15	15	90	90	300

Table 1. Importance factors assigned to different issues by the Buyer and Seller

	Good	F. good	Standard	Meager	None
BUYER	100	85	70	50	0
SELLER	30	65	80	65	100

Table 2. Evaluation given by each side for each qualitative value of the 4 issues: Tow hook, CD player, Extra speakers and Airco

As can be seen from Table 2, we assume a business model in which the Seller prefers to sell the car for a standard price – and not have to install extra accessories, but he is willing to do so in order to sell it.

Table 3 provides the complete trace of this negotiation from the perspective of the Buyer, while Table 4 does the same from that of the Seller. The vertical columns show the bids made by the two parties in successive rounds.

BUYER	1	2	3	4	5	Closing
bids						
price	18000	17450	17968	18047	18083	18083
tow hook	good	fairly good	fairly good	fairly good	fairly good	fairly good
airco	good	standard	standard	standard	standard	standard
speakers	good	meager	none	none	none	none
CD player	good	meager	none	none	none	none
utilities						
own bid	1	0.9203	0.9130	0.9094	0.9068	0.9068
seller's bid	0.7407	0.8782	0.8830	0.8864	0.8889	0.8889

Table 3. The negotiation trace: BUYER's perspective

Figure 7 provides a visualization of the negotiation progress in the joint utility space (as automatically produced by the implementation in our software environment). For clarity, only the first 3 bids of the Buyer and the first 2 of the Seller are shown. The rest lie in the straight line between these 2 points. An interesting effect is that, in this example, after establishing mutually agreeable values for the discrete-value issues (accessories), the agents seem to "walk" the Pareto-efficient frontier towards each other's bid. This corresponds to the haggling about the price from rounds 3-5 in Tables 3 and 4.

SELLER	round 1	2	3	4	5	accept:5
bids						
price	16900	18468	18404	18359	18325	18083
tow hook	none	fairly good	fairly good	fairly good	fairly good	fairly good
airco	none	standard	standard	standard	standard	standard
speak-ers	none	none	none	none	none	none
CD player	none	none	none	none	none	none
utilities						
own bid	1	0.9378	0.9296	0.9238	0.9195	0.8884
buyer's bid	0.3167	0.5932	0.8737	0.8838	0.8884	0.8884

Table 4. The negotiation trace: SELLER's perspective

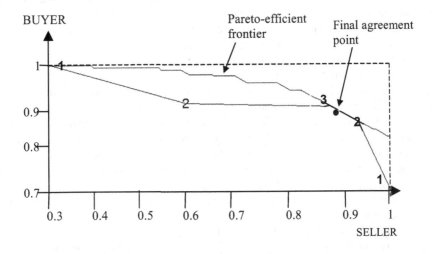

Figure 7. Utility space corresponding to the example trace from Tables 3/4

7 Related Work

This section discusses the literature on the analysis of negotiation processes. Moreover, it reviews automated negotiation systems that use incomplete information described in the literature and compares them to our own.

In the literature on negotiation a number of systems are described. Sometimes it is stated what properties these systems have, sometimes not. If properties are mentioned they can be of different types, and also the justifications of them can be of different degree or type. This section discusses the literature on properties of negotiation and analytical results of implemented systems and of human case studies.

Faratin, Sierra, and Jennings [2] concentrate on many parties, many-issues, single-encounter closed negotiations with an environment of limited resources (time among them). Agents negotiating using the model are guaranteed to converge on a solution in a number of situations. The authors do not compare the solutions found to fair solutions (Nash Equilibrium, Maximal Social Welfare, Maximal Equitability), nor whether the solutions are Pareto Efficient.

Klein, Faratin, Sayama, and Bar-Yam [6] developed a mediator-based negotiation system to show that conceding early (by both parties) often is the key to achieving good solutions. Hyder, Prietula, and Weingart [3] showed that substantiation (providing rationale for your position to persuade the other person to change their mind) interferes with the discovery of optimal agreements.

Weingart et al. [13] found that the Pareto efficiency of agreements between naïve negotiators could be significantly improved by simply providing negotiators with descriptions of both integrative and distributive tactics. Although Pareto *efficiency* was positively influenced by the tactics, Pareto *optimality* was only minimally affected. Compared to [8, 11, 12], the properties identified in this paper are geared towards the analysis of the dynamics of the negotiation process, whereas theirs are more oriented towards the negotiation outcome, rationality and use of resources.

In [19], a model for bilateral multi-issue negotiation is presented, where issues are negotiated sequentially. The issue studied is the optimal agenda for such a negotiation under both incomplete information and time constraints. However a central mediator is used and the issues all have continuous values. The effect of time on the negotiation equilibrium is the main feature studied, from both a game-theoretic and empirical perspective. In earlier research [20] a slightly different model is proposed, but the focus of the research is still on time constraints and the effect of deadlines on the agents' strategies. This contrast with our model, where efficiency of the outcome and not time is the main issue studied. This is because we found that, due to our cooperative assumption, a deal is usually reached in maximum 10-15 steps, if the negotiation speed and tolerance parameters are suitably calibrated.

A direction of work directly related to our guessing heuristic (introduced in Section 6) is represented by [17] and [18]. Like [17] we start from the perspective of distributed negotiation, which eliminates the need of a central planner. As in [17], we also take the heuristic approach and we model agents that are able to jointly explore the space of possible outcomes with a limited (incomplete) information assumption. In [17], this is done through a trade-off mechanism, in which the agent selects the value of its next offer based on a similarity degree with previous bids of the opponent. In our design, we do no explicitly model trade-offs, yet the same effect is achieved through the asymmetric concessions mechanism. An advantage of our model over [17] is that we allow agents to take into account not only their own weights, but also those of the opponent in order to compute the next bid. In this way agents may exchange partial preference information for those issues for which their owners feel this does not violate their privacy. Also the initial domain information for the issues with discrete ("qualitative") values is different. In [17], this consists of fuzzy values, while in our model it is a partial ordering of issue weights.

8 Conclusions and Future Work

The contribution of this work consists of a more systematic approach to the analysis of the negotiation process. Different types of properties are identified and for each class a number of properties are defined. The System for Analysis of Multi-Issue Negotiation (SAMIN) is presented and applied in two ways: to analyse human negotiation in a case study and to analyse the effectiveness of guessing and limited information exchange as implemented in a number of software agents. SAMIN consists of three components: an Acquisition Component to acquire the input necessary for analysis, an Analysis Component to perform the actual analysis, and a Presentation Component to presents the results of the analysis in a user-friendly format.

The system has proved to be a valuable tool to analyse the dynamics of human-human closed negotiation against a number of dynamic properties. Our analysis shows that humans find it difficult to guess where the Pareto Efficient Frontier is located, making it difficult for them to accept a proposal. Although humans apparently do not negotiate in a strictly Pareto-monotonous way, when considering larger intervals, a weak monotony can be discovered. Such analysis results can be useful in two different ways: to train human negotiators, or to improve the strategies of software agents.

The strategies tested using software agents showed that the original agents for closed multi-issue negotiation (used in the ABMP system, see [4]), when playing against each other, score better than the human subjects (in human-human negotiations). The software agents were subsequently augmented with a guessing strategy and with the ability to share a bit of information regarding their issue weights. The results show that both strategies increase the effectiveness of the negotiation.

Currently, SAMIN is being used to analyse the dynamics of humans negotiating against software agents of the ABMP system (with and without the guessing strategy, also in setting in which limited preference information is shared). Future research is to analyse the dynamics of other types of (e.g., more experienced) human negotiators. Furthermore, the system needs to allow heterogeneous agents, so that a competition of negotiating agents can be set up and the results of that competition formally analysed. In future, SAMIN will be extended with training facilities for human negotiators, allowing to test the effectiveness of training methods for negotiation. As a simple extension, for example, if a dynamic property checked in a trace turns out to fail, a more detailed analysis can be given of the part(s) of the formula that cause(s) the failure. Finally, we plan to extend SAMIN to provide feedback to a negotiator who is in the middle of a negotiation process, where SAMIN only has access to the same information as the negotiator.

References

[1] Bosse, T., Jonker, C. and Treur, J., Formalisation of Dynamic Properties of Multi-Issue Negotiations. Vrije Universiteit Amsterdam, Department of Artificial Intelligence. Technical Report, 2004.

[2] Faratin, P., Sierra, C., and Jennings, N.R., Negotiation decision functions for autonomous agents. In: International Journal of Robotics and Autonomous Systems, vol. 24(3-4), 1998, pp. 159 – 182.

[3] Hyder, E.B., Prietula, M.J., and Weingart, L.R., Getting to Best: Efficiency versus Optimality in Negotiation, In: Cognitive Science, vol. 24 (2), 2000, pp. 169 – 204.

[4] Jonker, C.M., Treur, J., An Agent Architecture for Multi-Attribute Negotiation. In: B. Nebel (ed.), *Proceedings of the 17th International Joint Conference on AI, IJCAI'01*, 2001, pp. 1195 - 1201.

[5] Jonker, C.M., and Treur, J., Compositional Verification of Multi-Agent Systems: a Formal Analysis of Pro-activeness and Reactiveness. *International Journal of Cooperative Information Systems*, vol. 11, 2002, pp. 51-92.

[6] Klein, M., Faratin, P., Sayama, H., and Bar-Yam, Y., (2001), Negotiating Complex Contracts. Paper 125 of the Center for eBusines@MIT. http://ebusiness.mit.edu.

[7] Kowalczyk, R, Bui, V., On Constraint-Based Reasoning in e-Negotiation Agents. In: Dignum, F, and Cortés, U., (eds.), *Agent-Mediated Electronic Commerce III, Current Issues in Agent-Based Electronic Commerce Systems*, Lecture Notes in Computer Science, vol. 2003, Springer – Verlag, pp. 31-46.

[8] Lomuscio, A.R., Wooldridge, M., and Jennings. N.R., (2000), A classification scheme for negotiation in electronic commerce, In: *International Journal of Group Decision and Negotiation*, vol. 12(1), January 2003.

[9] Pruitt, D.G., *Negotiation Behavior*, Academic Press, 1981.

[10] Raiffa, H., *Lectures on Negotiation Analysis*, PON Books, Program on Negotiation at Harvard Law School, 513 Pound Hall, Harvard Law School, Cambridge, Mass. 02138, 1996.

[11] Rosenschein, J.S., and Zlotkin, G., *Rules of Encounter: Designing Conventions for Automated Negotiation among Computers*. The MIT Press, Cambridge, MA, 1994.

[12] Sandholm, T., Distributed rational decision making, In: Weiss, G., *Multi-agent Systems: A Modern Introduction to Distributed Artificial Intelligence*, MIT Press, 1999, pp. 201-258.

[13] Weingart, L.R., Hyder, E.H., and Prietula, M.J., Knowledge matters: The effect of tactical descriptions on negotiation behavior and outcome. In: *Journal of Applied Psychology*, vol. 78, 1996, pp. 504-517.

[14] Jonker, C., Robu, V. – "Automated multi-attribute negotiation with efficient use of incomplete preference information", *Proceedings of the 3rd International Conference on Autonomous Agents and Multi-Agent Systems (AAMAS-04)*, New York, July 2004.

[15] Brazier, F.M.T., Jonker, C.M., and Treur, J. "Compositional Design and Reuse of a Generic Agent Model", *Applied Artificial Intelligence Journal*, vol. 14, 2000, pp. 491-538.

[16] Byde, A., Kay-Yut Chen – "AutONA: A System for Automated Multiple 1-1 Negotiation", *Fourth ACM Conference on Electronic Commerce*, pp. 198-199.

[17] Faratin, P., Sierra, C. and Jennings, N. Using Similarity Criteria to Make Issue Trade-offs in Automated Negotiations. *Journal of Artificial Intelligence* vol. 142 (2), 2003, pp. 205-237.

[18] Faratin, P., Sierra, C. and Jennings, N. "Using Similarity Criteria to Make Negotiation Trade-Offs", *Proceedings of ICMAS-2000*, Boston, MA., 119-126.

[19] Fatima, S. S., Wooldridge, M. and Jennings, N. R.. "Optimal Agendas for Multi-Issue Negotiation". In *Proceedings of the Second International Conference on Autonomous Agents and Multiagent Systems (AAMAS-03)*, Melbourne, July 2003, pp. 129-136.

[20] Fatima, S., Wooldridge, M. and Jennings, N. R.. "Optimal Negotiation Strategies for Agents with Incomplete Information" . In *Intelligent Agents VIII,* Springer-Verlag LNAI, vol. 2333, pp 377-392, March 2002

[21] Raiffa, H. – "The art and science of negotiation", *Harvard University Press*, Cambridge, Mass., 1982.

Tibor Bosse
Vrije Universiteit Amsterdam, Department of Artificial Intelligence
De Boelelaan 1081a
1081 HV Amsterdam
The Netherlands
e-mail: tbosse@cs.vu.nl

Catholijn M. Jonker
Radboud Universiteit Nijmegen, Nijmegen Institute for Cognition and Information
Montessorilaan 3
6525 HR Nijmegen
The Netherlands
e-mail: C.Jonker@nici.ru.nl

Lourens van der Meij
Vrije Universiteit Amsterdam
The Netherlands
e-mail: lourens@cs.vu.nl

Valentin Robu
CWI, National Center for Mathematics and Computer Science
Kruislaan 403
1098 SJ Amsterdam
The Netherlands
e-mail: robu@cwi.nl

Jan Treur
Vrije Universiteit Amsterdam
The Netherlands
e-mail: treur@cs.vu.nl

Software is available on the Internet as
 (X) Demo/trial version

Internet address for download:
 http://www.few.vu.nl/~wai/samin
Contact point for questions about the software:
 http://www.few.vu.nl/~wai/samin

FuzzyMAN: An Agent-based E-Marketplace with a Voice and Mobile User Interface

Frank Teuteberg and Iouri Loutchko

Abstract. The popularity of wireless devices stimulates widespread efforts to develop voice and mobile user interfaces for software systems in general and for e-marketplaces in particular. This paper focuses on conceptual foundations and the architecture of an agent-based job e-marketplace supporting mobile negotiations. The negotiation model is based on many negotiation issues, a fuzzy utility scoring method, and simultaneous negotiation with many negotiation partners in an environment of limited negotiation time. The design and implementation of voice and mobile user interfaces for accessing information on an e-marketplace called *FuzzyMAN* (Fuzzy Multi-Agent Negotiations) is described. A comparison of technologies for the development of voice and mobile user interfaces is given.

Keywords: software agents, e-marketplace, mobile negotiations, multimodal user interfaces, VoiceXML, J2ME, XHTML, XSLT.

1 Introduction

Recent advances in digital speech processing technologies and standards such as SALT (Speech Application Language Tags) [1] and VoiceXML (Voice Extensible Markup Language) [2] enable developers to enhance mobile applications with voice user interfaces to interact with e-marketplaces and other applications.

Mobile and especially voice-based access to e-marketplaces has several advantages in comparison to web-based access. Voice user interfaces enable users to directly access information via spoken commands instead of browsing through several drop down menus before coming to the desired information. Furthermore, handicapped persons (e.g. blind persons) who are unable to access e-marketplaces due to physical disabilities may gain access through voice-enabled mobile devices. The mobile and voice user interfaces described in this paper allow users to access applications such as e-marketplaces in a manner appropriate to the users' situation, for example, using speech, keyboard, web browser, or stylus.

In this paper, we also demonstrate the concepts of a multi-agent approach to electronic marketplaces using a prototype of a job e-marketplace called FuzzyMAN (Fuzzy Multi-Agent Negotiations). On the FuzzyMAN marketplace users create their individual agents that then act autonomously and proactively. Mobile, voice-enabled, and web-based user interfaces can be used to initialize the agents, manage them, and receive their feedback. Once initialized, the agents continuously search for new positions (employ-ees' agents) or for new employees (employers' agents). To achieve their objectives (in our case, to find an appropriate position or an appropriate employee) the agents negoti-ate about the conditions of a contract according to several criteria like salary per hour, working hours per week, and social benefits. As soon as a suitable position or a suitable candidate for a vacant position is found, the agents inform their owners about the condi-tions of the contract. Other useful features are that users can permanently monitor the performance of their agents and the situation on the marketplace, and that they may change their preferences for salary per hour, working hours per week, the negotiation tactics employed by their agents, the dates their agents expire, etc.

The remainder of this paper is organized as follows. In section 2, we describe Fuz-zyMAN's architecture. Section 3 discusses some essential features of the agents acting on the FuzzyMAN e-marketplace. Section 4 introduces the underlying multilateral ne-gotiation model. Section 5 focuses on the design and implementation of voice and mo-bile user interfaces based on VoiceXML and J2ME technology. In section 6 research efforts of other researchers related to our work are described. In the final section some experimental results, further research questions, and some concluding remarks are given.

2 FuzzyMAN's Architecture

The agent-based e-marketplace FuzzyMAN was developed in a research project sup-ported by the German Research Foundation and can be accessed through web-browsers as well as mobile devices.

The FuzzyMAN marketplace is a multi-agent system with the architecture shown in figure 1. In this section we describe the structure and functionality of the marketplace. The architecture includes both a specific mediator agent playing the role of a market coordinator and agents representing individual users with their own goals and tactics. The mediator is a centralized 'super-agent' handling the communication of other agents. Initially, all users have to register when entering the marketplace to create their own agents on the server. Employees' agents search for adequate jobs and employers' agents offer jobs. Each agent is uniquely identified by an agent-id. Users may access Fuz-zyMAN through mobile, voice-enabled, and web-based interfaces. Here the user can create an agent, set the agent's preferences, change personal settings, and access information provided by the agent.

An agent created by a user contacts the mediator agent to enter his profile, the user's data, and/or job offers or search requests into the database. The agents' preferences are used by the mediator agent to find and rank agents suitable for negotiations.

The mediator agent continuously seeks for pairs and/or groups of employees' and employers' agents with corresponding preferences. It initiates and manages the negotiations in different threads once suitable agents are found. After several rounds of exchanging offers and counter-offers, the negotiation process either ends with an agreement between an employer's and an employee's agent in the ideal case, or terminates without success. The mediator agent and the agents' owners are informed about the negotiation results.

The entire negotiation process comprises several stages, including:

- Discovery of potential negotiation partners in a pre-selection process with the help of the mediator agent.
- Determination of the negotiation issues through a communication process based on FIPA-ACL/XML (FIPA-ACL = FIPA Agent Communication Language [3]; XML = Extensible Markup Language).
- Automated negotiation by exchanging XML messages with values of negotiation issues generated by means of the agents' tactics.

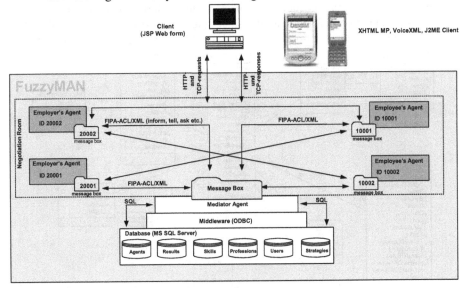

Fig. 1. Multi-agent system architecture

FuzzyMAN is a platform-independent application implemented in Java. In order to make FuzzyMAN widely accessible, the implementation was based on the following technologies:

- FIPA-ACL: Used as the agent communication language.
- XML: Used as the data interchange language for representing and processing fuzzy negotiation vocabulary from a syntactic and a semantic perspective. In XML domain-specific entities, attributes, and relationships between entities can be defined with tags like <salary>, <profession>, etc. The XML content of messages is constructed based on Document Type Definitions (DTDs). DTDs can be used as templates to define content models, the valid order of elements, and the data types of attributes.
- JDBC (Java Database Connectivity): Used to access FuzzyMAN's relational database from Java.
- MS SQL Server 2000: Used as database management system.
- JSP (Java Server Pages): Used for the generation of dynamic content from the database, writing to the database, and for the web forms to enter user data.
- XSLT, XHTML, VoiceXML, Java 2 Platform Micro Edition (J2ME): Used for realizing mobile and voice user interfaces.

FuzzyMAN is currently running on a server with a Windows 2000 operating system, 40 GB hard disk, Intel Pentium processor 1 Ghz and 256 MB DDR-RAM. The system was developed and tested using the following software versions: Java Software Development Kit 1.3, Tomcat Server 3.3, Internet Explorer 5.5 and 6.0.

The underlying database mainly stores information that is needed for the agents to do their work. This information includes, for example, preferences set by the users and statistical data about earlier negotiation results. Figure 2 gives an overview of the database tables and their interrelations in UML (Unified Modeling Language) notation.

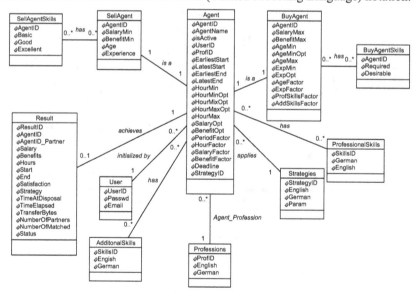

Fig. 2. Schema of the underlying database in UML notation

The multiplicity specifications used in figure 2 indicate how many elements (entities) of one database table (relation) may be connected to the elements of another database table. Multiplicity in UML is analogous to cardinality in other modeling languages. Professions, skills and strategies of agents (sell agents = employees' agents; buy agents = employers' agents) are stored in the database in both English and German to enable bilingual user interfaces.

3 FuzzyMAN's Agents

3.1 Employees' and Employers' Agents

In this section, some essential features of the agents acting on the FuzzyMAN e-marketplace are discussed. Two types of agents have to be considered:
a) *employees' and employers' agents* that communicate and negotiate with each other to achieve their respective objectives, and
b) a *mediator agent* responsible for managing the other agents, collecting statistical information, and selecting candidate agents for a specific negotiation process. We give a short overview of both agent types.
The architecture of employees' and employers' agents consists of three main modules: a communication module, a module for interaction with the agents' owners, and a negotiation module.
Whereas the communication module governs the exchange of messages between agents, the interaction module is responsible for communication between an agent and its owner. Interaction is bilateral: Users can manage their agents through the user interfaces (mobile, voice-enabled, and web-based user interfaces) and agents can contact their owners in certain situations (e.g. successful negotiation, approaching the deadline) via e-mail or SMS. A part of the web-based user interface is illustrated in figure 3. Users can manage their agents through this interface, including initializing, updating, and deleting agents.
For example, to initialize an employee's agent as in figure 3, the user has to specify the profession (e.g. "network administrator"), preferred employment dates, number of working hours per week, expectations about the salary per hour and social benefits, age, professional experience, and expiration date of the agent. Then information about professional skills (like knowledge of Unix, Java, SAP R/3) and additional skills (like foreign languages, driving license, flexibility), divided into three categories (basic, good, or excellent level of knowledge), has to be entered. Finally, the user specifies the tactic that the agent is supposed to employ in the negotiation process, and the weights for the negotiation issues, i.e. salary, employment period, working hours, and social benefits. The negotiation module consists of three components: negotiation object, decision-making model, and negotiation protocol.

New Employee Profile

1. Choose a profession from the list and enter a name for your agent:

    Network Administrator ▼   *Agent name: Bond007

2. Preferred employment dates:

    *Earliest start: 2005-02-01 (Use format yyyy-mm-dd)   *Latest start: 2005-06-01 (Use format yyyy-mm-dd)

    *Earliest end: 2005-12-31 (Use format yyyy-mm-dd)   *Latest end: 2006-12-31 (Use format yyyy-mm-dd)

3. Number of working hours per week:

    *Absolute minimum: 30 (A number between 1 and 40)   *Preferred minimum: 35 (A number between 1 and 40)

    *Absolute maximum: 45 (A number between 1 and 40)   *Preferred maximum: 40 (A number between 1 and 40)

4. Expectations about the salary:

    *Minimum salary: 30 €/hour   *Preferred salary: 40 €/hour

5. Expectations about social benefits:

    *Minimim benefits: 500 €/month   *Preferred benefits: 1000 €/month

Fig. 3. Part of the input form for initialization of a new employee's agent

The *negotiation object* is characterized by four issues: salary per hour, number of working hours per week, duration of the employment, and social benefits. We note that neither the specific types of negotiation issues nor their number are essential for the negotiation model under consideration; the same model can be used in other situations with different negotiation issues.

The *decision making model* consists of an assessment part (that evaluates an offer received and determines the corresponding action) and of an action part (that either generates and sends a counter-offer or stops the negotiation).

The value of negotiation issues is modeled by scoring functions. Larger scoring function values for particular issues reflect their suitability for negotiation. The scoring functions represent private information not known by and not given to other market participants.

For illustration, an example of a scoring function that can be used by employees' agents on the FuzzyMAN marketplace is presented in figure 4, where h_{Min}^n, h_{Max}^n, $h_{Opt\_Min}^n$, $h_{Opt\_Max}^n$ are the employee's minimal, maximal, and optimal number of working hours per week. The parameter n_h defines an employee's level of satisfaction with the worst case regarding the number of working hours per week.

In a real negotiation, different negotiation issues are of different importance to each partner. To model this situation, the notion of relative importance that a participant assigns to an issue under negotiation is introduced.

Using such scoring functions and the relative importance of issues under negotiation, a general scoring function is defined. The general scoring functions of FuzzyMAN's agents are additive functions [4] summing the scoring functions for individual negotiation issues multiplied by their weights (or their relative importance) that are kept in the interval [0, 1]. The sum of these weights is taken to be equal to 1. We note that this method of defining a general scoring function can only be used when the negotiation issues are independent, as they are in the FuzzyMAN marketplace.

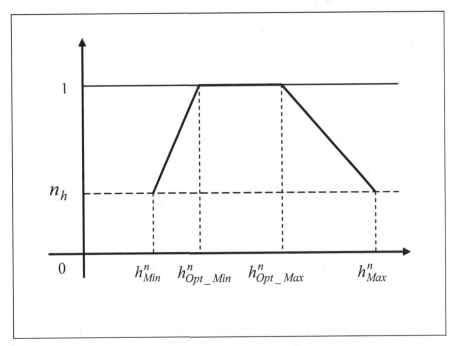

Fig. 4. Scoring function for negotiation issue "number of working hours/week"

The scoring functions are used both in the pre-selection procedure and in the negotiation process, in the latter case to evaluate the offers received from other agents. The pre-selection procedure is described in the next section.

3.2 Mediator Agent and Pre-selection Procedure

The most important functionalities of the mediator agent are management of other agents, collecting statistical information, and pre-selection of agents for a negotiation. In this part of the paper we focus on the pre-selection procedure that plays an essential role in the negotiation protocol.

Pre-selection means selecting and ranking those agents of the marketplace that will start a specific negotiation over certain issues with a given agent. In the pre-selection process, factors like profession, age, working experience, professional and additional skills of the potential employees are taken into consideration. The values of these factors are fixed on the employees' side and cannot be involved directly in the negotiation process although they are very important for the employment process.

For the ranking of employees' agents, additional scoring functions for age, working experience, professional and additional skills have to be constructed [5]. Then an extended set of weights (relative importance) of negotiation and pre-selection issues is defined for each employer's agent: In addition to the weights introduced before, this set contains the relative importance of the employee's age, of his or her working experience, and professional and additional skills.

For evaluation of an offer received by an employer's agent from an employee's agent, the extended scoring function in form of the sum of the general scoring function and the "fixed" scoring function is used. The "fixed" scoring function takes into consideration the fixed characteristics of the employees like their age, working experience, and professional and additional skills. Like the general scoring function described before, the "fixed" scoring function employed by the FuzzyMAN's agents is also an additive function.

For a given employer's agent an order of the set of all employees' agents is introduced according to the following rule:

An employee's agent y is more preferable for the employer's agent than another employee's agent z (or equally preferable) if and only if the value of the "fixed" scoring function for the agent y is greater than (or equal to) the value of the same function for the agent z. In this case, the relation between the two employees' agents is denoted by $y \succ z$ (or by $y = z$).

Using the above procedure, an ordered sequence n_1, n_2, n_3,..., n_l of employees' agents is determined for a particular employer's agent. This sequence is sorted according to the level of suitability as a negotiation partner for the employer's agent determined for each employee's agent:

$$n_1 \succ n_2 \succ n_3 \succ ... \succ n_l . \tag{3.1}$$

The results of the pre-selection procedure are heavily used in the multilateral negotiation protocol.

4 Negotiation Model

In this section, the negotiation protocol underlying the agents' negotiation on the FuzzyMAN marketplace is briefly presented. A detailed discussion of the multilateral negotiation protocol can be found in [5].

In general, there might be several employees who are interested in a position offered by an employer. Vice versa, several employers might be interested in a certain employee. So the negotiation model underlying a job marketplace should be a multilateral one.

First we discuss how the agents generate their offers and counter-offers, i.e. their negotiation strategies. A *negotiation strategy* consists of choosing an appropriate negotiation tactic depending on the time and other environmental conditions like the situation on the e-marketplaces, the number of negotiating agents, or the status of the current negotiations. The simplest negotiation strategy is a constant one, i.e. only one negotiation tactic is employed all the time. By a *negotiation tactic* a vector function with several components is understood. These components determine the way the agent changes the values of the negotiation issues (in the case of FuzzyMAN's agents: salary per hour, number of working hours per week, employment duration, and social benefits) over time.

In the literature various cases of negotiation tactics are discussed (see for example [6]). Families of tactics which can be employed by agents are time-dependent, resource-dependent, and behavior-dependent tactics. An important family of tactics consists of functions which are only time-dependent, i.e. neither the status of the marketplace nor the status of the negotiation influences the negotiation.

On the FuzzyMAN marketplace agents employ constant strategies with time-dependent tactics in the form:

$$f(t) = f_1 + \left(\frac{t - t_{Init}}{t_{Max} - t_{Init}} \right)^{1/\beta} (f_2 - f_1), \quad f : [t_{Init}, t_{Max}] \rightarrow [f_1, f_2]. \quad (4.1)$$

Tactics of this form are often used in the literature about agents' negotiations. Other approaches to define time-dependent tactics have also been proposed, but the formula (4.1) suited our purpose best because it describes the whole spectrum of time-dependent tactics. In formula (4.1), f_1, f_2 are user-defined values of the negotiation issue (minimal and maximal values of a certain negotiation issue for a given agent), $t \in [t_{Init}, t_{Max}]$ where t_{Init} is the time the agent was initialized by the user, t_{Max} is the time the agent has to complete the negotiation (deadline), and $\beta > 0$ is a parameter that determines how the agent changes the values for the given negotiation issue over time. The larger the value of the parameter β is, the sooner the agent is ready to make larger concessions in the negotiation process.

For multilateral negotiations in FuzzyMAN we employ a negotiation protocol based on the bilateral protocol described in [6] (see also [7] for an extended version of this protocol) and a partial order of the set of all employees' agents generated by the pre-selection procedure discussed in section 3.2.

The general idea behind the bilateral negotiation protocol is that two agents participating in the negotiation sequentially send each other offers and/or counter-offers. To generate the offers negotiation tactics are used. The decision to accept or reject an offer received from the other agent is based on scoring functions constructed according to the agents' preferences, restrictions, goals, and relative importance of negotiation issues. A negotiation is completed either if an offer is accepted by one of the agents (negotiation is successful) or if one of the agents reaches its deadline (negotiation fails). For a formal presentation of the protocol for bilateral negotiation see [6].

On the FuzzyMAN marketplace, a multilateral negotiation is modeled as a finite set of bilateral negotiations between employers' and employees' agents. However, these bilateral negotiations are not independent, but are influenced by other ongoing bilateral negotiations, just as they would be on a real marketplace.

In the following, the general idea of the multilateral negotiation protocol for multiple issues is outlined. The interested reader is referred to [5] for details. Suppose t_{Max} is the deadline of an employer's agent and n_1, n_2, n_3,..., n_l is the ordered sequence of the employees' agents suitable for negotiation with the given employer's agent and ranked by the pre-selection procedure: $n_1 \succ n_2 \succ n_3 \succ ... \succ n_l$. The idea behind the protocol is that the total value of offers the employer's agent sends at a particular time $t = t_i$, $i = 0,1,.....,n$ (n = number of negotiation steps) to the employees' agents it is negotiating with should be the same for all offers. The total value of an offer takes into consideration both the negotiation issues and the pre-selection issues (e.g. age, working experience, etc.) which are not involved directly in the negotiation.

If a new employer's agent comes to the marketplace, the mediator agent first performs the pre-selection procedure for it. Then the newcomer starts negotiation according to the multilateral negotiation protocol. When a new employee's agent comes, the pre-selection procedure is performed for every employer's agent once again. As a result, the newcomer may become involved in negotiations with one or several employers' agents.

In the case that an agent accepts an offer sent to it by one of the agents it is negotiating with, the agent stops negotiating with all other agents and informs those agents through a special message about the cancellation of the negotiation process. If such a cancellation message comes from one of the agents, that agent is withdrawn from the set of agents negotiating with the agent that received the cancellation message. Likewise at time $t = t_n$, $t_n \geq t_{Max}$ the agent stops the negotiation with all agents it was negotiating with and informs those agents about the cancellation of the negotiation process.

According to the bilateral negotiation protocol both employees' agents and employers' agents always send offers they themselves are satisfied with. Therefore, as soon as an offer is accepted by one of the agents, the agent that sent the offer and the agent that received the offer come to an agreement. Another point to mention is that the offers an agent receives are evaluated first-in-first-out: An offer received earlier than another one is evaluated first and corresponding actions are taken prior to the evaluation of the second offer.

Representing and processing negotiation vocabulary in electronic marketplaces is a difficult task. The explicit specification of common syntax and semantics of negotiation vocabulary is commonly referred as the ontology problem [8], which is still one serious problem in the area of multi-agent research. The problem is to ensure that the negotiation partner have the same understanding of the negotiation issues (e.g. "salary", "extra pay" etc.). On our marketplace we apply an XML-based approach for representing and processing fuzzy negotiation vocabulary from a syntactical and semantical perspective. The vocabulary is represented in a fuzzy way to make electronic negotiations more flexible. As a tag-based language for describing tree structures with a linear syntax, we use XML for the representation of ontologies and inter-agent communication during the negotiation process. XML provides the ability to define negotiation ontologies and to declare entities, entity attributes and relationships between entities. See [9] for details about the XML representation and its advantages in inter-agent communication.

Figure 5 illustrates our approach to represent an agent's fuzzy scoring function in a linear tree structure. An employee's agent searching for a specific job can apply an XML representation of a fuzzy scoring function to describe its preferences. In fuzzy set theory [10] a fuzzy set is described by a membership function, which can be approximated by a set of points. To each of those points a unique degree of membership is assigned. For example, a fuzzy term like 'average' of the linguistic variable working hours per week may have an attached degree of membership of 0 to 1 within the interval [30, 35]. Membership degrees between those specified points can be calculated by interpolation.

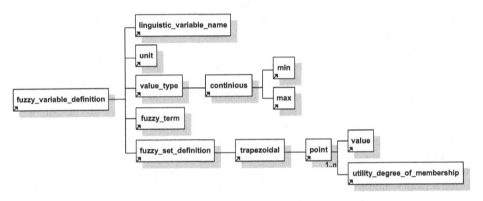

Fig. 5. Representation of a fuzzy scoring function in linear tree structure

5 Mobile and Voice User Interfaces

In this section, we describe the design and implementation of voice and mobile user interfaces for FuzzyMAN.

Mobile Negotiations (M-Negotiations) is an emerging research area that bridges the domains of Internet and Mobile Computing in order to provide time and location independent mobile negotiation services to users.

However, limited screen sizes or low data rates associated with mobile devices are some of the shortcomings which have to be addressed in this research area. Furthermore, mobile devices are equipped with different browsers that support various markup languages and media formats. Thus, the content has to be generated in different markup languages that fit the specific browsers. When delivering information it is necessary to address the diversity of mobile devices such as limited data input capabilities, small displays, limited graphical capabilities, small memory, limited processing power, etc.

Currently, we are doing research to present the XML formatted data of FuzzyMAN depending on the relevant features for different devices such as browser type, size of displays, graphical formats, etc. To realize device dependent transformations of the XML formatted data into formats such as WML and XHTML we apply XSLT stylesheets [11] and XPath [12]. XPath defines mechanisms for addressing specific elements in XML documents whereas XSLT specifies transformations on XML documents. In XSLT, rules are described for transforming the XML-based source document (also called source tree) into a new document structure (also called result tree). The transformation process is achieved by means of templates, which match some set of elements of the source document and then describe the transformation by associating patterns and styles with the templates to transform the XML-formatted data into multiple formats such as HTML, XHTML, WML, VoiceXML [13], etc.

One of our research goals in the FuzzyMAN project was to employ different technologies for implementation of the user interfaces on mobile devices, to analyze them and to compare them with each other.

FuzzyMAN's mobile user interfaces are available in the form of J2ME applications, voice user interfaces and dynamic pages displayed in different (mobile) browsers in HTML and XHTML to allow voice and mobile access to FuzzyMAN depending on the users' preferences and devices. Java 2 Micro Edition (J2ME) defines the minimum required Java technology components and libraries for small and resource constrained mobile devices. Java language, core libraries, input/output, networking, and security are the primary topics addressed by the J2ME specification [14].

In our approach, details about mobile devices such as the device manufacturer and the version of the mobile browser used are based on the HTTP headers (e.g. the UserAgent header). These HTTP headers are delivered when the user accesses the FuzzyMAN e-marketplace via the HTTP protocol. They help to automatically detect the most appropriate presentation form. Figure 6 shows the basic scheme for content presentation depending on the device type and browser.

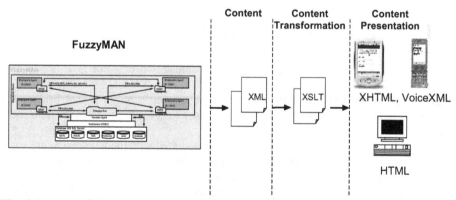

Fig. 6. Process of Content Transformation

In all cases the content requested by the user is first presented as an XML document. Using XSLT stylesheets [11] this document is then transformed into multiple formats such as HTML, XHTML or VoiceXML according to the information about the user's device and its browser. Finally, the content in the corresponding format is delivered to the user and presented on their end device.

5.1 Mobile User Interfaces

Fig. 7. FuzzyMAN's mobile front-end

Figure 7 illustrates FuzzyMAN's mobile front-end showing a selection of mobile user interfaces. Users can manage their agents through this mobile interface, including initializing, updating, and deleting agents as well as retrieving a statistical overview of the marketplace. The functionality of the mobile front-end is the same as the Web front-end which is described in section 3.1.

Figure 8 shows the presentation of FuzzyMAN's Login User Interface on a PDA.

Fig. 8. PDA with FuzzyMAN's Login User Interface

Figure 9 illustrates the mobile user interface of the German version of FuzzyMAN giving a statistical overview. This user interface is developed by means of J2ME technology, which inherits Java's rich graphic libraries and thus enables developers to present statistics as diagrams. The distribution of the 5 top positions that employees' agents are searching for is represented.

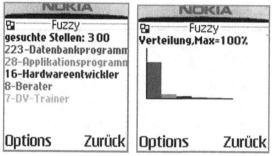

Fig. 9. Mobile User Interface with Statistical Overview

5.2 Voice User Interfaces

In this section, we describe a voice user interface for FuzzyMAN based on VoiceXML technology [2].

Voice enabled user interfaces have several advantages over traditional interfaces, for example:

- More convenient access to information on e-marketplaces in situations in which the interaction with graphical user interfaces via mobile devices is not possible (e.g. while driving a car).
- Voice enabled access to e-marketplaces is also possible by handicapped persons who are not able to use traditional user interfaces.
- Automatic voice-enabled services on e-marketplaces are available 24 hours a day and 7 days a week without the need for additional human operators (e.g. in call centers).

Automatic speech recognition technologies allow users to access e-marketplaces using their voice. A speech recognition engine processes speech as input to an application (e.g. an e-marketplace) and translates it into text. At present, even the best speech recognition engines do not achieve speech recognition rates of 100 %. Therefore, voice-based e-marketplaces have to cope with recognition errors and the dialog flow has to be considered very carefully.

A typical dialog between a user (**U**) and the FuzzyMAN e-marketplace (**F**) is illustrated in figure 10. The right window in figure 10 shows the dialog flow represented by means of VoiceXML.

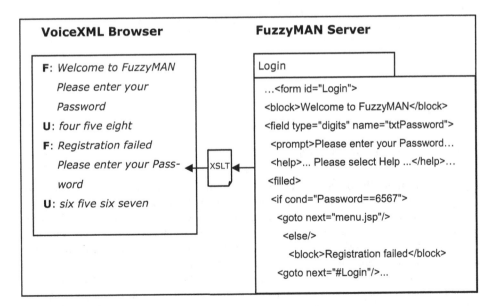

Fig. 10. Code Snippet in VoiceXML

VoiceXML documents such as a statistical overview were extracted from FuzzyMAN's database in XML format and were transformed into VoiceXML using predefined XSLT templates as illustrated in figure 11. Tags in the XML document (e.g. Dialog) are matched with templates that determine the corresponding processing of user data or the next step in the dialog flow that has to be taken.

```
<?xml version="1.0" encoding="ISO-8859-1" ?>
<xsl:stylesheet xmlns:xsl="http://www.w3.org/1999/XSL/Transform" version="1.0">
  <xsl:output method="xml" indent="yes" version="1.0" encoding="ISO-8859-1" />
- <xsl:template match="Dialog">
  - <vxml version="1.0">
    - <form id="Login">
      - <block>
          <xsl:value-of select="Title" />
        </block>
      - <field name="Password" type="digits">
        - <prompt>
            <xsl:value-of select="Form/Input[@name="txtPassword"]/@voice" />
          </prompt>
        - <help>
            <xsl:value-of select="Form/Help" />
          </help>
        - <filled>
          - <if>
            - <xsl:attribute name="cond">
                Password==
                <xsl:value-of select="Form/Input[@name='txtPassword']" />
              </xsl:attribute>
              <goto next="menu.jsp" />
              <else />
            - <prompt>
                <xsl:value-of select="Form/Error" />
              </prompt>
              <goto next="#Login" />
            </if>
          </filled>
        </field>
      </form>
    </vxml>
  </xsl:template>
</xsl:stylesheet>
```

Fig. 11. XSLT document for transformation

Figure 12 illustrates the process of a speech-based dialog with FuzzyMAN using a voice user interface via a mobile device. The user (U) dials the phone number of the VoiceXML interface, which answers giving the user the opportunity to choose between several options. By means of the speech recognition engine the VoiceXML interface interprets the user's answer (e.g. "Statistical overview") and makes an HTTP request to the FuzzyMAN server where the appropriate XML document contains the statistical overview. The speech recognition engine needs so-called utterances and grammars in order to process spoken input and translate it into statements that the underlying program can execute. Utterances are streams of speech delimited by two periods of silence (at the beginning and at the end of the stream). Grammars are finite sets of words expected as the user's spoken input.

The VoiceXML interface produces speech output based on the corresponding XML documents transformed by means of XSLT into a VoiceXML document. In order to realize the voice user interface for FuzzyMAN requests we used the IBM Voice Server Development Kit [15], which fully supports the VoiceXML standard. Additionally, grammars used as input to the Automatic Speech Recognition engine were developed.

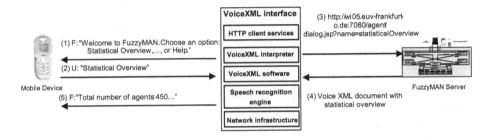

Fig. 12. Voice XML interface

5.3. Comparison of Technologies

In this section, we give a short comparison of the technologies we have applied to develop voice and mobile user interfaces for FuzzyMAN. Table 1 provides an overview of relevant criteria to compare the core technologies that can be employed to implement such user interfaces.

One of the main advantages of XHTML MP is that it enables precise positioning of text, graphics, borders, and other elements on the screen. In addition, colors can be used for better formatting of content on mobile devices with color capability.

J2ME inherits Java's rich graphic libraries and thus enables developers to significantly improve both the appearance and functionalities of the application's GUI on mobile devices. J2ME, for example, has a rich set of facilities allowing the presentation of diagrams based on statistics as described in section 5.1. Thus, J2ME is a good choice for visually representing numeric data.

VoiceXML can be used in situations where users might be simultaneously involved in several other activities (e.g. while driving a car) or where a task is complex and graphical user interfaces are not effective. However, flexibility and efficiency of using the VoiceXML technology is limited, because there is no possibility to speed up the interaction (e.g. to shorten the predefined dialog significantly).

At present, the use of voice user interfaces is not universally successful, because the dialog flow is a deterministic one. More flexible dialogs and sophisticated conversations would be desirable. Expert users have to use the voice interface in almost the same way concerning the dialog flow as the novice user.

During the test phase of the FuzzyMAN voice user interface we observed that correct voice recognition is heavily dependent upon the length of words and the similarity of words within a dialog. Therefore, it was necessary to replace similar words with less problematic synonyms (e.g. employee and employer agent replaced by buy and sell agent) to improve the recognition rate. Thus, we achieved quite good voice recognition rates of approximately 80 %.

In summary, the technology choice is heavily dependent upon the graphical aspects (e.g. diagrams have to be presented), the desired access mode (voice or mobile), and the application domain.

Criteria/Requirements	XHTML MP	J2ME	VoiceXML
Learning curve (Mobile and voice application development simplicity)	+++	+	++
Capabilities of designing graphical user interfaces	++	++	–
Ease of use (navigation through menus)	++	++	+
Extensibility	+++	++	–
Availability of code examples	++	++	++
Portability and Interoperability	++	+++	+
Flexibility and Efficiency of use	+++	++	+
Standardization of technology	W3C Standard	Proprietary standard developed and promoted by SUN	W3C Standard
Development environments (selection)	Nokia WAP toolkit, Openwave Mobile SDK	J2ME wireless toolkit, JBuilder	IBM Voice server development toolkit
Legend: +++: very good; ++: good; +: satisfactory; –: not available			

Table 1. Comparison of Technologies for Mobile and Voice User Interfaces

6 Related Work

In this section, we provide an overview of related work in the context of agent-based e-marketplaces focusing on systems that support the users' mobility.

Most of today's electronic marketplaces either do not use agent technology at all or they employ only restricted forms of this technology. For example, some online auctions can be regarded as multi-agent e-marketplaces. However, they are of a very simple type. The only issue under consideration is the price. Additional issues like terms and conditions, payment method, who will pay for shipment, timings, penalties, etc. are not taken into account. In the business-to-business area, for example, those issues play an essential role; sometimes they are even more important than the price. For such situations the agent models employed by today's marketplaces are not appropriate.

Several approaches to agent-mediated negotiation on electronic marketplaces have been introduced in the literature, see for example, [5-7] and [16-25]. In [26] a multi-agent system and analysis for multidimensional matchmaking in the human resources application domain is introduced. In [27] the negotiating environment Fuzzy eNAs (Fuzzy e-Negotiation Agents) is presented. Agents representing buyers and sellers can autonomously negotiate with fuzzy constraints and preferences in bi-lateral negotiations.

In fact, there is no single best approach or technique for automated negotiation. The negotiation strategies and protocols need to be set according to the situation and application domain. At present, the research activities in the area of agent-based e-marketplaces providing mobile and/or voice user interfaces are in an early stage [28]. We could not found any references to agent-based e-marketplaces with voice user interfaces in the literature. However, there are some agent-based e-marketplaces with mobile interfaces like Agora [29] (providing access to stationary agents via PDAs), Impulse [30], and MB (an agent-based framework for mobile commerce) [31].

Agora is a research project conducted at HP Labs where some applications of agent technology to mobile shopping are investigated. The mobile users of the Agora system can interact with the online store services through their personal digital assistants (PDA) from anywhere and anytime. The base of the Agora system is intelligent agents that represent both customers and the store. They participate in online auctions to bid for desired products based on customers' preferences. The agents have been implemented with a multi-agent system Zeus from BT Labs [32] and additional Java-based support software.

Impulse [30] is a project at MIT Media Lab that explores a scenario in which the buying and selling agents can run on wireless mobile devices and engage in multi-parameter negotiation for comparison-shopping at the point of purchase. In fact, the FuzzyMAN project uses the same approach differing only in that the point of sale is a fixed one, i.e. the FuzzyMAN e-marketplace.

MB, an agent-based framework for mobile commerce, provides a general architecture for developing applications employing mobile agents. MB agents can be of three different types. The device agent is a stationary agent that resides on a mobile device and provides access to wireless services such as location-based comparison-shopping. The service agents are owned by service providers and handle service requests from the users. The courier agents are lightweight mobile agents that can migrate from a service agent to a mobile device in order to establish communication with the user. MB has been implemented with the use of Java-based tools including Aglets SDK for service agents and KVM SDK for the device agent and courier agents.

For more examples we refer the interested reader to [28] where several other multi-agent systems using mobile agents/mobile devices are discussed and compared.

7 Conclusion, Future Work and Open Research Questions

7.1 Towards Efficiency Criteria

There is no single best negotiation protocol which is suitable for all negotiation scenarios. Standard ways to measure the efficiency of a negotiation protocol are, for example, symmetry, pareto-efficiency, and computational efficiency.

Our negotiation protocol is *symmetric*. No agent within both groups of agents (employers' and employees' agent) will be privileged with regard to others within these groups. However, the agents in both groups are treated differently. Employees' agents with low-ranking positions on the employers' agents' sequence lists must wait before they receive their first offers, because employers' agents start their simultaneous negotiation processes only with the highest ranked employees' agents. Therefore, the group of employers' agents has a superior position in our marketplace relative to the group of employees' agents. However, our proposed concept is comparable to real life employment situations. Employees also have to wait before they are invited to interviews with different employers.

A negotiation outcome is said to be *pareto-efficient* if there is no other outcome that will make at least one agent more satisfied without making at least one other agent less satisfied. Our proposed multilateral negotiation model is in most cases pareto-efficient but not in all: Assuming an employer's agent **A** receives two offers, one from employee's agent **B** (under deadline pressure) and one from employee's agent **C** (with a longer deadline) and both offers have equal utility values for the three agents **A**, **B** and **C**. In our proposed multilateral negotiation model, employer's agent **A** will choose the first offer in its message box. With regard to pareto-efficiency it would be better to choose the offer from employee's agent **B**, which has the earlier deadline, because the employee's agent **C** (with the longer deadline) has a better chance to reach an agreement before its deadline with another employer's agent and to achieve the same or even a better utility value. In the case that agent **A** chooses employee's agent **B** it is possible that agent **B** failed and due to its deadline pressure reach a utility value of 0 (e.g. no agreement). So in this special negotiation scenario there could be an outcome that will make employer's agent **A** and employee's agent **C** just as satisfied while making employee's agent **B** (under deadline pressure) more satisfied. However, in our multilateral negotiation protocol other agents' deadlines (as well as their tactics) are private information (as in real life negotiation situations for jobs). Therefore, we had to make a decision between pareto-efficiency in all negotiation scenarios and information privacy.

Agents are not *cooperative* or *benevolent* on our job marketplace, because each agent wants to get the agreement which satisfies its preferences best. If the negotiation tactic of agent **A** is known to agent **B**, agent **A** may be at a significant disadvantage.

An agent could get a better deal when putting negotiation partners under deadline pressure by not revealing his true negotiation deadline. However, on our job marketplace an employee's agent, for example, is unaware of the number of employees' agents simultaneously negotiating with one of its negotiation partners. Due to this lack of information agents on our marketplace reply to an offer immediately.

Concepts for concealing the agents' true preferences and deadlines or selfish negotiation behavior are not implemented yet. In this way the negotiation model can be extended. However, a negotiation model supporting selfish agents is not necessarily optimal with respect to reaching the best negotiation outcome for both negotiation parties (employees' and employers' agents) in terms of pareto-efficiency.

We have conducted a set of simulation experiments to evaluate our negotiation model.

The values and parameters for our simulation experiments were generated automatically, because we had no real employees and employers with real data available. Since there are infinitely many potential negotiation situations in which we can evaluate our negotiation model, we had to limit the possible values of the agents' utility functions for each issue. Therefore, we generated these values automatically based on empirical statistics. For example, to generate values for the issue working hours per week, we used empirical statistics from Germany's Federal Statistical Office, describing the distribution of German employees' working hours per week. 900 agents were initialized for our simulation experiments.

The main experimental results can be summarized as follows:

- The utility degrees of agreements achieved by agents only shortly before the end of their negotiation time (deadline) are on an average only 80 % of the utility degrees of agreements achieved by agents just at the beginning of their negotiation processes.
- Agents willing to make concessions early at the beginning of their negotiation processes have the best chance to achieve an agreement. Only a few deals were made when at least one negotiation partner was not willing to make concessions or both negotiation partners have applied divergent tactic functions.
- 'Extreme' tactical behavior (not willing to make concessions) results in a higher standard deviation with regard to achieved utility degrees. Agents unwilling to make concessions obviously have a higher risk of being unable to achieve an agreement during their disposable negotiation time. On the other side, when these agents achieve agreements the observed utility degrees were 20 % above the average utility degrees.

For more statistical results we refer the interested reader to [33] where simulation results of the FuzzyMAN marketplace were presented.

FuzzyMAN is a complete, robust, and working prototype of an agent-based electronic marketplace. In October 2002 the FuzzyMAN marketplace was made available for the scientific community in the Internet. Initially 200 employees' and 100 employers' agents were generated. Since then, 154 new agents were added by anonymous users from the scientific community to the FuzzyMAN marketplace. The current negotiation statistics are as follows: 116 out of 454 agents on our marketplace were successful and achieved agreements (contracts) before they reached their deadlines. The average utility value (in %) of agreements achieved by successful agents is 65 %. This low average utility value and low rate of matched agents is due to the divergent agent profiles initialized by their users. Most employees' agents failed in finding negotiation partners because the employers' agents looked for employees with different professional backgrounds.

7.2 Future Work and Open Research Questions

During the test phase of FuzzyMAN a number of starting points for improvements of its performance were observed. The following is a summary of these points:

Multimodality: At present, a mobile user has the possibility to interact with FuzzyMAN via either speech, web, or mobile browser. The next step to be considered in future work is multimodal access to the FuzzyMAN e-marketplace. Multimodal access means that content (e.g. a statistical overview) is displayed on the (mobile) browser and at the same time delivered and explained via speech. The main advantages of multimodal access via one (mobile) user interface are a better understanding and memorization of the delivered information [34].

Natural Language Understanding: The voice user interface presented in this paper is not capable of free speech input. The user can only choose one of the valid predefined responses specified by the corresponding grammar. More sophisticated approaches like Natural Language Understanding [35] could accelerate and improve the user interaction with regard to a natural way of communication.

Personalization: Personalization usually means adjustment of system functionalities to individual preferences. Adjustment of content display, output formatting, choice of exposed services, or creation of personal views on services that FuzzyMAN provides are some typical examples of personalization. By applying *XSL:FO* (XSL Formatting Objects), for example, it would also be possible to transform XML documents into formats such as PDF, RTF, SVG, etc., which are currently not supported by FuzzyMAN. More complex personalization concepts would require acquisition of the users' personal preferences and characteristics, e.g. competences, interests, preferred devices and browsers, or other relevant information with the aim to utilize them by interacting with FuzzyMAN. To take advantage of this extended personalization concept FuzzyMAN could use information stored in either static user profiles, which have been created based on the users' input, or in dynamic profiles, for which information is gathered through permanent observation of the users' behavior within the system. FuzzyMAN could use these profiles to personalize services according to user preferences.

Session management: Another concept closely related to personalization is the management and tracking of state and context of users' interaction with FuzzyMAN in the form of 'personalized' session management. FuzzyMAN provides mobile and voice-enabled access to its services. Thus, maintaining state spanning multiple connections is very important to avoid loss of information by almost uncontrollable breaks in wireless connections (e.g. by passing through a tunnel, transferring from one wireless hot-spot to another). It is personalized and persistent management of interaction state and context that would allow FuzzyMAN's users to resume their work at the next available opportunity.

Peer-to-Peer mobile communication infrastructure: FuzzyMAN's agents are not lightweight enough to directly operate and negotiate on mobile devices. At present, there are too many problems which have to be solved to realize a scenario of mobile agents migrating between a Peer-to-Peer communication infrastructure of mobile devices and negotiating on the mobile devices. In such a scenario, a central server would no longer pose a bottleneck. Furthermore, user sensitive data (e.g. user profiles/preferences) would be stored on various mobile devices and not in one central database, where such data could be misused by violating privacy issues. Issues that still have to be solved to realize such a scenario are, for example, security, bandwidth and performance issues. Furthermore, the heterogeneity and diversity of mobile devices must also be addressed.

FuzzyMAN is available at http://www.wiwi.euv-frankfurt-o.de/wi-www/agent.htm. Interested readers are welcome to create their own agents, send them out to negotiate, watch their behavior, and see if they are successful in their negotiations.

Acknowledgements

We are very grateful to the German Research Foundation that supported our work through grant no. Ku 569/15-1 and to Karol Fil for useful discussions concerning our implementation of voice and mobile user interfaces.

References

[1] SALT Forum, *Speech Application Language Tags 1.0 Specification*; available at: http://www.saltforum.org/saltforum/downloads/SALT1.0.pdf, 2003.

[2] VoiceXML Forum, *Voice eXtensible Markup Language*; available at: http://www.voicexml.org/specs/VoiceXML-100.pdf, 2003.

[3] FIPA – Foundation for Intelligent Physical Agents. *FIPA Specifications*, 2003; available at: http://www.fipa.org/specifications/index.html, 2003.

[4] Bichler, M. and Kalagnanam, J., *Bidding Languages and Winner Determination in Multi-attribute Auctions*, 2004. To appear in: European Journal of Operational Research. (IBM Research Report RC22478); http://ibis.in.tum.de/staff/bichler/docs/RC22478.pdf.

[5] Kurbel, K. and Loutchko, I., *Multi-agent negotiation under time constraints on an agent-based marketplace for personnel acquisition*. In: Dittmar, T., Franzzyk, B., Hofmann, R. et al. (Eds.): Proceedings of the 3rd Intern. Symposium on Multi-Agent Systems, Large Complex Systems, and E-Business (MALCEB), 2002, 566-579.

[6] Faratin, P., Sierra, C., and Jennings, N. R., *Negotiation decision functions for autonomous agents*. Robotics and Autonomous Systems **24** (1998), 159-182.

[7] Fatima, S., Wooldridge, M., and Jennings, N. R., *Multi-issue negotiation under time constraints*. In: Proc. 1st Int. Joint Conf. On Autonomous Agents and Multi-Agent Systems, 2002, Bologna, Italy, 143-150.

[8] Nwana, H. S. and Ndumu, D. T., *A perspective on software agent research*. The Knowledge Engineering Review **14** (1999) 2, 125-142.

[9] Glushko, R. J., Tenenbaum, J. M., and Meltzer, B., *An XML Framework for Agent-based E-commerce*. CACM **42** (1999) 3, 106-114.

[10] Zadeh, L., *Fuzzy Sets. Journal of Information and Control* **8** (1965), 338-353.

[11] W3C, *XSL Transformation*, Version 1.0; available at: http://www.w3.org/TR/xslt, 2003.

[12] W3C, *XPath*; available at: http://www.w3.org/TR/xpath, 2002.

[13] W3C, Voice *Extensible Markup Language (VoiceXML)*, Version 2.0; available at: http://www.w3.org/TR/voicexml20/, 2003.

[14] Sun Microsystems, *Java 2 Platform, Micro Edition* (2004); available at: http://java.sun.com/j2me, 2004.

[15] IBM, *Voice Server Software Development Kit*, (2002); available at: http://www-3.ibm.com/software/voice/, 2002.

[16] Adams, G., Rausser, G., and Simon, L., *Modelling Multilateral Negotiation: An Application to California Water Policy*. J. Economic Behaviour and Organization **10** (1996), 97-111.

[17] Aknine, S., Pinson, S., and Shakun, M. V., *An extended multi-agent negotiation protocol*. International Journal on Autonomous Agents and Multi-Agent Systems **8** (2004), 5-47.

[18] Anthony, P. and Jennings, N. R., *Evolving Bidding Strategies for Multiple Auctions*. In: van Harmelen, F. (Ed.), Proc. 15th European Conf. Artificial Intelligence, IOS Press: Amsterdam, 2002, 178-182.

[19] Faratin, P., *Automated Service Negotiation Between Autonomous Computational Agents*. PhD thesis, Univ. of London, Queen Mary College, 2000.

[20] Faratin, P., Sierra, C., and Jennings, N. R., *Using similarity criteria to make trade-offs in automated negotiations*. Artificial Intelligence **142** (2002), 205-237.

[21] Fatima, S., Wooldridge, M., and Jennings, N. R., *An agenda based framework for multi-issues negotiation*. Artificial Intelligence Journal **152** (2004), 1-45.

[22] Jennings, N. R., Faratin, P., Lomuscio, A. R., Parsons, S., and Wooldridge, M., *Automated negotiation: prospects, methods and challenges*. Group Decision and Negotiation **10** (2001), 199-215.

[23] Kraus, S., *Strategic negotiation in multi-agent environments*. The MIT Press, Cambridge, Massachusetts, 2001.

[24] Raiffa, H., *The art and science of negotiation*, Harvard University Press, 1982.

[25] Sandholm, T., *Agents in electronic commerce: component technologies for automated negotiation and coalition formation*. Autonomous Agents and Multi-Agent Systems **3** (2000), 73-96.

[26] Veit, D., *Matchmaking in Electronic Markets: An Agent-Based Approach towards Matchmaking in Electronic Negotiations*. Lecture Notes in Artificial Intelligence, Vol. 2882, Springer: Berlin, 2003.

[27] Kowalczyk, R. and Bui, V., *On Fuzzy e-Negotiation Agents: Autonomous negotiation with incomplete and imprecise information*. DEXA Workshop on e-Negotiation, UK, 2000.

[28] Kowalczyk, R., Ulieru, M., and Unland, R., *Integrating Mobile and Intelligent Agents in Advanced e-Commerce: A Survey*; available at: http://citeseer.nj.nec.com/551656.html, 2002.

[29] Fonseca S., Griss M., Letsinger, R., *An Agent-Mediated E-Commerce Environment for the Mobile Shopper*. HP Technical Report HPL-2001-157, 2001.

[30] Maes, P., Youll, J., and Morris, J., *Impulse: Location-based Agent Assistance*; in: Software Demos, Proc. of the 4th Int. Conf. on Autonomous Agents, June 2000; available at: http://citeseer.nj.nec.com/youll00impulse.html.

[31] Mihailescu, P. and Binder, W.: A Mobile Agent Framework for M-Commerce. Agents in E-Business (AgEB-2001), Workshop of the Informatik 2001, Vienna, Austria, 2001; available at: http://www.ifi.unizh.ch/events/GI/GI01/Proceedings/mihailescu.pdf.

[32] Nwana, H. S., Ndumu, D. T., and Lee, L. C., *ZEUS: A Tool-Kit for Building Distributed Multi-Agent Systems*. Applied Artificial Intelligence Journal **13** (1999), 129-186.

[33] Teuteberg, F., *Experimental Evaluation of a Model for Multilateral Negotiation with Fuzzy Preferences on an Agent-based Marketplace*. In: Müller, J., Maass, W., Schmid, B., and Pavlikova, L. (Eds.): Electronic Markets: The International Journal of Electronic Commerce & Business Media **13** (2003) 1, 21-32.

[34] Jankowska, A. M. and Dabkowski, A., *Voice User Interfaces for Mobile ERP System*. In: Branki, C. et al. (Eds.), MKWI 2004, Vol. 3, Duisburg, Essen, 2004, 44-53.

[35] IBM, *An Introduction to IBM Natural Language Understanding*, IBM White Paper, 2001; available at: http://www-3.ibm.com/software/voice/.

Frank Teuteberg
Research Center for Information Systems in Project and Innovation Networks (ISPRI)
c/o Department of Business Administration/E-Business and Information Systems
University Osnabrueck
Katharinenstr. 1, D-49074 Osnabrueck, Germany
e-mail: frank.teuteberg@uos.de

Iouri Loutchko
Department of Business Informatics
European University Viadrina Frankfurt (Oder)
POB 1786, D-15207 Frankfurt (Oder), Germany
e-mail: loutchko@uni-ffo.de

Information about Software

Software is available on the Internet as
(X) prototype version
( ) full fledged software (freeware), version no.:
( ) full fledged software (for money), version no.:
( ) Demo/trial version
( ) not (yet) available

Description of software:
FuzzyMAN is an implementation of an electronic marketplace where software agents negotiate, buy, and sell. The marketplace is open for public access. That is, you can create your own agents, provide them with your personal preferences, send them out to negotiate, and watch what they are doing. The application domain we chose is buying and selling "labour". Agents act for employers (looking for employees) and employees (looking for jobs). Negotiation models cover both bilateral and multilateral negotiations

about multiple issues, based on fuzzy logic. XML is used as the agent communication language. User interfaces for accessing information on the e-marketplace are web-, voice and mobile interfaces.

Access address:

http://www.wiwi.euv-frankfurt-o.de/wi-www/agent.htm

Contact person for question about the software:

Name: Frank Teuteberg

email: frank.teuteberg@uos.de

Efficient Agent Communication in Wireless Environments

Heikki Helin and Mikko Laukkanen

Abstract. In wireless environments, communication should be tailored to enable an efficient use of scarce and fluctuating data communication resources. In this chapter we consider software agent communication in such environments. We introduce a layered model of agent communication in the context of the FIPA agent architecture. We have designed and implemented efficient solutions for wireless agent communication for each layer of this communication stack. Further, we thoroughly analyze the performance of agent communication in slow wireless environments. The analysis shows that agent communication in wireless environments could be improved significantly as long as all communication layers in the agent communication stack are appropriately taken into account.

1. Introduction

The progress in wireless network technologies and mobile devices changes the ways in which people access services. A user may access the same services as she would using her desktop computer, but in the nomadic environment she is able to do so anywhere, at any time and even using a variety of different kinds of devices. Such an environment places new challenges on the architecture implementing the services. Nomadic environments differs from stationary environments in two fundamental ways. Firstly, the user may be situated in an environment, where multiple data communication networks may be available. Because of the different network types and characteristics of the networks, for instance the values of Quality-of-Service (QoS) parameters may change dramatically based on the network that the user is currently connected to. Secondly, the user may access the services using a variety of different mobile or stationary devices. The characteristics and limitations of a device dictates the constraints on how the user is able to access the services and what kind of content the user is provided with. Further, the other contextual parameters, such as user preferences, need to be taken into account. For instance,

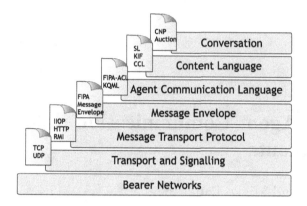

FIGURE 1. Agent communication layers

the user may prefer not having pictures at all, even if the terminal device and network connection would allow them.

We consider agent-to-agent communication over a wireless communication path. In wireless environments, the agents need to communicate efficiently and the communication should be reliable. Therefore, the communication stack should be tailored for the wireless environment. We will take a rather pragmatic view of agent communication. In particular, we neither consider why the agents are communicating, nor we consider the semantics of the messages. However, we assume that agents are communicating with each other and that at least a part of the communication path is implemented using wireless technology.

The rest of this chapter is structured as follows. In Section 2 we introduce a layered model of agent communication. Sections 3, 4, 5, 6, and 7 provide a performance analysis of message transport protocols, message envelopes, agent communication languages, content languages, and interaction protocols, respectively. Section 8 describes related research on using communicating agents in wireless environments. Finally, Section 9 summarizes our contributions.

2. Layered Model of Agent Communication

2.1. Overview of Agent Communication Stack

Figure 1 depicts a layered model of agent communication. The transport and signaling protocol layer should provide an efficient and reliable data transport service. Usually this layer should be transparent to agents. Therefore, the agents are typically unable to optimize anything at this layer by themselves. Given this, we will not discuss issues on this layer in more detail here. An overview of transport protocol issues in wireless environments can be found in [33], as an example.

A message transport protocol (MTP) defines the structure of messages sent using a transport protocol. Typically the MTP implicitly defines the transport protocol as well. Should this not be the case, the agents must agree on which transport protocol to use. FIPA has specified three message transport protocols: IIOP [10], HTTP [9], and WAP [11]. The transport layer and the message transport protocol layer do not necessarily differ at all from the communication in traditional distributed systems. What makes the agent communication different is how the communication above these two layers is modelled. Once the agents have agreed on these two protocols, they are able to transmit data between each other. However, to be able to exchange arbitrary data does not mean that agents can communicate meaningfully.

Given that several message transport protocols can be used, and these protocols can have different behaviour, FIPA has defined the concept of an envelope. The message envelope defines how the message should be routed, for example, among other parameters. The message envelope is sometimes independent of the MTP, but sometimes they are tightly coupled. An example of tight coupling is the IIOP protocol in the FIPA architecture. In this MTP, the message envelope is built-in to the protocol definition, that is, the IDL interface defines the structure of the message envelope. In this particular case, the tight coupling is well justified. In what follows, we assume that any concrete message envelope encoding can be used with any MTP with an obvious exception of IIOP MTP. This assumption gives us more freedom, but also introduces a problem that communicating agents should be able to agree on which concrete message envelope encoding to use. However, we do not consider that problem here.

Agent Communication Language (ACL) defines both the syntax and the semantics of agent messages. Several agent communication languages are developed, such as FIPA-ACL [13] and KQML [25]. The ACL layer consists of two sub-layers: An abstract layer that defines the semantics of the language and a concrete layer that defines the syntax of the language. For example, the abstract FIPA-ACL defines the message semantics, but is unconcerned with the encoding of the message; another layer defines the syntax of messages. FIPA has specified three encoding schemes for FIPA-ACL: String-based [5], XML-based [6], and bit-efficient [4].

Typically, an ACL lacks means for defining the content of the message. For example, by using the REQUEST communicative act in FIPA-ACL, the sender of the message applies to the receiver to perform some action. In ACL, the sender defines that the message is a REQUEST-message, but says nothing about the action that the receiver should perform. The action is described in the content language. FIPA content language library defines several content languages [14]. Each of these languages has one concrete encoding scheme, but in the future they may have different encoding schemes. To define the message content, the content language alone is insufficient, as it typically fails to define the terminology used in communication. Therefore, to have a common understanding of the message content, the communicating agents should share a common ontology.

The agent communication typically falls into common patterns. In FIPA specifications, these are called interaction protocols. Perhaps more typically in the literature these are called conversation protocols or conversation patterns. An interaction protocol defines a common pattern of conversations used to perform a task.

If only those choices defined by FIPA for various layers are taken into account, there are a total of 60 different possible combinations. If proprietary choices are taken into account, the number of possible combinations explodes drastically. Now, the problem is how the agents can efficiently agree on different issues. Usually, the environment reduces the appropriate possibilities. For example, when operating in a wireless environment, encoding schemes and protocols designed for these environments should be used. In these cases, the selection can be done using prior knowledge. On the other hand, even if the agent itself is operating in a wireless environment, the peer agent may be operating in a wireline environment and especially it may be unaware of the possibility of a wireless environment. In these cases, perhaps the best approach is to use a gateway that can perform necessary translations between incompatible choices [24, 27].

2.2. Analytical Performance Model

In wireless environments, the agents need to communicate efficiently and the communication should be reliable. Therefore, the communication stack discussed above should be tailored for the wireless environment. At the conversation layer communications patterns should be optimized so that agent message exchanges are carried out with a minimal number of round-trips. This is especially important when using a high-latency communication path. It is important to notice, that 'minimal' here does not necessarily mean the absolute minimal value; sometimes it is better to use more round-trips to achieve a better result. The encoding of the content language, the agent communication language, and the message envelope should be selected so that the scarce communication path is utilized as efficiently as possible. The MTP should be able to transfer messages over a wireless link reliably and efficiently. As noted earlier, selecting a message transport protocol may affect the selection of a transport protocol. For example, if the transport protocol is also reliable in wireless environments, the MTP implementation can be much simpler. Typically, however, this is not the case, and therefore reliability should be implemented into the MTP. In the following sections, we discuss these issues in more detail, and point out some optimization techniques.

The size of an agent message consists of six parts:

$$D_{msg} = D_{tp} + D_{mtp} + D_{env} + D_{acl} + D_{cl} + D_{ont} \tag{1}$$

To exchange messages efficiently, the D_{msg} should be minimized, which can be achieved by minimizing each component on the right side of the equation. Firstly, D_{tp} defines the overhead caused by the transport protocol. This component is typically dependent of other components. For example, one can easily determine the size of a TCP segment header. However, the total size of the other components defines how many TCP segments are necessary to transmit the whole message. Obviously, there are also other aspects that affect, such as the MTU size. Secondly,

D_{mtp} defines the overhead caused by the MTP. This is typically independent of other components; especially in each MTP defined by FIPA there is at most one MTP header by an agent message. Thirdly, D_{env} and D_{acl} define the overhead caused by the message envelope and the ACL, respectively. Fourthly, D_{cl} and D_{ont}, the overhead caused by the content language and the ontology, respectively. D_{ont} depends on D_{cl} because typically the content language defines how the terms in a given ontology are encoded into the message.

In the following sections, we consider reducing the overhead caused by each component. However, it is important to notice that although sometimes a minimal encoding of a given component is inappropriate. There are at least two reasons for this. Firstly, the computing power needed to encode the component may be too much compared to saving gained from efficient encoding. For example, assume the size of a given component is x bytes and the link bandwidth is $2x$ bytes per second. Now, if the component is encoded more efficiently giving the output size $3/4x$ bytes, but the encoding time is $1/2$ second, obviously the encoding was unnecessary and, more importantly, harmful. Such situation is likely when using mobile phones with very limited processing power. Secondly, having an efficient non-standard encoding scheme deteriorates interoperability. This is especially true in the transport protocol layer and in the message transport protocol layers, as usually network components that are not aware of agent systems must understand these layers. For example, although it is possible to define a transport protocol especially suitable for agent messages, such a protocol probably will not be widely accepted by the Internet community, and therefore it is an unattractive choice. On the other hand, the encoding of an ACL is an "agent-level" issue, and thus we have more freedom at that layer, as an example.

3. Message Transport Protocol Layer

In comparing the performance of the MTPs, we conducted exhaustive experiment in a simulated wireless environment. From possible MTPs, we selected IIOP, HTTP, Persistent HTTP (P-HTTP), WAP (CFW), Java RMI, and MAMAv2, which we will next analyze thoroughly. The IIOP and HTTP will used as specified by FIPA. The persistent HTTP (P-HTTP) is similar to that of HTTP protocol, but the sender does not close the TCP socket after receiving the reply, but uses the same TCP socket for subsequent messages. However, for each interaction protocol, two TCP sockets are needed, since the P-HTTP protocol allows only sending messaging to one direction over one TCP socket. The WAP implementation used in our evaluation is a WAP emulator in which message sequences are same as in WAP protocol. Therefore, we assume that the performance of our implementation and a real WAP are similar, since the protocol overhead as well as message sequences in these two protocols are about the same. Java RMI, although being a non-standard option, is taken into account because it is used in many FIPA-compliant agent platforms for intra-platform communication (e.g., in Jade [1]).

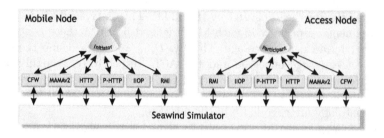

FIGURE 2. High-level overview of the MTP experiment configuration

The MAMAv2 protocol is designed by authors [26]. The objective of this protocol is to provide efficient and reliable agent message transport services over a (slow) wireless link for higher layers. As a basic service, the protocol offers a bi-directional semi-reliable message channel for the message transmission over a (wireless) link.

We use a typical client-server scenario to perform experiments, where the client (initiator) is executed at a mobile node and the server (participant) in an access node (see Figure 2). Each MTP we analyze using 8 different wireless network configurations (connection rates 9600bps, 28,800bps, 57,600bps, and 115,200bps; each with two propagation delay values (150ms and 300ms)), with three different conversation patterns (see Figure 3), and four different message payload sizes. The wireless link is simulated using the Seawind wireless link simulator [29]. Each experiment is repeated 11 times, but only 10 last repetitions are taken into account. The reason for this is that most of the software is implemented in Java and Java does some (heavy) initialization when particular classes are used first time.

In each case, four different payloads (message envelope + ACL) will be used. The smallest payload is about 0.5 kilobytes and largest about 10 kilobytes. Using a different size of ACL message generates different payload size, that is, the message envelope is constant through the experiment, about 250 bytes. However, the actual payload varies depending on the MTP. For example, in the IIOP protocol, the message envelope is expressed in terms of IDL. This means that fields are encoded using binary codes, and therefore the message envelope size in the IIOP protocol case is slightly smaller than with other MTPs. On the other hand, each MTP adds its own overhead. For example, in the HTTP protocol, the message headers are expressed using ASCII characters, which obviously increases the actual payload. This can be seen especially in those experiments where the message payload is small.

In the first test case, we initiate a FIPA-Query protocol [21] by sending a QUERY message to the participant. The participant replies by sending back an INFORM message to the initiator (see Figure 3 (a)). The purpose of this test is to measure the round-trip time in agent communication. In the second test case, we initiate a FIPA-Request protocol [22] by sending a REQUEST message to the

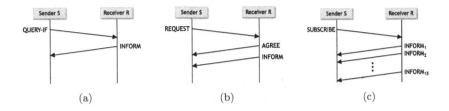

FIGURE 3. Message exchanges in interaction protocols used in the MTP evaluation

participant. The participant replies by sending back an AGREE message[1] and an INFORM message to the initiator (see Figure 3 (b)). Although this protocol is quite similar to that of the first case, this case is taken into account, as the FIPA-Request protocol is perhaps the most widely used interaction protocol in the FIPA archi-tecture. In the last test case, we use a subscription protocol, where the initiator first sends a SUBSCRIBE message, to which the participant replies by sending back a sequence (15) of INFORM messages to the initiator (see Figure 3 (c)).

3.1. Simple Round-Trip Case

Figure 4 compares the selected MTPs using FIPA-Query interaction protocol with 9600bps speed. Clearly, RMI protocol is the most inefficient. For example, having only 0.5kb payload and the slowest link, it takes more than 10 seconds to finish this interaction. Similarly, HTTP protocol is somewhat inefficient when the payload is small. This is due the fact that the protocol needs to open two TCP sockets, which takes most of the time when having small payload. However, for example in case (a) with 10kb payload, the HTTP is almost as efficient as MAMA and IIOP. In addition, the protocol overhead is bigger in HTTP, as HTTP headers are ASCII strings as well as MIME boundaries. MAMAv2 and IIOP protocols are about equally fast in these measurements. In the MAMAv2 protocol, no TCP sockets are opened during the interaction, but an existing TCP socket is used for all communication. IIOP protocol needs to open two TCP sockets. However, as noted earlier, the first interaction is not taken into account, and therefore IIOP performs reasonably well. The performance of the CFW protocol is the best in all cases, as was expected. However, it is important to note that the CFW protocol lacks sufficient reliability, and therefore its implementation is insufficient for real-life use, and therefore it is not directly comparable with other MTPs in this experiment. P-HTTP protocol is omitted in this case, as its performance would be exactly the same as HTTP protocol's. The results of FIPA-Query interaction using connection speeds 28,800bps, 57,600bps and, 115,200bps are similar to those of 9600bps.

Especially when the payload is small, an MTP that opens a new TCP socket for each message are highly inefficient. This was expected, because opening a TCP

---

[1] Although the AGREE message in the FIPA-Request protocol is optional, we use it here to show the negative effect of opening an "unnecessary" TCP socket in some MTPs.

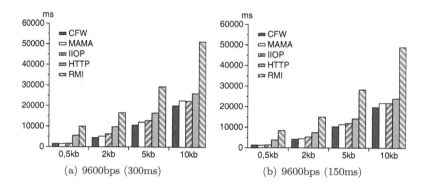

(a) 9600bps (300ms)   (b) 9600bps (150ms)

FIGURE 4. Comparison between MTPs using query interaction
with 9600bps connection speed

socket takes one round-trip, which is about 600 milliseconds when having 300
milliseconds propagation delay. Furthermore, in these cases, two TCP sockets are
needed for sending two messages, which means that almost 1.5 seconds is needed
just for opening the TCP socket. For example, when the payload is small, those
MTPs that do not need to open a TCP socket for each message can complete the
whole interaction in less than 1.5 seconds. Therefore, it is obvious that opening
a new TCP socket per message is highly inefficient in environments where the
propagation delay is relatively large.

3.2. FIPA-Request Case

Figure 5 compares MTPs using FIPA-Request interaction protocol using connection speed 28,800bps. As noted earlier, this interaction is quite similar to that of
FIPA-Query; the only difference is that the participant sends two replies instead
of one as in FIPA-Query interaction. Given the similarities of the interaction protocols, the results are also very similar. A difference to FIPA-Query case is that in
this experiment we also used P-HTTP MTP. As can be seen, the results P-HTTP
are quite similar to those of HTTP. This was expected, as the only difference between these two MTPs is that HTTP needs to open two TCP sockets for replies
where as P-HTTP needs only one. The results of FIPA-Request interaction using
other connection speeds are similar to those of 28,800bps.

3.3. Subscription Case

Figure 6 compares MTPs using the subscription interaction protocol using connection speeds 57,600bps and 115,200bps. In these results the effects of opening
a TCP socket for each message can be seen clearly. The performance of HTTP
and RMI is significantly worse than that of CFW, MAMAv2, IIOP, and P-HTTP.
The performance of P-HTTP is slightly worse than that of MAMAv2 and IIOP.
This was expected since the actual payload is larger in P-HTTP because of HTTP
headers. Furthermore, because of this, the relative difference is bigger when the

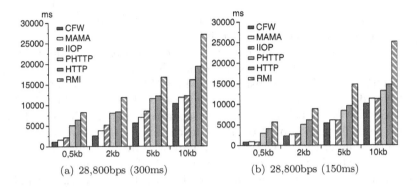

FIGURE 5. Comparison between MTPs using request interaction with 28,800bps connection speed

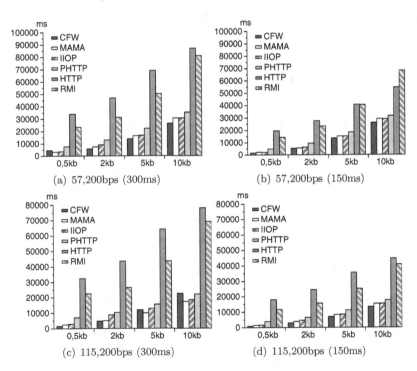

FIGURE 6. Comparison between MTPs using subscription interaction with 57,600bps and 115,200bps connection speeds

actual payload is smaller. For example, in 28,800bps connection speed with 300ms delay, the P-HTTP is about 2.2 times slower than MAMAv2 when the payload is 0.5kb, but only about 1.1 timer slower when the payload is 10kb. The actual time difference in both cases is about the same—about five seconds, which is due to more inefficient TCP socket usage in P-HTTP.

When there are more messages that just one or two in simple interactions between the mobile node and the fixed network, the difference between CFW, MA-MAv2, IIOP, and P-HTTP is insignificant. P-HTTP performs slightly worse the MAMAv2 and IIOP, mainly because of additional payload caused by HTTP headers and message envelope and ACL part separation mechanisms. On the other hand, the implementation of P-HTTP is much simpler than the other two protocols. Furthermore, the P-HTTP can be improved by carefully selecting which HTTP headers should be included in the message. If the communication is only between a mobile node and selected access node at the fixed network, not all HTTP headers mandated by FIPA specification [9] are necessary. Additionally, in such environments, the performance of P-HTTP can be improved by using the same TCP socket for messaging in both directions. Using HTTP or RMI is clearly not an option in such wireless environments we tested in this experiment, because of the bad performance.

4. Message Envelope Layer

In this section, we present a performance evaluation of message envelope encoding, and give a short analysis of the results. The selected encoding schemes are analyzed in number of output bytes needed for transmitting the message envelope.

We selected five different encoding schemes for the evaluation: IDL [10], Bit-efficient [7], XML [8], Binary-XML, and serialized Java object. In the FIPA-IIOP MTP [10], the message envelope is encoded to the GIOP message and all field codes are binary data. Therefore, this encoding is expected to be quite efficient in the number of bytes it produces. The syntax of the bit-efficient envelope is similar to that of FIPA-ACL [4]. This allows implementations to use (at least partially) same parser for envelopes as for ACL messages. XML DTD for message envelope is defined in [8]. This encoding scheme is expected to be highly verbose. Given the verbose syntax of XML, several binary-XML encoding schemes have been developed. For this evaluation, we choose the one provided by the WAP Forum [36]. This encoding allows two different ways to encode the message. Firstly, binary-XML can be used with or without special encoding tokens. We will evaluate both of these options, although neither of them is a FIPA standard. The last encoding scheme, serialized Java object, is not a FIPA standard, but it is widely used in intra-platform communication. The actual object we will use in this experiment is Jade's Envelope class [1].

All the experiments are conducted in a Linux environment using the Jade agent platform (version 2.5) [1] with JDK1.3. Here we do not analyze other aspects of concrete message envelope syntaxes, such as construction or parsing time of a message envelope. The main reason for this is that most of the encoding options used in this evaluation are experimental software, and therefore we believe that

TABLE 1. Comparison of FIPA message envelope transport encoding options

	Bit-Efficient	IIOP	bXML (w /codes)	bXML (plain)	XML	Object
Case 1	33	153 (464%)	90 (273%)	205 (621%)	346 (1048%)	1421 (4306%)
Case 2	179	337 (188%)	262 (146%)	473 (264%)	671 (375%)	1694 (946%)
Case 3	694	973 (140%)	843 (121%)	1154 (166%)	1844 (266%)	2790 (402%)

the results would not been comparable. We analyze construction and parsing times of ACL messages in the next section. As the encoding options for ACL are similar to those of message envelopes, similar results are expected.

We chose three different message envelopes for this experiment. The first case can be considered as a minimal message envelope. Additionally, the field values are minimal, that is, only a one byte in the most cases. This, obviously, is not a realistic message envelope, but was chosen to demonstrate the relative difference of the additional overhead caused by different encoding schemes. The second one is the same as the first one, but the field values are more realistic. The last case covers all the aspects of the message envelope.

Table 1 gives the number of bytes of message envelope transport syntaxes in three cases using all the selected encoding options. The bit-efficient message envelope is the most compact in all cases. This was expected. However, when the message envelope size increases, the relative difference decreases, especially when compared to IDL and binary XML. The reason for this is, that in the case of big message envelope, the ratio between additional overhead and the message envelope information content (i.e., the field values) increases. None of the selected encoding schemes handles the information content efficiently. As was also expected, the XML encoding and Java object serialization produces big message sizes. But, again, the relative difference decreases when the message envelope size increases. However, for example, in the case of Object serialization, the output size is still about four times bigger than the output size of bit-efficient encoding even in the case of big envelope. The binary-XML encoding shows its power in the case where the information content is small. In these cases using predefined tokens, the output size is much smaller than using the same encoding without predefined tokens. Also, using binary-XML with predefined the output is smaller than in the case of IDL encoding. Without predefined tokens, the output size of binary-XML is bigger than using IDL encoding.

5. Agent Communication Layer

In this section, we analyze the performance of different ACL encoding options. We selected four test cases to find out the performance of different encoding options. These test cases are the same as in message envelope experiment. Then, we selected five alternative methods to encode FIPA-ACL messages, which we compare against the bit-efficient encoding, totaling six different methods for ACL encoding. Firstly, the string-based FIPA-ACL encoding is measured. Especially we use the string encoding as provided by the Jade agent platform. Secondly, a standard XML-based FIPA-ACL encoding is measured. Thirdly, the binary-XML encoding is measured. As with the message envelope experiment, we use binary-XML both with special encoding tokens and without them. Fourthly, the standard Java serialization to output Jade's `ACLMessage` class is measured. Although this method is not a FIPA-compliant way to exchange ACL messages, it is, for example, used in Jade's internal communication when the agents are located on different hosts but belong to the same agent platform (that is, when Java RMI is used). Lastly, as the string-based messages are text information, we also analyze the deflate compression algorithm to compress the ACL messages. The implementation of this algorithm is the one included in JDK1.3 (`DeflaterOutputStream`). Notice that this encoding is not a FIPA-compliant solution. In this case, we also analyzed two different cases. In the first case, the message to compressed in encoded using the string encoding and in the second case using the XML encoding. In both cases, the message stream is reset after each message, which means that the same code table cannot be used in subsequent message. In the measurements, we use Intel Pentium II (366Mhz) laptop (Toshiba Portégé 7020CT) with 128Mb of main memory, Linux 2.2.14, JDK1.3 and Jade 2.3 Agent Platform.

5.1. Results Encoded Output Size

Table 2 shows the results of the output size measurement in bytes. In this case, we use the bit-efficient FIPA-ACL without a dynamic code table. We will analyze the effects of using the code table later. As can be seen in Table 2, the bit-efficient encoding gives the smallest output in all cases, as was expected. However, the difference between binary-XML with special tokens and the bit-efficient encoding is insignificant. Also, the difference between the deflate encoding and the bit-efficient is small. But, neither the deflate encoding nor the binary-XML are a FIPA-compliant solutions, and therefore cannot be used in a general case. The XML encoding output size is about twice as big as the string-based encoding. This was also expected. The serialized `ACLMessage` output size is notably big. This is because the Java serialization outputs the class description to each `ObjectOutputStream` to which the serialized objects are written. However, the class description is output only once to each stream, that is, if two or more objects are written to the same stream, the class description is written only once. In our measurements, we use a different stream for each message, and therefore several class descriptions are needed. While this may seem unfair, it is actually the most common case. For

TABLE 2. The output size in bytes

		Case 1	Case 2	Case 3	Case 4
Bit-efficient	Send	175	161	167	503
	Recv	371	168	1800	2339
bXML	Send	195 (111%)	182 (113%)	188 (113%)	565 (112%)
	Recv	409 (110%)	188 (188%)	2000 (111%)	2597 (111%)
bXML(plain)	Send	353 (202%)	342 (212%)	348 (208%)	1043 (207%)
	Recv	722 (195%)	345 (205%)	3570 (198%)	4637 (198%)
XML	Send	638 (365%)	626 (383%)	632 (378%)	1896 (377%)
	Recv	1294 (348%)	630 (375%)	6420 (357%)	8344 (357%)
String	Send	351 (212%)	339 (211%)	345 (207%)	1035 (206%)
	Recv	720 (194%)	343 (204%)	3550 (197%)	4613 (197%)
String (cmpr)	Send	204 (117%)	203 (126%)	211 (126%)	618 (122%)
	Recv	422 (113%)	208 (124%)	2165 (120%)	2795 (120%)
ACL Object	Send	1408 (805%)	1380 (857%)	1392 (834%)	4172 (829%)
	Recv	2854 (769%)	1394 (830%)	14144 (786%)	18384 (786%)

TABLE 3. Time to construct the messages (in milliseconds)

Bit-efficient		String		String (deflate)		ACL object	
Send	Recv	Send	Recv	Send	Recv	Send	Recv
Case 1							
3.24	4.42	4.22	6.30	9.40	12.64	107.62	117.92
		(130%)	(143%)	(290%)	(286%)	(3321%)	(2668%)
Case 2							
3.16	3.35	4.14	4.30	9.28	9.88	106.76	106.12
		(131%)	(128%)	(294%)	(295%)	(3379%)	(3168%)
Case 3							
3.32	11.68	4.32	21.46	9.24	38.30	106.36	149.82
		(130%)	(184%)	(278%)	(328%)	(3204%)	(1283%)
Case 4							
5.20	14.56	7.94	26.98	15.68	47.86	115.64	163.24
		(152%)	(199%)	(301%)	(329%)	(2223%)	(1121%)

example, when using Java RMI, a separate ObjectOutputStream has to be created for each invocation.

5.2. Constructing and Parsing Messages

In the second measurement, we analyze how long it takes to construct the output for different encoding schemes. The XML-based encoding schemes are left out in these measurements, as the parsers for these are too experimental for the results being comparable to other encoding schemes. Table 3 provides the results of these measurements. Each test is repeated 50 times and results (averages) are given in milliseconds. In these measurements we first create a Jade ACLMessage object of a

TABLE 4. Time to parse the messages (in milliseconds)

Bit-efficient		String		String (deflate)		ACL object	
Send	Recv	Send	Recv	Send	Recv	Send	Recv
Case 1							
16.14	18.32	24.70	31.08	27.48	40.48	144.88	151.58
		(153%)	(170%)	(170%)	(220%)	(898%)	(827%)
Case 2							
16.04	15.60	24.66	24.84	27.74	27.60	143.68	144.38
		(154%)	(159%)	(173%)	(177%)	(896%)	(926%)
Case 3							
15.42	41.24	24.88	93.08	27.68	186.76	144.02	211.22
		(161%)	(226%)	(180%)	(453%)	(934%)	(512%)
Case 4							
20.86	49.40	36.36	125.98	52.72	262.98	158.52	233.28
		(174%)	(255%)	(252%)	(532%)	(759%)	(472%)

FIPA-ACL message and then generate the encoded output of the message from this object. The time to create the `ACLMessage` object is not calculated in the results. As can be seen in Table 3, the bit-efficient encoding is the fastest in all cases, but the difference to the string-based encoding is insignificant. This was expected, since creating a string-based FIPA-ACL message is just outputting strings; there is little to optimize. The low performance of the deflate algorithm is due to a fact that after uncompressing the message, it still have to be parsed in order to create a Java object. This phase is included in the process of parsing the bit-efficient encoding. Furthermore, the deflate algorithm gives a slightly larger output than the bit-efficient encoding scheme (see Table 2). Creating serialized objects is also surprisingly slow. The reason for this is that creating a new `ObjectOutputStream` is a slow operation.

In the third measurement, we measure the parsing time of an encoded message, that is, how long it takes to create a Jade `ACLMessage` object from an encoded stream. In all cases, the data is first read into a memory buffer, and the time needed for this is excluded in the results. Table 4 gives the results of this measurement. Again, the bit-efficient encoding is the fastest. Further, in this measurement it is much faster than any other encoding scheme we measured. The main reasons for this are that (1) a very few string comparisons are needed to parse the message and that (2) our bit-efficient FIPA-ACL implementation, instead of allocating new memory, tries to reuse already allocated memory whenever possible. The method is an efficient method for optimizing Java programs.

5.3. Effects of Dynamic Code Table in Bit-efficient ACL

In all the cases analyzed above we used the bit-efficient FIPA-ACL encoding without the dynamic code table. Before the measurements, we believed that using the dynamic code table should give a better compression ratio, but the code table

TABLE 5. Number of bytes using different cache sizes

No cache		2^8		2^9		2^{10}		2^{15}	
Send	Recv	Send	Recv	Send	Recv	Send	Recv	Send	Recv
Case 1									
175	371	175	249	175	257	175	257	175	257
		(100%)	(67%)	(100%)	(69%)	(100%)	(69%)	(100%)	(69%)
Case 2									
161	168	161	168	161	168	161	168	161	168
		(100%)	(100%)	(100%)	(100%)	(100%)	(100%)	(100%)	(100%)
Case 3									
167	1800	167	792	167	864	167	864	167	864
		(100%)	(44%)	(100%)	(48%)	(100%)	(48%)	(100%)	(48%)
Case 4									
503	2339	354	1063	364	1152	364	1152	364	1152
		(70%)	(45%)	(72%)	(49%)	(72%)	(49%)	(72%)	(49%)

management might slow down both constructing the output and parsing the input as the code table is implemented in Java. However, as the result will show, the code table management slows down neither constructing time nor parsing time.

First, we analyze the size of the encoded message. As can be seen in Table 5, using the code table provides a more compact output, but only if there are enough messages to encode. This can be seen especially in the Case 4, where the coding scheme without the code table provides 2339 bytes of output in incoming traffic, while using the code table provides 1063 bytes of output. Using the code table with a larger size than 2^8 gives a slightly larger output, because of the two-byte cache indexes. However, when encoding a large number of messages, it is expected that using a larger code table give a more compact output.

Next we analyze how long it takes to construct the encoded output using different cache sizes. Table 6 shows the results of this measurement. A coding scheme without a code table is fastest when having only one or at most a few messages. This was expected, since when the code table is used, the encoder tries to find every string in the code table, which takes some time. However, when there are several messages and the encoder actually finds something in the code table, the process of constructing messages becomes faster. The reason for this is that when the encoder should output a string to the encoded message, it must copy it there, while if the string is found in the code table, it only has to output the corresponding index to the encoded message (one or two byte(s)). Similar results are also achieved when the parsing time is measured (see Table 7). The difference, however, is less significant than in constructing messages. The reason for this is that the code table lookups are much faster when decoding the message.

TABLE 6. Time to create messages using different cache sizes (in milliseconds)

No cache		2^8		2^9		2^{10}		2^{15}	
Send	Recv	Send	Recv	Send	Recv	Send	Recv	Send	Recv
Case 1									
3.40	4.40	4.12	4.96	4.22	4.98	4.28	5.10	4.20	5.24
		(121%)	(112%)	(124%)	(113%)	(125%)	(116%)	(124%)	(119%)
Case 2									
3.30	3.36	4.10	4.24	4.14	4.18	4.12	4.14	4.08	4.24
		(124%)	(126%)	(125%)	(124%)	(125%)	(123%)	(124%)	(126%)
Case 3									
3.28	11.78	4.24	9.92	4.18	9.96	4.20	9.98	4.12	10.00
		(129%)	(84%)	(127%)	(85%)	(128%)	(85%)	(126%)	(85%)
Case 4									
5.16	14.54	5.88	12.06	5.98	12.16	6.00	12.18	5.84	12.14
		(114%)	(83%)	(116%)	(84%)	(116%)	(84%)	(113%)	(83%)

TABLE 7. Time to parse messages using different cache sizes (in milliseconds)

No cache		2^8		2^9		2^{10}		2^{15}	
Send	Recv	Send	Recv	Send	Recv	Send	Recv	Send	Recv
Case 1									
13.78	15.14	13.84	14.68	13.90	14.76	13.88	14.64	13.94	14.74
		(100%)	(97%)	(101%)	(97%)	(101%)	(97%)	(101%)	(97%)
Case 2									
13.80	13.88	13.88	13.94	13.94	13.88	13.90	13.90	13.82	13.90
		(101%)	(100%)	(101%)	(100%)	(101%)	(100%)	(100%)	(100%)
Case 3									
13.80	25.12	13.92	19.26	14.00	19.64	13.90	19.78	13.92	19.76
		(101%)	(71%)	(101%)	(78%)	(101%)	(79%)	(101%)	(79%)
Case 4									
16.14	28.88	15.56	21.68	15.70	22.06	15.72	22.26	15.74	22.16
		(96%)	(75%)	(97%)	(76%)	(97%)	(77%)	(98%)	(77%)

6. Content Language Layer

A content language is used to express the actual content of a communication between agents. Each language specified in the FIPA-CLL [14] has only one concrete transport encoding syntax. Further, in each case either a string s-expression or XML is used. Given this, they are not in general suitable for environments where slow wireless links are involved. Obviously, having an efficient encoding of the message envelope and the FIPA-ACL does not help much, if the actual message content is expressed using a verbose encoding.

In following, we explore different options for encoding FIPA-SL and FIPA-CCL. We believe that the results can be generalized to any similar content language. In this experiment, we evaluate only the output size of different encoding options. Other features, such as the parsing time, are excluded because lack of mature enough implementations.

6.1. The Case of FIPA-SL

For FIPA-SL content language [23] evaluation we choose four different encoding schemes for FIPA-SL. Firstly, the standard s-expression is evaluated. This encoding option is the only one specified by FIPA. Secondly, we use deflate algorithm to encode the s-expression syntax. As the s-expression syntax is string, we believe that this option can give good results. Thirdly, we use XML encoding. Lastly, we use binary-XML. As with the message envelope encoding and FIPA-ACL encoding, we use binary-XML both with and without special encoding tokens.

For the experiment, we choose three FIPA-SL expressions, that is, message contents. The first two are simple and typical messages used with communication with the AMS. The third expression is a somewhat more complicated and contains more data than the other expression.

Table 8 shows the results of the output size measurements in bytes. The s-expression encoding and binary-XML with special tokens gives a similar performance; binary-XML being slightly better. Although s-expression encoding is plain text encoding, it does not contain that much additional overhead. On the other hand, the source format, that is XML, for binary-XML is so verbose, that even the binary version cannot produce small output. The output of the XML encoding is the largest, as was expected. The deflate algorithm gives better output if the message to encode is large enough. But even if the message is small, the deflate algorithm is only a slight worse than binary-XML and s-expression encoding schemes. Given this, it seems that using the deflate algorithm to encode the message content is the best solution when sending messages over a (slow) wireless link. Obviously, the deflate algorithm needs more processing power than the other options, because after the message content is decompressed, it still have to be parsed. Therefore, if the processing power is limited, the s-expression seems to be the best solution, assuming that the message content is relatively small.

6.2. The Case of FIPA-CCL

For FIPA-CCL content language [12] evaluation, we choose the same options as with the case of FIPA-SL. However, the s-expression encoding is excluded, as there is no s-expression syntax for FIPA-CCL. Obviously, we could define such syntax, but there is no real reason for doing so. Therefore, the encoding options we will use in the FIPA-CCL experiment are XML, binary-XML (with and without special encoding tokens), and deflated XML.

For the experiment, we choose three FIPA-CCL expressions, which are not semantically the same as in the case of FIPA-SL experiment. We could not use the same expression as in the case of FIPA-SL experiment, because these two

TABLE 8. Comparison of selected FIPA-SL encoding options in number of bytes

	S-Expression	bXML	bXML (plain)	Deflate	XML
Example 1	222	172	303	224	558
		(77%)	(136%)	(101%)	(251%)
Example 2	229	177	314	232	572
		(77%)	(137%)	(101%)	(250%)
Example 3	682	661	865	378	2275
		(97%)	(127%)	(55%)	(334%)
Total	1133	1010	1482	456	3405
		(89%)	(131%)	(40%)	(301%)

TABLE 9. Comparison of selected FIPA-CCL encoding options in number of bytes

	bXML	bXML(plain)	Deflate	XML
Example 1	335	548	297	885
		(164%)	(89%)	(264%)
Example 2	433	676	340	1125
		(156%)	(79%)	(260%)
Example 3	418	679	336	1122
		(162%)	(80%)	(268%)
Total	1186	1903	486	3132
		(160%)	(41%)	(264%)

content languages are developed for different purposes. The results of the output size measurements in bytes of the FIPA-CCL experiment are given in Table 9. The results are similar to those of the FIPA-SL experiment. The deflate algorithm and binary-XML with special tokens gives similar output. The binary-XML without special tokens is slightly worse and plain XML encoding is much worse than any other option.

7. Conversation Layer

Ongoing conversations between agents often fall into typical patterns, which can be described as a series of states linked by transitions. Given the certain state of a conversation, the participants can send and/or expect only certain messages. These patterns of message exchange are called interaction protocols [17]. FIPA has defined several interaction protocols, including simple ones such as FIPA Request [22] and FIPA Query [21], and more complicated ones such as FIPA Contract Net [18] and FIPA Auction English [16].

The use of interaction protocols eases the agent implementation, especially, when an agent is performing tasks that are irrelevant in achieving its goal, such

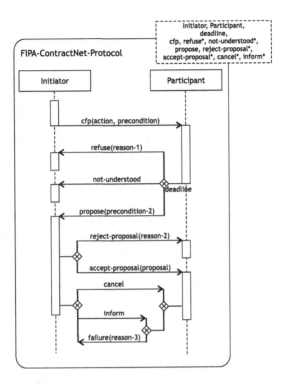

FIGURE 7. FIPA Contract Net interaction protocol

as the registration into a management system or into a directory service. In these cases, by carefully following the interaction protocol, an agent does not have be "smart" to take care of necessary administrative tasks.

The FIPA Contract Net protocol [15] is FIPA's version of the most well-known task sharing protocol called contract net [35]. In the FIPA Contract Net interaction protocol the initiator (contractor) sends a "call for proposals" (CFP) to several participants (contractees) requesting proposals to perform a given action (see Figure 7). The participants send their proposals back to the contractor. From these proposals, the contractor selects the most desired one, and sends an ACCEPT-PROPOSAL message to the sender of the selected proposal and a REJECT-PROPOSAL message to the others. Furthermore, the contractor can define a timeout for how long it will wait for proposals. If it does not receive all proposals in this time, it selects one from the received ones and rejects all subsequent proposals. Finally, the selected contractee sends an INFORM message to the contractor once it has performed the requested action.

Now, let us assume that the contractor resides at the mobile node, and n of the contractees resides in the fixed network. To finish the protocol, about $n * 3$ messages are sent over the wireless link. If we assume that one message contains

2 kilobytes of data and n is 10, more than 60 kilobytes of data is transferred over the link to accomplish the protocol. Having a slow link, such as a GSM data link, it takes more than one minute just to send these messages.

Interaction protocols could be improved for wireless environments. The main idea here is to reduce messages sent over wireless communication path. For example, the contractor can nominate a proxy agent in a fixed network to accomplish the interaction protocol, or using mobile agent technology the contractor can itself migrate to the fixed network and communicate with contractees over the fixed network. In both cases, some additional data is sent over the link. Nominating another agent to accomplish the interaction protocol needs some messages, and if the contractor migrates over the link, its code and state is transferred over the link.

The FIPA Propose protocol [20] was defined with slow wireless links in mind. In a way, it is a version of FIPA Contract Net protocol, where the CFP communicative act as well as the last INFORM communicative act are removed. In this protocol, the initiator agent sends a PROPOSE communicative act to the participant agent proposing that it (the initiator) will perform some action. The participant agent may either accept (ACCEPT-PROPOSAL) or reject (REJECT-PROPOSAL) this proposal.

The interaction protocol in a nomadic environment can be selected based on the current situation. For example, having a low-bandwidth connection, an agent can choose an interaction protocol that requires modest bandwidth, but therefore produces only sub-optimal results. Alternatively, when using more bandwidth is possible, an agent can choose an interaction protocol that requires more bandwidth and thereby produces better results. This selection, however, involves a careful analysis of the protocol; how many round-trips are necessary and how much data is needed. Additionally, some of this analysis must be done at the runtime, as it is impossible in general to predict the way possible opponents act.

8. Related Work

LEAP (Lightweight Extensible Agent Platform) [2] was the first FIPA compliant agent platform running on PDAs and mobile phones. For agent communication in wireless environments, the LEAP platform provides a protocol called JICP [3] for intra-platform communication. This protocol seems to be efficient in number of overhead bytes, but on the other hand, this protocol—even though designed for unreliable wireless communication paths—provides insufficient reliability. For example, messages might get duplicated during an unexpected disconnection, that is, the same message may get delivered to the ultimate destination more than once.

MicroFIPA-OS [32] is an agent development toolkit and platform based on the FIPA-OS toolkit. This system targets at medium to high-end PDA devices that have sufficient resources to execute PersonalJava compatible virtual machine.

The MicroFIPA-OS architecture is extensible by plugging in components that either replace or extend the architecture. An example of this kind of contribution is FIPA Nomadic Application Support [19], which provides support for wireless environments, including components for efficient message transport over slow wireless communication paths [31]. For example, The FIPA Nomadic Application Support incorporates the bit-efficient envelope and ACL messages discussed earlier.

Yet another example of providing an agent platform to wireless environments is A-Globe [34]. Unlike LEAP and MicroFIPA-OS, A-Globe is not FIPA compliant agent platform. However, this relaxation gives more freedom to design components for wireless communication and therefore more efficient solution can be made. The obvious drawback is that agent on A-Globe platform cannot directly communicate with agent residing on LEAP or MicroFIPA-OS platforms.

Several other attempts have been developed in order to enable agents in small devices (e.g., PDAs and mobile phones). However, very seldom the properties of wireless communication paths are taken appropriately into account, but these systems rely on communication solutions designed for reliable and fast wireline connections.

Another option for agent communication is to use Web Services standards for delivering ACL messages between agents [28]. However, when considering wireless communication paths, the same problems as with FIPA-style communication will remain (see for example [30]).

9. Conclusions

We performed a performance analysis of agent communication in wireless environments. At the lowest layer—transport and signaling layer—the agent communication should not be different from the communication in other distributed systems; hence we gave only a brief overview of this layer's issues. At the MTP layer, we examined the MTPs specified by FIPA and provided an exhaustive performance evaluation of various protocols. Further, we have designed and implemented a MTP called MAMAv2, which performs well in slow wireless networks. At the message envelope layer and the ACL layer, the most important factor in nomadic environments is efficiency, assuming that the MTP layer provides sufficient reliability as it should. We compared standard message envelope transport encoding options, and concluded that the bit-efficient encoding is the most efficient in number of bytes. The bit-efficient envelope encoding scheme is designed and implemented by us. The XML envelope syntax, as was expected, was the most verbose syntax. Similar comparison was made with ACL transport encoding options, providing similar results. Furthermore, we showed that bit-efficient ACL transport encoding is not only more space-efficient but also more efficient to process. For example, parsing bit-efficiently encoded messages is faster than parsing any other standard transport encoding. Space-efficiency is naturally an important feature in nomadic environments, but faster handling of messages becomes important when either the processing power is limited or a great deal of messages should be handled. The former is true in today's low-end mobile devices and the latter can be expected to happen in the future when agent technology is employed on a large scale. The bit-efficient ACL encoding scheme is designed and implemented by us, and it is freely available for Jade agent platform. Finally, we performed a similar performance analysis of two content languages, namely FIPA-SL and FIPA-CCL. For these languages, we have designed and implemented binary-XML encoding schemes,

References

[1] Fabio Bellifemine, Agostino Poggi, and Giovanni Rimassa. JADE — A FIPA-compliant agent framework. In *Proceedings of the 4th International Conference on the Practical Applications of Agents and Multi-Agent Systems (PAAM-99)*, pages 97–108, London, UK, 1999. The Practical Application Company Ltd.

[2] Federico Bergenti, Agostino Poggi, Bernard Burg, and Giovanni Caire. Deploying FIPA-compliant systems on handheld devices. *IEEE Internet Computing*, 5(4):20–25, 2001.

[3] Giovanni Caire, Nicolas Lhuillier, and Giovanni Rimassa. A communication protocol for agents on handheld devices. In *Workshop on Ubiquitous Agents on Embedded, Wearable and Mobile Devices*, Bologna, Italy, July 2002.

[4] Foundation for Intelligent Physical Agents. *FIPA ACL Message Representation in Bit-Efficient Specification*. Geneva, Switzerland, October 2000. Specification number XC00069.

[5] Foundation for Intelligent Physical Agents. *FIPA ACL Message Representation in String Specification*. Geneva, Switzerland, November 2000. Specification number XC00070.

[6] Foundation for Intelligent Physical Agents. *FIPA ACL Message Representation in XML Specification*. Geneva, Switzerland, October 2000. Specification number XC00071.

[7] Foundation for Intelligent Physical Agents. *FIPA Agent Message Transport Envelope Representation in Bit Efficient Specification*. Geneva, Switzerland, November 2000. Specification number XC00088.

[8] Foundation for Intelligent Physical Agents. *FIPA Agent Message Transport Envelope Representation in XML Specification*. Geneva, Switzerland, November 2000. Specification number XC00085.

[9] Foundation for Intelligent Physical Agents. *FIPA Agent Message Transport Protocol for HTTP Specification*. Geneva, Switzerland, October 2000. Specification number XC00084.

[10] Foundation for Intelligent Physical Agents. *FIPA Agent Message Transport Protocol for IIOP Specification*. Geneva, Switzerland, November 2000. Specification number XC00075.

[11] Foundation for Intelligent Physical Agents. *FIPA Agent Message Transport Protocol for WAP Specification*. Geneva, Switzerland, October 2000. Specification number XC00076.

[12] Foundation for Intelligent Physical Agents. *FIPA CCL Content Language Specification*. Geneva, Switzerland, October 2000. Specification number XC00009.

[13] Foundation for Intelligent Physical Agents. *FIPA Communicative Act Library Specification*. Geneva, Switzerland, November 2000. Specification number XC00037.

[14] Foundation for Intelligent Physical Agents. *FIPA Content Languages Specification*. Geneva, Switzerland, October 2000. Specification number XC00007.

[15] Foundation for Intelligent Physical Agents. *FIPA Contract Net Interaction Protocol Specification*. Geneva, Switzerland, October 2000. Specification number XC00029.

[16] Foundation for Intelligent Physical Agents. *FIPA English Auction Interaction Protocol Specification*. Geneva, Switzerland, October 2000. Specification number XC00031.

[17] Foundation for Intelligent Physical Agents. *FIPA Interaction Protocol Library Specification*. Geneva, Switzerland, October 2000. Specification number XC00025.

[18] Foundation for Intelligent Physical Agents. *FIPA Iterated Contract Net Interaction Protocol Specification*. Geneva, Switzerland, October 2000. Specification number XC00030.

[19] Foundation for Intelligent Physical Agents. *FIPA Nomadic Application Support Specification*. Geneva, Switzerland, November 2000. Specification number XC00014.

[20] Foundation for Intelligent Physical Agents. *FIPA Propose Interaction Protocol Specification*. Geneva, Switzerland, October 2000. Specification number XC00036.

[21] Foundation for Intelligent Physical Agents. *FIPA Query Interaction Protocol Specification*. Geneva, Switzerland, October 2000. Specification number XC00027.

[22] Foundation for Intelligent Physical Agents. *FIPA Request Interaction Protocol Specification*. Geneva, Switzerland, October 2000. Specification number XC00026.

[23] Foundation for Intelligent Physical Agents. *FIPA SL Content Language Specification*. Geneva, Switzerland, November 2000. Specification number XC00008.

[24] Foundation for Intelligent Physical Agents. *FIPA Messaging Interoperability Service Specification*. Geneva, Switzerland, August 2001. Specification number PC00093.

[25] Rich Fritzson, Tim Finin, Don McKay, and Robin McEntire. KQML — A language and protocol for knowledge and information exchange. In *Proceedings of the Thirteenth International Workshop on Distributed Artificial Intelligence*, pages 126–136, Seattle, WA, USA, July 1994.

[26] Heikki Helin. Supporting nomadic agent-based applications in FIPA agent architecture. PhLic. Thesis, Series of Publications C, Number C-2001-63, University of Helsinki, Department of Computer Science, Helsinki, Finland, December 2001.

[27] Heikki Helin and Stefano Campadello. Providing messaging interoperability in FIPA communication architecture. In Krysztof Zieliński, Kurt Geihs, and Aleksander Laurentowski, editors, *New Developments in Distributed Applications and Interoperable System. Proceedings of the Third IFIP TC6/WG6.1 International Working Conference on Distributed Applications and Interoperable Systems (DAIS'01)*, pages 121–126, Krakow, Poland, September 2001. Kluwer Academic Publishers.

[28] Michael N. Huhns. Agents as web services. *IEEE Internet Computing*, 6(4):93–95, 2002.

[29] Markku Kojo, Andrei Gurtov, Jukka Manner, Pasi Sarolahti, Timo Alanko, and Kimmo Raatikainen. Seawind: A wireless network emulator. In *Proceedings of 11th*

GI/ITG Conference on Measuring, Modelling and Evaluation of Computer and Communication Systems, Aachen, Germany, September 2001.

[30] Mikko Laukkanen and Heikki Helin. Web services in wireless networks—what happened to the performance? In Liang-Jie Zhang, editor, *Proceedings of the International Conference on Web Services (ICWS'03)*, pages 278–284, Las Vegas, USA, June 2003. CSREA Press.

[31] Mikko Laukkanen, Heikki Helin, and Heimo Laamanen. Supporting nomadic agent-based applications in the FIPA agent architecture. In Cristiano Castelfranci and W. Lewis Johnson, editors, *Proceedings of the First International Joint Conference on Autonomous Agents & Multi-Agent Systems (AAMAS 2002)*, pages 1348–1355, Bologna, Italy, July 2002.

[32] Mikko Laukkanen, Sasu Tarkoma, and Jani Leinonen. FIPA-OS agent platform for small-footprint devices. In John-Jules Meyer and Milind Tambe, editors, *Intelligent Agents VIII, Proceedings of the Eighth International Workshop on Agent Theories, Architectures, and Languages (ATAL-2001)*, volume 2333 of *Lecture Notes in Artificial Intelligence*, pages 447–460. Springer-Verlag: Heidelberg, Germany, 2002.

[33] G. Montenegro, S. Dawkins, M. Kojo, V. Magret, and N. Vaidya. Long thin networks. Request for Comments 2757, January 2000.

[34] David Šišlák, Milan Rollo, and Michal Pěchouček. A-globe: Agent platform with inaccessibility and mobility support. In Matthias Klusch, Sascha Ossowski, Vipul Kashyap, and Rainer Unland, editors, *Cooperative Information Agents VIII*, pages 199–214, 2004.

[35] R. G. Smith. The contract net protocol: High level communication and control in a distributed problem solver. *IEEE Transactions on Computers*, C-29(12):1104–1113, December 1980.

[36] Wireless Application Protocol Forum. *Binary XML Content Format Specification*, November 1999. Version 04-Nov-1999.

Information about Software

Software is available on the Internet as
    ( ) prototype version
    (•) full fledged software (freeware), version no.: N/A
    ( ) full fledged software (for money), version no.:
    ( ) Demo/trial version
    ( ) not (yet) available
Internet address:
    Description of software: Bit-efficient encoding of ACL messages for Jade
    Download address: http://jade.tilab.com/

Heikki Helin and Mikko Laukkanen
TeliaSonera Finland
P.O.Box 970
FIN-00051 Sonera
Finland
e-mail: Heikki.J.Helin@teliasonera.com, Mikko.Laukkanen@teliasonera.com

AMETAS – the Asynchronous MEssage Transfer Agent System

Michael Zapf

Abstract. AMETAS is a Java-based environment for creating and running mobile, autonomous agents. Some of its characteristic aspects are the 3-tier-oriented structure of applications, the restriction to pure message passing between the components, the security subsystem, and the flexible mediation subsystem which may employ declarative type descriptions for finding agents. In this article we will provide details about these aspects, also including application notes.

Keywords. Mobile autonomous agents, message passing, type system, security.

1. Introduction

AMETAS, an acronym for "Asynchronous message transfer agent system" was created at the University of Frankfurt as a platform for exploring concepts for agent type systems. Since 2002, AMETAS is distributed by the company *accsis GmbH* [1].

The latest versions of AMETAS requires the use of a Java Runtime Environment 1.4 or higher. All applications written for AMETAS are created within Java, including features like JNI (Java native interface) for specific solutions beyond the capabilities of pure Java programming.

The main target of AMETAS is not to provide an environment for lean, highly efficient, mobile agents. Instead, the system encourages a definite notion of *agent-oriented software engineering* which puts emphasis on the autonomy of each part of a multi-agent application.

AMETAS does not require agents to implement specific patterns of behavior, and it does not provide auxiliary components for supporting deductive algorithms for distributed problem solving. This does *not* mean that AMETAS may not be used to write *intelligent agents*. Neither is it required to write agents which *migrate* at some point of their lifetime. *Intelligence* and *mobility* are matters of design

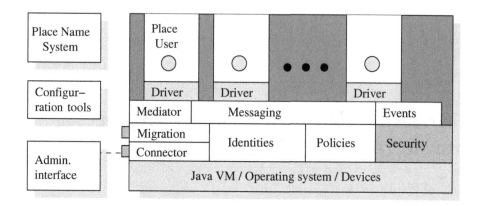

FIGURE 1. AMETAS components

and implementation of applications. To enforce autonomy, in our view the most important aspect of agent programming, the system provides a strict separation of the components and creates dedicated thread groups for each agent. Moreover, the system handles all mobility-related issues because Java does not offer suitable features for mobile code in current distributions. Implementing aspects like *beliefs*, *desires*, *intentions* is up to the individual application design.

For the following descriptions we assume that the reader is familiar with the basic ideas of agent theory and programming [16, 10], so we will keep the general basics short.

2. System Architecture

At first we provide some information about the general system architecture.

2.1. Components

Basically, the AMETAS architecture differentiates between

- *static parts*: These parts provide the infrastructure for the applications, but they are not part of any specific application. They comprise the core components as well as supporting services.
- *dynamic parts*: These are the applications, which may consist of user interfaces, software agents, services.

Creating an AMETAS application means to implement these dynamic components. The static parts are expected to be available during execution time and form the execution environment for any AMETAS application. Figure 1 shows the basic components of the AMETAS environment. On the bottom, the infrastructure is drawn, consisting of the hardware, the operating system, and the Java virtual machine which cares for a platform-independent operation of the agent system. The part which is located between the applications and the infrastructure is commonly called *place*, a term which has already been in use since early mobile agent system implementations like *Telescript*[1].

Places offer basic services to the application objects which are called *Place Users*[2]. Each of these Place Users is run by a driver which is equipped with an own thread group for allowing concurrent operation. Places offer the *post office* for maintaining the message system as well as an event system which may be utilized for notifying components about interesting changes in the environment. This is, for instance, useful for an efficient processing of Place Users which wait for incoming messages.

The security system is responsible for isolating the Place Users from each other, and to prevent illegal access of the Place Users on the place. The recent version applies various security features of the current Java 2 environment. The configuration is controlled by setting up *policies* which, for example, define the association of privileges and permissions to *identities*. The security subsystem is discussed in more detail in section 5.

If agents want to migrate, the places take care of the connection activities, marshalling and demarshalling and other protocol-related issues. Not only the code but also the state of the agent needs to be encoded and transmitted, and there are migration parameters concerning the security level and remote signing features. On arrival, the place resumes the execution of the agent.

Place addressing is organized by a dedicated naming system called *Place Name System*. This system abstracts from host-bound addresses and ports and allows to assign symbolic names to places. The Place Name System may also be dynamically updated.

Each place offers a *connection* point for attaching user and administration *interfaces*. These interfaces may be attached and detached during the runtime period of a place without interfering with the applications. Various configuration tools allow to create Place User code packages, to administrate the Place Name System, or to configure the security subsystem.

2.2. Place addressing

Place addressing is important in the situation

- when an administrator or user contacts a place using a user interface, and
- when agents migrate between places.

As the AMETAS infrastructure is based on separate processes on network locations – the places –, referencing cannot just rely on host adressing (like within DNS). Generally, one network node (i.e. one host) may run several places. These places are distinguished by the associated connection sockets. Thus, there is no single well-known port.

---

[1]Telescript is one of the first mobile agent systems, created by General Magic. Unfortunately, General Magic has completely dropped their engagements and do not offer any further information on Telescript.

[2]The term is capitalized in order to avoid confusion with "people using a place".

Dynamic IP addresses are another problem. Usually, IP addresses are dynamically assigned for dial-up connections. An agent system like AMETAS may consist of several components on different network nodes, some of them at locations without permanent IP address. This means that agents may fail to reach a node which has changed its address.[3]

Symbolic names are commonly used to solve the problem of changing identifiers (like network locsations). A mapping is used to associate the symbolic name to the network location and port number. This mapping is organized by the *Place Name System*, a mechanism similar to the *Domain Name System*. The symbolic name used in AMETAS is called *PNS name* or *fully qualified place name*.

There is one major difference between the (standard) DNS and the PNS systems. As places may change their network address because of dynamic IP address allocation, the PNS entries may be updated by the places on address change. Agents which try to reach a place will never get into contact with these details; they will just continue to use the PNS name.

The Place Name System is a hierarchical name space, similar to DNS, but is not depending on DNS naming. PNS domains need not be related to any DNS domain. The hierarchical structure is required to prevent a single point of failure, but also to control the propagation of changes of the mapping within a limited area of the name space.

Example. The place *first* shall be contained in a domain called *samples.ametas*. This yields the name *first.samples.ametas*. In PNS, there could be a mapping *first.samples.ametas.* → *myhost.ametas.de:1024*.

When an agent wants to travel to this place, it would use a command like

m_Driver.go("first.samples.ametas");

Technically speaking, the PNS is run by a collection of server processes, the *Place Name Servers*, which serve a part of the name space. Requests for name resolution are directed to one PNS server which may then attempt to resolve the name by itself, or delegate the request to another PNS server.

2.3. Message exchange

Components in client-server applications or object systems communicate by using procedure or method calls, or they utilize shared memory. Within object systems, this is often realized by variables of class scope.

As agent systems are mainly written in Java, and as Java runs applications as one single process, possibly with several execution threads, all components of an agent system may use one of these mechanisms to move information. For example, some systems allow the application programmer to subclass provided agent base classes, adding application-specific methods which are intended to be called by other components, notably also by other agents. In order to propagate the new agent methods, features like interface repositories may be used, or the Java Reflection API could serve to discover these methods.

---

[3]These concerns have lost some of their severity due to the success of the *DynDNS* system [4].

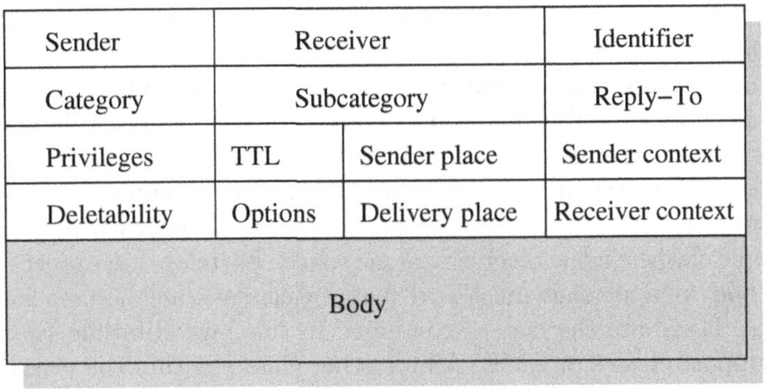

Sender	Receiver		Identifier
Category	Subcategory		Reply–To
Privileges	TTL	Sender place	Sender context
Deletability	Options	Delivery place	Receiver context
Body			

FIGURE 2. Message structure

AMETAS is not the only system to provide message passing between components, but it actually restricts the communication to message passing only. This delivers the name "Asynchronous Message Transfer Agent System". Unlike many other systems, AMETAS disallows agents to offer application-specific methods, while internal objects of the place certainly make use of all kinds of communication patterns. Thus, sender and receiver achieve a spatial and temporal decoupling. Figure 2 shows the structure of a message. Messages consist of two main parts, the *message header* and the *message body*. The header consists of the following fields:

Sender	ID of the sender of the message
Receiver	ID of the receiver of the message
Identifier	ID of this message
Reply-To	ID of another message which this message is (semantically) related to
Deletability	Determines which component may delete the message if it is addresses to a set of receivers
TTL	Time period after which the message is removed within the system
Privileges	Set of privileges which were granted to the sender at the time of sending
Category	Kind of message
Subcategory	Kind of message
Options	Options of message processing
SenderPlace	Place where this message has been submitted (for remote dispatching)
DeliveryPlace	Place where this message has been retrieved
Contexts	Sender and receiver contexts for conversations

Some of these header fields are automatically filled in by the system, especially to prevent spoofing attacks or illegal claim of privileges. These fields are *category*, *sender, identifier, privileges, sender place, delivery place.* The other fields may be set by the application.

The message body is nothing but an array of object references, technically speaking, *java.lang.Object[]*. This seems to provide a great amount of flexibility, but there is one important issue: As all components are loaded by their own classloader, there is no way of referencing the same class for different communication partners. Even if it were possible to transmit class definitions along with messages, there could be name clashes in the receiver's name space. Therefore, all objects which are sent in the body of a message must be defined by classes which are reachable for all components. These are the classes contained in the Java Runtime Environment, base and support classes of AMETAS, or other classes within the classpath.

Within the place, the *post office* is responsible for storing incoming messages in the mailboxes (which are simple queues) specified by the receiver address. When a message is sent to another component, the message is actually held within the local post office, and it is up to the recipient to get this message from the post office. In order to avoid polling, an event system may be utilized, but ultimatively, the recipient must actively retrieve the message. Messages may only be dispatched locally, so for dispatching across places, agents may be used (so-called *messengers*).

3. The Anatomy of AMETAS Applications

One basic feature of AMETAS is the distinction of application components in three categories: *agents*, *user adapters*, and *services*. All members of these categories are summarized under the term *Place User*, or *PU* for short, and share some important properties:

- the execution mechanism: Every Place User has a special method called *invoke* which is called by the place (by a newly created thread inside the place) to start it.
- the way they are maintained inside the place: All Place Users are managed and maintained by the place in the same way and at the same layer.
- the addressing scheme: Every Place User has a unique identifier (its *Place User ID*). Other Place Users and the place may identify and address it via this Place User ID.
- the way of communicating: Place Users use the post office of the local place to exchange messages.

3.1. Place User addressing

Each Place User is assigned a unique identifier. This identifier, called the *Place User ID* or *PUID*, is created using a timestamp and the local address (for providing uniqueness).

PUIDs provide a Place User with an identity within AMETAS. In that way, they could be considered to be like references for normal objects, but in this case,

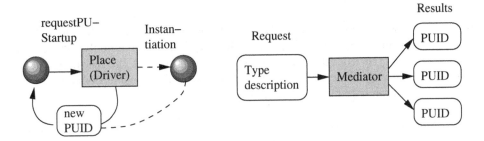

FIGURE 3. Getting the PUID

referring to a complete aggregation. The PUID is necessary to communicate with the Place User because it serves as the recipient identifier in AMETAS messages.

There are basically two ways to get the PUID of a Place User, as shown in Figure 3. In the first case, a new Place User is created. The Place User which initiates the creation gets the associated new PUID as a return value. This allows the "parent" to address the "child". After receiving a message from the parent, the child also knows the parent's ID.

In the second case, no new Place User is created, but there is a component called *mediator* which looks up a Place User using an abstract description. Thus, we have basically a local, internal directory service of Place Users. If the description is too general, the mediator possibly returns multiple PUIDs, and the requestor must decide which is the best fit.

3.2. Storing Place Users

Place Users consist of a well-defined set of classes which are aggregated during implementation time. These aggregations depend strongly on staying together – it would cause a fatal failure if an agent "lost" a class during migration. Therefore, in AMETAS, all classes belonging to a Place User are put into a data structure which may be stored and loaded from the file system, and also be sent through socket connections to allow for migration of agents.

These packages are called *Signed Place User Containers* or *SPU containers* or *SPUs*, for short. An SPU has a structure similar to a JAR file, but apart from storing class definitions and other plain data files, it has some important features:

- It may contain *more than one PU*: Agents may take other agent definitions with them and release (*spawn*) them at a remote location.
- SPUs contain *privilege lists* for starting and running this PU (see section 5.2).
- SPUs provide *type descriptions* for their contained PUs. These descriptions are used for mediation purposes (see section 4).

SPUs are cryptographically signed. These signatures are known as *author signatures*. It is possible to restrict the access to places to Place Users which are signed by known authors.

3.3. Agents

In the literature, the notion of *agenthood* has been widely discussed throughout the last years, but finally getting to no clear definition which is commonly accepted or even acceptable [16, 10]. Due to the different background of the researchers who are concerned with agent technology, each researcher has some domain-specific minimum requirements for entities to be agents.

3.3.1. Agenthood. One coarse distinction resulted from the two fractions of researchers coming from the AI (artificial intelligence) domain, and from the DS (distributed systems) domain. Agents coming from the former ones are sometimes called *intelligent agents*, while those from the latter are were commonly referred to *mobile agents*. Within AMETAS, both notions are just attributes for agents. AMETAS supports the notion of agenthood in two ways:

- *implementation-related*: by providing a base class for agents; so any entity utilizing this base class to derive a subclass is called *agent*;
- *paradigm-related*: agents are autonomous, self-contained components which communicate with other Place Users with the intention to fulfil a given task.

AMETAS follows a very strict notion of agenthood. The reason to split the application components in three different kinds of Place Users was to clearly define which parts can fulfill the agenthood property, thus eligible to be called agents, and which parts cannot.

The first and indispensable property of agents is *autonomy*.

By autonomy we describe the fact that an agent's behavior is completely defined within the agent itself and that the agent always keeps the power to decide how to continue with the plan. The agent need not explicitly define a data structure to be called a *plan*, but every agent must be written as if all initiative originates from within the agent's behavior, trying to achieve the goals of the plan.

The autonomy principle is the primary reason to restrict communication between components to a message passing pattern, because all other kinds of communication (like referencing and method invocation, sockets, pipes) establish a binding between the partners which limit the agent's choice of actions (like migrating away) until the communication is finished.[4]

3.3.2. Example. Programming an agent is pretty straight-forward. An agent may consist of one object or a collection of objects which are kept together as one well-defined aggregation. This aggregation gets an identifier and is, from now on, understood to be *the agent* as such. On the technical side, the agent must enclose exactly one instance of a class which is subclassed from *AMETASAgent*. Figure 4 gives an example of a simple agent.

---

[4]Various strategies have emerged to handle this problem; some agent systems introduce *proxies* to forward data, see also [3].

```
import AMETAS.agentdev.*;
import AMETAS.data.*;

public class MyAgent extends AMETASAgent {
    AMETASPlaceUserID m_idSender = null;
    public void invoke() {
        AMETASMessage[] ames = m_Driver.getMessages(true);
        if (ames!=null) {
            m_idSender = ames[0].getSenderID();
            Object[] aBody = { ''Going to place1'' };
            AMETASMessage mes = new AMETASMessage(m_idSender, aBody);
            m_Driver.depositMessage(mes);
        }
        try {
            m_Driver.go(''place1'');
            // This line after go is never reached
        }
        catch(Exception e) {
            m_Driver.output(''Migration failed.'');
        }
    }
}
```

FIGURE 4. Simple Agent implementation

The behavior of an agent is defined within its programming code, which is located within the *invoke* method. This method is automatically called after instantiating the agent.

- First, this agent gets all messages which are addressed to it – it reads its mailbox. It is assumed for this simple example that the topmost message (the first to be deposited) is the only interesting one.
- If there are messages, it gets the sender identifier of this message, creates a message containing the string "Going to place1" and sends it to the bearer of the identifier. If there are no messages, it skips this step.
- Now it migrates by calling the driver method *go*. Any exception (e.g. caused by an unreachable place) will be caught by the catch block, outputting a text to the log file.

When the execution thread leaves the *invoke* method (and when there are no more threads left), the agent is terminated and garbage-collected.

The *output* operation shown in Figure 4 actually creates a log file entry. This is only useful for demonstration and debugging purposes, because no other Place User may react on this output, and the place administrator may have decided to block outputting to the log. Information exchange should only happen using messages.

3.3.3. Migration mechanism. As can be seen in Figure 4, the execution never reaches the line after *go*: Either *go* succeeds – then the execution will resume with calling *invoke* again; or, if *go* fails, an exception is thrown. A successful *go* makes the place forcefully stop all threads[5] associated to this agent, serializing the state, retrieving the set of class definitions, and using a migration protocol to transfer these components to a remote place. This migration is only successful if the remote place actually accepts the agent; otherwise, the migration is aborted, and the agent may continue execution.

This kind of migration is commonly called *weak* migration [9]. AMETAS does not support *strong* migration; it is not possible to write an agent which continues execution right after the command which caused the migration. Using special programming patterns like *context-oriented programming*[6], handling weak migration may become as intuitive as handling strong migration.

3.4. User adapters

User adapters allow users and Place Users to interact. More than that, these components are used to integrate users and components from outside the agent environment into the system. For users, this is usually achieved by creating a *user interface*, while for components, the adapter defines an *application interface*. The structure of both interfaces is completely application-dependent, allowing to integrate existing external components into the agent system.

With user adapters, users get a tool for communicating with agents in exactly the same way as agents communicate among themselves. Different from agents, user adapters are entitled to access system resources like a graphics display or various input devices like mouse or keyboard. But they cannot migrate. In principle, the main application areas of user adapters are:

1. translating user actions into messages which are understood by Place Users; for instance, a click on a button is translated into an action which entails a message to be submitted to an agent;
2. translating Place User messages into a human-readable and interpretable form; an array of host names might be represented as a sorted list on a user interface.

User integration is fully transparent within the agent system. It does not matter for the agent application whether a message is sent to an agent or whether it should go to a user, because the details of presentation are completely encapsulated in a user adapter. Users might even choose a suitable adapter to represent the results of an agent computation without any changes in the application.

Invoking a user adapter is equal to invoking an agent: After instantiating the user adapter, the *invoke* method is called; the user adapter should then prepare and display a user interface. However, due to the nature of interactive user interfaces, user adapters must rely on event processing when processing user actions. The

---

[5] Forceful termination of threads is deprecated [15]. However, avoiding to externally kill threads puts the responsibility of cleaning up running threads to the application, which means some restructuring of currently running applications. The removal of forceful thread termination is scheduled for the next major release of AMETAS.
[6] See more on context-oriented programming on our web site [1].

```
public class WalkerAdapter extends AMETASUserAdapter
       implements AMETASNotifiable, WindowListener, ActionListener {

    /** Main method of the Place User. */
    public void invoke() {
        m_frmMainFrame = new JFrame("WalkerAdapter");
        m_frmMainFrame.addWindowListener(this);
        // ... further graphic programming
        m_frmMainFrame.show();
        try { m_Driver.registerEventListener(...); }
        catch (Exception ex ) {
            // could not register for events
        }
        // now wait here
        m_Driver.idle();
    }

    /** Invoked when there is an AWT event like button push. */
    public void actionPerformed(ActionEvent e) {
        if (e.getSource() == m_btnStart) {
            m_txfOutput.setText("Waiting for answer...");
            m_btnStart.setEnabled(false);
            // send the agent ...
        }
    }

    /** Invoked when there is an AMETAS event, like agent arriving. */
    public void notifyListener(AMETASEvent evt) {
        // called when there is an interesting event,
        // e.g. when the agent returned
    }

    /** When window is closed, terminate the user adapter. */
    public void windowClosing(WindowEvent e) {
        m_Driver.wakeup();
        // makes driver return from invoke
    }
    // further event handling methods
}
```

FIGURE 5. User adapter code

window system creates additional threads which poll input widgets and update screen display.

Again, when the user adapter driver leaves the *invoke* method, all threads belonging to the user adapter are forcefully terminated and all top-level windows are closed. Of course, the window system threads continue running.

Figure 5 shows an excerpt of the code of a sample user adapter. Within the *invoke* method, the graphical user interface is created and shown. In order to prevent the driver thread from leaving the *invoke* method, it should be put to sleep (using the *idle* method). From now on, the user adapter turns to event processing: Events from the window system represent user actions, and events from the agent system may, for instance, be incoming requests or replies from agents, or arriving and departing agents.

3.5. Services

The third kind of Place Users are called *services*. In general, a service is understood as a component which implements a specific functionality which it provides for other components *on request*. The usual processing is to receive the request, process it, and then formulate a response for the requestor. This communication pattern is referred to as the *request-response pattern*. AMETAS services consist of two parts,

- the service manager, and
- service objects.

3.5.1. Service managers and service objects.
The service manager is provided by the AMETAS system core, while the service objects contain the actual application-specific implementation. Unlike agents, services may not migrate; they are firmly installed within their execution environment. This allows to create services which provide platform-dependent functionalities to the rest of the agent system – by using native code or calling specific system services.

For creating a service, the application author does not write a Place User. The service manager is the subclassed Place User, provided by the core. The service object is subclassed from the *AMETASServiceObject* class. All service objects are instances of the same service object class.

The implementation differs in so far that instead of implementing the *invoke* method of a Place User, the *startService* method of the *AMETASServiceObject* class must be implemented which is executed whenever a message is received by the service manager and dispatched to this service object.The *initService* method is called when the service is initially started and is normally used for reading configuration data for the service.

Each Place User is run by one driver thread. For services which adopt a request-response behavior pattern, it is recommended to run additional threads which allow the service to accept further messages while still processing some messages from previous invocations. Threads may also be utilized to make the service become *initiative*, i.e. the service starts a communication with another component. This can be triggered by some background job while no message is coming in. These additional threads are also required if the service is intended to monitor some changes outside of the agent environment which shall lead to a reaction of the service.

3.5.2. Sharing and sessions.
The service manager resembles the *object adapters* of CORBA [11]. As such, it also controls the activation modes. Services may be used for information exchange between Place Users. There is only one Place User representing the service, so when multiple PUs want to communicate with the

```
public class TranslatorService extends AMETASServiceObject {
    private Hashtable m_htbDict;
    //
    public void initService(Vector vctServiceParams) {
        m_htbDict = new Hashtable();
        m_htbDict.put("Haus","house");
        m_htbDict.put("Hund","dog");
        m_htbDict.put("Katze","cat");
        m_htbDict.put("Maus","mouse");
    }
    //
    public void startService(AMETASMessage msgClient) {
        Object[] aBody = msgClient.getBody();
        if (aBody[0].equals("TRANSLATE")) {
            String sWordBack = (String)(m_htbDict.get(aBody[1]));
            if (sWordBack == null) {
                sWordBack = "No translation for \'" + aBody[1] + "\'";
            }
            String[] asAnswer = { "TRANSLATION", sWordBack };
            depositMessage(new AMETASMessage(msgClient.getSenderID(),
                msgClient.getID(), asAnswer));
        }
    }
}
```

FIGURE 6. Implementation of a simple translation service

same service, it is important to decide whether all these PUs consider this service as one service in a global scope (within the place), or as *their* service within a local scope. By the first meaning, there should be one common (*shared*) service object, while by the second meaning, there should be one service object instance per PU which issued a request to the service. Depending on the sender of the request, the service manager dispatches the request to the associated service object instance.

Interactions between PUs may consist of more than one request. In that case, the whole communicative act should be handled by the same service object. This is possible by establishing a *session* between the partners. The service object will be retained as long as the partner has not closed the session. Sharing and session establishment may be combined: SHARED (with no session), SHARED_SESSION, NON_SHARED, or NON_SHARED_SESSION. The mode is defined within the service type definition in the SPU.

3.5.3. Example. Figure 6 shows an example service. The *initService* method is used for initializing the service object before any request comes in. The *startService* method is called for each incoming message. This service should be implemented as a SHARED service.

For the sake of simplicity, we omit error handling and assume that the incoming request has the expected format, i.e. it always consists of two strings, the first one being the constant *TRANSLATE*, the second one the string to be translated. After looking up the corresponding translation, the service submits a reply message to the requestor.[7]

3.6. Interaction with the environment

We need to consider *external entities* which are not modelled as Place Users, namely the operating system and devices or other processes outside the Java environment. PUs normally may not get into contact with these external entities due to security restrictions. However, agent applications somehow need to get information from outside or change the configuration of the environment.

Most agent systems do not restrict the access of agents to external entities. For example, to get in contact with the user, some systems allow agents to open graphical user interfaces. In this case, user interactions may be described as *text input actions* or *button push actions* or the like for input, or *drawing graphs* for output. AMETAS hides all these different kinds of interactions by the user adapter concept.

Besides user interfaces, some data exchange may involve files or sockets. The communication with these external entities may be hidden within services, as described above. This means that all device-specific communication is effectively hidden as *Place User-internal communication*. To the outside, only AMETAS message exchange is visible.

For the message-based communication between the parts of the application, it is irrelevant which kinds of external entities are involved. Any other external application, even a complete CORBA system or .NET environment, may communicate with AMETAS-internal agent applications using a specific user adapter or service.

Another example of resource integration may be found in the implementation of *NetDoctor*[17]. Here, a side-band communication channel is established between places for immediate information transmission (if sending an agent is considered to be too costly). This is quite comfortable for network administrators when they want to get a current view on the network status. The communication endpoints (the sockets) are hidden inside specific services. That is, whenever a message is send to such a communication service, it transmits the contents to another communication service, depending on the destination information. The receiving service creates a new message, packing the received data into the message. Within the agent system, the transmitting service just looks like a data sink, while the receiving service plays the role of a data source. Within the agent system, the communication stays message-oriented.

---

[7]The requestor's address can be found within the header of the incoming message.

4. Mediation

In section 3.1, we already discussed ways to get the address of a Place User, the PUID. In most applications we encounter the problem how to find the right agents and services. Taking a look at the illustration of NetDoctor (Figure 8, later in this article), it becomes obvious that the *MobileManager* agent does not necessarily know the PUIDs of all components, because some might have been started at some time after the *MobileManager* was created.

When the *MobileManager* agent arrives at some place, it must at first determine the addresses of the other Place Users. One comfortable way to solve this problem is to let the application start the Place Users, which keeps newly created PUID for subsequent communication. Specifically, the methods

```
AMETASPlaceUserID requestPUStartup(...)
AMETASPlaceUserID spawnAgent(...)
```

are called by the parent PU, returning the PUID of the created PU (as described in section 3.1). This identifier is then passed by a message to the other agents.

The situation is a bit different with services. Services are sometimes started on start-up of the place itself, so no application gets the required PUIDs on the start event. Moreover, when applications are reconfigured by new components, these new components need to find out how to get the required addresses for communication.

AMETAS supports the discovery of components by *mediation*.

4.1. Mediator

Mediation, sometimes also known as trading [12], is a process which has the goal to get a concrete address from an abstract description, using some instance (called the *mediator* or *trader*) which is able to perform this translation. Actually, in practise, it means to find one or more objects that fit to some description and hence allow the requestor to get in communication with these objects. The more specific the descriptions are, the smaller the result sets become. We need to distinguish between two kinds of mediation:

- instance mediation, and
- type mediation.

Instance mediation delivers a set of identifiers of matching instances. In AMETAS, a list of PUIDs is returned after submitting a mediation request to the mediator. The result of a type mediation may be a set of new descriptions (e.g. PU package) which allow to create an instance; such an instance would then be discovered in the corresponding instance mediation process. For example, while the result in the first case would be the PUID of the (running) *SNMPService*, in the second case one would receive the *SPU name* (of the SPU containing the classes) in order to launch the *SNMPService*.

The AMETAS place registers the type descriptions enclosed within the SPU files and the types of the running PUs in a *type repository*. Services are registered using the description of the associated service object, which is mapped to the

```
public void invoke() {
   ...
   boolean bSearchInstance = true;
   AMETASMediationRequest mr = new AMETASMediationRequest(
      "SNMPService", bSearchInstance);
   AMETASMediationResult[] amrs = m_Driver.request(mr);
   if (amrs == null || amrs.length == 0) {
      m_Driver.output("SNMPService not found.");
   }
   else {
      AMETASPlaceUserID idSNMP = amrs[0].getPlaceUserID();
      // create a message for the SNMP service
      // ...
   }
   ...
}
```

FIGURE 7. Using mediation to find a service

PUID of the service manager. As soon as a PU is started, the PUID is registered, and the PU is available for mediation.

Mobility is a difficult issue for mediation. The requestor may not rely on the actual presence of an agent whose ID has been returned in a previous mediation response, because the agent might have migrated away in the meantime. For this reason, agent descriptions are stored for some predefined period of time, after which they are discarded. Messages sent to these addresses will be stored in the mailbox system, waiting for the agent to return. The client agent may also check whether the returned address refers to a present agent, but this is only a hint (the agent could still escape after the check). Agents which terminated at the local place (by themselves or by a forceful kill) cause the PUID to be immediately removed so that this outdated ID will not be returned as a mediation result any more.

4.2. Mediation process

In order to initiate a mediation process, the requestor formulates a *mediation request*. The request contains a *description* which is matched against the descriptions collected in the repository by the mediator. The matching procedure depends on the actual mediator implementation – the mediator may reject descriptions which it does not understand. The mediation request also informs the mediator whether instance or type mediation shall be used.

Figure 7 shows how to use mediation within a Place User implementation. In this example, the PUID of the *SNMPService* is requested. If there is no such service, an empty array is returned. If the mediation failed for some other reason, *null* is returned.

4.3. String types

The simplest descriptions for types are *string types*. A string type may be just the name of the Place User, for example, *KQMLService* or *SNMPQueryAgent*.

The mediation procedure only needs to check which Place Users have the same name in their string type. A string type contains an instance of the class *StringType*. To simplify, string types are always assumed when using strings in the description, so the following lines are equivalent:

```
mrq = new AMETASMediationRequest("SNMPService",bRunning);
mrq = new AMETASMediationRequest(new
     AMETASType(new StringType("SNMPService")),bRunning);
```

Strings are, in general, just a sequence of characters, without any specific structure. AMETAS defines a structure on string types which may be used for mediation. This structure defines a string type to consist of three parts. For example,

Name	Messenger
Instance	michael01
Group	SystemAgents

forms this string: *Messenger#michael01/SystemAgents*.

Using this substructure, mediation can become quite powerful. For example, the mediator may retrieve all instances of the same SPU, it may find all agents which belong to some predefined group, or – when setting the instance specification to be the starter identity name – you can find all Place Users of some specific user. For a mediation request, the wildcard symbol * may be used, and the string must be passed to the mediator within a mediation request.

- *Messenger#*/** will return all Place Users named *Messenger*, regardless of the group or the starter.
- **#michael/** will return all Place Users of any name or group, provided that they have the instance name *michael* (which could identify the starter).

4.4. Hybrid types

While strings are a very simple means of finding the desired Place User, there is a considerable drawback: How do you know which Place User does which job? In the case of a closed system, the situation is clear. You can just define that all services named *SNMPService* must provide some required functionality. But in an open system, new agents arrive, others depart, further agents come with familiar names but do quite different things. Who has the right to name his service *SNMPService*?

In AMETAS, a declarative type system was introduced, described in detail in my Ph.D. thesis [18]. The principle behind this type system is that

- structural compatibility of communication is a requirement for cooperative problem solving in a collection of agents, but
- semantic information is important to avoid unwanted matches of seemingly compatible requirements.

Abstracting from communication connection details (which is realized within AMETAS by enforcing message passing), the ways how the components communicate may be characterized. Actually, messages consist of message *items* which have some specific data type, so the first requirement for compatibility is that all received items have types compatible with the expectations of the recipient.

Moreover, as agents are expected to keep their state, they are stateful objects. This means that there is a protocol for communicating with the agent, considering incoming and outgoing messages.

Finally, most users may have no idea which messages are exchanged by the desired agents. They do not look for agents to comply to some protocol but to *perform some job*. This boils down to describing the *semantics* of the agent. Besides the overall meaning of the agent, it is possible to describe the meaning of agent states, incoming and outgoing messages, and senders and receivers which have been specified within the protocol description.[8]

5. Security

As AMETAS agents are mobile Java programs, they may perform any action that a Java program is able to do. If the underlying operating systems implements certain security policies, these policies may serve to restrict the possible actions caused by agents on the Virtual Machine. For example, when a place runs as a Unix process, the place and all objects on it will receive the exact set of privileges assigned to the owner of the process. This means that all agents are allowed to access the files of the place starter.

This kind of security is obviously insufficient, lacking an appropriate granularity. It cannot distinguish between the starter of a place and the agent owners. This could be disastrous when a place is started by the system administrator (root): The immigrated agents could perform administrative tasks and probably damage the underlying system. Obviously, there is a need for appropriate security precautions. The AMETAS security subsystem relies on the Java Security Architecture of Java 2 [14].

5.1. Basic principles

By the term *privilege* we define a property that must be assigned to a *principal* in order to let it perform a specified set of actions within the agent system. These actions are *starting, stopping*. and *communicating with* a given set of PUs.

A privilege is always referred to by a *name* and may imply *permissions* which are required to access resources via the Java Runtime Environment. Thus, having some privilege may imply to be able to write to a file if the appropriate permission is implied by the privilege. The following statements summarize the basic ideas of the security system:

---

[8]Describing the Hybrid Type System is far beyond the scope of this article. Please see [18, 19, 1] for more details.

- The system distinguishes between *user*, *author*, and *place identities*.
- It is the sole responsibility of the place to grant privileges at runtime. Each place decides by itself whether a privilege is granted or refused.
- Only users may be assigned privileges by places. Users must be known to the place.
- Places are entitled to reject Place Users from unknown authors.
- Users may delegate a subset of their privileges to Place Users.
- Place Users may restrict the set of privileges delegated to them.
- Place Users may require a minimum set of privileges in order to be started or used.
- Place Users may never possess more privileges than the user who started them. The granted privileges always depend on the set of privileges granted to this user at the current place.

All remaining aspects of the security system are based upon these principles.

5.2. Privileges of agents and user adapters

Privilege processing is equal for agents and user adapters. There are two sets of privileges called *start privileges* and *runtime privileges*.

In order to start an agent or a user adapter and become the owner, the principal (user) must have been granted at least the set of start privileges of this PU. This set is declared within the SPU container. If the user does not have these privileges, the start of the PU is denied.

By launching a Place User like an agent or a user adapter, the user becomes the *owner* of the PU. First, the owner automatically signs the code of the Place User so that the ownership can be determined at other places. Second, the set of available privileges is retrieved, according to the owner of the PU, from the local policy definition. Thus, it is irrelevant which privileges were active at other places: After arriving at a new place, the maximum set of privileges is never bigger than the set which is locally granted for this user.

After starting the Place User, all following actions – like launching further PUs – originate from within the Place User. As the PU acts on behalf of the user, it is reasonable to restrict the set of privileges of the PU to the set of privileges associated to the user. This is called *privilege delegation*.

The PU may restrict the set of delegated privileges. The maximum set of privileges which are in effect is called *runtime privileges*. This set is also defined within the SPU container. The *effective privilege set* is the intersection between the set of user privileges and runtime privileges.

It is possible to define a runtime privilege set which is bigger than the set of start privileges. This may be useful if an application shall be started by users with different privilege sets. If started by highly privileged users, the application gains more privileges; for normal users, the application gets fewer privileges. In fact, the set of runtime privileges and start privileges need not be related to each other in any way.

5.3. Privileges of services

Privilege handling of services is substantially different from the privilege handling of agents or user adapters. The reason is that services are considered to be started on behalf of the *place*, not of the user, although the user may trigger the launch of the service. Services are considered to be extensions of the place functionality.

Services also define two privilege sets, again called *start* and *runtime privileges*. Unlike the situation with agents or user adapters, the start privilege set does not determine whether the service is started; services are often automatically started at place startup. Instead, the start privileges control whether messages arrive at the service or not. A PU is only entitled to send a message to a service if the effective privilege set of the PU contains the start privileges of the service. Moreover, the runtime privileges play another role for services as well: The runtime privilege set is always the effective set for any requestor of the service.

The advantage is that it is not necessary to grant all kinds of privileges to a user who wants his agent to utilize a lot of services. Instead, the service acts like a *set-uid* program in UNIX: Using services, Place Users may get (indirect) access to facilities which they may not directly access.

5.4. Access control mechanism

There are two interesting situations which we take a brief look at: starting a Place User, and agents which arrive at a place.

5.4.1. Starting Place Users.

Each time a PU is requested to start, the place loads the SPU which is referred to by its file name, and uses this file in memory to set up a *codesource*. Each PU gets an own *ClassLoader* which retrieves all classes from this codesource, so agents are effectively isolated against each other: The classloaders create an implicit name space which prevents addressing of classes within other classloaders, i.e. within other PUs. That way, any kind of referencing is prevented. [9]

Each SPU is verified by its list of cryptographic signatures. There may be a set of signatures from different identities; if the *authentication policy* requires a *known author*, one of these signatures must be valid and coming from an identity known to this place. After this verification, the sets of start and runtime privilege names are retrieved and put into the *protection domain* of this PU.

The privileges of the user (who requested the start of the PU) are retrieved from the *access control policy* definition. Provided that they are a superset of the start privileges, the Place User class is loaded from the codesource and is finally instantiated. The runtime privileges as defined in the protection domain are intersected with the user privileges and form the effective privilege list. Just before start, the system signs the SPU on behalf of the user and transmits this signature along with the SPU. The signature allows to identify the user as the actual owner of this agent instance.

---

[9]This gives reason to the fact that you cannot send application-defined objects in messages: the receiver has no chance to get the class definition.

When a Place User attempts to access a resource which is protected by Java's security system, the *AccessController* of Java consults the associated protection domain of the Place User. The protection domain checks the required permission against the permissions set previously created from the effective privilege list, which is created using the mapping of privileges to permissions within the policy definition.

There are specific permissions which are forbidden for agents in order to prevent direct resource access. For example, agents may never access files, or sockets, or the window system. The protection domain of an agent will ignore any grant of such permission induced by a privilege definition.

5.4.2. Incoming agents. When agents immigrate from other places, they may have enjoyed a higher degree of freedom than at the new place. The reason is that the access control decision only depends on the current place's policy definitions, not on those from the place where the agent came from.

After instantiation, the agent SPU was signed by the user who started it. This signature is transferred to the new place by which that place determines the owner of the agent. Similar to the local start situation, the SPU is accepted at the new place and used to create a codesource instance, along with a new classloader. The place retrieves the definition of runtime privileges from the SPU and, by intersecting with the *local* access policy for this user, creates the new effective privilege set.

5.5. Signing of remote agents

Mobile AMETAS agents may carry other agent definitions piggy-backed with them. These agent definitions are contained within the SPU containers. When the agent is at a remote place, it may launch such an internal agent, which could, for instance, return to the initial place where the carrier agent started.

In this case, however, owners may not reliably sign the agent – because the signature would need to be done remotely. AMETAS allows to transmit the private key along with the agent – if this is desired. As the transmission of private cryptographic data is inherently dangerous to the security of the application, remote signing is not recommended. AMETAS places refuse the transmission of private cryptographic keys when the transmission channel is not encrypted. The built-in migration protocol may utilize common cryptographic algorithms as provided by the Java cryptography extension (JCE).

Unsigned agents cannot be associated reliably to some user. A possible trust model must enclose the remote places as trustful, which would lead to the conclusion that remote agent instantiation in a non-trusted environment must be generally discouraged.

6. Applications

The design principles for AMETAS applications resemble the three-tier principle [5]:

- User adapters provide the presentation logic.
- Agents are the data processing tier.
- Services are used as an interface to the system and deliver or store data.

One interesting feature is that, for example, the user adapter may be replaced, as long as the new one is compatible to the rest of the application in the way as expected from the original one. Speaking in terms of the mediation support (cf. section 4), any subtype instance of the expected Place User is applicable.

6.1. Sample application

For multi-agent applications, it is usually required to define a coordinating instance which controls the message flows between the application parts. While the AMETAS post office is suitable to store messages for some time, it is not intended for long-time storage. In addition, due to the nature of mobile and distributed applications, it is unclear whether an application has terminated in the meantime. It is advisable to have this control be done by a dedicated Place User. Which Place User kind to choose depends on the application scenario:

- Agents are not dependent on the presence and attention of a human user.
- User adapters may not only display results but also collect information and achieve control of the whole application.
- Services may be a good choice if the coordination also requires external data retrieval, and if the collected data are to be provided to requesting other Place Users.

Figure 8 shows an example of an agent application with some coordination tasks. This example refers to the *NetDoctor* project [17] which employed mobile agents for enhancing SNMP network management.

In *NetDoctor*, classic SNMP agents[10] communicate via services with AMETAS agents. These *SNMPServices* provide an interface which translates SNMP operations and data into AMETAS messages and vice versa. Instead of using one fully-featured AMETAS agent, there are specialized agents, each for handling one specific part of system management, e.g. checking memory usage, CPU load, network transmissions, or device access. One of the agents acts as a *coordinator* by collecting the data from the sub-agents and evaluating whether the given information shall be considered normal or alarming.

While the services are started together with the places, the agents are sent to the places by the user adapter, allowing a simple software deployment process, keeping the codebase updated. Note that the administrator who watches the system state on his user interface – provided by the user adapter – may log out and

---

[10]Note that the term "agent" again shows a different meaning.

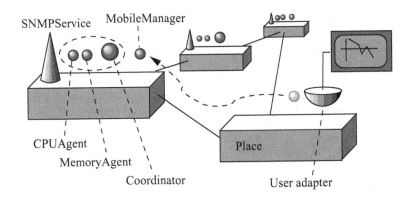

SNMPService   MobileManager

CPUAgent

MemoryAgent

Coordinator

Place

User adapter

FIGURE 8. Multi-agent application

close the user adapter, while the management system continues working. The task of coordination is up to the local coordinator agents.

The coordinator has a limited set of measures which may be applied if the system state requires corrections. If the coordinator fails, it sends a messenger agent back to the administrator, asking for help. The administrator may then decide to send a specifically prepared *MobileManager* which performs the required corrective actions. Failing again, the administrator may choose another *MobileManager* version or try to fix the problem by himself.

Agent applications should be designed to be multi-agent applications whenever some functionality shall be modularized, allowing to replace parts during runtime. It should be considered that migrations cause noticeable network load which, in turn, justifies the usage of smaller, specialized agents, even though this requires additional coordinating agents.

6.2. Using AMETAS in projects

We used the agent system successfully in several national and international projects. Some examples are listed below.

- The *IntraManager* [6] is an extension of the *NetDoctor* application for network management. It uses neural networks in mobile agents to detect patterns in the behavior of computer networks and tries to predict failures. This project was run by the University of Frankfurt in cooperation with Deutsche Flugsicherung.
- The *VOTEC* project [7, 8] was targeted towards creating new collaborative working environments with 3D user navigation in a VRML scene. Agents were used to handle personal profiles of members of this working environment. The project was run by the GMD institute SIT (now Fraunhofer SIT), using AMETAS as the infrastructure.

- The UNITE project [13], an IST project in the 5th EU Framework Programme, was also concerned with providing users with a virtual office environment. AMETAS was used as the implementation base. Here, the agent infrastructure was not only used to handle personal profiles but also to create a flexible, distributed middleware for plugging in collaboration tools and for dynamically adapting the group network topology. When users joined other users in some virtual office, their agents negotiated the appropriate communication channels.

7. Summary and Outlook

This article provided an overview on AMETAS, a development and runtime environment for the creation of mobile autonomous agents. A comprehensive system overview would be out of the scope of this article, so we refer to the web site [1] for up-to-date documentation.

AMETAS defines three kinds of application components: agents, user adapters, and services. While services are able to wrap system-dependent resource accesses and provide the place with a functional enhancement, user adapters integrate the human user into the agent environment. Communicating with users is not a special case anymore because this adapter makes users appear as Place Users. Finally, agents are implemented as being autonomous, and while they may migrate, they have the hardest restrictions concerning resource access. All these components, called Place Users, communicate solely via messages.

The benefit of this handling is clear: All resource usage is hidden within services (or user adapters), which avoids problems with remote resource access for agents. Finally, it is easier to replace components, especially to introduce new and enhanced versions of components.

AMETAS uses techniques of mediation to realize open applications (i.e. applications with an ever-changing set of components) by providing a means to determine the address of some Place User referred to by an abstract description. This description reaches from simple strings to complex declarative type specifications, using message format, protocol, and semantic information.

The security system prevents illegal access between Place Users and defines the access control to resources. However, there are no precautions to cope with places which attack agents (*malicious places*) – this is still an open research field, and, as quite some years have gone by, probably never gets to some generic solution.

In the past years up to now, AMETAS proved the applicability of its principles, even in some international projects. Currently, AMETAS still evolves; the next version is planned to allow to use more externally provided services, including external public key infrastructures, directory and naming services.

AMETAS is one of many approaches to support the creation of autonomous and mobile software agents, so a list of related work would quickly grow long.

A good overview may be found on the web page of the *AgentLink III European Coordination Action* [2].

References

[1] accsis GmbH: AMETAS web site, http://www.ametas.info/

[2] AgentLink III Coordination action in the 6th Framework Programme; http://www.agentlink.org/

[3] J. Baumann, K. Rothermel: The Shadow Approach: An Orphan Detection Protocol for Mobile Agents. In: Mobile Agents Second International Workshop, MA 98, Stuttgart 1998.

[4] Dynamic Network Services, Inc. http://www.dyndns.org/.

[5] W. Eckerson: Three-Tier Client/Server Architecture: Achieving Scalability, Performance, and Efficiency in Client-Server Applications. In: Open Information Systems 10 3 (1995), January, No. 20

[6] K. Herrmann, K. Geihs: Integrating Mobile Agents and Neural Networks for Proactive Management, Third IFIP WG 6.1 International Working Conference on Distributed Applications and Interoperable Systems, Krakow, Poland 2001.

[7] M. Hoffmann, M.-L. Moschgath, R. Reinema: A Security Infrastructure for the Virtual Project Office; Proceedings of the IEEE International Conference on Software, Telecommunications and Computer Networks (SoftCOM 2000) Split, Croatia, October 2000

[8] M. Hoffmann, R. Reinema: A Multi Agent Architecture for a Virtual Project Office; International ICSC Symposium on Multi-Agents and Mobile Agents in Virtual Organizations and E-Commerce (MAMA 2000), Wollongong, Australia; December 2000

[9] T. Illmann, M. Weber, F. Kargl, T. Krueger: Migration of Mobile Agents in Java: Problems, Classification and Solutions. In: International ICSC Congress: Intelligent Systems & Applications ISA 2000, Wollongong, Australia, Volume 1, ICSC Academic Press, December 2000.

[10] H. S. Nwana: Software Agents: An Overview. In: Knowledge Engineering Review 11 (1996), September, No. 3, pp. 1-40. http://agents.umbc.edu/introduction/ao/

[11] Object Management Group: The Common Object Request Broker Architecture and Specification. Revision 2.4.1. November 2000. OMG Formal Document 2000-11-03

[12] Object Management Group: Trading Object Service Specification. Version 1.0, May 2000. OMG Formal Document 00-06-27

[13] R. Reinema, S. Trpe, R. Wolf, M. Zapf: UNITE - An Agent-Oriented Teamwork Environment. Mobile Agents for Telecommunication Applications, 4th International Workshop (MATA 2002), Barcelona, Spain.

[14] Sun Microsystems: Java 2 Security Architecture. Located under Java documentation, http://java.sun.com/docs/

[15] Sun Microsystems: Why Are Thread.stop, Thread.suspend, Thread.resume and Runtime.runFinalizersOnExit Deprecated? Java 2 Platform Documentation, specifically

http://java.sun.com/j2se/1.5.0/docs/guide/misc/threadPrimitiveDeprecation.html, 2005.

[16] M. J. Wooldridge: Agent-based software engineering. In: IEE Proceedings on Software Engineering 144 (1997), No. 1, pp. 26-37

[17] M. Zapf, K. Herrmann, and K. Geihs: Decentralized SNMP Management with Mobile Agents. Proceedings of the International Symposium on Integrated Network Management (IM' 99) Boston/USA, 1999.

[18] M. Zapf: Typisierung autonomer Softwareagenten (Ph.D. thesis). Johann Wolfgang Goethe-Universitt Frankfurt/Main. Verlag dissertation.de; www.dissertation.de. ISBN 3-89825-402-X, 2001.

[19] M. Zapf and K. Geihs: What Type Is It? A Type System For Mobile Agents. 15th European Meeting on Cybernetics and Systems Research (EMCSR), Vienna 2000.

Information about Software

Software is available on the Internet as
( )   prototype version
(X)   full-fledged version (free for non-commercial use), version no.: 2.6
( )   full-fledged version (for money), version no.:
( )   Demo/Trial version
( )   not (yet) available

Internet address:

    Description of software: AMETAS run-time environment and software development kit, documentation, and samples
    Download address: http://www.ametas.info/, Download section

Contact point for questions about the software
    info@ametas.info

Michael Zapf
accsis GmbH
Kühhornshofweg 8
60320 Frankfurt
Germany
e-mail: zapf@accsis.de

Tracy: An Extensible Plugin-Oriented Software Architecture for Mobile Agent Toolkits

Peter Braun, Ingo Müller, Tino Schlegel, Steffen Kern,
Volkmar Schau and Wilhelm Rossak

Abstract. In this chapter we propose a software architecture for mobile agent toolkits and describe our Tracy toolkit as a reference implementation of this architecture. Agent toolkits mainly consist of a software system that forms an agency, which is responsible to host mobile and stationary software agents. In contrast to most architectures developed so far, which already define a large set of services for agent migration, communication, and security, we propose to employ a kernel-based approach. The kernel only provides fundamental concepts common to all agent toolkits and abstracts from any of these services. In particular, although Tracy was developed as a mobile agent toolkit, its kernel abstracts from all issues related to agent mobility, delegating this to an optional service implementation. This makes it possible to replace Tracy's migration service with another implementation and even to have two different migration services in parallel. Service implementations are developed as plugins that can be started and stopped during run-time. We have already developed almost a dozen plugins for agent migration, communication, authentication and authorization, and security solutions, only to name a few. We believe that this architecture is a useful foundation for research on agent-related topics as it allows research groups to implement their own results as a service which can be used by other groups running an agent system based on the same architecture.

1. Introduction

Mobile agents have been introduced as a design paradigm for distributed applications [35]. A mobile agent is a program that can migrate from host to host in a network of heterogeneous computer systems and fulfill a task specified by its owner. It works autonomously and can communicate with other agents and host systems. During the self-initiated migration, the agent carries its code and some kind of execution state with it. What comprises the execution state depends on the underlying programming language and is, in the case of most Java-based toolkits for example only the serialized agent (an agent is an object of a specific class) and does not contain information about the state of the Java virtual machine. On each host they visit, mobile agents need a special software that we name *agency*, which is responsible to execute agents, provides a safe execution environment, and offers several services for agents residing on this host. A *mobile agent system* is the set of all agencies together with agents running on these agencies as part of an agent-based application. To refer to a specific project or product, for example Aglets [23] or Grasshopper [3], we use the notion *agent toolkit*.

For some years, mobile agents have been a hot topic in the domain of distributed systems. Reasons were problems more traditionally designed distributed systems, especially client/server systems, might have to handle work-load, the trend to open large numbers of customers direct access to services and goods, and user mobility. Mobile agent technology can help to design innovative solutions in these domains by complementing other approaches, simply by adding mobility of code, machine based intelligence, and improved network- and data-management capabilities. We have seen tremendous research effort, for example, in the area of mobile agent security, where sophisticated security protocols were developed to solve the problem of malicious agencies (that try to attack visiting agents) and malicious agents (that try to attack hosting agencies) [17]. Other research topics are, for example, performance aspects of mobile agents [6], in which inherent drawbacks of mobile agents are tackled using sophisticated migration strategies, mobile agent communication [2], or control issues [1], which targets at the development of algorithms to trace mobile agents while roaming the Internet.

However, the interest in mobile agents as a design paradigm for distributed systems seems to have dwindled over the last years. The number of research groups working on mobile agent related topics is becoming smaller, some conferences and workshops cease to exist or are aligned with more general topics regarding mobility of code or mobility of devices. It is argued that mobile agents were not able to satisfy some of the main expectations, for example regarding their ability to reduce network traffic overhead. Vigna [34] states that mobile agents are very expensive and provide worse performance in the general case than other design paradigms, as for example remote procedure call or remote evaluation. Compare Vigna's early work regarding network load of different design paradigms [33] and a discussion of his approach in [6]. He also points to security problems, which are unlikely to be solved completely and will, therefore, impede the acceptance of mobile agents. Other authors try to get to the bottom of the problem of decreasing acceptance and discuss whether mistakes of the research community have caused the current disappointing situation. For example, Roth [29] questions Java to be the best programming language to cope with unresolved security problems. Johansen [19] points out that far too many groups have focused on the development of yet another prototype of a mobile agent toolkit with only small contributions to the fundamental research questions. In fact, the current situation is characterized by a few tens toolkits. Although this number reflects an enormous research output by different groups all over the world, it also reveals premature status of research and a not-existent coordination between projects.

We agree with Johansen about the high number of research prototypes and their negative effect to the research community. However, many research groups were obliged to develop their own prototype because of the lack of any reference architecture for mobile agent toolkits as well as the absence of an open and extendable implementation of a mobile agent toolkit. Therefore, each research group working on core research problems rather than application development was compelled to develop its own prototype and due to the high complexity and limited resources this prototype is more a proof-of-concept implementation focusing on a single research issue and leaving out elementary functional components necessary for a full mobile agent toolkit. Only to name two examples, we mention Semoa [30] as a system with a very strong focus on security issues and our first implementation of Tracy [7] which was designed around early ideas regarding high-performance migration protocols. At first, agent communication was not in the focus of neither of these systems–but added later in both of them. Other groups focused on agent tracing and communication problems, for example [25], but their algorithms are not adopted in other toolkits so far. We see these isolated islands of research as another obstacle for the acceptance of mobile agents as there is no single mobile agent toolkit available that provides at least an almost up-to-date set of features and research results.

To amend this situation, one of the most important challenges of our Tracy project is to develop a reference architecture for mobile agent toolkits. This architecture is leveraging off of previous work done by the Tracy team in designing the first Tracy architecture [7] and benefits from experiences learned when porting it to mobile platforms and investigating feasibility to use Tracy within an electronic commerce application [22]. Our model for agencies consists of a very small kernel which defines only imperative functions of an agency and the concept as well as the life-cycle of agents. As part of our model, we define the concept of services, which implement additional functionality on top of the kernel. The model does not define anything related to specific services, for example agent communication, agent migration, or agent tracing, except of an interface for services to communicate to the kernel.

The Tracy toolkit, which is the reference implementation of our new agency model, has a plugin-oriented software architecture. Each service in the meaning of our model is implemented as a plugin, which can be dynamically started and stopped at runtime. As part of the Tracy implementation, we have developed more than a dozen plugins for various services. An interesting result regarding mobile agent toolkits was that it is possible to design an agency without considering mobility of agents–and later to plugin this new service without any modification of the kernel.

The remainder of this book chapter is structured as follows: We start by giving a state-of-the-art overview of other approaches to build interoperable and component-oriented mobile agent toolkits. After that we introduce our agency model and describe the Tracy mobile agent toolkit, which is a reference implementation of our model. We will also introduce some of the most important software components that come along with Tracy already. Finally, we describe our experience with our agency model and the Tracy toolkit in building a mobile agent based application for mobile users.

2. Related Work

In this section, we will give a concise overview of the development of software architectures of mobile agent toolkits in the past few years. We choose this presentation style to demonstrate our kernel-based software architecture as the evolution of current mobile agent toolkit design.

In our opinion, the timely development of mobile agent toolkits can be roughly distinguished into an early, a current, and a next generation phase. The early phase from the mid 1990s till the end of the 1990s is characterized by the development of first complex mobile agent toolkits, such as AgentTcl [15], Aglets [23], and Grasshopper [3]. The main goal of these systems was to provide a basic set of functions and features for the development of mobile agent based applications. Therefore, early toolkits offer only a small but inflexible interface via a mobile agent class, which encapsulated access to the functionality of the toolkit. It is difficult to add (e.g. a tracking mechanism) or to change functionality (e.g. replace the existing mobility or communication model), or to adapt the toolkit to specific requirements (e.g. to downsize it for resource-limited mobile devices).

After the mobile agent community recognized the drawbacks from the early mobile agent toolkits, the current phase begun at the end of the 1990s [18, 30]. Now mobile agent toolkits are developed using a component-oriented architecture. Most systems still use a layered architecture, with a migration layer and communication layer below, a layer for agent management functionality in the middle, and a basic service layer on top [5, 20]. Each layer consists of a set of components, which implement the layer's functionality. Following this, the problems of first mobile agent toolkits with respect to flexibility, extensibility, and adaptability were improved. However, only for each mobile agent toolkit itself. For, the problem of exchanging functionality and interaction between different mobile agent toolkits still remains unresolved. The main reason for this problem is a high coupling between internal components and different definitions of component interfaces in these mobile agent toolkits.

Some mobile agent toolkits even implement standards to amend the interoperability problems, such as MASIF [24] or FIPA [26], originally developed for multi agent systems. Both standards do not solve the given problems in a suitable manner. MASIF has not been accepted because it relies too much on further OMG specifications such as CORBA and IDL, increasing the effort for the development of a mobile agent toolkit with aspects not belonging to the basic principles of mobile agents. FIPA, implemented for example by Jade [4], is also too complex because it defines a large set of system internal architectural and design constraints, for example regarding agent communication. This is a problem especially with respect to researchers who have their main focus on a single problem in the mobile agent domain not willing to implement all mandatory parts of the specification.

Thus, we are still looking for an approach that might solve the problems identified in the introductory section. This is the reason why we believe that mobile agent toolkits should enter a next generation phase in which the focus changes from trying to uniform system design to specify only a very small set of kernel functionality accessed through a lean interface, reducing the coupling between system components. Functionality can be added in a very flexible way with software components.

3. JAM – A New Model for Agencies

In this section we will introduce *JAM* (Java Agency Model), which is a new Java-based model for agencies for mobile and intelligent software agents. Our goal is to define a model that consists of the smallest number of interfaces and classes and only defines an imperative set of functional and non-functional requirements in order to execute software agents. In the following, we restrict ourselves to Java-based mobile agent toolkits, because Java has become the de-facto standard for programming mobile agents; almost all new toolkits developed in the last six years are programmed in Java. The reasons for this are many built-in functions, for example object serialization, dynamic class loading, and the sand-box security mechanism, which simplify the development of mobile agent toolkits. The restriction to Java makes sense, since we focus on the exchangeability of service components and the exchangeability of software agents on the level of implementations. Therefore, our model must be seen orthogonally to other models and standards, for example FIPA [26] and MASIF [24], which specify communication protocols and migration protocols, respectively.

Current models for agencies and collections of design issues for mobile agent toolkits [16, 21], already include design decisions for several high-level *services*. This notion will be used in the rest of this book chapter as synonym for optional functions offered by an agency and used by agents in order to fulfill their task. Services are for example migration, communication, agent tracking, persistency, region management, etc. We see as major drawback of these current agency model that they create many dependences between actually independent services. The resulting agency implementation is more monolithic, because services are not represented by independent software components. In fact, our model abstracts from these services and in contrast attempts to move as many functional requirements of a mobile agent toolkit into optional services.

As motivated in the introduction, we want to address the possibility to exchange research results between research projects in form of software components and software agents. Therefore, we propose to split an agency into a single *kernel* (compare [11] for an introduction to kernel-based software architectures) and several optional *service components*, each implementing a single *service*. The kernel only provides the basic environment for running agents, maintaining a directory of agents currently residing at this agency, defines and monitors an agent's life-cycle and defines a basic interaction model for agents and services. It might even be argued that maintaining an agent directory should not be part of the kernel but provided as a service. However, the kernel must maintain such a directory in any way, because it has to wait cooperatively for all agents to terminate, if the agency shuts down.

Upon that kernel, each software component provides an additional service that extends the functionality of the agency. The resulting model for an agency has, therefore, a layered design, where the kernel can be seen as lowest layer. On top of the kernel, all service components form the middle layer. Finally, agents are executed as part of the agency and form the topmost layer, where they can only access services but not the kernel anymore. Actually, it must be stressed that our model does not distinguish between mobile and stationary software agents. As a consequence, our system could be seen to be more a multi-agent toolkit instead of a mobile agent toolkit.

In the rest of this section we will define the basic concepts and functions of a kernel and we will define interfaces for services to communicate to the kernel. Finally, we will also explain how agents can communicate to services. We start with the description of the basic abstractions that form an agency, i.e. *kernel, services*, and *agents*. For the following, compare Fig. 1.

3.1. Kernel

We assume that every agency has a name, which comprises of a *logical agency name* and the full qualified domain name of the underlying host. For example, if the logical agency name is *goldeneye* and the host name is *fleming.cs.uni-jena.de*, then the *full agency name* is *goldeneye.fleming.cs.uni-jena.de*. The name of an agency must not change during runtime. It must be allowed to start multiple agencies on a single host but the model does not define how this is done in practice.

The kernel consists of two classes. Class *Kernel* is responsible to maintain a directory of all agents currently residing at this agency and all services currently connected to the kernel. Class *Context* is used as mediator for agents to access the agency and services (compare Sec. 3.2 and Sec. 3.3 for more information). The kernel retains several information about agents, for example name, time of creation, permissions, and owner.

The kernel is responsible to start and stop agents and to control an agent's life-cycle (which is explained later). The kernel is also responsible to generate agent names, which must be globally unique in the whole agent system. The model does not define *how* agent names are computed but enforces that they can be represented as *String* objects. The kernel must create a new class loader for each agent to ensure that agents cannot access each other via direct method calls and to assign each agent an individual set of permissions. In Java terms this is named

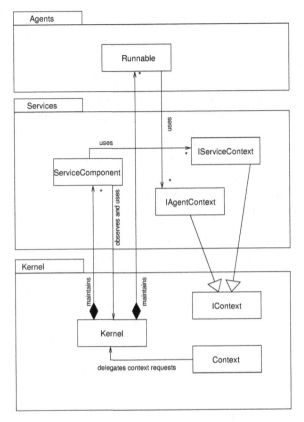

FigURE 1. Design of our agency model as UML class diagram.
For sake of simplicity, we omit methods and stereotypes.

a *sandbox*. Each agent is assigned an own thread of control when it is executed, which must be placed in an own thread group in order to prevent illicit access of agents to each other.

3.2. Services

On top of the kernel there are several *service components* that can be plugged into an agency. Each service component provides a specific service (which is identified by a *service name*) and extends the functionality of the agency. It bears a unique *name*, which is used to unambiguously identify a service component, if necessary. Usually, agents and other service components only use the *service name* to select a single component that provides this service. Assume for example the case, that an agency provides two migration components, both accessible under service name *migration*. To disambiguate components with the same service name, it is also allowed to address a service by its *full service name*, which is *name.servicename*.

When a service component is started, it is loaded using a new class loader in order to separate it from other components and agents. Note that the model does not define *when* a service component is started. It is possible to launch an agency with a predefined set of services or to allow to start dynamically on demand. Each service component obtains a reference to the kernel.

Service components can start and stop agents (simply by calling the corresponding kernel methods), request a list of all agents currently residing at this agency and a list of all services and service components. Our agency model also defines the reverse communication direction using the observer pattern. A service component can register with the kernel to become notified in case of specific events. A description of the most important events follows in the next section.

Our agency model defines a loose coupling between services components among each other and between agents and services. Direct method calls are prohibited and replaced by so-called *context* objects, comparable to proxies. Each service component has to provide two interfaces: an *agent context interface* and a *service context interface*. The first interface must extend interface *IAgentContext* (defined as part of the kernel package) and defines methods of this service to be used by agents, whereas the second interface must extend interface *IServiceContext* (part of the kernel package) and defines methods to be used by other service components. For example, a service for agent migration defines an agent context interface with methods to set the migration destination and a communication service defines an agent context interface with methods to post a message. The communication service also enables other service components to send messages to agents and, therefore, defines a service context interface, which includes a method to send a message.

The main advantage of this concept is that agents and service components do not hold strong references to another service component, which makes it possible to invalidate a context object, if a client must not use this service any more and to even exchange a service during runtime without giving notice to the agent or other services. In contrast to other agency models, we propose to use method calls rather than asynchronous messages as convenient means of communication between service components as well as between agents and service components. Our agency model is open to enable communication via asynchronous messages using an appropriate service component.

Finally, we have to describe how services and agents can obtain such a context object to access a service. For services this is straightforward, because the kernel provides a method to request a service context object of another service. In case of agents this is more complex, because agents do not have any reference to the kernel. We give an example of an agent requesting a service context object in the following section.

3.3. Agents

As common to all agency models, each agent must have a globally unique name or id which must not change during the life-time of an agent. As already mentioned above, our model does not define how to create such a name, but we recommend to use a combination of user given *agent nick names* and implicit names that are computed by the agency and that guarantee uniqueness. The full agent name must be representable as a *String* object.

Agents are represented by objects of a specific class, as in every agency model. However, in our model, agent classes must only implement interface *Runnable*, i.e. they must provide at least a single public method *run*, which serves as central starting point. Mobile agents must implement the *Serializable* interface too. We abstain from defining any base class for all agents, as for example class *Agent* or *MobileAgent* as done for example in the Aglets model. Such a base class already defines several methods to access services, for example methods to communicate or methods to initiate the migration process. Although this might simplify agent programming, it also creates a dependence between agents and services that we want to avoid. Such a base class also prevents to add new services for agents as this would entail to modify the base class which would then lead into an incompatibility between agents migrating to other agencies. The consequence of agents as *Runnables* is of course, that an agent is unaware of itself and its environment. It does know neither its name nor its hosting agency and must use services to obtain these information.

The life-cycle of an agent actually consists only of two states. The first one is *Running* which is characterized by assigning a thread to this agent that executes agent's *run* method. After this method has terminated, the agent might switch to state *Waiting* where no thread is assigned to this agent or the agent's thread is waiting to become activated again. Thus, the agent is now only a passive object that is waiting for a message or another external signal or event. Details about the life-cycle will be presented in the following section, when we introduce the basic functions of an agency.

If an agent wants to communicate to a service, a similar technique is used as for services. As an agent object does not have a reference to any object of the agency, there must be a static method which is provided by class *Context* and which is named *getContext*. Consider the following example:

```
public class MyAgent implements Runnable
{
  public void run()
  {
    IAgentMessageContext cxt;

    cxt = (IAgentMessageContext)Context.getContext("message");

    cxt.sendMessage( ... );
  }
}
```

The agent requests a context object of a service that has registered itself under
service name *message* and uses it to send a message. We omit to discuss problems
that arise from many service components providing the same service and we also
omit to print parameters of method *sendMessage* for sake of simplicity.

Method *getContext* delegates the task of requesting an agent context object
to class Kernel, which first identifies the agent that has requested a context by
determining the current thread (the kernel maintains a directory for this). Second,
the kernel asks the agency, which itself selects the service component that provides
the requested service *message* and asks this component for an agent context object,
which is then returned to the agent. If the agent requests a context object from this
service component for the first time, it is created. In the other case, the component
must return the same object as before.

We face two problems with this first example. First, if there is no service component providing a service under the given name, then class *IAgentMessageContext*
does not exist. Second, the service registered under the given name *message* does
return a context object that is not assignable to variable *cxt*. The first problem can
be solved by Java's dynamic class loading concept. The class of type *IAgentMessageContext* is not loaded until it is accessed, which is in the above example not
before the type cast. If the agent first verifies that a service with the given name
exists, then this problem can be solved. The second problem can be solved by
comparing class names. The following example shows the resulting code sequence:

```
public class MyAgent implements Runnable
{
  public void run()
  {
    IAgentMessageContext cxt;

    if( Context.existsContext("message", "IAgentMigrationContext" ))
    {
      cxt = (IAgentMessageContext)Context.getContext("message");

      cxt.sendMessage( ... );
    }
  }
}
```

We omit to print full qualified package names in this example. First, the agent
verifies that there is (i) a component providing service *message* and (ii) this component has created a context object which is assignable to an object of class
IAgentMessageContext (we omit package names here).

3.4. Functions of an Agency

In this section we will define how kernel, service components, and agents interact with each other. We will describe the basic functions according to the agent's life-cycle.

3.4.1. Registering an Agent. Registering an agent can be done by services in two ways. In the first case, an agent (as Java object) has not been instantiated yet. To register an agent, a nick name, the name of the agent's main class and a URL where the agent's classes can be found must be specified. The agent object is instantiated and a full agent name is computed. In the second case, the agent has already been instantiated by a service component and must now be registered with the kernel. In this case, the agent already has a full name. In both cases, the agent is finally enrolled with the agent directory and then started (explained below).

Before an agent is registered, all service components are informed that have been registered a listener for this event. Each service can access all information about the agent and is now able to vote against registering. For example, a service that scans an agent's code for pattern of malicious behavior, is able to prevent registering and starting of this agent. If no service has voted against, the agent is registered with the local agent directory. Finally, a second event is fired, by which registered services are informed about the finalization of the registering process. For example, a graphical user interface can now update its list of agents.

Finally, the agent switches to state *Running*, which is described in the next section.

3.4.2. Running an Agent. When an agent is started, its *run* method is invoked within an own thread of control. The model does not define, whether it must be same thread that executes the agent during its whole life-time, or thread-pooling is allowed. The latter technique is preferred due to performance reasons. As agents must be strongly separated from each other, no two agent threads must be member of the same thread group. While the agent is running, it can request context objects from services as shown above.

3.4.3. Termination of Agent's Main Method. Every time, an agent's method *run* terminates, it is decided whether the agent should be killed (i.e. deleted from the agent directory and finally garbage collected) or remain as passive object. It is important to note that this decision is not only up to agents but is influenced by the service components. The protocol that is proposed for this can be seen as a voting protocol that works as follows (compare Fig. 2). The kernel asks all service components sequentially about the local status of the agent by calling method *getState*. A component might announce that it wants the agent to be immediately restarted again (return value *restart*), or to continue to live without restart (*passivate*), or raise no objection to kill the agent (*terminate*).

If there is at least one service component that wants the agent to be re-started, then agent's method *run* is invoked immediately again. If no service component wants the agent to be restarted, but there is at least a single one that wants the agent to continue to live, then the agent's thread might terminate or wait and the agent continues to live as passive object waiting to become started again. For example, as long as an agent has pending messages, a communication service should prevent the agent from being terminated. If no component raises an objection to kill the agent, the agent is removed from the agency and is eventually garbage collected.

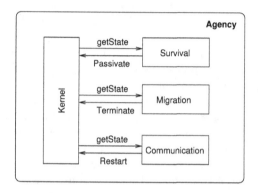

FIGURE 2. This figure illustrates the voting protocol that is used by the kernel to decide on the next state of an agent. The figure shows three service components to show the three different agent status results. In this case, the result of the voting protocol will be *restart*.

We want to mention two consequences of this protocol. First of all, if an agent wants to survive termination of its *run* method, then it must have registered with some service by requesting a context object. Second, as long as an agent possesses at least a single context interface, it cannot die.

3.4.4. Agent Termination. If the voting protocol results in terminating an agent, all registered observers are notified about this event to perform some final clearance and then de-register the agent. This notification process is implemented as a transaction using a two-phase commit protocol. In the first phase, each service component is *preparing* to delete the agent's context object. Only if all service components are ready to delete, the agent's context is deleted and the transaction is *committed*. Otherwise, if any component raises an exception, the transaction is *rolled back* and the agent is re-started again.

Figure 3 shows as an example the case of three service components, amongst others a migration component. During the first phase of the two-phase commit protocol, the migration component starts the migration process, if the agent has defined a migration destination in its context object. It uses the information stored in the agent's context object in order to open a network connection to the migration destination. After that, the agent's code and data are sent to the destination agency. On the destination site, the migration component might inform the kernel (named *lock* in the figure) about the in-migration, for example to let the kernel validate the agent name. During this first phase of the protocol, the migration process is not finalized and the network connection between sender and receiver agency is not closed. In case of any error during the migration process, this service throws an exception. When the transaction is then committed, the migration component sends a command to the destination which finalizes the migration process and starts the agent. Otherwise, in case of an error during the first phase of the protocol, a different command is sent to roll back the whole migration process at the destination agency.

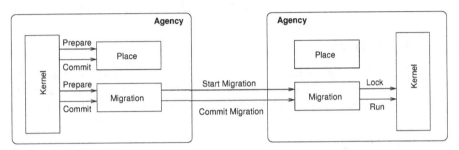

FIGURE 3. This figure illustrates the two-phase commit protocol that is used to stop agents.

3.5. Summary

In this section we have defined basic principles of our new agency model. Our aim was to identify the smallest common denominator of typical functions of an agency. The model specifies that an agency consists of three entities, i.e. the kernel that is responsible to execute agents and control their life-cycle, service components that provide high-level functions of the agency, and finally defines the main interface that all agents have to implement. Further, the model defines how these entities communicate to each other. The model does deliberately not define any high-level functions of an agency, as for example migration or communication and it does define only basic requirements related to security.

We see as main advantages of our new approach the following aspects.

1. Agent toolkits that conform to our new agency model are *compatible* to each other which actually has two aspects. First, it means that service components developed for one toolkit are applicable in all other agent toolkits too. We believe that it will be possible to enable exchange of research results on the basis of such software components in future. Second, agents and therefore complete agent-based applications are executable on every other toolkit too. The only requirement is that both toolkits provide the same set of high-level services.

2. A second advantage of our approach is that agent toolkits become very modular, as there is only a very small imperative kernel which forms the basis for

many service components to be added on. This modular architecture makes it very easy to port an agent toolkit to other devices, as components no longer needed can be simply removed. If it is too heavy-weighted for a resource limited mobile device for example, it can replaced by another component with less functionality and of less size.

3. Finally, every research group working on core research problems of mobile agents can implement their research results, for example new protocols for location-transparent communication as a service component and distribute it with other research groups. It is not necessary for them to implement other service components or even a complete agent toolkit by themselves.

4. The Tracy Toolkit

Tracy is a mobile agent toolkit designed according to the model defined in the last section. In this section, we will mention details of the Tracy implementation and especially describe several service components that have already been implemented.

4.1. The Tracy Kernel

The kernel of Tracy mainly consists of an implementation of the *Context* class mentioned in the previous section, classes for agent and service management (ASM), and a thread pool. In total, the kernel only consist of about 3000 lines of Java code.

If an agent switches from state *Waiting* to state *Running*, a sleeping thread from the thread pool is activated to execute the agent. After agent's method *run* has terminated, this thread is responsible to carry out the voting protocol. If the agent is not started immediately again (transition back to state *Waiting*), the thread is given back to the thread pool. The thread pool is initialized with a predefined number of threads (this number can be configured) and adapts dynamically to load variances.

The ASM classes are responsible to maintain a directory of all agents and service components. These classes communicate with the thread pool in order to execute agents. Agent names are defined to consist of the agent's nick name and a hash value that is computed over the agent's classes, the home agency's name, and the start time, to which the name of the home agency is appended. The ASM classes are also responsible to initiate the start of service components, which are named *plugins* in Tracy, because they can be started and stopped dynamically during runtime. Important functions of the kernel are guarded using Java permissions, so that it is possible, for example to prohibit plugins to start or kill agents.

4.2. Tracy Plugins

As part of the Tracy project, we have already defined several high-level service components and correspondent interfaces for context objects. They range from very simple plugins that provide agents access to the hosting agency to complex services to manage overlay networks of agencies. In our opinion, this makes Tracy a comprehensive agent toolkit that can be used for the development of real-world applications yet. For each of these services, Tracy provides a default implementation as plugin. In Tracy, a plugin is deployed as JAR file, which contains a manifest to define the service name, version and author information, and dependences on other plugins, which are then started automatically before. In the following, we describe some of the most important plugins.

4.2.1. Place. The Place plugin provides agents an interface to the hosting agency to obtain information about themselves, their environment, and other agents. As already mentioned above, agents are innately blind, i.e. they are not aware of their environment and do not even know their name. Using this plugin, an agent can retrieve its name, name of its home and current agency and a list of all other agents and services currently residing on this agency.

4.2.2. Survival. The most important feature of the Survival plugin is to prevent an agent from being disposed after its *run* method has terminated. This plugin can also be used to schedule agent execution in the future. For example, an agent can define that it wants to be started once at a specific time or after some time interval. Additionally, an agent can also define that it wants to be started periodically.

4.2.3. Migration. The migration plugin that is used in Tracy is based on the Kalong migration component that is the result of a research project on high-performance mobility models and migration protocols [6, 9]. The main difference of Kalong as compared to other mobility models is that it provides a flexible and fine-grained migration protocol, which leads to a higher migration performance of mobile agents and to a flexible implementation of security protocols.

Current mobility models only offer a single *migration strategy*. For example, in Grasshopper the agent migrates only with its data but without any code, which is then dynamically loaded on demand (pull migration strategy). Other systems always transmit the agent as a package of code and data to the next destination agency (push migration strategy). In [8], we proofed that none of these simple migration strategies leads to an optimized network load and transmission time and proposed in the thesis that mobile agents should be able to adapt their migration strategies according to specific environmental parameters, as for example, the code size of each class, the probability that a class is used at the next destination, network bandwidth and latency, etc.

Therefore, Kalong defines a virtual machine for agent migration with a small set of methods to fully conduct the migration process by the agent or by the agent programmer. A program for this virtual machine is called *migration strategy* and we have already implemented several migration strategies, where the simplest ones just implement the simple migration techniques of Aglets and Grasshopper and the most sophisticated ones take several parameters into account, for example code execution probability, which is determined by static program analysis, and network bandwidth and latency information. In [6] we presented results of several experiments, where mobile agents migrate in wide-area networks using Kalong and need about 30% to 50% less execution time for a complete round-trip than using simple push or pull-based strategies.

The Kalong component defines hot spots within the migration protocol, where each message that is sent or received via network is processed by a pipeline of so-called *protocol extensions*. Every protocol extension can modify network messages, for example compress, sign, or encrypt it. In [6] we already presented first protocol extensions for agent authentication, code signing and protecting data items against illicit tampering. We are currently working on adapting more sophisticated security protocols, especially path history [27], execution tracing [32], environmental key generation [28], and state appraisal [14].

The migration plugin also provides the possibility to use various network transmission protocols and we have already implemented support for TCP and SSL. As a feature provided in order to make programming of mobile agents more convenient, we have implemented transparent agency name resolution. The programmer of a mobile agent can address a destination agency using the full agency name *without* a port number on which the destination agency is listening for incoming request–instead of the full qualified domain name together with a port number as it is used in most other agent toolkits.

4.2.4. Agent Authorization.
Security is a non-functional requirement of software systems and therefore cannot be implemented in a single software component, but is distributed over the kernel and several services. Some basic requirements concerning agent security were already introduced in the *kernel* and we mentioned that some security protocols can be implemented as extensions of the migration component.

Another component that is considered with security is *agent authorization*, which defines which permissions are granted to an agent. This service is an example of a component that might vote against starting an agent, if, for example, the agent is included on some black-list of possibly malicious agents. Otherwise, this service assigns permissions to the agent with regard to the agent's name and owner, its path history [12] and the result of code inspections done in the Kalong component.

4.2.5. Communication.
The communication service developed as part of the Tracy toolkit supports the transfer of asynchronous messages between agents and services. Every agent has a message box in which new messages are stored. The agent can decide on its own how to handle these messages. It can decide to accept messages or not by closing its message box (even temporarily). So, the autonomy of an agent can be preserved. To send a message, the agent needs to know the name of the receiving agent.

This service does not support any kind of remote communication, i.e. an agent cannot send messages to another agent residing on a different agency. Even if both agencies were to reside on the same host sending messages between them would not be possible. We are currently working on an extension of this plugin

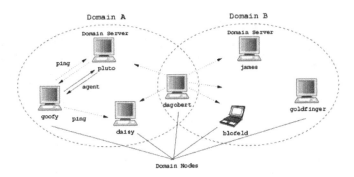

FIGURE 4. Example of two Tracy domains: Each contains a domain server and several domain nodes. Each node is registered
at exactly one domain server. Agent server dagobert resides in
the intersection of two domains and could be either registered at
pluto, or at james.

which also allows remote communication using a forwarding pointer concept as
already proposed by [25].

4.2.6. Tracy Domain Service. To manage logical Tracy networks we implemented
the *domain management service*, which is completely implemented using stationary and mobile agents. A *domain* is a set of agencies that are connected in a
local subnetwork. All agencies in one domain must be pairwise reachable by a
UDP multicast. However, not all pairs of agencies in one local subnetwork must
be member of the same domain—several logical Tracy networks can exist in one
subnetwork independently. The domain management service is the basis for a comprehensive directory service in which each agency publishes services it offers for
mobile agents [13].

A logical Tracy network consists of several agencies, which can either be in
the role of the unique *domain server*, or in the role of a *domain node*. A domain
server is responsible to manage a list of all registered domain nodes, whereas a
domain node only knows its domain server. When a domain service is started, it
first sends a UDP multicast message to all computers in the local subnetwork, see
Fig. 4. If there already exists a domain server, this one will answer by sending
a UDP package to the sender. This package contains the name of the agency on
which the domain server resides. In a second step, the new agency sends a mobile
agent to the domain server with the task to register it over there. If no domain
server exists in the local subnetwork the new agency will become a domain server
itself. As can be seen in Fig. 4, an agency (dagobert) can be in the intersection
of two domains. The UDP multicast would be answered by more than one domain
server. In this case the new agency is registered at the domain server which has
answered the UDP multicast first. This makes sense, because Tracy domains should

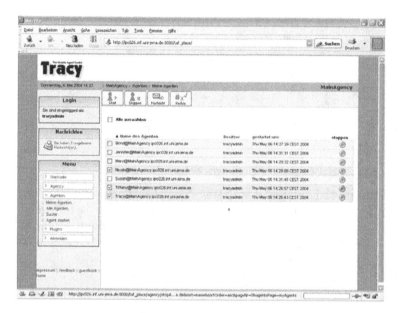

FIGURE 5. The screen shot shows an example of the Tracy Web interface, showing the list of agents currently residing at agency *MainAgency*.

contain servers that are situated locally and request time is a good indicator for this metric.

To build larger Tracy networks, domain servers can be connected dynamically. At the time, this process must be performed manually. For the future, we plan to build up larger Tracy networks by using mobile agents that explore the agent system and connect domain servers according to quality of services and quality of network connections. Note, that for an agent it is not necessary to follow this domain server connections to migrate to another agency–this can be done directly, as in a peer-to-peer network. The structure of a Tracy network is only important to explore new agencies in an unknown environment. The Tracy system contains all agencies, even if they could not find each other because they are in different logical Tracy networks–nevertheless it is possible for them to exchange mobile agents.

4.2.7. Other Services. Other services that are already defined and implemented as part of the Tracy project allow

- to send emails to arbitrary users using the SMTP protocol,
- to send short messages via a SMSC (using a SOAP Web service),
- multi-user management including dynamic permission management,
- to administrate an agency using a text-based user interface via Telnet protocol,

- to load public keys from a LDAP server (this is used by some security enhancements of the migration plugin),
- to launch agents automatically when an agency starts,
- to administrate an agency using the SOAP protocol.

As an application of the last service, we have already implemented a Web-based user interface, where Java servlets communicate to an agency using SOAP. Fig. 5 shows a screen shot of the Tracy Web interface.

5. Proof-of-Concept

This section describes an application scenario to mainly express two things: First and most significant to give evidence that our service-based approach does work and second to emphasize the applicability of well-structured mobile agent frameworks in production.

Thus, we have designed and implemented an application offering mobile services for customers of a fictive railway company on top of our mobile agent toolkit Tracy. The main goal of that application is to provide a passenger while traveling with in-time information about schedules and state of potential or prospective trains he is going to use during his journey. That passenger can use mainly two functions with our application directly from his mobile device. On the one hand he is able to compose complete time tables including departure and arrival times, transfers, platform numbers, etc., and on the other hand the application can be configured to observe train states to provide the passenger with latest information regarding train delays or breakdowns giving a passenger an opportunity to react on those incidents and to keep his journey efficient.

When we have a closer look at our application it can be recognized that two different types of agencies are needed. On the railway company's side we need a high performance and high scaling agency able to host thousands of concurrent agents, each represents a single user. Additionally, the company's agency offers services for mobile agents to access the time table database and to compose schedules. Finally, it offers a service for mobile agents to register with some kind of notification manager in order to retrieve information about train latencies.

In contrast, a small agency is needed on the customer's side, which easily adapts to the restricted resources, such as low processor performance and limited memory. That client agency has to provide also additional services, i.e. to connect to other local applications (e.g. PIMs) and to enable communication with the user via a graphical interface. We have chosen a PDA as basic hardware for our application in the first phase because it offers sufficient resources for running Java programs and hosting mobile agents. In a next step our client agency could be further downsized to another version which can be executed on even smaller Java-capable devices, for example mobile phones.

Mobile agents are used as information carriers between passenger and company agency in order to transmit schedules and delay information from the company agency to the client agency and to transmit schedule requests and observation configurations from the client agency. Additionally, mobile agents offer additional functionality to passengers, such as the opportunity to re-plan a journey if a train delays. Following this, both agencies need to implement a migration service.

At this point the advantages of a fully service-based approach for designing agent toolkits are brought to bear. Obviously we have two different implementations of our agency model both able to run the same migration service. The only service running on the PDA agency is the migration service that we were able to adopt to the restrictions of the mobile device and new Java version successfully.

Let's have a look at a concrete scenario. Imagine a salesman to plan a business trip by train from Jena to Hamburg. We presume he is already a customer of our fictive railway company and has yet a Tracy agency installed on his PDA. A day before traveling the salesman assigns a mobile agent via the graphical interface of our application to obtain the schedule for his journey. Therefore, he parameterizes the mobile agent with details about start location and destination, date, and prospective departure and arrival time. Then the mobile agent migrates to the railway company's agency, interacts there with appropriate services for composing the schedule, and returns back onto the PDA for presenting the information to its owner. We assume the salesman has got a connection with two transfers.

The salesman creates a mobile agent and configures it to observe the state of all trains involved in his journey and starts it in the morning before the travel begins. The mobile agent determines the unique train identifiers and migrates again to the railway company's agency. This time the mobile agent subscribes to a certain service for being provided with information regarding to all incidents influencing the salesman's trip. If an event occurs, for example the second train delays 15 minutes, the mobile agent receives a notification from the service, migrates back onto the PDA and presents that information audio-visually. Thus, the salesman can react on this event, for example by notifying his business partners about his delay or even by looking for other transport opportunities to keep the time loss to a minimum. Of course, the scenario is a simple one. However, behind that idea there is much potential for further more sophisticated services for mobile users.

6. Conclusions

The main motivation for the work presented in this chapter was the lack of any widely accepted implementation of a mobile agent toolkit that can be used by researchers to implement and test their own research results. Our thesis is that research on mobile agents will benefit from our kernel-based approach, in which we only define basic concepts and functions common to all toolkits. Core services, for example agent migration, communication, management of logical agency networks, and parts of security issues are implemented as software components. All research groups still working on core research topics related to mobile agents are invited to contribute to our idea by implementing their own research results as plugins for Tracy.

In our opinion, our Tracy approach differs from already existing models for mobile agent toolkits in the following aspects: Current models for agencies [3, 16] include design decisions for several core services already. We see as major drawback of such an agency model that it creates many dependences between actually independent services. In fact, our model abstracts from these services and in contrast attempts to move as many functional requirements of a mobile agent toolkit into such services. To extend the discussion of related work started in Sec. 2, we mention two mobile agent toolkit that also claim to employ a kernel-based approach, namely JavaSeal [10] and MobileSpaces [31]. In both toolkits a kernel is defined comprising of core functionality and additional basic services. In JavaSeal these services are migration, communication, and security–in MobileSpaces it is mainly migration, as services are implemented as mobile agents in this toolkit. Our approach goes a step further by defining core services such as migration and communication as exchangeable components that are not part of the kernel. Besides, services are clearly distinguished from agents.

Finally, we mention Semoa [30] as an example of another extendable toolkit. Agents are also represented as *Runnables* in Semoa and the concept to decouple agents and services using context objects is comparable to our approach. Agents offer application-specific services by registering a service object with the single *environment*. We see as main difference to our approach that Semoa handles application-specific services and the two *core services* for agent migration and communication differently. Whereas the first class of services can be plugged into the system during runtime, core services seem to be strongly coupled into the design of the whole toolkit. In Tracy, we do not distinguish between these two classes of services and migration and communication are both optional services.

References

[1] Joachim Baumann. *Mobile Agents: Control Algorithms*, volume 1658 of *Lecture Notes in Computer Science*. Springer-Verlag, 2000.

[2] Joachim Baumann, Fritz Hohl, Nikolaos Radouniklis, Kurt Rothermel, and Markus Straßer. Communication concepts for mobile agent systems. In Kurt Rothermel and Radu Popescu-Zeletin, editors, *Proceedings of the First International Workshop on Mobile Agents (MA'97), Berlin (Germany), April 1997*, volume 1219 of *Lecture Notes in Computer Science*, pages 123–135. Springer-Verlag, 1997.

[3] Christoph Bäumer, Markus Breugst, Sang Choy, and Thomas Magedanz. Grasshopper — A universal agent platform based on OMG MASIF and FIPA standards. In Ahmed Karmouch and Roger Impey, editors, *Mobile Agents for Telecommunication Applications, Proceedings of the First International Workshop (MATA 1999), Ottawa (Canada), October 1999*, pages 1–18. World Scientific Pub., 1999.

[4] Fabio Bellifimine, Giovanni Caire, Agostino Poggi, and Giovanni Rimassa. Jade – A White Paper. *EXP in search of innovation*, 3(3):6–19, 2003.

[5] Diego Bonura, Leonardo Mariani, and Emanuela Merelli. Designing modular agent systems. In *Proceedings of Net.ObjectDays, Erfurt (Germany), September 2003*, pages 22–25, 2003.

[6] Peter Braun. *The Migration Process of Mobile Agents–Implementation, Classification, and Optimization.* PhD thesis, Friedrich-Schiller-Universität Jena, Computer Science Department, May 2003.

[7] Peter Braun, Jan Eismann, Christian Erfurth, and Wilhelm R. Rossak. Tracy – A Prototype of an Architected Middleware to Support Mobile Agents. In *Proceedings of the 8th Annual IEEE Conference and Workshop on the Engineering of Computer Based Systems (ECBS), Washington D.C. (USA), April 2001*, pages 255–260. IEEE Computer Society Press, 2001.

[8] Peter Braun, Christian Erfurth, and Wilhelm R. Rossak. Performance Evaluation of Various Migration Strategies for Mobile Agents. In Ulrich Killat and Winfried Lamersdorf, editors, *Kommunikation in verteilten Systemen (KiVS 2001), 12. Fachkonferenz der Gesellschaft für Informatik (GI), Fachgruppe Kommunikation und verteilte Systeme (KuVS) unter Beteiligung der VDE/ITG, Hamburg (Germany), February 2001*, Informatik Aktuell, pages 315–324. Springer Verlag, February 2001.

[9] Peter Braun, Ingo Müller, Sven Geisenhainer, Volkmar Schau, and Wilhelm R. Rossak. Agent migration as an optional service in an extendable agent toolkit architecture. In Ahmed Karmouch, Larry Korba, and Edmundo Madeira, editors, *Proceedings of the First International Workshop on Mobility Aware Technologies and Applications (MATA 2004), Florianopolis (Brazil), October 2004*, volume 3284 of *Lecture Notes in Computer Science*, pages 127–136. Springer Verlag, 2004.

[10] Ciaran Bryce and Jan Vitek. The JavaSeal mobile agent kernel. In Dejan S. Milojicic, editor, *Proceedings of the First International Symposium on Agent Systems and Applications (ASA'99)/Third International Symposium on Mobile Agents (MA'99), Palm Springs (USA), October 1999*, pages 103–116. IEEE Computer Society Press, 1999.

[11] Frank Buschmann, Regine Meunier, Hans Rohnert, Peter Sommerlad, and Michael Stal. *Pattern-oriented Software Architecture: A System of Pattern.* John Wiley and Sons, 1996.

[12] Guy Edjlali, Anurag Acharya, and Vipin Chaudhary. History-based access control for mobile code. In Jan Vitek and Christian D. Jensen, editors, *Internet Programming – Security Issues for Mobile and Distributed Objects*, volume 1603 of *Lecture Notes in Computer Science*, pages 413–432. Springer-Verlag, 1999.

[13] Christian Erfurth, Peter Braun, and Wilhelm R. Rossak. Migration Intelligence for Mobile Agents. In *Artificial Intelligence and the Simulation of Behaviour (AISB) Symposium on Software mobility and adaptive behaviour. University of York (United Kingdom), March 2001*, pages 81–88, 2001.

[14] William M. Farmer, Joshua D. Guttman, and Vipin Swarup. Security for mobile agents: Authentication and state appraisal. In Elisa Bertino, Helmut Kurth, Giancarlo Martella, and Emilio Montolivo, editors, *Proceedings of the Fourth European*

Symposium on Research in Computer Security (ESORICS 1996), Rome (Italy), September 1996, volume 1146 of Lecture Notes in Computer Science, pages 118–130. Springer-Verlag, 1996.

[15] Robert S. Gray, George Cybenko, David Kotz, and Daniela Rus. Agent Tcl. In William R. Cockayne and Michael Zyda, editors, Mobile Agents: Explanations and Examples, pages 58–95. Manning Publications, 1997.

[16] Dieter K. Hammer and Ad T. M. Aerts. Mobile Agent Architectures: What are the Design Issues? In Proceedings International Conference and Workshop on Engineering of Computer-Based Systems (ECBS'98), Maale Hachamisha (Israel), March/April 1998, pages 272–280. IEEE Computer Society Press, 1998.

[17] Wayne A. Jansen. Countermeasures for mobile agent security. Computer Communications: Special Issue on Advances in Research and Application of Network Security, 23(17):1667–1676, 2000.

[18] Mehdi Jazayeri and Wolfgang Lugmayr. Gypsy: A component-based mobile agent system. In Proceedings of the 8th Euromicro Workshop on Parallel and Distributed Processing (PDP), Rhodos (Greece), January 2000, 2000.

[19] Dag Johansen. Mobile agents: Right concept, wrong approach (panel). In Anupam Joshi and Hui Lei, editors, IEEE International Conference on Mobile Data Management (MDM'04), Berkeley (USA), January 2004, pages 300–301. IEEE Computer Society Press, 2004.

[20] Neeran M. Karnik. Security in Mobile Agent Systems. PhD thesis, Univeristy of Minnesota, Department of Computer Science, 1998.

[21] Neeran M. Karnik and Anand R. Tripathi. Design Issues in Mobile Agent Programming Systems. IEEE Concurrency, 6(6):52–61, 1998.

[22] Ryszard Kowalczyk, Bogdan Franczyk, Andreas Speck, Peter Braun, Jan Eismann, and Wilhelm R. Rossak. InterMarket: Towards Intelligent Mobile Agent-based e-Marketplaces. In Proceedings of the 9th Annual Conference and Workshop on the Engineering of Computer-based Systems (ECBS-2002), Lund (Sweden), April 2002, pages 268–275. IEEE Computer Society Press, 2002.

[23] Danny B. Lange and Mitsuru Oshima. Programming and Deploying Java Mobile Agents with Aglets. Addison-Wesley, 1998.

[24] Dejan S. Milojicic, Markus Breugst, Ingo Busse, John Campbell, Stefan Covaci, Barry Friedman, Kazuya Kosaka, Danny Lange, Kouichi Ono, Mitsuru Oshima, Cynthia Tham, Sankar Virdhagriswaran, and Jim White. MASIF: The OMG Mobile Agent System Interoperability Facility. In Kurt Rothermel and Fritz Hohl, editors, Proceedings of the Second International Workshop on Mobile Agents (MA'98), Stuttgart (Germany), September 1998, volume 1477 of Lecture Notes in Computer Science, pages 50–67. Springer-Verlag, 1999.

[25] Luc Moreau. A Fault-Tolerant Directory Service for Mobile Agents based on Forwarding Pointers. In The 17th ACM Symposium on Applied Computing (SAC'2002) — Track on Agents, Interactions, Mobility and Systems, Madrid (Spain), March 2002, pages 93–100, 2002.

[26] Paul O'Brien and Richard Nicol. FIPA – towards a standard for software agents. BT Technology Journal, 16(3):51–59, 1998.

[27] Joann J. Ordille. When agents roam, who can you trust? In *Proceedings of the First Conference on Emerging Technologies and Applications in Communications, Portland, Oregon (USA), May 1996*, 1996.

[28] James Riordan and Bruce Schneier. Environmental key generation towards clueless agents. In Giovanni Vigna, editor, *Mobile Agents and Securtiy*, volume 1419 of *Lecture Notes in Computer Science*, pages 15–24. Springer-Verlag, 1998.

[29] Volker Roth. Obstracles to the adoption of mobile agents (panel). In Anupam Joshi and Hui Lei, editors, *IEEE International Conference on Mobile Data Management (MDM'04), Berkeley (USA), January 2004*, pages 296–297. IEEE Computer Society Press, 2004.

[30] Volker Roth and Mehrdad Jalali. Concepts and architecture of a security-centric mobile agent server. In *Proceedings of the Fifth International Symposium on Autonomous Decentralized Systems (ISADS 2001), Dallas, (USA), March 2001*, pages 435–442. IEEE Computer Society Press, 2001.

[31] Ichiro Satoh. An architecture for next generation mobile agent infrastructure. In *Proceedings of International Symposium on Multi-Agent and Mobile Agents in Virtual Organizations and E-Commerce (MAMA'2000)*, pages 281–287, 2000.

[32] Giovanni Vigna. Protecting mobile agents through tracing. In Christian Tschudin, Joachim Baumann, and Marc Shapiro, editors, *3rd ECOOP Workshop on Mobile Object Systems: Operating System support for Mobile Object Systems, Jyvälskylä (Finland), June 1997*, 1997.

[33] Giovanni Vigna. *Mobile Code Technologies, Paradigms, and Applications*. PhD thesis, Politecnico di Milano (Italy), February 1998.

[34] Giovanni Vigna. Mobile agents: Ten reasons for failure (panel). In Anupam Joshi and Hui Lei, editors, *IEEE International Conference on Mobile Data Management (MDM'04), Berkeley (USA), January 2004*, pages 298–299. IEEE Computer Society Press, 2004.

[35] James E. White. Mobile agents. In Jeffrey Bradshaw, editor, *Software Agents*, pages 437–472. The MIT Press, Menlo Park, CA, 1996.

Information about Software

Software is available on the Internet as
  ( )   prototype version
  (x)   full fledged software (freeware), version no.: 1.0.1-40
  ( )   full fledged software (for money), version no.:
  ( )   Demo/trial version
  ( )   not (yet) available
Internet address: http://www.mobile-agents.org
Description of software: Tracy mobile agent toolkit
Download: http://www.mobile-agents.org
Contact point for question about the software:
Name: Peter Braun
Email: braun@mobile-agents.org

Peter Braun
Faculty of Information and Communication Technologies
Swinburne University of Technology
Hawthorn, Victoria 3122, Australia
e-mail: pbraun@ict.swin.edu.au

Ingo Müller
Faculty of Information and Communication Technologies
Swinburne University of Technology
Hawthorn, Victoria 3122, Australia
e-mail: imueller@ict.swin.edu.au

Tino Schlegel
Faculty of Information and Communication Technologies
Swinburne University of Technology
Hawthorn, Victoria 3122, Australia
e-mail: tschlegel@ict.swin.edu.au

Steffen Kern
Friedrich Schiller University Jena, Computer Science Department
Ernst-Abbe-Platz 2, 07743 Jena, Germany
e-mail: steffen.kern@informatik.uni-jena.de

Volkmar Schau
Friedrich Schiller University Jena, Computer Science Department
Ernst-Abbe-Platz 2, 07743 Jena, Germany
e-mail: volkmar.schau@informatik.uni-jena.de

Wilhelm Rossak
Friedrich Schiller University Jena, Computer Science Department
Ernst-Abbe-Platz 2, 07743 Jena, Germany
e-mail: rossak@informatik.uni-jena.de

The Packet-World: A Test Bed for Investigating Situated Multi-Agent Systems

Danny Weyns, Alexander Helleboogh and Tom Holvoet

Abstract. Research on situated multi-agent systems investigates how to model a distributed application as a set of cooperating autonomous entities (agents) which are situated in an environment. Many fundamental issues remain unrevealed in this research area. A profound understanding of these issues, however, is necessary before situated multi-agent systems can be applied to industry-strength applications. We use the abstract application called the Packet-World quite extensively as a test bed for investigating, experimenting and evaluating fundamental concepts and mechanisms. Examples are active perception, decision making of situated agents, synchronization of simultaneous actions and indirect coordination. The Packet-World has direct connections with real-world applications, such as the decentralized control of a warehouse transportation system through unmanned vehicles. In this article, we describe the Packet-World and we give an overview of our research for which we have used the Packet-World as a test bed.

Keywords. test bed, situated multi-agent system, environment, perception, action selection, protocol-based communication, synchronization, simultaneous actions, stigmergy, automated warehouse transportation system, automatic guided vehicle.

1. Introduction

In the last 15 years, multi-agent systems (MASs) have been put forward as a paradigm to tackle the increasing complexity of distributed applications. An agent as an autonomous entity, capable of interacting with other agents in order to satisfy its design objectives, is a natural concept to manage complexity in a decentralized manner. Agents encapsulate their own behavior and are able to adapt to changes in

This work was completed with the support of the Concerted Research Action on Agents for Coordination and Control project and the Egemin Modular Controls Concept project.

their environment. Although MASs have already been applied with success in practice, many issues remain open for further research. One thing that researchers and application developers have made clear is that MASs are very complex systems. Test beds are important for investigating, experimenting and evaluating fundamental concepts and mechanisms of MASs. In the end, however, the benefits of obtained research results should/must be demonstrated in real-world applications.

Our research focusses on situated MASs, i.e. MASs in which agents are explicitly placed in an environment. In this article, we present the Packet-World. The Packet-World is a test bed for investigating situated MASs, developed in Java. We show how the Packet-World has inspired our research during the last three years, and we explain how we have used the test bed for the evaluation of our work. Examples concepts and mechanisms we discuss are active perception, decision making of situated agents, synchronization of simultaneous actions and indirect coordination. In a current research project with an industrial partner, we investigate how the paradigm of situated MASs can be applied to the control of automated transportation systems that use automatic guided vehicles (AGVs) to transport loads through a warehouse. In this project, we can validate many of our research results obtained in the Packet-World in a complex real-world case. The AGV case shows that the Packet-World can serve as an abstract application that represents a family of real-world applications for which situated MASs may be a suitable solution.

This article is structured as follows. Section 2 briefly introduces situated MASs. In Section 3 we present the Packet-World. Section 4 discusses the underlying reference architecture of the Packet-World. Next, we elaborate on the main architectural concerns in the Packet-World in Section 5. Section 6 zooms in on advanced forms of collaboration. In Section 7, we illustrate the analogy between the Packet-World an an automated warehouse transportation system. Finally, we draw conclusions.

2. Situated Multi-Agent Systems

A situated MAS is a computing system composed of a (distributed) environment populated with a set of localized agents that cooperate to solve a complex problem in a decentralized way. Situated agents are entities that encapsulate their own behavior and maintain their own state. They have local access to the environment, i.e. each agent is placed in a local context which it can perceive and in which it can act and interact with other agents. A situated agent does not use long-term planning to decide what action sequence should be executed, but instead it selects actions on the basis of its position, the state of the world it perceives and limited internal state. In other words, situated agents act in the present, "here" and "now". Intelligence in a situated MAS originates from the interactions between the agents, rather then from their individual capabilities.

The approach of situated MASs has a long history. R. Brooks [6][7] identified the key ideas of *situatedness, embodiment* and *emergence of intelligence*. L. Steels [25] and J. L. Deneubourg [11] introduced the basic mechanisms for agents to co-ordinate through the environment: *gradient fields* and *marks*. P. Maes [19] adopted the early robot-oriented principles of reactivity in a broader context of software MASs. K. Rosenblatt and D. Payton [23], T. Tyrrell [26], T. Balch and R. Arkin [3] and many others explored the underlying fundamentals of reactivity and sit-uatedness and developed new architectures for situated agents that enable better adaptive behavior and support more flexible design than the early-days hard-wired stimulus-response structures. A. Drogoul [12], M. Dorigo [9], V. Parunak [20] and many other researchers drew inspiration from social insects and adopted the prin-ciples in situated MASs.

Situated MASs have been applied with success in practical applications over a broad range of domains. Some examples are: manufacturing control [21], supply chains systems [24], network support [5] and peer-to-peer systems [2]. The benefits of situated MAS are well known, the most striking being efficiency, robustness and flexibility. In [35], M. Wooldridge points to a number of limitations of situated MASs. Wooldridge argues that situated agents take into account only local, current information and thus inherently must take a "short-time" view for decision making. However, complex problem domains suitable to apply agent-technology, such as manufacturing control or ad-hoc networks, are by their very nature distributed and highly dynamic. In such domains it is questionable whether it is feasible or even useful for agents to collect global information or to have a "long-term" view on the situation. Another problem raised by Wooldridge is that there is no principled methodology to engineer situated agents, in particular with respect to desired overall behavior of the system. The relationship between the local interactions of agents and the global behavior of the MAS is indeed a complex open problem in need of extensive further research.

3. The Packet-World Test Bed

In [17], M. Huhns and L. Stephens propose a research exercise to tackle a number of open research questions regarding situated MASs. The problem domain of this exercise is composed of a two-dimensional grid consisting of packages and destina-tions. In this domain, robots must move the packages to the correct destination. The goal of the exercise is to investigate under which conditions the robots will develop social conventions and how the robots can take advantage of information communicated with each other. This exercise was our inspiration for developing the Packet-World.

3.1. Basic Setup of the Packet-World

The basic setup of the Packet-World consists of a number of differently colored packets that are scattered over a rectangular grid. Agents that live in this virtual world have to collect these packets and bring them to the correspondingly colored

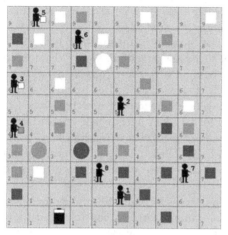

(a) A Packet-World of 10x10.

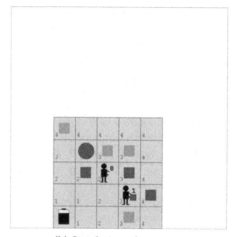

(b) Local view of agent 8.

FIGURE 1. Example of the Packet-World.

destination. We call a *job* the task of the agents to deliver all packets in the world. Fig. 1(a) shows an example of a Packet-World of size 10x10 with 8 agents. Colored rectangles symbolize packets that can be manipulated by the agents and circles symbolize destinations.

In the Packet-World, agents can interact with the environment in a number of ways. Agents are allowed to make one step at a time to a free neighboring cell. If an agent is not carrying any packet, it can pick up a packet from one of its neighboring cells. An agent can put down a packet it carries at one of the free neighboring cells, or of course at the destination point of that particular packet. Finally, if there is no sensible action for an agent to perform, it may wait for a while and do nothing. Besides acting in the environment, agents can also send messages to each other. In particular agents can request each other for information about packets or destinations, or ask to set up collaborations. Performing actions requires energy. Therefore agents are equipped with a battery. The energy level of the battery is of vital importance to the agents. The battery can be charged at one of the available battery chargers. Each charger emits a gradient. The gradient values of all battery chargers are combined into a single gradient field. To navigate towards a battery charger, the agents follow the field in the direction of decreasing gradient values. In the example of Fig. 1 there is only one charger, indicated by a battery symbol. The value of the gradient field is indicated by a small number in the bottom left corner of each cell. The intensity of the field increases further away from the charger.

It is important to notice that each agent of the Packet-World has only a limited view on the world. The *view-range* of the world expresses how far, i.e. how many squares, an agent can perceive its neighborhood. Figure 1(b) illustrates the limited view of agent 8, in this example the view-range is 2.

The goal of the agents is to perform their job efficiently, i.e. with a minimum number of steps, packet manipulations and message exchanges. We monitor the Packet-World via two counters that measure the efficiency of the agents in performing their job. A first counter measures the energy consumed by the agents. Stepping with a packet or without a packet, picking up a packet or putting it down and communicating messages all have an energy cost. As a default, when an agent makes a step without carrying a packet it consumes one unit of energy, stepping with a packet requires two units of energy. The energy required to pick up a packet or to put it down is also one unit. Finally, waiting and doing nothing is free of charge. The second counter measures the number of messages sent. By default, this counter simply increments for each message that is transferred between two agents. The overall performance can thus be calculated as a weighted sum of all energy-consuming activities.

3.2. Objectives of the Packet-World

In the past, several other test beds for MASs have been developed. The most famous is probably the "Tileworld" [22]. The original Tileworld consists of a grid of cells on which an agent has to pick up and move tiles toward holes. The tiles and holes appear and disappear at rates determined by parameters of the simulator. These parameters enable the user to tune the experiments in order to examine particular aspects of interest. The Tileworld has been used for evaluating several kinds of agent architectures, see e.g. [18].

In contrast to the Tileworld, in which only one agent operates, in the Packet-World a collection of agents has to solve the problem. Central to the Packet-World is global problem solving using local interaction between the situated agents. The focus of the Packet-World is on "conceptual exploration" of situated MASs, rather than on "testing". During the last three years, we have applied the Packet-World as a test bed for investigating the following issues in situated MASs: (1) perception of the environment; (2) (simultaneous) actions; (3) direct and indirect communication; (4) timing issues and execution control; (5) different forms of collaborations; and (6) adaptability. In the course of this research, we have introduced several extensions to the Packet-World, such as "heavy packets" that must be manipulated by two agents simultaneously, or pheromones, flags and gradient fields to enable agents to coordinate indirectly, etc.

4. Underlying Reference Architecture of the Packet-World

In this section, we discuss the underlying reference architecture of the Packet-World. First we clarify the main characteristics of the reference architecture. Then we give a graphical overview of the architecture and briefly explain the essential building blocks and their interrelationships.

4.1. Characteristics of the Reference Architecture

The early school of reactive MASs originated from the rejection of classical agency based on symbolic AI. Nowadays, the original opposition tends to evolve towards convergence and integration. A pioneer of this synergetic vision on MASs is J. Ferber [13]. In line with this evolution we developed a new perspective on situated MASs, resulting in a reference architecture with the following main characteristics:

1. The environment is modeled as a first-class entity with its own processes that manage the state of the environment. The environment is observable to the agents and serves as a regulating entity, i.e. it defines the rules for, and enforces the effects of, the agents' (inter)actions.
2. The situated agents as well as other processes can be active in the environment, asynchronously as well as simultaneously.
3. The situated agents are approached as social entities capable to commit to one another in their situated context.
4. The reference architecture is developed according to state-of-the-art software engineering principles and complies with the rules of separation of concerns and reuse-ability.

4.2. Overview of the Reference Architecture

Figure 2 depicts a high-level overview of the reference architecture for situated multi-agent systems [30]. We use a model for action that is based on Ferber's theory of influences and reactions [13]. According to this theory, agents produce influences in the environment and subsequently the environment reacts by combining the influences to deduce a new state of the world from them. The reification of actions as influences enables the environment to combine simultaneously performed activity in the system.

The architecture integrates three primary abstractions: agents, ongoing activities and the environment. First we look at the agent architecture. The $Perception_i$ module maps the local state of the environment onto a percept for the agent. We use a model for active perception that enables an agent to direct its perception at the most relevant aspects in the environment according to its current task. We discuss perception in the Packet-World in Section 5.2. The $KnowledgeIntegration_i$ module uses the most recent percept to update the current knowledge of the agent. The $Decision_i$ module is responsible for action selection. The decision module is set up as a free-flow activity tree. To enhance the social behavior of the agents, we extended free-flow trees with the concepts of a role and a situated commitment. A role maps on a subtree that covers a logical functionality of the agent. A situated commitment enables an agent to bias its action selection towards the actions of the role it plays in the commitment. We elaborate on agent's decision making in the Packet-World in Section 5.3. The $Communication_i$ module takes care of the communicative interactions. The communication module processes incoming messages and produces outgoing messages according to well-defined communication protocols. Agents typically modify their state (current knowledge and/or situated

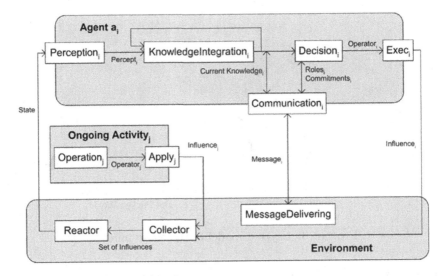

FIGURE 2. Overview of the Reference Architecture.

commitments) based on the commutative interactions. We discuss communication in the Packet-World in Section 5.4.

Next to agents, the architecture integrates the concept of an ongoing activity to model other processes that may produce activity in the system. Examples of ongoing activities are moving objects, evaporating pheromones or environmental variables such as temperature. An ongoing activity is defined by an $Operation_j$. Ongoing activities produce influences in the environment depending on the current state of the environment. We discuss several kinds of ongoing activities in the Packet-World in Section 6.2.

The *MessageDelivering* module of the environment handles message transport. The *Collector* module collects the influences of agents and ongoing activities in the MAS and passes sets of simultaneously performed activity to the *Reactor* module. The *Reactor* calculates, according to a set of domain specific laws, the reaction, i.e. state changes in the environment. Dealing with actions in the Packet-World is the subject of Section 6.1. To determine the simultaneity of actions, the architecture supports three forms of synchronization: (1) global synchronization, i.e. all agent act in lock step; (2) regional synchronization, i.e. agents form synchronized groups on the basis of their current locality; and (3) fine-grained synchronization based on logical time. We elaborate on synchronization in the Packet-World in Section 5.5.

5. Architectural Concerns in the Packet-World

In this section, we discuss the architecture of the Packet-World. The architecture of the Packet-World is a concrete instantiation of the reference architecture for

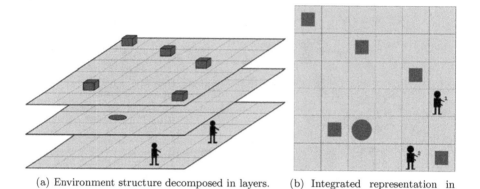

(a) Environment structure decomposed in layers.   (b) Integrated representation in the Packet-World.

FIGURE 3. Layered model of the environment.

situated MAS as presented in the previous section. Subsequently, we zoom in on the following concerns: structure of the environment, perception, agent's decision making, communication, execution control and timing.

5.1. The Structure of the Environment

A first concern we have investigated with the Packet-World is the structure of the environment. The environment of the Packet-World has a grid structure. We have modeled the environment as a collection of grid layers [27], see Fig. 3(a). Each layer hosts a particular kind of item[1]. Examples are an agent-layer, a packet-layer, a pheromone-layer etc. Relations can be defined between items in different layers, e.g. an agent in the agent-layer can hold a packet in the packet-layer. The aggregate of layers populated with items and their interrelationships represent the state of the world as it can be perceived by the agents. Each layer defines a set of constraints on the items for that layer, e.g. two packets can not be located on the same location in the packet-layer. In addition, the combined locations of items in different layers can be constrained. An example of an inter-layer constraint is: an agent can not be located on the same position as a destination (since agents are not allowed to move across a destination).

The layered structure of the environment has several advantages. First of all, it improves extensibility and re-usability. It is relatively simple to add a new layer to the environment when needed, and layers can be reused over different versions of the Packet-World. Second, the layered structure simplifies the generation of agent's perception and the calculation of effects of actions. Since we allow an agent to perceive its environment selectively, only the corresponding layers of the environment have to be taken into account to generate a perception. The laws that apply when agents act in the environment are made explicit by means of the

---

[1] Item is the generic type for objects and agents in the Packet-World.

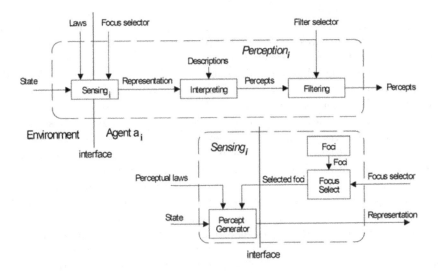

FIGURE 4. *Perception$_i$* module at the top, with a detail of *Sensing$_i$* module at the bottom.

constraints defined for each particular layer, and the constraints defined between layers. We further elaborate on these issues in the next sections.

5.2. Perception

Perception in software MASs is a relatively unexplored research domain. We investigated perception in the Packet-World and developed a model for active perception that enables an agent to direct its perception according to its current tasks. Figure 4 gives an overview of the perception module of an agent [33]. The module for perception is decomposed into three functional modules: sensing, interpreting and filtering.

Sensing$_i$ maps the state of the environment to a representation. The mapping of state to a representation depends on two factors. First the agent can select a set of *foci*. Focus selection enables an agent to direct its perception, it allows the agent to sense the environment for specific types of information. Examples of foci in the Packet-World are *see*$(a_i, range)$ and *smell*$(a_i, range)$. The focus *see*$(a_i, range)$ expresses that agent a_i intends to perceive all "visible" items within a distance defined by *range* measured from its current position. Examples of visible items in the Packet-World are packets, destinations, battery chargers or other agents. With the *smell*$(a_i, range)$ focus, the agent expresses its intention to smell its neighborhood, typically to sense pheromones (see Section 6.2). Second, the representation of the environment state is composed according to a set of *perceptual laws*. A perceptual law constrains the composition of a representation according to the requirements of the modeled domain. As such, perceptual laws are an instrument for the designer to model domain-specific constraints on perception. Contrary to physical sensing that incorporates such constraints naturally, in virtual environments we have to model the constraints explicitly. An example of a perceptual law in the Packet-World is a law that specifies which items agents are able to "see" in their neighborhood. If e.g. an agents a_i requests a perception with a focus $see(a_i, 5)$ and the general view-range is four, the law will cut off the perceived area to a range of four cells relative to the agents current location. But if the agent requests a perception with focus $see(a_i, 2)$, the returned representation will contain all visible items within a range of two cells. The generation of a representation is a responsibility of the environment and is handled by the *PerceptGenerator*, see Fig. 4.

The second functionality of perception is *Interpreting*. Interpreting maps a representation to a percept. To interpret a representation, agents use *descriptions*. Descriptions are blueprints that enable agents to extract percepts from representations. Percepts describe the sensed environment in the form of expressions that can be understood by the internal machinery of the agent. An example is a representation that contains a number of packets in a certain area. The agent that interprets this representation may choose a description to interpret the distinguished packets or another description to interpret the group of packets as a cluster.

The third and final functionality of active perception is *Filtering*. By selecting a set of *filters*, an agent is able to select those items of a percept that match specific selection criteria. Each filter imposes conditions on the elements of a percept. These conditions determine whether the elements of a percept can pass the filter or not. For example, an agent that has selected a focus to visually perceive its environment and that is currently interested in the agents within a range of two cells can select an appropriate filter *select("Agent", 2)*.

5.3. Agent's Decision Making

Another architectural concern we have investigated with the Packet-World is decision making. The model for agent's action selection in the Packet-World is based on free-flow trees [23]. Since existing free-flow trees are designed from the viewpoint of individual agents, they lack support for *explicit* social behavior. To enable explicit social behavior for situated agents, we have extended free-flow trees with the concepts of a *role* and a *situated commitment* [31]. Fig. 5(a) depicts a simplified partial action selection model for an agent in the Packet-World.

The tree is composed of *nodes* which receive information from internal and external stimuli in the form of *activity*. The activity values of internal stimuli are directly derived from the agent's current knowledge, the values of external stimuli are indirectly derived from perception, via the *KnowledgeIntegration* module. The nodes feed their activity down through the hierarchy. When the activity flow arrives at the *action nodes*, i.e. the leaf nodes of the tree, a winner-takes-it-all process decides which action is selected. Fig. 5(b) depicts in detail how the *DeliverPacket* node collects its activity from a parent node and the "carry packet"" stimulus, and feeds the combined activity down in the hierarchy.

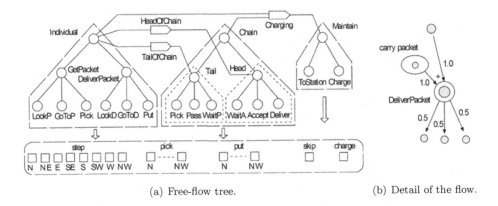

(a) Free-flow tree.   (b) Detail of the flow.

FIGURE 5. Action selection for an agent in the Packet-World.

We define a role as a subtree in the hierarchy that covers a logical functionality of the agent. The root node of such a subtree is denoted as the *top node* of the role. A role is named after its top node. A role may consist of a set of sub-roles, and sub-roles of sub-sub-roles, etc. All roles of the agent are constantly active and contribute to the final decision making by feeding subsets of actions with activity. However the contribution of each role depends on the activity it has accumulated from the affecting stimuli of its nodes. In the example, there are three roles demarcated by dotted triangles. In the role *Individual*, the agent searches for packets and brings them to the destination. The role of *Chain* is composed of two sub-roles: *Head* and *Tail* denoting the two roles of agents in a collaboration to pass packets along a chain. Such a collaboration enables these agents to deliver packets more efficiently at the destination. Finally, in the role of *Maintain* the agent recharges its battery.

A situated commitment defines a relationship between one role, i.e. the *goal role*, and a non-empty set of other roles of an agent, i.e. the *source roles*. Each link between a source role and the commitment has a *weight factor* that determines the extent of influence of the associated role on the situated commitment. Situated commitments have a name. Explicitly naming the commitments enables agents to set up mutual commitments in a collaboration. However, a single agent can also commit to itself. The connector *Charging* in Fig.5(a) denotes the situated commitment of an agent to itself to recharge its battery. The connectors *HeadOfChain* and *TailOfChain* denote the mutual situated commitments of two agents to collaborate in a chain. The situated commitment *HeadOfChain* in the example, connects the single source role *Individual* with the goal role *Head*. *Charging* on the other hand connects two source roles with one goal role.

Besides a name, each situated commitment is characterized by a *relations* set, a *context*, an *activation condition*, a *deactivation condition*, a *status* (activated or deactivated) and an *addition function*. To illustrate these characteristics, consider agent 6 in Fig.1(a) that commits to be $HeadOfChain$ in a collaboration to pass yellow packets along a chain with agent 5. The relations set contains the identity of the related agent(s) in the situated commitment. The relations set of agent's 6 commitment is the singleton containing agent 5. The context describes contextual properties of the situated commitment. Applied to the example, the context of the situated commitment denotes that yellow packets are passed along the chain. Activation and deactivation conditions are boolean expressions based on internal state, perceived information and/or received data of a message. When the activation condition becomes true, the situated commitment is activated. The situated commitment then injects an additional amount of activity in the goal role defined by the addition function. The weight factors of the links from the source roles determine the fraction of the activity level of the top node of each source role that is taken into account by the addition function. The top node of the goal role combines the additional activity of the situated commitment with the regular activity accumulated from its stimuli. The activation condition for the situated commitment of agent 6 in the example, is the receipt of agent's 5 confirmation to collaborate. As soon as the deactivation condition becomes true, the situated commitment is deactivated. Then the situated commitment no longer influences the activity level of its output node. The deactivation condition of the commitment of agent 6 is a change in the environment that indicates that the collaboration has finished, e.g. agent 5 has left its post to recharge its battery.

In general, one agent can be involved in different situated commitments at the same time. The top node of one role may receive activity from different situated commitments and may pass activity to different other situated commitments. Activity received through different situated commitments is combined with the regular activity received from stimuli into one result.

Summarizing, agents typically agree on mutual situated commitments in a collaboration via direct communication, which is discussed in the next section. Once activated, the situated commitment will affect the selection of actions. The situated commitment induces extra activity in the hierarchy, favoring action selection described by the goal role of the situated commitment. Traditional approaches of commitment oblige agents to communicate each other explicitly when the conditions for a committed cooperation no longer hold. For a situated commitment it is typically the local context in which the involved agents are placed that regulates the duration of the commitment. This approach fits the general principles of situatedness and robustness of situated multi-agent systems.

5.4. Protocol-Based Communication

Communication in multi-agent systems is traditionally based on speech act theory [1]. Speech act theory treats communication as actions and these communicative acts are considered in isolation. In practice, however, speech acts are mostly part of series of logically related communicative acts. We used the Packet-World to study communication in terms of protocols. Communication protocols emphasize the relationship between the exchanged messages in communicative interactions.

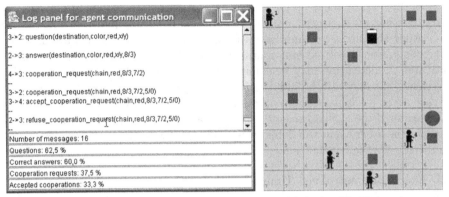

(a) Communication log.   (b) Packet-World situation.

FIGURE 6. Communication in the Packet-World.

We define a *communication protocol* as a set of *protocol steps* [32]. A protocol step is a tuple *(conditions,effects)*, with *conditions* a set of boolean expressions that determine whether the protocol step is applicable. Conditions are based on received messages, the agent's available roles, and the agent's state (i.e. its current knowledge and the status of its situated commitments). *Effects* are the results of the application of the protocol step, i.e. the composition of a new message and/or the modification of the agent's state. A communicative interaction (conversation) is initiated by the *initial* step of a communication protocol. At each stage in the conversation there is a limited set of possible protocol steps. Terminal states determine the end of a conversation.

As an example, let us look at the communication protocol to set up a chain for passing packets in the Packet-World, see Fig. 6. In the depicted situation, the conditions for agent 4 to set up a chain are fulfilled. Therefore it sends a *cooperation_request* to agent 3, the candidate tail. *cooperation_request* is the initial step of the communication protocol. In the Packet-World agents use a simple FIPA-ACL-like communication language. The basic version of this language allows agents: (1) to request each other for information about packages or destinations, and (2) to set up chains to pass packets to each other. The third line in Fig. 6(a) depicts the cooperation request of agent 4. *chain* refers to the kind of cooperation that is requested, *red* is the color of the packets to be passed, 7/2 are the current *x/y*-coordinates of agent 4 and 8/3 are the coordinates of the destination for red packets. Agent 3 then investigates the proposal. Since it is able to pass two red packets to agent 4, agent 3 sends an *accept_coopeartion_request* and activates the situated commitment *TailOfChain*, as shown in Fig. 5(a). The fifth line in Fig. 6(a) shows that agent 3 accepts the request for cooperation. After receiving the acceptance, agent 4 activates the situated commitment *HeadOfChain*. In the mean time, agent 3 itself has requested agent 2 to cooperate in the chain, see line

4. But, since agent 2 has no packets to pass, it refuses the cooperation and sends a *refuse_cooperation_request*, see the bottom line in the log panel.

After the mutual commitments between agent 4 and agent 3 are activated, the cooperation is settled and continues until the situated commitments get deactivated. Deactivation may be communicated explicitly by "end of cooperation" messages, but may also be induced by changes in the environment. For example, in case agent 3 has passed all packets and leaves its position to find new work, or in case one of the agents runs out of energy and leaves its position to recharge its battery, the other agent will detect this change and will *terminate* the conversation and that ends the cooperation.

5.5. Execution Control and Timing

A radically different concern investigated in the Packet-World, is execution control and timing for situated MASs. The relative timing and order in which various agents perform activities in the Packet-World, is completely arbitrary due to thread scheduling, message transport delays and variable processor loads in the execution platform. Providing execution control mechanisms is necessary to enforce requirements with respect to relative timing and order, e.g. for enabling repeatable simulation results and reliable testing. Three different approaches of execution control are supported in the Packet-World: global synchronization, regional synchronization and synchronization based on logical time.

5.5.1. Global Synchronization.
Global synchronization enforces all agents in the Packet-World to act at one global pace. All agents are synchronized with each other and perform actions simultaneously. In each cycle, each agent performs one action, after which the actions of all agents are processed and the cycle restarts. The main advantage of this approach is its simplicity. However, global synchronization severely limits the agent's autonomy, since agents cannot decide themselves when to perform an action. Moreover, as all agents are forced to act at the pace of the slowest agent in the entire MAS, the efficiency of acting is low. Finally, in a distributed setting this approach scales badly since the centralized synchronizer is a bottleneck and a single point of failure.

5.5.2. Regional Synchronization.
Compared to global synchronization, regional synchronization [28, 8] allows synchronization to be more selective, increasing the efficiency of acting for the agents. Regional synchronization is based on the characteristic that agents within a situated MAS typically perceive and act locally. In the Packet-World, a regional synchronization algorithm allows each agent to synchronize with all agents within its perceptual range, and in turn, these agents synchronize with all agents within their perceptual range, and so on. Applied to an example: with a view size of 2 in Fig. 7, we have three regions of synchronized agents, indicated by different colors: region 1 consisting of agent 1, agent 4 and agent 5, region 2 consisting of agent 2, agent 3 and agent 6, and finally agent 7 forms region 3 on its own, since it is currently out of range of all other agents. All

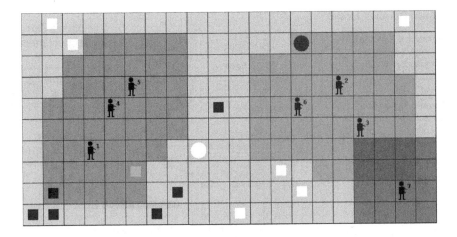

FIGURE 7. Regional synchronization in the Packet-World.

agents within the same region are synchronized with each other and act simultaneously, performing actions at the same pace. Different regions on the other hand are asynchronous: the agents within region 1 act at their own pace, independent of the pace of the agents in region 2 or region 3. Note that the regions are dynamic and have to be kept up-to-date as agents move. For instance, if agent 7 performs a step in the northern direction, it enters the perceptual range of agent 3, and hence regions 2 and 3 merge. The cost of regional synchronization is an overhead of communication to maintain regional groups of synchronized agents. The advantage of regional synchronization is its scalability, as no central synchronizer is employed. However, since the execution of different regions is asynchronous, the relative timing and order of actions performed by agents belonging to different regions is not guaranteed. For a quantitative evaluation of regional synchronization we refer to [28].

5.5.3. Synchronization Based on Logical Time. Global and regional synchronization does not take into account the nature of the actions agents perform, the handling of (simultaneous) actions does not reflect the characteristics of the actions in the real world. For example, suppose that in the real-world a step represents travelling a distance of 10 meters at a speed of 1 meter per second, and picking up a packet takes 5 second. In this case, it takes an agent 2 times longer to perform a step than to pick up a packet. Synchronization based on logical time [16] allows the developer to customize the timing for each action and for each agent, such that the characteristics of the real world are reflected in the model.

In the Packet-World, synchronization based on logical time is supported by means of (1) *semantic duration models* which allow the developer to describe the desired timing characteristics for the Packet-World, and (2) a mechanism that integrates all synchronization functionality *transparently* into the MAS. Consequently,

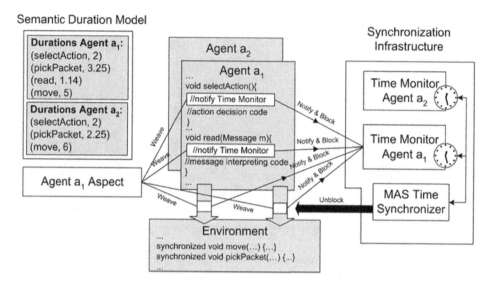

FIGURE 8. Synchronization based on logical time. The white parts of the infrastructure are hidden from the developer.

the timing of the Packet-World can be changed without requiring changes in the agents. Moreover, the complexity of all underlying synchronization infrastructure can be hidden from the developer.

We explain the working of a prototype [15] that was developed and that uses AspectJ to integrate this approach of synchronization in the Packet-World, see Fig. 8. First, the developer specifies a particular *Semantic Duration Model* for each agent within the MAS. Semantic duration models enable the developer to express a duration for each of the activities[2] the agent can perform. The duration of an activity of an agent is the period of logical time it takes until the effects of that activity are noticeable. For each agent a_i, the semantic duration model is described in terms of a list of (c_j^i, r_j^i)-tuples, with c_j^i mapping to a Java method that the agent executes to perform a particular activity with semantic meaning, and r_j^i a constant denoting the logical duration of that activity. For example, in Fig. 8, the model specifies that performing a move action in the Packet-World takes a logical time of 5 units for agent a_1, compared to 6 units for agent a_2.

Based on a semantic duration model of all agents within the MAS, an *Aspect* and a *Time Monitor* are generated for each agent (see Fig. 8). The *Time Monitor* of agent a_i contains a logical clock for that agent. At the start of the simulation, the logical clocks of all agents are zero. The goal of the *Aspect* on the other hand is to notify the *Time Monitor* of all activities the corresponding agent executes.

---

[2]With the term *activities*, we refer to all internal deliberation an agent can perform, as well as all actions on the environment and all perception of the environment, insofar they are considered semantically relevant for the simulation.

Therefore, the *Aspect* weaves code into all methods that are defined as activities c_j^i of the agent. The goal of the inserted code is to block the execution of the agent as soon as it decides to perform an activity c_i^j and to notify the *Time Monitor*, which then advances the agent's logical clock with a value of r_i^j. For example, a simulation starts and agent a_1 performs a move action while agent a_2 picks up a packet. Both actions are intercepted and blocked, causing the logical clock of agent a_1 to be advanced to 5 and that of agent a_2 to 2.25. The notification of the *Time Monitor* and the blocking of an agent's execution by the inserted code is represented graphically for agent a_1 by the arrowed lines in Fig. 8. The *MAS Time Synchronizer* ensures that all activities are not executed out of logical clock order. The *MAS Time Synchronizer* continuously inspects the logical clocks of all agents, and unblocks agents for which it is safe to proceed. In our example, agent a_2 has the smallest logical clock and hence is allowed to proceed. Consequently, agent a_2 is allowed to perform the pick-up packet action that was previously blocked, and a_2 continues by performing a move afterwards. This causes the execution of agent a_2 to be intercepted again, and its logical clock to be advanced to 8.25. The *MAS Time Synchronizer* compares this value with the logical clock of agent a_1, which still has a value of 5. This causes the execution of agent a_1 to be unblocked while agent a_2 remains blocked. Consequently, agent a_1 performs the move, followed by picking up a packet. At this moment, the logical clocks of both agents are 8.25. Both agents are unblocked and hence the pick-up packet action of agent a_1 and the move of agent a_2 are simultaneous actions as they occur at the same moment in logical time. Note that, to allow agents to perform simultaneous actions deliberately, agents must have an activity at their disposal to wait for a particular logical duration without action. This fine-grained level of synchronization comes at the cost of a scalability comparable to that of global synchronization.

6. Advanced Collaborations in The Packet-World

In the previous section, we discussed several forms of simple collaborations between agents in the Packet-World. Examples are the exchange of information about packets and destinations, or the formation of chains to deliver packets more efficiently. In this section, we zoom in on more advanced forms of collaboration in the Packet-World. First we illustrate collaborations based on simultaneous actions, after that we elaborate on different forms of collaborations based on stigmergy.

6.1. Simultaneous Actions in the Packet-World

Introducing the possibility for agents to act simultaneously opens up new perspectives on collaboration. We extended the Packet-World in several ways to enable agents to act simultaneously. One extension is the possibility for two neighboring agents to transfer a packet directly to one another. An example in Fig. 9 is agent 1 that passes the packet it carries to agent 8. Such a transfer only succeeds when the involved agents act together, i.e. agent 1 has to pass the packet *while* agent

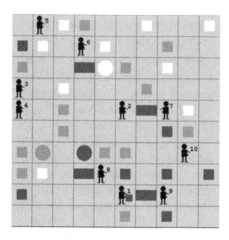

FIGURE 9. Simultaneous Actions in the Packet-World.

8 accepts the packet. Another extension is the introduction of "heavy" packets, denoted in Fig. 9 by the larger rectangles. Contrary to regular packets, to pick up a heavy packet, two agents have to lift up the packet *together*, each of them at a short side of the packet. Agents that carry a heavy packet can only move together in the same direction. As for regular packets, heavy packets can be put down at any free cell or at the delivering point of the packet. However, to put down a heavy packet, both agents have to release the packet simultaneously. An example in Fig. 9 are agents 2 and 7 that make a step with the large packet they carry. Such a step only succeeds when both agents step in the same direction. In the depicted situation, this could correspond to a direction southwest towards the destination of the packet they carry.

6.1.1. Support for Simultaneous Actions. To avoid race conditions, all access to shared state must be controlled. Current mechanisms for access control (locks, semaphores, monitors, etc.) provide support for interleaving concurrent access to shared state. As such, additional support is needed for simultaneous actions whose combined effect differs from performing these actions sequentially. To enable simultaneous actions: (1) agents must be able to act together and (2) the outcome of simultaneous actions must be in accordance with the laws of interaction that apply for the MAS.

Enabling agents to act together requires (1) a model that prescribes the conditions to determine which actions happen simultaneously, i.e. the synchronization model; (2) support to reify actions; and (3) a runtime mechanism that resolves which actions satisfy these conditions. In Section 5.5, we discussed three different models for synchronization we have applied in the Packet-World: global synchronization, regional synchronization and synchronization based on logical time.

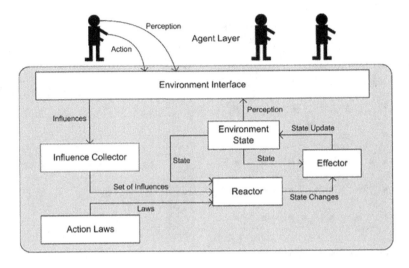

FIGURE 10. Dealing with Simultaneous Actions in the Packet-World.

Ensuring the correct outcome of simultaneous actions requires additional support of the environment. Fig. 10 depicts the model we have used to deal with simultaneous actions in the Packet-World [29]. When an agent invokes an action in the environment, that action is reified as an influence and collected by the *influence collector*. When the collector has received a complete set of influences from a set of simultaneously acting agents[3], it passes the set to the *reactor*. The reactor combines the influences with the valid action laws. The resulting effects are passed to the *effector* that updates the state of the environment. For a detailed discussion on the infrastructure for simultaneous actions we refer to [29][30].

6.2. Stigmergy: Flags, Gradient Fields and Pheromones

The concept of stigmergy was first introduced by P. Grassé [14] to describe the indirect communication among individuals in social insect colonies. In the context of MAS, stigmergy is applied as various forms of indirect communication by means of markers in the environment. Stigmergy enables agents to influence each others behavior indirectly through manipulation of the state of (marks in) the environment, while in learning approaches such as [4] agents modify their own internal state based on feedback received from the environment. To evaluate the applicability of stigmergy as a means for communication between situated agents, we studied the use of three kinds of environmental markers in the Packet-World: flags, gradient fields and synthetic pheromones [10].

---

[3]For global synchronization, a set contains an influence of each agent in the MAS; for regional synchronization a set contains the influences of all agents of a region; for synchronization based on logical time all the influences with the same logical time belong to a set.

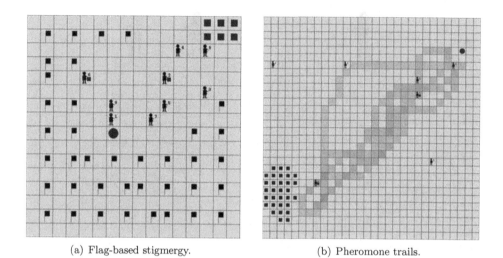

(a) Flag-based stigmergy.   (b) Pheromone trails.

FIGURE 11. Stigmergic communication in the Packet-World.

6.2.1. Flags. A first and most simple form of indirect communication are flags which the agent can place in the environment. In the Packet-World, the use of flags was studied as a means to solve the "sparse world" problem. The sparse world problem arises when only a couple of packets are left. The behavior of the agents then becomes inefficient. Most agents keep searching aimlessly for packets, wasting their energy. When several agents detect one of the few packets remaining, all of them run towards it, while in the end only one of them is able to pick it up. To cope with the sparse world problem, agents can use flags to mark a part of the world in which no more packets are present. By placing flags, the agents divide the world in two zones: a marked and an unmarked zone. Agents avoid the marked zone, and only consider the unmarked zone for further exploration. The agents' behavior for placing flags had to satisfy two requirements. First, the destinations must at all times be part of the unmarked zone. Otherwise, the agents would forever try to search for the unmarked zone, even if all packets were collected. Second, and for the same reason, there can only be one unmarked zone: all cells belonging to the unmarked zone are connected. We tested various behaviors for the agents with different strategies for placing flags. The best results were obtained with a behavior maintaining an unmarked zone which always has a convex shape, see Fig. 11(a). To obtain this solution, agents start placing flags in empty corners. Extra flags are placed between other flags or between (flags and) the borders of the world. The shortest path between the remaining packets on the one hand and the destinations on the other hand always lies entirely within the unmarked zone (because of its convex shape) and hence is never excluded.

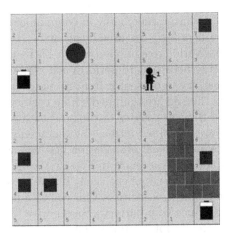

FIGURE 12. Gradient field emitted by battery chargers.

6.2.2. Synthetic Pheromones. A second important form of indirect communication is the use of synthetic pheromones, see Fig. 11(b). Analogous to flags, pheromones are markers that agents can place in the environment. However, pheromones exhibit a number of additional characteristics: evaporation, aggregation and diffusion. Evaporation means that the strength of pheromones diminishes over time. Aggregation on the other hand means that different pheromones at the same cell are combined into a single pheromone with increased strength. Finally, diffusion means that pheromones deposited at a particular cell are spread to neighboring cells over time, making it more likely that agents further away can perceive them. Evaporation and diffusion are examples of ongoing activities, see Section 4. In the Packet-World, the use of pheromones is studied to construct trails between clusters of packets on the one hand and destinations on the other hand. The agents first search for the destination, and then start forming a pheromone trail while searching for packets. In this way, the pheromone trail will lead from the destination towards the packet cluster. Once a packet has been found, the agent can easily deliver the packet by following the pheromone trail back to the destination. In this way, pheromones provide a means for stigmergic coordination between the agents which goes beyond the limitations of the agents' locality in the environment. On the way back from a packet cluster towards the destination, the pheromone trail is reinforced. Shorter trails are reinforced more regularly than longer trails, and hence tend to be more attractive. In the Packet-World, three different types of pheromones are supported: undirected pheromones, unidirectional pheromones and omnidirectional pheromones. *Undirected pheromones* are only characterized by a strength. *Unidirectional pheromones* contain a strength as well as a static direction pointing to one of the neighboring cells. *Omnidirectional pheromones* on the other hand are not limited to a single direction, but contain a probability distribution for all (eight) possible directions.

6.2.3. Gradient Fields. A third form of indirect communication are gradient fields. In the Packet-World, gradient fields are used by agents to retrieve battery chargers. All agents in the Packet-World are equipped with a battery. The battery provides each agent with the energy necessary to perform actions. At regular times, agents have to recharge their battery to prevent it from running out of energy. In order to do so, particular cells on the grid are equipped with a battery charger. Each battery charger emits a gradient that propagates throughout the environment. The effects of all battery chargers are combined into a single gradient field. Gradients fields are constructed only relying on local propagation between neighboring cells, while taking the effect of obstacles into account. In Fig. 12, the value of the gradient field is depicted in the bottom left corner of each cell. The value of the gradient field on each cell represents the minimal distance of that cell to a battery charger. Agents compare the minimal distance to a battery charger with their remaining battery level to estimate the urgency for charging the battery. To navigate towards a battery charger, the agents follow the field in the direction of decreasing gradients.

7. From the Packet-World to an Automated Warehouse Transportation System

The results of our study of the Packet-World as a test bed for situated MAS are currently being validated in a research project in cooperation with Egemin[4], an industrial expert in automating warehouse transportation systems using automatic guided vehicles (AGVs) [34]. An AGV is an unmanned, computer-controlled transportation vehicle that uses a battery as energy source. AGVs have to perform transportation tasks. Such a transportation task consists of picking up a load at a particular location in the warehouse and bringing it to a particular destination. To move from one location to another, AGVs use a complex network of predefined road segments and crossroads. The problem context is highly dynamic. First, the environment continuously changes, as road segments can get congested or blocked because of fallen products or broken down AGVs. Second, the task stream continuously changes as transportation tasks are created on demand. Third, AGVs can become temporarily unavailable for reasons of maintenance or battery charging. The responsibilities of the AGV-system thus are: (1) allocating transportation tasks to AGVs; (2) completing those tasks; (3) avoiding collisions and deadlock; and (4) charging the batteries of AGVs on time.

Today, the design of automated warehouse transportation systems is based on a centralized control system for the AGVs, using one planner which controls all AGVs. The central system gathers all relevant information and controls the actions of each AGV. The goal of the project is to investigate the feasibility of decentralize system control using a situated MAS, aiming to improve flexibility.

There is a clear connection between the Packet-World and an industrial automated warehouse transportation system. First, AGVs as well as agents in the

---

[4]http://www.egemin.com

Packet-World are situated in an explicit environment. Second, the AGVs as well as the Packet-World agents have to perform transportation tasks in that environment. Third, the automated warehouse transportation system as well as the Packet-World are decentralized systems; both AGVs and Packet-World agents only have a limited, local view on the environment. Fourth, both AGVs and Packet-World agents use a battery as an energy source that has to be recharged at regular times. Fifth, both applications have a constrained topology. Whereas a grid is employed in the Packet-World, the automated warehouse transportation system has a graph-like topology consisting of nodes (crossroads) and edges (road segments). The main difference between both systems is that AGVs have to deal with the ongoing problem associated with a continuous stream of transportation tasks, whereas in the Packet-World, the stream of transportation tasks is finite and arises as agents detect packets and destinations.

8. Conclusions

In this article, we presented the Packet-World. We illustrated the use of the Packet-World as a test bed in our research to explore and evaluate a broad range of fundamental concepts and mechanisms for situated MASs. We elaborated on the structure of the environment, agents' perception, flexible action selection, protocol-based communication, execution control and timing, simultaneous actions and several forms of stigmergy.

The Packet-World can be considered as an abstract application for a family of complex distributed applications. We illustrated the direct connections of the Packet-World with an industrial automated warehouse transportation system. Currently, our research results obtained from the Packet-World are applied in this real-world application.

A Java implementation of the Packet-World is available[5] under GNU General Public License (GPL).

Acknowledgment

We would like to thank the members of the AgentWise task force at DistriNet labs, K.U.Leuven for their contribution to the work presented in this article. Many thanks also to Eva Weyns for the graphical design of the Packet-World.

References

[1] J. L. Austin, *How To Do Things With Words.* Oxford University Press, UK (1962).
[2] O. Babaoglu, H. Meling and H. Montresoret, *Anthill: A Framework for the Development of Agent-Based Peer-to-Peer Systems.* 22th International Conference on Distributed Computing Systems, Vienna, Austria (2002).

---

[5] https://sourceforge.net/projects/packet-world

[3] T. Balch and R.C Arkin, *Communication in Reactive Multiagent Robotic Systems.* Autonomous Robots 1(1) (1994), 27–52.

[4] H.R. Berenji and D. Vengerov, *Cooperation and Coordination Between Fuzzy Reinforcement Learning Agents.* 8th IEEE Conference on Fuzzy Systems, Korea (1999).

[5] E. Bonabeau, F. Hnaux, S. Gurin, D. Snyers, P. Kuntz and G. Theraulaz, *Routing in Telecommunications Networks with Ant-Like Agents.* IATA (1998), 60–71.

[6] R.A. Brooks, *Intelligence Without Representation.* Workshop in Foundations of Artificial Intelligence, Dedham, MA (1987).

[7] R.A. Brooks, *Intelligence Without Reason.* MIT AI Lab Memo No. 1293 (1991).

[8] L. Claesen, *Regional Synchronization in the Packet-World.* Master thesis Katholieke Universiteit Leuven (2004), available in English.

[9] M. Dorigo and L.M. Gambardella, *Ant Colony System: A Cooperative Learning Approach to the Traveling Salesman Problem.* IEEE Transactions on Evolutionary Computation 1(1) (1997), 53-66.

[10] J. De Meulenaere, *Stigmergy Applied in the Packet-World.* Master thesis Katholieke Universiteit Leuven (2003), only available in Dutch.

[11] J.L. Deneubourg, A. Aron, S. Goss, J.M. Pasteels and G. Duerinck, *Random Behavior, Amplification Processes and Number of Participants: How they Contribute to the Foraging Properties of Ants.* Physics 22(D) (1986), 176–186.

[12] A. Drogoul and J. Ferber, *Multi-Agent Simulation as a Tool for Modeling Societies.* Decentralized A.I. 4, Elsevier (1992).

[13] J. Ferber, *Multi-Agent Systems, An Introduction to Distributed Artificial Intelligence.* Addison-Wesley, Great Britain (1999).

[14] P. Grassé, *La theorie de la Stigmergie: Essai d'interpretation du Comportement des Termites Constructeurs.* Insectes Sociaux, Vol. 6 (1959).

[15] A. Helleboogh, T. Holvoet and D. Weyns, *Time Management Support for Simulating Multi-Agent Systems.*, AAMAS Workshop on Multiagent and Multiagent-based Simulation, New York (2004).

[16] A. Helleboogh, T. Holvoet and D. Weyns, *Towards Time Management Adaptability in Multi-Agent Systems.* AISB 2004 Fourth Symposium on Adaptive Agents and Multi-Agent Systems, (2005).

[17] M. Huhns and L. Stephens, *Multiagent Systems and Societies of Agents.* Multiagent Systems, A Modern Approach to Distributed Artificial Intelligence, MIT Press (2000).

[18] D. Kinny, *Measuring the Effectiveness of Situated Agents.* Technical Report 11, Australian AI Institute, Carlton, Australia (1990).

[19] P. Maes, *Modeling Adaptive Autonomous Agents.* Artificial Life Journal 1(1-2), MIT Press, Cambridge, MA (1994), 135–162.

[20] V. Parunak, *Go to the Ant: Engineering Principles from Natural Agent Systems.* Annals of Operations Research 75 (1997), 69–101.

[21] V. Parunak, A.D. Baker and S.J. Clark, *The AARIA Agent Architecture: From Manufacturing Requirements to Agent-Based System Design.* Workshop on Agent-Based Manufacturing, ICAA98, Minneapolis, MN (1998).

[22] M. Pollack and M. Ringuette, *Introducing the Tileworld: experimentally evaluating agent architectures*, Eighth National Conference on Artificial Intelligence, CA (1990).

[23] K. Rosenblatt and D. Payton, *A fine grained alternative to the subsumbtion architecture for mobile robot control*. IEEE Joint Conference on Neural Networks, (1989).

[24] J.A. Sauter and V. Parunak, *ANTS in the Supply Chain*. Workshop on Agent based Decision Support for Managing the Internet-Enabled Supply Chain, WA (1999).

[25] L. Steels, *Cooperation between distributed agents through self-organization*. First European Workshop on Modeling Autonomous Agents in a Multi-Agent World, Elsevier Science Publishers, Holland (1990), 175–196.

[26] T. Tyrrell, *Computational Mechanisms for Action Selection*. PhD dissertation, University of Edinburgh (1993).

[27] B. Vandeweerdt, *A Model for the Environment in Reactive Multi-Agent Systems*. Master thesis Katholieke Universiteit Leuven (2003), only available in Dutch.

[28] D. Weyns and T. Holvoet, *Regional Synchronization for Simultaneous Actions in Situated Multi-Agent Systems*. 3rd International/Central and Eastern European Conference on Multi-Agent Systems, Czech Republic, LNCS 2691 Springer (2003).

[29] D. Weyns and T. Holvoet, *A Model for Simultaneous Actions in Situated Multi-Agent Systems*. 1st International German Conference on Multi-Agent System Technologies, Germany, LNCS 2831 (2003).

[30] D. Weyns and T. Holvoet, *A Formal Model for Situated Multi-agent Systems*. Fundamenta Informaticae 63(2-3) (2004), 125-158.

[31] D. Weyns, E. Steegmans and T. Holvoet, *Combining Adaptive Behavior and Role Modeling with Statecharts*. 3th International Workshop on Software Engineering for Large-Scale Multi-Agent Systems, ICSE, Scotland (2004).

[32] D. Weyns, E. Steegmans and T. Holvoet, *Protocol Based Communication for Situated Multi-Agent Systems*. 3th International Joint Conference on Autonomous Agents and Multi-Agent Systems, New York (2004), 118–127.

[33] D. Weyns, E. Steegmans and T. Holvoet, *Towards Active Percption in Situated Multi-Agent Systems*. Journal on Applied Artificial Intelligence 18(8-9) (2004), 867–883.

[34] D. Weyns, K. Schelfthout and T. Holvoet, *Decentralized Control of E'GV Transportation Systems*. 4th Joint Conference on Autonomous Agents and Multi-Agent Systems, Industry Track, Utrecht, (2005).

[35] M. Wooldridge, *An Introduction to MultiAgent Systems*. John Wiley and Sons, England (2002).

Information about the Software

The software of the Packet-World is available on the Internet as full fledged software (under GNU General Public License), version no.: 1.0. The Internet address is: https://sourceforge.net/projects/packet-world/
The Packet-World is a 100% Java test bed for investigating situated multiagent systems. The tool allows users to experiment with various aspects of multiagent systems, incl. agent architectures, stigmergy, communication, etc. For questions about the software, please email : danny.weyns@cs.kuleuven.ac.be

Danny Weyns
Katholieke Universiteit Leuven
Department of Computer Science
Celestijnenlaan 200A, 3001 Leuven
Belgium
e-mail: danny.weyns@cs.kuleuven.ac.be

Alexander Helleboogh
Katholieke Universiteit Leuven, Belgium
e-mail: alexander.helleboogh@cs.kuleuven.ac.be

Tom Holvoet
Katholieke Universiteit Leuven, Belgium
e-mail: tom.holvoet@cs.kuleuven.ac.be

Decommitment in a Competitive Multi-Agent Transportation Setting

Pieter Jan 't Hoen, Valentin Robu and Han La Poutré

Abstract. Decommitment is the action of foregoing of a contract for another (superior) offer. It has been analytically shown that, using decommitment, agents can reach higher utility levels in case of negotiations with uncertainty about future opportunities. We study the decommitment concept for the novel setting of a large-scale logistics setting with multiple, competing companies. Orders for transportation of loads are acquired by agents of the (competing) companies by bidding in online auctions. We find significant increases in profit when the agents can decommit and postpone the transportation of a load to a more suitable time. Furthermore, we analyze the circumstances for which decommitment has a positive impact if agents are capable of handling multiple contracts simultaneously. Lastly, we present a demonstrator of the developed model in the form of a Java Applet.

1. Introduction

Multi-agent systems (MASs) have emerged as an important paradigm for modelling decentralized, real-time optimization problems. Several lines of work have addressed the application of multi-agent systems (MASs) [21, 8, 16, 27] in the logistics of the transportation sector, a challenging area of application. The transportation sector is very competitive and profit margins are typically low. Furthermore, the planning of operations is a computationally intensive task which classically is centrally organized. Such centralized solutions can however quickly become a bottleneck and do not lend themselves well to changing situations. For example, a centralized planner may not be well suited for incident management, or exploiting new profitable opportunities. This last issue is of great importance as a large proportion of the orders for transportation originate in the course of operation. MASs can overcome these challenging difficulties and offer new opportunities for profit by the development of robust, distributed market mechanisms [5, 25]. In this paper, we use as model online, decentralized auctions where agents bid for cargo in a MAS logistics setting. We study a bidding strategy which is novel for such a large scale setting.

In [23, 2, 24], a leveled commitment protocol for negotiations between agents is presented. Agents have the opportunity to unilaterally *decommit* contracts, at the price of a prenegotiated penalty. That is, they can forgo a previous contract for another (superior) offer. Sandholm *et al.* have shown formally using a game theoretical analysis for a constrained number of agents that by incorporating this decommitment option the degree of Pareto efficiency of the reached agreements can increase. Agents can escape from premature local minima by adjusting their contracts. In this work, decommitment is the possibility of an agent to forgo a previously won contract for a transport in favor of a more profitable load.

We show in a series of computational experiments that significant increase in performance (profit) can be realized by a company with agents who can decommit loads, as opposed to a company with agents that only employ the option of regular, binding bidding. As a necessary precondition for this gain, the experiments show that decommitment is only a clearly superior strategy for an agent close to the limit of its capacity. This is a new, general result for agents capable of handling simultaneous tasks. Furthermore, we claim that the increase in performance for our (abstract) model can be seen as a lower bound for expected increased performance in practice. We substantiated this statement through experiments in [18] that show that the relative impact of a decommitment strategy increases with the complexity of the world. We hence expect a decommitment strategy to be very effective in highly stochastic environments, i.e the real world.

The remainder of this paper is organized as follows. Section 2 presents the transportation model that we use in this paper. The market mechanism is described in Section 3. Section 4 briefly discussses other multi-agent systems applied in logistics, focusing on market-based approaches. Section 5 presents a Java applet build to visualize the problem domain and online bidding complexity as presented in Sections 2 and 3. Section 3 details our application of decommitment in a market setting. Section 7 discusses a required precondition for a successful decommitment strategy by an agent capable of handling multiple tasks concurrently. The computer experiments are presented in Section 8. Section 9 contains concluding remarks.

2. The Logistics Model

In this section, we present the transportation model that is used in this paper. We have kept the transportation model, the market mechanism, and the structure of the bidding agents relatively simple to keep the analysis as transparent as possible. Some extensions of the basic model are further discussed in Section 8, where we show that performance can increase significantly when a decommitment strategy is used. We expect the (positive) effect of decommitment to increase when the complexity of the transportation model increases as the uncertainty of possible future events consequently increases. In [18] we investigated some venues to further substantiate this claim.

2.1. Overview

The world is a simple n by n grid. This world is populated by trucks, depots with cargo, and competing companies. The trucks move over the grid and transport cargo picked up at the depots to destinations on the grid. Each truck is coupled with an agent that bids for cargo for its "own" truck.[1] The trucks are each owned by one of the companies. The performance of a company is measured by the total profits made by its fleet of owned trucks. We consider (for simplicity and to facilitate the analysis of the model's results) that all companies consist of the same number of (identical) trucks.

2.2. Performance Indicators

Poot *et al.* [19] give an extensive list of performance measures for the transportation of cargo found in literature. The indicative performance measures from this list that we consider are (i) the profit made as a function of the total number of transported loads, (ii) the profit as a function of the bulk of the transported loads, and (iii) the costs as a function of the distance traveled for the made deliveries. We have used profit as the most important indicator for measuring the outcome of our simulations. Here we assume that the raw profit made by a transportation company provides a good overall indication of how efficiently it organises its operations.

2.3. Cargo

Loads for pickup prior to delivery by the trucks are locally aggregated at depots. Such an aggregation procedure is for example used by UPS,[2] where cargo is first delivered to one of the nearby distribution centers. Warehousing, where goods from multiple companies are collected for bundled transport, is another, growing example. This aggregation can take place over relatively short distances or over more substantial distances (e.g., in case of international transport). In general, the origin of loads will not be randomly distributed but clustered, depending on population centers and business locations [14]. We thus also consider depots as abstractions of important population or business centers. Section 8 presents such a model.

Like most regular mail services (e.g., UPS) and many wholesale suppliers, we employ a model of "next day delivery". In the simulations, each depot has a number of loads available for transport at the start of the day. Furthermore, new orders can also arrive for transport in the course of the day.

According to [29], transportation is dominantly limited in one dimension for roughly 80% of the loads. In Europe, this dimension is volume; in the United

---

[1] In the text, we sometimes blur the line between the agent and its truck.
[2] See www.ups.com.

States this dimension is weight.[3] We hence use a model where we characterize the cargo (and the carrying capacity of the trucks) in only one dimension, which we, without loss of generality, call weight.

2.4. The Transporters

The trucks drive round trips in the course of a day. Each individual truck starts from the same initial location each day, to return to this location at the end of the day. Multiple round trips on the same day are allowed, and taken into consideration in the planning, as long as sufficient time remains to complete each trip the same day.

Alternative distributions of the trucks (e.g., dynamically changing over time) can of course occur in practice. Such distributions, however, significantly complicate the analysis of the model's results, especially over multiple days. Furthermore, a repeating pattern is common as population and business centers do not change dramatically overnight. In our simulations, the trucks start their trips at the depots. This is in line with the tendency of companies to base their trucks close to the sources of cargo (to maximize operational profits).

Legal restrictions typically limit the number of hours that truck drivers can work per day. There may also be a maximum distance which can be driven in one day. In addition, speed limits need to be taken into account. We set the length of a typical working day of eight hours. We also assume (for simplicity) that the trucks travel with a constant "average" speed. These two assumptions determine that the total distance on the grid which can be travelled by any truck in a simulation "day" is limited.

2.5. Computing the Cost of Routing

The costs of the trucks, are in our model, strictly dependent on the distance which the truck needs to cover in a day to deliver commited loads. Supposing a truck agent is already commited to delivering n loads, the cost of a (n+1)th load is computed as the additional cost of modifying its path to consider the new load. In the general case, this problem is NP-complete, even for a single truck, since it is equivalent to a Travelling Salesman Problem.

An insertion algorithm (where we attempt to insert the new load at each point in the existing plan) provides a reasonably good heuristic for this problem in many cases. However, it may be the case that after obtaining a new order, by modifying the path for already existing loads, an agent may obtain lower costs. In order to overcome this, we make the following choice: if the number of loads to plan by the truck is at most 8, then we compute, by brute force, the best possibility for the ordering of the load pickup and deliveries, which guarantees the most efficient route. If the total number of cargo to consider in the route exceeds 8 loads, then

---

[3]Private communication with E. Tempelman, author of [29].

the insertion heuristic is used for the current plan, since computing all re-ordering possibilities becomes computationally prohibitive. [4]

The value of the cost of acquiring a new load computed by the truck is an important measure in our model, because it is used by the truck agent to compute its bid in the distributed auctions (as shown in Section 3).

3. The Market Mechanism

Each piece of cargo is sold in a separate auction. Auctions for loads are held in parallel and can continue over several rounds. The auctions continue until all cargo is sold or until no further bids are placed by the agents in a round. After a load is sold, it awaits pickup at its depot and is no longer available for bidding.

Agents are not allowed to bid for bundles of cargo. Such a combinatorial auction type is as yet beyond the scope of our research because the number of different bidding options is huge (at peak 300 pieces of cargo are offered in the experiments, yielding an intractable number of bundles for each of which traveling salesman problems have to be solved.).[5] We also do not allow agents to participate simultaneously in multiple auctions with all implied complications [20, 4, 28]. An agent's valuation for a load is typically strongly dependent on which other loads are won, and at what cost. For this reason, and for the sake of computational feasibility, we allow each agent to place a bid for at most one load in each round of auctions. Our agents can thus be seen as computationally and rationally bounded, although they repair (some of) their non-optimal local decisions through a decommitment strategy (see Section 3).

Each piece of cargo is sold in a separate Vickrey auction. In this auction type, the highest bidder wins the contract but pays the second-highest price.[6] In our model, neither the number of participants nor the submitted bids are revealed by the auctioneer.[7] An attractive property of the one-shot (private-value) Vickrey auction is that it, for certain restrictions, is a (weakly) dominating strategy to bid the true valuation for the good [32, 10].[8] Another attractive property of the Vickrey auction is that a limited amount of communication between the auctioneer

---

[4]We acknowledge other heuristics for this problem could be implemented, but we leave this to future research

[5]Determining the winners of a combinatorial auction is NP-complete. There has recently been a surge of research in this area, however. A fast algorithm for winner determination has for instance been proposed in [26].

[6]Ties are broken at random.

[7]We do not use or reveal sensitive business information in our market mechanism. When extensions of the model are considered (e.g., models where companies receive information about their competitors' actions and behavior) privacy issues should be taken into account.

[8]It is important to note here that the Vickrey auction has some known deficiencies. Furthermore, limitations of the protocol may arise when the Vickrey protocol is used for automated auctions and bidding is done by computational agents [22]. These aspects deserve further attention for future implementations.

and the bidders is required (as opposed to, for example, the "open-cry" English auction).

The agents use the following strategy in each bidding round. First, they determine the valuation of each piece of cargo which is offered in an auction. The valuation of an added load is equal to added profit for this load (the amount of money which the truck receives when the load is delivered minus the additional costs associated with the new path). The application of more elaborate valuation functions can also be useful. For example, the value of a load can increase when the truck, by transporting the extra load, can move cheaply to an area of the grid with a high density of depots. Another venue of research is in the line of COIN [33], where the aim would be to modify the agents' valuation function to let them more efficiently cooperate as one company. Such refinements of the agent's valuation function form an interesting topic for further studies.

There is however obviously an incentive for a company to avoid competition between its own trucks. As part of its strategy, the agents of each company therefore makes a pre-selection that determines which agents are allowed to bid for the company in each auction. In this pre-selection phase, the company compares the valuations of the company's agents for the available cargo. The agent with the highest valuation (overall) then bids (its valuation) in the proper auction. This auction is then closed for other agents of the same firm. In this manner, we eliminate the possibility that the no. 2 in the auction, who determines the price, is an agent from the same company. The agents then repeat this procedure to select a second agent, which is allowed to bid in another auction, etc. Using this strategy, the agents of a company distribute themselves over a larger set of auctions than would otherwise be the case. This, in general, also increases the competition between the trucks of different companies.

4. Market-Based Approaches in Logistics Problems: A Review

Although there are many agent platforms have been proposed for automating transportation logistics and supply chain management [9, 11, 13, 30], many consider the problem from the perspective of software design or design of the communication protocols used, while others take a more hierarchical approach to planning, using more conventional OR techniques. By contrast, our work is focused on simulating bidding strategies and/or different market mechanisms which can be present in such a setting. We provide a tool to simulate and visualise the effect of market-based planning in a distributed transportation scenario.

A line of work related to ours is that of holonic agent systems [3, 11]. In this approach, the domain is modelled through holonic agents or holons, composed of several sub-agents performing different tasks. The agent representing the head of the holon has the task of coordinating the activities of the other sub-agents, negotiating on behalf of the holon etc. (for example, a company agent can be modelled to coordinate and optimize the plans of individual truck agents). By contrast, our approach is more decentralised: each truck agent is responsible for optimizing its own plan based on local order information, while overall coordination between these plans is assured though distributed market mechanism (i.e. the auctions). The idea of using micro-markets to coordinate activities within a company (as well as between companies) has also been employed in [15]. This paper succesfully shows, in the context of the supply chain trading agent competition, that subdividing decisions within a company into smaller agents and coordinating them through internal markets can lead to better performance than more hierarchical planning approaches. Another succesful application of market-based scheduling [16] proposes an auction-based design applied to decentralized train scheduling.

Other lines of research related to ours are those which propose extensions of the Contract Net Protocol (CNP) [8, 17, 1]. The work of Aknine et all [1] proposes an extended multi-agent negotiation protocol (an extension of the original CNP), and applies it to negotiations over tasks between managers and contractors. Perugini et al. [17] propose a decentralised approach to transportation scheduling in military logistics. A Provisional Agreement Protocol (PAP) is proposed in order to facilitate negotiation between manager agents, which contract out transportation tasks to actual transportation agents. There are some differences between the approaches discussed above and the one discussed in this paper. First, these approaches (at least [8, 1]) refer mostly to the cooperative case, and in this setting the problems of self-interest or strategic behaviour by the agents does not need to be considered. Second their main focus is on bid syncronisation issues (which can appear in distributed settings), while our approach is mostly focused on efficiency of market mechanism and bidding strategies.

The next section introduces an applet demonstrator of the concepts introduced in Section 2 and the online auctions. The behavior of the trucks and the results of their bids can be interactively studied.

5. The Visualisation Environment

In order to get a more tangible impression of the complexity of the domain and the routing decisions of the agents, we have developed a graphical front end for our simulator, as depicted in Figure 1. This has the form of a Java Applet.

5.1. Overview

The visualisation space is partitioned into several panels (see Fig. 1):

- A central panel which shows the movement of *all* the trucks in the simulated "world".
- A side panel (leftmost) which shows detailed information about the route of one of the trucks, as selected by the user.
- Two smaller information panels (rightmost), which provide details about the general state of the simulation and the degree to which the trucks are filled at any point from their existing capacity.

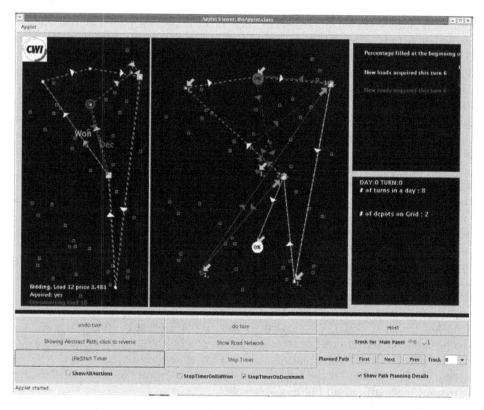

FIGURE 1. Overview of the software visualisation environment. The central panel shows the routes taken by 2 trucks during the day, while the left side panel shows the detailed route calculation performed for a truck selected by the user.

- A control panel, featuring a combination of buttons, check-boxes and drop-boxes to control the simulation.

The demo can be run in one of two modes. The first of these is interactive: the user explores the evolution of paths of different trucks through the buttons provided. This allows a more fine-grained exploration of the strategies used by the trucks. The second is more dynamic: the simulation runs independently in a loop, controlled by a system timer. This allows a more general impression of the functioning of the system.

5.2. The information panels

Figure 1 illustrates the whole visualisation tool, Figure 2 gives a view of the central panel with paths for 3 trucks shown, while Figure 3 illustrates the evolution of paths (i.e. re-routing) computations taken by a single truck, as a result of winning several loads in auctions.

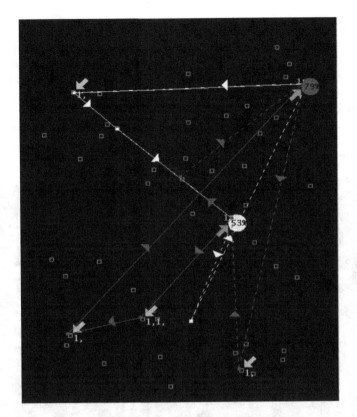

FIGURE 2. The central panel showing the paths taken during a turn by 2 trucks. The coloured dots represent the current positions of the trucks.

All figures contain several elements. Small, green, open boxes represent the basic location units (i.e. drop off points of cargo) available in the system. The depots are represented by larger, filled in boxes. A depot is yellow by default unless the agent is currently located at the depot in which case the box is colored white.

Arrows are used to indicate pickup and delivery of items of cargo. As defined in Section 2, all cargo originates at depots and pickup is represented by a green arrow (pointing up). A drop off of a load is represented by a yellow arrow (pointing down). The current location of each truck is given by a large coloured circle, which also gives the percentage of filling capacity. The route of the agent during the course of the day is depicted by an individually colored line (different for each truck) that is either solid or dotted. A solid line represents a part of the path already traversed during a simulation "day". A dotted line represents the *planned route* (i.e. that part of the route which the truck plans to still traverse, given the auctions it has won so far).

5.3. Evolution of the path for one truck

As described in Section 3, the agents acquire cargo by participating in a sequence of online auctions. After each won auction the planned path of the truck evolves (i.e. is expanded), to incorporate the newly won loads. The truck which has the lowest cost of expanding its path in order to include a new load wins the respective auction. In Figure 3, we show how a user can explore the evolution of the path step by step, for one truck, after a number of loads (in this case 4) has been won. The user can visualize how the truck computes the extension of its path - which gives an important insight into the routing algorithm.

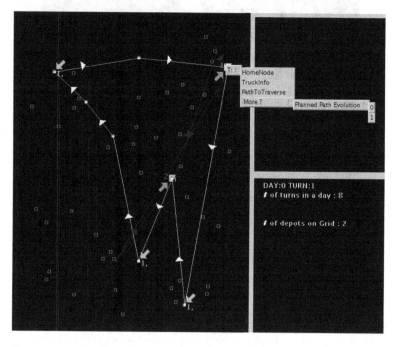

FIGURE 3. Exploring step-by-step the evolution of the route for one truck

6. The Decommitment Strategy

Contracts are typically binding in traditional multi-agent negotiation protocols with self interested agents. In [23, 25, 2], a more general protocol with continuous levels of commitment is proposed and analyzed. The key ingredient of this protocol is the option to break an agreement, in favor of, hopefully, a better deal, at the possible cost of a prenegotiated penalty. We refer the interested reader to [31] for an execellent overview of the literature on the decommitment concept. Furthermore, this work addresses an interesting application of the decommitment concept in a collaborative setting, as opposed to the more competitive setting we consider, for a multi-agent sytem where decommitment is used to repair use of detectors to reflect new conditions.

In our experiments, an agent with a decommitment strategy can improve its immediate profits by bidding for a new load with the additional possibility to discard a load to which it committed earlier. The agent is hence more flexible in the choice of loads to choose to bid on, at the cost of discarding a previously won bid. This allows an agent to avoid delivery of a previously won load which has become less than optimal due to results of continuing auctions. Furthermore, it allows an agent to consider loads earlier not available for auction while an agent without the decommitment option may not be able to adapt to new opportunities. Figure 4 illustrates such a situation, visualised by our software. This shows both the original path planned by a truck agent, and the extended path computed in order to reach a new load. The load to be delivered at the location shown in a red double circle was decommitted.

Trust and reputation are however of importance in the world of (electronic) contract negotiation [12, 6]. A bad track-record can, for example, lead to the shunning of a party in negotiations. How an auctioneer or a client will change its attitude towards a party which in the past has decommitted from a negotiated contract has to be quantified for specific areas of application. For example, for many bulk transports, a delayed delivery is not too detrimental as another transporter can easily be found and the transport does not have a tight delivery schedule. This is however not the case for expensive, quickly perishable goods.

In our market mechanism, we circumvent the above quantification issue. We achieve this by delivering decommitted cargo by a truck of the same company as the truck that decommitted the load (with consideration of delivery constraints). We thus "hide" the process of rejecting deals from the customer who offered the load at auction: a truck only postpones the transport of decommitted cargo until another truck of the same company becomes available. A company that uses a decommitment strategy in this fashion retains its reputation and performs according to the contract. For more complex scenario's (not considered here) where there is no "hiding" the decommitment and where a good cost function is available to quantify the impact of decommitment on trust, we however expect the benefits of a decommitment strategy to increase. The agents then have more options available to optimize their choice of loads.

The "hiding" of the decommitment strategy is achieved by internal reauctioning of loads. Decommitted cargo is once again offered in a Vickrey auction. This auction is, however, only accessible for agents of the company which should deliver the load. The auctions for decommitted cargo thus serve as internal re-sale markets for companies. Effectively, through a "hidden" decommitment strategy, tasks are redistributed between the agents of one company. Implicitly, the agents renegotiate their concurrent plans.

The bids for decommitted cargo, calculated as for "regular" auctions, are made in terms of "blue"(i.e., fake) money as the contract for transportation has

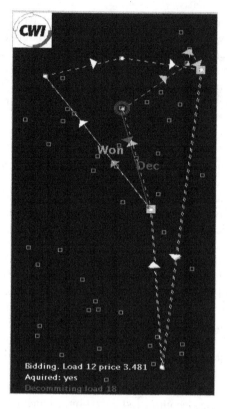

FIGURE 4. View of a decommitment situation. The truck agent decommits from the load shown through a red circle in favour of another opportunity further away (the direction marked by green arrow)

already been won by the company. Full competition between all agents of one company is allowed and all agents of the same company can enter a bid for transporting the previously decommitted load. This system ensures that the most viable agent of the company transports the load. A high bid price is not an issue as the internal auctions for decommitted loads are held with "blue" money, and the costs are fictional. We however require that new bids for decommitted cargo (in terms of blue money) exceed the original bid costs (in terms of real or "green" money). This rule is used to ensure that the original bidding costs for winning the decommitted load in the original auction are covered. The internal resale auctions of decommitted loads are held in parallel with the public auctions as experiments showed that this as a good approach to maintain a sufficient degree of competition with the other companies on the auctions for publicly available loads. As an alternative, a decommitted load could be offered in a public auction to other companies, i.e. outsourcing, a common practice in the transportation world.

For simplicity and from a computational viewpoint, we allow agents to discard only one load in each round of bidding. Furthermore, only loads which have been won but are not yet picked up can be discarded, to avoid the possible extra cost of unloading. Decommitment is hence an administrative action.

Furthermore, we do not allow agents to decommit cargo which must be delivered today (see Section 2.1) to minimize the chance of a too-late delivery. Additionally, we have constrained the possible backlog of decommitted loads by only allowing a decommitment by an individual truck if the total number of currently unassigned, decommitted loads does not exceed the number of trucks in the company.[9] This approach leads to good results: In the computational experiments less than 0.2% of the decommitted loads were delivered too late. Penalties for too-late delivery will hence have to be exorbitant in order to offset the benefits of decommitment presented in Section 8.

7. Conditions for Decommitment

We observe in the computational experiments that decommitment of a load occurs predominantly when trucks are close to filling their maximum capacity. To understand this result, it is useful to first consider two extreme situations: (i) an extreme shortage of available cargo and (ii) an extreme excess of available cargo (relative to the carrying capacity of the trucks).

In case of an extreme shortage of loads, a truck will not decommit a load as it has a large excess capacity: it is more profitable to add a load to a relatively empty truck than to replace one load by another one. In the other case of a large selection of loads to choose from, a new load, which (closely) fills the remaining capacity of the truck is mostly available. Again, decommitment does not occur as adding a load which fits is more profitable than fine tuning profits at the cost of another load which is dropped.

Figure 5 illustrates the impact of decommitment for a range of offered loads for a single truck to bid on. We plot the number of transported loads as a function of the number of loads presented. On the far left, the number of available loads is low. As a consequence, the available loads are almost all picked up and transported. If the production rate increases, we move to the right in Figure 5. The (positive) effect of decommitment then increases, until the trucks reach their capacity limits. On the far right in Figure 5, the number of offered loads is very high. In this case (an excess of cargo), the added value of decommitment also decreases as the maximum number of tasks that the truck is able to handle can be achieved. Note that for specific scenario's a slightly higher performance can be reached than without the use of a decommitment strategy, but in the limit of available loads (tasks) the added benefit of decommitment will disappear.

---

[9] Alternative, more sophisticated heuristics are a topic of research.

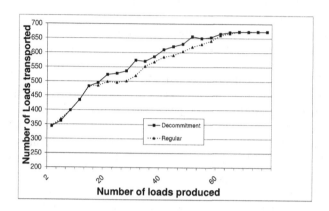

FIGURE 5. The added value of decommitment for a wide range of number of offered loads for one truck. The decommitment strategy only has a strong impact for a subset of the range of number of offered loads.

Hence, we hypothesize a decommitment strategy is most beneficial when a truck is close to reaching its maximum capacity and has a limited number of extra tasks to choose from. We believe this is a general result for an agent capable of doing multiple tasks in parallel. This hypothesis must be kept in mind when evaluating whether to apply a decommitment strategy in novel settings.

In our experiments, we observe for a company with multiple trucks, the use of a decommitment strategy only has a strongly positive effect when a significant fraction of its trucks actually decommit loads. When the supply of loads during one day approximately matches the carrying capacity of the trucks, the above condition is met. We note in real-life situations that there are often economic incentives which drive the market to such a balanced situation, if supply and demand do not match. Hence, a decommitment strategy can be expected to have an impact in real markets.

In our simulations, we keep the number of companies and trucks constant when observing the performance of the companies over a number of days. In case of a balanced market, this implies that the amount of cargo which is transported per day is relatively constant. To this end, we search for an equilibrium "production" of new cargo. In a sense, this is a reversion of the normal market operation. The addition or removal of a truck is however an operation with a large impact. It is not straightforward to formulate criteria in terms of profits which make the addition/removal of a truck an issue, especially over a short time period. Furthermore, differentiation between the various companies in composition makes evaluation of the experiments non trivial. We hence set the production level at a good initial estimate and adapt towards the equilibrium for the strategy used.

In our experiments, this equilibrium of supply and demand is achieved by setting the production level of loads to match the approximate carrying capacity of the trucks, while as yet not using a decommitment strategy. An initial number of loads is generated and new loads are produced in the course of the day. The level of production is chosen so as to arrive at a constant number of loads available for transport the next day (within 5% of the initial number of loads available). When this constraint is met, the number of loads and the carrying capacity of the trucks on the grid are in equilibrium over the days of the simulation. With the derived production schedules, we rerun the experiments, but with the additional possibility of a truck to decommit an earlier won bid. The performance of the regular bidding strategy versus the decommitment strategy can then be calculated.

8. Experimental Results

In this section, we study the performance of companies that use a decommitment strategy relative to companies which do not. Section 8.1 contains results for a Sugarscape-like model. In this model, the edges of the transportation grid are connected (to suppress boundary effects). In Section 8.2 we consider a finite-size model with a Gaussian distribution of the production. In Sections 8.1–8.3, we further investigate the effect of decommitment for these two models (as a function of the number of depots and the number of trucks per depot. Special cases of the models are further presented in [18]. We conclude with Section 8.4 on performance of the decommitment strategy for domains with larger uncertainty. Similar results for the above two models were also found using benchmark data from www.opsresearch.com and www.sintef.no/static/am/opti/projects/top/vrp/ for location of depots and scheduling of loads. We feel that our results hence hold for a wide scheme of settings as long as the number of offered loads meets the requirements given in Section 7.

In the experiments, the performance of the bidding strategies is tested over a period of days (15) in order to measure not only immediate performance but also the effect of a bid (or decommitment) over a longer time period. All companies place an equal number of trucks at each depot for fair competition. Unless stated otherwise, we use one truck per depot per company. We refer to the full paper [18] for the experimental setting details.

8.1. A Sugarscape-like Model

We first consider a "Sugarscape-like" grid [7]. Like in Sugarscape, we connect the edges of the grid (to suppress boundary effects). In addition, trucks can only move along the grid lines (i.e., they cannot move diagonally). We place the depots with equal spacing on the grid (the distance is 2 nodes); each depot also has the same production rate. With these assumptions, we obtain a highly symmetric "transportation world".

The performance of the Sugarscape model for one company without and with a decommitment strategy is summarized in Table 1 for respectively 4, 9, and 25 depots. We consider two companies in these experiments of which only one can use a decommitment strategy. In Table 1, we report the number of transported loads and the profit that is generated (in 1000 monetary units), with and without use of a decommitment strategy. Note that the grid is already filled densely in case of 25 depots (out of 100 possible locations). Competition between the two companies then becomes intense and profit margins drop as competition in the auctions increases.

TABLE 1. Results for a Sugarscape model.

depots	decommitment?	loads	profit
4	no	940	91
4	yes	987	99
increase		5%	8.7%
9	no	1826	420
9	yes	1920	446
increase		5.1%	10.6%
25	no	3704	585
25	yes	4197	627
increase		10.6%	7.1%

8.2. A Gaussian Distribution Model

The Sugarscape transportation model of Section 8.1 is highly stylized. For example, boundary effects are suppressed by using a toroidal grid, depots are equally spaced, production is uniform, and trucks can only move along the grid lines. We investigate in this section whether the decommitment strategy also works for a transportation model which does not make these limiting assumptions.

This alternative model consists of a plain square grid. The trucks can move in arbitrary directions on the grid, as long as they do not exceed the grid's boundaries. The depots are placed at random locations on the grid. Furthermore, we do no longer assume that production is uniform. Instead, we assume that the spatial production rate follows a Gaussian distribution (with its peak in the center of the grid) and then assign each new load to the nearest depot for transportation[10]. Such a model is representative of a large city or a major business center which is surrounded by smaller cities or businesses [14]. The remainder of this paper discusses results obtained for this model.

Figure 6 shows the profits made by a company (with and without the use of a decommitment strategy) as a function of the number of depots on the grid. Note

---

[10]Production is maximized by maximizing the standard deviation of the Gaussian.

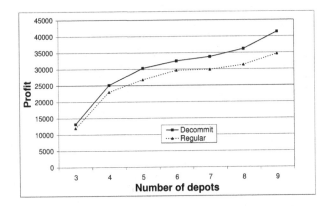

FIGURE 6. Profits made by a company (with and without decommitment) as a function of the number of depots on the grid.

the positive effect of decommitment on a company's profit. This effect becomes especially large in case of a densely filled grid. In the experiments, we observed on average one decommitment per truck per day, increasing to a maximum of three per day for a densely filled grid. Results for more than two companies show similar trends for the decommitting company. Figure 7 shows that the number of transported loads also increases when a company uses a decommitment strategy.

It is also important to note that the use of decommitment by one company can decrease the performance of the non-decommitting companies. This loss can amount to half the increase in profit of the company who uses a decommitment strategy. This effect is of importance when the margin for survival is small and under-performing companies may be removed from the field.

8.3. Multiple Trucks at Depots

In the previous experiments, only one truck per company was stationed at each depot. Figure 8 shows how a firm's profit depends on the number of trucks per depot, with and without decommitment. Note that the effect of the decommitment strategy clearly increases as the number of trucks on the grid increases.

8.4. Decommitment With Larger Uncertainty

In this final section, we investigate two changes in the transportation model which further increase the impact of the decommitment strategy. We first consider a price function for which the correct prediction of future loads becomes more important due to a greater difference in the price of individual loads. Secondly, we investigate the impact of restricting the available information to the agents by limiting the distance over which an agent can sample the grid for available loads.

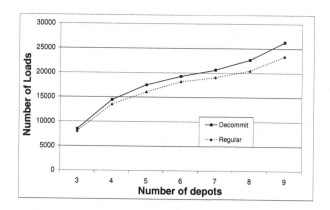

FIGURE 7. Number of transported loads as a function of the number of depots on the grid. Decommitment has a clear positive effect: the number of carried loads increases significantly.

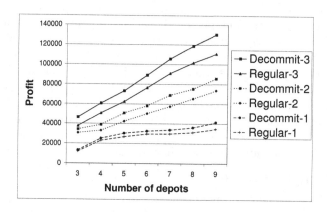

FIGURE 8. Influence of the number of trucks per depot on the profit made by a company, with and without decommitment. The number of trucks per depot is indicated in the figure's key.

In Figure 9, we show the strong relative increase in profits when a quadratic price function is used.[11] A similar effect as visible in Figure 9 occurs if the price

---

[11]The price for a load l is $40 + weight(l)^2 + distance(l)$ as opposed to the usual $40 + weight(l) + distance(l)$.

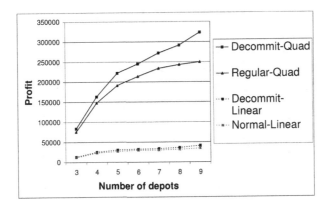

FIGURE 9. The effect of decommitment in case of linear and non-linear (quadratic) price functions.

for delivery increases sharply as the deadline for delivery approaches. In both cases there is a strong incentive for agents to correctly anticipate which profitable loads will still appear.

Additional experiments also show that the effect of decommitment increases if the truck's agents are more "myopic". Truck agents can decide to limit their bidding range due to communication overhead or a lack of computational resources. In Figure 10, we show the impact of decommitment when an agent only considers loads for pickup which are not too far away from its current location.[12] This figure shows that the absolute and relative impact of decommitment increases in this case, as an agent is less able to observe the available loads and thus makes less optimal choices in the course of time, which need to be repaired.

9. Conclusions and Discussion

We study the use of a decommitment strategy in case of on-line bidding for cargo by agents in a multi-company, multi-depot transportation setting. In our model, an agent bidding for a truck can decommit a load in lieu of a more favorable item of cargo. We observe significant increases in profit that scale with the size of operations and uncertainty of future prospects. The observed profit margins are significant in the competitive market of transport where a 4% profit is considered exceptional. For example, the average profit margin before taxes for the Dutch road transport sector (from 1989 to 1999) was only 1.6% [29]. Adoption of a decommitment strategy can thus give a company a significant edge.

---

[12]We use an operating range of one quarter of the size of the grid.

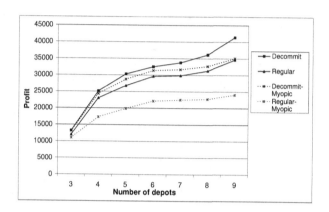

FIGURE 10. The role of decommitment in case of "myopic" bidding agents.

For specific applications beyond that of our model and for novel areas, the added value of decommitment, and the circumstances where it can be applied successfully should be studied further. However, based upon our computational experiments, we hypothesize that the positive impact of a decommitment strategy increases with the complexity of the operating domain, as it then becomes of greater importance to have the opportunity to roll-back a previous sub optimal decision [24]. Furthermore, we currently shield the reputation of a company by hiding the decommitment strategy by internal resale of decommitted loads. Without this hiding, the impact of a decommitment strategy can further increase, of course dependent upon the possible penalties incurred for specific domains.

We also observe that decommitment has the highest impact when an agent is close to its maximum capacity for handling multiple contracts in parallel. With sufficient capacity, it is often more beneficial to add an extra contract than to replace a won contract in favor of a superior offer. Hence, for multi-agent systems where agents are capable of handling several tasks simultaneously, a decommitment strategy can be expected to have its largest impact when the agents are operated at (almost) full capacity.

The efficient routing of cargo has a long history within Operational Research (OR). Classical OR techniques with their centralized coordination and computation are however not as well suited to cope with the dynamics of incidence management or for exploiting new opportunities on-line as an agent-based approach can be. A non trivial, but fruitful line of future research is a full combination of both worlds. Issues which then to be addressed are the intertwining of optimizations by individual agents and the capabilities of OR to (re)calculate efficient schedules for (a subset of) the agents. We expect the application of a decommitment strategy in such a complex world to have a clear, added benefit.

References

[1] S. Aknine, S. Pinson, and M. F. Shakun. An extended multi-agent negotiation protocol. *Autonomous Agents and Multi-Agent Systems*, 8(1):5–45, 2004.

[2] M. Andersson and T. Sandholm. Leveled commitment contracts with myopic and strategic agents. *Journal of Economic Dynamics and Control*, 25:615–640, 2001.

[3] H.-J. Bürckert, K. Fischer, and G. Vierke. Teletruck: A holonic fleet management system. In *Proceedings of the 14th European Meeting on Cybernetics and Systems Research*, pages 695–700, 1999.

[4] A. Byde, C. Preist, and N. R. Jennings. Decision procedures for multiple auctions. In *Autonomous Agents & Multiagent Systems*, pages 613–622, part 2. ACM press, 2002.

[5] S. Clearwater, editor. *Market based Control of Distributed Systems*. World Scientific Press, Singapore., 1995.

[6] C. Dellarocas. Goodwill hunting: An economically efficient online feedback mechanism in environments with variable product quality. In W. Walsh, editor, *Proceedings of the 4th Workshop on Agent Mediated Electronic Commerce at AAMAS 2002. Lecture Notes in Artificial Intelligence from Springer-Verlag volume 2531*, pages 238–252. Springer, 2002.

[7] J. Epstein and R. Axtell. *Growing Artificial Societies: Social Science From The Bottom Up*. Brookings Institution, 1996.

[8] K. Fischer, J. P. Müller, and M. Pischel. Cooperative transportation scheduling, an application domain for DAI. *Journal of Applied Artificial Intelligence, special issue on intelligent agents*, 10(1), 1996.

[9] T. R. Fox M. S., Barbuceanu M. Agent-oriented supply-chain management. *International Journal of Flexible Manufacturing Systems*, 12:165–188, 2000.

[10] P. Klemperer. Auction theory: a guide to the literature. *Journal of economic surveys*, pages 227–286, 1999.

[11] M. Klusch and A. Gerber. Casa: Agent-based integrated services network for timber production and sales. *IEEE Intelligent Systems*, 17(2), 2002.

[12] L. Mui, A. Halberstadt, and M. Mojdeh. Notions of reputation in multi-agents systems: A review. In *Autonomous Agents & Multiagent Systems*. ACM press, 2002.

[13] S. Ossowski, A. Fernández, J. M. Serrano, J.-L. P. de-la Cruz, M.-V. Belmonte, J. Z. Hernández, A. García-Serrano, and J.-M. Maseda. Designing multiagent decision support system - the case of transportation management. In *Proceedings of the Third International Conference on Autonomous Agents & Multiagent Systems (AAMAS), New York*, pages 1470–1471, 2004.

[14] H. S. Otter, A. van der Veen, and H. J. de Vriend. ABLOoM: Location behaviour, spatial patterns, and agent-based modelling. *Journal of Artificial Societies and Social Simulation*, 4(4), 2001.

[15] F. D. P. Keller and D. Precup. Redagent-2003: An autonomous supply-chain management agent. *Proceedings of the Third International Conference on Autonomous Agents & Multiagent Systems (AAMAS), New York*, pages 1182–1189, 2004.

[16] D. C. Parkes and L. H. Ungar. An auction-based method for decentralized train scheduling. In *Proceedings 5th International Conference on Autonomous Agents (Agents'01)*, 2001.

[17] D. Perugini, D. Lambert, L. Sterling, and A. R. Pearce. Agent-based global transportation scheduling in military logistics. *Proceedings of the Third International Conference on Autonomous Agents & Multiagent Systems (AAMAS), New York*, pages 1278–1279, 2004.

[18] P.J. 't Hoen and La Poutré, J.A. A decommitment strategy in a competitive multiagent transportation setting. In *Proceedings of the 5th Workshop on Agent Mediated Electronic Commerce at AAMAS 2003*, volume 3048 of *Lecture Notes in Artificial Intelligence*, pages 56–72. Springer, 2003.

[19] A. Poot, G. Kant, and A. Wagelmans. A savings based method for real-life vehicle routing problems. Technical Report EI 9938/A, Erasmus University Rotterdam, Econometric Institute in its series Econometric Institute Reports, 1999.

[20] C. Preist, C. Bartolini, and I. Phillips. Algorithm design for agents which participate in multiple simultaneous auctions. In *Proceedings of Agent Mediated E-Commerce, LNAI 2003*, page 139 ff, 2001.

[21] T. Sandholm. An implementation of the contract net protocol based on marginal cost calculations. In *Proceedings of the 12th International Workshop on Distributed Artificial Intelligence*, pages 295–308, Hidden Valley, Pennsylvania, 1993.

[22] T. Sandholm. Limitations of the vickrey auction in computational multiagent systems. In *2nd International Conference on Multiagent Systems (ICMAS-96)*, pages 299–306. AAAI Press, 1996.

[23] T. Sandholm and V. Lesser. Issues in automated negotiation and electronic commerce: Extending the contract net framework. In *Proceedings of the First International Conference on Multiagent Systems.*, pages 328–335, Menlo park, California, 1995. AAAI Press / MIT Press.

[24] T. Sandholm and V. Lesser. Leveled-commitment contracting, a backtracking instrument for multiagent systems. *AI Magazine*, Fall 2002:89–100, 2002.

[25] T. Sandholm and V. R. Lesser. Leveled commitment contracts and strategic breach. *Games and Economic Behavior*, 35:212–270, 2001. Special issue on AI and Economics. Early version: *Advantages of a Leveled Commitment Contracting Protocol* in the proceedings of the National Conference on Artificial Intelligence (AAAI), pp. 126–133, Portland, OR, 1996.

[26] T. Sandholm, T. Suri, S. Gilpin, and A. Levine. CABOB: A fast optimal algorithm for combinatorial auctions. In *International Joint Conference on Artificial Intelligence (IJCAI)*, 2001.

[27] J. Sauer, T. Freese, and T. Teschke. Towards agent-based multi-site scheduling. In *ECAI 2000 European Conference on Artificial Intelligence 14th Workshop, New Results in Planning, Scheduling and Design (PUK2000)*, 2000.

[28] P. Stone, R. Schapire, J. Csirik, M. Littman, and D. McAllester. ATTac-2001: A learning, autonomous bidding agent. In W. Walsh, editor, *Proceedings of the 4th*

Workshop on Agent Mediated Electronic Commerce at AAMAS 2002. Lecture Notes in Artificial Intelligence from Springer-Verlag volume 2531, pages 143–160. Springer, 2002.

[29] E. Tempelman. Daf-trucks- where materials make money. In *Second Workshop on Cold and Hot Forging of Light-Weight Materials, Delft, from the ICFG (International Cold Forging Group)*, 2002.

[30] I. J. Timm, editor. *Proceedings of the Workshop on Agent Technologies in Logistics.* ECAI, 2002.

[31] M. van Dyne. *Negotiated Decommitment in a Collaborative Agent Environment.* PhD thesis, University of Kansas, 2003.

[32] W. Vickrey. Counterspeculation, auctions and competitive sealed tenders. *Journal of Finance*, 16:8–37, 1961.

[33] D. Wolpert, K.Tumer, and J. Frank. Using collective intelligence to route internet traffic. In *Advances in Neural Information Processing Systems-11*, pages 952–958, Denver, 1998.

Software is available on the Internet as
( ) prototype version
( ) full fledged software (freeware), version no.:
( ) full fledged software (for money), version no.:
( ) Demo/trial version
(*) not (yet) available

Internet address for description of software:
http://homepages.cwi.nl/ robu/netobjectdays2004/NetObjectDaysPresentation.ppt

Pieter Jan 't Hoen
CWI, Centre for Mathematics and Computer Science
P.O. Box 94079, 1090 GB Amsterdam, The Netherlands
e-mail: hoen@cwi.nl

Valentin Robu
CWI, Centre for Mathematics and Computer Science
P.O. Box 94079, 1090 GB Amsterdam, The Netherlands
e-mail: robu@cwi.nl

Han La Poutré
CWI, Centre for Mathematics and Computer Science
P.O. Box 94079, 1090 GB Amsterdam, The Netherlands, and
TU Eindhoven,
De Lismortel 2, 5600 MB Eindhoven, The Netherlands.
e-mail: hlp@cwi.nl

TeamWorker: An Agent-Based Support System for Mobile Task Execution

Habin Lee, Patrik Mihailescu and John Shepherdson

Abstract. An organization's mobile workforce is a vital asset, as it is in the front line liaising with customers, and driving the sale of an organization's products and/or services. Despite this, the IT support provided to mobile workers is often inferior to that available to office-based workers. Mobile workers operate in an unreliable environment, and as such require differing types of support. Within this paper we present a multi-agent based computer cooperative support system known as TeamWorker which can help overcome the difficulties faced by mobile workers. Within this system, each mobile worker is assigned a personal agent that can assist her/him during the working day through appropriate service provision (based on current work context), and through monitoring work progress to anticipate and undertake required actions on the user's behalf. A detailed presentation of the TeamWorker system is given, including the benefits provided for a real life mobile business process.

1 Introduction

A mobile workforce differs significantly from an office-based workforce. Mobile workers operate within an uncertain computing environment where both network and computational resources are lower, when compared to an office-based workforce that typically works within a reliable computing environment [2]. Mobile workers also behave differently to office based workers due to their frequent movements, and physical isolation from other workers. As a result mobile workers require additional IT support, as they are typically in the front line interacting with customers and driving the products/services offered by an organization.

Despite this, the support provided for a mobile workforce is often substandard when compared to that given to an office based workforce. Agent technology has been used to support business processes for the last decade. Huhns and Singh [3] summarize the state of the art in agent-based workflows. Jennings et al. [4] insist that a multi-agent system has the necessary features for the support of modern dynamic business processes and propose a suitable multi-agent system architecture. Khoshafian and Buckiewicz [5] highlight some of the limitations faced by a mobile workforce. Firstly, the intelligence of an agent can be used to transparently monitor the actions of the user, and determine an appropriate course of action based on the current work context. Secondly agents have the ability to support different types of interaction protocols that can be used to coordinate the activities of distributed users. Finally, the autonomy of an agent can be used to increase the usability of a system for a user by optimizing the interaction types based on the constraints of the mobile computing device.

This paper proposes a multi-agent based Computer Supported Cooperative Work (CSCW) system called TeamWorker that supports the coordination of mobile workers. A personal agent plays a central role within the TeamWorker system, in that each mobile worker is assigned their own personal agent which assists them during their working day. Each personal agent is deployed on a mobile computing device which enables a mobile worker to access the system regardless of his or her location. In this paper we will discuss all aspects of the TeamWorker system, including both technical and non-technical details such as how the system improves the working practices of mobile workers.

In the following section we will introduce the TeamWorker system, and follow up in section three with a discussion of the mobile business process which this system supports. In section four we present an architectural overview of the TeamWorker system, and provide technical details such as the structure of the personal agent. In section five we provide a detailed explanation as to how the TeamWorker system supports the specified mobile business process, and then we conclude this paper.

2 Introduction to the TeamWorker System

The TeamWorker system has been designed to support a business process where mobile workers are the primary participants. Mobile workers are grouped together into teams to complete jobs within a certain geographically area. Each team has a leader who oversees the progress of their team, ensuring that jobs are completed, and acting as the first point of contact for team members. Each mobile worker is assigned their own personal agent which will guide them during the execution of their jobs during the working day. A personal agent resides within a mobile computing device and provides a number of services such as job retrieval, job update, and job closure. The TeamWorker system has not been developed from scratch, rather it has been derived from a platform called mPower [6]. The mPower platform is a component-based framework that can be used to support a mobile business process by modeling the interactions amongst participants via a linked set of conversational messages. The mPower platform has been implemented using an existing multi-agent system called JADE-LEAP [1] that has been designed to operate on a variety of mobile computing devices, such as a cell phone or a personal digital assistant (PDA). The mPower platform is composed of four layers:

1.   Foundation: This layer provides infrastructure support for the upper three layers. It
     relies on the functionality provided by the JADE-LEAP platform such as message

composition, message delivery, ontology/language support, and agent management.

2.   Component: This layer provides reusable components known as conversational components (C-COMs) which provide a common set of functionality that can be used within any type of application domain. For example, a C-COM that provides the ability to retrieve and add information from/to a knowledge source regardless of the information type. A C-COM is made-up of two parts, an interaction protocol that defines the sequence of asynchronous messages between participating roles, and role components that undertake the necessary actions to fulfill the provided service. Further information on C-COMs can be found within [7].

3.   Generic workflow: This layer provides a generic set of pre-defined high-level workflows that can be applied to business processes in similar domains. Each generic workflow aims to complete a higher-level business goal as opposed to an individual C-COM which completes a specific service, and as such a generic workflow is composed of a set of linked C-COMs.

4.   Application: This layer is where applications can be composed such as the TeamWorker system. An application can be developed by selecting only the required features (such as ontology support, used to devise domain-specific ontologies) from each of the lower three layers.

Further information on the mPower platform can be found within [6].

3 Mobile Business Process

Within this section we will present an overview of a real life mobile business process within British Telecommunications plc (BT) and discuss how TeamWorker has been applied to support it.

3.1 Telecommunications Service Provision and Maintenance

BT operates a large mobile workforce to maintain its network and provide telecommunications services to residential and business customers across the UK. Every day thousands of engineers perform tens of thousands of tasks. The process begins when either a customer or an engineer requests the provision of a new service, or repair of an existing service. Once a new job is created (either manually by a call centre operator or automatically) it is placed within a job pool. This job is then assigned to a particular engineer by a centralized workflow management system, based on criteria such as the skills required to complete the job, and the location of the job. In some cases a job may require two or more engineers, and may also involve multiple locations such as a telephone exchange and the customer's premises.

Engineers receive their jobs by connecting to the centralized workflow management system using a laptop, at the start of the working day either via a GSM or PSTN connection. Once a job is completed, the engineer closes the job with the appropriate information such as the cause of the fault, equipment used, hours worked, etc. If new jobs arrive during the day they are kept in an engineers queue until they are manually retrieved, otherwise a phone call is made to inform the engineer that s/he has new work (depending on the urgency of the new job).

As engineers infrequently use their laptops due to network (high access cost, slow network access, etc), and physical factors (size of laptop prevents use during job execution), a number of issues arise. Firstly, engineers often have an out of date view of their assigned work, and do not have visibility as to what other engineers within their area are working on. Therefore if the engineer's schedule has been altered s/he will only be aware of the change when s/he connects to the centralized workflow system, or by a phone call. Secondly, if an engineer knows that they cannot complete an assigned job, his/her only recourse is to initiate several mobile phone calls to other engineers (which increases costs). There is no support within the current system to transparently trade jobs amongst engineers. Finally, the inability of engineers to update their progress in real time limits the visibility management have, and therefore hampers their ability to respond to changes such as informing customers as to the progress of their requests (i.e. when an engineer will arrive), and assigning new urgent jobs to the appropriate engineers.

3.2 Application of the TeamWorker System

The TeamWorker system was designed to improve many of the working practices of BT field engineers. Improvement falls into three areas:

1. Team working/coordination: Currently, in principal engineers are assigned to teams, however due to the limitations of the current system (as discussed in the previous section), they typically work alone. The TeamWorker system addresses this issue by providing a set of coordination services such as job trading, job assistance, and organizing meetings (work or social) that enable engineers to interact with each other in real time.

2. Work visibility: As the TeamWorker system supports the ability to communicate over a GPRS network, engineers can benefit from the always-on aspect. Therefore, engineers not only have the ability to access the latest job information, including any changes to their schedules (which can be automatically pushed out to them), but also be able to update their progress in real time. In addition, management has greater visibility as to what is occurring in the field, and can respond to changes more quickly.

3. Work flexibility: As the TeamWorker system has been developed for use within mobile computing devices, engineers can take the device with them regardless of whether they are at a customer's premise, or up a pole. This not only enables engineers to access the system at any time and any place, but also increases their reachability when other engineers or management need to get in touch with them.

4 Technical Overview of the TeamWorker System

Within this section we firstly provide a high level architectural overview of the TeamWorker system, followed by a brief technical overview in section 4.1. Finally in section 4.2 the internal structure of the personal agent is discussed.

4.1 Architectural Overview of TeamWorker

The TeamWorker system is split into two parts: 1) a front-end part that executes within a mobile computing device (one for each engineer), and 2) a backend part that executes within a server, or set of servers (for all engineers). Both parts communicate securely over a network such as GPRS, via a VPN connection. Each front-end part contains a single agent, while the backend part contains a number of agents that may be distributed on a set of servers (depending upon the deployment options). Each agent provides a specific type of service. When an engineer wishes to access a service, a request is sent from her/his front-end agent to the corresponding backend agent which fulfils the service request by accessing resources within the Corporate Intranet such as a database, or a legacy system. Figure 1 provides the architectural overview of the TeamWorker system.

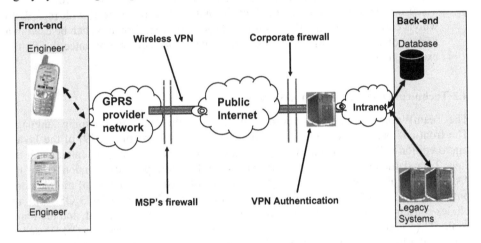

Fig. 1. Architectural overview of the TeamWorker system.

Within the front-end part of TeamWorker, JADE-LEAP runs in split-container mode, which reduces both the level of computing resources required and the time taken to register the agent with the agent management system (AMS) of the main container. Using this runtime configuration mode, a single TCP socket connection is established from the front-end to the back-end, and maintained for the duration of the application. All requests and responses are transmitted over this TCP socket. Both push and pull communication modes are supported. If a network disconnection occurs (i.e. no network coverage), messages are buffered at both-ends, and re-connection occurs automatically. Both the buffering and re-connection timings are configurable. Finally, only a single instance of the front-end is permitted, to not only conserve computing resources, but to also reduce the level of confusion for users as to which instance of the application they were using when they return from using other external applications. The backend part is comprised of approximately six agents, each of which provides a set service. Those services are:

1. User authorization: Before an engineer is able to access any other services s/he must firstly be authenticated. Once authenticated, an engineer is assigned a role that determines which services s/he can access.
2. Job management: This is the most frequently used service, as it enables engineers to retrieve their jobs, and also update job progress.
3. Job trading: This service enables an engineer to trade her/his jobs within the team. There are two types of job trades: 1) mini, and 2) maxi.
4. Notification: As new jobs enter the job pool during the day, this service ensures that they can be notified to the appropriate engineer. There are two types of notifications: 1) new job, and 2) urgent job.
5. Subscription: Once an engineer is authorized s/he is automatically subscribed to a number of services such as notification, based on her/his assigned user role.
6. Team list: This service keeps track of the status of each engineer, with regards to who is currently logged into the system. This presence information can be used in a variety of ways such as when an engineer wishes to request assistance during the execution of a job.

4.2 Technical Overview of TeamWorker

The TeamWorker system has been developed using the Java programming language. The front-end part has been implemented using the Foundation profile [9] of the Java 2 micro edition (J2ME) platform, while the backend part has been implemented using the Java 2 standard edition (J2SE) platform version 1.4.1. Both parts use version 3.2 of the JADE-LEAP platform. The front-end part has been tested on a number of mobile computing devices that operate on the Microsoft Pocket PC 2002, and 2003 OS. This includes consumer devices such as the Compaq IPAQ, the O2 XDA I and II, and the Panasonic P2 (a non-consumer device). The underlying Java virtual machine (VM) used to execute the front-end part is the IBM J9 version 2.1 VM. A number of optimizations as discussed in [8] have been applied to the front-end part of the TeamWorker system in order to improve performance. Table 1 provides a breakdown summary of the total size of both the front-end and backend part of the TeamWorker system, including the size of the mPower and JADE-LEAP runtime libraries.

A modular approach has been employed to both simplify the maintainance and installation of new features such as C-COM services to the front-end part of TeamWorker. For example, each C-COM service is deployed independently within its own individual jar file. Using this approach, if a C-COM service needs to be updated, only the jar file needs to be replaced, and not the entire front-end part of TeamWorker. There is no fixed limit on the number of C-COM services or user interface screens that can be used within TeamWorker, instead it is dependent on the available computing resources.

4.3 Internal Overview of Personal Agent

The core of the TeamWorker system is the personal agent which is responsible for assisting an engineer during her/his working day by not only providing access to useful services, but also by monitoring the engineer's progress and taking autonomous action. To achieve this the personal agent is comprised of three specific roles:

1. User manager: The user manager is responsible for managing a user's preferences by monitoring her/his interaction with the user interface. Through observing a user's interaction behavior over a period of time, the user manager can build an interaction profile, and is better able to tailor the application's functionality to meet the needs of the user. For example, if the user manager observes that the user seldom views the routing information for a job, it may decide to only download this information on demand and not when the job details are first downloaded. All interaction with the user interface pass through the user manager.

2. Coordination manager: The coordination manager is responsible for fulfilling a service request by selecting a goal plan that meets the requirements of the requested service from a list of available goal plans. Each goal plan contains details of the tasks involved and their execution sequence. Typically a task will execute one or more C-COMs, or access a resource from the Resource Manager or interact with the user during its execution. An exception handler is provided within the coordination manager that will process any failures that occur during the goal-achieving phase of a goal plan.

3. Resource manager: The resource manager is responsible for managing all the resources required to support the execution of the personal agent, and any application-specific components such as user jobs, C-COMs, and third party programs.

Front-end Component name	Physical size
TeamWorker	
• Personal agent	84 kb
• User Interface	209 kb
• C-COM (services)	118 kb
mPower	138 kb
JADE-LEAP	309 kb
Total	**858 kb**
Back-end Component name	
TeamWorker	241 kb
MPower	138 kb
JADE-LEAP	1593 kb
Total	**1972 kb**

Table 1. Runtime size of TeamWorker system.

In order to increase the autonomy of a personal agent, a clear separation between itself and the underlying user interface was created. This provides a number of development and runtime benefits, such as: 1) the user interface can be developed independently from the internal workings of the personal agent by a non-agent developer; 2) the personal agent is capable of operating on a diverse set of mobile computing devices; and 3) during its execution the personal agent could move to another mobile computing device if a failure occurs (e.g. a battery runs flat). As both the personal agent and the user interface run within separate threads, an asynchronous event-based mechanism is used for communication. There are four standard events that can be generated. These are:

1. Goal event: This is generated when a goal plan needs to be created in order to fulfill a service. For example when an engineer wishes to retrieve work assigned to her/him.
2. User interface event: Whenever an action on the user interface needs to be performed this type of event is generated. For example, when the results from a service call are available they are sent back to the user interface to be displayed to the user.
3. Resource event: This is generated whenever a resource needs to be accessed or modified. For example, when the coordination manager needs to execute a C-COM to complete a goal plan.
4. System event: This represents a system level event that typically is generated externally from the personal agent. For example, when the network has been disconnected.

All events are captured by the personal agent, which acts as a sensor that collates, records, and forwards the events to the appropriate destination, as shown in figure 2.

5. Support for Mobile Business Process

Within the remainder of this paper we discuss step by step how the TeamWorker system supports the lifecycle of an engineer's job from its inception to its completion.

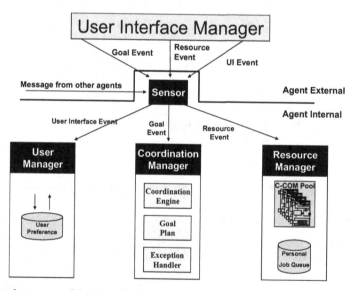

Fig. 2. Internal structure of the TeamWorker system personal agent.

5.1 Job Creation

When a new job is created (usually as the result of a Customer request), it is placed within a job pool where it is scheduled overnight by a centralized workflow management system. At the start of the day, a job agent from the TeamWorker system retrieves these scheduled jobs, including a list of engineers who have been roistered to work for the day. The job details and engineer data are stored within a relational database, ready to be sent to an individual engineer as they log into the system. To compliment the job creation process, a future enhancement of the TeamWorker system will include the ability for engineers to create new jobs, e.g. on noticing damage to a network element. We will now discuss how jobs are delivered to engineers.

5.2 Job Delivery

Jobs are delivered to engineers using two well-known communication modes: 1) Push, and 2) Pull. In the push mode, jobs are dispatched transparently to an engineer from the backend part as they become available, while in the pull mode jobs are dispatched (if available) to the engineer when requested manually. When an engineer logs into the system at the start of the day (as shown on the left hand side of figure 3), a list of any jobs assigned to her/him are delivered once s/he are authenticated (push mode). In addition to this, if the engineer is assigned the team leader role, s/he will also receive the list of jobs assigned to the team. The right hand side of figure 3 shows the view an engineer has available to them to view the jobs assigned to them. This view is identical when viewing both personal jobs and team jobs.

Currently within the TeamWorker system there are two business rules that determine how and when jobs are delivered to engineers. Either jobs are delivered directly to engineers, or via the team leader. When jobs are delivered via the team leader, the team leader has the ability to check the job assignments, and perform job re-allocation at her/his discretion. This is useful if a team member is absent as typically the team leader will be notified and s/he is then able to immediately make the necessary job reallocations to ensure that jobs are completed on time. New business rules for job delivery may be added to the TeamWorker system at any time based on the working practice of the targeted organization.

An engineer is able to refresh her/his job queue manually, by selecting the refresh menu item from the queue menu. There are two types of refresh modes available:

1. Heavy refresh: This mode retrieves all the job details from the backend part regardless of the job list that is currently available locally. This type of refresh is performed automatically when an engineer logs into the system.
2. Light refresh: This mode only retrieves new job information from the backend, by comparing what is available locally and at the backend part.

5.3 Job Execution

A number of services are provided within the TeamWorker system that assist an engineer during the execution of her/his work. Within the following subsections we discuss four such services beginning with how the TeamWorker system provides engineers with the required knowledge to complete their assigned jobs.

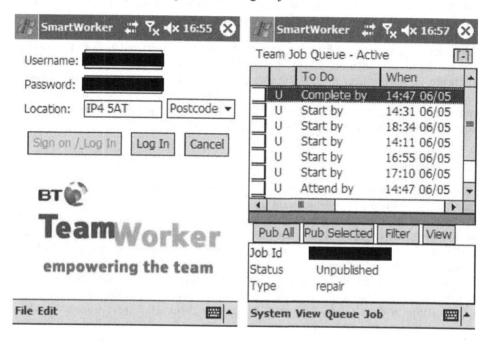

Fig. 3. Screenshots of the user authorization and job queue screen.

5.3.1 Job Details

Each job contains a set of information that provides an engineer with the knowledge that helps them to complete it. This information is broken down into a number of categories, such as customer information, routing information, and job summary. Within the TeamWorker system this information is presented to the engineer using tabbed folders, where each category is presented to the user in an individual tab as shown in figure 4. The lower right arrow buttons enable the engineer to scroll through the available information categories. The majority of the information presented is read only. However there are a few fields available that can be edited such as the status of a job, and when a job has been completed. An engineer is able to view the job details via the job queue screen as shown in the right hand side of figure 3.

In addition to viewing job information, an engineer is also able to enter notes for a job. This information can be specific to a job or to a location. For example, an engineer may add a note that a cable at the job location needs to be replaced soon. This information is useful for other engineers who may in future receive a job in the similar location. A future enhancement of the note taking function is to enable engineers the ability to add a digital photograph or small video clip instead of a plain text note.

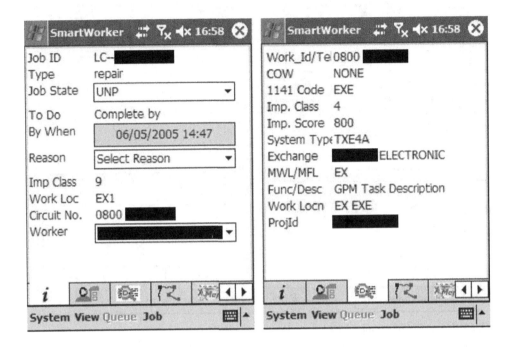

Fig. 4. Screenshot of the job details screen.

5.3.2 Job Trading

Job trading enables engineers to trade jobs amongst themselves. This is very useful when an engineer realizes that s/he cannot complete an assigned job, and rather than missing the appointment time, s/he can instead ask if a colleague is willing to complete the job. Two types of job trading services have been implemented, 1) mini trade, and 2) maxi trade. In a mini job trade an engineer offers a job to other engineers within their team who meet certain criteria. For example, an engineer who has the right skills to complete the job, or an engineer who is within close proximity of the job. New criteria may be added depending upon the working practice of the organization. An engineer can trade a job by selecting it from the job queue screen, and then choosing the mini trade menu item as shown on the left hand side of figure 5. Once an engineer has initiated a mini job trade, s/he can keep track of the progress of this trade by switching to the coordination view screen as shown on the right hand side of figure 5.

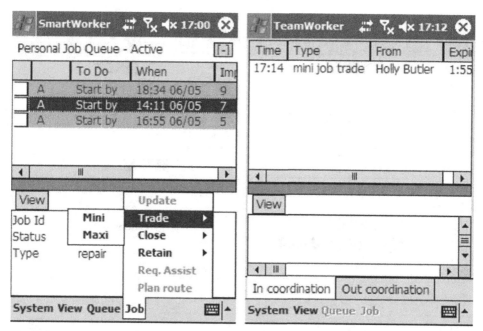

Fig. 5. Screenshot of a mini job trade.

An engineer who receives a mini job trade offer is able to view the offer within the same coordination view screen as shown on the right hand side of figure 5. From this screen an engineer is able to view the job details and decide whether or not s/he is willing to accept the job. To view the jobs, an engineer highlights the job proposal and selects the view button, then is presented with a dialog that shows all the job details as per figure 4, with the exception that an engineer cannot edit any fields. Once an engineer accepts a mini job trade proposal, all the other engineers who received the same one will receive a notification informing them that it has now been withdrawn.

A maxi job trade is an alternative job trading option for an engineer, as instead of sending an offer to several of their peers, a single offer is sent directly to their team leader, who will be asked to re-assign the job on their behalf. This can be useful when an engineer's mini job trade repeatedly fails. When a team leader receives a maxi job trade offer s/he can view the job details in the same way as with a mini job trade. However s/he will have the ability from within this view to reassign the job. As with both job trade types, there is a time limit on the offer. Finally additional business rules may be added to the job trading process that determines how it operates. For example, one such rule could be that jobs cannot be traded more than three times, or an engineer who already has four jobs is not able to accept or receive a job trade.

5.3.3 Request Assistance

When a job requires two or more engineers to complete, engineers are able to request assistance from their colleagues. This coordination service is similar to the job trading service in that engineers who require assistance send a request that contains such information as the job type and location, and when assistance is required to their peers. Once an engineer receives a job assistance request it appears within their coordination view screen (as shown in the right hand side of figure 5), where s/he can view the details and decide if s/he is willing to assist. As with the mini job trade service, once an engineer accepts this request, the job assistance request will be withdrawn from other engineers.

5.3.4 Job State Update

To provide greater visibility as to the progress of jobs within the field, engineers are able to update the progress of their assigned jobs. There are six available job states:

1. Unpublished: This is the initial job state of a job when it enters the TeamWorker system.
2. Published: Once a team leader publishes a job, its job state changes to published which enables an engineer to retrieve the job or for it to be pushed out automatically.
3. Activated: Once a team member receives a job its state is set to activate, to indicate it has been received.
4. Executed: This job state is used to indicate that an engineer is currently executing a job.
5. Negotiated: This job state is used to show that a job is currently under negotiation (that is either a mini or maxi job trade is occurring).
6. Closed: This job state is used to represent that a job has been completed.

An engineer can change the status of a job by firstly viewing the details of the job and then selecting the appropriate job state from a combo box as shown on the left hand side of figure 6. Once the progress of a job has been changed, a team leader is able to view these changes by refreshing the team job queue. A sample screenshot of this view is shown on the right hand side of figure 6.

5.4 Job Closure

Once an engineer has completed a job s/he is able to close the job and capture closure information such as the time taken to complete the job, the cause of the fault, materials used etc. In addition, an engineer is also able to capture customer feedback. Information such as if they were satisfied with the level of service received, consent for an engineer to dig, and the cost of non-contractual work can be captured directly by an engineer once a job is completed.

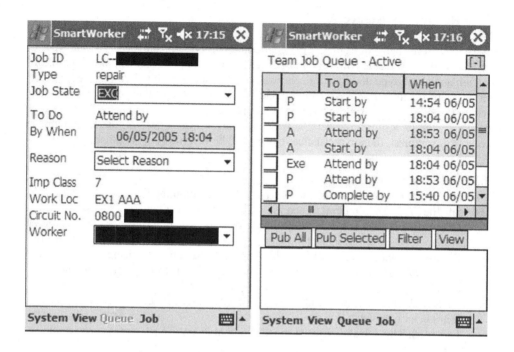

Fig. 6. Screenshot of job state update.

5.5 Job Injection

Within the course of the day new jobs may arrive in the job pool, which need to be delivered to engineers. The TeamWorker system supports two forms of job injection:

1.   Normal: In normal job injection mode, jobs have already been assigned to engineers and only need to be delivered. As with the job delivery (discussed in section 5.2), there are two business rules that determine how jobs are delivered to engineers: 1) directly to engineers, or 2) via the team leader. The left hand side of figure 7 shows job injection when the business rule is set to 'via the team leader', and the right hand side of figure 7 shows direct job injection to team members.

2.   Urgent: In urgent job injection mode, jobs have not yet been assigned to an engineer rather they have been assigned to a team. In this case a mini job proposal is generated automatically by the system and sent to members of the team that meet certain criteria. If no one accepts this urgent job after the expiry time, its priority will be raised, resulting in a maxi trade request being generated.

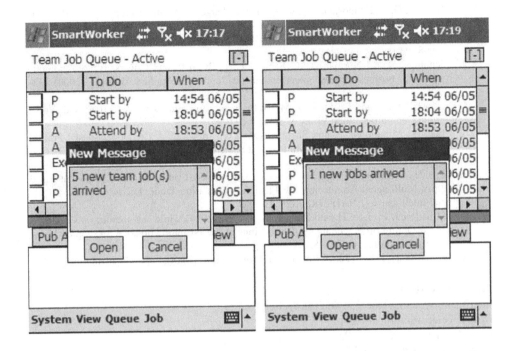

Fig. 7. Job injection screenshot.

Conclusion

This paper provides details about an agent based computer supported cooperative system known as TeamWorker, which supports mobile business processes. Agent technology plays a key part in the TeamWorker system, as each mobile worker is assigned a personal agent, which negates some of the problems experienced within the mobile computing environment (in particular usability, device adaptability, communications efficiency and computing resource requirements). A technical overview of the TeamWorker system was presented, and a detailed description as to how the system supports a real life telecommunications mobile business process was given. An internal trial of the system has been conducted in order to assess the technical qualities and potential business benefits of agent technology in general and the TeamWorker application in particular.

References

1.   Berger, M., Rusitschka, S., Schlichte, M., Toropov, D., and Watzke, M. (2003). Porting Agents to Small Mobile Devices - The Development of the Lightweight Extensible Agent Platform. EXP in search of innovation special issue on JADE, vol. 3, no. 3, pp. 32-41.

2. Forman, G. and Zahorjan, J. (1994). The Challenges of Mobile Computing. IEEE Computer, Vol. 27, No. 4, pp. 38-47, April.
3. Huhns, M.N. and Singh, M.P.: Workflow Agents. IEEE Internet Computing, 2 (4), (1998) 94-96.
4. Jennings, N. R., Norman, T. J., Faratin, P., O'Brien P. and Odgers, B.: Autonomous agents for business process management. Int. Journal of Applied AI 14(2), (2000) 145-189.
5. Khoshafian, S. and Buckiewicz, M.: 'Introduction to Groupware, Workflow, and Workgroup Computing', John Wiley & Sons, Inc (1995).
6. Lee, H., Mihailescu, P. and Shepherdson, J.W.: mPower: A Component-based Framework for the Development of Multi-Agent Systems, BT Technology Journal, 23 (3), Oct. 2003..
7. Lee, H., Mihailescu, P. and Shepherdson, J.W. (2003). Conversational Component-based Open Multi-agent Architecture for Flexible Information Trade. Lecture Notes in Artificial Intelligence (LNAI) 2782, 109-116.
8. Mihailescu, P., Lee, H. and Shepherdson, J.W. (2004). Hold the sources: A Gander at J2ME Optimisation techniques, Proceedings of the 1st International Workshop on Ubiquitous Computing, pp 73 – 82, April.
9. Sun. (2002). JSR 46 J2ME Foundation Profile. http://jcp.org/en/jsr/detail?id=46.

Author Affiliations

Intelligent Systems Research and Innovation Centre
British Telecommunications plc
B62 MLB1/pp12, Adastral Park
Martlesham Heath, Ipswich
Suffolk, IP5 3RE, UK
Ha.lee@bt.com
patrik.2.mihailescu@bt.com
john.shepherdson@bt.com

Information about Software

Software is available on the Internet as

( ) prototype version
( ) full fledged software (freeware), version no.:
( ) full fledged software (for money), version no.:
( ) demo/trial version
(X) not (yet) available

Contact person for question about the software:

Name: John Shepherdson
Email: john.shepherdson@bt.com

Author Index